A TALENT FOR GENIUS

The Life and Times of Oscar Levant

Villard Books / New York / 1994

A TALENT FOR GENIUS

The Life and Times of Oscar Levant

Sam Kashner and Nancy Schoenberger

Library of Congress Cataloging-in-Publication Data

Kashner, Sam.
A talent for genius : the life and times of Oscar Levant / by Sam
Kashner and Nancy Schoenberger.
p.   cm.
Includes bibliographical references.
ISBN 0-679-40489-9
1. Levant, Oscar, 1906–1972.   2. Musicians—United States—
Biography.   I. Schoenberger, Nancy.   II. Title.
ML417.L64K37   1994
780′.92—dc20   93-40647

9 8 7 6 5 4 3 2
First Edition
Book design by Jo Anne Metsch

To our parents
Betty and Dutch Schoenberger
Marion and Seymour Kashner
with everlasting gratitude
And to the memory of Jonathan Lieberson
(1949–1989)

"To live life to the end is not a childish task."

—"Hamlet," from the poems of Yurii
Zhivago by Boris Pasternak
(translated by Bernard Gilbert Guerney)

"It's not what you are but what you don't become that hurts."

—Oscar Levant, as Sid Jeffers,
in *Humoresque*

Contents

Prelude

AT THE HEIGHT OF HIS POWER, OSCAR LEVANT WAS THE HIGHEST-PAID concert artist in America, eclipsing Vladimir Horowitz and Artur Rubinstein. He appealed to a mass audience in a way that few of his contemporaries ever did, and his wit and eccentric personality as they came across on radio and film (and later on television) were as fascinating to the public as were his superb renditions of George Gershwin's piano works. He was known variously as Gershwin's best friend and the supreme interpreter of his music, and as the bad boy of radio and film, whose witty, often outrageous remarks were as insulting to himself as they were to those around him: "I knew Doris Day before she became a virgin"; "An evening with George Gershwin is a George Gershwin evening"; "Zsa Zsa Gabor has learned the secret of perpetual middle age"; "I'm controversial—my friends either dislike me or hate me."

Yet Levant was deeply cynical about success: "I hate that word—functioning is the important thing" he said on television in the late 1950s, after drug addiction and manic-depressive illness had taken their toll on him. Levant would abandon several successful careers in his time—composer and songwriter, radio personality, stage and film actor, television host, author. His concert works, written under the tutelage of Arnold Schoenberg, one of the century's major figures in music, were admired for their "high seriousness" by men like Aaron Copland. Levant's three autobiographical books were best-sellers. Yet Levant was plagued by self-doubt. He became increasingly dependent on an elaborate system of rituals and superstitions just to be able to perform. Rather than expand his concert repertoire, Levant limited himself to playing mostly Gershwin, thus ensuring himself a provincial career. He was so enamored of Gershwin's songs that he gave up writing popular songs himself, though he had written a number of hits and at least one standard, the haunting "Blame It on My Youth." He felt his serious compositions could not compete with Gershwin's nor those of his mentor Schoenberg, so he gave up a promising composing career. Levant would pay a high price for his honesty, and for his attraction to high and low culture, from the concert hall to the boxing ring. He was criticized for being a dilettante and "a man of fragments." Though he was often called a "genius" in the media, Levant anguished over whether he possessed true genius or mere talent.

The story of Oscar Levant is in part the story of his troubled friendship with George Gershwin, which was far more ardent on Levant's part than on Gershwin's. It is also a love story: Levant's second wife, June, would keep him alive through countless drug withdrawals and hospital incarcerations.

Levant was the first public figure to announce his barbiturate addiction to the world and to talk about his experiences with psychiatry and mental illness. In an era when every television talk show casually offers up the confessions of reformed substance abusers, it is hard to realize how shocking that information was in the mid-1950s, when Oscar Levant went on *The Jack Paar Tonight Show* and talked candidly about the shock treatments, drug withdrawal, and group therapy he had undergone. "There is a thin line between genius and insanity," Levant once said. "I have erased that line."

Many feared Levant's acerbic wit, yet Levant inspired many lifelong friendships. Through his thirteen films and what little remains of his over one hundred recordings, Levant's outrageous persona and artistry have appealed to a whole new generation, from Michael Tilson Thomas to Michael Feinstein and Eddie Van Halen.

None of this mattered to the twenty thousand music lovers who used to gather on brilliant summer nights at New York's Lewisohn Stadium half a century ago to hear Levant play. The all-Gershwin programs were no longer simply a memorial to a vanished era but a celebration of Oscar Levant, America's favorite *enfant terrible*.

PART I

An American in Pittsburgh

1

The Unmentionable City

"I've always been a baby,
but this is how it started."

PITTSBURGH IN 1906, THE YEAR OSCAR LEVANT WAS BORN, WAS
nothing to be afraid of. The youngest of four sons born to industrious
Russian Jews, Oscar spent his first fifteen years roaming the immigrant streets of the Hill district, a once-prosperous area that is now
pockmarked by dilapidated tenements, pool halls, liquor stores, and
weedy vacant lots. Bordering the Hill district was Colwell Street, a
notorious neighborhood where workingmen went on weekends to
sate their sexual appetites. The story goes that when young Jewish
men were bar mitzvahed on Saturday morning, on Saturday night
they were taken to Colwell Street for their real initiation into man-
hood.

Years later, at the height of his renown, Oscar Levant developed a
phobic loathing of Pittsburgh. Merely to say the word in front of him
meant banishment. "I paid thousands of dollars to psychiatrists to forget my childhood" was a famous Levant quip, but he never did forget
it. His early suffering was always with him, just under the surface. In
fact, his phobias were complex and trenchant, especially for one who
would accomplish so much in his lifetime.

The Hill district was once one of the most picturesque sections of

Pittsburgh. In the early 1800s, the district had been a residential section where many of the city's famous families lived. By the late 1870s, it became less fashionable as the gentry moved out and immigrants began to pour into the district. Eastern European Jews, followed by Italians and Syrians, moved in, strengthened by a younger wave of Jewish immigrants.

It was with this second wave of immigration that Oscar's father, Max Levant, arrived in Pittsburgh, in 1891, at the age of twenty-two. Born in St. Petersburg, Max Levant, unlike many of the immigrants arriving from Russian *shtetls* with their attendant poverty and narrowness, was cosmopolitan. His skill as a watchmaker had given him a tradesman's entree into other cities, and he had already tasted life in European capitals before emigrating to America. A wiry man of diminutive height, sporting a neat black mustache, Max spoke several languages.

Settling in Pittsburgh allowed Max to escape the more extreme hardships of life in New York City's Lower East Side, with its infamous sweatshops, stultifying tenements, and outbreaks of tuberculosis. Since Jews were barred from working in Pittsburgh's steel factories, Max Levant and his young family were spared the substandard housing called "Painter's Row," where the poverty-stricken Slavic families who worked for the steel companies lived. Life was less hard on men like Max, who had a marketable skill, who learned English quickly, and who found a transplanted culture already thriving in the Hill district, with its *cheders* and *shuls;* its Jewish bathhouses; its *landsmanschafts;* its lively debates among Zionists, socialists, and various labor movements; and—most happily for Max—access to free music concerts at Schenley Park and inexpensive recitals at Carnegie Music Hall and the Alvin Theatre.

Whatever the hardships, the Hill district was full of vitality: Peddlers hawked their wares through the vivid streets, horse-drawn wagons rattled by the dry-goods shops, and markets spilled their fruit onto the sidewalks from overflowing bins. Jewish socialist and Zionist groups were active, arranging meetings and holding demonstrations.

By the turn of the century, the Americanization of Hill district immigrants was well under way. Many Jews began speaking English instead of Yiddish.

In 1894—three years after arriving in America—twenty-six-year-old Max Levant met and married twenty-one-year-old Annie Radin in a ceremony held at the Radin home at 9 Marion Street and presided over by Annie's father, Rabbi Abraham Radin.

Inflexibly devout in matters of religion, Annie's mother, Sarah

Radin, raised five children. She had emigrated to Pittsburgh in 1890 from Biyalik-Grodno, a Russian city famous for its cantors and its onion rolls. Her husband, Abraham, had arrived earlier, first settling in Boston and eventually following a nephew to Pittsburgh. He quickly sent for his first son, Oscar Radin, who traveled alone from Russia by way of Canada with his violin tucked under his arm. Six years later Abraham sent for his wife, Sarah, and the rest of their children. When Sarah Radin and her brood first passed through Warsaw on their way to the new world, they were dazzled by the city's beauty. Sarah—called Sadie by her family—turned to her eldest daughter, Annie, and exclaimed, "If Warsaw is this beautiful, can you imagine what Pittsburgh is like!"

Having arrived in America as an impressionable teenager, Annie was caught between the Old World and the New. If Max had wanted an Americanized wife to share his modest American success, Annie changed all that: She was religiously observant, keeping a kosher home and attending her father's synagogue. She was a good-looking, good-humored girl with an hourglass figure, and in the neighborhood she was considered quite a catch.

On December 27, 1906, Oscar Levant was born into this crucible of old- and new-world values vying for dominance. Oscar's Russian Jewish background, like that of two of the great composers of popular music in the first half of the twentieth century, Irving Berlin and George Gershwin, provided him with a love of music coupled with the status of an outsider. That status gave him the boldness, the *chutzpah,* and the irony to attack the cultural mainstream; it also provided him with a lifelong sense of inadequacy and resentment against the status quo.

Max Levant was an autocratic figure who was strict with his four sons. He wanted them to become either doctors or dentists. When his eldest son, Harry, defied him, Max was implacable, and his silent rage filled the cramped house at 1420 Fifth Avenue.

Annie was also a force with which to be reckoned, as were Oscar's formidable grandparents Sadie and Abraham. Annie's three brothers and sister were colorful personalities as well. His aunt and uncles shaped Oscar's sense of how one could live in the world and offered, by example, an alternative to the dutifully Orthodox existence his parents demanded of him.

When Abraham and Sadie's eldest son, Oscar Radin, displayed a virtuosity on his beloved violin, they set aside weekly portions of Abraham's income to pay for music lessons. The lessons paid off handsomely. While barely out of his teens, he became second violinist for the house orchestra of the Pittsburgh Stock Company. The company's director went on to stage most of the Shubert brothers' musical productions, bringing the young violinist with him to New York. Radin eventually became influential in the Shubert Organization as music director for many of their Winter Garden Theatre productions. To theatregoers of the 1920s, Radin became well known as Al Jolson's music conductor.

Oscar Radin's success stirred the sediment of his nephews' ambitions, making it easier for Max and Annie's eldest son, the self-assured, womanizing Harry, to leave Pittsburgh and find his way in New York's burgeoning theatrical world.

Samuel Radin, the second of Annie's doted-on brothers, inspired in Oscar a lifelong admiration for all debunkers. Samuel, a physician, was the most secularized of the brothers, rebelling against Abraham's strict Orthodoxy, refusing to keep a kosher home. "He ate ham and bacon," Oscar remembered, "which to us was unheard of." Oscar's father refused to set foot in Samuel's house because it was *treyfe*. He would go to the door and holler "Shmuel" (Yiddish for Samuel), rather than cross the threshold.

"That kind of freedom made him seem to us a strange adventurer," remembered Oscar. "He was the only sophisticated man we knew, completely emancipated from the strictures of religion and the insularity of provincialism." For Oscar he became a figure to emulate.

Annie's youngest brother, Mickey Radin, remained a bachelor. It was Mickey who introduced his nephews Harry and Oscar to the rites of Priapus—he was a notorious Don Juan and a frequent visitor of Colwell Street brothels, so much so that the Radins and Levants were accorded family rates, as Oscar would later joke.

This triad of uncles—Mickey Radin, the man-about-town who became a Broadway boulevardier; the brilliant conversationalist and apostate Samuel Radin; and Oscar Radin, gifted prodigy and rising star of Broadway's musical theatre—served as beacons for Oscar Levant, who desperately needed an alternative to his father's duty-bound, oppressively respectable household.

Annie Levant once confessed to her son Oscar that she was the least glamorous member of her family, that her siblings were charming and popular but that, as she was the eldest, most of the household drudgery had fallen to her. She was reserved about expressing affection, as was her husband. In fact, an icy formality ran through their marriage. "My mother was inarticulate about expressing affection," Oscar would one day write. "She even confessed to me once that she didn't particularly like her mother, which was quite a confession for those pre-Freudian days." Oscar later observed that he felt at home with the Gershwins because they were "the most undemonstrative people I'd ever met," much like his own parents.

Max and Annie both loved music. Max firmly believed that "no man can be great unless he loves music." Annie had a lifelong passion for Tchaikovsky, whose symphonies seemed the only thing capable of moving her to rapture. Max was an opera addict who managed to see the first American performance of Wagner's *Parsifal* in a pirated version staged in 1903 in New York City. He was an admirer of Enrico Caruso—a new Caruso recording for the gramophone was a great occasion in the Levant household.

Three things were stressed in the Levant home: good education in preparation for a profession, observance of all Jewish rituals, and a love of music.

A shrewd, intelligent man, Max Levant was probably attracted to Samuel Radin's brand of iconoclasm, but he believed that Jews should not assimilate; rather, they should pursue a profession which would protect them from persecution by the dominant culture. Unfortunately, his insistence on forcing his sons into the professions backfired when it came to the eldest and the youngest, and Max did not have the temperament to allow them to find their own way.

Max showed "a derisive contempt for displays of emotion in other families," Oscar remembered. His aloofness at home, combined with his high expectations for his sons and his terrible temper when crossed, made Max the undisputed patriarch of the family. He was an excellent jeweler but often found the work tedious, preferring to take his daily afternoon nap on the couch behind the store. During these naps, silence prevailed in the household and—or so it seemed to Oscar—out into the streets. His boisterous sons stayed out of his way in the quiet afternoon gloom.

Annie Levant was taller and heavier than her husband. Her photographs show a woman with a full, round face, well-molded lips, and eyes like spoonfuls of dark tea. Her dusky hair coiled on top of her head and her splendid posture gave her a dignified air.

What the photographs fail to reveal is Annie's cutting humor and sharp, biting wit. The Radins and the Levants shared in the brisk exchange of sarcastic remarks. Beginning with Sadie Radin, they all had quick tongues. It was a sword that cut both ways, and Oscar often found himself on the receiving end of cruel jests. He felt particularly vulnerable because he hadn't inherited the natural grace and manly presence his brothers and uncles possessed; he was a knock-kneed, round-faced, big-eared boy.

Max and Annie's was a compatible if restrained marriage. They disagreed, however, on one crucial point. Max was absolutely opposed to his sons becoming professional musicians. As much as he loved music, he considered professional musicians little more than ne'er-do-wells, itinerants. Annie felt differently. She revered Tchaikovsky and worshiped Paderewski. After all, her own brother had become a professional musician. Music was almost as dear to her as were her sons, and she secretly cherished ambitions for her youngest that she dared not confide to her husband. She would have to work surreptitiously, subverting Max's influence, because Oscar's talent outshone even that of his gifted brothers. She would see to it that, despite Max, Oscar would have a concert career.

Throughout his life, Oscar was overly devoted to his mother. Indulgent but remote, loving but aloof, she inspired her youngest child's extreme neediness. She gave little of herself, but that portion was strong and it endured.

2

The Making of
a *Chuchum*

"*Chutzpah*—that quality which enables a man
who has murdered his mother and father to throw himself
on the mercy of the court as an orphan."

MAX ESTABLISHED HIS JEWELRY SHOP ON PITTSBURGH'S BUSTLING
Fifth Avenue, with the family quarters behind the store. He often
worked in the small showroom beneath his sign, "M. Levant, Jewelry
Manufacturer, Diamonds, Watches, Clocks and Silverware," so pass-
ersby could see the watch-repair department and appreciate his dili-
gence in a trade he increasingly found tedious. Behind the shop was
the Levant living room, with a secondhand upright piano by the door;
one had to squeeze by the showcases against the wall to get through.
Oscar and his brother Honey shared their parents' bedroom until the
older boys moved out of the house. Because of the lack of space,
Oscar slept in a crib until he was eight years old, his feet sticking out
"like bamboo shoots," an early humiliation he remembered throughout his life.

Max and Annie's first son, Harry, was born in 1895, ten months
after their marriage. A second son, Benjamin, was born in December
1897. Howard, nicknamed "Honey," came along in 1904. Max Levant was disappointed when Honey arrived because he had wanted a
girl. When in 1906 Oscar was born, Max was inconsolable. Annie

seemed to share his disappointment, setting the tone for a sense of inadequacy that haunted Oscar's life.

Oscar's earliest conscious fear was one of abandonment. His parents were in the habit of going out in the evenings, locking their youngest son alone inside the house. In a fit of anger and frustration, Oscar once smashed a hole through the glass-paned door with his right hand. His parents ignored their small son's plea to be taken with them on their nightly strolls, and a week later he smashed his left hand through the glass. This time he came close to cutting off one of his fingers.

The walls of the Levant house were adorned with the sepia-toned photographs of dead ancestors, patriarchs with enormous beards and dark, stiff coats. These stern shades added a somber tone to the shop and living quarters. Oscar would often wake in the middle of the night, terrified, and grab Honey's neck in a chokehold. "Are you still here, Honey?" he'd whimper.

When Oscar was seven years old, he wrote a letter to his mother, who had gone to New York to visit her sister, Leannette. The letter suggests some of the small boy's sensitivity and loneliness. He began by proudly telling his mother that he had passed the first grade:

> My Dear, Dear Mamma:
> I past to room four on the second floor. I am glad that you went to New York, but when you will come back home I will be more glad, So will be papa and Hony and every body will be glad to have you home. I am not crying and not fighting with Hony but I would rather have you home.
> good by My dear Mamma.
>
> > Your loving
> > son Oscar

His loneliness was of course lessened by the company of his brothers. In a house full of older, vigorous boys, Oscar was quick to grow up. The Levant boys and their cousins played makeshift baseball games in the streets and alleys behind Beimer's Candy Factory. Baseball became Oscar's first passion. His earliest ambition was to play for the Pittsburgh Pirates, and from a tender age he memorized box scores and dreamed of Forbes Field.

All the Levant boys were given music lessons at an early age. Each was assigned an instrument to study, alternately the violin or the piano. Annie Levant explained years later that "the eldest was given the violin, the second the piano, and so on. . . . If [Oscar] had been the first or third child, he probably would have been a violinist."

Harry studied the violin with such success that when it was time for him to put it away and take up the study of medicine, he rebelled against his father, bailing out of his second year of premedical studies to become a professional musician. Benjamin, the second son, studied piano and was Oscar's first piano teacher. Always the good son and Max's favorite, he became a urologist, though he composed music for the Pitt Cap and Gown shows at his alma mater, the University of Pittsburgh, as well as the music for their team's fighting song. One of his Cap and Gown shows featured another famous son of Pittsburgh, the young Gene Kelly.

It was felt that Honey had the true gift for music and would have made a world-class violinist, but it was not to be. He simply did not have the temperament to rebel against his father, so he reluctantly became a dentist. Though he would continue to play the violin as an amateur, Honey was bitter at having been bullied out of a musical career.

Oscar at first hated to practice and had to be coerced. A relative recalled that Annie literally tied him to the piano bench to force him to practice. Honey remembered, "Sure, he could play the piano like nobody's business, but you almost had to drag him out of the alley where he was playing with the other kids, to get him to come in and practice or play for some visitor. He'd howl and bawl, the little bum."

There was no denying Oscar's extraordinary skill and quickness. Becoming his brother Benjamin's pupil, he soaked up Chopin's Ballade in A-flat and Schumann's "Faschingsschwank aus Wien." In only twelve weeks he mastered the Beethoven symphonies for four hands with his brother, who, incredulous, advised his parents that Oscar was ready for another teacher.

Martin Miessler was no stranger to the Levant home, having given Harry instruction on the violin. A tyrannical teacher, Miessler had received his training at the Leipzig Conservatory and was a proponent of the Czerny rigid-finger technique. Oscar would later complain, "I never quite overcame the limitations of this method, because the main characteristic of my youth was literalness. I had the same reaction when I was taught the Old Testament."

Karl Czerny, the Austrian pianist and teacher of Liszt, described his method: "The thumb must never be placed on the black keys. Never strike two or more keys one after the other with the same finger. In runs, the little finger must never be placed on the black keys." The method was so hard on the fingers that Oscar's right thumb would swell up and bleed after his practicing.

Proud of their talented boys, Annie and Max frequently showcased them in family recitals held in the narrow quarters behind the store. Oscar would usually play Liszt's Second Hungarian Rhapsody or Twelfth Rhapsody or a transcription from a movement of a Bach orchestral suite, the program selected entirely by his father.

Annie was proud of her youngest son's pianistic gifts, and she was determined—despite her husband's opposition—that Oscar be groomed for a concert career. However, she worried that he didn't have the physical presence to be one of the greats. She frequently told him, "You'll never be a Paderewski," adding cryptically, "but you'll never be lonely." The remark haunted him. In later years, he would parody it when he supplied his own dialogue for a number of films.

What deepened their relationship was their shared love of music. Oscar and his mother spent the early summer of 1913 close to the Victrola, listening to Tchaikovsky. Her records were sacred objects, heavy as dinner plates. Oscar—who had a reputation for being accident prone—was forbidden to touch them.

That summer Annie took her son to an outdoor concert in Schenley Park offered free of charge by the Pittsburgh Symphony. It was a beautiful summer evening, and, surrounded by a vast crowd of concertgoers, seven-year-old Oscar and his mother found their places on Schenley Park's lawn. Annie was thrilled that one of her favorite pieces, Tchaikovsky's *1812 Overture,* was on the program. Enthralled by the heroic dimensions of the overture, the two music lovers were startled out of their reverie by a loud thunderclap. With a streak of lightning the sky opened up and rain drenched the panicked crowd. Oscar and Annie ran through the ranks of howling children and soaked concertgoers. Suddenly Oscar, afraid he would lose his mother in the crowd, began to suffocate. He dug his fingers into her arm. Eventually they made their way to a storefront awning several blocks from the park, but the evening was ruined. Oscar would never forget the trauma of his breathless panic. This early memory, which Oscar later recorded, may have been the first of many associative phobias that would torment him most of his adult life. From that day on, Oscar could never hear the *1812 Overture* without cringing.

By the time Oscar reached nine years of age, he had outgrown Martin Miessler. In an effort to find another teacher for her prodigy, Annie took Oscar to Philadelphia. The events surrounding this excursion are hazy, but Oscar confided to a friend years later that his mother left him alone in Philadelphia for several days, having rented him a room in a boardinghouse and given him money for meals. In actuality, it may only have been a few hours, but Oscar, overwhelmed by his sense of abandonment, remembered it as days. Oscar cowered in the room until Annie returned to rescue him. This time he did not smash his fist through a pane of glass; instead, the forlorn boy returned to Pittsburgh with his mother.

When Harry defied his father and abandoned his premed studies, Uncle Oscar Radin took him under his wing, getting him his first job playing the violin at New York's Winter Garden Theatre. Uncle Oscar had a favor to ask of his nephew: to keep an eye on a beautiful young chorus girl named Pearl Eaton in whom he was interested. Harry did as he was told, and within weeks he wooed and married her, further alienating Max Levant and infuriating his Uncle Oscar. By defying Max and marrying a glamorous chorus girl—Pearl Eaton was said to have the best legs on Broadway—Harry became a hero to his youngest brother.

Harry's triumph was a serious blow to Max's authority. To see his son break away from his sphere of influence was a wound from which he never fully recovered. When Benjamin, halfway through medical school, eloped with a German Jewish girl, Max's frustration was compounded by his antipathy to Germans and he couldn't bring himself to sanction the marriage.

Perhaps it was to shore up the authority of the family unit against the influences of the outside world—particularly women—that Max made a point of telling each of his sons a Grand Guignol fable of mother love:

> A son murders his mother and cuts her heart out to present to his sweetheart. With the heart in his hand, he rushes off to present it to his fiancée. In his hurry, he stumbles, and the disembodied heart that he clutches in his hand cries out, "Did you hurt yourself, son?"

"No analyst I ever had found a fable to equal that," Oscar later wrote.

What his sons did not know when they were listening to this ghoulish tale was that their father was not well. His naps behind the store were lasting longer than usual, and his irritability and temper increased as his energy and endurance flagged. Yet he continued to exert his authority over his youngest son's musical life, choosing the selections Oscar would play at family recitals. Out of fear and respect, Oscar dutifully performed his father's selections.

One evening when extra chairs were squeezed into the smoky living room to accommodate an overflow of guests for a recital, Oscar decided to defy his father. Max had instructed him that for his encore he must perform Chopin's "Military" Polonaise. His beloved Radin grandparents were there, as was his favorite uncle, Samuel Radin, whose independent-mindedness he tried to emulate. Oscar stood before the piano and accepted applause for a precocious performance, basking in the approval of his family and neighbors. Returning to the piano for an encore, he announced in his high, squeaky voice that he would play the second movement of Beethoven's "Pathétique" Sonata. His father, disturbed by his son's disobedience, said nothing. But when it was over and everyone burst into spontaneous applause, Max strode up to his youngest son and slapped him full across the face.

From that moment Oscar's love of performing would be undercut by a sense of dread, and he would lock horns with his father over possession of his music, a battle he would fight in various guises for the rest of his life.

A good boy who faithfully attended Hebrew school at his grandfather's synagogue, eight-year-old Oscar was sometimes shocked by the stories of the Old Testament, which he diligently read in Hebrew. Of all those that troubled him, he was most disturbed by the story of Jacob and Esau, of how Jacob cheated Esau of his birthright and his father's blessing. He couldn't have been immune to the fierce competition among his brothers for Max's approval.

Oscar reacted to his after-school Hebrew classes and to his mother's orthodoxy by becoming slavish in his adherence to Jewish ritual. As a young boy he was fascinated by Kaddish, the Jewish prayer for the dead, a fascination that would take another form in adulthood: a phobic dread of any mention or thought of death. When, at the suggestion of his psychiatrist, he finally gave up the ritual of reciting Kaddish, he felt he was betraying not God but his mother, at whose knee he had first learned to observe all the Jewish rituals.

Oscar had another difficulty: Despite his grace at the piano, he was developing into a clumsy, accident-prone child. His ears stuck out, and his hair hung in strands over his forehead; his dark eyebrows and full lips gave him a perpetual scowl. He was knock-kneed and so apt to drop things that the insult "Butterfingers!" followed him around the house like a Greek chorus. A Butterfingers candy wrapper would later fill him with dread. Hypersensitive, Oscar felt that his clumsiness was an affliction. He learned to cover up his social ineptitude and physical awkwardness with smart remarks, trading insults with his family, because the best defense is a good offense. Oscar learned to be offensive, but because he was truly funny, his offensiveness became a kind of charm.

By the age of eight he had developed an interest in books and an ability to remember anything he read. He particularly loved Greek myths—he was fascinated by monsters and was soon identifying with the monsters in *Bulfinch's Mythology*. Another favorite book was Ring Lardner's *You Know Me, Al*, whose wisecracking hero became something of a role model for the young *chuchum* (Yiddish slang for "wise guy.")

Oscar was becoming known in the neighborhood as a prodigy on the piano, a reputation he tried to keep hidden from his circle of friends; schoolboys who were regarded as exceptional were usually given a sound drubbing in the schoolyard. With his smart mouth and bantam swagger, Oscar made sure the other boys would accept him as one of them.

As a pupil at Forbes Elementary School, Oscar played at school functions. His playing was remarkably accomplished for one so young, and he quickly became the accompanist for every youthful aspiring violinist in the city. He began performing at the Kaufman Settlement on Center Avenue, a leading Jewish center in Pittsburgh, and he played recitals at the YMHA, as well as in private homes in the fashionable suburbs of Pittsburgh.

On one memorable occasion, Oscar was summoned to play for the aging music-hall star Lillian Russell while her teeth were being worked on by an upscale Pittsburgh dentist who kept a baby grand in his waiting room. When the recital was over, the stately diva gave Oscar the then princely sum of one dollar. Oscar was exhilarated, and his appetite grew for stories about Broadway actors, chorus girls, musicians, and gangsters, a hunger that was fed by his uncle Oscar Radin and, a few years later, by his oldest brother, Harry, whose beautiful new wife, Pearl Eaton, would appear, resplendently blond, with marcelled curls, in all the newspapers.

Max's health continued to decline. He had always had a persistent smoker's cough but was now plagued by exhaustion and was experiencing a weight loss his wiry frame could ill afford. His sons knew not to bother him, leaving the house at first light and remaining outdoors as long as possible. Even Hebrew school was a welcome change from 1420 Fifth Avenue when Max was in one of his moods.

But the gloom was often relieved by Uncle Samuel Radin, who was a welcome guest at Annie's table. Oscar remembered his frequent visits as great events in his childhood, for Samuel was a raconteur of the first magnitude, equally at home discussing "Balzac, Gilbert and Sullivan, and the Kneisel Quartet." He could discourse on any subject, or so it seemed to his young nephew, who thirsted after the knowledge and experience his worldly uncle represented.

• • •

In 1918 Uncle Oscar returned to Pittsburgh to conduct the orchestra for a new musical comedy called *Ladies First,* showcasing the popular vaudevillean Nora Bayes. Radin had begun to make a name for himself in New York conducting shows and revues at the Winter Garden. When he returned to Pittsburgh, he was a hero to all the Levant sons. This was Oscar's first live theatre experience, and he was thrilled to be sitting with his parents in the crowded hall.

The musical was something of a blur to Oscar, except during the second act when the show stopped and Nora Bayes came down front to perform what amounted to a song recital. "After one chorus of the first song," Oscar later recalled,

> my attention left Bayes and remained fixed on the playing of the pianist. I had never heard such fresh, brisk, unstudied, completely free and inventive playing—all within a consistent frame that set off her singing perfectly.

The pianist was a barely twenty-year-old composer by the name of George Gershwin. He had patterned this "free and inventive playing" on that of the black musicians he had observed performing in Harlem nightclubs, but none of this would have mattered much to twelve-year-old Oscar, for whom Gershwin's playing opened a door to thrilling, transcendental possibilities. Oscar's playing would never be quite the same afterward, though it would be six years before the two pianists would meet. Oscar was inspired by hearing Gershwin play, but the inspiration stirred another emotion that living with three talented siblings had made familiar: envy. He would later write, somewhat facetiously, of the incident: "Thus were established the two characteristics I have nurtured ever since as the dominating influences of my life—jealousy and revenge."

3

The "Paderooski" of Colwell Street

Jack Paar: "What did you want to be when you were a kid, Oscar?"

Oscar Levant: "An orphan."

AT THE TRADITIONAL AGE OF THIRTEEN, OSCAR LEVANT WAS BAR mitzvahed on a Thursday morning at eight o'clock, in a service attended only by his grandfather and the few regular inhabitants of the synagogue at that hour.

Grandpa Radin met his grandson in front of the house and walked him to *shul*. Once inside, Grandpa Radin, who was in charge of the service that morning, pointed to the appropriate passage in the Torah, which he chanted and which Oscar dutifully repeated in his high, nervous voice. There was no speech paying tribute to his parents, which is customary on such occasions. The Torah was rolled up and put back into the ark, and the two returned home in silence. No other family member had attended.

Back at 1420 Fifth Avenue, Max and Abraham celebrated with a glass of schnapps while Oscar waited for his bar mitzvah gift. The family sat down to dinner. Oscar listened for clues about his present. Even as he got ready for bed he held out the slim hope it would be there waiting for him in the morning. But there was no gift for the boy everyone said was so gifted. Oscar was stunned. He left for school the next morning, perplexed and miserable.

Perhaps Oscar's bar mitzvah was the first opportunity Max had to show his displeasure over his youngest son's rebelliousness. If he neglected to attend Oscar's bar mitzvah, then he might also have refused to allow Annie to give her son a bar mitzvah gift, the traditional fountain pen or wristwatch. Oscar received nothing.

A marked difference in Oscar's behavior followed his uncelebrated bar mitzvah. Discipline was rigid at Fifth Avenue High School, a few blocks from Oscar's house. Graduates from the school say that "it was unheard of to sass a teacher. Students were monitored as they marched between classes in a single file according to class academic rank." Into this strict regimentation stepped Oscar Levant. A dutiful student at Forbes Elementary School, Oscar the good son would be replaced by Oscar the maverick as he increasingly defied his teachers and turned his back on his family.

To begin with, Annie kept Oscar in short pants long after other boys his age were allowed to wear trousers. To compensate, Oscar started smoking five-cent cigars at the tender age of twelve. The sight of this scowling boy in short pants with a stogie in the corner of his mouth must have astonished his teachers.

The Fifth Avenue High School was a four-story, Gothic-style, yellow-brick structure, considered at the time a building of rare beauty. In 1919, when Oscar entered its halls, its student enrollment was predominantly Jewish. Oscar's report cards were poor, consistently showing D's and C's. He earned B's only in music. He did manage to earn two A's, in orchestra. His poor grades were a reflection of his even poorer attendance record: In the first quarter of the twelfth grade, which is as far as he got, he had forty-five absences and was tardy twenty-eight times. In a school where students did not "sass their teachers," Oscar gained a reputation as a troublemaker and wise guy, even when it came to the school's most popular teacher, Oscar Demmler, who taught music and orchestra and who early recognized Oscar's gifts.

Demmler gave private music lessons on the piano and violin and in fact became Oscar's teacher for a while, replacing Martin Miessler. Still preferring playing ball to practicing, Oscar had to be dragged in from baseball games for his weekly lesson with Demmler. Oscar's pals would see the music teacher coming around the corner looking for Oscar, who was usually one alleyway ahead of him.

Demmler—with his pleasant, round, open face and thinning hair over a very pink pate—was a born pedagogue. Most of his students adored him, remembering him with admiration, except for Oscar, for whom the double whammy of having Demmler as his teacher both at home and at school was simply too much. Displacing some of the anger and frustration he felt toward his father, Oscar behaved badly toward his genial mentor.

Their first meeting was memorable. It was on the day before a much-anticipated recital to be given by a pianist who had become a god in the Levant household and in music-loving households across the country—Ignacy Jan Paderewski. The concert program had been advertised for weeks in advance. On Oscar's first day of high school, the twelve-year-old boy in knickers sauntered into Demmler's class-room and asked, "Do you want to hear what Paderewski is going to play tomorrow night?"

Demmler expected him to rattle off the program. Instead, Oscar proceeded to the piano in the corner of the room and played through Paderewski's whole recital.

Demmler was astonished, immediately warming to this cocksure boy, and he encouraged him to join the student orchestra; he later programmed a piece of Mendelssohn's for piano and orchestra to showcase Oscar's talent.

Demmler often took his students to concerts given by the Philadel-phia Symphony Orchestra conducted by Leopold Stokowski, who quickly became one of Oscar's heroes. Each program was discussed and illustrated beforehand, with Demmler on the violin and Oscar on the piano.

Oscar would later write about his indebtedness to Demmler in *The Etude,* a magazine for music students and teachers:

> I got to know a great deal of piano literature—vocal, chamber, orches-tral, everything . . . also, I accompanied the school glee club and orchestra. That was a great advantage, particularly for a pianist. Or-chestral playing can be learned only through orchestral playing—and a lot of it. . . . You have to adjust yourself to other standards of rightness; you learn to think, to question, to weigh values; most of all, to cooper-ate.

But his cooperation would be short lived.

Under Demmler's guidance Oscar experienced the absolute joy of being featured in an orchestra. However, as he progressed through Fifth Avenue High his behavior worsened, and his frequent truancies got him into trouble with the school authorities. Oscar began to dis-place his frustrations onto all the authority figures around him, in-cluding his patient and dedicated music teacher. Oscar failed to show up for rehearsals, and in a final act of rebellion he quit the orchestra, announcing in front of his music appreciation class that Demmler was forced to attend because he was paid to show up, but Oscar Levant wasn't!

It is significant that Oscar's relationship with Demmler was inaugurated by a Paderewski recital. The adored Paderewski—or "Paderooski," as he was called by his vast public—was one of the most romantic figures of his day, rivaling Liszt in his ability to attract legions of female admirers, who on occasion stormed the concert stage during his performances. In spite of his tremendous popularity, he was not always taken seriously by his fellow pianists. Critics complained about his wrong notes and inaccurate rhythms, but the public continued to heap adulation—and money—at the feet of this *artiste,* who fulfilled the popular romantic notion of what a great pianist should be like. Paderewski earned an estimated $10 million from his frequent concert tours in America. The pianist Moritz Rosenthal went to hear the phenomenon in London and came out shrugging his shoulders, commenting wittily, "Yes, he plays well, I suppose, but he's no Paderewski."

The specter of Paderewski—Everyman's idea of a musical genius— was raised by Oscar's mother, whose own taste in music was Romantic and for whom any feeling of nobility and grandeur were the ingredients of great art. That Oscar had astonishing technical ability but lacked physical grace pained her. Oscar instinctively knew how Annie felt, and he came to loathe his own gawkiness, developing an exaggerated self-consciousness. He was growing taller and long legged, and his skin had begun to blossom into an adolescent's complexion, sprouting "like a radish garden" overnight.

In his junior year of high school, an incident occurred that would lay the groundwork for one of Oscar's most enduring phobias. His wit and conversation were just beginning to develop, but they were better suited to the alleys and pool halls of Fifth Avenue than to a genteel school mixer. One evening he slunk into the gymnasium, where a school dance was under way.

Too self-conscious to ask the more glamorous girls in his class to dance, he approached a rather plain girl who stood off to the side. A contest was announced, and Oscar found himself waltzing with his partner, solemnly guiding her in simple steps, concentrating on each move. One by one, couples were tapped on the shoulder by a chaperone, thereby eliminated from the dance floor. Oscar began to think the unthinkable: Knock-kneed Levant was still waltzing! Just two couples were left. Finally, the only other couple remaining was escorted from the dance floor. Oscar stood with his dancing partner, beaming, astonished that he had won the contest.

The school coach, a man named Briggs, strode forward and presented Oscar and his partner each with a lemon while the rest of the dancers laughed at the winners of the booby prize for being the worst dancers on the floor.

In later years, Oscar would never allow a lemon to be served to him, its image conjuring up his adolescent humiliation. He would heap imprecations on any hapless waiter who served a wedge of lemon with his meal.

It was not long before Oscar felt his first romantic stirrings. Rose—her last name is not known—was a radiant girl who was in Demmler's music appreciation class with Oscar. True to his tough-boy façade, Oscar was ashamed of the tender feelings she inspired in him. He was habitually tongue-tied in her presence, though he arranged many "chance meetings" and even managed to walk her home once. Their romance never got beyond that point, but she would return to haunt him in other ways.

In the middle of Oscar's third year of high school, on December 24, 1921, just three days before Oscar's fifteenth birthday, Max Levant died. The cause of death stated on his death certificate was lobar pneumonia. He had recovered before from debilitating coughing spells, but his wheezing filled the house, and in the last year of his life he would often have to take to his couch after only an hour or two of work. But the bronchial condition that had plagued his adult years was not the cause of his painful and lingering death. Max Levant suffered from rectal cancer.

Pneumonia may have carried him off, or, in the absence of any cure for cancer but the knife, the doctor may have left Max's pneumonia untreated to allow him a more merciful death. It is also possible that pneumonia was written on the death certificate because in the early years of the century, cancer was still regarded with dread and shame. As late as 1914, cancer was believed to be highly contagious, and families of cancer victims often burned the clothes and bedding of the deceased patient, hiding the cause of death from relatives.

Besides the vast array of quack remedies that proliferated at the turn of the century, the only medical treatments for cancer were surgery and the masking of pain by opiates. Opium and morphine were palliatives against acute pain, insomnia, and diarrhea. In 1921, the year of Max's death, morphine, the only treatment sanctioned to ease Max's remaining weeks and days, was still freely available. Oscar would have witnessed Pfaff's Drug Store delivery boys arriving at all hours with vials of morphine, but it is unlikely that he was told why his father was so sick and why Annie retreated deeper into the sickroom, unable to cope with her intractable youngest son.

Max's death was a terrible blow to Oscar. His brothers Ben and Harry had by now left home and were doing well, having weathered the storms caused by defying their implacable but loving father, but Oscar would never be able to resolve his differences with his father now. Instead, he would carry an unresolved anger toward all authority figures. Max died before Oscar was able to find his own direction and force his father—like Jacob wrestling with the angel—to bless him. The shock of Max's death was so intense that Oscar could not even mourn his passing. "My father was a great man," he would write years later, though he would never be able to speak about his father's illness and death.

Oscar virtually dropped out of school after Max's funeral, unable to concentrate, unable to control his behavior. His father's death wrought profound changes in the household, and Oscar was the most affected. How could Annie control her youngest son's growing fascination with bookmakers, his inveterate crapshooting, his truancies from school? Was this tough-guy son going to be her one failure?

Times were now hard for Annie. Max had left her property on Greenfield Avenue that he had invested in, but she still had Oscar and Honey to look out for. She managed to get Oscar a job selling ladies' shoes, but that was a short-lived endeavor, as Oscar couldn't muster the smooth manner so essential to the successful shoe salesman.

Annie felt she had to get her son out of Pittsburgh and away from the bad influences of Colwell Street. Oscar would later claim that he had convinced Annie to send him to New York, but it is more to the point that school was no longer an option for this brilliant, troubled, and sensitive boy.

Music was Oscar's only refuge from the street and from the sad sight of Max's empty shop, the watches with their works open, the dozens of stopped clocks. But with Max gone, Annie could at last carry out her plan for her youngest and most gifted son. Hadn't Miessler told her that Oscar was an outstanding student, that he had already developed "a personal approach and a mature grasp of the music he was playing"?

So it was decided. They would take the train to New York, where he would continue with his piano study. In a move reminiscent of their earlier trip to Philadelphia, Annie packed their bags and they left the house at 1420 Fifth Avenue. Oscar would never live in that house again.

No doubt the prospect of New York was thrilling, with its theatres, nightclubs, Carnegie Hall, and Broadway, but Oscar was angry with his mother for forcing him to leave home. In short, he felt abandoned, and before the train even pulled out of Union Station, his exultation turned to despair. Failing to secure his father's blessing on his new career, he had wrestled with the angel and had lost.

PART II

The Emperors of
Broadway

4

The Main Stem

"Integrity is a lofty attitude assumed by someone
who is unemployed."

IN FEBRUARY 1922 ANNIE ACCOMPANIED OSCAR TO NEW YORK AND
stayed with him for a week, anxiously settling him into a furnished
room before she departed for Pittsburgh. Though Harry Levant was
not around to ease Oscar's loneliness, he put him in touch with what
would be the first of a long parade of Oscar's shadier companions—a
bookmaker named Benny Kaplan, twelve years Oscar's senior, who
took the adolescent boy under his wing. He introduced Oscar to
three other fellows who became his roommates in a brownstone
apartment on West Eightieth Street.

Ironically, Oscar found himself in a situation mirroring that of his
childhood: He was sharing two rooms, dominated by a baby grand,
with three older males, just as he had with his brothers. One of them
was Rabelaisian, one "a gentlemanly homosexual," the third an Italian who ran a Western Union office and who would later run afoul of
the law.

Fifteen-year-old Oscar was desperately homesick, and he begged
his mother to let him return to Pittsburgh, but to no avail. At great
personal sacrifice she was sending Oscar money to pay for his piano
instruction, and Harry was helping out by sending him five dollars

each week. It was obvious to Annie that her youngest son was destined for a concert career and it was her duty to see that he got there.

The means by which she would achieve her goal was through the Polish pedagogue Sigismond Stojowski, a highly regarded teacher and disciple of Paderewski. Unfortunately for Oscar, however, Stojowski's resemblance to Max Levant in appearance and manner, not to mention his connection to his mother's hero, Paderewski, guaranteed that their relationship would be brief.

Stojowski looked like Central Casting's idea of a piano teacher with his penetrating, deep-set eyes, his expertly manicured beard bristling above an immaculate cravat, his head carried as if it were already a bust on a pedestal. Stojowski was in his early fifties when he accepted Oscar as a pupil. His reputation had been established with a series of published compositions and by a fruitful relationship with his countryman and mentor Paderewski, who had performed Stojowski's Prologue, Scherzo, and Variations. In 1916 Stojowski's *Prayer for Poland* had debuted at Carnegie Hall with the New York Symphony Orchestra. After having concertized widely in Europe, Stojowski now wrote extensively on piano teaching and devoted his life to pedagogy.

Stojowski was a shrewd and demanding taskmaster. As if condemned to repeat the past, Oscar was immediately put to work on Czerny exercises. "There are a certain number of things without which no pianist can do—scales, five-finger exercises, and arpeggios," Stojowski believed. "Czerny is the first and indispensable source of study." He felt that the structure of the hand was not suited for the piano, so finger-strengthening exercises were *de rigueur*. He was fond of quoting Paderewski on this point: "Among the various kinds of memory—aural, visual, and so on—the most reliable at the piano is the muscular memory of the finger."

Stojowski warned Oscar of the perils of composing, which he deemed "a career of luxury" since music copyists charged so much. But Oscar would eventually wonder whether playing the piano was also "a career of luxury," as he would find himself unable to make the transition from giving recitals arranged by his teacher to competing with the conservatory-trained pianists. He would soon find that without financial support, or the backing of a conservatory, he would have no entree to the concert stage.

In his first lonely months in the city, Oscar was comforted by a correspondence initiated by his former schoolmate Rose, the "radiant girl" from his music appreciation class. Oscar was at first delighted to hear from her—here was another link to Pittsburgh—but his growing habit of rejecting that which he most craved asserted itself, and he abruptly broke off the correspondence. "As enthralled as I was," he later confessed, "this correspondence intruded on my solitary and bleak attitude that writing to a girl betrayed indulgence and weakness of character." More to the point, however, snubbing Rose was his way of lashing out at those who had hurt him, using Rose as a surrogate for his mother. She had, after all, abandoned him, and Max had abandoned him, too, by dying. Feeling rejected and angry, Oscar declined the one innocent offer of friendship that had come his way, punishing Rose and himself. He would later bitterly regret it.

Oscar had time to brood—and to read. He read voraciously and indiscriminately, becoming the kind of vastly read youth whose references to history, poetry, and music were erudite and surprising and hid great gaps in his education.

Oscar landed in New York in 1922 during Prohibition, in the era of the flapper. That year, George Herman "Babe" Ruth became an outfielder for the New York Yankees. On Broadway, a comedy about East Side immigrant life called *Abie's Irish Rose* began its record-breaking run of 2,532 performances. Eugene O'Neill's *The Hairy Ape* and Luigi Pirandello's *Six Characters in Search of an Author* also opened during 1922. Silent films of note included *Nanook of the North*, *The Prisoner of Zenda*, *Robin Hood* with Douglas Fairbanks, and a D. W. Griffith picture starring the Gish sisters, *Orphans of the Storm*. The Fatty Arbuckle scandal rocked Hollywood, leading to the creation of the censorious Will H. Hays office to oversee production codes in the industry. T. S. Eliot's "The Waste Land" was published, as well as Sinclair Lewis's *Babbitt* and F. Scott Fitzgerald's *The Beautiful and Damned*. Popular songs of the day included "Toot, Toot, Tootsie, Good-bye" from the Broadway revue *Bombo,* a "Negro convict song" titled "Water Boy," Irving Berlin's "Some Sunny Day," and a musical rendition of Joyce Kilmer's poem "Trees."

New York City's Broadway—sometimes called "the main stem" by its denizens—reveled in an unprecedented flowering of theatre, music shows, and revues.

Go *shpatzerin,* Harry would write to Oscar (Yiddish for "Go! Walk! Discover!"). Oscar did so, often in the company of his book-maker friend Benny Kaplan. Benny would take bets in unusual locales, with Oscar tagging along—in a woman's lingerie shop at 1607 Broadway, for example, a building that also housed the music publishing firm owned by Irving Berlin. Oscar hung around their offices, later remembering:

There was much action among song pluggers, song demonstrators, vaudeville acts, and sometimes great celebrities. I once had the opportunity to hear the two great Negro pianists of the period, Lucky Roberts and Jimmy Johnson; the latter was to write the immortal Charleston for a show called "Running Wild."

The rare appearances of Irving Berlin were accompanied by "noisy genuflections" among the staff, the song pluggers, and the starstruck hangers-on.

On other jaunts Benny would take Oscar to Forty-fifth Street and Seventh Avenue, where the buses would languish before starting their runs. A clutch of bookies would wait there, taking bets before the departure of the Chinatown bus. On a few occasions Benny involved Oscar in gin deliveries to the Pennsylvania Hotel. After each of these forays into the gin-running business, Benny would perform a set ritual that mesmerized Oscar: "He would urinate into a glass and study it intently for the 'tortuous threads' indicating gonorrhea."

Though Oscar was at first too lonely to notice it, the Jazz Age—F. Scott Fitzgerald's term—was busting out all over the city, in lavish nightclub openings and in jubilant speakeasies. With Harry's five dollars in his pocket, Oscar began to experience the kingdom of Broadway. Not only did he discover a glorified, expanded version of Colwell Street, but he was immersed in a whole other realm of music that would compete for his heart and soul with the classical and Romantic music he had imbibed at home.

At 1420 Fifth Avenue, popular music had been forbidden. Annie and Max had made it clear that the discipline of music meant mastering the great European composers. The syncopated tunes pouring out of Colwell Street dives—like Irving Berlin's "Alexander's Ragtime Band"—were considered a dangerous influence. But like all things forbidden, the popular tunes of the day were siren songs to the developing ear of Oscar Levant.

One of Broadway's greatest attractions was Florenz Ziegfeld's *Midnight Frolics* at the rooftop garden of the New Amsterdam Theatre. Dancing, inter-table telephones, and after-theatre suppers were featured in the rooftop garden; the *Frolics* was a forerunner of the modern floor show. It flourished until 1922, so Oscar would have seen the show in its final, extravagant year. He was dazzled by the stunning Ziegfeld showgirls. Will Rogers was one of Ziegfeld's biggest attractions, along with Gilda Gray, who introduced the "Shimmy" in 1922.

Convinced that he was too ugly and awkward ever to be loved by a pretty girl, Oscar hungered for the beautiful, powdered darlings of Ziegfeld's *Follies* and *Frolics*. He felt that his own worth could only be proven by the attentions of a nymphlike showgirl. He would one day describe his taste in women as tending toward the empty-headed-but-gorgeous type:

> I always liked girls who were shallow . . . girls who had no personality or emotional depth, and who were temperamentally bloodless. This enabled me to endow them with all kinds of mystery.

Oscar lived for Harry's weekly letters and the five-dollar bill that would flutter out of the envelope, landing on the worn carpet of his rented room. He was always hard up for cash, now that he was obliged to rent a practice room, pay a succession of sour-faced landladies, and still have something left over to get him into the *Midnight Frolics*. He needed to fill his senses with the sight of a dozen girls in feathers and ruffled French knickers kicking in unison. Of all his needs, keeping himself fed was the lowest priority. On occasion he was reduced to stealing a sandwich, slapping an empty palm on the counter as if it concealed a coin. The mere sight of a delicatessen, with its salamis, smoked fish, and pastrami sandwiches, "looked like the Louvre" to the famished boy. But it bothered him that Annie was sending him money; it hurt his pride. He felt he should be sending her money instead.

Oscar hungered for a chance to take part in Broadway's musical world. He would soon have that opportunity, thanks to Harry Levant, who returned to New York to conduct the last two weeks of the run of *Spice of 1922,* a Shubert revue designed to compete with Ziegfeld's *Follies* and Irving Berlin's *Music Box Revue*. The revue featured the silent film star Valeska Suratt and two chorus girls who would go on to bigger things—Nancy Carroll and Joan Crawford. Harry took his baby brother backstage to meet Miss Suratt, where he was asked to give an impromptu recital for the silent film star.

Counting on Oscar's remarkable ability to sight-read music, Harry arranged for him to play in the pit orchestra during the show's final week. Oscar, however, was not familiar with the technical terms for orchestration, and he blew his big opportunity. At one point in the show, a male dancer was supposed to toss his partner high over his head; the accompanying music read "Tacit," signifying complete silence as the dancer sailed through the air.

"I ruined it," Oscar remembered, "by playing 'oom-pah-pah' while the dancer, Midgie Miller, was catapulted up into the houselights." Oscar remembered the incident as "the great catastrophe of that week," though it didn't diminish his appetite for Broadway musical shows. It did, however, add an edge of anxiety to his feelings about performing. If he was being tempted away from his classical training by the siren call of popular music, this incident sent him fleeing back to the rented practice room where he embraced his Stojowskian lessons with the fervor of a convert. Perhaps his father had been right all along—to make your living as a musician was to cheapen yourself.

By wintertime Oscar did not have the luxury of choice. He needed money. He was barely able to cover his rent, his practice room, his meals. Despite his embarrassing faux pas in the pit orchestra of *Spice of 1922,* Oscar made up his mind to try his luck with the theatrical booking agents in order to get work playing the piano.

The booking man's office was a brutal place, particularly for a classically trained pianist. Oscar sat, hour after hour, in a succession of agencies on Broadway, watching a parade of "toothy tenors, lady hoofers, twin acts, clog dancers, acrobats, and comedians" filing in and out. He was eventually given his first job playing with a violinist for a banquet at the swanky Hotel Astor, just west of Times Square.

When Oscar arrived at the hotel, he was bowled over by its opulence. The Hotel Astor, a $7 million extravaganza built to be the finest hotel in the world, had opened its doors in 1904. A ten-story edifice of red brick and limestone, the hotel boasted in its advertising more than five hundred rooms and "the most Recently Invented Safeguards Against Fire, Bad Air, and All Forms of Discomfort."

Ascending by an express elevator near the Forty-fourth Street entrance, Oscar and the violinist entered a ballroom where the banquet was under way. It was actually a stag party—the revelers, bootleg drunk and raucous, were oblivious to the arrival of their hired musicians. Oscar was terrified of playing for a roomful of drunken men.

Unfortunately, the first request was for "East Side, West Side," New York City's theme song and a favorite of Governor Al Smith's. Oscar had never even heard of it.

"How does it go?" he timidly asked the reveler who had made the request. "Can you hum it?"

Incredulous, the crowd booed its disapproval. "My ignorance was a frontal attack on New York culture," Oscar later wrote. Luckily the violinist was also an adept pianist, and he was able to rescue Oscar from the surly crowd. But the ordeal was not over. The two musicians were handed some sheet music to accompany a dancing girl hired for the evening. After the opening trills, she appeared at one end of the ballroom, completely nude. Oscar had never seen a naked woman before, and he nearly fainted.

Despite his less-than-spectacular debut, Oscar continued to get bookings at some of the city's fancier hotels. His second engagement was with a trio at the Ambassador, the grand hotel that dominated Park Avenue at Fifty-first Street. Walking past the green stone walls and marble columns of the main floor, Oscar and his fellow musicians were led into the hotel's restaurant, a splendid room with gilded Roman moldings. Here Oscar's knowledge of chamber music was more in keeping with the atmosphere, and the trio alternated chamber music with popular tunes during matinee and lunch hours. This pleasant engagement would not last long, however. One evening when he was playing Mozart, a diner requested "a livelier tune," and Oscar responded by playing Bach. It cost him his job.

But he soon got other bookings, and Oscar found he was able to make good money as a pianist, as long as he introduced popular music into his repertoire. He continued to study with Stojowski, but he doubted he would ever make as much money playing Beethoven as he did playing Berlin. He wondered at the futility of trying to become a concert artist, without conservatory backing or the sponsorship of a *grande dame*. For that he would need serious money: enough to rent a concert hall, pay for publicity and promotion, and sustain himself during the long years it would take to build a reputation in arguably the most competitive field in all of the arts.

After several months in New York, Oscar could scarcely think of anything but returning to magnetic Pittsburgh, to see what had become of his old Colwell Street pals and, like Coleridge's Ancient Mariner, describe what he had seen and heard to anyone who would listen. Oscar was beginning to doubt he would ever have a concert career, and he wanted to go home.

5

Stairway to Paradise

"It didn't really affect me,
except for the rest of my life."

OSCAR MADE PLANS TO RETURN TO PITTSBURGH, BUT SOMETHING IN-
tervened to delay his departure. To the delight of thousands of music
lovers, Paderewski announced his intention to return to America for
a concert tour, promising seventy concerts in two dozen major cities.
Stojowski arranged for his students to attend Paderewski's Carnegie
Hall concert on December 7, 1922, followed by a private recital at the
Plaza Hotel by twelve of his best pupils. Oscar was to play Paderewski's "Légende." At last Oscar would have a chance to go before the
maestro himself and learn from the source whether or not he had the
potential for a concert career.

Paderewski's five-year tenure as premier of Poland had led to ru-
mors that he could no longer perform, that he had lost his health and
his fortune. But his triumphant concert tour of America, undertaken
when he was in his sixty-third year, proved the rumormongers
wrong. The tour was a tremendous success.

At the recital arranged by Stojowski, Paderewski sat impassively
through the parade of nervous students who performed his compositions. Oscar later recalled:

[At] the end of the piece, Paderewski, who had an imposing, magnetic personality, would congratulate the performer with a handshake and some words of praise. A girl who had cried when she made a mistake got a special kiss on the forehead—something she wouldn't have received if she'd played it correctly. This was my first personal contact with a world-famous artist.

It's hard to know what really took place after Oscar performed "Légende." Oscar belittled the experience in his memoirs: "As Paderewski patted me on the head, he restrained his foot from kicking me." What actually happened, according to one of Oscar's cousins, is that Paderewski had said to Stojowski that no one could teach Oscar anything about technique, but "he doesn't have the soul of a concert pianist."

So Oscar was kicked by Paderewski after all. Like the slap laid across his cheek by his father, Paderewski's remark would always be a reminder that no matter how beautifully he played, someone would rise up to shame him.

Six months after Oscar first landed in New York, he managed to raise enough money to return to Pittsburgh. It happened that his brother Harry was also in Pittsburgh at the time, as the conductor for an Al Jolson vehicle called *Bombo.* Jolson was at the height of his form and was considered by many—including himself—to be the world's greatest entertainer. For Oscar Levant, Al Jolson would always represent an antidote to the burden of Paderewski: a performer who was as famous and as adored as Paderewski but in the parallel universe of popular culture. Jolson's exuberant performances in blackface had made him the most popular box-office attraction in New York. Oscar, his brother Harry, and his uncle Oscar Radin were kinder than most in their remarks about Jolson, who was as disliked by his professional colleagues as he was adored by his fans. There were the stories about Jolson's monumental ego: his habit of stopping a show in the middle of a performance and, pointing to the rest of the astonished cast, telling the audience "These folks have been working hard tonight—why don't we tell them to go home and just let Jolie sing!" Jolson insisted that the Shuberts tear out precious aisle seats in the Winter Garden to make room for a runway down which Jolson would prance and caper. (The promenade would become known as the "Bridge of Thighs" when long-legged showgirls sashayed out into the audience.)

Oscar admired Jolson's *chutzpah;* he was impressed by the level of

Jolson's ambition and by his monomania. As Irving Howe has written in *World of Our Fathers,* his study of Jewish life in America, Jolson was "emblematic of the energies, ambitions, and yearnings unleashed by the Jewish immigrant experience." In some ways, Oscar, the classically trained young pianist, must have felt an affinity with Jolson's sense of abandon. The critic Gilbert Seldes in *The Seven Lively Arts* observed in Jolson and his female equivalent, Fanny Brice, qualities of "daemonic abandon." He attributed this to their status of being outside the mainly Protestant business community that rules most of America. "Jolson and Brice," he wrote, ". . . gave something to America which America lacks and loves . . . both are out of the dominant class. Possibly this accounts for their fine contempt for artificial notions of propriety."

The Yiddish performer as a blackface minstrel struck a chord in the American public. In Irving Howe's phrase, Jolson brought together "Yiddish schmaltz and blackface sentiment":

> some deeper affinity [was] also at work. Blackface became a mask of Jewish expressiveness, with one woe speaking through the voice of another. Gershwin's biographer Isaac Goldberg . . . found a musical kinship between the Negro blue note and the blue note of Chasidic chant.

The daemonic spirit would be embraced by Oscar with increasing fury, and his admiration for Jolson would remain intact throughout his life.

On his return to Pittsburgh, Oscar relished feeling like a big shot, lording it over his young cousins and Colwell Street buddies. He was reluctant to return to New York; he dreaded the loneliness of his life in the great metropolis. Although he appreciated his lessons with Stojowski, his face still burned at the memory of Paderewski's assessment. But he dreaded disappointing his mother.

One of his earliest jobs after returning to New York was to play for his sister-in-law Pearl Eaton's tap-dancing class, which she conducted in a Broadway studio. He was paid a dollar for each class, not a lot of money, but Oscar had a crush on his sister-in-law and would probably have played for nothing. Pearl's quick wit and intelligence dazzled Oscar, and the dance studio was frequently visited by Pearl's sister Mary Eaton, whose appearance that year in *Kid Boots* had made her one of Broadway's darlings. The sound of a roomful of tap shoes thundering in Oscar's ears sweetened his return to New York.

One of the tunes used to put Pearl's fledgling dancers through their paces was a new Gershwin song called "(I'll Build a) Stairway to Paradise." Oscar had never heard of it, and he may not have recalled that the composer was the same lively pianist who had accompanied Nora Bayes four years earlier in Pittsburgh. "Stairway" was Oscar's first introduction to a Gershwin jazz-inspired Broadway tune.

Oscar's first extended engagement as a paid musician was in a roadhouse along the Hudson River called the Mikado Inn, an establishment presided over by a corpulent Japanese who was known as "Admiral Moto." Oscar was hired to play popular tunes with a three-piece orchestra on the weekends and classical music with a violinist during the week.

Roadhouses sprang up in the early 1920s as a result of Prohibition, usually fronting as a restaurant and sometimes offering a stage show or an orchestra—a phonograph in the smaller joints—but the main business was conducted in the back room with a full supply of liquor. As Jimmy Durante and Jack Kofoed said in their book *Nightclubs*, "nearly all had rooms for rent—and you could either bring your own girl or get one there." Many roadhouses dotted the countryside and suburbs of New York, from Yonkers to the farmlands of Long Island. Some were little more than honky-tonks in the midst of potato farms.

Oscar, who probably got the job at the Mikado Inn through a booking agent, played those crowded nights on an upright piano with a horizontal string across it—"a not too subtle hint for tips." As the evenings progressed and the clientele grew more boisterous and drunk, the most popular requests were the spiritual "Show Me the Way to Go Home," followed by "Yes, We Have No Bananas."

After the roadhouse closed for the night, Oscar would sleep in the cellar with a legion of Japanese waiters. As he read his letters from home in the drafty cellar, it wasn't long before homesickness again began to dog him. After six months of the Mikado Inn and Pearl Eaton's tap-dancing classes, Oscar again fled to Pittsburgh.

He returned to Pittsburgh in June, a month when even the grim light of that city takes on a hopeful, heavenly hue. This time he would see Rose and maybe bring himself to speak to her. For the last three days of the school year, Oscar waited unsuccessfully outside Fifth Avenue High for Rose to appear. It was only later, as he walked the Hill with a friend, that Oscar discovered that Rose had died. His first reaction upon hearing the news was not to betray the fact that he had known the dead girl. "I thought [it] would be a sign of weakness and unmanliness," he later recorded. "So I greeted his news with poker-faced rigidity." But Rose's death left him deeply shaken.

There is no record of how Rose died, though Oscar's cousin remembered that influenza, which had been epidemic five years earlier, was still claiming victims in Pittsburgh. In any event, Rose's death came too soon after the death of Oscar's father, and it reopened his wound.

A bewildered Oscar returned to New York and went back to work at the Mikado Inn. It was now summer, the height of the roadhouse season. Rose's family had sent him a picture of their daughter, which Oscar would take out of his wallet and study as he lay sleepless on a cot in the roadhouse cellar among twenty snoring waiters. One night he simply tore up the photograph. As with the other painful episodes in his life, a new phobia was taking shape: a dread of roses, which would culminate in a refusal to allow that flower in his home, even during the happier years of his married life.

On a trip home to Pittsburgh later that summer, ostensibly to play an engagement with a dance orchestra—by now his roadhouse experience had provided him with a "fluid, agile technique"—Oscar joined his brother Harry and his uncle Maurice ("Mickey") Radin in a pilgrimage to a Colwell Street whorehouse.

Harry inaugurated his youngest brother. "I loved Colwell Street," Oscar later recalled. "I was as devoted to that street and its madams and whores as I later became to Beethoven's Ninth Symphony."

Every prostitute had a pan of bichloride of mercury at her bedside, in which, to prevent the spread of venereal disease, customers would wash their genitals before having sex. It was a potent mixture, and it served as an unpleasant reminder of how one's recreational hours were spent. With his Uncle Mickey and brother Harry leading the way, Oscar underwent his baptism of bichloride of mercury. "They charged $1 straight, $2 French," Oscar remembered.

Oscar befriended the brothel's caterer, a boxer who had achieved local fame by beating Tony Canzoneri in the Olympics. Ever since Oscar had been a scrappy boy growing up in the Hill district, he had admired boxers for the qualities he felt he most keenly lacked: physical grace and confidence. On more than one occasion he had been forced to tangle with gangs of Irish toughs who chased Oscar and his cousins on their way to synagogue on Saturday morning. Proud that he had come up from the streets, Oscar would always revel in the company of boxers, gangsters, and other tough-guy characters.

Except for the occasional baseball game and boxing match and the serious work of studying with Stojowski, Oscar's life in New York was defined by steady employment at the Hudson River roadhouse, where he was bored by most of the music that was demanded of him. "Since I had been oriented to a different musical background," Oscar recalled, "I had an unhealthy contempt for most of the tunes we played." Oscar would have had to play, or fake, most of these popular tunes, though he found them repetitious and inane.

But he was discontented as well with the concert offerings of the day. He was impatient with the prevailing styles of music at both ends of the spectrum, and he felt a vague longing to collide with something new, original, and soul-stirring, something "worthy of envy."

Oscar described musical tastes in New York concert halls as "a slothful, degenerate, sybaritic, undiscriminating, post-war hysteria of enthusiasm for such pianists as Paderewski, Rachmaninoff, Hofmann, and Rosenthal." He felt the public was content to be "entertained rather than disturbed."

A case in point was Josef Stransky, the Czechoslovakian-born conductor of the New York Philharmonic Orchestra, who served in that post for twelve years before resigning amid a storm of widely differing critical opinion. Oscar would record his disillusionment with the mediocrity of Stransky's conducting, particularly in comparison with that of Leopold Stokowski, whom Oscar had heard conduct the Philadelphia Orchestra with his high school music class. (As a boy he had been struck by Stokowski's "beautiful hands and exquisite gestures.") About Stransky, Oscar observed, "his limitations are boundless."

But that was all about to change. On February 12, 1924, in a concert at Aeolian Hall, the Paul Whiteman Orchestra presented an "all-jazz" program, ambitiously and shrewdly billed as "An Experiment in Modern Music." Whiteman was attempting to satisfy the public's curiosity about the syncopated "Negro" music called jazz. The unequivocal hit of the program was George Gershwin's *Rhapsody in Blue*. Although some critics attacked the *Rhapsody*'s form as being "top-heavy" in the piano part, it was singled out as the most spectacular contribution to Whiteman's concert.

In 1924 jazz was controversial, denounced by the Vatican as "one of the causes of flagrant immorality," yet it was heralded by musicians and some critics as "the folk music of America," embodying American hopefulness and vitality. Much of the violent reaction against jazz was racist, attacking the "primitive" origins of jazz in "ignorant" African music. In Europe, however, composers had already begun experimenting with ragged time and jazz rhythms, such as Stravinsky's "Rag-time" for eleven instruments, Debussy's "The Golliwog's Cakewalk," and Darius Milhaud's *La Création du monde*. (Milhaud had actually lectured Americans on jazz during his 1920–21 tour of the United States.) Although in 1921 John Alden Carpenter's popular ballet *Krazy Kat* introduced jazz into concert music, the impact of Gershwin's *Rhapsody* was such that, in music historian Vivian Perlis's words,

> Jazz was considered a new discovery, as though it had just happened on the scene in time for white composers to use its lively and danceable rhythms in their concert music. Composers [like George Gershwin] made forays into Harlem to hear the way real jazz was played . . . and they suddenly began to talk about "riffs," "blue notes," and "breaks." . . . "Negroes" played jazz in nightclubs, but most of them could not read music, and therefore jazz was only art when incorporated into rhapsodies, symphonies, and ballets by white composers . . . for a brief time it seemed possible that our popular and concert musics, so hopelessly divided, might have found a way of blending.

Paul Whiteman was just the musician to pull off this feat of jazz and symphonic hybridism. And, as Perlis has observed, "black Americans puzzled over all this, including the question of how a bandleader with the incredible name of Whiteman had come to be called 'The King of Jazz.' "

Oscar probably responded not so much to the *Rhapsody*'s jazz effects and embellishments—in part provided by Whiteman's in-house arranger, Ferde Grofé—but to the melodies reminiscent of the Russian music Gershwin had heard in his youth. Oscar had heard those melodies, too. Never a true convert to jazz, Oscar would always prefer concert music and Broadway show tunes, but with *Rhapsody in Blue* Gershwin had forged a music that combined all three forms. The *Rhapsody* would resolve the conflict raging in Oscar's breast between classical and popular music.

For Oscar Levant, the "febrile tornado" that followed the premiere of the *Rhapsody* shattered his disdain for the saxophone players and drummers with whom he had been making his living, transforming it into excitement for the possible. Though Oscar does not record being present at the epochal Aeolian Hall concert, he heard the *Rhapsody* played by Paul Whiteman's Palais Royal Orchestra soon thereafter— it became the jewel in the crown of Whiteman's nightclub repertoire—and Oscar immediately committed it to memory. Here, he thought, was something worthy of envy.

Oscar had no way of knowing at the time that George Gershwin

had created the means by which Oscar Levant would become re-
nowned. Gershwin had brought into being Oscar's opportunity and
his torment: Levant's playing of the *Rhapsody* would bring him fame,
but it would also be an obstacle to his achieving anything like it on his
own.

Oscar's studies with Stojowski had enhanced his ability to pick up the
popular tunes of the day quickly and play them with great style: "I had
developed into what was called a flash pianist, full of technical ornamentation, appoggiaturas and cascading frills, but in the jazz lexi-
con, signifying absolutely nothing." Stojowski put Oscar to work
learning Debussy, but during one such lesson he confided in his pupil
his own fears about performing. He said that the mere thought of a
student who had stumbled at a particular passage could throw him off
balance during a recital. The maestro's words cut deep into Oscar's
mind, and he dove into the more advanced piano compositions of
Debussy with a new fear nibbling at him: that he might be one of
those students who stumbled during a concert, though he learned and
rehearsed each piece flawlessly. He worried that playing dance music
was eroding his concentration and undermining his technique. But
the development of his talent suited him perfectly to Gershwin's
compositions, which were often, like the *Rhapsody,* essentially conventional in structure but overlaid with jazz effects and flourishes.
    But when Oscar broke into a chorus of Gershwin's "Fascinating
Rhythm" in the middle of a session with Stojowski, the composer of
"Auf Sturm und Stille" was not amused. True to the pattern of behavior he had developed in adolescence, Oscar was chafing under
Stojowski's tutelage, convinced that whatever his gifts, he could not
satisfy the expectations of his elders. Oscar would soon quit his lessons, convinced that Paderewski was right—he would never achieve
a concert career.
    Years later, Oscar would write glowingly of his old teacher, under-
playing his struggle to be free of Stojowski's autocratic influence:

> a good deal of what I know of music and also what I feel about it owes
> its origin to Sigismond Stojowski (*please,* not Stokowski) who is not
> only a brilliant pedagogue but a warmly sympathetic human being.
> The several years I spent studying piano in New York with him re-
> main among the most profitable and worth remembering in my life.

By 1926 Stojowski would be completely supplanted by Oscar's
new hero, George Gershwin. Oscar was smitten, not only with

Gershwin's genius but with the possibilities of composing music that would encompass the old-world tastes of Annie and Max Levant while capturing the excitement and verve of Broadway and its environs—a realm that included Irving Berlin, Al Jolson, Duke Ellington, the Ziegfeld revues, and the sound of a dozen pretty girls tap-dancing in unison. Now that Broadway, jazz, and Tin Pan Alley had been lifted to symphonic heights, Oscar would be inspired to use his own classical training to compose popular music. He realized he didn't have to be another Paderewski—but could he be another George Gershwin? He might as well try, now that Colwell Street had come to the concert hall.

6

The Emperors of Broadway

"When I was young, I looked like Al Capone but I lacked his compassion."

BY JANUARY 1925 OSCAR WAS BEGINNING TO FEEL MORE AT HOME IN New York than in Pittsburgh. Harry Levant came back to town and took up residence at the Congress at 161 West Fifty-fourth Street with his wife, Pearl, and young daughter, Doris, inviting Oscar to move in with them. Life was once again sweet. The loneliness that had plagued Oscar during his first three years in New York at last subsided. In 1925 he would begin to come into his own, not as a concert pianist but as a dance band musician and man-about-town.

The Congress was a popular apartment building among musicians. Many well-known entertainers lived there. George White (the dancer and producer who had created the annual *Scandals* revues) occupied the penthouse apartment, and Mary Eaton lived one floor below the Levants. The parties were nonstop, and Oscar frequently headed downstairs to Mary Eaton's, where a group of Broadway celebrities would sing around the piano until dawn. Fanny Brice, Billy Rose, Gertrude Lawrence, Clifton Webb, and Marilyn Miller were among the luminaries attending these late-night soirées. Oscar began to develop the nocturnal habits that would remain with him the rest of his life. He stayed up all night to play the piano, rising in the afternoon, when eight-year-old Doris—nicknamed "Dossie"—would bring him the New York newspapers. He would then read the sports pages to Dossie while consuming two soft-boiled eggs and potfuls of coffee. Oscar was grateful to be part of a family again, and he was frequently moved to tears. On Monday mornings, when Dossie had to return to boarding school, Oscar would cry when the car came to pick her up. The sight of his little niece with her suitcase in tow must have stirred his own fear of abandonment.

Oscar soon landed a job with a big dance orchestra at the Knickerbocker Hotel. By now he could play just about anything; his training and talent were beginning to make themselves felt, restoring his old Pittsburgh cockiness. But Oscar chafed at the intrusiveness of his job, resenting the time it took away from reading, theatregoing, and attending concerts at Carnegie Hall. Without warning, Oscar quit, bidding farewell to the tuxedoed swells and swanky dames of the Knickerbocker.

No sooner had he hung up his tuxedo than another offer came—a job at Wallack's Theatre in a four-piece orchestra for a dramatic show called *Hell's Bells*. The play was forgettable except for the facts that Shirley Booth was making her theatrical debut as the ingenue and Humphrey Bogart played the juvenile lead. Oscar's sense of superiority to the music and to the rest of the orchestra was so palpable that he was fifteen minutes late on opening night, inexcusably delaying the curtain and infuriating the producers. He would often, during the run of *Hell's Bells*, sneak out of the theatre to participate in a secret dice game run by the McManus brothers, professional gamblers, returning just in time to play during the intermission.

Oscar had begun to drift back into his old Colwell Street habits, prowling a growing list of haunts along Broadway and fraternizing with gangsters. One of his new friends was an underworld figure known as "Big Frenchy" DeMange, whose resemblance to Babe Ruth endeared him to sports-loving Oscar.

Big Frenchy was a dangerous fellow—he had been one of the ringleaders of the infamous Hudson Dusters gang. He used his ill-gotten gains to invest in Broadway shows and nightclubs. Another gangster Oscar rubbed shoulders with was the sumptuously dressed Larry Fay, owner of the El Fey Club and possibly a role model for F. Scott Fitzgerald's Gatsby. Fay had gotten his start by smuggling bonded Canadian whiskey across the border. Impressed by Big Frenchy's style, Fay opened some of the fanciest nightclubs to flourish during Prohibition. He hired the best entertainers—Ruby Keeler, Barbara Stanwyck, and George Raft all started out as dancers in the El Fey.

The El Fey Club was Larry Fay's most popular speakeasy, featuring "Texas" Guinan, a hard-drinking, brassy blond and ex-singer who greeted each customer with a raucous, "Hello, sucker!" Celebrities poured through its doors—politicians, actors, debutantes, and newspapermen like Walter Winchell, who, introduced by Larry Fay, would soon befriend Oscar Levant. Fay aspired to high society, and his Great Neck, Long Island, mansion was filled with glittering guests who drank his bootleg liquor and partook of his fabulous repasts while snubbing their host. Fay wandered among his guests, an aloof, horse-faced but splendidly dressed loner, surrounded by silent, hulking bodyguards. His fortunes eventually collapsed and he was murdered, not by a rival gangleader but by a disgruntled doorman at one of his own nightclubs. Oscar described his death as "one of the ironies of the jungle in which [Fay] was one of the royal figures."

It is true that nightclub life in the twenties was rife with underworld figures. Why was Oscar so attracted to them? The presence of a burly bouncer with gangland connections must have made him feel safe. These older, more powerful men who were content to treat him like a kid brother evoked the camaraderie of his youth. Or maybe he was attracted to "the realm of high audacity" in which most gangsters operated.

The Mirador was one nightclub which went out of its way to shed its gangster image. "If you had a graduate course in Emily Post etiquette, proper evening attire, and an A-1 rating in Bradstreet, you could get in," wrote Jimmy Durante and Jack Kofoed in *Nightclubs*; ". . . even the waiters and busboys were supposed to come from noble families and talk three languages without errors."

Besides the Mirador, other popular nightclubs of the day were Jimmy Durante's Club Durant, the Trocadero, where Fred and Adele Astaire danced their brand of elegant "society" dancing before they broke into musical comedy, and the Club Alabam', which took advantage of the trend toward black music and black performers. The Cotton Club, the most famous of the Harlem night spots, introduced Duke Ellington to a white audience. At Small's, in Harlem, waiters danced the Charleston carrying loaded trays. There was the Cave of Fallen Angels, on Forty-sixth Street, and the Casanova, which featured singer Morton Downey. The notorious blues songbird Libby Holman—tried and acquitted for allegedly murdering her millionaire husband Smith Reynolds—sang at the Lido in 1929.

In spite of the clubs' efforts to maintain a façade of aloof elegance and sophistication, nightclub life could get wild. As gangsters invested heavily in the lucrative clubs, it would be impossible not to make the acquaintance of a mobster or two.

Oscar got a job working with a six-piece "society orchestra" at Ciro's, which many considered to be the smartest nightclub in New York. Oscar described this stint as his "first job with any status." The orchestra conductor was Dave Bernie, brother of Ben Bernie, a popu-lar bandleader at the Roosevelt Hotel. Oscar was making $100 a week with Dave Bernie's band and was now able to send money home to his mother—a source of enormous pride to him.

Impressed with Oscar's vigorous dexterity and style, Ben Bernie wanted him for his own orchestra and thought nothing of hiring him away from his brother. Oscar, always bored with routine and looking for an opportunity to thumb his nose at the boss, jumped ship. So in the spring of 1925, Oscar quit Dave Bernie's orchestra to join Ben Bernie's "Lads" at the Roosevelt Hotel. In doing so—though his pay was the same—he took a step up in the world of nightclub orchestras. Ben Bernie was a fearless promoter, a big personality, and a successful popularizer of the toned-down "jazz" style of dance music. He invented the much-copied bandleader ejaculation "Yowsuh!," which may have been a slurred imitation of black speech since white musicians were copying the slang of Harlem musicians.

When not in residence at the Roosevelt Hotel, the garrulous Bernie and his orchestra played the Palace and Rialto theatres on the same bill with performers like Ray "Rubberlegs" Bolger and George Raft, who did a show-stopping Charleston to "Sweet Georgia Brown." Ray Bolger was still just a kid in his teens, and he befriended Oscar. "You were not only in the orchestra," Bolger told him, "you *were* the orchestra." When they played the Winter Garden, where Harry Levant and Oscar Radin had had such success, Oscar couldn't help but feel—at least in the arena of popular music—that he had arrived. When *Variety* noted young vaudeville performers on their way up, their list for 1925 included Clifton Webb in a dance act with Mary Hay; a baritone named Walter Pidgeon; an ex–scholastic swimming champ turned hoofer, James Cagney; and in the midst of this litany: "The name of the piano player in Ben Bernie's orchestra at the Rialto Theatre, N.Y., is Oscar Levant."

Despite their frequent tiffs (Bernie fired and rehired Oscar several times), Ben Bernie appreciated Oscar's ability and recruited him to play piano for a Vocalion recording session of "Yes, Sir, That's My Baby" and "Collegiate" on August 10, 1925. It was the first record on which Oscar Levant appeared.

But except for the opportunity to play the *Rhapsody,* Oscar grew impatient with Ben Bernie's soft, slightly syncopated dance music, particularly when the members of the band were required to dress up in various national costumes—Swiss, Russian, or German. "This made me rather ill, particularly the Swiss Alpine hat," Oscar remembered.

Despite Oscar's reluctance to dress up in costume, Ben Bernie took a special interest in him and delighted in his combination of brashness and innocence. When the married bandleader started seeing a woman on the sly, it was Oscar whom he asked to come along as the "beard." Oscar did so, escorting Dorothy Wesley, who would become Bernie's second wife, to Reuben's restaurant nearly every night until "the old maestro" would show up, feign surprise, and pull up a chair to join them.

But Oscar was not always the beard. At eighteen, he was a good listener, he was funny, he had a growing reputation as a hot musician with a popular orchestra, and he loved women—particularly showgirls and their "pound cake beauty." That in itself, combined with his shy manner around women, was an appealing combination, and Oscar was soon taken over by a number of Ziegfeld beauties. Their attentions made him feel desirable for the first time in his life.

"Sax-o-phun"

"Long before I ever met George Gershwin
he had begun to impinge on my life."

PHIL CHARIG WAS ANOTHER OF BEN BERNIE'S FAVORITE SONS—OSCAR
called him a "coprotégé." Charig was an aspiring songwriter who had
landed the plum job of rehearsal pianist for Jerome Kern's 1925 musical comedy *Sunny*. Kern was one of the biggest names on Broadway—"the composer's composer" whose extraordinary melodic gifts
had modernized musical comedy. But it was George Gershwin whom
Phil Charig worshiped, and he ingratiated himself into the Gershwin
circle as the rehearsal pianist for two Gershwin musicals that season. In
late November 1925, Phil Charig had advanced to carrying Gershwin's briefcase and scores. He would tenderly place the Concerto in F
manuscript, which Walter Damrosch had commissioned for the New
York Symphony earlier that year, on the piano for Gershwin during
rehearsals at Carnegie Hall. It was Phil Charig who would teach Oscar
how to get started writing popular tunes for Broadway shows.

Charig first met Oscar in a cafeteria on Forty-third Street near
Broadway. Oscar struck him as a brash young upstart. With his feet up
on the table while leaning back dangerously in his chair, Oscar implored the dark-haired songwriter to introduce him to George Gersh-

win. Charig at first resisted—he jealously guarded his connection to his favorite composer, whose face would appear that summer on the cover of *Time* magazine. But if this was going to be a battle of devotions, Oscar had already demonstrated his special affinity for Gershwin music, having mastered the *Rhapsody* not only for Ben Bernie's orchestra but for occasional sit-ins with Paul Whiteman's Palais Royal Orchestra as well. Finally Charig agreed to introduce them.

The Gershwins were still living in the family's West 110th Street apartment when Charig brought an eager young Oscar to meet his new hero. When Charig arrived with Oscar in tow, George was working on the first movement of the Concerto with William Merrigan Daly, one of George's closest associates. Oscar felt that he was being "exposed, first hand, to history in the making," and he stammered some since-forgotten remark. George simply ignored him and continued with his work. Abashed, Oscar left, returning to his old room in Harry's apartment at the Congress, where *he* was often the center of attention at the piano in a room full of admirers. It would be months before the two men met again.

Charig was probably relieved that Oscar bombed in his first meeting with Gershwin—less competition in that intense inner circle—and thus he could afford to let his affection for Oscar flourish. Charig was soon talking up his young friend to other members of Gershwin's coterie, praising Oscar's ability to play Sibelius and "(I'll Build a) Stairway to Paradise" with equal confidence. Charig brought Oscar along on a visit to Emily and Lou Paley's, where Oscar would come into his own as a quick and dangerous wit.

At their brownstone on West Eighth Street in the heart of Greenwich Village, the Paleys held a lively salon on Saturday nights. Frequent guests included the Gershwins, Emily Paley's sister, Leonore Strunsky (soon to become Mrs. Ira Gershwin), the playwright S. N. Behrman; lyricist Howard Dietz, composer Vincent Youmans; and Buddy De Sylva; actors Sam Jaffe, John Huston, and Edward G. Robinson; Phil Charig, of course; and eventually, through Phil's good graces, Oscar Levant.

Emily and Lou Paley were a rather dashing couple in an unpretentious, bohemian way. Emily was a windswept, down-to-earth beauty, while Lou was solidly built and graceful, with a high forehead and light, thinning hair. He was a lyricist and a high school English teacher, and he collaborated with George Gershwin on a handful of songs.

Despite George's ubiquitous presence at the Paleys', he was not there during Oscar's debut at their salon. On subsequent visits Oscar harbored a secret hope that George might show up and allow him a chance to make a better impression.

Oscar was immediately welcomed into the lively "Saturday nights." "As good hosts, the Paleys felt it incumbent to ask me to play the piano," Oscar recalled. "It was my custom to expect this request and I obliged with a furious alacrity. I played the Chopin étude *Winter Wind,* Opus 25, No. 11 with carefree virtuosity." Oscar tried out a new style of playing that he copied from Irving Berlin, who had a habit of "leaning forward over every bar he played, with great yearning, while he [sang] rather passionately in a thin, sweet voice." Howard Dietz, who happened to live in the apartment below the Paleys', remembered that Oscar was frequently asked to play, usually, however, as a substitute for George Gershwin.

At the age of eighteen, Oscar would begin to make his name at the Paleys' as a talented pianist and wit. With his quick retorts, in fact, he was becoming someone to be reckoned with. He soon learned that he could make his presence known by a memorable insult, a skill he had honed since childhood.

"It was the scene of many a verbal battle about songs and scores, librettos and operas," Dietz wrote about the Paley circle, and

> Oscar could crush with a phrase. Of Sigmund Romberg, the operetta balladeer, he said, "He writes the kind of music you whistle on the way *into* the theater." Norman Levy, the light verse lawyer-poet, asked Oscar if he thought Gershwin's music would be played a hundred years hence. "If George is around, it will."

At the Paleys', Oscar also met the playwright S. N. ("Sam") Behrman, who would become a lifelong friend. After their first meeting Oscar described Behrman as "an unprepossessing, reticent man with incredibly good manners. I was told that the Theatre Guild was going to produce his first play—news I greeted with utter disbelief." Behrman, for his part, thought the young pianist "a shambling Mercutio," but from their first meeting the thirty-year-old, Harvard-educated playwright became friends with the eighteen-year-old high school dropout.

Oscar's relationship with Howard Dietz was a little less sanguine. Dietz later wrote:

> I was fond of Oscar, but there was something about our twin natures which made us exchange insults. I told him that I wanted to make a

date with him every day so that I would know where he was and could avoid the place.

Oscar enjoyed playing the *enfant terrible,* but his naughtiness would turn to nastiness regarding Phil Charig, his first real friend in the music business. Oscar would turn on Charig, eventually taking his place at the second piano in George Gershwin's penthouse.

Though Oscar was now casting his lot with Broadway composers and songwriters, concerts and recitals were still the lifeblood of his musical interests; it had become a necessary part of his life to hear everything. He heard Rachmaninoff at the Brooklyn Academy of Music, saw Siegfried Wagner—son of Richard—conduct, and followed George Antheil's frenzied attempts to become America's answer to Stravinsky through his mechanized music (which would culminate in the disastrous performance of his *Ballet mécanique* at Carnegie Hall in 1927).

But it was still easier to get a job playing in a nightclub or vaudeville than with a symphony orchestra. Oscar's playing in the Ben Bernie band brought him to the attention of an intense, bespectacled man named Nat Finston. Finston, the musical director of the Balaban & Katz movie theatre chain, wanted to hire Oscar to play the piano before and after the featured film.

Oscar took advantage of Ben Bernie's frequent firings to accept Nat Finston's offer to work for Balaban & Katz. Finston and his boss, Sam Katz, were obsessed with controlling every aspect of their movie house operation; every time Oscar showed up at the Paramount Theatre for his job, a memo awaited him as to what music he should play and for how long. Typically, Oscar reacted badly. If he was commanded to play selections from four light classical pieces during the course of a single show, he might play Chopin's "Minute Waltz" four times and then go home. Or he might decide to play a concerto, urging the audience to hum the orchestral parts.

No account exists of how many bicarbonates of soda Sam Katz had to swallow before they decided to send their star pianist out of town. "I'd love to fire him," Finston confided to a friend, "but I can't afford to"—Oscar was fast becoming their most popular pianist. They finally decided to send him to Boston with the Eddie Elkins Band, a job Oscar enjoyed for the camaraderie of the other musicians. Before the first week was over, however, Oscar missed the Friday-night show. He overslept, and an empty piano graced the stage. The following night, Elkins, the bandleader, missed the show. "My example of self-discipline is often contagious," Oscar offered by way of an apology, but his Balaban & Katz career was over.

When Gershwin's Concerto in F premiered on the afternoon of December 3, 1925, Oscar was supposed to be rehearsing a run-through of Ben Bernie's new show, which was to begin that evening at the Roosevelt Hotel. Instead, Oscar called in sick that afternoon and the following evening so he could attend both performances. He arrived in the midst of a sweeping winter rain; the performance was sold out, and crowds thronged the concert hall. A favorable critical response to the Concerto was in no way assured: Days before, the music critic for *The New York Times,* Olin Downes, had asked, "Can dance rhythms be employed for three movements of a concerto, and is Mr. Gershwin, in his present state of musical development, the man to do it again?"

For Oscar, the premiere performance was a singular, difficult, yet exquisite event. As far as he was concerned, the Concerto in F was more than "just one or two good melodies" (as had been said about the *Rhapsody*) but a gushing of wonderful ideas, refreshing in their contrasting idioms and moods. Oscar was ravished by its "wistful melody." It was apparent to him that Gershwin had crossed over to "a more astute, more musical" way of working, a more self-assured musical sensibility than that of the *Rhapsody.*

In the concert hall Oscar was surrounded by Gershwin's admirers; he wanted to join this scintillating group. But he would have to content himself with hearing from Phil Charig about the party given in George's honor at conductor Walter Damrosch's home on West Seventy-first Street, and he would later read about it in Franklin P. Adams's weekly diary column, "The Conning Tower":

> The place swarmed with Gershwin's friends and admirers, the praises gushed as freely as the liquor. . . . Then George Gershwin, the composer, came in, and we did talk musique, and about going ahead regardless of advice, . . . that one saying, Study, and another saying, Write only jazz melodies, and another saying, Write only symphonies and concertos.

Gershwin's triumph did not inspire unalloyed joy in Oscar. It was time, he decided, to pursue his own compositions, and even to try his hand at songwriting. Hadn't the critics noted Gershwin's lack of musical training? Well, Oscar was better trained and was probably the better pianist; he knew more about music than George. Whereas *Rhapsody in Blue* had seemed daunting to Oscar, the Concerto in F now bolstered his confidence. Gershwin, Oscar would later write, would not merely be "a subject for aesthetic envy, but in my youthful bumptiousness, a business competitor." The Concerto in F was a call to industry, its "orgy of rhythm" a gauntlet thrown down to Oscar Levant.

Ben Bernie wanted to go to Europe. By the end of 1925, most of the dance bands in London had taken up George and Ira's song "The Man I Love." Paul Whiteman, the Gershwins, and Irving Caesar had all been to Europe. In 1926 a wildly enthusiastic crowd of ten thousand filled the Royal Albert Hall to hear Paul Whiteman conduct the *Rhapsody*. The Prince of Wales, no less, had helped create a fashionable interest in jazz bands, occasionally sitting in on drums during Whiteman's sessions at the popular Kit Kat Club.

Whiteman's success abroad had aroused envy in Ben Bernie's heart, and he planned a European tour. Oscar was excited at the prospect of touring England with Bernie's band, but the Old Maestro's plans were dealt a lethal blow by the British Minister of Labour, who refused his application for a visa on the grounds that there was not enough parity of employment between American and British musicians—Whiteman's band had already tipped the balance.

Seeing how difficult it was for American musicians to work overseas, Oscar was about to give up the idea completely when he met a man in a cowboy hat who billed himself as "the world's greatest saxophonist." His name was Rudy Wiedoeft, and while his appellation is now obscure, he was a noticeable figure in the dance band world of New York in the 1920s. It was a tribute to Oscar's growing reputation that Rudy Wiedoeft invited Oscar to join his band on their way to Europe. Wiedoeft had been recording music since the beginning of World War I and was already well known in Europe as a soloist on the saxophone in songs like "Crazy 'bout Daddy in a Uniform" and "Saxophobia." A popular music paper of the day, *The Metronome*, called Wiedoeft "the Paderewski of the Saxophone."

So Oscar accompanied the author of "The Saxophone—With Hints on How to Play It" on a tour of England. The association would prove profitable. A year after Oscar's first recording date with Ben Bernie, he joined up with "the pioneering pitchman of the saxophone" to record "Sax-o-phun" and "Valse Mazanetta," on the Columbia label.

And so it was with Rudy Wiedoeft (from whom Rudy Vallee, the famous crooner, took his name) that Oscar Levant crossed the Atlantic. As a pianist touring with an internationally known musician, Oscar would be treated with the respect he couldn't quite command at home.

8

One of the Boys

"I had an affair with almost every girl in the club
except the one I liked."

OSCAR WAS THE FIRST MEMBER OF HIS FAMILY TO CROSS THE ATLANTIC
since his mother and grandmother had sailed to America years earlier.
By 1926 Oscar had filled out; with his dark hair, and full lips, and
somewhat heavy-lidded, hazel-green eyes, he was turning into an attractive young man. His intelligence and sardonic wit lit up his sensu-
ous face. He was nearly six feet tall (all of his height being in his legs,
which supported a short, round torso). Oscar's growing confidence
was apparent.

Rudy Wiedoeft and his musicians were installed at Prince's, the
hotel where they were booked for a six-week engagement. Oscar was
featured playing a solo variation of Irving Berlin's "What'll I Do?," a
song Oscar described as "one of the spate of sentimental waltzes composed by Irving Berlin when he was surreptitiously courting Ellin
Mackay." Berlin's marriage to the New York socialite—against her
father's wishes—was the talk of Tin Pan Alley. "It was," wrote Irving
Berlin's biographer Laurence Bergreen, "the supreme act of assimila-
tion." The example set by Berlin's marriage would not be lost on
Oscar.

Word of the Wiedoeft band and their talented, unpredictable pianist soon got around town. The café was filled with music-mad patrons crowding the stage. Oscar's playing of the *Rhapsody* was the highlight of the evening. One night after the last set, Oscar found Nora Bayes—the musical comedy star who had first caused him to notice the piano playing of George Gershwin—waiting for him in his dressing room and offering him charming compliments. Oscar was also introduced to Frank Fay, the Irish American vaudevillian who was appearing at the London Palladium at the time. Oscar was fascinated by Frank Fay and his aura of shabby worldliness. True to form, Oscar fell in with characters who were colorful, bumptious, and a little shady, despite his own private reservations about their character. Fay introduced Oscar to the pleasures of London club life.

In March 1926 in England—a time when the expatriate poet T. S. Eliot and his wife, Vivian, were about to move into a new home near Sloane Square and Eliot was wondering if he would ever write another poem after "The Hollow Men"—Oscar spent much of his time in the British recording studio of Columbia Records, recording Rudy Wiedoeft's compositions, which were entirely works for the classical saxophone that Wiedoeft promoted at every opportunity.

By the time Rudy Wiedoeft's band had fulfilled its contract at Prince's, the management offered Oscar a contract of his own. Oscar refused—he found that he balked at too much routine: "I always managed to break off my jobs at a certain interval. It was the same principle Noël Coward used." His dislike of the repetitious life of the performer was to stay with him his entire career.

When Wiedoeft left England, Oscar was on his own. He was in London without a boss, a mentor, or a family member to remind him of who he was supposed to be. During these weeks he transformed himself into an English fop, buying a cane and bowler hat and an entirely new wardrobe made by a fashionable English tailor. He insisted on outlandish colors for his suits, running toward the purples, while Harry's old hand-me-down suits hung abandoned in his closet in the new flat he rented on Duke Street.

Oscar's success with the Wiedoeft band began to "bear social and sexual fruit"; Frank Fay introduced him to the Forty-Three Club, an after-hours club at 43 Gerrard Street where illicit drinking took place. (The Forty-Three Club was later immortalized as "The Old Hundredth" in Evelyn Waugh's *Brideshead Revisited.*)

"The club was famous for its well-mannered bawdiness," remembered Oscar. He claimed that he had affairs with just about every girl at the Forty-Three Club except the one he fancied, a young woman named Mimi. When Mimi invited him to her flat and insisted he spend the night, Oscar slept with her but they did not make love. Years later, when one among Oscar's legion of psychiatrists heard this story and asked why he didn't have an affair with her, Oscar replied, "I couldn't, I liked her." It would be many years and many women before he could bring desire and admiration together.

Frank Fay invited Oscar to play piano for him onstage at the London Palladium. Oscar's appearance on that legendary stage was brief, but an enthusiastic claque of young women from the Forty-Three Club greeted the performance with lusty applause and cheers. (This would be re-created years later in *The Barkleys of Broadway,* a Fred Astaire–Ginger Rogers film in which Oscar's performance of the "Sabre Dance" is cheered by a bevy of glamorous showgirls.)

In England Oscar began to find the shape of his personality. He was becoming more comfortable with the role of performer, though he was often haunted by the sense of having disappointed someone—the ghost of his father, Stojowski, his mother. "I always felt that somehow I did not fulfill the dream of my mother," he would write balefully, years later. Oscar brought his hat and cane back with him to America, but it was the uncut diamond of his personality that he had discovered in London that would help make him famous in New York.

Oscar was twenty-one when he published his first song, "Keep Sweeping the Cobwebs off the Moon" (with lyricists Sam Lewis and Joe Young). Though Jerome H. Remick & Co. published his first two songs, it was Max Dreyfus, the driving force behind the music publishing firm of T. B. Harms, Inc., who nurtured Oscar's career as a songwriter. In a business "about as friendly as a drama critic," Dreyfus was loved and respected. By 1927 Dreyfus was already something of a legend in the music business, having discovered Jerome Kern. Kern's brilliant career gave T. B. Harms, Inc., the cachet to attract some of the biggest musical talents in New York—Harms would publish George and Ira Gershwin, Cole Porter, Rodgers and Hart, and Vincent Youmans.

Dreyfus's acumen was due in part to his own abandoned talent as a composer. He was perhaps the only figure in the music publishing business who was also a musician. As Sam Behrman noted in a *New Yorker* profile, "it was his early training and ambition which enabled him to distill a profession from a racket." Harms soon became a second home to Oscar Levant. He spent hours in its West Forty-fifth Street offices, where young composers flocked to try out their unpublished songs.

"Keep Sweeping the Cobwebs off the Moon" was recorded by

Nick Lucas for Brunswick Records (and subsequently by Vaughn DeLeath and Fred Waring). The song was arranged for ukelele accompaniment. The lyrics are typical of the optimist school, so prevalent during the years just before and during the Depression: "Change all of your gray skies / Turn them into gay skies / And keep sweeping the cobwebs off the moon."

Lyricists Young and Lewis had also written the words for "Rock-a-Bye Your Baby with a Dixie Melody" and "My Mammy," two of Al Jolson's greatest songs, a fact that delighted Oscar. Oscar remembered that Joe Young had a habit of snapping his fingers in rhythm, a style of keeping time that would be much copied in later years. That the lyricists for two of Al Jolson's greatest songs would write the words for his first published song delighted Oscar. Songs would soon follow with collaborators such as Edward Heyman and Billy Rose, and, during the twelve years of his songwriting career, Oscar would team up with some of the most successful lyricists in the music business, including Irving Caesar, Sidney Clare, E. Y. "Yip" Harburg, and Stanley Adams.

Like Stojowski, the music publisher Max Dreyfus bore many similarities to Max Levant. Both men had old-world manners and loved music (except that Dreyfus loved popular songs and show tunes as well as Strauss, Beethoven, and Mozart). Dreyfus showed a noticeable preference for Oscar, as Behrman noticed in his *New Yorker* profile:

> Discussing his fondness for a young composer and pianist who is now one of the "boys" under his aegis, Max admitted to me his predilection for this irresistible *enfant terrible* and said with a faint smile: "I admit it's a weakness and may cause a little bad blood among the other boys, but why shouldn't I be allowed a little weakness?"

Oscar Levant was the *enfant terrible* in question, and Max Dreyfus would develop into one of Oscar's most important paternal figures. "He was like my father," Oscar wrote years later in a tender, confessional letter to the woman who would become his second wife.

In the early 1930s Dreyfus transported his movable feast to his baronial estate in Brewster, in upstate New York. Here Oscar enjoyed his status as the youngest and favorite of Dreyfus's "boys." The Dreyfus household was like the Paley salon, but in a country setting. There were two pianos and a bowling alley that competed for noisy supremacy. Oscar sharpened his wit over the Dreyfus billiard table. He even learned to ride a horse. "I couldn't canter because I had no strength in my knees," Oscar recalled, "so I would post for hours, going up hills and down mountains on a full gaited horse." Oscar never really developed horsemanship:

> I could never get [my horse] to a complete halt and I would yell at him, "Stop, you dirty son of a bitch! Stop, you bastard, you lousy bastard!" Mr. Dreyfus was always shocked and would quietly explain, "You don't talk to horses like that."

The gatherings in Brewster were riotous and packed with songwriters, composers, and musical comedy stars. But Oscar also shared more serious pleasures with Dreyfus, such as playing all the new compositions for him. Dreyfus was impressed with Oscar's ability to see a score for the first time and play it unerringly.

Dreyfus seemed to look upon Oscar as a son, and he wouldn't allow anyone else to publish his music. When a rival music publisher was about to bring out an Oscar Levant–Stanley Adams song, Dreyfus was quick to respond. "They printed the orchestration and the sheet music and planned to give it a major plug, until Max came back to work and heard about it," remembered Adams. "He was absolutely furious. He called them up and said, 'You can't publish anything of Oscar's! I'm the only one!' "

Adams liked Oscar, but he found his brand of humor "a little bit sadistic." He was present when the composer Vernon Duke dropped by Oscar's room one day to get his opinion on a concerto he had just written. (Vernon Duke, best known for his songs "April in Paris" and "Autumn in New York," also composed serious music under his real name, Vladimir Dukelsky.) At the end of the first movement of his concerto, he asked Oscar, "So, what do you think of it?"

Oscar replied, "For a man who's destined for obscurity, why do you need two names?"

Oscar's own songwriting career would produce eighty songs, a number of which became popular, like "Keep Sweeping the Cobwebs off the Moon" (1927), "If You Want the Rainbow (You Must Have the Rain)" (1928), "Lady, Play Your Mandolin" (1930), "Wacky Dust" (1938), and one song that would become a standard, "Blame It on My Youth" (1934).

The father-son relationship that flourished between Dreyfus and his young protégé threatened neither Oscar's productivity nor his self-esteem, but there was a darker side to it. Dreyfus treated Oscar like a "Teutonic father, sometimes rather brutally." Oscar was Dreyfus's pet but was expected to perform certain household duties, as if he

were a servant. After Max Levant and George Gershwin, Max Dreyfus became the most important figure in Oscar's youth. As for Dreyfus, toward the end of his long life (he died at the age of ninety-one),
he once confided in Ira and Leonore Gershwin that his happiest years
were the ones spent with Oscar Levant, "because, among other
things, Oscar made me laugh."

9

Burlesque

"Gee, Mazie, it's great to see you."

OSCAR CONTINUED HIS MAD RUSH TO ESCAPE THE FATE ANNIE HAD
laid out for him. When he returned to the States from his extended
stay in England, he made a short visit to Pittsburgh to see his mother,
who by then had moved from 1420 Fifth Avenue to one of the row
houses on Greenfield Avenue that Max had left her. Oscar spent most
of his time visiting his mother, but he managed to hang around his old
haunts long enough to learn about the fates of some of his former
cronies. He discovered that several of his Colwell Street friends had
been sentenced to jail terms for stuffing ballot boxes in the last mayor-
alty race.

Oscar briefly saw his brothers Ben and Honey, the "good" sons
who had stayed behind to practice medicine and dentistry and look
after their mother. Ben was now a urologist practicing in a Pittsburgh
office; he was married, with a young daughter and a son on the way.
And Honey was still playing the violin—exquisitely—but only when
he wasn't pulling teeth or peering into the mouths of his patients,
who often asked their dentist for news of Oscar, "the wandering minstrel."

Oscar's pastimes on his visit home were not entirely familial. His younger cousin, Oscar Radin, remembers Levant at this time "bragging to me that when he was just fifteen he was already earning his own living . . . he grew up fast, with Ben Bernie, in Europe, with the freedom that gave him. . . . he started making good money, and he started spending. He would spend fifty dollars a night," Radin remembered, "on a streetwalker for an hour's time." His carousing at the Forty-Three Club in London had created a habit that Oscar was loath to break.

Annie was unimpressed with Oscar's accomplishments. She advised him to send his money home and she'd invest it for him. And, as always, she sent him back to New York with admonishments to keep practicing the piano. Oscar resented Annie's riding him whenever he saw her. He resolved to get even, to undermine her adulation of the great composers and show her that musicians were human, too.

Oscar had brought with him to Pittsburgh the first recording of the Tchaikovsky Piano Concerto No. 1 in B-flat Minor, played by Mark Hamburg. With his head resting on one of Annie's antimacassars and the room filling with the Concerto's strains, Oscar watched his mother's transports of joy. Annie waltzed around the room hugging the air, proclaiming her love for Tchaikovsky. During one such rapturous moment Oscar told his mother, "You know, Ma, Tchaikovsky was a fairy."

Annie didn't quite understand Oscar's cryptic remark, but she knew her son was deflating one of her heroes. Oscar had learned to fight back verbally against those who hurt him. Annie, for her part, continued in her indifference toward every success of Oscar's that drew him away from a concert career, including his debut as an actor in a successful Broadway show.

During the time Oscar had been in England, a Times Square stage manager–turned–writer by the name of George Manker Watters and the formidable producer Arthur Hopkins had been working on a play called *Burlesque*. It was similar in theme to the previous year's hit play, *Broadway*—a backstage look at the mounting of a Broadway show, with its long food chain of agents, stage managers, temperamental stars, chorus girls, and hoofers.

Burlesque is the story of Skid Johnson, a song-and-dance man specializing in pratfalls, and his stoic music-hall wife. The play evokes the grueling circuit of one-nighters among the lowest level of vaudeville performers, who await a George White or a Flo Ziegfeld to discover them and send a telegram inviting them to play Broadway. When in the first act the telegram comes inviting Skid to join the cast of

Charles Dillingham's show *Manhattan Follies,* Skid's martyred wife, Bonnie, is left behind. Skid wows them on Broadway but abandons his faithful wife to take up with a no-good chorine, all the while sinking deeper into the bottle. "Maybe some of us are only happy when we ain't treated well," Bonnie laments halfway through the play.

Watters, a former Times Square house manager with roots in the Broadway demimonde, knew the world of vaudevillians, low comics, and hoofers. He was adamant that his play present the "putty nose comedians, pulchritudinous chorines and cigar chomping stage managers as he knew them."

While working on the rewrite of the second act, the two men decided to make one of the characters a songwriter who would spend most of his time onstage noodling on the piano and breaking out with a few popular tunes. The rewritten second act, which became known as "the party scene," would prove popular with audiences and would help to establish the fame of *Burlesque.*

By the summer of 1927, with the play nearly complete, it was obvious to Hopkins that the part of Jerry Evans, a songwriter, would require a real piano player. Watters suggested engaging Oscar Levant for the part, in an effort to cast the play with "actors, [who] for once have a chance to be themselves." In 1927 one needn't have been a denizen of the Broadway demimonde like George Watters to have heard of Oscar Levant. His first published song, "Keep Sweeping the Cobwebs off the Moon," was becoming something of a hit, and musically savvy New Yorkers would have known his playing of *Rhapsody in Blue* with Ben Bernie.

What made him especially appealing to Arthur Hopkins, however, was his personality. Here was the genuine article—not an actor pretending to be a musician but a musician who had only to be himself in order to act his part. *Burlesque* would establish a remarkable pattern in Oscar's life of acting in roles based on his own personality, playing himself or a version of himself.

Burlesque was set to open at the Plymouth Theatre on September 1, 1927, after an out-of-town run at a number of summer resorts. The role of Skid was played by Hal Skelly. And Hopkins's choice for the part of Bonnie, Skid's long-suffering wife, would make a bona fide star out of Ruby Stevens, a Brooklyn orphan who just the year before had won a featured role in her first Broadway play, *The Noose.* By this time she was calling herself Barbara Stanwyck.

Hal Skelly was like a composite of all the performers living picaresque lives that Oscar Levant had met during his years in New York City. Skelly had already had a long and colorful career, but his performance as Skid in *Burlesque* would finally make his name.

By the time Hopkins cast Skelly as the rubber-limbed vaudevillian, Skelly had been in and out of theatre most of his life. He had once been a tumbler with a circus tour, and his tumbling had prepared him well for the pratfall life of comic actor/song-and-dance man. He possessed an uncanny grace and flexibility. Oscar admired him.

When Oscar was first given a copy of the *Burlesque* script, he pored over his handful of lines, the most prominent of which was "Mazie! It's great to see you. Give us a little kiss." Oscar practiced his line everywhere, as if it were a soliloquy. He would greet Irving Caesar or Max Dreyfus or a favorite waiter at the Hunting Room or Dinty Moore's with his line. Once when he was introduced to Ethel Barrymore he tried it out on the stage diva, asking her advice as to how to read it.

Hopkins also needed Levant to score the music for the second act, with certain songs cueing dramatic scenes. "Cherie, I Love You," "Ain't She Sweet," "Sometimes I'm Happy," and "Here in My Arms" set the mood for a night of revelry that is undercut by Skid's desperate realization that Bonnie has left him for good and is about to marry her "breath of Wyoming air," a stagestruck rancher named Harvey. Levant then plays Gershwin's "Someone to Watch Over Me" and also manages to get in a few phrases from his signature piece, the *Rhapsody,* finishing up the scene with a demented, madcap rendition of "The Wedding March," while poor Skid, now soused, dances a mad jig.

When the play opened and Oscar began to feel comfortable in the role, he would often change songs, switching a new Gershwin or Jerome Kern number for one of the set pieces, sometimes interpolating refrains and melodies which he might have heard only that afternoon on a brief visit to T. B. Harms.

Burlesque was soundly paddled by the critics, but it nevertheless became a success and ran for over a year. The 1927–28 theatre season was truly a spectacular year. Among the memorable plays presented were Dorothy and DuBose Heyward's *Porgy;* Eugene O'Neill's *Strange Interlude* (which won the Pulitzer Prize that year); Sean O'Casey's *The Plough and the Stars;* Jerome Kern and Oscar Hammerstein II's *Show Boat* (which featured the fabulous Helen Morgan and which made veteran journalists Robert Benchley and Marc Connelly weep); *Diamond Lil,* starring its author, Mae West; and George Kaufman and Edna Ferber's *The Royal Family,* a takeoff on the royal family of theatre, the Barrymores. As if that weren't memorable enough, Gershwin musicals were subdividing everywhere: *Oh, Kay!* had burned brightly for 256 performances the previous season; *Rosalie* boasted a Romberg-Gershwin score; and Gershwin's *Funny Face,* starring Fred and Adele Astaire, was at the Alvin Theatre. It seems remarkable that *Burlesque,* a play by a novice playwright, did as well as it did that season and brought notice to a couple of newcomers, Barbara Stanwyck and Oscar Levant, as well as making Hal Skelly a star.

Oscar was elated to be in this Broadway show that was turning out to be such a hit. Though he had never had any serious ambitions to become an actor, he loved Broadway and had been a devotee of its vaudeville shows, musicals, comedies, and dramas ever since he could scrape together the money to buy half-price tickets.

Unlike his fellow actors who went home after the show to try to catch up on their sleep, Oscar would go out on a solitary round of his favorite nightclubs and all-night delis in search of a sympathetic heart or at least some diverting company. One of the nightclubs Oscar frequented at this time was his friend Frank Fay's club, which was currently in vogue. Fay, the companionable if mean-spirited comic with the fast wit, was smitten by Barbara Stanwyck and had asked Oscar to introduce them. According to Oscar, Stanwyck fell madly in love with Fay at their first meeting.

What was a triumph for Fay turned out to be a disaster for Stanwyck. Onstage, Fay was handsome, elegant, and suave; offstage he was a drinker, a brawler, and a womanizer.

The marriage between Stanwyck, who had started out as a hoofer, and the devil-may-care Fay was uncannily similar to the plot of *Burlesque.* Stanwyck's career flourished, beginning with her tremendous popularity in *Burlesque,* while Fay's withered on the vine. By the time she divorced Fay in 1935, Stanwyck's devotion had turned to hate— she refused ever to speak to him again. "I always felt guilty about serving as the catalyst in this romance," Oscar later admitted.

But Oscar's taste in friends was beginning to improve. He renewed his friendships with a number of people he had met prior to going to England. In April 1927, six months before the opening of *Burlesque,* Sam Behrman invited Oscar to the premiere of his new play, *The Second Man,* which was being presented by the prestigious repertory company the Theatre Guild.

Since first meeting Behrman at one of the Paleys' Saturday nights, Oscar had been taken with the playwright, who was known as "Berrie" by a wide coterie of friends. Oscar liked this restless, short, compact, balding man with the owlish countenance and talent for gentle mockery. In conversation Behrman was a character out of his own plays—epigrammatic, sophisticated, amusing.

When they first met, Behrman was still living on the fringes of Broadway as something of an intellectual itinerant. He reviewed books, wrote short stories and articles, collaborated on two failed plays, toiled as a press agent for the producer Jed Harris, made friends with the Gershwins, and had, like Levant, just taken his first trip to England. So the two men had much to talk about.

The Second Man opened to ecstatic reviews. The play went on to be an equal success in London with Noël Coward as its star.

Behrman had taken an instant delight in Oscar, who at twenty years of age was some twelve years Behrman's junior. He liked Oscar's almost total lack of formality, his hard-bitten integrity which, in Behrman's words, aroused "the maternal impulse" in all men, including himself. He took impish glee in Oscar's provocativeness and introduced Oscar to many distinguished people over the course of their long friendship.

After each performance of *Burlesque,* Oscar would walk Barbara Stanwyck home to the Knickerbocker Hotel on Forty-fifth Street, then walk the thirteen blocks to the Park Central Hotel on Sixth Avenue, where he had moved when he left his brother Harry's apartment. Oscar would then begin his late-night circuit of "niteries" and cabarets: the House of Morgan, where Helen Morgan, fresh from her triumph in *Show Boat,* would cross and uncross her legs from her perch on top of the piano; the Cotton Club, where Duke Ellington had held court since the early twenties; the Hollywood, the first no-cover-charge establishment on Broadway; the Plantation, where Sophie Tucker was featured; or Frank Fay's nightclub, where cronies besieged Oscar with requests for an introduction to Barbara Stanwyck, who even before her appearance in *Burlesque* had caused a stir as the "display girl" who used to walk the Shubert gangplank wearing little papier-mâché nothings. Before long, Oscar found himself on the "A" list of New York's chic party givers.

Jules Glaenzer's parties, for example, were as glittering as the wares he sold at his exclusive jewelry store, Cartier's. The parties were a kind of open house for celebrities, businessmen, entertainers, producers, and various celebrity hangers-on. The more gifted guests, such as George Gershwin, and Richard Rodgers, would often entertain. A typical guest list might include Florenz Ziegfeld, Paul Whiteman, Noël Coward, Vincent Youmans, Fred and Adele Astaire, Fanny Brice, Charlie Chaplin, Marilyn Miller, Irene Bordoni, and, in Oscar's words, "half a dozen piano players, all the popular show girls in New York, and a generous smattering of High Society." Oscar invited Barbara Stanwyck to accompany him, but she always refused. A Flatbush orphan still working on her accent, Stanwyck loathed such gatherings, telling Oscar to be wary of phonies.

A frequent guest was Fanny Brice. Oscar was getting to know her through his acquaintance with Fanny's suitor, the producer and songwriter Billy Rose.

By 1927 Billy Rose was primarily a lyricist writing words for songs like "A Cup of Coffee, a Sandwich, and You." Fanny Brice's marriage to Billy Rose would do much to elevate Rose's songwriting career. Brice sang his songs in her first talking picture, *My Man*. The film's theme song, a lovely, bittersweet ballad called "If You Want the Rainbow (You Must Have the Rain)," was written by Oscar Levant, with lyrics by Billy Rose and Mort Dixon.

Oscar was paid only a hundred dollars for this composition, while Rose and Dixon each received a thousand. This would be the last time Oscar published his music with Jerome H. Remick's music company. With friends like Billy Rose, Oscar would need a Max Dreyfus to look out for him.

Nevertheless, Oscar was proud of his friendship with Rose and therefore endured his abuse. And Rose liked Oscar, often picking him out of an afternoon crowd on Seventh Avenue, calling to him from inside Fanny Brice's chauffeur-driven Mercedes-Benz.

Oscar's nocturnal habits were developed and honed as *Burlesque* ran through its 372 performances at the Plymouth Theatre. By his own account, he never went to bed before eight in the morning, walking home to his hotel room while the newspaper trucks roared by and an army of street cleaners scrubbed the sleep from the city's long avenues. He would finally doze off under a mountain of morning papers, the ashtray beside the bed a haystack of cigarette butts. And so the Broadway boulevardier, actor, and songwriter was born, while Oscar's ambitions for a concert career were indefinitely postponed.

10

The Widening Circle

**"Oscar, I've been hearing a lot of
nice things about you."**

"They're all lies."

But of course if a guy is looking for trouble on Broadway along toward
four o'clock in the morning, anybody will tell you that the right address is nowhere else but Mindy's. . . .

When Damon Runyon wrote about "Mindy's," his readers knew
that he meant Lindy's, the Broadway delicatessen at 1626 Broadway
just below Fiftieth Street. From 1921 until its closing in 1957,
Lindy's restaurant was the meeting place of mobsters, vaudeville
stars, politicians, and horse players. Al Jolson, Eddie Cantor, Jack
Benny, Fred Allen, Irving Berlin, Sophie Tucker, Damon Runyon,
and Walter Winchell were all regular customers, and the notorious
gangster Arnold Rothstein made Lindy's his headquarters, over the
protests of its genial owners, Leo and Clara Lindemann. (Arnold
"Mr. Big" Rothstein was at Lindy's when he got the call to head
over to the Park Central Hotel, where he was gunned down minutes after eating a sturgeon sandwich, a Lindy's specialty.) The
Times "obituary" about the closing of Lindy's described the restaurant's early success:

Lindy's sandwich shop prospered from the start. He got the half-starved little dancers from the near-by Winter Garden and from other hits in the neighborhood. It was Al Jolson, an early customer, who suggested that Lindy put in small tables for people instead of making them stand up.

Lindy's was the primal home of a number of underworld types who were transformed into fictional characters by Damon Runyon: people with the enchanting sobriquets of Harry the Horse, Spanish John, Nicely-Nicely Johnson, Milk Ear Willy, Sorrowful Jones, and Sleep-out Louie. It was Runyon who came to the rescue when Rothstein's murder attracted unfavorable publicity. He quickly wrote that "the same thing might have happened to a man who had left a church," thereby earning the gratitude of Clara Lindemann, who would, years later, in 1946, bring "great bowls of crushed strawberries smothered in rich cream and sugar" to Runyon's bedside at the Buckingham Hotel, where Runyon was dying of throat cancer.

"Sandwiches in glorious combinations, sturgeon, gefilte fish, pickled herring, apple pancakes, and strong-minded waiters"—here was the menu of Oscar's youth, the same dishes Annie Levant had served her four sons. Oscar became a Lindy's regular.

At Lindy's Oscar rubbed shoulders with another habitué whom he had met a few years earlier at mobster Larry Fay's El Fey Club—the gossip columnist Walter Winchell. Whenever he saw Oscar, Winchell would grab his arm and ask for a line or a gag for his column. The two men became pals in the late twenties and early thirties, and it was partly through the offices of Winchell's newspaper column that Oscar's reputation as a Broadway wag became established. The relationship would later turn sour, but Winchell would remain an important figure in Oscar's life, for two reasons: He helped create Oscar's reputation as a caustic and unpredictable wit, and he introduced Oscar to his first wife, Barbara Smith.

At Lindy's or the Stork Club or "21," Winchell would rush up to celebrities or personalities on the rise, grab an arm or coat lapel, and demand, "Got an item? Gimme a gag." Playwright Arthur Caesar, whom Oscar met at his first night at the Paleys', "used to jeer at [Winchell] openly with considerable venom. 'Look at him!' he would say when Winchell came up to his table, 'the mental mendicant.' " A controversial figure, Winchell was described by one source as "bewitching," his voice and manner "charged with an inner excitement"; another described him as "a thrilling bore."

But his influence and power were immense, and politicians, celebrities, writers, actors, even stockbrokers and underworld figures,
would try to get their names printed in his column, often hiring public relations experts to hang around his table at the Stork Club, hoping
to slip in an item.

Winchell was also famous for his uses and inventions of "slan-
guage"—H. L. Mencken credited Winchell with creating more
neologisms than any other newspaper columnist around. He was
first to use the words "baloney," "palooka," and "belly-laugh" in
print. His phonetic spellings captured New York's streetwise pro-
nunciations: "Moom pitcher" for moving picture, "Joosh" for
Jewish, "phewd" for feud (and his phewds were legion). His own
jargon for Broadway said it all: "Hard Times Square" and "Two
Times Square," "The Hardened Artery" and "Baloney Boulevard"
for Broadway, and "Heart-Acre Square" for Longacre Square.

Maybe it was at Lindy's or the Stork Club where Winchell heard
Oscar's quip about the Russian-born songwriter Vernon Duke,
whose affected accent and Continental airs led Oscar to remark that
"Vernon Duke talks with a monocle in his throat." That crack would
be the first of many Oscar tidbits to go into Winchell's column.
Oscar's impulse to talk jibed perfectly with Winchell's impulse to
overhear. They were a good match, for a while, anyway, with Oscar
making a kill and feeding it to Winchell. Winchell's column gave
Oscar an audience of thousands who would read his quips and feel
that they were there at the small table at Lindy's or in the swanky
embrace of the Stork Club, sharing inside jokes and the often mali-
cious laughter.

Indeed, it may be said that the gossip column, with its penchant for
popularizing witty remarks, helped create the idea of the modern wit.
Without someone to record and make available the *bons mots* that
dropped from the lips of the Broadway boulevardiers, celebrities, and
wise guys who flocked to New York's eateries and nightspots, those
apposite remarks would pass from our collective memory. But with
the advent of the gossip column, witticisms were given a shelf life, and
one could indeed become known for a quick tongue. It is no accident
that the Algonquin Round Table adopted Walter Winchell as their
pet and that its illustrious members included at least seven who wrote
for newspapers and magazines—Robert Benchley, Dorothy Parker,
Alexander Woollcott, F. P. Adams, George S. Kaufman, Heywood
Broun, and Herbert Bayard Swope. In the heady days just prior to the
stock market crash, and lasting into the early thirties, Winchell did his

part in helping to create a few legends, Oscar Levant among them. Like the playwright Oscar Wilde, Levant would became famous for his conversation—at least in New York circles—before achieving fame in any other arena.

This quickly became a sore point for him. By the late thirties, he would complain to the press,

> I don't want to be known as a wag. . . . I want to be known as a serious musician. But there I go. Jokes. Silly stories. It's a disease. Beethoven was deaf, Mozart had rickets and I make wisecracks.

But Oscar would soon discover that along with his growing reputation as a wag, he was also developing a genuine gift for friendship— unexpected, perhaps, in a figure whose name became synonymous with caustic wit.

George S. Kaufman became a friend of Oscar's and also helped popularize some of his remarks. Kaufman was already something of a legendary figure by 1929, when the two men met toward the end of Oscar's run in *Burlesque.*

"George was tall, dour, and solemn," Oscar observed, "with the slightly forbidding look of a startled egghead." Though Kaufman's rather formal, standoffish manner made others uncomfortable, Oscar had no trouble with the incessantly punning playwright. Kaufman dreaded outward displays of affection, particularly of the backslapping, hand-pumping variety, but Oscar was used to this demeanor— his father had also been phobic about physical displays of affection. A withering wit without so much as a dollop of sentimentality, George S. Kaufman (like Max Levant) conducted himself with utmost propriety at all times.

Oscar was no doubt drawn to the older man in part because they both hailed from Pittsburgh. Kaufman told Oscar about his current play, a collaboration with one of Oscar's early heroes, Ring Lardner. The play, called *June Moon,* was a jaundiced view of Tin Pan Alley and would become one of the big successes of 1929 on Broadway.

Kaufman had little use for music, but he was very interested in Oscar's stories about his first few years in New York hanging around at Irving Berlin's music publishing company. Oscar told Kaufman about his perambulations among the song-plugging offices of Tin Pan Alley while his bookie roommate, Benny Kaplan, took bets along Broadway. Kaufman was especially attentive when Oscar told him about an Irving Berlin company arranger working in a cubbyhole where he proudly displayed a portrait of Beethoven that had been embellished by the hardworking hack with the inscription, "To a swell little arranger—[signed] Ludwig van Beethoven."

Kaufman's dry sense of humor didn't allow him to laugh out loud, but he saw in Oscar's story the encapsulation of Tin Pan Alley's craving for acceptance and legitimacy, and its lowbrow respect for high culture. Kaufman put the song arranger with the inscribed portrait in *June Moon,* and it was greeted every night with laughter and applause.

The pope of the Algonquin Round Table, Alexander Woollcott, and Dorothy Parker, perhaps its most quotable member, adopted Oscar Levant as a kind of unofficial mascot. This enclave of troubled, hypochondriacal, mostly hard-drinking writers and journalists was breaking up by the time of Oscar's ascendancy in 1929, but the Round Table's legend was so powerful that the group was believed to be alive as long as fifteen years after its demise, according to Dorothy Parker's biographer, Marion Meade. "In the minds of the nostalgic, it lasted even longer," she observed. "Edna Ferber realized the party was over when she arrived at the Rose Room in 1932 and found the big table occupied by a family from Newton, Kansas."

Of the Round Table's charter members, Oscar would know them all—Woollcott, F. P. Adams (known as F.P.A.), Ring Lardner, Robert Benchley, George S. Kaufman, playwrights Marc Connelly and Robert Sherwood, *The New Yorker*'s founding editor Harold Ross, Herbert Bayard Swope, and Dorothy Parker, as well as the occasional members—Irving Berlin, Tallulah Bankhead, Jascha Heifetz, Harpo Marx, critic and composer Deems Taylor, novelist and socialite Alice Duer Miller, playwright Laurence Stallings, and novelist Edna Ferber, who was one of Kaufman's collaborators, having cowritten *The Royal Family* in 1927 and *Dinner at Eight* in 1932.

Oscar was especially fond of Dorothy Parker. He noted that she had such a reputation as a wit that she was credited with every funny remark going around. " 'Why, it got so bad,' [Dorothy] said resentfully, 'that people began to laugh before I opened my mouth!' " After Parker's death in 1967 (her heart gave out after a lifetime of Scotch and Chesterfields), Oscar would remember her with genuine affection as

a tiny woman, fragile and helpless, with a wispy will of iron. She loved dogs, little children, President Kennedy, and lots and lots of liquor. Even her enemies were kind to her; she brought out the maternal in everyone. At her cruelest, her voice was most caressive—the inconstant nymph. She was one of my favorite people.

During the next twenty years Oscar's contacts with many of the members of the Round Table would be extensive. He worked with Kaufman on radio and became an eternal houseguest of Harpo Marx in the thirties. But for Oscar, the Round Table essentially had little meaning beyond its mythic status—he knew its members as individuals. Its founder and guiding spirit was the drama critic Alexander Woollcott, who was a compulsive talker and, as Oscar observed, "could not tolerate loquacity in others." Woollcott apparently had the same opinion of Oscar, complaining shortly after meeting him that "arguing with you is like fighting a man who has three fists instead of the regulation two." Oscar had been upbraiding Woollcott for taking a few shots at Gershwin in an article about the composer for *Cosmopolitan* magazine (Woollcott, among other things, said that Gershwin's paintings were "godawful," though he softened this a bit by admitting his own distaste for all modern painting).

Oscar's reputation was growing not just among the wits and intelligentsia of New York but in music circles as well. One May morning in 1928 as he continued to sleep his way toward noon, he was awakened by a sharp, insistent ringing in his ears. The hotel switchboard operator knew better than to put through such early calls, but Frank Black, soon to be the resident conductor of the NBC Radio Orchestra, had browbeaten the hotel operator into putting through his call. He needed Levant, and he needed Levant now.

On this particular morning Frank Black was in the Brunswick recording studio with, in Oscar's description, "an orchestra on his hands, wax waiting to be scarred and indented—but without a pianist." Black was scheduled to record *Rhapsody in Blue,* but his pianist was on a bender. In casting around for a replacement, Oscar Levant's name quickly came up—everyone knew his ebullient playing of the *Rhapsody.* Frantic, Black pleaded with Oscar to fill in for the missing pianist.

No pleading was necessary. Practically before Black had hung up the phone, Levant was at the recording studio sitting at the piano, waiting for his cue. He didn't even require any rehearsal time, so well did he know Gershwin's music. For nearly four years since its debut at Aeolian Hall, the *Rhapsody* had been a part of Oscar's life. He did not even ask what he might be paid for the recording session—it was an intoxication just to be invited. After all, Gershwin would hear this recording and would have to acknowledge Oscar as a pianist worthy of his friendship and recognition.

Oscar Levant was paid union scale for the recording session, but his heart leapt at the sight of his first Brunswick record, with its purple-and-white-filigree label, his name appearing just under "Frank Black and His Orchestra." Oscar's first recording of the *Rhapsody* was light, brisk, confident, and almost casual, its pace underscoring the "modern times" theme of the piece while capturing its urbane, mercurial passions. Oscar was going to make sure George Gershwin heard it.

Meanwhile, the expanding family of Gershwins—Ira had by now married Leonore Strunsky—had moved from the 110th Street apartment into a five-story house at 316 West 103rd Street, just off Riverside Drive. George may well have been aware of the first recording of the *Rhapsody* with the piano solo performed by someone other than himself, but he didn't jump to acknowledge it. Oscar, perhaps wounded by Gershwin's silence, decided to beard the lion in his den, so he called him on the telephone. Gershwin graciously summoned the young upstart to his new home to listen to Levant's version.

Gershwin played the Brunswick recording while Oscar suffered the tortures of awaiting his hero's verdict. At last Gershwin got up and said, "I like mine better."

"George was quite firm in his preference for his own version on Victor," Oscar would recall years later. "He was unstinting in his declaration of the superiority of his performance over mine."

Oscar had recorded the *Rhapsody* in fifteen minutes, without rehearsal, "tossing it off" as he once said, but he couldn't have been thrilled with George's response to his recording. Oscar was, and would always be, so protective of George Gershwin that he would often say that George's own recording was indeed the better of the two. But Oscar's deft handling of the piece was unmistakable, and if he couldn't satisfy himself with a morsel of praise from George, he at least knew that he was the first pianist after Gershwin himself to record the *Rhapsody*. And the Brunswick recording of the *Rhapsody* was soon being heard all over the country, bringing Oscar Levant's name to the attention of a growing number of radio stations, many of which were now banding together in a network reaching from one end of the country to the other. The Brunswick recording was frequently requested and frequently played. Oscar's reputation as pianistic purveyor of the *Rhapsody* was now secure, and his recording helped to further popularize the work. While George Gershwin was busy composing and performing, Oscar Levant was being asked to play the *Rhapsody* again and again. In fact, each time his mother would hear Oscar playing the *Rhapsody* on the radio, she would call him and, in exasperation, say, "Again, the *Rhapsody?*"

In the next decade, when the two men became friends, Oscar passed on Annie's comment to Gershwin: "Again, the *Rhapsody?*" It became a standing joke.

Not long after Oscar Levant made the Brunswick recording, he was contacted by a reporter from *The New York Times.* Word had gotten around—from Winchell's column, from gossip at the Round Table, from his favorably received performance in *Burlesque*—that Levant might make good copy. An article called "The Piano Player of *Burlesque*—Considering Several Musical Show Folk" appeared in the Sunday *Times'* entertainment section on June 17, 1928. It was the first major coverage of a man whose later life would, for all intents and purposes, be played out in the media.

> Levant hails from Pittsburgh. He once thought of himself as a potential concert pianist, and studied for a while under Stojowski, at whose request he played several times for Paderewski. The dictaphone fails to record exactly what the former Polish Premier said, but soon thereafter young Levant accepted an offer to play with Ben Bernie's orchestra at the Hotel Roosevelt. He accompanied Bernie into vaudeville . . .

The article was the beginning of a lifelong, sometimes mean-spirited, symbiotic relationship between the press and Levant. Even in this appreciation, some of Oscar's responses are characteristically casual and undercutting, making much of the accidental nature of his career while treating his serious work as not worth talking about. He had begun to make light of the disappointment at playing for Paderewski. And he had already, at the tender age of twenty-one, relegated his hopes for a concert career to a failed ambition. Yet the piece ends, insouciantly, on a promising note: "If he likes a new tune he plays that—Gershwin and Rodgers tunes come tinkling out as soon as he hears them—and upon occasion even new Levant melodies have pleased Plymouth audiences. It's all very exciting."

But if Oscar thought that he had finally buried the concert pianist and resurrected the Broadway entertainer in its place, he would find that the ghost of suppressed ambition haunted him, poisoning his other successes and troubling his peace of mind. Even if he pleased himself, his friends, and his audiences, he knew he had stopped pleasing his mother. Cursed, perhaps, with too many talents, Oscar hid his sense of failure, at least for a while, by basking in the flattering lights of Broadway.

Two weeks after his twenty-second birthday, Oscar Levant had yet another Gershwin work to admire and to envy. This time his response to Gershwin's newest symphonic effort, *An American in Paris,* had the salutary effect of awakening in Oscar the desire to compose music— not the Tin Pan Alley tunes he had tossed off so far but concert music. Inspired by George's example, Oscar returned to the serious study of piano and theory. Once again, he must have felt that the disparate avenues of his own life and talents were being brought together in the fabulous accomplishments of George Gershwin.

By the close of the 1920s, Oscar's enthusiasm for George's music had become, in his own words, "a neurotic love affair." The composer David Diamond, who became a friend of Oscar's in the thirties, described it as "an obsession" with the composer and his works, which Oscar would quickly learn, tossing them off like child's play. George Gershwin seemed to hold out to Oscar the possibility of a new kind of freedom, in which the pianist, by becoming a composer, would have complete control of his music. There would be no Annie, no Max, no Demmler, no Stojowski to tell him what to play or how to play it, and no Paderewski, whose unfeeling pronouncement continued to haunt him.

If Gershwin represented the possibilities of a bridge between the vulgar, tuneful culture of Broadway and the purity of the classical piano literature Oscar had studied since boyhood, there was yet another element in Gershwin's work and personality that dazzled Oscar: his unabashed, unparalleled self-confidence. Gershwin's most recent biographer, Joan Peyser, has suggested that Gershwin was a solemn man, hurt by American and European composers who did not take his work seriously and wounded by his mother's indifference. But to the world—and to Oscar Levant—he seemed supremely self-confident.

"There was nothing frustrated about George," Oscar would remark in later years. "There was no gap between his dream and his doing."

As a boy in Pittsburgh, Oscar had feared that his gift as a classical pianist would sissify him in the eyes of his Hill district chums. It was too Old World, too studious, perhaps even too Jewish for a young boy who wanted to be part of the burgeoning American culture embodied in moving picture shows and Tin Pan Alley music. Yet Oscar loved Chopin, Liszt, Beethoven, even his mother's beloved Tchaikovsky, and could not give them up. In Gershwin he found the resolution of this conflict. In remarks prepared for a later recording in tribute to George Gershwin, Levant would say:

> [Gershwin's] music summed up his Time. Part of our Time. The Rhapsody ties up an era as no musical work has ever done. It's the Scott Fitzgerald Time. The fabulous Twenties. Dempsey and Tunney, and million dollar gates, Tilden, Bobby Jones, Babe Ruth, Red Grange, the old New York *World,* "What Price Glory?," Mencken, and the old Ziegfeld. Oh, well, those are just words. Mr. Kostelanetz, again, the Rhapsody!

PART III

The Dance of Life

11

The Dance of Life

"In 1929, every songwriter who could play
one chord was hired by Hollywood."

ON AUGUST 16, 1927—TWO WEEKS BEFORE OSCAR LEVANT WAS DUE
to appear on the stage of the Plymouth Theatre in *Burlesque*—Al Jolson sang "Dirty Hands, Dirty Face" in a downtown Los Angeles studio where one of the first talking motion pictures, *The Jazz Singer,*
was being made. Jolson broke the sound barrier with his portrayal of
Jakie Rabinowitz, a cantor's son, thus changing the nature of the motion picture industry forever. Dozens of Tin Pan Alley–bred songwriters and composers flocked to Hollywood to find lucrative work
writing songs and scores for the movies. Once the Depression hit, a
steady paycheck was enough to lure the most hardened urbanite
across the country to live among the oleanders and fraying date palms
in the relentlessly glaring sunshine of southern California.

Oscar Levant would soon join their ranks, though he clung to his
Pittsburgh–New York urban habits longer than most. It would be a
half-dozen years after first arriving in California before Levant would
bother to take a look at the Pacific Ocean, which he eventually visited
in the company of Harpo Marx, dressed in his usual rumpled blue suit
and hard shoes—leisure clothes were anathema to him. They drove to
the Palisades and looked out at the unspoiled, tranquil vista— "no

boardinghouses, bathhouses, refreshment stands, or boardwalks anywhere in sight." Oscar gave it a long look. He gave a whistle of disbelief. He said, "What do you know—a Gentile ocean!"

The 20th Century Limited run from New York to California was
beginning to take on a lot of talented passengers. By 1929 all of Hollywood had converted to sound. Some feared the new industry would
destroy Broadway. The invention of the "talkie" had reached a level
of sophistication that made it possible to film and record Broadway
musical shows such as *Burlesque*. Rights to the play were quickly
bought by Paramount Studios, thereby altering the destinies of a
number of its players, including Oscar Levant's.

Paramount bought the play for the movies, as it was leading the
pack in buying up Broadway musicals to transform into film. Stage
actors flocked to Hollywood to replace veteran film actors, whose
careers were wrecked by the new requirement of speech—they simply didn't have the trained voices, or, as in director D. W. Griffith's
case, they were wedded to the silent form, whose day was now over.
They had nothing but contempt for the new talkies.

Paramount opened up an outpost studio in Astoria, Queens, enabling it to more easily feed off Broadway hits. Paramount's founder
and chief mogul, Adolph Zukor, was fascinated by stage performers.
The studio's stars would be largely culled from Broadway hits:
the Marx Brothers, Helen Morgan, Maurice Chevalier, Jeanette
MacDonald, Gertrude Lawrence, Walter Huston, Claudette Colbert,
Fredric March, and Mary Eaton.

Hal Skelly had achieved great popularity through *Burlesque,* and the
star and the play were right down Paramount's alley, not to mention
the added attraction of the promising beauty Barbara Stanwyck. Stanwyck, however, would not reprise her role of Bonnie King in the film
version of *Burlesque*—her husband, Frank Fay, already fearful that her
success would eclipse his own, forbade Stanwyck to join the other cast
members when they assembled in New York City for their Paramount screen test.

In 1929 Harms was bought by Warner Bros., as all the Hollywood
studios rushed to buy up the big music houses. Warner Bros. gobbled
up Harms, Remick's, and Witmark. Feist and Miller Music were
bought by Metro. Dreyfus sold T. B. Harms's catalog to Warner Bros.
for $9 million, which included an agreement to refrain from publish-
ing music for several years. But one of Max Dreyfus's last acts as head
of the company was to put Oscar Levant on the payroll.

It didn't surprise anyone when Dreyfus offered Levant a songwriting contract. Levant had always been Max's pet. Max believed in Oscar's pianistic gifts and his instincts about melody. The contract was lucrative enough for Levant to stop having to dress up for dates with dance orchestras. Dreyfus knew that any day now Levant would be called to travel to California for the filming of *Burlesque,* but he hoped to keep him in New York a little longer. And Oscar, reluctant to leave Max Dreyfus and his "boys," felt ambivalent about the move west.

However, Levant typically repaid Dreyfus's faith in him by hopping a train for the West Coast. The money he was offered to appear in *Burlesque* was twice what Dreyfus's songwriting contract offered. Levant would spend the next two decades shuttling back and forth between Hollywood and New York.

Levant embarked on what he would one day describe as one of his most memorable years: "I had the two best times of my life in London in 1926 and in Hollywood in 1929." His appearance in the film version of *Burlesque* would give him a chance to be present at the creation of a new art form: the Hollywood musical.

Paramount producer David O. Selznick was put in charge of filming *Burlesque.* It was the fledgling mogul's first chance to actually produce one of the studio's "specials" (this was intended to be Paramount's first "talking-and-musical" production). He was given a large budget and the opportunity to be as lavish as he wished, particularly now that one of the musical numbers—the *Ziegfeld Follies*–like production number—would make use of a new, two-color process called Technicolor.

One of Selznick's first acts as the producer of *Burlesque* was to get rid of the title. Fearing that the word "burlesque" would sound too gamey to American family audiences, Selznick searched for a replacement. Ironically, the new title, *The Dance of Life,* came from a 1923 sex study written by Havelock Ellis that the studio had purchased just to be able to use the title.

Selznick suggested a popular young contract player, Nancy Carroll, to replace Barbara Stanwyck in the role of the loyal, suffering wife, Bonnie King. (Levant had met and liked Nancy Carroll a few years earlier, when he had been introduced backstage by his brother Harry during the run of *Spice of 1922.*) She had made a big hit in the film version of *Abie's Irish Rose* in 1928. Carroll had an almost kewpie-doll prettiness animated by genuine warmth and vivacity. But the Broadway cast of *Burlesque* snobbishly turned up their noses at the movie star interloper—she had already been in ten films—and treated her rather badly.

The Dance of Life, adapted for the screen by its original author, would take its place as one of the most important early film musicals, due in part to its portrait of the now-vanished age of vaudeville and certainly for the deeply affecting performance by Hal Skelly. Film historian Miles Kreuger described Skelly in the film:

> In his screen debut, Hal Skelly gives one of the most emotionally chilling performances in the history of cinema. The simple, unaffected manner in which he speaks and moves, the old face of the young man who has struggled for so many years to survive, the intermingling of pathos and humor, and the almost virginal innocence with which he permits his own weakness to toss him around are almost too moving to comprehend in one viewing.

The unending toughness of the vaudeville circuit, reducing its most ardent performers to ground-down workhorses, is accurately reflected in *The Dance of Life*. And Hal Skelly's portrayal, toward the end of the film, of a benumbed, stiff-jointed alcoholic underscores the film's essential realism. *The Dance of Life* also accurately contrasts the worn-out, blowsy chorus "girls" on the vaudeville circuit—out-of-shape, middle-aged women with hard lives—with the elegant, thoroughbred beauties of Broadway's *Ziegfeld Follies*.

The night before Oscar Levant and the cast of *The Dance of Life* were scheduled to appear on Paramount's newly equipped sound stage, the studio burned to the ground.

The devastating fire destroyed the expensive construction and threatened to bring all filming to a halt. The production manager decided to shoot on an old silent stage, but only at night because of traffic noises during the day. What was a vast inconvenience to crew and actors was a boon to Levant, however, since he could keep the same late hours he had become accustomed to in New York. This may be why he seems so relaxed onscreen, so well rested. His "Jerry Evans, piano player" is indeed insouciant, spirited, and natural. Compared to Levant's later films, when he was called upon to simply play himself, his Jerry Evans suggests potential as an actor that Levant would never fully develop. As in the play, he has few lines in the film, but he has presence—he comes across as youthful, dapper, and charming. He holds his own in the company of more seasoned actors, even in his two scenes with the unforgettable Hal Skelly.

Levant didn't need much direction from directors John Cromwell and Edward A. Sutherland. Cromwell in particular had a special affinity for his actors and a knack for drawing their best work from them, most likely due to his vagabond years working in the theatre. He must have thought Oscar didn't need much tampering with, because the only advice he gave the novice actor was "Don't put your hands in front of your face."

The Dance of Life was released in August 1929, and the early Selznick film was embraced at the box office by a public clamoring for the novelty of sound. It also garnered favorable reviews from the critics. *The New York Times* praised Skelly's "talking film bow" and the film's technical advances.

Levant greatly enjoyed his first six months in Hollywood. Here, too, he flourished, elaborating on the bad-boy-about-town personality he had developed in England, although at first he found little about Los Angeles that appealed to him. Levant rarely used his Beverly Hills Hotel swimming pool, preferring to recline in a dark suit and tie, his black wing tips looking even scruffier in the brilliant California sun.

He kept up his persona of the disgruntled wiseacre, nurtured by a growing audience of admirers.

In his first few months in Hollywood, Levant immersed himself in a new community of hopeful performers and songwriters in an attempt to re-create his life in New York. Everyone in Hollywood went to a different place on certain nights of the week, Levant recalled:

> On Sunday nights, it was the Cotton Club in Culver City, where I first saw Jean Harlow. She was ravishingly young and beautiful and was with the ubiquitous Howard Hughes. Other popular places were the Cocoanut Grove, the Roosevelt Hotel, and late at night, the newly opened Brown Derby. On Tuesday nights it was the Club Montmartre, where the songwriters gathered.

Levant soon found a new tutor in hedonism, filling the role recently vacated by Frank Fay in London and earlier by Benny Kaplan and "Big Frenchy" DeMange in New York. Lew Brice—Fanny Brice's brother—became the big brother Levant was lucky he never had. It was a common Bricean ruse to have "girls denude themselves of their clothes, by telling them that he could forecast their future by what he called Body Reading," a ploy Levant disdained, in part, perhaps, because it seemed unnecessary: "Pretty girls were available with such superabundance," Levant remembered, "that they would obligingly fulfill the most sophisticated sexual acts with bland virtuosity."

About this time Levant perfected a party act similar to telling fortunes. He would sit down at the piano and create a characterization in music. At one party, the influential society writer Clare Boothe—who would soon add *Time* and *Life*'s "Luce" to her name—begged Oscar to sketch her in notes. Observing that she indulged in what he termed "intellectual baby talk," Levant created a tiny glissando effect, which she understandably found insulting. "Clare is always capable of speaking my mind," Oscar added to the insult.

One afternoon when Oscar was sleeping late in his Beverly Hills Hotel room, he was awakened by a call from Nancy Carroll, the shop-girl heroine with the heart-shaped face. She was down in the lobby, and she asked if she could come right up. Surprised, Oscar said yes. The two had barely spoken during their nighttime shooting schedule. Carroll was married to playwright Jack Kirkland, but she found Oscar sexy and exciting. Oscar soon found himself involved in an affair with the star of *The Dance of Life*.

They met frequently in the afternoons, when Carroll could slip away from her other responsibilities. Oscar fell madly in love with her, but he began to feel guilty about the adulterous aspect of their relationship. He didn't know that Carroll's marriage was already foundering and that she would file for divorce the following year. Oscar broke off the romance; he may also have felt that he didn't deserve his good fortune. But the two parted friends, making a pact to meet again in ten years—a pact Carroll would fulfill but Levant would not. In any case, the affair gave him proof that he was developing the one thing left to the outsider: personality. And while he didn't have John Gilbert's profile or Cary Grant's way with a suit, he had that quality both men and women ultimately respond to—the sexiness of personality.

After filming was over for *The Dance of Life,* Levant appealed to Max Dreyfus to find him work writing music. Dreyfus interceded with William Le Baron, a songwriter by trade who had become the newly created RKO studio's vice president in charge of production. (Before coming to Hollywood, Le Baron had written the libretto for the 1919 operetta *Apple Blossoms,* which had helped make Broadway stars of its principal dancers, Fred and Adele Astaire.) Le Baron gave RKO its first major success in a film called *Rio Rita* and its only Best Picture Academy Award for *Cimarron.*

Le Baron liked having Oscar Levant around and was glad to see this brash kid from New York out among the swaying palms of Hollywood. He hired Levant to write, with lyricist Sidney Clare, the songs for one of RKO's first musical pictures, *Street Girl*.

Levant described the primitive state of sound production in 1929, when "talking-and-musical pictures" were practically made out of spare parts, as Hollywood entered the mad rush to supply America's new demand for movie musicals:

> Inasmuch as "Street Girl" was an early venture by R.K.O., they had no actual music department for the film. The producer just hired Gus Arnheim's band to play the score because it happened that he was playing at the Cocoanut Grove in Los Angeles at the time. All that was done was to map out a routine for the band on the tunes. . . . Then the same sound track was repeated over and over, as many as a half-a-dozen times in the picture. . . . They certainly got their money's worth out of that one chorus.

Levant and Sidney Clare wrote three songs used in the film: "Broken Up Tune," "My Dream Memory," and the most successful of the three, which became a minor hit for Levant, "Lovable and Sweet." "However," as Levant was quick to add, "in those days anything that got into a picture was a big hit."

Levant would eventually write more than a dozen songs for RKO with Sidney Clare. Clare was fourteen years older than Levant and a veteran of vaudeville with a passion for baseball, golf, and boxing. He and Levant often talked shop while sitting at ringside during American Legion Hall boxing matches, which were popular with the film community. In spite of Levant's often-abrasive personality, Sidney Clare got along well with him.

Between work sessions with Clare, Levant would rove the RKO lot in search of a soundstage that needed a rehearsal pianist. On such occasions, he would sit at the piano and work with the performers on their routines or musical numbers. Dorothy Lee, the pert sidekick to RKO's house comedy team Bert Wheeler and Robert Woolsey (featured in *Rio Rita*), recalled that "the man who played piano for all of [our] rehearsal sessions was a very young Oscar Levant. We could hardly rehearse because he was such a riot." Levant loved having the run of the studio, working on songs, acting as a wisecracking, troubleshooting rehearsal pianist, making time with the chorus girls and ingenues languishing between shots.

In the space of six months, Levant composed tunes for six RKO films, following the trend to feature a musical component in each production. The second film for which he wrote music was RKO's 1929 feature *The Delightful Rogue;* he and Clare provided the song "Gay Love" (at a time when "gay" had only one meaning). Produced by William Le Baron, *The Delightful Rogue* was about a "ruthless sea rogue and the titian-haired dancing girl in a throbbing tropic love duel," in the words of the studio publicity department. The film was not a hit.

In 1929 alone, the Levant-Clare team wrote songs for four films: *Jazz Heaven* and *Tanned Legs,* both pretty insubstantial pieces of fluff though not without some charm, and the melodramas *Half Marriage* and *Side Street.*

In *Jazz Heaven,* star-crossed lovers on Tin Pan Alley risk everything to compose a successful song together. When they do so after much hardship, it's with a song called "Someone"—written, of course by Levant and Clare. In *Tanned Legs,* they provided a number of snappy tunes to accompany the hijinks of a spunky but troubled family at a seaside resort, most notably "You're Responsible," a good-natured tune of mock indignation.

Half Marriage deals with a secret marriage, accidental death, a jealous suitor, and recalcitrant parents; the Levant-Clare songs "After the Clouds Roll By" and "You're Marvelous" help to relieve the heavy melodrama. The only other notable aspect of *Half Marriage* is that the bride's mother is played by future gossip columnist Hedda Hopper.

"Take a Look at Her Now" is the Levant-Clare song featured in the melodrama *Side Street,* the story of the three O'Farrell brothers, which was designed to showcase three Irish silent film actors, the Moore brothers.

All of these RKO films using Levant's music were William Le Baron productions, and the songs were published by T. B. Harms, though RKO retained the copyrights. In fact, in later years RKO would use some of Levant's tunes as background music in other films. The singer and music archivist Michael Feinstein has noticed that:

> In *Shall We Dance*—because RKO owned the rights to the songs Levant had written for the studio—before Fred [Astaire] and Ginger [Rogers] sing "Let's Call the Whole Thing Off," the background music that they're playing is [a 1935 Levant tune,] "I Got a New Lease on Life."

Levant and Clare were considered one of the hot songwriting teams in 1929, although their RKO songs are not much more than average, workmanlike tunes. Feinstein, who worked as Ira Gershwin's assistant before becoming a successful performer, believes:

> There are only a couple of songs in those early musicals that I think are really good. Most of them are rather average. . . . There's not a whole lot of inspired stuff in them, but the movies are not inspired, you know. They're just not very good movies, and they probably were under the gun, where they had to write a lot of material and were just churning it out, and [Levant] probably didn't take it very seriously. . . . It probably didn't mean all that much to him, even though he had, of course, a song, "If You Want the Rainbow (You Must Have the Rain)," in a Fanny Brice movie. And I think that's a better song, probably because it was written for Fanny Brice. And, of course, there's a little bit of it played in the background of *Funny Lady*.

The Levant-Clare team would provide one more song for RKO, for a film called *Leathernecking,* released in 1930. It was an unsuccessful adaptation of a Rodgers and Hart stage musical, but without the Rodgers and Hart score. "Mighty Nice and So Particular" is the Levant-Clare song; the only other notable feature of *Leathernecking* is the debut of its star, Irene Dunne.

Oscar was lucky to have had this flurry of film work just prior to the stock market crash, an opportunity he appreciated but couldn't help commenting on in his typically self-denigrating way:

> Since RKO had just been put in competition, it got all the dregs of the songwriting world. I, it seemed, had been hired to raise the tone of the establishment. That was the first mistake of many in RKO's career. . . .

But Levant is too hard on RKO, which was, after all, the first studio created to market the talkie that had no background in silent films. RKO's lack of history does, however, help to explain how the bumptious twenty-two-year-old Oscar Levant virtually became its music department in 1929, and how he graduated to become William Le Baron's unofficial aide-de-camp. Indeed, Levant seemed to be all over the lot, wearing different hats—sitting in on production meetings, being asked to read properties, playing the piano for visiting dignitaries from America's growing chain of movie houses, assisting Le Baron in various ways. Without a Mayer, a Goldwyn, or a Zanuck at the helm, a gap was left open in management for an upstart like Levant to be brought into the decision-making process. And Levant,

a well-read autodidact, was better informed about literature and culture than many of the moguls-in-the-making at RKO.

He enjoyed his RKO work for other reasons—it gave him a
chance to exercise his hyper sexual appetite:

> My job had a lot of facets, and one of the best was picking the girls to
> sing the songs I wrote. I will not say that I romanced all of them but I
> certainly tried.

Levant also claimed that he helped start George Raft on his movie
career: "He was in a line of extras when I suggested to the assistant
director that he be given a few lines of dialogue."

Levant's role at RKO established a pattern in which leading
producers and production executives of the major film studios all
seemed to enjoy having him around. The antithesis of a yes-man,
Levant was more like an "are you kidding?" man. He had intelligence, wit, and he made the moguls laugh. Having spent so many
hours of his young life at the *Follies* and *Midnight Frolics,* in the peanut
galleries of legitimate theatres, in Carnegie Hall, not to mention the
hours spent reading alone in boardinghouse rooms, Levant had a solid
background in the prevailing forms of high and low culture of his day.

And so he became the *enfant* consultant who didn't care enough to
pander to the big shots, thus earning their respect. He didn't really
care whether or not he got another acting job, and since the nascent
soundstages needed Levant more than he needed them, he was protected by his lack of Hollywood ambition. The ambitions he still
nursed, secretly, could never be satisfied by Hollywood.

In 1930, a year after he broke off his affair with Nancy Carroll, Oscar
became involved with another beauty, the actress Virginia Cherrill,
who made her luminous screen debut as the blind flower girl in
Charlie Chaplin's silent picture *City Lights.* However, a nasal, twangy
voice with a pronounced upper-crust midwestern accent would prevent her from successfully crossing over into talking pictures. No
matter—Virginia Cherrill, a socialite from Chicago, was bred to
marry well, and marry well she did, several times. In 1930 she was
making the rounds of all the smart parties in Hollywood. Louella Par-
sons described her as "Hollywood's greatest beauty." One evening
the slim, flaxen-haired actress found herself at a dinner party seated
next to Oscar Levant.

"I'm sorry they sat me next to you," was Oscar's opening gambit.

He had actually meant to commiserate with her that she was not given a more famous or handsome dinner partner, but Cherrill took it the wrong way and became incensed. Still, Levant managed to overcome her pique, and by the time dessert was served they had made a date.

The two embarked on a passionate affair, although Oscar wasn't Cherrill's usual type—for one thing, he wasn't rich. Oscar later admitted that he actually found her "a little dull": She worried constantly about her face. But the romance was heated to a fast boil by the entrance of another suitor—the impeccable Cary Grant, who claimed that he had fallen in love with Virginia the first time he saw her. From that moment she used her relationship with Oscar to make Cary Grant jealous.

It was a strange courtship all around—Cary Grant on a date with Virginia Cherrill, dragging along his housemate, Randolph Scott. The two—Grant and Scott, that is—were inseparable, working out every morning in their private gym or taking a long swim before heading over to Paramount. Virginia saw in Cary Grant the superior catch. His popularity was surging at the box office, he was well liked in Hollywood society, his new film *I'm No Angel* was breaking box-office records—but she seemed to prefer Oscar with his sexy, irreverent personality to the perennially tanned Englishman.

But Cary Grant was not about to have his time beaten by the rumpled-looking fellow from Pittsburgh. One night, furious with Virginia over her liaison with Oscar, Cary Grant took his revenge—not on Oscar Levant but on his car. Levant's car was parked in front of Virginia's house in Hancock Park, so Grant repeatedly rammed it, tattooing it with dents, while the two lovers slept. "The one thing I got out of our love," Levant later wrote, "was a bill for damages to my car. I thought it was a peculiar way of anyone's showing his strength, even though I sympathized with his mood." Soon after, Virginia married Cary Grant, though the marriage would not last.

In 1930 Levant became involved in the decision-making process on Le Baron's successful RKO feature *Cimarron,* based on the Edna Ferber novel. Luckily for the studio and the career of Irene Dunne, his advice was not taken. Levant had gotten to know Irene Dunne on *Leathernecking* and had liked her—she would often serenade visiting dignitaries while Levant played the piano—but he felt that she was wrong for the lead role of Sabra. He sat in on endless casting conferences and emphatically opposed the selection of Irene Dunne. When the film was finally made and released in 1931, *Cimarron* won an

Academy Award for best picture and Irene Dunne was nominated for best actress. It would be the only Best Picture Academy Award RKO ever received in its twenty-eight-year history.

Although the movie was enormously popular, it lost money due to its astronomical expenses. As for Oscar Levant, he soon found himself on the Super Chief, hurtling back to New York.

12

Penthouse Beachcomber

"An evening with George Gershwin is a George
Gershwin evening."

OSCAR LEVANT DIDN'T PICK A VERY AUSPICIOUS MOMENT TO MAKE HIS
debut as the composer for a Broadway musical. With the stock market
crash on October 24, 1929, banks failed and hundreds of thousands of
families lost their life savings. After the boom years of the twenties,
Broadway felt the impact of the Depression and began to take on a
decidedly down-at-heels look.

Despite the caution of the early months of 1930, Oscar made his
Broadway debut as one of the composers of a musical whimsy called
Ripples, a Charles Dillingham production built around the legend of
Rip Van Winkle. The book was written by a distinguished librettist,
William Anthony McGuire, and Dr. Albert Sirmay (T. B. Harms's
music editor) cowrote the score with Levant. Irving Caesar and Gra-
ham John wrote the lyrics. It was an exciting opportunity for Levant,
but he would experience his debut as a defeat.

Charles Dillingham was a highly successful producer of Broadway
plays and lavish musical productions that were second only to Florenz
Ziegfeld's for sheer glory and popularity. Dillingham was known for
his dapper, gentlemanly appearance—he was always seen wearing his
trademark derby hat. The Depression would bankrupt Dillingham,

but not before he managed to produce *Ripples,* giving the twenty-three-year-old Oscar Levant the chance to compose the show's score with Sirmay. It was in fact a Dreyfus–Le Baron–Dillingham connection that provided Levant with this opportunity.

The city Levant returned to in 1930 was markedly changed from the one he had left in 1928. Tin Pan Alley had been bought up by Hollywood, so the streets around West Twenty-eighth Street that had once reverberated with the clamor of song pluggers and fast pianists were now silent. The breadlines on Times Square, the empty hotels and vacant stores along Broadway, the plethora of out-of-work actors, the famous New York City skyline that darkened as lights went out across the city—the once-thriving metropolis was locked in the deadly embrace of the Great Depression.

Levant had grown noticeably during his West Coast hegira. He had gained in confidence and was now returning to his adopted city as something of a Hollywood veteran. He would remain relatively unscathed by the Depression. His career continued to thrive—he was hired for *Ripples* almost as soon as he arrived in New York. The most cataclysmic event of his generation never rattled him, though it shook the confidence of more established performers. Groucho Marx, for example, admitted that after the Depression, he never had an untroubled night of sleep. Levant would continue to host other demons, but financial insecurity would never be one of them. He was protected by his youth—and by his ability to endear himself to the rich.

The chance to write a Broadway musical had lurked in Oscar's mind ever since his envy had been stirred by George Gershwin. He knew that the success of even one song in the show would be an enormous boon to his reputation. Unfortunately, reality would fall short of his expectations.

One of the two lyricists for *Ripples* was none other than Irving Caesar, another Lindy's habitué and a gifted songwriter. Caesar, who had written "Swanee" with George Gershwin, billed as "Al Jolson's Greatest Song," was already something of a legend among songwriters.

With his crushed porkpie hat and ever-present cigar screwed into the side of his mouth, Caesar was in some ways a perfect collaborator for Oscar Levant, though their brief association would produce only one successful song from *Ripples,* the popular "Lady, Play Your Mandolin."

Introduced to the public by the ukelele-toting Nick Lucas and taken on the road by Blossom Seeley (whose earlier fame was as a "red hot mama" in what was called "coon shouting"), the song became a much-requested novelty in vaudeville. The song is a lighthearted, playful rumba with a Spanish flavor. Early versions, such as the Havannah Novelty Orchestra's 1930 recording on the Victor label, feature the mandolin only in the introductory passages. Later, more appealing versions feature the mandolin throughout. In the Havannah Novelty Orchestra's recording, the song comes across as pretty typical late-twenties nightclub fare—a catchy and likable tune, but nothing to inspire dreams. Frank De Voll and the Friendly Tavern Boys' recording on the Columbia label is far more pleasing—smoother, more fully orchestrated, with the mandolin heard throughout the song. Ironically, the last extant recording of "Lady, Play Your Mandolin" would be made in 1974 by the first person to record it, Nick Lucas, in an obscure comeback album called *Rose Colored Glasses* (Accent LP). By then the song had mutated into a highly embellished vocal solo accompanied only by ukelele and piano.

Dreyfus's boy had finally produced a bona fide hit, and Dreyfus was proud of his *enfant terrible*.

On the cold February night of *Ripples'* opening, Levant picked up the early-morning newspapers and read the reviews of the show. The consensus was that it was an entertaining comeback for its comedy star, Fred Stone, who had recently survived an airplane crash, but its appeal was too unsophisticated for Broadway audiences. The reviews would go from welcoming to lukewarm to final pronouncements over the dead body. "A Fred Stone Show Flops!" announced the *New York Telegram* on March 22, 1930. "Comedian, Outmoded Today on the Broadway He Helped Make Glamorous, Will Close 'Ripples' Next Week," the headline continued. The show was simply too wholesome for contemporary Broadway, and its small audience of families with children couldn't sustain the run. The show closed after only eight weeks at the New Amsterdam Theatre.

Though *Ripples* fell short of Oscar Levant's ambitions, it would bring him closer to George Gershwin. Across the street from the New Amsterdam Theatre, Gershwin's political satire *Strike Up the Band* was playing at the Selwyns' Times Square Theatre—geographically opposed, as Levant noted, to *Ripples*. Levant quickly became one of the show's biggest fans, though an earlier version of the musical had bombed in its first out-of-town production three years earlier. "I . . . acquired a fondness for the score of 'Strike Up the Band,' " Levant would later reminisce.

As quickly as the score of "Ripples" palled on my audience, it palled on me more. Hypnotically, I would find myself at the rear of the Selwyn [sic], resentfully transported by the fresh rhythms and humors of the Gershwin lyrics and music. . . . Ironically, just as I had my first musical show produced . . . George emerged with a wholly new concept of musical comedy writing. Up until this time his librettos had not encouraged any departure from the clichés of boy-meets-girl songs. For the first time he was provided by George S. Kaufman and Morrie Ryskind with a book whose wry satiric wit illuminated a new facet of Gershwin's talent.

But Oscar was, in his usual fashion, too hard on himself. Unable to enjoy his own seemingly modest success—which was in actuality a terrific undertaking for a twenty-three-year-old song composer—Oscar instead tortured himself with the more sophisticated melodies pouring out of the Times Square Theatre.

One afternoon, during a matinee performance of *Ripples,* Oscar, as was his habit, found himself drifting across the street to the Times Square Theatre. While he was standing at the back of the theatre and listening, spellbound, behind a knot of ushers, his reverie was broken by a tap on the shoulder. A slim figure asked him, "How's your show doing?" When the curtain came down on the first act, Oscar invited the young woman across the street to see for herself. Oscar had immediately recognized his inquirer as Leonore (Lee) Gershwin, Ira's wife and Emily Paley's sister.

Lee was typically gracious to Oscar, but she did little to allay his fears about the success of his own score bursting forth from the pit orchestra. "After she had seen a few numbers of 'Ripples,'" Oscar remembered, "she developed in me a scorn for my own music almost equal to hers."

Oscar made apologies for his work to Lee, noting that the fairy tale was not his genre. She rather agreed and encouraged him to come with her to watch the conclusion of *Strike Up the Band.* Oscar would dolefully recall their crossing the street, which was beginning to seem like an unbridgeable distance: "Like a missionary after office hours, she led me back, symbolically, to the Selwyn [sic], where I remained in spirit for the next nine or ten years."

Lee asked if Oscar would like to come by the penthouse and spend the evening with the Gershwins. Before she tapped him on the shoulder, Oscar had been no more than a distant satellite in the Gershwin constellation. Now he was brought crashing into the center of their universe.

"I escorted her back to the apartment," he wrote calmly years later, but one can feel the restraint in that sentence. For Oscar, the doors of a new life were about to open, though other doors would slam shut. After *Ripples,* Levant would become trapped in the Gershwin orbit and would never again write a Broadway musical score.

Leonore Gershwin remains an ambiguous figure in the life of Oscar Levant. She liked to think of Oscar as *her* discovery, and throughout his life he would consider Lee a good friend and confidante. Yet there was a darker side to Lee Gershwin.

Leonore Strunsky Gershwin and her sister Emily were both attractive, intelligent women with a gift for hospitality. It is not surprising that Ira Gershwin was attracted to the assertive, strong-willed Leonore. Sam Behrman had seen in Ira a deep reclusiveness. As nature abhors a vacuum, Lee rushed in to fill that reserve.

But Oscar liked her: "Leonore was a gracious hostess and the first person to tolerate my unresolved social dissonances." Through this friendship, Oscar was soon spending days and weeks in Ira and Lee's apartment. Since their penthouse adjoined George Gershwin's at 33 Riverside Drive, Oscar was soon wandering between the two households through the short passageway that allowed the brothers to work easily together, their apartments like two chambers of the same heart.

A different portrait of Lee Gershwin emerges from other sources. In Truman Capote's book-length essay *The Muses Are Heard,* he describes accompanying Lee and the cast of *Porgy and Bess* on a tour through Russia undertaken some twenty-four years after Oscar's first meeting with Lee. Capote observed her, bedecked with diamonds, in her role of the surviving *grande dame* of the Gershwin family. When asked if her accommodations on their way to Leningrad were comfortable, she answered,

> "Darling, please. It's not important, not the tiniest bit. If they'll just put me somewhere. I wouldn't dream of moving," . . . [though she] was destined, in the course of the next few days, to insist on changing her accommodation three times.

She emerges from Capote's description as vain and pretentious, but there is still another side to this woman who would devote herself to the preservation of the Gershwin legacy. Her amiability and graciousness were threaded with an instinct for ferreting out the vulnerabilities of those around her. Something of this is caught in the Warner Bros. film *Rhapsody in Blue,* the romanticized 1945 version of the life of

George Gershwin, when the actress portraying Lee turns to Ira and says, "Do me a favor, Ira—don't ever turn out to be a genius like your brother." Lee was master of the subtle insult, made so silkily that it wasn't felt until much later, when it was too late to defend oneself. Though Oscar jokingly described Lee's reaction to his score during their first encounter, for a man struggling with a tremendous amount of self-doubt Lee's attitude was subtly undermining.

Within a few years, Lee Gershwin would give Oscar a sleeping pill, Alenol, to help his insomnia—his first, slippery step down a nightmare path of drug dependency. But for now, his friendship with George Gershwin at last truly blossoming, Levant was wallowing in ambrosia. He would put his own ambitions aside while he played at being Gershwin's acolyte, favorite pianist, and penthouse court jester.

Though both were from Russian Jewish immigrant families and were high school dropouts, Gershwin and Levant couldn't have been more different—Gershwin with his impeccable grooming, his elegant walk, his spats, his cultivation of high society, his apparent self-confidence, and Oscar Levant, unruly-haired, knock-kneed, unkempt, yet more fluent than George on the piano, able to run through all of Chopin, for example, whereas "Gershwin couldn't run through a Chopin prelude," as their friend the composer David Diamond once observed. Gershwin affected an upper-class accent, which Levant never bothered to acquire. Gershwin was a health faddist with a personal trainer, barbells, and a tremendous zest for Ping-Pong. Levant, his black shoes in need of polish and his blue suit jacket creased like a map of the world, eschewed all forms of physical activity except sex and playing the piano.

The confident, cigar-smoking composer and the insecure snapping turtle of Lindy's developed a kind of friendship: Levant adoring, Gershwin tolerant and aloof—really too busy composing music to put a lot into a friendship.

Oscar Levant's unmannerly behavior must have been a constant reminder to George of a skin he was trying to shed—the rough hide of the immigrant working class. Oscar dragged that carapace around with him like a hermit crab its shell. George was like the favored older brother, Esau, in the biblical story that haunted Oscar, receiving the paternal blessing and approbation of the world while the younger brother coveted his blessing. Oscar would try to steal Gershwin's blessing by truncating his own composing career to serve as second pianist and sidekick for Gershwin. Still in search of an authentic self, Levant wanted to *be* George Gershwin. *Ripples* would soon end with a whimper, and Levant would put his own ambitions on hold while he basked in the brilliant, reflected glow of Gershwin's risen star.

But Levant didn't submerge all of his talents in Gershwin's shadow. One of the areas in which Oscar felt he could compete was in dating chorus girls (he preferred the chorus girls in Gershwin's show to the ones in his own, who, he decided, were off limits). Levant complained that George's name recognition tipped the friendly rivalry too much in his favor. Characterizing himself in typically unflattering terms, he described the competition:

> My tactic . . . was to appeal to the mother instinct, latent even in a chorus girl, as a social misfit, an irresponsible lad, an example of talent wasting for want of the proper guidance. I kept hinting that these veins could be tapped by the right woman, that I could go far with the proper girl. (I might go even farther with the wrong girl.)

Ira and Lee, a childless couple, virtually adopted Oscar, and Oscar happily settled into the pattern of competing and performing music within an immensely talented family. Here was another household of brothers, looked after by an intelligent, emotionally reserved woman capable of encouraging and squelching simultaneously—just the kind of nurturing Oscar was used to.

In their familial embrace Levant nearly forgot about the closing of *Ripples* and the songwriting he had recently rededicated himself to. How could he do his own work when he spent all of his time at the Gershwins', when George was composing the insouciantly wonderful music for *Girl Crazy* and for his first Hollywood film, *Delicious*?

The advantage of having a pianist with Oscar's gifts at the ready was not lost on Gershwin. "The two pianos in George's apartment," Oscar wrote, "made it possible for us to play his music together as it was written, for it was his custom to sketch his large works for two pianos before scoring them." But what really ensured that the doors would be kept open for Oscar was his wit. Gershwin didn't even seem to mind when he was the butt of Oscar's jokes. "An evening with George Gershwin is a George Gershwin evening," Oscar said about Gershwin's penchant for hogging the piano all night at every gathering. His swipes at Vernon Duke and Sigmund Romberg must have pleased Gershwin, who was intensely competitive but generally kept his opinions of his fellow composers to himself.

Soon Oscar was taking all his meals with the Gershwins, and since their two apartments remained an open house to a vast coterie of friends and relatives, no one really noticed that Oscar had virtually moved in (though he kept his room at the Park Central Hotel, to which he would return late at night to sleep). The heady atmosphere of music and talk stimulated his volubility. The longer he stayed, the more he had to say. In his own words, Oscar became the Gershwins' "penthouse beachcomber," and his room at the Park Central—like his composition notebooks—remained mostly empty.

With the fabulous, romantic melodies and lyrics of the *Girl Crazy* score—"Embraceable You," "But Not for Me"—running through his head, Levant would soon find someone who would satisfy his stirred feelings. In 1930 he ran into a young woman he had briefly met a few years earlier in the company of Walter Winchell at one of the seamier nightclubs in the city. The crusty gossip columnist had approached Levant and said to him in his staccato, tommy-gun voice, "There's a lovely girl here. I want you to sit with her and look out for her. She's a friend of mine."

The young woman, who was about eighteen at their first meeting, was a dancer and aspiring actress from Lewistown, Illinois. At the time of their second meeting she was appearing in the Cole Porter revue *The New Yorkers*. Her name was Barbara Smith, but she was working as a dancer and actress under the stage name of Wooddell, which was her grandmother's name. Her mother's maiden name, Oscar would note, was Jones. The sheer Americanness of Miss Barbara Smith-whose-mother's-name-was-Jones was a delight to Oscar, as was the athletic, redheaded young woman's extreme attractiveness.

Barbara loved tennis, golf, and horseback riding—all physical activities Levant loathed. She had gotten a job with the *Follies* her first day in New York. Though she tended to be quiet and insecure about her intellect—she felt she was saddled with the "beautiful but dumb" label—she exuded a kind of midwestern vitality and beauty that never went unnoticed. Oscar was impressed. He fell in love with Barbara Wooddell, née Smith, whose mother's name was Jones.

Through 1930 and early 1931, whenever Levant wasn't at the Gershwins' he was squiring Barbara around. She received all of his romantic attentions and began to meet his circle of writers, composers, newspapermen, bookies, gangsters, and horse players at Lindy's, where she was welcomed as Oscar's girl, Oscar cutting a path through the crowded tables and busy waiters like the parting of the Red Sea. When *The New Yorkers* closed, Barbara joined the chorus of Ziegfeld's *Follies of 1931*. Oscar would walk her to nearly every show at the Ziegfeld Theatre and meet her when it let out, giving her an earful about George, Ira, Lee, Sam Behrman, and a host of Broadway big-timers along the way. Most of Oscar's buddies liked Barbara Smith—the waiters at Lindy's would carve a generous slab of cheesecake for the young woman with great cheekbones and long legs whenever she came in, proudly, on Oscar Levant's arm.

13

Various Debuts

"Who goes to debuts? Relatives and enemies."

THOUGH T. B. HARMS HAD BEEN SOLD TO WARNER BROS., MAX Dreyfus still held court at his upstate retreat in Brewster, New York. In 1930 Oscar met the composer and gifted orchestrator Robert Russell Bennett, who had entered the Dreyfus circle by becoming T. B. Harms's chief arranger. He had launched a tremendously successful career orchestrating musicals, a talent that would earn him the sobriquet "the Beethoven of modern orchestration."

Bennett had observed Oscar playing four-handed piano pieces with Dreyfus and Gershwin. It would have been hard *not* to run into Oscar at the Gershwins' in those days, as his presence seemed to galvanize the household around his uninhibited nervous energy.

Bennett was tall, fair, and craggy, with a high forehead that gave him a brainy, ascetic look. He had just completed a work for two pianos and orchestra and was anxious about its upcoming premiere at the Hollywood Bowl. In casting around for a second pianist, he realized he had to look no further than his own circle of friends. Oscar excelled at piano duets, and, though he had not yet set foot on the concert stage, he clearly had the ability and musicianship to do justice to the piece. Bennett asked Levant to accompany him to California.

At long last Oscar Levant would have his concert debut, performing Robert Russell Bennett's March for Two Pianos and Orchestra at the Hollywood Bowl in Los Angeles on July 19, 1930.

The first musical season at the Hollywood Bowl had opened just eight years earlier, establishing the amphitheatre as a center of musical and dramatic arts in Los Angeles. Built into the Hollywood hills just outside the Los Angeles city limits, the Bowl was a natural amphitheatre and was beginning to be known as "the place to be," though some were put off by the challenges of conducting and performing in the open air.

Robert Russell Bennett had high expectations for the premiere of his work, hoping that it would be the highlight of a rather crowded Hollywood Bowl program that evening. In fact, Levant confessed, the two men spent more time rehearsing their bows than practicing the piece. They were slated for the eighth program in a series of summer music offerings that would be held under the stars on a balmy California night.

Unfortunately for Bennett and Levant, the conductor, Karl Krueger, a somewhat humorless fellow, was not an appreciator of the Great White Way nor of orchestral music inspired by Broadway themes. To make matters worse, the evening's program was an overcrowded mix of contrasting musical styles. It was so long and unwieldy that half the audience had disappeared by the time Levant and Bennett took their places at the two pianos.

Krueger's own lack of enthusiasm for the piece and his dislike of the Broadway style (which was, after all, what Bennett was driving at despite his having studied with Nadia Boulanger in France) caused him to botch the coda. The two pianists fled the stage when their performance ended, taking their practiced bows with them. For Levant, his debut was another humiliation, and the Sunday and Monday Los Angeles papers would only rub salt in his wounds. Writing in the *Los Angeles Times,* Isabel Morse Jones mentioned "the monotonous New York cacophony of the young Mr. Bennett's march," not bothering to mention Levant's performance. The *coup de grâce* was the misspelling of Oscar's name as "Lavant" on the program. Oscar retreated to New York.

The following year he would have a second chance to display his pianistic skills in Bennett's March, coincidentally at another outdoor stadium—this time at the Lewisohn Stadium at 138th Street in Manhattan. As part of its season of summer concerts it had scheduled an all-American program of music for August 10, 1931. To Oscar's delight, he and Robert Russell Bennett were on a program that included George Gershwin performing the piano part of *Rhapsody in Blue.*

Throughout the Depression, one could hear symphonic music at Lewisohn Stadium's summer concerts for twenty-five cents for the cheapest seats. The stadium concerts were a highly popular event that drew leading artists and became a summer tradition. The series was organized by an irrepressible and indefatigable socialite, Mrs. Charles Guggenheimer, known as "Minnie" to her legions of friends and admirers. The stadium itself, dedicated in 1915, was the gift of Adolph Lewisohn, a German-born Jew who came to America as a young man and eventually accrued enormous wealth as head of several mining companies.

The structure, built entirely of concrete, was meant to evoke the semicircular, rock-hewn theatre on the Trasteverine Hill overlooking the city of Rome, though critics would come to call its concrete look "the municipal disposal plant" style of architecture. The acoustics were not the best, and its cold stone seats were uncomfortable and treacherous to clothing. But stadium events were popular, and the summer music series flourished.

Gershwin's circle was featured prominently in the August 10 program: Not only did the evening's roster include Bennett and Levant, but Gershwin's friend and co-orchestrator William Merrigan Daly would conduct the *Rhapsody.*

The afternoon before the concert, Levant dressed in his tuxedo and joined the Gershwins for an early dinner. A light rain began growing heavier and heavier as the afternoon progressed. Just before he left with the Gershwins for Lewisohn Stadium, the downpour turned into a summer thunderstorm, drenching the stadium. The concert was postponed.

The following day the ritual was repeated, and again a steady downpour drowned the musicians' scheduled concert, which was postponed a second time. When the third day brought a third consecutive rainstorm, biblical allusions were being made at dinner. After each cancellation, Levant would make a date with Barbara Wooddell. Barbara would bring a friend for George, and the four of them would go out on the town.

The first clear night that permitted the concert to be held—August 14, 1931—brought Oscar a sickly feeling of panic. Suddenly he was gripped by nauseating stage fright—something that had been much milder at his Hollywood Bowl debut. Perhaps it was the memory of the poor reviews that worried him, or possibly the incessant rain and the outdoor venue stirred up an earlier memory: the summer rain that had sent him into a breathless panic when he and his mother had gone to listen to Tchaikovsky's *1812 Overture* at Schenley Park, out under the gloomy skies of Allegheny County. The weather—and, it seemed, even the music—had turned against him then. Once he sat down at the piano and began to play, however, his panic subsided.

The concert reviews tended to focus on the event rather than the individual performances. The all-American concert presented three generations of composers in a program that was considered a novelty in 1931. *New York Times* critic Olin Downes's concert preview reminds us that Gershwin, despite his tremendous popular success, was still having to earn his stripes from the serious music critics:

> Mr. Gershwin is a city composer. His music comes from the bricks, the cabaret, the theatre. It is music of which it could be said that like Topsy it has "just growed." . . . It is still short, from the symphonic angle, on the technical side . . .

Downes concluded his preview with a brief mention of Levant: "Thus three generations of musicians contribute to the Stadium program tomorrow night, including Oscar Levant as pianist, and a crowd will not be lacking for the occasion."

Despite the disappointingly scarce mention of Levant at the piano, it had been an auspicious New York debut for the young songwriter. Levant had, at the relatively young age of twenty-four, fulfilled a secretly nurtured ambition: He had appeared on the concert stage with George Gershwin.

Levant would soon make a debut of a different kind—this time in a more personal arena. One evening as Oscar and Barbara Wooddell strolled up Seventh Avenue toward the Ziegfeld Theatre on West Fifty-fifth Street, the insecure Pittsburgh prodigy asked the young midwestern showgirl, "Why don't we get married?"

Barbara was appearing in one of the last editions of the *Follies*—truly the end of an era for Broadway aficionados of the twenties and for Oscar in particular, who had first fallen in love with Ziegfeld's *Midnight Frolics* as a young boy fresh in the city. In 1931 Florenz Ziegfeld was exhausted, ailing, and nearly bankrupt—broken on the big wheel he had helped to create. His 1931 *Follies* was a desperate fling at restoring past glories, and it featured, in Oscar's opinion, the most breathtakingly beautiful women he had ever seen, including his own Barbara Wooddell. The Joseph Urban sets, Helen Morgan singing Noël Coward's "Half-Caste Woman," and Ruth Etting singing

"Shine On, Harvest Moon" were completely eclipsed, as far as Oscar was concerned, by the stunning showgirls. Despite these glories, the 1931 *Follies* failed, so it may have been the added appeal of nostalgia that prompted Oscar to propose marriage.

In any case, Oscar rather casually proposed, the midwestern beauty responded with "Wonderful," and so Barbara Wooddell walked into the theatre an engaged terpsichorine while her future husband rushed down to the Paramount Theatre to tell Ben Bernie and his second wife, Wes, of his plans.

"You're out of your mind" was Wes Bernie's response to Oscar's news. "You don't want to get married, you're a kid!" Ben Bernie agreed. The more they spoke against the marriage, the more terrified Oscar became.

Oscar left the Paramount in confusion. He scrambled back to the Ziegfeld Theatre, making his way through the backstage props and showgirls adjusting their shimmering costumes, to find Barbara. But before he could locate his fiancée, Barbara's girlfriends in the chorus surrounded him, congratulating him and covering him with lipstick kisses.

Oscar found Barbara backstage and told her the marriage was off, that he had changed his mind and she should, too—it was all a big mistake. Barbara was humiliated. With the strains of the overture and the dimming houselights, she traipsed onstage, going before an unsuspecting audience that couldn't guess at her disappointment.

Desperate to escape his own machinations, Oscar fled back to what was left of his real family, all the way back to Pittsburgh.

When Harry Levant had married Pearl Eaton, the family had been outraged. When Oscar's brother Bennie—ten years older than Oscar and their father's favorite son—eloped with a German Jewish girl, Max was said to have fainted. An anxious gloom had settled on the household the afternoon of Bennie's elopement. Annie enlisted Oscar's help in calling all of Bennie's friends to try to find out what had happened. She became so distraught that Oscar had tried to comfort her: "I said that I would not only never marry a Gentile—I would never get married at all." At a tender age, Oscar concluded that "girls were obviously insidious and bad and I made up my mind I would do without them."

By the time Oscar returned to Pittsburgh in 1931 to escape marriage to Barbara Wooddell, his older brother Bennie had two children. Harry was divorced from Pearl Eaton, Honey was still married to his first wife, and Annie was still living alone in one of the Greenfield Avenue row houses Max had left her. A lot had changed in the Hill district. It had begun to steadily lose its Jewish character after the First World War; Jewish cultural life continued to diminish. The synagogues on the Hill were still Orthodox but had smaller congregations. There were fewer kosher markets, and the sounds of children reciting in Hebrew no longer filled the streets. The only aspect of Oscar's old neighborhood that seemed unchanged was Colwell Street.

Oscar didn't even discuss his problematical engagement with Annie. It was enough to be home again and to be reminded of his solemn boy's promise never to marry. In any case, his three-week hiatus in Pittsburgh did little to calm his mind. Annie would express her opinion of Oscar's marriage in her own way, after the fact.

Having found neither encouragement nor discouragement for his wedding plans, a confused Oscar returned to New York and confessed his intentions to Max Dreyfus, who remained chief among his father substitutes in New York. Dreyfus's reaction was to hustle his young protégé off to London immediately, to discourage his romantic attachment.

"You're not in love, you only think you're in love," he stated (a line almost good enough to be a T. B. Harms song title), putting his foot down on Oscar's shaky plans. He was convinced that the young man's marriage to a *Ziegfeld Follies* girl could only mean disaster. He arranged for Oscar to accompany him and his wife to London, where, among other enterprises, he was involved in a musical show slated for the Hippodrome called *Out of the Bottle*. Oscar could work on the score with its English composer, Vivian Ellis, a song composer and lyricist, thus keeping him out of trouble and his mind off his inamorata.

Out of the Bottle was a forgettable affair. It would open briefly at the Hippodrome the following year but would never make it across the Atlantic to Broadway. The most successful number to come out of the show was a fox-trot titled "We've Got the Moon and Sixpence," which Levant described as "a rather successful la-de-da song." The song was recorded by Ray Noble and became a hit in 1932, long after Levant had left England. Dreyfus's newly formed music publishing venture, Chappell & Co., published the song, though Levant would never be paid royalties for it. It is probable that Dreyfus—always fatherly but always a good businessman—deducted Oscar's expenses, so that Oscar, in lieu of royalties, was presented with a bill for one pound, for use of a piano. This particular trip to England would not turn out to be a lucrative one.

Levant and the Dreyfuses stayed at the Carlton Hotel in London during their six-week visit. It just so happened that residing on the same floor as Oscar were two luminaries: Charlie Chaplin and Oscar's *bête noire,* Ignacy Paderewski. "You can imagine what kind of service *I* got," Oscar groused, and he avoided running into Paderewski in case the Lion of Paris recognized him. The specter of Paderewski still haunted Oscar's peace.

One night he attended a performance of a Dreyfus-backed operetta. The next morning—after having turned in at his customary dawn hour—he found he could not get out of bed. "I could not wake up for ten days," he later recalled. "I was luxuriating in somnolence. It may have been nerves but I still attribute it to the soporific 'The Great Waltz.' "

It was more likely a deep depression rather than an aversion to operetta that felled Levant—the first, but not the last, psychosomatic spasm he would suffer in his life. Lovesick for Barbara, unhinged at the proximity of the terrifying Paderewski, unable to work well with Vivian Ellis, Levant simply checked out for ten days. It bothered him that no one approved of his nuptial plans. Oscar sorely missed Barbara—at least he knew where he stood with her. He had been following her movements from his exile, noting that by now she would be in Boston with the tryouts of the Gershwin musical *Of Thee I Sing.* Oscar longed to go home. Finally giving in to his lovesickness, he put in a transatlantic call to his Ziegfeld sweetheart and took the next boat back to New York.

When Oscar returned to the city he was reunited, in his words, with an "apoplectically indifferent" young woman who was understandably miffed at Oscar's fast backtracking. No doubt she was a bit numb—if not frostbitten—at having been exposed to Oscar's emotional sleigh ride. Still, they decided to go ahead with it. Oscar took Barbara out to dinner the night before the wedding ceremony, when he suffered a final reversal in his resolve to marry. Suddenly Barbara's forehead seemed to Oscar to be too low. He instantly decided to call the whole thing off again.

It is a testament to Barbara's enduring patience that she put up with his shenanigans. He went flying off to his friend George Backer, the good-looking, aristocratic intellectual Oscar socialized with who would one day hold positions of power as editor of the *New York Post* and as New York governor Averell Harriman's chief adviser.

"George, Barbara's forehead isn't high enough!" Levant complained. Backer, who had agreed to be Levant's best man should the wedding ever take place, waited a long, Solomonic moment before answering. "You can't have everything." Levant married Barbara Wooddell the following day, at the attorney general's office in New York City. None of Barbara's family attended the ceremony.

Nor did any member of the Levant family attend on that crisp January day in 1932. None of the Gershwins were present, though the ceremony was postponed briefly while Oscar entrusted George Backer with his bride-to-be so he could dash over to Grand Central Station and see off George, Ira, and Lee Gershwin. They were on their way to Canada for a vacation "of skiing and playing Canadian pianos." (Oscar would, in retrospect, describe his nuptials as "a feeble effort to escape the Gershwin thrall by getting married.") After the ceremony, the threesome went to the Ritz Carlton Hotel for coffee and brioche.

Once the knot was tied, Oscar immediately called his mother. The other knot, the Gordian one, still bound him to Pittsburgh. Screwing up his courage to tell Annie of his virtual elopement with a *Ziegfeld Follies* showgirl—following in the footsteps of his two eldest brothers in choice and in method—Oscar spoke first: "Ma, I just got married."

There was a long silence at the other end of the phone. Finally, Annie demanded of her freshly espoused son, "That's nice, Oscar. But did you practice today?"

Annie's dismissal of her son's marriage was preceded by another insult from an unexpected quarter. A few weeks before the wedding actually took place, Walter Winchell carried a snide announcement of Levant's nuptials in his *New York Daily Mirror* column. Winchell may have felt personally involved in Levant's life, having already printed a number of his ripostes. After all, it was he who had first introduced Barbara Wooddell to Oscar, and he might have been sweet on her himself. And so late one night when Oscar was reading the daily papers, he turned first to the sports page (as had been his habit since the age of six) and then to Winchell's column. There he read, "Barbara [Wooddell], who is lovely and nice, is marrying Oscar Levant, who isn't."

Levant finally caught up with Winchell at one of the columnist's regular hangouts. Restraining himself from punching the older man, Levant peered down at Winchell and yelled, "Don't ever print anything about me again!"

Winchell shrugged. "So I'm a shitheel" was his cool response. He was used to such abuse and took it as a sign that he was doing his job. But from then on, Levant's firsthand remarks were left out of the Winchell column.

Barbara and Oscar moved into a hotel in the West Fifties, near

Carnegie Hall, and settled into married life. Oscar preferred hotels to apartment houses. "As a hotel dweller," Oscar once observed, "I had acquired an imperishable respect for the maternal instincts of bellboys and elevator operators." Somehow residing in a hotel was a friendlier way to live—the percolations of travelers and guests, the bustling lobbies with their comings and goings, gratified his need to be surrounded by people and activity. Since childhood Oscar had hated to be alone, and a big residence hotel was calming for him, an antidote to the crushing solitude of his first lonely years in New York.

Now Oscar would have to adjust to the terrifying intimacy of the newly married. He was passionate about Barbara, but, like many men of his generation, he was trapped in the dichotomy of his idealized feelings for his wife and his sexual desire for her. During their courtship, Oscar used to walk Barbara to the theatre in the evening, and, while she was dancing in the *Follies,* he would "walk about three doors over toward Broadway to a hotel, go upstairs to what they called the 'pay broad,' and get my ashes hauled." Later he would meet Barbara after the show. The practice apparently continued even after they were married. ("It relieved the tension of my marriage," he later wrote.)

Barbara, for her part, almost immediately felt that she had made a mistake. During the first dinner they shared alone, she felt a tremendous heaviness. She had come to New York to be a dancer and an actress, and now she was trapped.

Oscar must have sensed her ambivalence. He was genuinely in love with Barbara, and he tried to delight her with gifts and funny little love notes he would leave around the hotel suite for her to find. He had won her over with his wit and his music—humor is a great aphrodisiac—and he continued to offer her a life of entertainment, great parties, important friends, and the music he played constantly at home and which they both loved. He especially enjoyed listening to music on the gramophone and conducting along with it. It was almost enough.

Oscar struggled with his ambivalent feelings about sex and love, and Barbara continued to feel trapped in the marriage, although she enjoyed their exciting circle of friends. Unfortunately, Barbara's popularity with Oscar's crowd gave rise to a new worry. Oscar was a jealous man when it came to the women in his life, and Barbara's acceptance by his crowd made him feel even more insecure. Exposed to his witty, urbane friends, would Barbara find him somehow inadequate, uncouth, undesirable? These were some of the undercurrents of their shaky marriage.

•••

In 1932 America was still in the grip of the Depression, although Oscar and his circle were cushioned by their royalties from their musical and theatrical successes. Life at Lindy's and at the Gershwins' matching penthouses went on as usual. Much of the rest of the country suffered. But all was not gloom. Radio City Music Hall, the largest indoor theatre in the world, opened at the end of the year. Ira Gershwin's lyrics and Moss Hart's book for *Of Thee I Sing* won a Pulitzer Prize. Heavyweight boxer Jack Sharkey defeated the German heavyweight champion Max Schmeling in fifteen rounds on a decision, bringing the championship back to America. Popular songs of the year included "April in Paris," by Vernon Duke and E. Y. "Yip" Harburg; "I Gotta Right to Sing the Blues," from the Earl Carroll *Vanities;* Cole Porter's "Night and Day"; and "Willow, Weep for Me," written by Ann Ronell and owned by the Irving Berlin company. That year would also see the premiere of George Gershwin's *Second Rhapsody* in Boston under the baton of Serge Koussevitzky and the Boston Symphony Orchestra.

The *Second Rhapsody* would prove significant in the relationship between Levant and Gershwin for two reasons. First, Gershwin was asked to play his as-yet-unorchestrated composition for the legendary Arturo Toscanini, principal conductor of the New York Philharmonic–Symphony Orchestra, in the hope that Toscanini would agree to conduct the work in its New York premiere. The critic Samuel Chotzinoff, a friend of Gershwin and Toscanini, arranged a meeting between the two men at his home.

Of all his friends, Gershwin chose Oscar Levant to accompany him to the Chotzinoff home to play alongside him in what amounted to an audition of both Gershwin rhapsodies. Levant was the perfect choice to bridge the gulf between the two strata of culture represented by La Scala's famed conductor and the composer of "I Got Rhythm."

But it was an awkward encounter. Gershwin was thrown off his game from the start when he learned that "Toscanini had never even heard the *Rhapsody in Blue* . . . can you imagine a man living in the last seven years—being connected with music—and never hearing the *Rhapsody in Blue?*" Gershwin wrote incredulously to a friend. Toscanini spoke warmly of the works he heard that evening but would not conduct the premiere of the *Second Rhapsody*—nor would he ever conduct any Gershwin music during the composer's lifetime.

The coveted role of Gershwin's friend and second pianist would show its dark side at the New York premiere of the *Second Rhapsody* on February 5, 1932. Levant accompanied Gershwin to the performance, which Serge Koussevitzky would conduct. Alone with Levant in the greenroom before his performance, Gershwin was noticeably nervous about how the critical establishment would respond. Levant tried to take his friend's mind off the job ahead, and, noticing a piano in the greenroom, he asked Gershwin to play some of the tunes they both liked. Knowing that "George at the piano was George happy . . . like a gay sorcerer celebrating his sabbath," Levant involved Gershwin in a half hour of running through their favorite songs on the piano.

Suddenly, a boy knocked on the door and yelled, "Ready, Mr. Gershwin!"

George turned to Levant and, with his long, dark face growing longer and darker, scolded the younger man: "Now look what you've done, Oscar, I haven't had time to warm up!"

The idea that Levant might have spooked Gershwin into a bad performance was anathema to Oscar—or was it? Oscar was performing his usual role of amusing and relaxing the celebrated composer. But the role was beginning to undermine his already shaky confidence in his own abilities, and if he could express his resentment by playing that role to the hilt, then so be it. George's outburst of anger also underscored the inequality of the friendship—George being more loved than loving. Oscar must have been deeply hurt by the incident, as he recorded it in his memoirs more than thirty years later.

Levant soon turned his thoughts to his own serious composing. It was about time he put his sketches and ideas down on paper. Whether it was Gershwin's influence, Levant's own sense of competition, or the temporary security his marriage afforded him, he was finally able to return to his own composing. In 1932 he completed the first movement of his Sonatina for Piano.

Composing did not come easily to Levant. First he had to throw out the influence of Gershwin melodies crowding his head, as well as the daunting achievements of contemporary composers he admired like Maurice Ravel. Once when his cousin Oscar Radin visited him in his New York apartment while he was working on the Sonatina, Levant became so frustrated he threatened to throw both his composition and his young cousin out the window. Although Levant had had training in classical piano literature, he had never studied harmony and composition, and so, in composing as in life, he had to teach himself.

Unlike the gregarious nature of songwriting, composing serious music is a solitary business, and for a soul fearful of being alone, work-ing in solitude was perhaps the most difficult aspect for Levant. How-ever, there was an oasis in the desert complete with a caravan of young, ambitious composers—Americans all—who shared many of Oscar's aspirations and surpassed him in ambition. At the head of this caravan was Aaron Copland, a wiry, bespectacled man who would come into Oscar Levant's life and give him the faith in himself as a composer that George Gershwin was never able to give.

14

Oscar Among the Composers

"... to the next festival, please!"

OSCAR LEVANT FIRST MET AARON COPLAND AT ONE OF THE GERSH-wins' "miscellaneous evenings." Levant had certainly heard of the Brooklyn-born composer, whose 1926 Piano Concerto had seen him paired critically with Gershwin, though Copland and Gershwin had had little contact. Gershwin seemed to have increasingly resented Copland's ascendancy in serious music circles. Both men had studied with Rubin Goldmark, and both were obsessed with incorporating indigenous American idioms into their music, but Copland had had European training (with the famed teacher Nadia Boulanger in Paris) and would soon lose interest in the jazz idiom. "We *must* have been aware of each other," Copland later recalled, "but until . . . the Thirties, we moved in very different circles. On one occasion, when we were finally face to face at some party, with the opportunity for conversation, we found nothing to say to each other!"

It is significant that Copland expressed an interest in hearing Levant's Sonatina for Piano at a Gershwin gathering. Levant had recently completed the first movement. For once he was proud of his achievement, and he played it with his usual strength. In his own words:

> The musical structure [of the Sonatina] was quite academic—it was a grafting of jazz into a classical mold. Although I had not studied composition, the piece displayed remarkable form. It was jocose, lively and light in texture.

The first movement, which was the only part of the Sonatina Levant ever recorded, expresses two moods that are not entirely resolved: fast, Broadway-inspired themes reminiscent of Cole Porter and Gershwin, interspersed with slower, lush, Chopin-like passages. The first movement seems unable to make up its mind which direction to follow; but what it lacks in conviction it makes up for with effervescence.

Copland was quite taken with the piece, admiring its temperament and hybridism. He encouraged Levant to complete his Sonatina for a premiere at Yaddo, the Spencer Trask estate in Saratoga Springs, New York, a retreat for artists, poets, novelists, and composers.

Aaron Copland, as the central figure in the recently organized League of Composers, was planning a festival of contemporary music to take place at Yaddo. The festival would be held on April 30 and May 1, 1932, in an effort to focus attention on new American composers who were being overlooked by the critical establishment. Copland was moving among the composers in America and those studying abroad like a young Demosthenes, looking for composers who were using a quintessentially American idiom. He had already written to Virgil Thomson and Paul Bowles in Paris and to Roy Harris in California, requesting pieces from them all. From the Young Composers' Group, he had invited Henry Brant and Vivian Fine to submit work. Copland planned on drawing from the League of Composers, which he had helped spearhead in 1924, and from Nadia Boulanger's former students. That other *enfant terrible,* the bad boy of American music George Antheil, was also scheduled to put in an appearance at the festival.

In many ways Aaron Copland was the perfect agent for championing the work of new American composers. Like most serious composers of his day, he had gone to Europe to study and had there discovered his own roots. When European composers like Debussy, Ravel, Stravinsky, and Milhaud began to work with American jazz idioms and ragtime, it was certainly time for Americans to make use of what was happening right under their noses. At last American composers had access to new themes that would put them on a par with the Europeans.

Since Copland's return to America in 1924, one thing had not changed in the musical world: the critical establishment and its chilly response to new American composers. The First Festival of Contemporary American Music Copland was organizing at Yaddo was an attempt to challenge the critics to take note of the music being created by Americans, utilizing American themes, rhythms, and sounds.

Levant was acutely aware of this critical deafness, an awareness that would percolate for several years until he addressed it headlong in his first book, which would be published in 1940. He agreed with Copland that the audience for serious American music was coolly apathetic. "A new generation of composers was emerging," he would write about the Yaddo festival, "which inevitably would be subjected to the same cycle of mild patronizing interest and essential indifference as that which preceded them." What the situation needed, Levant recounted, was a strong central figure who would attract public interest in America's emerging composers. Levant observed,

> There was on the horizon no critic of sufficient influence to occupy the position of Edwin Evans, in England . . . Jean Cocteau in France, Einstein in Germany—all of whom had a profound effect on the emerging new talents in their countries. . . . The interested critics were not influential, and the influential critics were not interested. . . .

Now, through the intervention of Aaron Copland, Levant was invited to take part in the seminal gathering of American composers who would help define serious music in the decades to come. But was Oscar capable of belonging to the proverbial club that would have him as a member? Or would his own private group of phantom critics cut him down to size, tell him he didn't belong in this group of serious composers? "You'll never be one of the greats, but you'll never be lonely," his mother had long ago cautioned him.

Levant left the Gershwins' that night to return to Barbara and their honeymoon hotel suite, although the shine on the couple's domestic life had already begun to tarnish. Now he had a compelling reason to complete the second movement of the unfinished Sonatina, to prepare it for Copland's music festival, which was to occur in less than three months.

If Levant had known the history behind the Trask mansion in Saratoga Springs in upstate New York, he might not have shown up at all. "How strange the name [Yaddo] sounds to those not familiar with it," Copland later wrote. "In fact, the story behind Yaddo is a strange and tragic tale resembling an opera in which all the main characters mysteriously expire before the final curtain." The Trasks' infant son had died there, and the original house had burned to the ground. The very name "Yaddo" was their daughter's mispronunciation of "shadowed," after hearing her mother say that the grounds were shadowed.

Into these beautiful surroundings traipsed the composers, performers, and guests of the first Yaddo festival. The printed program begins with a listing of "Assisting Artists" that includes soprano Ada MacLeish (the wife of poet Archibald MacLeish), baritone Hubert Linscott, and flutist George Laurent. The Hans Lange Quartet is listed right above the League of Composers Quartet, and beneath them on the program, under the heading "Composer-Pianists," are George Antheil, Vivian Fine, Aaron Copland, and Oscar Levant. Charles Ives, Henry Brant, Roger Sessions, and Paul Bowles were also represented—eighteen composers in all, scheduled for three concerts on Saturday and Sunday, with a "Conference for Critics and Composers" to take place on Sunday morning. When Antheil canceled at the last minute, Copland replaced him with a performance of his own Variations, which garnered the highest praise of the festival, along with Sessions's Sonata for Piano and seven songs by Charles Ives. The only music critics present were Arthur Berger, Paul Rosenfeld, Alfred H. Meyer, and Irving Kolodin, who would later take a special interest in Levant's career.

Levant traveled with his music and a haphazardly packed overnight case on the train from New York City to Saratoga Springs, a serene five-hour ride along the Hudson River flanked by the freshly greened trees of late April. Levant arrived the first evening of the festival. He felt like an interloper from Broadway among this enclave of European-trained composers, although he was thrilled to have been invited. But the longer he dwelled on the concert and the reactions his serious colleagues might have to his Sonatina, the more uncollegial he began to feel. Levant could not imagine that he was traveling toward a possible triumph.

Saratoga Springs was wilderness to Oscar Levant, city boy. He had no interest in the scenery, the miracle of the underground springs, or any of the flora and fauna surrounding the Trask mansion. "I must recount my impressions of that Yaddo interlude," Oscar wrote eight years later. "Added to my constitutional aversion to the country was the annoyance I had built up during the five-hour train trip, alone, from New York to Saratoga." It is telling that he made the trip alone, without Barbara, without his brother Harry, without Sam Behrman. Lacking the confidence of a Gershwin, Oscar preferred to slink out of town, alone with his self-doubt, rather than be exposed to possible disgrace in front of his friends and loved ones.

His spirits were buoyed by the sight of his friend Robert Russell Bennett, whose close ties with Broadway made Oscar immediately feel more at home. Bennett had recently been in residence at the Gershwins', working with George on the music for *Of Thee I Sing* in preparation for its road company production. "All that saved the situation as far as I was concerned," Oscar would recall, "was the presence of Russell Bennett, in a sense an interloper from Broadway as I was, but a musician of firm foundation and sound development, which I was not." Despite his feelings of being undertrained for the company he was about to keep, Levant felt that Bennett's presence gave him the passport he was looking for, in which a Broadway association would not rob him of credentials for serious work. Now Levant would test the waters for his own acceptance as a concert composer among the most difficult of audiences—his fellow composers.

The odor of self-protection sent out by artists who feel they are being overlooked and have something to prove was in evidence that evening of April 30, 1932, at Yaddo. The petulant, backbiting criticism of fellow artists was in full sway. "Before the concert," Levant noted, "we all sat down to dinner in an atmosphere whose preciosity exceeded anything in my experience." Here was Levant, who spent his life surrounded by great talkers, by supreme and loquacious egoists, suddenly feeling outdone:

> The air was full of jeer for everything and everyone outside the closed shop of those present. . . . This startled me somewhat, and I was at a further disadvantage because I was the only one present who had not either studied in Paris with Boulanger . . . or was not scheduled to leave for France as soon as the festival was over.

Jittery about performing and defensive about the possible reception of his music, Levant still had his wits about him enough to survey his new colleagues. One fellow in particular Levant noted with dislike was Marc Blitzstein, a young composer whose three-movement string quartet *Serenade* preceded Levant's on the program. (Five years after the Yaddo festival, the Philadelphia-born composer would create a sensation with his controversial propaganda musical *The Cradle Will Rock*.) Following their performances, the two men exchanged insults.

Blitzstein's string quartet was not well received by the audience, but Levant's Sonatina was. The assembled guests enjoyed it, and it would be one of the few pieces mentioned favorably in the scanty reviews of the festival. When Levant's piece came to an end—the "lively and jocose" first movement followed by, in Levant's own estimation, the less successful second movement ("pure dross and banality")—enthusiastic admirers of the Sonatina crowded the off-stage room where the composers were assembled. Blitzstein crabbily greeted Levant with the remark "Now try to write a little *music.*"

His wife, Eva, would later agree with her husband, describing the Sonatina in her diary as "Broadway (lower & noise)." But Levant would have the last word. He would articulate his opinion of the Blitzstein *Serenade* eight years later in his first published book, after trying out his remarks on his friends in the intervening years:

> [*Serenade*] reflected one of the greatest presumptions toward an audience that I had ever encountered in any composer. Each of the movements was a largo, in which the contrasts were to be supplied by altered sonorities rather than a change in tempo. It was like a meal consisting entirely of stained glass, with different dressings.

Levant was, perhaps, merely defending himself. Five years after the festival he would praise Blitzstein's music for *The Cradle Will Rock* but criticize its libretto as "surprisingly unsubtle and heavy-handed . . . its pseudo-virility I felt to be forced and artificial."

Blitzstein, a married but active homosexual, would see in "pseudo-virility" an attack on his sexuality. Levant, who once referred to ballet as "the fairies' baseball," was an unenlightened creature of his time when it came to the subject of homosexuality. His unthinking homophobia may have been a defense against his own powerful attraction to Gershwin, whose looks and style he admired as much as he admired George's music. Though he would have enduring friendships with gay men such as Virgil Thomson and David Diamond, he was not above making wisecracks. Any possibility of a rapprochement between the two went up in smoke with the phrase "pseudo-virility."

The final performance of the festival was Aaron Copland's Variations. "This was a departure from his usual self-effacement," noted Levant with the stirrings of envy; "it was a work already enshrined as something of a legend, in the estimation of the devout—a legend with a halo."

The critic Alfred H. Meyer enthusiastically reviewed the Yaddo festival in *Modern Music:* "American music need no longer step aside for Europe . . ." When Copland expressed his anger that so few critics had bothered to show up, that bit of news—not the festival itself—was forwarded by an Associated Press dispatch to *The New York Times:* "The long-standing feud between composers and critics flared into the open at a conference in Yaddo, the Spencer Trask mansion." Angry letters were aired in the *Times,* with critic Olin Downes having the last, churlish word. But the First Festival of Contemporary American Music—though it did not rouse a legion of critics to champion the cause of American music—helped to establish a new acceptance of native composers.

Among the reviews, Irving Kolodin praised Levant's Sonatina. The piece was indeed singled out as one of the festival's successes by the music critics who bothered to attend.

In a photograph taken at the Yaddo festival, the group portrait includes Lehman Engel, Roy Harris, Paul Bowles, Aaron Copland, and Vivian Fine. In this portrait of genius and aspiration in a country setting, Oscar Levant is among the missing. His own insecurity and cynicism caused him to banish himself, unable to find a family among America's serious composers. Too many knives had been drawn, too much was at stake.

Levant's only friend there, the ascetic-looking Bennett, had contributed to the program songs with a string accompaniment entitled *Captivity, Rejection, Escape*—a fitting description of Levant's unhappy sojourn into the land of the composers. Out of sheer gratitude for his presence there, he dedicated his Sonatina to Robert Russell Bennett.

15

A New York Divorce

"Besides incompatibility, we hated each other."

OSCAR LEVANT MAY HAVE FELT LIKE A BROADWAY INTERLOPER AT Yaddo, but the festival spurred him to renew his efforts to establish himself as a concert composer. Though he would belittle the favorable reception of his Sonatina at the festival, it ultimately bolstered his confidence.

His experience at Yaddo also established a relationship with Aaron Copland. Knowing that Copland was planning a second festival for October 1933, Levant set to work on a new composition, hoping he would be invited back to preview the new work. Unfortunately, Levant would undermine his chances in a typically self-defeating move:

> After I had been working on [the new composition] for some time, Copland came to my place one day, and I began to play it for him. He characterized it, after hearing a dozen bars of the first movement, as "A cross between Scriabin and Berg." When he left I tore it up. I liked it, though.

Levant turned instead to what he felt he did best: humor. He began work on a light piano composition which he mischievously titled "A

Slight Touch of Tiflis," associating Tiflis with Josef Stalin's birthplace. Other parodistic titles flew through his head, all of them designed to deflect and camouflage his serious ambition as a composer.

Levant made some attempt to improve his increasingly frustrating marriage. He and Barbara argued a lot, mostly about trivial things such as how best to cook an egg. When things got too hot Barbara would move to another hotel and Oscar would go out looking for her. But just as often their fights would dissolve in humor, with Oscar making a crack and Barbara roaring with laughter. "I loved his brand of humor," she would later recall:

> In the middle of a fight sometimes I'd guffaw. It's just his humor, his kind of humor. Then he'd say, "That's the real me!"

But Barbara was also becoming aware of how moody Oscar was, how given to self-doubt, especially when he was bereft of a boisterous circle of friends. She sensed in Oscar a tremendous sadness that she supposed sprung from having lost his father at so early an age.

Levant had not given up his habit of frequenting prostitutes while married, but Barbara's real rival was George Gershwin. The Gershwin ménage continued to hold him in thrall. Its energy and competition were a welcome contrast to Oscar's frequently gloomy moods when left alone with his bride. When he was invited to accompany the Gershwins to Chicago to oversee the road company tour of *Of Thee I Sing* (Barbara had a small role in the New York production), Oscar jumped at the chance. George S. Kaufman's book and Ira Gershwin's lyrics had won the Pulitzer Prize the previous year —the first time a musical was cited—but George Gershwin's music had not been cited for the award. Levant would call this "an unforgivable and cruel oversight."

The trip to Chicago in the summer of 1932 was Levant's only ride with George Gershwin on the 20th Century Limited. He was ecstatic to be accompanying the Gershwins, and the men had a great time in Chicago. Opening night would prove to be a family affair: His brother Harry Levant was conducting the orchestra (after opening night, which Gershwin conducted). Harry, who chain-smoked and imbibed coffee at a rate to rival his baby brother (Oscar was drinking an astonishing forty cups of coffee a day and was never seen without a cigarette), was by now a sought-after conductor of Broadway musicals. His light, engaging manner endeared him to his fellow musicians as well as to a legion of female admirers. The two brothers would find themselves competing, in Chicago, for the attentions of a young woman. Oscar recalled:

> I had my eye on one girl. (I was married at the time.) Barbara was in New York and I didn't think she cared. I was supposed to pick up this girl and take her home, but when I looked for her she had disappeared. She wound up with my brother.

If Oscar thought that Barbara didn't care, he was wrong. Though she chafed at being married, she would later describe Oscar as "a beautiful lover—he was tender." And she greatly enjoyed her evenings out with the Gershwins, or Sam Behrman, or spending the evening with Jascha Heifetz and his wife.

Upon his return to New York, Oscar charged an expensive, tailored coat with a silver mink collar for Barbara from the exclusive department store Bergdorf Goodman. If he couldn't keep Barbara happy and warm during the New York winter, then Bergdorf Goodman would. When Max Dreyfus's wife advised Barbara to keep the coat in a cold room at all times, the young woman insisted on maintaining their suite at a cool sixty degrees. She kept the coat in the second bedroom with all the windows open. "So the coat was on display like a throne and I froze for that entire winter," Oscar complained, while he scrambled for a way to pay for it.

He hit upon a solution. He had recently begun work on a light piece, a Sinfonietta, that he hoped would efface the painful effects of having ripped up the work he had played for Copland. Oscar wrote a letter—lost now in the ghostly files of Accounts Receivable in the basement of Bergdorf's—that recounted the proud history of musical patronage and offered to complete the "Bergdorf Goodman Sinfonietta" in exchange for Barbara's coat. The august department store politely but firmly refused his offer. Oscar paid for the coat and froze for the rest of the winter.

On May 14, 1932, Morris Gershwin—George and Ira's father—died. Oscar was affected by Morris Gershwin's death but found no way to talk about it with George, who was not able to express his grief. Both men were limited by a certain superficiality in their relationships with those around them. Emotions were expressed in music but were never spoken of. Gershwin's letters and public utterances at the time speak only of his work and future plans, and despite the two men's friendship, Gershwin was unable to confide in Levant about so painful a subject. Levant later wrote:

> I can lay no claim to a special access to [George's] feelings . . . we merely had a healthy, extrovertial intimacy, born . . . of mutual interests. Excluding the members of his family, the only man who could possibly be said to have enjoyed such a special affection from George was Bill Daly, . . . an enthusiasm we shared.

William Daly figured largely in Levant's next music concert, which would cement Levant's relationship with Gershwin and point the direction his concert career would ultimately take.

In the summer of 1932 Gershwin made Levant an offer he couldn't refuse: He asked Levant to perform his Concerto in F at the Lewisohn Stadium's first all-Gershwin program. The concert would premiere Gershwin's newly finished *Cuban Overture.* What would become a tradition began as a necessity. Levant noted that Gershwin's offer was

> conditioned by the fact that [he] was planning on playing both the "Rhapsody in Blue" and the "Second Rhapsody," and finally decided that he could not undertake the "Concerto" also.

Nothing could have prepared Levant for the experience of playing the music of George Gershwin in the open-air theatre on the night of August 16, 1932—certainly not his fleeting appearance the year before at the Hollywood Bowl, when a dwindling audience and a botched finale had robbed Levant of his bows, nor his appearance with Bennett at Lewisohn Stadium's all-American program. The Gershwin evening would begin with the overture from *Of Thee I Sing,* after which Levant would take the stage with Bill Daly at the podium.

While waiting in the wings for his cue, a wave of fear and nausea overcame Levant. He had consumed a full dinner with Gershwin and Daly that afternoon, and now he gave it all back in the not-very-private dressing room behind the stage. It was the first, but certainly not the last, time that Levant suffered the paroxysms of performer's nerves. Still fighting nausea, Levant took his place at the piano.

What he saw when he strode onstage must have astounded him: "17,000 persons, an all-time record crowd for these [summer] concerts, jammed into all the available seating and standing room, including aisles, ramparts, towers, stairs and colonnade," reported *The New*

York Times the following morning. In addition, more than 4,000 souls had been turned away, "protesting bitterly." (One of those without even a twenty-five-cent ticket who tried to sneak in through the back gate was Adolph Marx, who—sans curls, sans hat, sans oversized trench coat—little resembled his cinematic persona of Harpo Marx. Levant recognized the great screen comedian before the program began and managed to secure him a ticket.)

It was clear that the public had come to adore Gershwin's music, and Levant's performance was swept up in their adulation. "The audience was enormously enthusiastic," the *Times* reviewer reported, ". . . giving warm and prolonged applause to the music and all the performers."

For Oscar Levant, performing the Concerto in F (which would become his favorite Gershwin piece, surpassing in his affection the *Rhapsody*) had been torturous. He had never played for an audience of that size, and he discovered that he did not like it. His stage fright was nearly incapacitating.

Though he was not paid for his performance—there was never any discussion of remuneration—Oscar was proud to have been asked to participate. As at every other significant moment in his young life, his family was conspicuously absent. He and Barbara hadn't seen each other for several days. Barbara had more than once gone to stay with friends or to visit her mother, leaving Oscar alone at their hotel, from which he would call her a dozen times a day. She was now absent from the crush of well-wishers who surrounded the musicians. Oscar noticed enviously that the crowd around George far outnumbered his own circle of admiring strangers.

Despite his bout of intense stage fright and his lack of family support, Levant basked in the success of the evening. Here at last he had found a musical niche that filled his hunger for approval and satisfied his need to worship and emulate Gershwin.

A few days later, he showed up at his customary place at the Gershwins', full of talk about the tremendous success of the all-Gershwin evening. George greeted him with "a small boy smile . . . his hands clasped behind his back."

He asked Oscar, "What would you rather have: money or a watch?"

There had never been any mention of paying Levant for his part in the concert. As George asked the question, he simultaneously handed Oscar a strikingly handsome wristwatch that was simply inscribed

From George to Oscar
Lewisohn Stadium
August 15, 1932

Nothing could have given Oscar as much joy. The art deco watch had a rectangular face and tiny numbers like those in an Otis elevator. "It is by this watch," Levant liked to say, "that I have been late for every important appointment since then. But I'm grateful now that I didn't get what I would have preferred then—the money." Levant would wear the watch until its numbers became an indistinguishable blur.

Despite the favorable reviews and the excitement of being part of the all-Gershwin program, Levant did not pursue his concert career for the next five years. The stage fright he had experienced had been nearly incapacitating. Just when he was getting started and getting his name known in the right circles, he found he couldn't go on with it.

Luckily, he found he could keep the momentum of his performing career going by playing in a radio orchestra, where he did not have to confront tremendous audiences and suffer bouts of humiliating stage fright.

Back in 1927, when he had been invited to play the *Rhapsody* on several radio music programs, he had dismissed radio as an industry "with a questionable future." But in 1933 and 1934 he renewed his association with radio. For one thing, it paid the bills.

In many ways Levant was ideally suited for radio broadcasts. His reputation as a fine pianist had preceded him: first, from the 1928 Brunswick recording of *Rhapsody in Blue;* second, from his popularity in *Burlesque;* and more recently from his inclusion in the record-breaking all-Gershwin program at Lewisohn Stadium. In addition, he was astonishing in his ability to sight-read anything thrown at him. In the early thirties, radio was hungry for programming, and Levant found there was a demand for his services beyond simply playing the *Rhapsody.*

The Columbia Broadcasting System, created in 1927, sent out music programs throughout the United States. Many were symphony concerts, although jazzed-up dance music was added in the late twenties. After 1930, especially with the success of two white men doing minstrel-show dialect in *Amos 'n' Andy,* comedy and then drama came to occupy more and more airtime. But music remained the staple; it made performers like Bing Crosby and Kate Smith famous, and it played a crucial role in the careers of Benny Goodman, Tommy Dorsey, and the swing bands to come.

The accessibility of music through radio and the disappearing pay-check during the Depression closed down nightclubs and cabarets. In November 1930 *Variety* announced, "Dance halls all starving." The thriving New York nightlife Oscar had cut his teeth on during his first years in the metropolis was a mere ghost of its former self. Instead of going out, people stayed home and huddled around the radio. Programs were broadcast from hotels and the nightclubs that had managed to stay open, but more often than not orchestras gathered in radio studios to perform live on the air.

One orchestra conductor who found success on the radio was Gershwin's friend Bill Daly. Since 1926 the thatch-haired, bespectacled "Irishman" (as his friends called him) had been conductor for the National Broadcasting Company Grape Nuts Orchestra (named for its sponsor).

Levant looked up to Bill Daly. Daly was George's close friend, and the young pianist admired Daly's literary background as well as his sound musicianship. Daly and Levant had something else in common: As young men both had performed for Paderewski, though in Daly's case, Paderewski had urged the young man to put aside literature and concentrate on music.

Levant was soon hired as pianist for the NBC Grape Nuts Orchestra under Daly's baton. He played a piano solo each week. Despite the presence of such brilliant young musicians as Artie Shaw and Benny Goodman, the Grape Nuts Orchestra played practically no jazz and "little popular music of any kind, unless you consider the 'Kashmiri Love Song' or 'In a Persian Garden' popular music," remembered Levant. They played standard works, such as Liszt's Hungarian Rhapsodies and various operatic excerpts.

Levant soon found himself bristling under Daly's conducting, his old "boss-hating attitude" rising up. He was bothered by Daly's obvious preference for a flute player in the orchestra and took a special delight one afternoon when the flutist stepped toward the microphone for his solo in "The Flight of the Bumblebee" and, obviously drunk, produced "an indistinguishable smear of noise."

Levant worked for a number of radio orchestras in 1933–34, and they all seemed to have the same musicians in them. Several weeks into playing with one radio orchestra, Levant was asked to take his usual solo. While still on the air, Levant grabbed the sheet music off the piano stand and tore it up in front of the microphone. He let the confetti fall to the floor. It was his "salute of contempt" before jumping ship. The routine of a weekly performance had done him in. Unable to take being dictated to week after week, he bolted. He told the startled conductor, "I quit!" and marched out of the studio, leaving a stunned orchestra in its wake. Artie Shaw, however, remembered that Levant had been fired for his insolence and that he, Shaw, had intervened to get him his job back. Typically, Levant never thanked Shaw—he hated to feel beholden to anyone. One of his favorite sayings at the time was "Do me a favor—don't do me any favors."

On September 6, 1933, Oscar Levant's marriage to Barbara Wooddell was officially terminated by divorce. She had regretted the marriage almost from the start, but what finally ended it was her unexpected, and unwanted, pregnancy.

"I refused his child," was how she described her abortion years later. "I don't think Oscar ever got over that."

Whatever Levant's private feelings about starting a family in the midst of the Depression while still feeling like a kid himself, Barbara's decision to end the pregnancy hurt him deeply. He took it as a denial of his love for her. When she then asked for a divorce, he was crushed.

"I always felt guilty. I thought I had been very cruel," Barbara recalled years later.

> I remember him standing in the door. We were talking about the divorce. I made him get the divorce in New York . . . adultery was the only thing you could get it on. I remember this sadness again, it was almost like the sadness of when we were married. It was a kind of sad, sad hurt . . .

Fourteen days later, Barbara Wooddell married Arthur M. Loew, son of Marcus Loew, the movie theatre mogul and founder of the Loew's theatre chain. It was an indication of how far apart the couple had drifted that Levant knew nothing about Loew's courtship of his wife. He had thought he was entirely to blame for the breakup of the marriage; he was surprised to hear at their divorce proceedings that Barbara, like himself, had failed to remain faithful to their vows.

They made plans for Barbara to come to his hotel room, where he would supply her with the evidence she needed to divorce him, since New York law at that time required explicit evidence as grounds for an uncontested divorce. Oscar would hire one of his "pay broads" to be present, "in flagrante delicto," when Barbara burst into the room with her lawyer.

A posse of city newspapermen had gathered at the hotel in anticipa-
tion of a juicy story. The distinguished lawyer Morris Ernst, retained
by Oscar at the last minute, made the reporters wait in the lobby
while he presided over the divorce proceedings. The divorce was
granted, the woman paid for the afternoon was sent home, and the
gaggle of disappointed newsmen hanging around the lobby was given
the bum's rush.

In an effort to undercut his sense of failure at the occasion, Oscar
later told his friends, "I was a little distressed that I wasn't allowed to
be caught. I believe in the strict letter of the law at all times."

Oscar Levant and Barbara Wooddell had been married less than
nine months. To Oscar's surprise and disappointment, he found that
many of the same friends who had cautioned him not to marry Barbara in the first place ended up siding with her after the divorce. Max
Dreyfus and his wife, who both strongly disapproved of divorce, had
come to adore Barbara, and they chastised Oscar for ending the marriage. Even Lee Gershwin, whom Oscar considered one of his good
friends, inexplicably sided with Barbara. Oscar felt he couldn't do
anything right—he couldn't even get divorced without alienating his
friends, and the divorce had been Barbara's idea!

Oscar had a little revenge, however, when he learned about his
former wife's hasty new marriage. In an exploit that would become
one of his most notorious examples of *chutzpah,* he called up his ex-
wife and her new husband on their wedding night, at two in the
morning.

"What's playing at Loew's State and what time does the feature go
on?" he demanded when Barbara answered the phone.

As a display of arrant nerve, Oscar's prank became famous. Barbara's response was to laugh. "I roared," she admitted years later.
"That's his idea of a joke—he'd go to any length for a joke." Levant
would go further in covering up his hurt with humor. When asked
later about the breakup of his marriage, he quipped, "Besides incompatibility, we hated each other." Which was simply not true—he was
still drawn to Barbara Smith Wooddell Loew.

The day after Levant's divorce, Dreyfus accompanied the depressed
and angry young man to Grand Central Station, where he was scheduled to depart for California on the 20th Century Limited. He was
accompanying his friend Sam Behrman, who was also recuperating
from a romance that had ended badly. Train stations usually awoke in
Levant a memory of his early banishment to New York by his

mother, and he sulked all the way to the station. Unable to locate Behrman at the crowded terminal, Oscar suddenly let his bags drop like dead weights and he banged his head against the marble archway, shrieking at the top of his voice. It took Behrman's appearance to calm him down, and the two friends boarded the train.

16

Exiles and Moguls

"Sorry, I didn't get the name."

—Oscar Levant to Greta Garbo

MANY LEADING GERMAN AND EASTERN EUROPEAN FILMMAKERS AND composers were fleeing to America to escape Hitler's tyranny. One of the notables forced to emigrate by the rising tide of Nazism was the distinguished composer and inventor of the twelve-tone system, Arnold Schoenberg, who in 1933 had been cautioned not to return to his lifetime appointment of professor at the Berlin Academy of Music. In an effort to safeguard his career, he had early on converted to Lutheranism, but one of his last acts before leaving Europe was to reconvert to Judaism. With his wife and daughter in tow, Schoenberg began his exile in America. Virtually unknown and unappreciated in the United States, the proud composer and teacher would subsist on charity until a professorship at UCLA was finally offered him. Feeling bitterly outcast, Schoenberg could not have realized that he landed in Los Angeles just as it was becoming the musical center of the world.

The twenties had seen the migration to Hollywood of Broadway actors and performers eager to act in the new talkies. In the thirties, with sound becoming more sophisticated, composers and musicians flocked to Los Angeles, where their work would be heard by millions and recompensed far more generously than any mere commission could offer. Leopold Stokowski, Igor Stravinsky, Dmitri Tiomkin, Vladimir Horowitz, and Sergei Rachmaninoff were some of the distinguished names who would draw paychecks from movie moguls. Whereas the studios of the twenties had wanted popular, Tin Pan Alley–style songs, by the thirties, lush, heavily orchestrated scores on a multitude of themes were being sought.

Levant's and Behrman's 1933 trip to California began in gloom but picked up after Chicago, when they bumped into Berthold Viertel on the train.

Berthold Viertel was a well-known European poet and film director who had emigrated with his wife, Salka, then an actress hoping to find work in this new paradise called Hollywood. Salka's brother, Eduard Steuermann, was an accomplished pianist who had been a devotee of the Schoenberg school in Berlin. When Levant met Berthold on the train, the Viertels were already known for hosting one of the most interesting salons in Los Angeles.

Salka had become close friends with Sam Behrman and Greta Garbo, having worked with Behrman on the script for one of Garbo's great films, *Queen Christina*. She had become so trusted an adviser to the eccentric Swedish beauty that it was said that Garbo would not commit herself to a project unless Salka Viertel first approved of it. In 1935 Salka would adapt Tolstoy's *Anna Karenina* as a vehicle for Garbo.

Behrman had already filled Berthold and Salka's ears with Oscar Levant stories, so when they met him it was like welcoming a familiar face. Stories about Oscar—his all-night carousing, his unfettered conversations, his phenomenal capacity for cigarettes and coffee—had begun to blow across the plains to the poolsides and cottages of Hollywood.

When they arrived in California, Oscar stayed at Behrman's house for six weeks. When things got dull at Behrman's, the movable feast would continue at the Viertels' salon on Maberry Drive in Santa Monica.

As more and more Europeans fled to America, "the great house for all German refugees in Southern California," Levant would recall, "was that of Salka Viertel. All Germans who got past Ellis Island in those days made a beeline for the hospitality of the Viertels." One of those refugees was Dmitri Tiomkin, who was having a hard time getting any work at all as a composer. He bemoaned his plight to Salka, who comforted him with the ambiguous words, "Dmitri, that is the way of all genius. I can prove it. Take my husband, Berthold, who is a *real* genius."

Salka described these gatherings in her 1969 memoir, *The Kindness of Strangers*. Sundays in Maberry Road were like the musical Sundays they had attended, a world ago, in Berlin. The gatherings became a "sacred rite" with Ping-Pong matches and friends ranging from Johnny Weissmuller of *Tarzan* fame, who kept the Viertels' son Tommy enthralled, to

the "enfant terrible," Oscar Levant, [the British novelist] Clemence Dane, [the actress] Miriam Hopkins, the MGM musicians Dmitri Tiomkin and Bronislaw Kaper from Warsaw and Lola his wife, both very Polish and nostalgic. Schoenberg and his wife would come, and Otto Klemperer, the conductor of the Los Angeles Philharmonic Orchestra. . . . Silver-haired and charming, [director] Max Reinhardt arrived to stage "A Midsummer Night's Dream" in the Hollywood Bowl and as a film for Warner Bros.

Max Reinhardt's son, Gottfried, added his volatile presence to the ongoing political discussions.

They all came—Maxwell Anderson, Laurence Stallings (cowriter of *What Price Glory?*), William Faulkner, a thin man with a dark, drooping mustache who was, as Salka described him, "reserved, polite, and taciturn" and had just published his tour de force, *As I Lay Dying*. One night Faulkner turned to Oscar and described his recent meeting with Alexander Woollcott: "I didn't know I'd have to sit and listen to a fat man talk all night."

Besides the interminable Ping-Pong matches (Schoenberg would invariably arrive with his own paddle), a chess tournament was usually in progress. "As for conversation," Levant recalled, "the theater was only a preliminary to literature, painting, sculpture and music."

While working with Salka Viertel on the adaptation of *Queen Christina,* Behrman had told Greta Garbo about his friend Oscar Levant, whom he described as "a kind of legend." Two years later, at a small gathering after the preview of *Anna Karenina,* Oscar would be summoned to meet the film goddess and the two were introduced.

Oscar, usually so self-possessed when meeting the famous, was overcome with shyness in the face of such understated glamour.

"Sorry, I didn't get the name," was all he managed to stammer.

Garbo turned to Behrman and said, "It is better he remain a legend."

They would have one other memorable meeting, some twenty years later, when a much more assured Levant saw Garbo dining at Le Pavillon in New York. Levant recalled, "When the inaccessible actress came in, I called the headwaiter over and said, 'Please tell Miss Garbo to quit staring at me.' " She laughed and invited Levant to join her. Oscar explained that he was leaving the next day for a concert in Emporia, Kansas, and he urged the legendary recluse to come with him.

"What time does the train arrive?" she asked.

"Eleven in the morning."

"Ah," replied the actress enigmatically, "too late for breakfast."

It was Salka Viertel's salon that inspired Levant to write a "mock French opera," *Le Crayon est sur la table,* in Levant's words "using all the Debussy clichés from 'Pelléas'—the descending fourth in the voice parts, the parallel seventh chords and the interrogatory 'Pourquoi?' " He loved to regale the Viertel guests with enthusiastic performances of his opera, which drove the German refugees crazy.

Levant was soon hired by Metro-Goldwyn-Mayer, probably through Sam Behrman's intervention, where he was teamed up with lyricist Gus Kahn. Like Levant, Kahn was strictly a city boy who never got used to the palm trees, desert climate, and poolsides of Los Angeles. He had clung to his native city of Chicago long after other songwriters had headed west, until the movies finally lured him to Los Angeles. The two urban souls did not produce much music together. The one song to make it into Levant's discography was "I'd Do It Again"—a misleading title as the two didn't do much composing together after that. Levant's career at MGM was altogether brief, thanks to the presence of a music department head and mogul-in-the-making from Levant's past: Nat Finston. Now Levant had to appear in his office to seek continued employment at the studio. Levant had defied Nat Finston's memos on what to play when he was the house pianist for the Balaban & Katz theatre chain, leaving Finston with an ulcer the size of a fedora. Fearlessly putting the past behind him, Levant walked into Finston's headquarters.

I found him in a commodious office, hung with charts which were his most absorbing possession. Within a few minutes he had led me to a wall (which they covered completely) and begun to explain their significance. Each chart represented a film, and each bore the name of a composer who had been assigned to write the score for it. . . . A Commissar of Music for the M.G.M. enterprises, Finston was as closely in touch with the activities of his vassals as the tovarich in charge of a salt mine in the Ukraine.

To an anarchist like Oscar Levant, the mere sight of Finston's obsessively maintained charts spelled disaster.

"I tell you," Finston barked at Levant, pacing the room with supervisory strides, "it's running like a well-oiled machine. Every man a cog in the wheel." Levant gave Finston the scores he had written a few years earlier for a half-dozen films at RKO and promised to return the next day. When he returned to Finston's office, the music mogul shook his head at the composer—his former *bête noire*—and said the inevitable: "I don't think you fit into this well-oiled machine."

Back at the studio lot, Levant realized that his musical scores had been returned to him unopened. Finston had never even looked at them. Levant would later characterize Finston's methods as emblematic of the sometimes mechanistic way music was commissioned for Hollywood movies, whittling down existing classical themes to fill in various dramatic slots, counted out by the minute. It was an approach to composing designed to thwart a contrary-minded artist like Levant.

But Finston was a minor setback, and Levant's life among the moguls continued.

His love life continued as well, this time with an aspiring actress of a different sort than Nancy Carroll or Virginia Cherrill. Whereas Carroll's brief reign as a film star was already beginning to slip when Oscar was involved with her, and Cherrill's career never outlasted her first and last silent film, Oscar met and became involved with Jean Arthur just before she found fame as a film actress.

The raspy-voiced actress was different from most of the women Oscar sought out. He was used to dating chorus girls, showgirls, and pretty actresses who got by on their looks and hid their intelligence. Arthur's tomboyish quality and obvious, frank intelligence challenged Oscar, but she didn't have that devastating *femme fatale* quality that he was such a sucker for.

Oscar still felt burned by Barbara Wooddell, and he wouldn't feel safe enough for a deep involvement until more time had elapsed. He still held out the hope that Barbara might inform him that she had made a terrible mistake and take him back.

Once Levant's desultory work at MGM had concluded, Behrman

moved him into the Beverly Wilshire Hotel and helped get Levant a job with Sol Wurtzel, a producer of B pictures at Fox Film Studios.

Behrman had a special, though incomprehensible, affection for Sol Wurtzel—incomprehensible because Wurtzel seems to have been universally disliked. The Texas showgirl Jean Howard had called him "a boor" and "an ugly, mean little man." Salka Viertel also found the studio mogul "incredibly boorish." Levant would describe Wurtzel as "an unbenevolent tyrant saved by his lack of humor."

Perhaps Behrman was fond of Wurtzel despite his gruff manners because he had a genuine appreciation for writers—rare among production chiefs. "He was one of the few Hollywood producers who read," remembered Behrman; "he had tremendous tenacity and he ploughed through books."

It was a job not unlike the one Levant had held in 1931 when he worked for William Le Baron at RKO—a job without any real responsibilities. "My duties were very vague; but I was always on time," Levant recounted with a touch of pride.

One day a large gathering of studio executives and visitors on their way out of a meeting happened to overhear Levant playing the piano in an empty projection room. One eavesdropper swore the music was Brahms, another, Bach, but all were impressed by the confidence and beauty of his playing. This solitary recital could only have added to their confusion about his role at Fox. It was soon obvious to Levant, however, that Wurtzel, like most of the studio producers in town, possessed the proverbial tin ear when it came to music; thus Levant's duties embraced all aspects of production—except music. (André Previn, another composer who would sit at Hollywood's lavish table in the fifties and sixties, also found producers curiously blasé about their film composers. He observed, "the music department was no more nor less important than the Department of Fake Lawns.")

One of the duties Wurtzel assigned his young assistant was to accompany him to Las Vegas, where he indulged in marathon gambling sessions. Wurtzel was an obsessive gambler.

Oscar's training on Colwell Street stood him in good stead with his boss. Just about every night during his tenure as Wurtzel's assistant, Oscar accompanied him to a gambling casino. As soon as he started to lose money, Wurtzel would toss him a hundred-dollar chip. The next morning, Oscar would receive a memo reminding him that he owed his boss a hundred dollars and he'd better pay up. Then the two men would spend the rest of the day in companionable silence, watching the dailies from the previous day's shooting.

Wurtzel would never rise above his status as a producer of B pictures, but, to his credit, throughout his career at Fox he hired a lot of directors and actors from the silent era, giving new work to movie people who were wiped out by sound. He would also be responsible for giving Oscar his first—and only—job as a screenwriter, adapting the British novelist Graham Greene's *Stamboul Train.* The film was retitled *Orient Express,* and Greene, who often reviewed films, gave it a thumbs down:

> the direction was incompetent, the photography undistinguished, the story sentimental . . . by what was unchanged I could judge and condemn my own novel: I could see clearly what was cheap and banal enough to fit the cheap banal film.

Needless to say, *Orient Express* was a hit.

Carl Hovey, Levant's writing partner who did most of the adaptation, was a far more experienced wordsmith than Levant. Hovey had been an editor of the well-respected *Metropolitan Magazine* in New York. He liked to impress Oscar with stories about his writers, such as H. G. Wells and Scott Fitzgerald. Always fascinated by literary figures, Levant sopped up such stories, and he hung around Carl Hovey for another reason: He was mad about Hovey's wife, the screenwriter Sonya Levien.

Sonya was a striking, dark-haired woman with a thick European accent. Sinclair Lewis had once been in love with her. "She was warm, overflowing with vitality, an instant darling," Behrman had said. Her friends good-naturedly made fun of her English—she was constantly saying, "That's exactly!" As early as 1930, during Levant's previous trip to Los Angeles, he had made himself a member of Levien and Hovey's household.

During the thirties Oscar would develop close relationships with a number of older married women who maternally took him under their wing but who were at the same time alluring and flirtatious. Chief among them were Salka Viertel and Sonya Levien in California, and Beatrice Kaufman and Maggie Swope in New York. Behrman had once observed that Levant brought out the maternal instinct in men, but he did so in women as well, with his unruly hair, rumpled suits, and general air of having been orphaned at an early age. Oscar basked in their attention.

Though *Orient Express* was successful at the box office, it did not lead to more screenwriting jobs for the two men. Wurtzel didn't really trust Hovey—he felt that the somewhat somber, decidedly highbrow literary man was "too educated" to make a good story editor or anything else at Fox Film Studios. As for Oscar, Wurtzel gave the young pianist a daunting task that would put an end to his screenwriting career.

Wurtzel greatly admired Fyodor Dostoevsky, not merely for his literary genius but possibly also for his reputation as a compulsive gambler. One morning Oscar received two memos, one the customary sucker's memo reminding him that he owed his boss a hundred-dollar gambling debt, another asking him to see Wurtzel to discuss a new idea.

Levant slouched in a chair in Wurtzel's office—he had a habit of making himself so comfortable in a chair or couch that he seemed to slide half out of it—and lit a cigarette. Wurtzel asked his young aide-de-camp if he would write a screen treatment of Dostoevsky's classic 1866 novel of sin, remorse, and redemption, *Crime and Punishment*.

"That's a rather weird assignment for an embryo writer," Levant chided his boss.

Waving his protestations aside, Wurtzel was convinced he had just given the kid another routine job and saw him to the door. Levant decided to overlook the impossible assignment in the hope that his boss would eventually forget about it. But he had no such luck.

Not long thereafter Wurtzel sent word to Levant that he wanted to see the screen treatment. In a panic, Levant rushed out to MGM, where Sam Behrman was working with Salka Viertel on *Queen Christina*. Speeding through the studio gates, Levant implored his experienced friend to help him. He also appealed to a new acquaintance at MGM, the young Charlie Lederer, whose first screenplay, an adaptation of Charles MacArthur and Ben Hecht's stage play *The Front Page,* had already made his reputation in Hollywood.

Lederer was the nephew of Marion Davies, the inamorata of the newspaper mogul William Randolph Hearst. He was a charming, puckish young man with bright blue eyes and thinning brown hair. He had a tremendous sense of fun and was game for working up a treatment of the Russian novel from memory. The two screenwriters dictated their ideas to Oscar, who wrote it all down in longhand.

Levant handed the treatment to Wurtzel the following day. The mogul's only comment was that it was not very professional of Levant to present a treatment in longhand. Insulted at this response, Levant retorted, "If you wanted me to quit, you've succeeded!"

It was just as well. Levant, in his own words, always managed "to break off his jobs at a certain interval"—what he called his Noël Coward principle. A free man again, Levant took the next train back to New York.

17

Crimes Without Passion

"Mine was the kind of piece in which nobody knew what was going on—including the composer, the conductor and the critics. Consequently, I got pretty good notices."

DURING 1934, THE YEAR FOLLOWING OSCAR'S DIVORCE, HE WAS AT loose ends. He hung out at a number of famous households in New York and desultorily composed music. His divorce had left him rudderless, and he flitted from project to project, from one surrogate family to another.

In the spring of 1933, George Gershwin had moved into what would be the last of his New York City homes—at 132 East Seventy-Second Street. Levant noticed that among the fourteen rooms there was no guest room, but he was one of the small circle of friends to be given a key to the duplex.

It was in this apartment that Gershwin would embark upon his most ambitious project yet: Here he would compose the folk opera *Porgy and Bess,* based on DuBose Heyward's novel *Porgy,* about the Gullah blacks of South Carolina. Oscar watched as a third Steinway grand was hoisted up and came sailing through an open window.

George interrupted his work on the opera to make a tour of several city orchestras with his friend Bill Daly, in celebration of the tenth anniversary of *Rhapsody in Blue.* The reliable Daly was scheduled to conduct, but he was unable to leave New York in time to rehearse, so

Gershwin invited Levant to accompany him to Pittsburgh to rehearse the *Rhapsody* and the Concerto in F with the Pittsburgh Symphony. Levant accompanied Gershwin by overnight train, returning to the city of his birth at the side of one of the emperors of Broadway. The two men took a late train and shared a drawing room. When it was time to go to bed, Gershwin eased himself into the lower berth; there was no question in his mind as to who rated the more comfortable space. After casually offering Gershwin a sleeping pill with "the air of a man offering a friend an after-dinner mint"—by now Levant usually took two Alenols before bed in order to sleep—Levant tried to stretch out in the compartment's upper berth:

> I adjusted myself to the inconveniences of the upper berth, reflecting on the artistic-economic progression by which Paderewski has a private car, Gershwin a drawing room, and Levant a sleepless night. At this moment my light must have disturbed George's doze, for he opened his eyes, looked up at me and said drowsily, "Upper berth—lower berth. That's the difference between talent and genius."

Levant felt the remark characterized "a certain undertone in our friendship, in which there was always a small element of nastiness, a fondness for putting the blast on each other."

Levant would repeat Gershwin's witty insult to all their friends, though it certainly underlined the difference between the two men in terms of the music they had brought into the world. Gershwin didn't mean to be cruel; it was simply unthinkable that anyone around him should not acknowledge his genius. Levant never recorded whether or not his family met Gershwin or even attended the concert—after all, Levant was appearing in Pittsburgh only as Gershwin's rehearsal pianist.

The irony is that it was Levant, not Gershwin, who was being courted by the new American composers epitomized by Aaron Copland—a rarefied group of serious musicians who would dismiss Gershwin as essentially a composer of show tunes. Gershwin craved their acceptance of his music.

Their competitiveness would surface over the composer and theorist Joseph Schillinger, with whom Gershwin was enthusiastically studying and whom he praised to Levant. Like a man who has discovered a new diet or a painless dentist, Gershwin proselytized Schillinger's compositional theories until Levant decided he must find out for himself.

Schillinger had a decidedly mathematical bent, and his exercises were mapped on graph paper weighted with titles like "Rhythmic Groups Resulting from the Interference of Several Synchronized Periodicities." Schillinger's "reduction of all musical procedures, from the most formidable to the least imposing, to a mathematical system . . . [was the] compositional equivalent of playing the piano in six easy lessons," in Levant's opinion, but his desire to share his friend's enthusiasms led him to begin a course of study with the Russian-born pedagogue.

At first Levant did not tell George of this new venture, perhaps because he had made fun of Schillinger's methodology too often. Levant manned the second piano alongside Gershwin nearly every day throughout the sweltering summer in New York, while Gershwin attempted to put his lessons to good use on *Porgy and Bess*. Finally, one afternoon Levant casually informed Gershwin that he, too, had been studying with Schillinger.

Gershwin exploded. "He wrathfully accused me of jealousy, of imitating him." Levant soon ended the lessons, having been neither harmed nor helped by the Schillinger method.

Gershwin also accused Levant of imitating him when, in 1934, Levant began to undergo psychoanalysis for the first time. It was true; Gershwin's foray into the mire of analysis had emboldened Oscar and made psychotherapy "the thing to do" among the Gershwin circle. But Levant's psychiatric initiation would be a sore spot with George.

Levant's first psychiatrist was Dr. Dudley Shoenfeld, who specialized in the criminal mind, a fact that appealed to Levant's highly developed sense of guilt, or so he joked. Dr. Shoenfeld's book on the Lindbergh baby kidnapping case, *The Crime and the Criminal,* was a study of its alleged perpetrator, Bruno Hauptmann. "I chose him because he was a criminologist," Levant would later write, adding enigmatically, "which proves something." Levant also wrote that he had begun psychoanalysis not only because George Gershwin had done so but because he had been traumatized by a case of gonorrhea contracted the year following the breakup of his marriage:

> I was still in my twenties when I went to my first psychoanalyst. One of the less familiar songs from *Porgy and Bess* would keep recurring to me. Its title was, "It Takes a Red-Headed Woman to Make a Fool of Me." It was only logical. My first analysis was brought about because of a case of gonorrhea I had contracted from a redhead.

The event so traumatized Levant that he protected himself "so fulsomely that every time I had an affair, I dressed like a paratrooper—a rubber paratrooper." He would continue to see Dr. Shoenfeld throughout the rest of the 1930s.

The score of *Porgy and Bess* completely absorbed Gershwin's attentions for most of 1933 through 1935. Levant never warmed to Gershwin's ambitious opera. He detected in the music not only the handprints of Schillinger but the klezmer music of their mutual boyhoods: *Porgy and Bess,* Oscar remarked sardonically, was the greatest Jewish opera ever written.

How much of this opinion was laced with envy is hard to discern, but Levant felt inspired enough to continue his own composing in the popular vein. In 1934 he would write what would prove to be his most enduring melody, the bittersweet ballad written with Edward Heyman called "Blame It on My Youth." The song was something of a breakthrough for Levant: A lovely ballad with a haunting melody, it stands out from the dozens of typical Tin Pan Alley–inspired tunes he had written thus far.

The song, published by T. B. Harms, was first recorded by the Jan Garber Orchestra on the Victor label, with vocals by Lee Bennett. It was subsequently recorded in 1935, on Decca Records, by two acquaintances of Levant's from his radio days: the Dorsey Brothers. A long list of recording artists would add "Blame It on My Youth" to their repertoire—Bing Crosby, Rosemary Clooney, Nat "King" Cole, Frank Sinatra, and, most recently, Michael Feinstein. Feinstein has described "Blame It on My Youth" as

> . . . a beautiful song. It has a very clear, well-constructed melody that is not in any way contrived—a very natural flow and a logical progression. It doesn't seem perspirational; it's a very inspired melody.

The melody has had an enduring appeal for jazz artists: Chet Baker, Art Farmer, and Keith Jarrett have recorded the song. Nat "King" Cole's and Chet Baker's renditions are particularly haunting, and the song, with its unstressed elegance, has survived as a minor masterpiece. Set to the plangent, melancholy tune are sweet lyrics by Edward Heyman. "Lady, Play Your Mandolin" is little more than a museum piece today, but "Blame It on My Youth" was recently named in a poll of cabaret artists as among their most-requested songs.

Alec Wilder's classic study *American Popular Songs, The Great In-*

novators, 1900–1950 mentions Levant's two hits, "Lady, Play Your Mandolin" and "Blame It on My Youth," noting that the latter "is the better of the two by far." He goes on to make the case, however, that Levant finds a way to subtly spoil the song's melodic flair by undercutting it with a weak measure and final phrase:

> I am, I admit, puzzled how Levant, after such sinuous writing, could allow such a measure as fifteen to slip by him.

> And I feel the same way about the final phrase.

> Why the b flat in twenty-nine? Why not, in that 1st triplet, c, d, and e flat? Is the b flat there in order to keep a stricter imitation with the previous measure? The song is so finely fashioned that any phrase less polished than the rest stands out that much more.

It seems that Levant's penchant for undercutting himself was present even when he was at his best. Nonetheless, the melody succeeds—its bittersweet mood suggests that Levant allowed more of himself into the composing process; the melody is more expressive, more tender, than his usual fare (with the possible exception of the lovely "If You Want the Rainbow [You Must Have the Rain]").

Though Oscar provided neither the lyrics nor the title of the song, its theme is curiously appropriate to its composer, who would go through life feeling like the youngest member of any group in which he found himself and who would struggle on Dr. Shoenfeld's couch in an attempt finally to throw off the lamentations of that youth.

In 1934, perhaps the roughest year of the Depression, Levant was between Hollywood assignments. He stuck mainly to New York, making daily calls at T. B. Harms "to sneer at everybody who had hits," though he hadn't done too badly that year with "Blame It on My Youth." At Harms, Levant ran into Bernard Herrmann, one of the malcontents at Copland's first American music festival at Yaddo.

Herrmann nursed fierce ambitions to become a conductor. He found backing for a series of concerts to be held at Town Hall, and he suggested that Levant compose a piece for one of the programs. Levant at first demurred, telling the stocky, bespectacled composer that he had never written anything for orchestra. Herrmann tried to convince him that "orchestration was a push-over":

> He gave me daily pep talks, complete with brief biographical sketches of composers who became famous overnight on the strength of one piece. Then he sent me a score. . . . On my own, I had purchased a small book on clefs. This was my preparation for orchestrating.

What Oscar didn't tell Herrmann was that he had already begun his Sinfonietta during the final stages of his marriage to Barbara. So the aborted "Bergdorf Goodman Sinfonietta," pulled out of the crushed hat of his brief marriage, would have a life after all.

The program at Town Hall was a bit more theatrical than musical, typical of many League of Composers gatherings. Aaron Copland's Prelude from the First Symphony was on the program, as well as Charles Ives's Prelude and Fugue from the Fourth Symphony. Dana Suesse, Ernest Bloch, Roy Harris, Henry Cowell, Percy Grainger, and Herrmann's partner-in-discontent at Yaddo, Jerome Moross, were all represented.

The program notes for the February 25, 1934, concert described the Sinfonietta as "not deliberately in the jazz idiom, although, like the majority of American, even European works, [it] manifests a number of its devices, notably rhythmic."

> The Sinfonietta is in three movements; Toccata—fast; Adagio; Rondo—vivace. There is much interesting motive development too intricate to enlarge upon here in the absence of musical illustrations. . . . Levant's music is highly contrapuntal and altogether in a modern idiom.

Though Oscar's piece was well received, the program did not go well, due to Aaron Copland's sudden defection in midstream. During the intermission, Copland denounced the entire project. Drawing a crowd of attentive disciples, he "tiraded eloquently on the failings of the conductor, the meager talents of the orchestral players and the presumption of both in playing difficult contemporary music," as Levant later described the evening. The critics took their cue from Copland, although Levant's Sinfonietta got favorable notice.

For Levant, the 1930s would establish a pattern of alternating serious composing with writing film scores and popular music, but with his concert works finding increasing acceptance. Yet whenever he found his serious music being praised, he retreated from the scene and turned his attention to the less-challenging, less-intimidating forms of popular music.

In 1934 Levant was hired by the brilliant playwright and screenwriter Ben Hecht, who with his fellow playwright Charles MacArthur had recently embarked upon producing the first of three films contracted under a special arrangement with Paramount Studios in Astoria, Queens. Hecht and MacArthur would produce, write, and direct films at the Long Island studio, having the Astoria outpost almost entirely to themselves. George Antheil, the avant-garde composer who looked like an angelic boxer—his sweet blue eyes, his straw blond hair in a bowl cut, his blunt broken nose—was brought in to score the films.

A spirit of fun and mockery overtook the enterprise, with Hecht and MacArthur satirizing Hollywood by giving everyone associated with their productions an inflated title. Office boys were all made members of the Board of Directors; the porter was "Supervisor in Charge of Sanitation," and Levant was installed as "Assistant President of the Music Department."

Part of Levant's job was to play duets with the violin-toting, music-mad Ben Hecht. "My association with Hecht," Levant remembered, "arose from the fact that I was at liberty, and he played the violin very badly."

It was a rather cruel joke to hire Levant at the embarrassingly low salary of $15 per week. But Hecht and MacArthur were obsessed with bringing in their first film on the impossibly low budget of $150,000, and they found ingenious ways to cut expenses (such as using mostly unknown actors, shooting nightclub scenes in nightclubs rather than building sets, and sliding their scanty backdrops on wheels so each scene could be shot in the same, already lit corner of the studio). Hiring Levant at $15 a week to accompany Hecht on the violin, and maybe score a movie in addition, was Hecht's idea of a funny way to stay under budget. Oscar went along, though he had by now accumulated a great deal of experience writing film music and certainly could have made himself a better arrangement.

Levant's good fortune in being at the right place when something innovative and fresh was coming together compensated for his low salary. *Crime Without Passion* would prove to be the most interesting of all the Hecht-MacArthur collaborations—a defining moment, for some critics, in film noir—and it would launch the career of Claude Rains. The music director, Frank Tours, was so busy on other projects that he gave Levant a number of scenes to score. Without intending to, Levant once again found himself fully employed and underpaid by Paramount, the studio that had first taken him to Hollywood in 1929 to help turn *Burlesque* into *The Dance of Life*.

Levant's score for this strange, melancholy film, which opens with a surreal montage of three gauze-draped Furies hovering over Manhattan, is eerie, clangorous, and evocative, probably inspired by Antheil.

As much as he was enjoying the chaotic camaraderie of the Astoria studios, it dawned on Levant that he was being shamelessly exploited. His cab fares from his midtown hotel to the Astoria studio were higher than his salary. He was forced to tell Hecht that he was actually losing money working for him. "With a generous gesture," Levant later wrote, Hecht "nominally doubled my salary each week, though my paycheck still called for only $15.00. . . . Hecht kept sending a steady stream of memos announcing increases in my wage. One day I was drawing 350 dollars a week . . ." Eventually, Hecht increased Levant's salary to $1,200 per week, but only on paper—his pay envelope continued to contain only fifteen dollars. "Before long," Levant complained, "I was in the hysterical [tax] brackets, but still only drawing my fifteen dollars."

Levant finally marched into Hecht's office and said, "I can't afford any more of these raises. I'm starving to death as it is." But Hecht was either unable or unwilling to pay him what he was worth, and Levant soon quit the enterprise.

From 1933 through 1937 Oscar Levant spent his time shuttling between New York City and Los Angeles. These were years of bachelorhood in which he made himself a kind of permanent guest at a series of different households and salons, ranging from the theatrical to the aristocratic to the notorious. In these years he befriended George S. Kaufman's wife, Beatrice, whose best friend was Maggie Swope. Through Maggie Swope's son, Ottie (Herbert Bayard Swope, Jr.), Oscar became a perennial houseguest of the Swopes on Long Island. Oscar's friendship with Bea Kaufman took him frequently to their

Bucks County home in Pennsylvania. In New York City he could always be found at the Gershwins'. In Los Angeles there was Salka and Berthold Viertel's salon and the comfortable home of Sonya Levien and Carl Hovey.

Then there were the houses that weren't homes. Levant frequented one of the great brothels of New York, the infamous house of Polly Adler. Polly Adler's (known by the name of its famous madam) was the meeting place of all of Broadway. It was once said that if a bomb exploded in Polly Adler's house, the political and cultural life of the city would be wiped out. Polly Adler's was a salon like Hovey and Levien's, the Viertels', or even the Swopes', with the added attraction of sex for sale.

But many of its clients, including Levant, went to Polly Adler's more for camaraderie than for sex. Levant liked the *gemütlichkeit* of the place—a gang of swells, actors, and politicians milling around, talking, laughing, reading the newspapers, standing around the kitchen drinking coffee, grabbing a bite and listening to the fights on the radio. Levant and a pal, the newspaper reporter Curly Harris, often visited Polly Adler's. "About five in the morning," Levant recalled, "we'd go there and drink tea. No business, we never bothered." Occasionally Polly would get fed up with their hanging around and throw them out.

Oscar's work for the Hollywood studios brought him into contact with plenty of willing young women—nascent glamour girls and starlets, healthy young women in search of a good time. And Oscar, though not handsome, exuded a comforting kind of sexuality, as testified to by his affairs with women like Nancy Carroll and Jean Arthur. So Oscar went to Polly Adler's to dine, and to Hollywood restaurants for sex.

While Levant was enjoying himself at Polly Adler's and making the rounds of his various favorite households, Arnold Schoenberg—the autocratic, distinguished composer of *Verklärte Nacht* and *Pierrot lunaire*—was fleeing Germany. Embittered by his forced exile, Schoenberg took the only job he could find in America, teaching a music composition course at the Malkin Conservatory in Boston. No one registered for his class. Finally, in September 1935, USC invited him to lecture, and UCLA countered with the offer of a full professorship. Schoenberg accepted the UCLA post, though he would complain that his students were inadequately prepared, that teaching them was "as if Einstein were having to teach mathematics at a secondary school."

The year 1934 was memorable for Oscar for "Blame It on My Youth" and *Crime Without Passion,* but 1935 ushered in the last of his father figures, Arnold Schoenberg. Levant began his studies with the ex-Viennese Jew who had sought refuge in the sun-drenched outpost of Los Angeles. Under the strict tutelage of the sixty-year-old, balding, gruff lion, Levant would begin to flourish as a serious composer.

18

The Lion in Exile

"We had endless dialogues. I characterized it as
exchanging his ideas with him."

LEVANT RETURNED TO LOS ANGELES IN 1935 TO STUDY WITH ARNOLD
Schoenberg, but his path to the great teacher was routed through the
Fox and RKO studios, where he was again hired to write popular
tunes for a number of films. For the next three years Levant would
rely on his film work to support his study with Schoenberg. It was a
typically Levantian juxtaposition of high and low culture.

Levant was rehired by Sol Wurtzel at Fox Film Studios, where he
was again paired with lyricist Sidney Clare to write songs for a number of mostly forgettable B movies. For a shipboard melodrama about
a professional gambler entitled *Black Sheep,* the songwriting pair wrote
"In Other Words I'm in Love." Levant and Clare also provided the
title song for *Steamboat 'Round the Bend,* notable as Will Rogers's last
picture, made shortly before his untimely death in an airplane crash.
Oscar was proud of having worked on the film, simply to have been
associated with the legendary humorist, who had been a hero of his
youth. For their third Fox film, *Music Is Magic,* starring Alice Faye,
Levant and Clare wrote "Love Is Smiling at Me" and "Honey
Chile."

Levant drifted over to the RKO studios and was hired by Pandro S.

(Pan) Berman, whom he had known when Berman was just a film cutter during Levant's earlier stint with RKO in the late twenties. Pan Berman's meteoric rise at RKO was responsible for Levant's second phase of work for that studio. The film *In Person* was meant to demonstrate the abilities of a rising young actress, Ginger Rogers, without the partnership of Fred Astaire, with whom she had just scored a hit in *Top Hat*. Levant was hired to write a handful of danceable tunes with Dorothy Fields, the most successful woman lyricist of her day ("I Feel a Song Comin' On," "I'm in the Mood for Love," "The Way You Look Tonight")—quite an achievement in the macho world of song-writers in which women were sorely underrepresented. ("Ladies don't write lyrics" was the prevailing attitude, as expressed by Dorothy's own father, the vaudeville comedian Lew Fields.) One unimpressed movie critic, however, wrote "The Levant-Fields songs are basically deficient, but Miss Rogers makes reasonably good use of them vocally and for her taps."

Despite its poor reviews, the film was highly profitable and would prove Ginger Rogers's box-office appeal as a solo actor. *In Person* opened on December 12, 1935, two weeks before Levant's thirtieth birthday, but he was not at the premiere.

Before the edit of *In Person* was even complete, Levant left Hollywood and briefly returned to New York. He did manage to see the film in a preview just prior to its opening at the RKO-owned Radio City Music Hall. Pan Berman was also in town, and Levant invited him to dinner after the preview. "How did you like the picture, Oscar?" Berman asked him.

"Frankly, Pan, I was disappointed."

Berman flung down his napkin and yelled, "Who in hell are you to be disappointed?" Levant and his former boss spent the rest of the evening arguing over "who had to be who to be disappointed."

William Le Baron, Sol Wurtzel, Pan Berman—Levant worked for all three men. They were of a type—"Type A" personalities, stressed-out and often abusive, used to getting their own way. They fit into Oscar's pattern of ingratiating himself with father substitutes and then finding some pretext to break with them or get himself fired. But he enjoyed his outsider status in Hollywood, and he continued to play the bad boy. After all, none of the work that was demanded of him tapped his real resources. But working with Arnold Schoenberg would.

Schoenberg and his family had finally settled in Hollywood, then moved to the upscale suburb of Brentwood to be closer to UCLA once he began his tenure there. Almost from the moment of his arrival in Los Angeles, Schoenberg began conducting small, private classes in composition. Film composers and arrangers flocked to his classes. It was considered the thing to do, and among his early disciples were Alfred Newman, Franz Waxman, and David Raksin.

Schoenberg was plagued by financial worries during most of his life in America, complaining bitterly that his major works, written according to his twelve-tone system, were being ignored by the leading orchestra conductors of the day. The solution to his financial worries was staring him in the face: Why not compose scores for the movies? One film score could bring in $25,000, more than five times the meager professor's salary he received at UCLA. Schoenberg was in fact tempted when MGM producer Irving Thalberg approached the great man—after noting that he had an entry in the *Encyclopaedia Britannica*—to write music for *The Good Earth,* the epic film adapted from Pearl S. Buck's equally epic novel and starring Paul Muni and Luise Rainer.

Thalberg, who had been impressed with a broadcast performance by the New York Philharmonic of Schoenberg's *Verklärte Nacht,* knew that Schoenberg came with a reputation for greatness, and he wanted greatness for his grand, sweeping film. He engaged Schoenberg's countrywoman and friend Salka Viertel to help with the negotiations.

The meeting between the young mogul Thalberg and the lion-in-exile Schoenberg, as recounted in Otto Friedrich's *City of Nets,* was a classic clash of wills:

> Brought finally to Thalberg's imperial office, Schoenberg took a seat in front of the producer's desk. He kept both hands clasped on the handle of an umbrella, which he refused to give up. Thalberg began explaining his idea.
> "Last Sunday, when I heard the lovely music you have written—"
> "I don't write 'lovely' music," Schoenberg interrupted.

Confused by this response, Thalberg began explaining the plot and sweep of *The Good Earth,* asking the composer if he could supply music expressing the themes of Chinese peasant life. At one point he described a scene in which O-lan gives birth in a wheat field:

> "Think of it! . . . There's a terrific storm going on, the wheat field is swaying in the wind, and suddenly the earth begins to tremble. In the midst of the earthquake Oo-Lan [*sic*] gives birth to a baby! What an opportunity for music!" "With so much going on," said Schoenberg mildly, "what do you need music for?"

Schoenberg would work on *The Good Earth*, he said, but only if he were given complete control of the dialogue as well as the music.

> "What do you mean by complete control?" Thalberg asked in wonderment.
>
> "I mean that I would have to work with the actors," Schoenberg said. "They would have to speak in the same pitch and key as I compose it in. It would be similar to *Pierrot lunaire*, but of course less difficult."

Thalberg couldn't believe that anyone would turn down a lucrative MGM contract, and he felt confident that he could eventually get Schoenberg on his own terms. But he was impressed with the composer's nerve, especially in "a threadbare professor," and he gave him a copy of the novel and the script to study before their next meeting. After he showed Schoenberg the door, he confided to Salka, "This is a remarkable man."

But Schoenberg did not change his mind. He instructed Salka to demand that in addition to complete control over the film's dialogue he be paid $50,000. In amazement at the professor's *chutzpah*, Thalberg refused.

Though Levant was composing for the studios at the time, he came to Schoenberg as a student of serious music, determined at last to make his reputation as a composer. Schoenberg was of course known for his twelve-tone system, but he taught his students to use traditional tonal methods; only the advanced students were allowed to try to compose atonally, though he never insisted upon it. By many accounts, he was an inspired teacher, always allowing his students to find their own way. Levant noted that "from the beginning, [he was] an outstanding and prophetic teacher. His students did not merely study with him but became his disciples." His models were from the classical repertory: Bach, Beethoven, Mozart, Schubert, Schumann, and Brahms.

But Schoenberg's "search for truth" did not sit very well with some of the young movie composers who had signed up for short stints, often more for the cachet than for direction or help with compositional problems. As Levant observed,

> . . . most of the boys wanted to take a six weeks' course and learn a handful of Schoenberg tricks. They were sorely disappointed when they discovered that it was his intention to give them instruction in counterpoint, harmony and chorale, which meant that they would have to expend considerable effort themselves in doing assigned work.

A friend of Oscar's, the composer David Raksin, took one of his problems to Schoenberg, hopeful of a quick, concise solution. He had been assigned to write some music for an airplane sequence and was not sure how he should go about it. He posed the problem to Schoenberg, who thought a moment and then said, "Airplane music? Just like music for big bees, only louder." Schoenberg would afterward always refer to film music as "big bee music."

In Levant's three books, in the countless articles and stories that would be written about him in his lifetime, and in the recollections of friends and family, only two people among his vast acquaintanceship would Levant ever call "great"—one was his father, the other Arnold Schoenberg. If George Gershwin was a kind of older brother he could worship, yet still feel competitive with, Schoenberg became the ideal father who would finally bless Levant's yearnings to create his own music. At their first meeting, Schoenberg took one look at Levant and told him, "You have a very talented face." In one sentence, Schoenberg did much to mollify a quarter of a century of insecurity and sadness.

In other ways, however, Schoenberg was like Max Levant: a Jewish émigré with European manners who, at sixty-one, was the same age Max would have been had he lived. Like Levant's long-deceased father, Schoenberg was given to making emphatic pronouncements ("No man can be great unless he loves music," Max had warned his sons). "I can see through walls," Schoenberg once announced to a startled Levant. Schoenberg also had Max Levant's arrogance. When Schoenberg wrote a violin concerto for Jascha Heifetz that the younger man rejected, Levant asked him, "Who will play the piece now that Heifetz has turned it down?"

"In a hundred years, everybody," was his instant reply.

On another occasion, Levant informed Schoenberg that he liked his second quartet the best of his four quartets. The composer sniffed. "I am above comparisons."

Levant found ample opportunity to discuss music and personalities with his teacher—what he referred to as "exchanging his ideas with him." Though never a great driver, Levant chauffeured Schoenberg around town in a battered secondhand Ford he had acquired, or hung out in the kitchen of the beautiful Schoenberg house in Brentwood. As always, Levant was the insatiable student; he had a gift for asking the right questions and eliciting discourses on a number of subjects. One subject that came up often was Schoenberg's opinion of contemporary conductors. About Toscanini, he pronounced, "I do not consider any man great who refuses to play my music."

The Schoenberg appointment books (kept today behind the heavy steel doors of the Arnold Schoenberg Institute on the USC campus—a kind of hermetically sealed, modern, architectural homage to pantonal music) record sporadic appointments with Levant, usually on Tuesdays and Fridays, from April through September 1935. The appointments resume in October 1936 and continue through November 1937, during which time the two men met from one to eight times a month. Levant found himself blossoming under Schoenberg's influence, and he spent as much time with him as possible.

Like many performers and artists, Schoenberg had a deeply superstitious side. One of his enduring interests was numerology, which would translate into triskaidekaphobia, a morbid dread of the number thirteen. Whenever he was unable to complete a composition, he found that he had stopped at a measure that was a multiple of the number thirteen. Toward the end of his life, he avoided writing the number whenever possible. For example, in his late composition "Dreimal tausend Jahre," the measures are numbered 12, 12a, and 14. He became convinced that he would die on his sixty-fifth birthday, in 1939, because sixty-five is a multiple of thirteen.

During his three years of on-again, off-again study with Schoenberg, Levant completed three works: a piano concerto premiered in 1942 with the NBC Symphony; a string quartet that was performed by the Kolisch Quartet in Denver and in a League of Composers concert in New York in 1938; and an orchestral piece, *Nocturne,* which was performed in a Federal Music Project symphony concert in Los Angeles on April 14, 1937, at Trinity Auditorium. This concert featured Schoenberg's symphonic poem *Pelleas und Melisande* and works by four of his students—Adolph Weiss, Oscar Levant, Gerald Strang, and Anton von Webern—and was conducted by Schoenberg and his student Gerald Strang, with Levant conducting his own piece.

It seems that Levant was finally able to throw off the shadow of George Gershwin, but he was unable to quell his own instinct for contrariness. As much as he admired Schoenberg, the demon father-killer in Levant rose up in all its perversity. While working on the string quartet, for example, Levant confessed that

> the constant acerbity which tonally characterized the piece forced me suddenly to rebel, so I inserted two bars of rather agreeable harmony and counterpoint which didn't germinate from what had preceded them.

When Schoenberg saw these "two innocent bars," he asked Levant suspiciously, "How did this evolve?"

Levant answered, "Your system doesn't work for me."

Schoenberg's enigmatic reply was, "That's the beauty of it—it never works!"

Of the three compositions, Levant's *Nocturne* is the most modern in sound. It would be published in 1936 by *New Music Editions,* the first, experimental, publisher of young modern composers, under the editorial directorship of Henry Cowell and Charles Ives.

The piano concerto is less successful in throwing off the influence of Gershwin, using Gershwin-inspired rhythms combined with Schoenbergian dissonance and developing variation. In Levant's description:

> When I studied with Schoenberg, I wrote a piano concerto. It was in three movements. I wanted to make it palatable to popular taste so I inserted a boogie-woogie strain in the middle of it. It spoiled the whole thing.

Unlike many of his contemporaries, Levant was not an aficionado of jazz and felt it had serious limitations, though he was capable of using jazz effects in his compositions. Levant would disparage his own work when looking back on the composition of the piano concerto:

> This concerto is fourteen minutes long, mostly in fast tempo, relieved with an all-too-short slow section. Composed in the late Thirties, this music reflects an arrogance and a pretentiousness, based on an economic and emotional insecurity. However, those are days we now look back on as happy.

The critic and composer Virgil Thomson, however, would find merit in the piece: "The concerto is, beneath its schoolboy homage to Gershwin and Schoenberg, hard and lonely and original music, full of song and solitude."

Despite their divergent musical wellsprings, Schoenberg respected Levant and maintained a friendly mentor-student relationship with him throughout the mid-1930s. He seemed indeed to have greatly enjoyed Levant's company and once advised the young composer that "[your] relentlessly serious music . . . could use a little of your humor." Eventually Schoenberg accorded Levant the honor of asking him to be his teaching assistant at UCLA.

Surprisingly, given Oscar's admiration for the man and his hunger for a father figure, Oscar turned him down. "I didn't think I qualified," he later admitted, though Schoenberg was fond of saying that the teacher learns from the student. It could be that Levant was just too sensitive about his own lack of formal education ever to accept such a post.

The insecurity of the autodidact may have prevented him from accepting the opportunity to work side by side with the great man. But on the other hand, Levant was already studying with Schoenberg, he was making money writing popular tunes and themes for the studios. What was the incentive to become a teacher's assistant? Perhaps Levant was right to continue his rogue course, in full knowledge that by studying with Schoenberg he was taking his place in a noble lineage. "Schoenberg was very proud," Levant writes, "of producing two such disparate exponents of his style as Alban Berg and Anton von Webern"—two composers Levant greatly admired.

Not only that, but Schoenberg—as he was fond of telling Levant— "had once had the excitement of standing next to Brahms at a concert hall in Vienna, and if Brahms had lived six more months they would have both belonged to the same musical club." Here was a lineage that linked Oscar Levant with Arnold Schoenberg, who had breathed the same air as Johannes Brahms—heady stuff for a high school dropout.

From his room at the Beverly Wilshire Hotel, where Jerome Kern was also in residence, Levant would head for work; then, after his studio work was done for the day, he would dash off to the Schoenberg home in Brentwood. Sundays at the Schoenbergs' were especially festive: there were always visitors, and while the children played, Schoenberg's wife would serve "sandwiches, little sausages, large, openface fruit cakes, cheese tarts, and all manner of drinks."

As with some of his other brilliant students in Vienna and Berlin, Schoenberg had gotten through to Levant—he had pierced Levant's coat of mail and found the wounded core of the *enfant terrible*. Like Oscar, Schoenberg had lost his father when he was fifteen, so he may have recognized in him that need for a mentor. Perhaps because he was used to public humiliation himself—his difficult, pantonal music had been met with boos and catcalls on many occasions—Schoenberg never humiliated his students. He was demanding but not cruel. Levant would have his brief flowering as a composer under Schoenberg's paternalistic tutelage.

Schoenberg entered Levant's life like the moon passing in front of Gershwin's heat and brilliance. But Gershwin was planning to move to Hollywood in 1936 to work on a film score. How long would Schoenberg's presence eclipse Gershwin's?

During Levant's trip to New York City in the fall, he attended the opening night of Gershwin's folk opera *Porgy and Bess* at the Alvin Theatre on October 10, 1935. For the first time, Levant could listen to Gershwin's latest achievement not as an acolyte but more as a fellow composer.

Levant was sitting beside the critic John Weaver as the curtain went up on Catfish Row. By the time the opera was half over, Levant was squirming a little in his seat—there were too many Broadway endings for this newly converted Schoenberg pupil. He turned to Weaver and said, "It's a right step in the wrong direction."

Almost as soon as the words were out of his mouth, Levant felt a pang of remorse. The opera had cost his friend the past three years of his life, and Levant's remark would come back to haunt him. "I have felt tremendous remorse for that remark," Levant later wrote, "as I have for many of my other soundings and phrases about my best friend's work"—such as referring to the opera as "a glorious paean to American Jewish music."

But Levant's remarks to the critic while both men were seated in the audience anticipated Virgil Thomson's waspish criticism in the *Herald Tribune,* which set the tone for other negative assessments: "Gershwin does not even know what an opera is."

Levant would not stay long in New York. Curiously enough, it was his old idol from Tin Pan Alley, Irving Berlin, who would get him a job working, again, for the Fox studios—now known as 20th Century–Fox after its merger with Darryl F. Zanuck's 20th Century Studios. And of all the projects to be involved with in Hollywood, Levant was asked to compose an opera.

Levant had never liked Darryl F. Zanuck. The mogul had, in Levant's opinion, a somewhat sadistic sense of humor and was given to making practical jokes, a form of humor Levant detested. In any case, Zanuck lost no time in assigning the young composer—still under Schoenberg's tutelage—to write an operatic sequence for the next Charlie Chan movie, called *Charlie Chan at the Opera.* The idea came about because the studio had acquired a rather magnificent Mephistophelian costume that it wanted to use. Boris Karloff had been signed to star opposite the Scandinavian actor Warner Oland, whose impersonation of the inscrutable Chinese detective was very popular.

Charlie Chan at the Opera, released in October 1936, was regarded by most reviewers as the best of the series, an opinion that still holds true today, for a few reasons. First, the production values were superior. The Chan series were B movies, which meant limited budgets (usually between $250,000 and $275,000), but the director, H. Bruce Humberstone, had managed to use sets built for an A movie titled *Café Metropole,* which gives this film a classier look. The costumes were an added boon, as was Boris Karloff's restrained but suitably spooky performance as an amnesiacal baritone recently escaped from an insane asylum. (The scriptwriters were not above using the line "This opera is going on tonight even if Frankenstein walks in!," capitalizing on Karloff's most famous role.)

Warner Oland is particularly persuasive in *Charlie Chan at the Opera.* Humberstone had apparently discovered that if he let Oland get drunk before a performance, his stumbling and groping around for his lines convincingly approximated a man speaking in an unfamiliar language, and it added a relaxed quality to his performance.

When Zanuck saw the finished product, he was so impressed that he fumed, "This son-of-a-bitch Humberstone is making my 'A' directors look sick turning out a 'B' that looks like this."

The opera Levant wrote, titled *Carnival,* is in some ways emblematic of his musical career in Hollywood. Levant actually consulted with Schoenberg for advice on how best to proceed. Schoenberg advised his pupil to study the score of Beethoven's *Fidelio.* Levant commented wryly that "Since this is one of the most unoperatic of all operas it was just what I didn't need." And it wasn't lost on Oscar that he was playing second fiddle to a costume: "I had heard of music being written around a singer, but never for a costume." Still, he was commissioned to write an operatic sequence, and write one he did.

Without a libretto to work from, Levant composed the music first, and the studio assigned a songwriter named William Kernell to write the libretto. Kernell wrote, in Levant's estimation, some "silly English words" which were then translated by the studio linguists into Italian.

Michael Feinstein has described *Carnival* as the most memorable of Levant's film scores, noting that the operatic sequences were composed for a bass baritone played by Boris Karloff but dubbed by Tudor Williams:

> The music had to be tailored to fit the dramatic context, one point of which was an aria leading up to the stabbing of a soprano with a knife thought to be a prop but actually lethal. According to the composer, his score was "a potent mingling of Mussorgsky and pure Levant." Much of the opera was cut from the film . . .

In addition to the baritone aria, Levant also wrote an affecting soprano passage and a rhythmic little march for soldiers who suddenly appear onstage. Pan Berman and associate producer John Stone apparently liked the soprano aria because, they felt, "it had a good tune." In keeping with this approach to composing music, Levant made one demand of 20th Century–Fox, that he be allowed to use the word *silencio* in the opera. They concurred.

Levant produced sixteen minutes of perfectly good opera; it is both serious work and a kind of ironic quotation of the real thing. But the irony for Levant was that when given the chance to create a serious piece of music, it was trapped inside a Charlie Chan picture. Coming as it did after Gershwin's *Porgy and Bess,* it was almost as if Levant existed in a kind of parallel universe—a parodistic version—of Gershwin's.

Levant himself expressed more amusement than frustration over the composing of *Carnival.* After all, it allowed him to continue to study with Schoenberg, where he was writing real music for real symphony orchestras. But he was slowly developing a contempt—shared by his mentor—for the run-of-the-mill movie music that was being demanded of him. Before long, Levant dropped out of sight, becoming a missing person on the 20th Century–Fox lot.

19

The Great Houses

"During the Depression, I made it a point
to make friends with the rich."

LEVANT SPENT THE MID-1930S DASHING BACK AND FORTH FROM HOL-
lywood to New York, living mostly in hotels. The Beverly Wilshire
in Los Angeles and the Park Central Hotel in New York City were
his two regular habitats. He liked hotel living, and anyway most of his
waking hours were spent in the great houses of a number of his famous friends, such as the Herbert Swopes' Sands Point, Long Island,
estate; George and Beatrice Kaufman's Bucks County retreat; and
Harpo Marx's Hollywood mansion. Driven by his desire to re-create
the boisterous, musical household of his youth and by his dread of
being left alone, Levant made sure that his hours were spent surrounded by friends.

In 1917 Herbert Swope, Sr., had won the first Pulitzer Prize ever
awarded in journalism, for his war coverage. He rose through the
ranks of the *New York World* until he achieved the position of executive editor, turning the declining newspaper into one of New York's
liveliest dailies. He virtually invented the op-ed page. Wealthy on a
grand scale, statesmanlike, and a brilliant conversationalist, Swope entertained lavishly during the Depression years.

The Swopes hosted continuous parties, entertaining on a scale that was nothing short of miraculous: "tea at six, dinner at midnight, supper at three o'clock in the morning, and champagne nearly all the time." The guests played all manner of games, from poker and whist to lawn tennis and croquet, games that were lit at night by the headlights of their expensive cars.

Levant was invited to the Sands Point estate by the Swopes' tall, good-looking, college-aged son, Herbert Swope, Jr., known as Ottie to his friends. Ottie had met Oscar Levant through Dorothy Parker. She had been a frequent houseguest throughout his childhood years, and he adored her.

Ottie, now a grown-up Princeton man, accompanied Dorothy Parker to Tallulah Bankhead's apartment in the Elysee Hotel, known affectionately as "The Easy Lay." Around 10:30 P.M., Parker said, "Let's all go over to see Oscar Levant."

"Who's he?" asked Ottie.

"Well, he's delightful. Come over."

They taxied to the Park Central Hotel, which still hadn't quite gotten over its bad reputation of having been the site of gangleader Arnold Rothstein's bloody demise in 1928. Swope remembered:

> Anyway, we went up to the hotel . . . and Oscar was lying on the bed. He looked up as we came in. . . . He'd already taken his two sleeping pills, so we'd invaded his privacy. And then he stayed up until about 2:00 A.M.

Oscar had a little upright piano in his hotel room, and, after rousing himself from his pill-induced lethargy, lighting a cigarette, and gulping down some hotel coffee, he started playing the piano for his guests, to their delight. Swope was impressed by how vivaciously he played in his drugged state. "He played so ecstatically and so brilliantly, it was wonderful. He always seemed to resent it when he finished."

Despite almost ten years' difference in age, the two men would become good friends. Ottie was used to having companions older than himself, having grown up in the extraordinary social whirl of the Swope household. The only rule at the Swopes'—besides standing when Swope, Sr., entered the room—was never to be boring.

Levant's irreverence was a refreshing change from the politesse of the business, government, and publishing worlds Swope inhabited. But Herbert Swope, Sr., never really took to Oscar. According to Dorothy Hirshon, a frequent guest who was married to CBS chief William S. Paley at the time, "Herbert wasn't the least bit interested in Oscar. . . . Herbert's interests were very different. But Maggie [Margaret Swope]—she was entertained by Oscar and he felt quite comfortable in the house. Although I don't think he felt included by Herbert." The sentiment was apparently shared by William Paley. These two powerful, influential men who made a virtue of hiding their weaknesses were, perhaps, made uncomfortable by Oscar's raw neediness. Here was a man who made a virtue of his neuroses, his loneliness, his need to be coddled and attended to. "It was the women who appreciated him," remembers Dorothy Hirshon.

> My husband [William Paley], for instance, couldn't bear him. He didn't want to have any part of Oscar. And I think that was not an uncommon feeling with men. . . . I think they didn't take Oscar seriously. I won't say that they thought of him as a buffoon, because they knew better than that—but they still didn't take him seriously. He was not of their world in a curious way. . . . He was friendly with men in music—that was different. Those were the men who were really his friends.

Despite Herbert Swope's lack of interest, Levant flourished in the literate hot air of the Swopes' three-story structure of twenty-seven rooms and eleven and a half baths—"almost fifty rooms," Swope would say when feeling especially seignorial. The Swopes also had a quarter-mile of beachfront, but this latter detail failed to impress Levant, who felt much more secure thumbing through the first editions in the enormous library or loping over to the piano, his movements enveloped in a fog of cigarette smoke.

Levant greatly enjoyed his friendship with Maggie and Ottie Swope—in part delighting in the ironies that placed a Pittsburgh Hill district son of immigrants in this wealthy, prominent—and incidentally Jewish—household on the East Coast.

Though few people, including his children, were aware of it, Swope was Jewish. As Swope's biographer E. J. Kahn has observed, Swope "didn't care whether he was known as a Jew or a non-Jew. There was nothing in his experience to make him feel Jewish." This was not true, however, of some of Swope's other rich Jewish friends such as Raoul Fleischman, cofounder of *The New Yorker* magazine, about whom Levant remarked, "He can afford every luxury except anti-Semitism."

Oscar always traveled alone to the Swopes'. In the months following his divorce, he couldn't bring himself to seek other women. But he found himself drawn to two older married women who could make him feel appreciated and fussed over but who offered little threat of serious entanglement: Maggie Swope and Bea Kaufman.

Like Lee Gershwin, Maggie was an excellent hostess, and she took to Oscar right away, lavishing her maternal interest on the disheveled young composer. "She used to rule him with an iron hand," recalled Ottie. His churlishness found a place at the Swopes', but when he found that he had gone too far with an insulting remark, Maggie would retaliate by banishing him temporarily. "The iron gate is down," she would tell him.

Despite the many guest bedrooms and invitations to stay over, Levant's insomnia prevented him from spending the night; he always insisted on taking a taxi back to the city, even at four in the morning, and returning to Sands Point the next day. In the mid-thirties each trip cost nine dollars—"nine tears," Oscar would say—a luxury the Swopes found terribly extravagant.

While the Swopes' guests were gossiping or playing card games or croquet, someone would invariably be at the piano—George Gershwin, Deems Taylor, or Irving Berlin. Levant would take his place there as well, but only when no one asked. He was sensitive about being urged to play the piano—perhaps it was too close a reminder of the family recitals at which he had been made to perform as a youth. He would play only when he felt like it—never on demand—but when he did he would play beautifully.

Back in New York and spending a lot of time at the Swopes', Levant renewed his friendship with Beatrice Kaufman, the somewhat melancholy wife of the playwright. Bea Kaufman was Maggie Swope's best friend. The two women were similar in that they both developed a wonderful wit and sense of humor as survival strategy in their marriages to brilliant, famous men. Friends drawn into their circle by their husbands' reputations often ended up gravitating toward the two wives—certainly this was the case with Oscar. Oscar would often accompany Bea Kaufman to Sands Point as a stand-in for George Kaufman, who usually preferred to stay in the city. The two developed an extremely close relationship.

Her maiden name, curiously for a woman who would marry a successful playwright, was Bakrow. Through her rich social life and varied connections, Bea was able to avoid the back-row life of being married to a successful writer. But her life was soon marred by tragedy: Her first and only child with Kaufman was born deformed and stillborn. As a result, her husband, who was already considered by many to be a germophobic cold fish of a man, found he could no longer make love to his wife. The rest of their married years were spent companionably but without passion. Kaufman would carry on affairs with a great many women other than his wife, including one of the most popular film actresses of the thirties, Mary Astor, whose private diaries were entered into evidence at her child custody trial. They depicted Kaufman as her most indefatigable lover. Bea would eventually carry on affairs of her own—one of her friends claimed that she started to have affairs even before her husband did.

Throughout their mutual infidelities, Bea Kaufman—brilliant, warm, loquacious—remained her husband's partner and champion in nearly every other aspect of their marriage. It was an unusual arrangement, and Oscar Levant was sometimes caught in the middle.

Bea had a sense of style, though no one would call her beautiful and an uncharitable view saw her as unattractive. She had frizzy hair, a full, sullen face, and a heavy torso. She had a tragic look about her, with sad, ewelike eyes. (Moss Hart and Harpo Marx called her "lamb girl.") She was smart and charming, and somewhere between Rochester, her hometown, and New York City, she had developed an impressive sophistication. She was one of the first women in New York society to bob her hair and wear slacks. She chain-smoked cigarettes from a long, elegant cigarette holder. She even had a job, as fiction editor for *Harper's Bazaar.* When Bea and George Kaufman were both profiled, separately, in *The New Yorker,* Bea's profile, written by Ring Lardner, appeared first, on July 7, 1928.

After the Mary Astor debacle, the Kaufmans retreated to a fifty-seven-acre farm in Bucks County that they purchased for $45,000. Oscar was a frequent visitor, though he hated country living. He would endure the summer heat, mosquitoes, and deafeningly chirping birds just to hang around Beatrice, whose brand of maternal-but-sexy solicitude filled a gap in Oscar's emotional life. Despite their closeness, Bea enjoyed teasing and insulting Oscar—turning the tables on him. Her pet name for him was "Idiot Boy," and when she became irritated with him she introduced him to people as "undiscovered and deservedly so." Yet Oscar loved her.

What may have cemented their friendship was their complex about being unlovely and unlovable. Their friends and admirers found them attractive, but they were convinced otherwise. Certainly Bea had the proof right in her own marriage.

Oscar's friendship with Harpo Marx began on the opposite coast, in a household that was a Hollywood version of the Swope soirées at Sands Point.

Shortly after completing work on the Marx Brothers' 1933 romp *Duck Soup,* which Harpo remembered as "the hardest job I ever did," the film comedian moved permanently to California, where he leased a Beverly Hills mansion from a former silent screen star. The house was so tremendous, Harpo joked, that he never actually counted all the rooms. It wasn't long before his household began to fill up with Algonquin Round Table alumni—Moss Hart, the Kaufmans, Ruth Gordon, Dorothy Parker—and writers like Sam Behrman, Charlie Lederer, and Ben Hecht. After the Gershwins moved out to California in 1936, they were frequent guests. The house also became a retreat for vaudevillians George Burns, Jack Benny, Al Jolson, Eddie Cantor, Georgie Jessel, and the Ritz Brothers; Harpo called it "a combination Retreat for Retired Vaudevillians and Hillcrest Annex" (referring to the only Jewish country club in Los Angeles).

One evening in the middle of a small dinner party, Harpo was interrupted by a phone call.

"Harpo? I'm coming over," said the nasal voice on the other end, a voice Harpo described as sounding like an oboe under a blanket.

"Who the hell is this?"

"This is Oscar Levant, is who the hell this is. I'm coming over. Now."

"Oscar who?"

"*Levant,* you musical illiterate."

Harpo pleaded with Oscar to come another night as he was in the middle of entertaining guests.

Oscar wailed inconsolably. "Look, you son of a bitch. You can't leave me here alone!"

Harpo gave up and Oscar appeared at his door in five minutes. "He stayed for one year and one month. . . . I lost a house, but I gained a friend."

Oscar lay claim to Harpo's gigantic house and his equally gigantic hospitality, eating his food, running up his phone bill, and monopolizing his guests. Harpo complained, "He was a leech and a lunatic—in short, a litchi nut. But I loved the guy."

Levant, for his part, described Harpo Marx as "in reality a person of complete conventionality" (despite his penchant for receiving guests while playing the harp in his underwear), and he marveled that Harpo was "the most beloved man among the intelligentsia of show business." He noted that Charlie Chaplin and Harpo Marx topped the list of movie personalities every visiting dignitary wanted to meet:

One can only conclude that there must be some subconscious attraction in their silence. Naturally, also, everyone wonders what a man who never says anything sounds like.

Intrigued by Levant's studies with Arnold Schoenberg (Harpo was, after all, an accomplished if unconventional harpist), he asked Levant to invite his mentor to dinner. The only other guests were Fanny Brice and her friend the English music-hall comedienne Beatrice Lillie.

Schoenberg was rather mystified by his dinner companions, having little idea who they were. The two famous performers felt the same way about Schoenberg, but to make conversation, Fanny Brice asked the composer what "hits" he had written. After dinner she coaxed him with "C'mon, professor, play us a tune." The professor did not oblige.

It is clear that by the mid-thirties, Levant had turned his anxieties into topics of conversation—he had begun to invent the character of Levant the Neurotic, an invention based on his real neuroses. He was, in essence, playing himself, but the line between the real and the acted would always remain blurred.

Harpo noticed and seemed to have completely accepted two troubling aspects of Oscar's personality that were beginning to manifest themselves. First was his insomnia and ever-increasing reliance on sleeping pills. Harpo also noted that Oscar did not know how to accept generosity. He took Harpo's endless hospitality as his due. Except for his friendship with George Gershwin, Harpo noted, Oscar was "unable to enjoy an equal relationship with anybody. It had to be one-sided, on his side. . . . Once I understood this and accepted it, I found Oscar to be one of the most rewarding men I had ever known."

Oscar was also given to brooding, his depressions settling on him like a miasma. Harpo tried to respect his guest's moods. "He had wit and talent to burn," Harpo recalled in his memoirs. When Oscar fell into one of his sullen moods, drinking steaming coffee and smoking furiously, "he might have been burning off excess talent, along with the witticisms he'd never have time to make."

Harpo indulged Oscar's moods, knowing enough to stay out of his way when his depressions hit, partly because he was struck by Levant's intelligence and verbal audacity. "The amount of knowledge Oscar carried in his head," remembered Harpo, "was fantastic." Harpo was also impressed with Oscar's ability to do a number of things simultaneously—that is, when he wasn't brooding. Once Harpo came downstairs and walked in on Oscar reading a book propped on the piano rack while simultaneously playing Bach and listening to a Beethoven recording on the phonograph. He would sing along with the phonograph in his rasping baritone. Harpo wrote, ". . . in the middle of this triple performance he'd say, without looking away from the book, 'Harpo, why don't you loathe me like everybody else? Don't you like me?' " Part of what the two men shared was a love of music. One evening Harpo invited a well-known concert ensemble to play for his guests after dinner. Unannounced, Oscar joined the ensemble and astonished his host and the members of the Kapinsky Trio with his ability to flawlessly sight-read through Mozart, Schubert, and Brahms.

Harpo, who created the most pixilated character in American cinema, recognized in Oscar Levant another original. Oscar felt close enough to Harpo to reveal his wounded side, his terrible insecurities. Both men had spent most of their lives in show business; Oscar had been supporting himself by his piano playing and songwriting since the age of fifteen. Both had grown up in a household of talented, rambunctious brothers ruled over by a strong, determined mother. Both came from immigrant Jewish families that had known difficult times. Both had sensitive, gentle natures, though Oscar's was buried under an aggressive slugger's personality. Harpo preferred to have his friends do his tongue-lashing for him, and, though his stock-in-trade was silence, he seemed to love the company of fast-talking wits. But Harpo saw the darker, sadder side of Oscar Levant.

"The rarest gift Oscar had to offer," Harpo wrote, "was not his virtuosity, but something few people were fortunate to receive—his smile. . . . Oscar, for all his sarcasm and sullen cracks, didn't really mean to hurt anyone except himself."

20

Concert of Missed Notes

"Whenever anybody turns me down they tell
me how talented I am."

DURING HIS WORKING VISITS TO HOLLYWOOD, LEVANT USUALLY
stayed at the Beverly Wilshire Hotel, but by 1936 he had taken an
apartment on South Roxbury Drive. Among all the New Yorkers
gathering in Hollywood, topping the list as far as Levant was concerned were the Gershwins, who had been hired by RKO to compose music for *Shall We Dance,* a Fred Astaire–Ginger Rogers vehicle.

The Gershwins found a spacious house, on the high-class end of
Roxbury, North Roxbury Drive. Many of their friends—Eddie Cantor, Edward G. Robinson, Irving Berlin, Jerome Kern, Harold Arlen,
Yip Harburg—lived on the same street. Here, in this Hollywood
Spanish-style house, Oscar Levant picked up where he had left off as
the court jester of the Gershwin household—its most frequent, as well
as its most uninhibited and loquacious, guest. Levant resumed the
rigors of playing intense, life-or-death Ping-Pong matches with
George and Ira. "George was a much better player than I," Levant
remembered, "but due to sheer will I would sometimes hold him
even." George Gershwin also loved golf and tennis. Oscar, convinced
that tennis was detrimental to his pianist's wrists, would clomp down
to the tennis courts in his dark suit (a "subtlely spotted business suit,

suitable for all Fahrenheits from 0° to 212°") and heavy shoes, to watch George briskly dominate the court in his dazzling tennis whites, which looked all the whiter against his dark, suntanned skin. "His chest," Oscar teased, "was the hairiest since Beethoven's. I used to make fun of it. I'd say, 'Cut off a lock and give it to a girl.' "

Levant resumed his place of honor at the piano, next to George, playing the new scores Chappell's publishing house sent out to its favorite sons. "A lot of good songs were coming out then," remembered Oscar. Things were changing fast on the Broadway musical scene during the years George had devoted himself to *Porgy and Bess.* Levant noticed that Gershwin had become acutely aware that "such men as Cole Porter and Richard Rodgers had made a considerable advance into the territory once indisputably his."

Oscar was thrilled to have his friend with him in Hollywood, out among the suspicious-looking palms. When Gershwin arrived in August 1936, Oscar was nearly thirty years old and had known George for ten years.

Gershwin was keenly interested in Schoenberg and had apparently met him in New York. Perhaps it was Oscar's connection to Schoenberg that made George more interested in Oscar's music. Levant's struggles with the opera *Carnival* entertained and interested Gershwin; he even offered to pay for an orchestral reading of one of Oscar's highly complex, harmonically involved symphonic works—probably *Nocturne*—a generous offer that Oscar nevertheless could not bring himself to accept. Gershwin may have envied his friend's acceptance by Schoenberg and Copland—an acceptance by serious composers that Gershwin felt still eluded him.

Levant was abashed about showing his work to Gershwin and was, perhaps, a little distrustful of his friend's enthusiasm. He had once nervously shown George the piano concerto he was composing under Schoenberg's tutelage. After examining the piece for a while, Gershwin had exclaimed, "It looks so confused . . ." Baffled and hurt, Oscar shot back, "Didn't you know? I've just been offered the chair of confusion at UCLA."

During that long, strange year—the last year of their complicated friendship—Levant and Gershwin would often play Brahms quartets together, occasionally staying up all night, away from the endless stream of Gershwin's visitors.

Schoenberg and Gershwin became tennis partners. Schoenberg would usually arrive on the same day each week, with an entourage of "string-quartet players, conductors and disciples." Oscar, in his street shoes and crumpled blue suit, was good-naturedly banned from the court—but it was banishment nonetheless, Oscar's reward for having reintroduced the two men.

Levant was present when Gershwin and Schoenberg were driven from the tennis court by a sudden burst of rain. As they all huddled for shelter, Schoenberg announced that his wife had just given birth to a son. George suggested that he name the boy "George," because it was a lucky name. None of them knew it at the time, but the luck of the name George, at least for Gershwin, was about to run out.

Arnold Schoenberg might have been imperious; he might have intimidated his students, scaring some of them into inactivity; but he was fully committed to his fledgling composers and to their continuing development. Much like Paderewski had before him, Schoenberg had brought with him to America the tradition of encouraging performances of his students' works. It was a tradition he fought to maintain, despite a certain amount of audience disruption that frequently occurred during his recitals. The controversial nature of the music he was propounding had often caused Schoenberg, during his early years in Vienna, to lose both collegial and financial support. Still, he insisted that his students present their works to the world, and he arranged performances for them.

Schoenberg tried to interest his fellow émigré Otto Klemperer, the principal conductor for the Los Angeles Philharmonic Orchestra, in Levant's music. Levant, though usually performance-shy since his last furious bout of stage fright at Lewisohn Stadium, was eager to have his recently completed piano concerto heard.

Klemperer was a singularly impressive figure. Born in 1885 in Breslau, he was a man of prepossessing height, called "Dr. Klemperer" by all who knew him in deference to his great dignity. Like Schoenberg, he was an intense, formidable man, and his tremendous physical size added to his grandeur. Levant called him "the tallest conductor in the world" and quipped that he looked as if he carried the podium with him wherever he went.

Like Schoenberg, Klemperer had been forced to flee Germany when the Nazis rose to power. (It is one of the ironies of show business that Klemperer's son, Werner, became an actor and won two Emmy awards for his comic portrayal of a Nazi on the popular sixties television show, *Hogan's Heroes*.) Like Schoenberg, Klemperer was Jewish by birth, but he had converted to Catholicism, reconverting toward the end of his life.

One night at Salka Viertel's, Schoenberg, desiring to help his pupil, suggested to Levant that he play his piano concerto for Klemperer.

Levant later wrote plaintively about the occasion that "this was the opportunity that would have meant so much to me." Yet when he sat down at the piano to begin to play, to everyone's astonishment "When Irish Eyes Are Smiling" came out instead. His pal Charlie Lederer, not quite catching on, provided a lusty tenor in accompaniment. The *coup de grâce* was a spirited version of that old party pleaser "Chopsticks."

Klemperer and Schoenberg were horrified.

"To this day," Levant wrote, "I am perplexed by my own behavior. My impulse for self-condemnation is my only clue." In an effort, perhaps, to leaven the situation with humor, Levant promptly asked Klemperer if he liked Beethoven. Since his conducting of Beethoven was legendary, considered among the greatest of his day, the question reverberated with its obviousness. "That's like asking me if I believe in religion," was Klemperer's measured reply before turning on his heel and stalking out of the room.

In short, Levant's impromptu recital for the conductor was a debacle, brought about by his now deeply entrenched penchant for undermining himself. Being asked to play on demand in the context of a social gathering was already a problem for Levant; no one who knew him well ever asked him to sit down and play. He had long struggled with his resentment over being made to perform on cue by his parents, and anything that smacked of that raised his hackles.

And then there was Dr. Klemperer's sheer impressiveness. Most musicians were in awe of him, and Levant wasn't about to put himself in harm's way by being judged by this formidable figure. What if his piano concerto had been found wanting? Now he would never have to know. "It was a cheerless victory," Levant wrote a few years after the event, "because I had postponed the moment of truth concerning my abilities as a serious composer. This strange pattern kept me free and pristine."

For weeks following the incident, Levant repeatedly called Klemperer at home to try to make amends for his boorish behavior. Each time he called he was told, "Dr. Klemperer is walking in the garden." Eventually Levant would restore himself to Klemperer's good graces. He sought the conductor out in the greenroom following a Los Angeles Philharmonic concert. He managed to ingratiate himself with the esteemed conductor, who not only forgave Levant but agreed to look at the scores of his piano concerto and his orchestral *Nocturne* as well. At last, an opportunity to have his work performed by the maestro was in his grasp.

However, Levant recalled, "When he had completed his study of the scores . . . he looked at me severely with those powers of sustained concentration and said, 'You are undoubtedly very talented.' "

Oscar recognized that comment as the kiss of death, and so replied, "That means you're not going to play my music."

"How did you know?"

"For years now," Levant replied,

> whenever anybody turns me down they tell me how talented I am. If a man is going to hire me he says, "Come in Monday morning at nine o'clock." If a conductor is going to play a piece of music the first thing he asks for is a "few changes here and there." But if it's thumbs down, I always am praised for my talent.

Klemperer saw Levant's vexation. He offered consolingly, "What's your hurry? Bruckner was fifty before his first symphony was played," and he advised Levant to play the Beethoven piano sonatas every morning. So Oscar's music was rejected after all, but at least it was turned down privately, with encouragement and respect, and not in the noisy confines of the Viertel salon, in front of Schoenberg and Oscar's friends.

On yet another occasion Levant would find himself barely able to perform at one of the Viertel gatherings. This time he was traumatized not by the patriarchal Klemperer but by one of Schoenberg's most treasured disciples, Salka's brother, Eduard Steuermann. Steuermann was something of a thorn in Levant's side. As a student of Schoenberg's in Berlin since 1912, Steuermann had so impressed his teacher that Schoenberg began to make use of him as a performer and interpreter of his own controversial twelve-tone music, which Schoenberg believed would secure the supremacy of German music into the next century.

A small crowd of the usual suspects had gathered at the Viertels'. Levant approached the piano and extinguished his cigarette before starting to play. Steuermann, for whom Levant was ostensibly performing, sat behind Levant on a divan.

But just as Levant took his seat at the piano, an excruciating pain shot through his back, temporarily paralyzing him. The Viertels quickly called for a doctor, who arrived shortly and taped up Levant's entire torso. Levant managed to play his piano concerto, but his performance was sufficiently upstaged by his catastrophic and no doubt psychosomatic back pain. It was virtually impossible for him to resume playing for the next three weeks.

When the tape was finally removed, Levant complained that he felt a sense of loss. "I liked the constricted, crippling effect it had had on me," he confessed. It had certainly given him a good excuse not to perform his best for Steuermann. What disabled Oscar seemed almost to comfort him. Feeling like a failure gave him a kind of reassurance, perhaps because failing seemed easier than being judged.

Levant was now poised on the brink of a successful film-composing career, like his friend David Raksin, a fellow student of Schoenberg. But where Raksin embraced film music and did marvelous work within its confines (*Laura* in 1944, *Force of Evil* in 1948, *Separate Tables* in 1958), Levant began to chafe at the very notion of composing for the "moom pitchers." He began to feel that composing movie music was a cheapening of his talents and a waste of his time.

There was some truth to his observations about the formulaic nature of writing for the movies, but his reaction was another example of his "Noël Coward syndrome": quitting a venture when it had become too routine—or, in Oscar's case, when success beckoned.

First of all, it bothered him that movie composers were paid by the minute—that is, by each minute of music actually used in the film. This seemed inordinately anticreative. Little attention, Levant believed, was paid to the character of a score as a whole, and he winced at the overly lush orchestrations, the constant use of musical clichés, the undeviating devotion to formula. For example, he complained, there were several species of fog music: "Ordinary fogs are invariably Ravel-Debussy. . . . A few of the recondite figurations from Dukas's *L'Apprenti Sorcier* are put into play for special or particular kinds of fogs, such as prison breaks or bank robberies." He noticed how the members of the 20th Century–Fox music department, with whom he had once shared "tea [marijuana] breaks," were able to utilize Frederick Delius not only for walks in the garden but for bicycle rides in the country as well. All train music, Oscar noticed, seemed to come from Honegger's *Pacific 231*. The orchestral pattern of all carousels, he complained, was derived from Stravinsky's *Petrouchka*.

In contrast to American film music, Levant was impressed with the work of Russians and Europeans. Their often-inspired film scores made the fate of American composers seem even more bleak and frustrating to Levant.

All musical sequences were channeled into four categories: main titles, inserts, montages, and end titles. This amounted to his old *bête noire*—being told when and how to make music. The fact that he had little respect for the musical discernment of the typical studio chief made this prospect all the more galling.

> If a composer . . . appeared at a studio with an opening sequence scored for [only] one, three or five instruments, the producer would think that he was not getting a proper return for his investment.

Levant convinced himself that it was impossible to assert his individuality as a composer in this milieu, as he came to realize that the requirements of producers, directors, and accountants were quite different from those of serious composers. He took Schoenberg's relief at escaping from *The Good Earth* as a cautionary tale, and, after completing the mini-opera for *Charlie Chan at the Opera* as well as a few days' work on an Alice Faye picture, Levant rebelled. He simply stopped showing up at 20th Century–Fox.

He left the studio, just as he had left Aaron Copland's first music festival at Yaddo. As a result, he succeeded in cheating himself out of what would prove to be a golden age of film music. Bernard Herrmann would auspiciously cut his teeth on Orson Welles's groundbreaking *Citizen Kane* in 1940 before becoming Alfred Hitchcock's favorite film composer in the fifties and sixties, producing the chilling score for *Psycho* and other Hitchcock films. David Raksin would evolve from notating Charlie Chaplin's whistling in *Modern Times* to composing a film score for *Force of Evil* that would rouse Levant's envy.

It was William Goetz, an executive at 20th Century–Fox, who finally fired Levant. Goetz—who had married one of Louis B. Mayer's daughters and thus owed his job to his father-in-law—had harbored a grudge against Levant ever since Levant had one-upped him in a battle of insults at a Hollywood party. Goetz had snidely asked Levant to "play us a medley of your hit"—referring to Levant's one big hit at the time, "Lady, Play Your Mandolin." Levant had countered with, "Why don't you play us a medley of your father-in-law?" successfully shutting up the young man whose career had been launched by nepotism.

Though Levant would later score two more films, *Nothing Sacred* and *Made for Each Other*, for Selznick International Pictures in 1937 and 1938, he virtually shut himself out of a career as a film composer. Some years later, when David Raksin dropped in on Levant one balmy afternoon and showed him his new score for *Force of Evil*, Levant was impressed and envious, an emotion that always expressed itself in anger. He threw Raskin out of the house and refused to speak to him for a few weeks. It was only later that Raksin heard Levant's appraisal of his new score and understood his rage—"that's what *I* should have been writing," Levant had moaned.

• • •

In 1936, the year the Gershwins moved to California, Moss Hart and George S. Kaufman completed one of their most enduring stage plays, the hilarious comedy *You Can't Take It with You*. The inspired, zany depiction of a family of eccentric misfits would win the Pulitzer Prize for Kaufman and his thirty-two-year-old collaborator.

Moss Hart's impoverished Bronx boyhood had given a brooding undercurrent to his otherwise sunny personality. Like Levant, Hart was funny and clever, and he appreciated a good joke and a sardonic remark. Both men seemed to feel an obligation to entertain their friends.

As a result of his desperately impoverished childhood—one spent in grimy apartments where it was necessary to take in boarders—Hart became extravagant in his tastes once he could afford it. He bought himself gold cuff links, gold cigarette cases—everything gold. But for a long time, the one accoutrement he did not acquire was a wife.

"He was programmed," remembered one friend, "forever to be single." The young playwright's bachelorhood was so well known that one night in New York at a dinner party, Moss Hart came in with the stately, beautiful actress Edith Atwater on his arm. "Ah," Oscar exclaimed in his performing baritone, "here comes Moss Hart and the future Miss Atwater." The remark made the rounds of all their friends; it seemed to perfectly sum up the fate of every one of Hart's female companions—all except for Kitty Carlisle, who would eventually marry the playwright. She had met him on the set of *A Night at the Opera;* it was Oscar Levant who had gotten her the part in the Marx Brothers film.

Kitty Carlisle was a young singer from Shreveport, Louisiana, when she met George Gershwin. George invited Kitty to the Gershwins' for a Passover seder, where she first encountered Levant.

"Oscar Levant," Kitty remembered, "was wonderfully funny and almost frighteningly articulate." It was Levant who presided over the seder service, and he performed the whole ceremony "in a kind of mad jazz rhythm." George, not to be outdone, chimed in.

On February 10 and 11, 1937, Gershwin was scheduled to play two concerts in Los Angeles as part of a northwest concert tour. The concerts, with Alexander Smallens conducting the Los Angeles Philharmonic, would be Gershwin's first appearance in that city as a soloist. Levant attended both performances.

But on the second night, as Levant sat and listened to his friend begin the first movement of the Concerto in F—a piece he had seen

Gershwin perform effortlessly at countless gatherings—nothing could have prepared him for what he suddenly, startlingly, heard.

> I noticed that he stumbled on a very easy passage in the first movement. Then in the andante, in playing the four simple octaves that conclude the movement above the sustained orchestral chords, he blundered again.

Levant was nearly jolted out of his seat. Gershwin was always an impeccable performer—"not terribly expressive but very rhythmic and ingenious." What was happening?

Backstage after the concert, where Levant had gone to congratulate his friend, he debated whether or not to mention the muffed notes. But it was Gershwin who first spoke, greeting Levant with "When I made those mistakes, I was thinking of you, you bastard."

It was not that Levant's presence unnerved Gershwin, but he knew that among all of his friends, Oscar would have been the one to detect the marred passages. He was annoyed with himself, not with Levant. Still, the remark haunted Oscar.

Gershwin later said to Levant that he had experienced a sudden dizziness and the disagreeable odor of something burning. No one considered it important, however, including Gershwin and the friends and admirers crowding Lee's gala party later that night, where Levant played his usual role of Mephistophelian jester.

No one suspected in February 1937 that George's impaired motor function, as evidenced by the missed notes, his dizzying headaches, and the burning smell in his nostrils, were a triad of symptoms that suggested a brain tumor.

Gershwin's remark reverberated in Levant's psyche. Levant had long nursed a vague sense that his father's disappointment in him had contributed to his fatal illness. And now a major figure in Levant's life was sending him a similar message: Because of you I stumbled. Those words resonated as Gershwin's mysterious symptoms worsened.

21

Someone to Watch Over Me

*"You have an unawakened face but your mouth
has possibilities."*

THE FIRST TIME OSCAR LEVANT SAW JUNE GALE SHE WAS SEATED
at a piano in a Darryl F. Zanuck film called *Sing Baby Sing* starring
Adolphe Menjou. "That's the best-looking pianist I ever saw," Oscar
remarked to a friend when the preview ended and the lights came on.

In fact, June Gale didn't play the piano at all. The film orchestra
was faked, with actresses pretending to play their instruments while a
recording of a big band was heard on the sound track. Perhaps some
sort of weird transference was taking place in Oscar's soul: The kid
who had always felt unattractive, whose prowess at the piano had
robbed him of that mythic entity—a happy childhood—now saw
before him a fresh, lovely young woman seated at the piano, his beloved instrument of torture. From the moment Levant saw this
image—the ineffable juxtaposition of piano and beautiful girl—he
was a goner.

A few nights later at the popular Trocadero nightclub on Sunset
Boulevard, Levant spotted the piano-playing ingenue out with her
date. The "Troc," as it was familiarly called, had by 1937 become a
focal point of Hollywood glamour to which both stars and hopefuls
flocked. Though Hollywood still lacked a Lindy's, a "21," or a Stork

Club, it was beginning to compete with New York City in exciting nightspots. For a nocturnal creature like Levant, that was an important development.

As June and her date, Allan "Pinky" Miller, got up to leave, Pinky recognized Charlie Lederer seated over in a corner with a group of friends. June recalled the evening:

> I'm standing waiting for Allan Miller to finish his talk with Charlie. Somebody in the background got up, walked around to me and said, "Can I have your phone number?" and I said "No," and he said to me, "Oh, please, would you?" So as we're walking out, I told him about this young man who came out of the dark and said he wanted my phone number. I asked, "Who was he?" Pinky said, "His name is Oscar Levant."

The name didn't mean anything to June Gale; in any case, she wasn't about to give her phone number to a complete stranger, and she made sure Pinky wouldn't give it out, either. At nineteen, June was still living with her mother, Sayde, and her sister Jean in the Canterbury Apartments across from Musso and Frank Grill, the popular Hollywood Boulevard restaurant. She was dating a lot of men, but what she wanted was an acting career. Now that she was a contract player at 20th Century–Fox, marriage was the furthest thing from her mind.

June Gale preferred to date much older men—older than Oscar, who was thirty at the time—probably because she had been emotionally deprived by her own father, a darkly handsome Irishman named John Gilmartin whose drinking had put his family in jeopardy. "He would just show up at night," June remembered,

> with a little plaster in his hair [he worked as a plasterer] . . . and then he would go off, and I'd have a feeling he wouldn't come home, and I knew he was out on a drunk. . . . My mother suffered terribly, so I had no feeling for him. We took care of him. . . . He just backed away from life.

June's mother was a schoolteacher devoted to her remarkable offspring—two sets of pretty, talented twins, all girls, born fourteen months apart. With her husband too often staggering home drunk, Sayde resolved that a life in show business would be more dependable than life with John Gilmartin. The twins were adept at their dancing lessons, so Sayde made them fetching little costumes and billed them as dancing quadruplets, adopting the stage name of Gale. "We were always terrified," June remembered, "that somebody would find out we were two sets of twins, not quadruplets." They reached the pinnacle of their success when they appeared as a featured act in George White's *Scandals.* June was the driving spirit of the Gale Sisters, forcing them to practice their routines. June's sister Jean never quite got the choreography down, but she faked it beautifully—audiences thought she was the best dancer of the four.

Vaudeville was on its way out as the Gale Sisters—June, Jean, Jane, and Joan—tapped and somersaulted at the Paramount and Palace, so their appearing on Broadway in *Scandals* was a godsend. They had been supporting the family since they were children, and now that they were in their teens, they wanted what every other teenage girl wanted—to have fun, to live a more normal life. June and her sister Jean decided to try to break into the movies, so they moved with their mother to Los Angeles. Joan and Jane got married.

The day after June refused to give Levant her phone number, Oscar looked it up in the phone book and began calling her. He called the next day and the day after that. He called three times in three days, so June finally phoned her sister Joan's husband, Lou Schreiber, who was a casting agent and knew everybody in town. June explained the situation, and Schreiber told her, "He's a crazy musician, but he's harmless."

The next time Oscar called, he managed to make her laugh, so June agreed to go out with him.

On their first date, Oscar seemed acutely aware of June's youth and inexperience. ("When I was really young," June remembered, "I was terribly shy and always kept my trap shut. . . . I had no personality that I can remember at all.") Their early dating life followed a curious pattern. Levant would usually spend his evenings with the Gershwins and then meet June later, around eleven P.M., just as she was returning from her first date of the evening. He would then take her to a movie or out for a late supper. The first night this happened, he drove his battered Ford to the Canterbury Apartments and watched in discomfort, like a Hollywood detective, as she kissed her other date good night. Yet Levant would rather endure that indignity than give up spending his evenings with the Gershwins or his other friends. "In those days I had so many interesting friends," Levant wrote later, "that I found it torturous and dismaying to spend the whole evening with my empty-headed picture actress."

Nonetheless, Levant was smitten. June recalled:

I guess I looked rather appealing to him because he used to take me to the movies and then he'd stare at me and not watch the movie. He liked me. He really fell for me in a big way. . . . at Armstrong-Schroeder's [a late-night eatery], he looked at me and said, "You have an unawakened face but your mouth has possibilities." That was quite a line. . . .

"Oscar was sexy," June says, "and women instinctively knew he'd be good in bed . . . particularly if they were a little thwarted in that department with their [husbands]." Many of his big affairs were with married women, however, which suggests his reluctance to repeat the brief, painful marriage he had had with Barbara Wooddell. But he quickly made up his mind about June, and from their first few dates he knew he wanted to marry her.

The appearance of Aaron Copland in Los Angeles in June 1937 was a major event for Hollywood composers who had been at the first Yaddo music festival, such as Jerome Moross, Bernard Herrmann, and Oscar Levant. George Antheil, who had been a no-show at Copland's festival, had successfully made the transition to Hollywood, where he was writing film scores and his wife was running the Antheil Gallery, which also hosted musical evenings. Copland had come west to try his luck at breaking into the lucrative film market. He had been following Antheil's column in *Modern Music,* "On the Hollywood Front," where Antheil had written,

> Something is going on in Hollywood. Composers may remain aloof to it, but only at the peril of being left behind, esthetically perhaps as well as financially.

Having heard that Stravinsky and Schoenberg had been invited to write scores for Paramount, and Honegger for RKO's *Joan of Arc,* Copland headed west. Antheil tried to warn him that Hollywood was a "closed corporation," and that "no one should attempt to come out unless he can write piano scores at the rate of fifteen to thirty pages a day," speed being "one of the main requisites of the picture business."

Nonetheless, Copland arrived and Levant took him over to the Gershwins'. Copland was impressed with the spacious house, the wide, tree-lined block, the swimming pool and tennis court. "It was hard for me to realize," he would later recall, "that you could get all that for writing songs and lyrics!"

Levant took advantage of Copland's presence in Hollywood and asked him to listen to his new string quartet, written under Schoenberg's influence. Copland was pleased with what he heard. Levant recalled:

Copland expressed his pleasure with the progress I had made in the formal aspects of composition and offered his approval of the seriousness of the work, the good contrapuntal structure and solidity of the writing.

However, he did offer the composer some criticism; he said that Levant's harmonic style was excessively chromatic. Hearing this, Levant exploded: "But your 'Variations' are completely lacking in harmonic style—and full of dissonant clichés as well!"

The two men argued, and Copland left in a huff. To aggravate matters, Levant ran off to Schoenberg and fabricated a case in which Copland had demolished Schoenberg, with Levant's work as a pretext. He justified his attack by reasoning that any criticism of his work was an implicit criticism of Schoenberg's methods.

When Schoenberg a short time later made an appearance at a meeting of the League of Composers, he coolly rebuffed Copland. Baffled, Copland couldn't understand what he had done to elicit such behavior. Feeling guilty, perhaps, Levant took Copland out to the most expensive restaurant in Los Angeles and confessed what he had done. Copland was furious.

It is a testament to Copland's level-headedness and his respect for Levant's talents that he soon forgave Levant and invited him to participate in the all-Copland program planned for the Antheil Gallery on Sunset Boulevard. Copland asked Levant to join him in playing the two-piano arrangement of his Piano Concerto. He later wrote that Levant played brilliantly. Levant felt guilty about his treatment of the composer, especially when Copland arranged for the very string quartet he'd heard—and liked—to be performed on a League of Composers radio broadcast two years later, in 1939.

The Works Progress Administration—known by its initials, WPA— was established by an act of Congress on April 5, 1936. It funded a range of activities, from repairing and building bridges to sponsoring musical, theatrical, and literary projects, including the writing of guidebooks and the creation of murals that can still be seen in various public buildings across the country. Among the many programs it sponsored was Schoenberg's student concert given on April 14, 1937, at the Trinity Auditorium on Grand Avenue and Ninth Street in Los Angeles.

The program showcased an early Schoenberg piece, his symphonic poem *Pelleas und Melisande*. Adolph Weiss, Gerald Strang, and Anton Webern were all represented, with Levant's *Nocturne* appearing second on the program. Schoenberg had encouraged Levant to conduct his own piece.

The evening loomed as a great and terrible night for Levant. Many of his friends were in the audience: Harpo Marx, George Gershwin with his date, the British actress Benita Hume, the formidable Otto Klemperer, and June Gale, who arrived with her sister Jean at Oscar's invitation.

June had not known Oscar for very long when she and her sister found their seats in the Trinity Auditorium and waited for Oscar to approach the podium. He took the stage in his usual nervous, apprehensive state. He stood in front of the orchestra and tapped the music stand, signaling the start of the piece. At the first light tap the music stand collapsed. For a moment it looked as though a Marx Brothers routine was about to unfold, but the mishap succeeded in breaking Oscar's stage fright. "It was pure gold," June remembers, for such slight accidents have the happy result of relieving the unbearable tension of stage nerves.

Nocturne had been completed only two months before its premiere. Scored for full orchestra, the music proceeded flawlessly under Levant's baton. After the performance, Otto Klemperer came backstage and offered Levant his congratulations. It seemed Levant had finally overcome the bad impression he had made at Salka Viertel's. Levant shook his hand, formally closing the book on his earlier hijinks. In the midst of congratulating Levant, Klemperer noticed June Gale standing quietly beside her sister.

Suddenly a huge shadow fell over the Gale sisters—it was Klemperer, who found himself drawn to June like a giant magnet. Levant sidled over and insinuated himself between June and the tall conductor, all his old insecurities kicking into gear.

Klemperer reacted to Oscar's show of possessiveness by telling him, "You don't know how to bow—you must learn how to bow."

Oscar shot back, "You bow beautifully. I'd rather watch you bow than hear you conduct."

Afterward, Oscar took June to the Brown Derby, where George Gershwin and Benita Hume were waiting for them. June recalled:

I remember how George looked and how he laughed at everything Oscar said, because Oscar was a little bit embarrassed about his piece, and he was defending it in a way. And was squirming a little bit. . . . And George was laughing. . . . Everything went so well.

That April evening at the Brown Derby would be one of Gershwin's last carefree nights out with Levant. Several days later he experienced another episode of dizziness, and the odor of burning rubber filled his nostrils. Levant was baffled by Gershwin's physical decline, as were his family and friends. Visitors to the Gershwin home found the composer a changed man. His friends and family blamed his frequent, debilitating headaches on the anxieties of working in Hollywood. Lee Gershwin even told their friends not to indulge George's "artistic temper tantrums."

In the two months following the WPA concert, George became increasingly fatigued and began to lose his temper, becoming hypercritical of everything around him. For the first time in his life he developed a strange compulsion. Seated in the back of his chauffeured car, Gershwin would call out the name of each street he passed. If he skipped one, he made his driver go back and start over again.

Lee and Ira finally brought a doctor and a neurologist to the house and George underwent a complete physical. He was given a clean bill of health, and they all retired to the garden to have lunch. Levant remembered Gershwin coming downstairs after undergoing the examination:

> When George came down and shuffled over in his beach robe and sandals I called to him facetiously, "What did the doctors say?" He laughed, as in relief, and said, "Well, before they told me anything they wanted to rule out the possibility of a brain tumor."

The frightening word in that description is "shuffled." The sight of George Gershwin—who "had lived all his life in youth," in Sam Behrman's phrase—shuffling over in his beach togs must have been chilling. On one occasion, Oscar was sent to the drugstore to have a prescription filled for Gershwin. Oscar noticed that the prescription was for "one-fourth or one-half a grain of phenobarbital, an inadequate anodyne for anyone in exquisite pain." Like the young boy who was sent to Pfaff's Drug Store to fill Max's prescription for morphine, Oscar was sent on a drug mission to help ease George's suffering.

Whereas Ira and Oscar seemed at a loss as to how to react to George's troubled moods and increasing lack of motor control, Lee Gershwin's reactions devolved from concern to annoyance, from embarrassment to revulsion. One day June accompanied Levant on a brief visit to the Gershwins' North Roxbury Drive house. Lee took them aside and confided, "It's disgusting. He's drooling out of the side of his mouth."

There are different schools of thought about Lee Gershwin's behavior. There was speculation in the Gershwin circle that Lee had originally been in love with George and had only married Ira because she couldn't have George. Perhaps she was taking out her resentment when George was most vulnerable. It's also possible that Lee envied the close ties between the two brothers, whose intimacy born from a life of collaboration naturally tended to exclude her. Their collaboration was like a marriage that diminished all other relationships the two men had.

By mid-June, when Oscar visited George he would make the painful pilgrimage up to his bedroom only to find him crouched between the two beds holding his head, wracked with pain.

"People thought that he was suffering from a nervous breakdown," Oscar later wrote, "which was nonsense. They even said he had an inferiority complex about Hollywood. George Gershwin knew his just worth at all times." This theory drove Oscar crazy. Gershwin was producing terrific music for Sam Goldwyn, and though he would complete only five songs, two of them—"Love Walked In" and his last song, "Love Is Here to Stay"—are among his finest compositions. Levant felt that "George had never written anything better than the songs in his recent films."

Levant, however, on first hearing "Love Is Here to Stay," thought its melodic line too complex, and he complained of

> its lack of breathing space in the second eight bars, its too-long contours . . . George spent two days trying to rephrase the melody and simplify the line, eventually returning to the original form of it. Ira was quite annoyed with me, and rightly.

But Ira would later call on Oscar Levant to help him reconstruct some of the melodic verses of "Love Is Here to Stay," when Vernon Duke was brought in to complete the score for the *Follies*. Though Duke would take credit for composing the verses for this and two other Gershwin songs, the Gershwin biographer Edward Jablonski has noted:

. . . there is reason to doubt him—he must share credit with Oscar Levant and Ira Gershwin. Both heard George play possible verses for these songs, and though they had not written them down they remembered how Gershwin had played them. Levant recalled the distinctive Gershwin harmonies of "Love Is Here to Stay."

Gershwin's physicians asked a psychiatrist, Dr. Ernest Simmel, to search for an emotional cause of the headaches. "In those days," Sam Behrman wrote, "everybody was going to psychoanalysts." The headaches increased in frequency, and despite the normalcy of all of Gershwin's vital signs, Dr. Simmel became convinced that George's problem was organic, not emotional.

Behrman was in Los Angeles that July of 1937. He, too, noticed the alarming changes in George Gershwin. Before leaving for New York, where he would begin rehearsal of a new play, Behrman went over to say good-bye to his friend. "All the time," wrote Behrman, "I wanted to break through and ask him if there was anything on his mind—he did not seem as carefree as usual." The two men agreed to meet on July 5 at the Biltmore Theatre, where Behrman's new play, *Amphitryon 38,* was to open.

Not long after, George was moved out of the Gershwin house on North Roxbury Drive into Yip Harburg's house nearby. Jablonski wrote that Dr. Simmel had ordered the move, to secure more peace and quiet for his suffering patient and to keep George out of the way of "Hollywood's parlor psychiatrists." Others have suggested that it was Lee's idea; George's falling on the stairs, spilling food, and dribbling water out of the corner of his mouth were disgusting to her.

Most of George's friends were denied admittance to this last, depressing house. Oscar Levant arrived one afternoon with June. Only George and his male nurse were at home. "Oscar and I were seated in the living room," June recalled, "and George came walking down the stairs. He walked into the room and said hello to us. He was in a robe and pajamas." Oscar went over to the piano and began to play passages from *Porgy and Bess*—they each had different favorite songs from the opera. Oscar always liked to sing the part of Crown in his deep, chesty baritone. Gershwin's favorite at the time was Porgy's first entrance.

Oscar was playing the part where Crown sings, and George Gershwin had his arm around me. . . . George was looking at my face and peering into my eyes and hugging and patting me. It made me very uneasy. . . . Oscar would have been furious. . . . I don't even know if he noticed it, he was so busy singing away.

But Levant must have noticed, because years later he would confide:

> George kept moving toward her. It was very strange. I don't know if it
> was part of the syndrome of sickness or not. Anyway, to use an old
> fashioned phrase, he was horny, as sick as he was. That didn't bother
> me. I loved George.

Levant was present at Sam Behrman's final visit with George
Gershwin. Behrman recorded in his diary that George came downstairs with his male nurse. "I stared at him," he wrote. "It was not the
George we all knew. The light had gone from his eye. He seemed
old."

> He came to a sofa near where I was sitting and lay down on it. He tried
> to adjust his head against the pillows. The nurse hovered over him. I
> asked him if he felt pain. "Behind my eyes," he said, and repeated it:
> "Behind my eyes." I knelt beside him on the sofa and put my hand
> under his head. I asked him if he felt like playing the piano. He shook
> his head. It was the first refusal I'd ever heard from him.

"I had to live for this," Gershwin complained to Behrman, "that
Sam Goldwyn should say to me: 'Why don't you write hits like Irving
Berlin?' "

Behrman asked Lee, "How long has he been like this?"

"For several weeks. He seems worse tonight. Maybe it's seeing
you—reminds him of the past."

The friends left the house and got into Behrman's car, driving off in
silence. Finally, Oscar asked, "You think George is very sick, don't
you?"

"Yes. I think he's very sick."

Behrman had to return to New York, but he asked Levant to call
him daily to report on George's condition. On his second call, Levant
informed Behrman that George had fallen in the bathroom and had
been taken to the Cedars of Lebanon Hospital and that he was in a
coma.

It was after midnight when the five-hour surgical procedure began.
Neurosurgeon Dr. Carl Rand performed the operation, with an eminent surgeon, Dr. Howard C. Nafziger, as consultant.

Gershwin's family and friends had dinner and then went to the
hospital, where they gathered anxiously on the fourth floor. When
word first came back that the doctors had discovered an operable cyst,
the gathering was tremendously relieved. However, once the cyst was

taken out, Dr. Rand found a tumor embedded deeply in Gershwin's brain—too deep to remove. It was a glioblastoma, an extremely malignant type of tumor. If Gershwin survived the surgery, he would be blind and his entire left side would be paralyzed. He would never play the piano again.

Around six-thirty on Sunday morning, July 11, 1937, a distraught and weary group returned to North Roxbury Drive. Around seven that morning Gershwin was wheeled from the operating theatre to his hospital room. Levant and Moss Hart left the hospital and walked through the dawn light to the back of Harpo Marx's house, where they talked through the early hours. Levant then returned to his suite at the Beverly Wilshire.

A few minutes after nine A.M., Gershwin's temperature rocketed to 106.5 degrees. Sometime just before eleven A.M., the phone rang in Oscar's hotel room. It was Moss Hart.

"George is dead."

Levant called June and passed on the terrible news, desperate to share his stunned grief with the young woman he had become so attached to in such a short period of time.

George Gershwin was just thirty-eight years old when he died. "The time of his illness and death were bewildering to me," Levant would write. "I had never once entertained the dismal thought that he was not insuperable. I didn't know what to think."

Levant had been plunged into loneliness and isolation at his father's early death; how could he cope with the shocking death of George Gershwin?

From now on, he would devote himself to Gershwin's music, even to the detriment of his own gifts as a composer and pianist. As Gershwin dominated Oscar in life, he would dominate him in death.

There had been a falling off of interest in Gershwin's serious music, particularly after the poor critical reception of *Porgy and Bess*. Levant's brilliant renditions of *Rhapsody in Blue* and the Concerto in F would help give those works a posthumous life. Levant's quip that Gershwin's music would be around in a hundred years if George were around to play it, was being fulfilled. But now it was Levant's being around that would make all the difference.

PART IV

Love and Fame

22

"Dear Junie"

"God knows, Christ knows, and even the mob knows
I love you."

NOW THE REMEMBERING BEGAN. OF ALL THE TRIBUTES EULOGIZING George Gershwin, none would sum up the richness of Gershwin's achievements better than the concert being planned for September 8, 1937, at the Hollywood Bowl.

The first and last time Levant had played the Concerto in F in public was at George's request, at the Lewisohn Stadium all-Gershwin concert a few years earlier. He had played so well that when he had finished, George and Ira's mother, Rose Gershwin, had gone up to Oscar, looked him straight in the eye, and said, "Promise me you won't get any better." Now he was asked to play the Concerto in F at Gershwin's memorial.

The concert was a herculean undertaking. The program involved "seven conductors, a half dozen singers, two piano soloists, and full symphony orchestra," and it was to be broadcast live throughout the world, courtesy of CBS's founder, William S. Paley.

Levant was tortured by the thought of the upcoming concert. Now that June Gale had landed a part in the road company of *Stage Door* and had left for New York to begin rehearsals, Levant had to face his insecurities alone. It was as if great hopes were being realized by terrible means—the death of Gershwin giving him this opportunity to be heard worldwide. His fear of failure and his dread of the stage fright that had poisoned his last concert tormented him. For the first time, Levant took extra doses of Alenol not to sleep but to calm him down and "ease his emotional tension."

Twenty-two thousand souls crowded into the Hollywood Bowl on the night of the concert. Traffic was backed up on Highland Avenue, and many of the performers needed police escorts to make their way to the concert stage. Concertgoers were still arriving and finding their seats when Otto Klemperer began the program with Gershwin's Second Prelude for Piano, which he had arranged as a funeral march. Halfway through the program, conductor Charles Previn took his place at the podium and Levant crossed the stage to the piano.

Levant played the Concerto in F with sensitivity and brilliance—he emerged as one of the trimphs of the evening. "Our" concerto, Oscar had called it when he used to take the second piano at George's side. His performance over, Levant received a deafening ovation.

"Levant might profitably give an all-Gershwin piano program indoors some time. He is the best Gershwin exponent heard out here so far," wrote music critic Isabel Morse Jones in the *Los Angeles Times*.

Levant's triumph, however, did not cure his stage fright. When the performance was over and he left the stage, he thought, "I don't want this. This isn't for me. To go through that! My God!" For those of Oscar's friends who had forgotten what a fine pianist he was, the Hollywood Bowl concert put an end to their doubts. The audience's response that evening suggests that passage in *Remembrance of Things Past* in which Proust describes the piano playing of Vinteuil:

> . . . one is no longer aware that the performer is a pianist at all . . . his playing has become so transparent, so imbued with what he is interpreting, that one no longer sees the performer himself—he is simply a window opening upon a great work of art.

One writer compared Levant to a latter-day Philoctoctes, the wounded Greek warrior and friend of Hercules upon whom the honor fell of lighting Hercules' funeral pyre, "when the flames rushed up and [Hercules] was seen no more on earth."

The weeks following Gershwin's memorial concert found Oscar adrift. He remained devoted to Lee and Ira. Ira would retreat into mourning, virtually transforming their North Roxbury Drive house into a George Gershwin shrine, and he would unstintingly dedicate himself to preserving the music of his brother (though he would write lyrics with other composers). At the time of George's death, it was not clear to anyone what the fate of his orchestral music would be.

Despite his defensive cynicism about composing for the movies, Levant allowed himself to be seduced back by David O. Selznick, who hired him to score two films. He also went back to work on his Piano Concerto, determined to complete the orchestration and prepare it for publication. But it was June Gale who dominated his thoughts. It was as if Levant were determined to fill the void left by Gershwin's death with a new devotion. His infatuation with the fledgling actress was deepening into something more.

When June had received the telegram notifying her that she had been cast in the part of Jean Maitland in *Stage Door*, she was delighted. This would be her first acting role onstage, and to be cast in a Kaufman-Ferber play was indeed an auspicious debut. But it meant that she would be involved first with rehearsals in New York and then with a six-month tour—in other words, a long absence from Oscar Levant. It was hard for Oscar to share June's enthusiasm; everywhere he looked, his losses seemed to be piling up.

In 1936 Selznick had announced that he was leaving Metro-Goldwyn-Mayer to set up an independent production company that would bear his name: Selznick International Pictures. Levant knew Selznick from *The Dance of Life* days; Selznick, then a fledgling producer for Paramount, had been heavily involved in the transformation of *Burlesque* into *The Dance of Life*. A Paramount production chief described Selznick as "the most arrogant young man I've ever known" but hired him as his assistant nonetheless. In a pattern that established itself with *The Dance of Life* and continued through the apotheosis of the producer's career, *Gone With the Wind*, Selznick involved himself with every aspect of production.

Selznick developed a congenial feeling for Levant. "He had a weakness for me," Levant later wrote, "perhaps because I came from Pittsburgh" (Selznick and his two brothers had been born in Pittsburgh). When Selznick married Louis B. Mayer's youngest daughter, Irene, much against her father's wishes, Oscar could claim a distant relationship to the Selznicks (Louis B. Mayer's first wife, Margaret, had been a Radin cousin). Not that this connection impressed Oscar. If anything, he didn't want it to be known among his fellow musicians and friends. Irene Mayer Selznick, in her memoir *A Private View*, recalls a meeting with Oscar in the late 1920s at their beachfront home:

The beach was a magnet for all sorts of people. . . . only occasionally would Mother yield to temptation and sneak a relative in. One Sunday there was a reverse twist: a fellow absolutely loathed the idea. Inasmuch as he was quite funny, it will come as no surprise if I say it was Oscar Levant, my mother's cousin. He kept shaking his head and finally said, "If this ever gets out, I'm ruined!"

Levant found the Columbia University–educated Selznick a hopeless middlebrow where music was concerned. "If I appeared at the studio with anything even faintly modern, Selznick's invariable comment was, 'It sounds Chinese,' " Levant complained. He also objected if Levant wrote something for the orchestra without a hummable melody.

"You're not writing for the Bowl," he'd say. "You're writing for fifty million people."

Despite their disagreements, Levant had an amiable relationship with the producer. The first film Selznick hired Levant to score was *Nothing Sacred,* the screwball comedy starring Carole Lombard and Fredric March.

Selznick had hired Ben Hecht to write a comic vehicle for Carole Lombard, but Selznick hadn't liked his ending, so the two had quarreled and Hecht had walked off the picture. Selznick then hired Ring Lardner, Jr., and Budd Schulberg (son of Paramount's chief mogul) to devise an acceptable climax. Selznick didn't particularly like their ending either, but as shooting was well under way, he went along with it, bringing in Dorothy Parker as a last resort to polish up the dialogue. Two of Oscar's acquaintances turned up in the picture—his old pal Frank Fay and ex-boxer "Slapsie" Maxie Rosenbloom.

Nothing Sacred began shooting in June 1937. In a final act of friendship, Levant composed a score in tribute to his late friend. Levant's score is lively and lush, full of Gershwinesque melodies. Like *Rhapsody in Blue,* his score is a paean to city life. The opening phrases rise like a New York City skyscraper in the establishing shot. Levant's score deftly matches both the effervescence and the black humor of the film, a tale about Hazel Flagg, a small-town girl who seems to be dying from radiation poisoning and is exploited for her human interest value by a large New York newspaper. Levant's music is at turns aspiring and cynical, celebratory and wistful.

After completing the score for *Nothing Sacred,* Levant continued to compose, helped out by Selznick's largesse. The producer was impressed with Levant's credentials as a serious composer, and he put him on a small stipend which allowed Levant to work on his compositions, with the stipulation that Selznick could use his occasional music for other films, should he so desire. By this arrangement, Levant would later comment, Selznick became "a patron of the arts," a moniker that would certainly have appealed to him. The stipend, however, did little to defray the enormous phone bills he was racking up as he pursued June across the country. Like a military campaigner, he lay siege to every city she appeared in as Jean Maitland in *Stage Door.* "He had enormous phone bills," June recalled—"hundreds and hundreds."

> He couldn't control himself. He had to call me all the time and talk. . . . And then he'd write me a letter and then he'd say, "Send me a telegram as soon as you get this." . . . I would get seventy-five telegrams, and he expected me to do the same thing, which I did. I was caught up in the whole frantic thing.

In those phone calls and letters—many of them written on Beverly Wilshire Hotel stationery in a schoolboy's big, sloppy hand—Levant poured out his soul to June Gale. His daily routines are only glancingly mentioned; the real content of his letters is his love for June and his sadness at her absence.

With June away, Oscar would visit her mother, Sayde Gilmartin, and her sister Jean. It was the smart thing for a suitor to do, knowing how devoted June was to her mother, but it also gratified Oscar's need to be part of a family. In one letter he wrote:

> Every so often I feel a certain emptiness accompanied by a twinge of pain and I feel helpless. This, my ambitious and predatory rat, is due to you. . . .
>
> Thursday night I was driving Susan Marx [Harpo's wife] home and the moon was shining with what I thought was a sneer on its face. As I missed you by my side, I felt there was no necessity for this gloat on the moon's part. I looked up and shouted "Screw, moon".
>> Answer me with the speed of my heart beat,
>> Good 'Avenin' my darling. Love,
>> Osc.

Oscar's letters, besides being obsessional, reveal some resentment about the power June had over him. Though he praises her and longs for her, he also delights in calling her insulting names—"my ambitious and predatory rat," "you foul wretch," "my smug darling." The letters also reveal Levant's need for constant company—he mentions the Berlins, the Marxes, the Gershwins. He also confides a little of his frustration about composing for Selznick and later readying his String Quartet for a scheduled performance in Denver by the Kolisch Quartet, and preparing *Nocturne* for publication.

As much as he resented June leaving him, he encouraged her acting career, shoring up her confidence and seeing in her a resemblance to comedienne Carole Lombard, the irrepressible star of *Nothing Sacred,* whom June Gale did indeed physically resemble. Her way of speaking had something of Lombard's breathless, rapid-fire delivery.

Levant continued to suffer through June's absence, plunging into a fitful depression interrupted only slightly by the sometimes frantic nature of his work for Selznick.

> Dear June—
> . . . I am, as you probably guessed by my last letter, in a funk. My work is of such an uncertain nature that I'm a little jittery. By that I mean I will not be able to get a finished negative until the last moment and then hurry—faster, faster, etc. makes me nervous.
>
> I've had to get up early these last few days and consequently with the added coffee, cigarettes and no sleep I really feel like hell. As this job will probably not take over a few weeks I may make tentative plans to go away.
>
> I took Leonore Gershwin to a picture tonight and she thought I looked like hell. She also said that I've been here much too long, etc.—I don't know what to do at the moment.
>
> > Love
> > Oscar

Levant's most frequently used slang expression—reserved mostly for describing himself—is "full of crap." His letters reveal a tendency toward the scatalogical, tucked in among his tender endearments. His letters also reveal his self-contempt, particularly in contrast to the pedestal he builds for June.

As Oscar continued to cling to his long-distance relationship, he found himself confiding in June on levels deeper than he had ever been able to plumb with his male cronies.

Once the score for *Nothing Sacred* was completed, Levant decided to return to New York to be closer to June during her three-week stint in Boston. On November 5, 1937, he headed east and moved back into the Park Central Hotel.

Finally, Oscar and June met in New York and became lovers. They would meet again the following week in Washington, D.C. But June was still not entirely won over: "I had a wonderful time with him, and

I just loved him, but I didn't know what I wanted." Oscar attended the evening's performance of *Stage Door,* but his presence so unnerved June that she became self-conscious and gave her worst performance.

Levant was not the only suitor pursuing the ingenues of *Stage Door.* In real life, as on the stage for two hours each night, the actresses in the production were being courted, wooed, and romanced by a passel of eager admirers. Joan Bennett's understudy, Marian Edwards, was being pursued by the young playwright and novelist Irwin Shaw. Producer Walter Wanger was courting Joan Bennett. Actor Richard Conte was wooing Ruth Story, while Wilma Francis was sleeping with George S. Kaufman.

June, pursued by this banshee from Pittsburgh, was not about to marry him, but she was unable to send him packing: "There was something inside me, I guess, that said, 'He'll be a problem, but it might be worth it.'"

In October 1937, the Kolisch Quartet participated in a festival held in honor of Arnold Schoenberg at the Denver Art Museum. Two of the concerts were given over entirely to Schoenberg's music, while the third featured work by four pupils: Alban Berg, Anton von Webern, Gerald Strang, and Oscar Levant. It was on this occasion that Levant's String Quartet was to be performed.

Rudolf Kolisch's interest in Oscar Levant's music came about from his association with Arnold Schoenberg, who happened to be his brother-in-law. (In 1924 Schoenberg married Gertrud Kolisch after the death of his first wife, Mathilde, in the previous year.) Kolisch, a violinist, became one of Schoenberg's most devoted pupils and was considered a brilliant interpreter of his works. In 1922 Rudi Kolisch formed the Kolisch Quartet, which eventually earned an international reputation for specializing in modern works.

Schoenberg would attend the festival, not only to hear and approve the concerts but to deliver a lecture with the provocative title "How One Becomes Lonely," a topic that would certainly have interested Oscar if he had bothered to attend.

Levant never gives any reason for his failure to attend the three-day festival in honor of his esteemed teacher. It doesn't seem likely that his duties as a film composer would have prevented a short hiatus to hear his own work performed. Levant hated to fly and relied on the trains, so that would have lengthened the journey. But it does seem puzzling that he would be so cavalier about the performance of his String

Quartet, written under Schoenberg's tutelage and now presented on the same program as the music of Berg and Webern, two composers he greatly admired.

Though he mentioned the performance in a couple of his letters and he attended the rehearsals in Los Angeles, by late 1937 Levant seems to have drifted away from his intense mentor-apprentice relationship with Schoenberg. Not only did he fail to attend the concert, he waited for Rudi Kolisch to provide him with a review of the program, which was entirely favorable to Levant's composition:

> The short Andantino of Oscar Levant was in many ways the surprise of the festival. It shows great talent, a feeling for string writing, strong sense of form, and the composer apparently had something to say before starting to say it. This thoroughly refreshing work shows Schoenberg influence only in warmth of feeling, soundness of form . . . and in some of the thematic material.
>
> Both Schoenberg and the quartet shared the tumultuous ovation of the audience.

In any other composer, such inattention to a major performance of his work would be inexplicable; in Oscar's case, it was probably his old sense of inadequacy that kept him from being in attendance. He would complain sporadically when he felt his identity as a composer was being overlooked, but he publicly slighted his own compositions and did not exhibit that keen, overriding interest in promoting his serious work that, for example, Copland, Gershwin, and Schoenberg displayed in abundance.

Levant's String Quartet found another champion in his old friend Robert Russell Bennett, who would, three years later, in December 1940, present the Andantino on one of his "Robert Russell Bennett's Notebook" radio programs on WOR. Bennett's "Notebook" showcased work by new American composers and usually included an interview. In a lively and genial interview with Levant, it is clear that Bennett has faith in Levant's gifts and high seriousness as an artist, despite Levant's penchant for trivializing his own efforts. Bennett described the String Quartet as "one of the most profound works he has so far produced."

Through the course of the interview, the two men reminisced about the Yaddo festival and their disastrous performance of March for Two Pianos and Orchestra at the Hollywood Bowl. Levant then managed to jokingly disparage the very String Quartet that Bennett had taken pains to hold up as an exemplar of Levant's seriousness:

"I wonder if you remember the impression the work made on its first performance?"

"Violently. It not only brought me obscurity but many enemies."

Once Levant resettled in New York City, his pursuit of June again took center stage. But he had other motives for abandoning Los Angeles for New York besides wanting to be closer to June during her *Stage Door* tour. First, there was the terrible emptiness left by Gershwin's death. Levant also needed money—the Selznick stipend was not enough. Maybe things would pick up in New York.

In November 1937, he traveled to Pittsburgh to meet June, whose tour had brought her there. Pittsburgh became their third trysting place. Levant introduced June to his brothers Bennie and Honey—the doctor and the dentist—and to his mother, whom June remembered as "a sweet lady in precarious health." June liked Annie, and it seemed to be mutual, much to Oscar's relief. Annie must have realized the intensity of Oscar's feelings for the young woman and felt that something might come of this relationship. But at one point during their visit, Annie took June aside and warned her about Oscar's dark moods.

Levant tried to pick up the threads of his old New York life, hanging out at Harms and Lindy's when he wasn't composing music or writing to June Gale. He would work fitfully with lyricist Stanley Adams through the rest of 1937. His entreaties to June to take him seriously and consider what he called "the big question" (his offer of marriage) sometimes became violent. They argued passionately—June on behalf of maintaining her independence, Levant in an effort to persuade her to marry him.

Levant's often-frantic letters alternated with support given to June's fledgling career. Throughout his letter-writing campaign to woo June, he kept up a hectic pace of writing songs, readying manuscripts, and dining out with old friends. Though he called himself "a café society bum" Levant was, as usual, belying the amount of work he had undertaken to keep his songwriting and composing careers on track. After all, June had early on suggested that Levant wasn't rich or famous enough for her to take him seriously as a suitor. June wasn't necessarily being mercenary; she was still supporting her mother and had real financial concerns. Nonetheless, Levant bristled at her demands. June also suggested that Oscar buy himself a nail brush in an effort to spruce up his usually unkempt appearance. Eager to oblige her on this small point, he complied.

On December 27, 1937, Irving Berlin's wife, Ellin, threw a party for Oscar on his thirty-first birthday. He described it to June in one of his love letters:

> Ellin Berlin threw a hell of a party for me. After theatre a hell of a lot of people dropped in that I assure you are not terribly close friends of mine. However, Ellin poured it on plenty—birthday cake, champagne, dinner, supper (the last for about 30 guests). She gave me one of those men's travelling kits (you know, like Dorothy Paley gave me, only larger). Moss Hart gave me a gold tie clasp from Cartiers.
>
> I liked by far the best your telegram—no crap, I did. Irving Berlin and Harpo both phoned me from the coast.
>
> From now on I got to buckle down and really go to work. I just finished 2 hours work after I got home from Ellin's. That's enough holiday for me. . . .
>
> I really love you in the nicest and the worst way.
>
> All my love,
> Oscar

If Oscar needed any more proof that he was no longer the boy who had felt orphaned in his first years in New York, certainly Ellin Berlin's lavish party provided that for him. But without June it was not enough.

Levant's letters to June provided a kind of therapy for him; here he could drop his guard and not be embarrassed to reveal his longing and occasional despair. For the first time since his disastrous marriage, Levant revealed himself as fully as he was able:

> Allow me to clarify what may appear as hysteria to you. During my entire life, I have been rootless both as to emotion and geography. Having left a rather dispersed and, at about that time, depleted remains of a home. I was fourteen [*sic*] at the time, completely unequipped not only financially but educationally, etc. Being of an hyper-sensitive nature as well as overladen with love, I had no one to lavish these on. I had no friends. Not one. I was in New York at this infantile age for some years before I could emerge even with an acquaintance.
>
> My talents lay in music. This is a rather abstruse art. Understand that in my pursuit of this muse (my racket) I went through uncertainties, torturous doubts. Understand that I pursued this with more than a little idealism. In the gradual diffusion of idealism into reality (economic reality too) I underwent something other people go through just as much. I know, however, when you say I have no guts, I resent it. The temper and battle of one's vocation conditions one's sensitivity. . . .
>
> During all this I was looking for an anchor; for stability; for, as I said before, roots.

I want to go on but the hell with it. You may think I'm full of crap and I don't want to expose myself as I am battle-scarred enough as it is. . . .

Don't forget that when I met you I was practically loveless, emotionless, cynical, full of skepticism. You were that "home" I was unconsciously looking for all my life. So give me a chance to emerge from a whole, previous, stinking, nasty lifetime of instrinsic bitterness. . . .

Please forgive me my excesses and extravagances for they are the penalty of my deep love for you. . . .

All my love,
Oscar

Levant at last shows some insight as to where his loneliness and his sudden changes of mood came from. Perhaps it was June Gale's unavailability that elicited Levant's confessions. Though the strength of her personality would reveal itself over the years, in the first stages of their courtship June was a beautiful cipher, an unknown quantity, a void into which Levant could rush with all the ailments of his soul.

The last stop on the *Stage Door* tour was Chicago, and Levant made plans to meet June there and celebrate the close of the show. Though June agreed to see him, she had begun to put limits on his phone calls, feeling, as ever, fascinated but uneasy with the intense outpouring of emotion coming from her lover. She made him promise not to phone her in St. Louis, a promise Oscar was unable to keep.

When June Gale's six months with *Stage Door* came to a close, the young actress returned to Los Angeles to be with her mother and to pick up where she had left off in her pursuit of her film career. She was soon offered a new contract at 20th Century–Fox, working in Sol Wurtzel's unit. June would appear in three films in the next three months, cast in what she dubbed "buddy blond pictures," beginning with *Pardon Our Nerve* with Lynn Bari, a light comedy about two women who manage a boxer.

Levant continued to write to June, his letters and telegrams now crossing hers from east to west. However, a year would elapse before the two would meet again.

In February 1938, Levant wrote to June that he had completed "some of the toughest orchestration in my whole suite—which is not only fiercely difficult but probably unpleasantly incomprehensible as well. Did it with a certain Olympian (God-like to you, my one and only Goddess) ease and superiority." On April 1, he wired June: "MONDAY AFTERNOON 345 NEW YORK TIME WABC BROADCASTING MY LIFE AND MY POPULAR SONGS . . ."

But by the end of April there would be a decided change in their relationship, instigated by June, who felt that Oscar had become enormously dependent upon her: "the responsibility was too heavy, my pedestal was too high." By now, many of their meetings and telephone conversations were now being ruined by unpleasant scenes. For every "unprecedented, magical" call, there were quarrels, fierce words, and tears. Oscar lashed out whenever he felt he was being ignored, and now June was withdrawing from him. Even June's abilities as an actress would be fair game for Levant when he felt abandoned. Levant proposed a trip to California to see June one more time, but she rebuffed him. His letters soon began to reflect the role of rejected suitor. A rueful letter written at the end of April confirms their "open break":

> Dear June,
> . . . First I want you to know that in no way have you committed any wrong toward me. There is no reason for you to feel any contrition. Your conservative reaction to my proposed trip to see you is after all no crime. . . .
> In today's conversation I did no probing. I was conciliatory, sweet, affectionate and loving. . . . I was reluctant for us to recede into a memory. However your reaction to every proposal, every attempt for us to get together, has been consistent and identical. I feel sure that you think you can do better than what I am and have.
> I do not condemn you for this. It is your prerogative. I feel sure that I'm not the man you are looking for. It is absurd for me not to accept this reality. I now accept it.
> Forgive any behavior that smacked odious on my part. It was only a desperate attempt to have us survive. That I was in love with you, you must have realized. That my intentions were of the best and consummate, please believe me they were. That you are not willing to accept me . . . I am now entirely convinced. . . .
> That this, our relationship, which in my opinion attained those rare heights, is at an end causes in me deep regret.
> Well, you can't say I didn't try my damndest.
>
> Oscar (Levant)

With the formality of grief, Levant forgoes his usual signature, "Osc," and offers up his last name, in parenthesis, as if to remind June of the name of her failed suitor.

Levant struggled in solitude over the weeks and months to complete the orchestration of a Suite for Orchestra, which he had begun shortly after Gershwin's death. His old life called to him, but he preferred to stay in and work on his compositions. He did, however, continue to drop in on Max Dreyfus's publishing house, Chappell & Co.

On one of his sorties into Chappell's, Levant met the Russian composer Sergei Prokofiev. Levant admired Prokofiev's film scores for *The Czar Sleeps* and *Alexander Nevsky,* which he thought "good enough to be separated from its scenario and converted into a concert suite." Several years earlier he had heard Prokofiev perform his Third Piano Concerto at Carnegie Hall.

Prokofiev had come up to Chappell's to secure a copy of the *Porgy and Bess* score, which he planned to take back with him to the Soviet Union. Levant was thrilled to meet the pianist and composer whose "savage playing" had made a deep impression on him, and he asked Prokofiev to play the second movement of his Third Piano Concerto.

The Russian composer was reluctant at first, but Levant urged him to play. With a deep sigh Prokofiev sat down at the piano and began the piece. When the composer could not remember it sufficiently to continue, Levant practically pushed him off the piano bench and played it himself.

23

The Unknown
Celebrity

"I was only famous among the high and mighty."

TWO MEN WHO BEFRIENDED LEVANT IN THE 1930S WERE ASSOCIATED with the innovative, socially conscious Group Theatre in New York—playwright Clifford Odets and actor John Garfield. Levant and Odets would have a long but volatile friendship. Odets would find much in Levant's personality that corresponded to the noncon-forming, bitter characters he created in a series of triumphant plays produced by the Group Theatre.

Like Levant, Odets shuttled back and forth between New York and Hollywood in the thirties and forties. The thirties was really Odets's decade. *Waiting for Lefty, Awake and Sing!, Till the Day I Die, Paradise Lost, Golden Boy,* and *Rocket to the Moon*—six plays in four years—established his reputation as a controversial and brilliantly gifted playwright. His successes earned him a *Time* magazine cover, and his celebration of working-class heroes debunking establishment mores earned him the role of "conscience of a generation." But by 1940, when he was thirty-three, Odets's greatest successes were be-hind him.

The Group Theatre was the first to present Odets to New York theatregoers. Though the part of Jerry Evans in *Burlesque* would be

Oscar's only stage role, Oscar had always felt at home in the theatre and by 1939 had met many of the leading theatrical producers, directors, and actors of his day. His friendships with Behrman, Moss Hart, and George S. Kaufman gave him an entree to that world. Though Oscar would never be officially involved with the Group Theatre, Odets was attracted to the very qualities in Oscar that his own work embodied: the outsider cynical about success, the rough-hewn city boy dripping with talent and heart who snarls his way through life, throwing away his opportunities. It was a new, modern personality that found its way onto stage and screen in the late thirties: the persona now defined as the antihero.

Odets would describe Levant in his journals as "an unhappy, rambunctious boy, a startled clumsy Jewish faun from Pittsburgh." He would later become somewhat bitter about Levant, especially after Odets's marriage to the beautiful actress Luise Rainer failed and he increasingly saw his once-brilliant career shrivel on the vine. "Success is the jinni who kills," Odets once wrote—a belief Levant would echo nearly twenty years later in front of a bewildered Los Angeles television audience.

The opinion that Levant was ruining his own talent was shared by other members of the Group. Odets's wife, Luise Rainer, wrote to Odets from Hollywood, "I am tired of hearing about how Oscar Levant is wasting his talents."

Odets and Levant would work together in Hollywood in 1946, in a film called *Humoresque* for which Odets wrote the screenplay, John Garfield played the lead, and Levant appeared in a supporting role. At the end of his once-brilliant career, deeply depressed, Odets wrote a screenplay for Elvis Presley, in which the King commits suicide at the end of the picture. Naturally, it didn't fly (the preview audience was horrified), and Odets was compelled to rewrite the ending. Levant would find it heartbreaking that Odets had to work on such a project in the first place, he who was considered the leading playwright of his generation. "Everything he was against in the beginning of his career," Levant later wrote after Odets had written a number of bad films and had shamed himself by naming names at the House Un-American Activities Committee hearings, "he wound up doing himself."

Julius Garfinkle—aka John Garfield—was another story. Garfield, known as "Julie" to his friends, joined the Group Theatre in 1934 and appeared in Odets's *Awake and Sing!* before emigrating to Hollywood. (He left the Group Theatre in 1937, when the lead role of Joe Bonaparte in *Golden Boy* went to Luther Adler.) He had a successful career in Hollywood throughout the forties, including electrifying leading roles in *The Postman Always Rings Twice* and *Body and Soul.* He was later blacklisted in the early fifties, as was Odets, by the House Un-American Activities Committee.

Seven years Levant's junior, Garfield embodied the role of the embittered, eternal outsider—a persona that could have been scripted by Levant. In fact, his first screen performance, the part of Mickey Borden in the 1938 Warner Bros. film *Four Daughters,* was modeled after Levant, as the gossip columnist Hedda Hopper revealed in an interview with the actor:

> "Well, when I saw you in 'Daughters,' I gasped and said: 'There is Oscar Levant.' "
>
> Garfield replied: "You're the first person who's recognized it. When I read the script, that mad, sardonic genius of music flashed through my mind. And I based my character on him.
>
> "Tried to figure out how he'd behave under like circumstances. Always keeping uppermost the frustration, and knowledge, that I myself was a failure. Try to pick out a living character, because from them you learn how to tick."

Bosley Crowther in *The New York Times* described Garfield's film debut as "the most startling innovation in the way of a screen character in years." It is clear from the wrinkles in his suit to the limp curl hanging over his forehead that Garfield had imagined Mickey Borden as Oscar Levant.

By June 1938, Levant's notoriety was limited to the theatrical cognoscenti, socially prominent New Yorkers, Hollywood musicians, and the Broadway demimonde that congregated at watering holes like Lindy's. To the proverbial man in the street, Oscar Levant was still an unknown quantity. But in 1938 two newspaper articles appeared, having the effect of widening Levant's reputation as a wit and composer. Michael Mok's article for the *New York Post* crowned Levant "the wag of Broadway." Gossip columnist Dorothy Kilgallen's article for her *New York Journal* column, "The Voice of Broadway," devoted a piece in a series called "Young Men in Manhattan" to "Town Wit—Oscar Levant." The publicity was favorable in both articles, but each described Levant as a wit who sometimes composed, whose very personality kept him from being taken seriously as a composer. It was an idea about Levant that took hold, as it accurately reflected his own ambivalence and defensiveness about his musical career.

The two articles were the beginning of the media's long fascination with Levant, a kind of love affair that began sweetly enough but in time would grow bitter. Levant's quickness with a one-liner or a put-down made for good copy, and over the years his quips would be repeated in newspapers all over America. His surprising intellect combined with a cabdriver's street smarts and his role as the late George Gershwin's "best friend" made him an irresistible subject.

Dorothy Kilgallen wrote,

> He refers to himself always as a neurotic, but when someone asked him, "Are you really neurotic or is it just a pose?" he looked up blandly and said, "I guess it's just a pose."

This is astute of Kilgallen. She senses that Levant's neurotic mien is part pose, that he has created a personality based in truth but exaggerated for effect.

Once he had been translated into a "personality," the thousands of articles that followed about Levant over the next three decades would sound very much alike. Though future journalists began to cover his pianistic accomplishments throughout the rest of the 1930s and 1940s, the press would basically write and rewrite the same view of Levant first presented by Dorothy Kilgallen and Michael Mok.

Michael Mok's article appeared in the *New York Post* on June 27, 1938. It was accompanied by a large photograph of Levant next to a dark-eyed caricature drawn by George Gershwin in 1931, immediately establishing the connection between the two men. The most revealing comment occurs about three quarters of the way through:

> In Hollywood I was always with George Gershwin. George and I were close friends. You must have read it in the Broadway columns. The columns are always quoting me. If it weren't for them, somebody, some day, might take me seriously as a musician.

Here is Levant still holding on to his connection to Gershwin, which he feels legitimizes him as a musician and composer. But he had created a public persona he could no longer step out of. Levant and his character—the neurotic Broadway wag who takes nothing seriously—were now fused.

It was Dan Golenpaul's idea. Golenpaul, an aggressive radio salesman turned producer, was searching for a new format when he came up with the idea for a radio quiz show called *Information, Please!* Its originality would lie in the reversal of the usual quiz show format: The public would write in questions in an effort to stump a panel of celebrity journalists, critics, musicians. Golenpaul argued that "by reversing the ordinary quiz program by letting the public badger a board of experts with baffling questions, the 'average' listener was made to feel equal in erudition to the college-educated experts."

Golenpaul's program was simply the latest development of the quiz show and book chat craze that was sweeping radio in the late thirties. Golenpaul had earlier produced a program in which the newspaperman and Algonquin Round Tabler Heywood Broun interviewed literary figures, so the producer was experienced with the kind of cultural-cum-entertainment shows that *Information, Please!* took as its point of departure.

After some initial resistance from NBC executives, who feared the show would be too highbrow for mass audiences, the program was scheduled to go on the air May 17, 1938, on WJZ in New York. Its regular time slot would be Tuesday evening at eight P.M.

But Golenpaul and his young assistant—a capable, twenty-year-old graduate of Hunter College named Edith Schick—soon discovered that it was not easy to get well-known personalities to appear live on radio and subject themselves to possible humiliation. However, Golenpaul's true gift as a producer turned out to be assembling his board of full-time experts. Franklin P. Adams—known as FPA—whose "Conning Tower" column in the *New York Herald Tribune* was well known, was asked to audition for Golenpaul. John Kieran, a journalist and popular sportswriter for *The New York Times* (where he wrote the first daily, signed column ever published in that newspaper) was soon hired to join FPA on the panel. Kieran fit the criterion as well as anyone of having more than one area of expertise: At home with boxing argot, he was also a Latin scholar and something of an expert on Shakespeare, as well as an amateur ornithologist. He would quickly earn the sobriquet "Mr. Know-it-all."

The show's tremendous popularity was due as much to Golenpaul's choice of a moderator as it was to the show's unusual format. Clifton Fadiman appealed to Golenpaul because he was witty and knowledgeable, and, as book critic for *The New Yorker,* he projected a professorial air without sounding stuffy or pretentious. Fadiman, who had been a ship's chandler among other things in his picaresque youth, seemed like both an intellectual and a regular guy, setting just the right tone for the program. Fadiman had an appealing radio voice as well, one that undercut the broadcast's potential for formality with flashes of playful humor. "The program was a conversation, disguised as a question-and-answer show," remembered Fadiman. Fadiman made a point of calling each of the panel members and special guests by his or her surname in the belief that people would appreciate hearing the "experts" addressed in respectful tones. "People liked it," Fadiman believed. "They wanted to feel a certain distance between themselves and the panel." The presumably nonintellectual pop audience "seemed to like an occasional suggestion of intellectual good manners."

Practically from the start of the program, about five thousand letters a week—each one replete with questions for the panel of experts—poured into the *Information, Please!* offices. Publishers such as Bennett Cerf of Random House were soon asking Golenpaul to have their authors appear on the program. Before long, celebrities, writers, and various "novelties" who were on the lecture circuit made guest appearances on the show. Some of the personalities who appeared alongside the regular panel were Gracie Allen, Lillian Gish, Boris Karloff, Christopher Morley, Cornelia Otis Skinner, Alfred Hitchcock, Moss Hart, Beatrice Lillie, Wendell Willkie, Mayor Fiorello La Guardia—even Harpo Marx in a disastrous, silent appearance in which he whistled and mimed.

Canada Dry came forward as the first of many corporate sponsors. Golenpaul was a difficult man to work with, and his insistence on controlling every aspect of the broadcast, even the commercials, would alienate a number of sponsors. Lucky Strike would come along during the war years, and finally Heinz Foods.

Golenpaul became desperate when the music expert he had hired to join the panel left the country to take a teaching assignment in Hawaii. The composer and critic Deems Taylor was quickly hired as his replacement but was soon let go when it became apparent that Taylor lacked the quick wit and verbal sharpness that made the show exciting. Irving Kolodin, music critic of the *New York Sun* who had earlier been recruited by Golenpaul to serve on the editorial board of *Information, Please!,* was brought in to help the frantic producer find a suitable replacement. Kolodin had been one of the few critics to attend the first Yaddo music festival in 1932, and he told Golenpaul about Oscar Levant. He referred him to Michael Mok's article in the *New York Post.* Golenpaul was impressed by what he read and summoned the "wag of Broadway" to his office for an interview.

"We talked with him," Edith Schick remembered,

but not at length, because Kolodin said, "this is a very bright, very funny, very talented man." . . . Oscar was a snap wit. He came back so fast and it was so to the point. His satire was very clean and sharp. So Oscar was asked to make a guest appearance as the program's music expert.

Levant told Lee and Ira Gershwin he would be appearing on the program, but prior to his debut he couldn't bring himself to listen to the show. In fact, he studiously avoided becoming familiar with it as a way of diminishing any stage fright that lay in wait for him. So Levant went to the NBC studio still unaware of exactly what the program was all about. He wore his usual dark blue suit, a white shirt, and a red tie with white horizontal stripes. He first stopped at the Radio City coffee shop and gulped down a cup of coffee, leaving a dime tip before getting up to go. On his way to the station he noticed a legless man sitting on a board fitted with skates, selling pencils among a group of mendicants gathered on Fifty-ninth Street, not far from NBC and Rockefeller Center. He reached into his pocket and pulled out a crumpled bill to give to the unfortunate fellow.

The sound of a rooster crowing, followed by "Wake up, America! It's time to stump the experts!" signaled the start of *Information, Please!*

Each time a panel member muffed a question, the sound of a cash register was heard and the person who sent in the question would receive five dollars, and two dollars was sent to anyone whose question was used on the air. (Later the amounts were raised to ten dollars and five dollars respectively; an *Encyclopaedia Britannica* was eventually added as an extra incentive.) Levant performed brilliantly on his first guest appearance. He understood immediately that it wasn't as important to have the right answers as it was to be funny and fresh on the air. At certain moments a wickedly uncontrolled giggle—unmistakably Levant's—could be heard emanating from his end of the table.

The response to Levant's first appearance on *Information, Please!* the night of July 5, 1938, was phenomenal. Letters flooded the station demanding his return. Levant's spontaneous wit had finally found its perfect showcase. Curiously, his success on the show didn't endear him to Golenpaul, whose jealousy was aroused by Levant's tremendous popularity. Golenpaul's proprietary feelings about the program led him to resent even those he had handpicked to help make the broadcast a success. But Levant's popularity could not be ignored, so he arranged for the witty composer with the fast comeback to appear every other week on the show, paying him $200 for each half-hour stint.

Levant was stunned by his success on the program. He had gone on the show as a lark; the last thing he expected was to make a career out of it. But whether he knew it or not, *Information, Please!* was just what he needed at the time. At its peak the broadcast would boast a weekly audience of 12 million listeners. Here, at last, was fame.

In an article commissioned by *Harper's Magazine* in 1942 about the inner workings of *Information, Please!,* Franklin P. Adams aptly described Levant on the show as "unpredictable":

> . . . there is a "perhaps" about him which there is not, alas! about Kieran or me. A pair of veteran newspapermen, when we have nothing to say we say nothing, while Oscar is at his wordiest, and sometimes his best, under those conditions.

Fadiman, who would become a good friend of Oscar's as a result of working with him on *Information, Please!,* described Levant as "a bit of a loose cannon. . . . He just didn't have much of a censor in the depths of his ego."

The show gradually developed a decreasing educational appeal and an increased display of "personality"—"its style belonged to the theatre and the Algonquin Hotel dining room," as one scholar of popular culture has observed. Oscar Levant, who was uncensored and funny and who, incidentally, correctly answered a high percentage of the questions, fit right into that format. And his identification with Hollywood and Broadway added a certain glamour to the show's image.

Levant's various interests and his prodigious memory fascinated the growing audience of *Information, Please!* He was not merely an expert on music but, like Kieran, on sports as well. He was re-creating his boyhood pattern in which his interest in ballplayers made his proficiency at the piano less suspect in the eyes of his peers. By reducing his musical training to a parlor game, Levant appealed to cabdrivers, milkmen, cops—they all read the sports pages and marveled at Levant's memory for World Series statistics. Levant epitomized what *Information, Please!* was all about—culture without elitism, a bridge between highbrow conversation and popular sensibilities.

On one broadcast that summer, Levant correctly identified three musical compositions based on one-chord clues played by the house pianist, Joe Kahn. "That's Beethoven," Levant responded to the first chord.

"Correct," intoned Fadiman.

The next chord was played, and Fadiman called on "Mr. Levant," whose hand had shot up as though he were still a schoolboy in Demmler's music appreciation class. "I have a revolutionary answer. It's Chopin's 'Revolutionary étude.' "

"Bravo, Mr. Levant," responded Fadiman.

When the final clue was played, Fadiman again called on Oscar, who, with a grin in his voice, piped up, "There's no other sound quite like that. It's Rachmaninoff. The second piano concerto."

Swept up by his three bull's-eyes, Levant added, "Did you know Rachmaninoff had a nervous breakdown in Russia when he was nineteen years old? That I can understand. But they brought in Tolstoy to cheer him up. That I cannot understand."

The audience in the tiny studio burst into laughter and applause. Whether or not Levant meant to be funny with that last remark, the audience took to him completely. Sitting before the microphone on Tuesday nights, Oscar Levant began to avenge his past.

There was, however, one drawback to Levant's rousing popularity on the radio program. By the time he had to show up for his second appearance, he had begun to worry that his success was purely accidental.

Levant was continuing to see his psychiatrist, Dr. Shoenfeld. On one visit, he asked the psychiatrist whether or not he should continue to appear on the program. Shoenfeld urged him to stay with it.

"It fits the family constellation," he told Levant. Because Oscar had been the youngest of four intelligent brothers, his being the youngest of the four *Information, Please!* regulars was a recapitulation of his earliest and most familiar role. "The program will be great therapy for you," he assured his patient. But Dr. Shoenfeld's reassurances did not prevent Levant from fretting.

To ensure a successful performance, Levant decided that everything he had done casually before the first show would have to be repeated before each subsequent broadcast. Because he had stopped off at the Radio City coffee shop before his first appearance and had left a dime tip for a cup of coffee, that now became a ritual to be repeated: the same coffee shop, the same counter, the same swivel seat, the same dime tip. He had given a dollar to a legless beggar on the street before his first broadcast; now he searched for that same fellow and repeated the gesture.

Soon these rituals meant to ward off failure were performed not just on Tuesdays but on a daily basis. "I had to give the man the same tip every day," Levant later wrote. If the beggar was busy with strangers and didn't see him, Oscar would elbow his way through the crowd to reach him. The more popular *Information, Please!* became and the funnier Levant was on the show, the more his dread of failure increased. He decided to wear the same clothes for each broadcast without spoiling his luck by having them cleaned. Like a ballplayer on a winning streak, he refused to bathe as long as his luck held out. Every broadcast day, he'd call Dr. Shoenfeld for reassurance. Soon his soiled tie and stubborn lack of grooming were beginning to be noticed by his friends. (June's prolonged absence also contributed to his personal neglect.)

He simply couldn't trust his own success. Adept at snatching defeat from the jaws of victory, Levant was sure public humiliation awaited him, were he not vigilant in maintaining his rituals. Success, for Levant, was an ill-cut suit.

He began calling Golenpaul's assistant at home after each broadcast, "at all hours of the day and night" she remembered, racked with doubts about his performance and plying her with questions: "How'd I do?" "Did I goof that one?" "Was I too smart?" "Was I too fresh?"

"He was insecure all the time," Edith Schick recalled. "It didn't bother me because I knew where it was coming from, and I knew Irving Kolodin had so much respect and affection for him and so did the others."

Though he usually came across on the air as relaxed and confident, at times Levant would be so paralyzed with fear that his mind would drift and he'd appear to blank out. "I felt he wasn't paying attention sometimes," Schick remembers.

> If there'd be a musical piece that he was supposed to identify, sometimes you would feel that he wasn't really listening. . . . He was so afraid he wasn't going to get it, and maybe he would say something unpleasant. Then maybe John Kieran, who was also very musically alert and aware, would give the answer, and he would feel that somebody had taken away his property, his claim, his territory.

John Kieran looked upon thirty-one-year-old Oscar as an underprivileged boy with a lot of talent. "He felt sympathetic towards him and never wanted to upset him," Schick remembered. Franklin P. Adams, on the other hand, was "very caustic, and sometimes the sparks would fly. He had some minimal amount of tolerance for Oscar's quirks." Adams was especially contemptuous of Levant's facility for answering questions about the movies, which he considered a debased medium. But Levant admired the older man and was an avid reader of FPA's "The Conning Tower."

When Levant felt that his performance on *Information, Please!* was not up to snuff, he could relax sufficiently to bathe and change his shirt. But, to the satisfaction of Golenpaul and the show's various sponsors, Oscar rarely disappointed. Radio audiences had never heard anyone quite like Oscar Levant before. His unvarnished urban accent came right through. It soon became clear that he would say anything on the air. The panel was once asked to name common household expressions. "Please pass the salt" and "The front doorbell's ringing" were FPA's and Kieran's responses. Levant piped up with "Are you going to stay in that bathroom all day?"—a risqué remark in the forties, when radio considered itself a medium of gentility.

Within the show's first year, *Information, Please!* had become radio's most-talked-about program. The man who was once only "famous among the high and mighty" had become a celebrity to the 12 million who tuned into the quiz show each week.

24

Distant Music

> "I'll have to hang up now or I'll be too sleepy
> to take my sleeping pill."

"I WILL PROBABLY DO A SHOW," LEVANT HAD WRITTEN TO JUNE GALE in the spring of 1938. Despite his disappointment over *Ripples,* Levant had agreed to venture back into the theatre. For one thing, he needed the money. His $400 a month for the biweekly broadcasts was good money in 1938, but he still hadn't entirely given up the idea of persuading June to marry him, and she had already questioned his ability to support both her and her mother. And then there was his lifelong intoxication with Broadway, though his romance with the theatre would remain unrequited.

Levant was hired to be the music director for George S. Kaufman and Moss Hart's *The Fabulous Invalid.* It was to be Kaufman and Hart's valentine to the American theatre. Broadway and Times Square had slumped into tawdriness after the stock market crash, and the two playwrights hoped that by reprising excerpts from twenty-six past Broadway productions they would convey the message that theatre never dies. The ghosts of an actor and actress preside over the play, kept alive, like two Tinkerbells, as long as the theatre lives.

The Fabulous Invalid opened on October 8, 1938, at the Broadhurst Theatre, with Harry Levant conducting the orchestra. After opening night, Harry handed the baton over to Oscar, who had worked with the musicians throughout rehearsals. But the production ran for only eight weeks, closing after a total of sixty-five performances and sending the presiding ghosts of live theatre back into purgatory. The play's biggest drawback was its form: It was a cavalcade, and it was too big and unwieldy to travel. Out-of-town tryouts had been impossible.

Undeterred, however, by the closing of *The Fabulous Invalid,* Levant allowed himself to be talked into composing a score and conducting another Kaufman-Hart extravaganza called *The American Way.* It would prove to be a gargantuan undertaking.

A patriotic cavalcade meant to celebrate the fortunes of a German immigrant—modeled on Kaufman's own grandfather—as he rises to riches and then goes bankrupt during the Depression, the play's action spans three generations, with a warning against the rising tide of Nazism. The only theatre large enough to house the production, which required a cast of 250 and a total of 2,200 costume changes, was the cavernous Center Theatre, part of Rockefeller Center. The theatre, which held 4,000 seats, was variously described as a white elephant and the eighth blunder of the world. One critic wrote that it made him feel like Jonah, writing his notes in the belly of a whale. To make this behemoth even more complicated, the stage of the Center Theatre had to be enlarged, which was accomplished by covering the orchestra pit. Now a solution had to be found as to where to put Levant and his orchestra.

When *The American Way* finally opened, on January 21, 1939, Levant was conducting a small band of musicians in a seventh-floor studio, his music piped into the theatre and cued by means of flashing lights.

Levant greatly enjoyed the task of conducting, but the technical aspect of playing on cue for a drama that was unfolding six floors below was another matter. As far as Levant was concerned, Kaufman's well-known dislike of music was evident in the music direction, which was under the control of Kaufman's technical director. The whole procedure had the effect of trivializing the music's contribution to the experience of the play. It was just the kind of highly technical, split-second operation that was designed to make Levant feel not like an orchestra conductor but more like a technician in the pump room of a dirigible.

"The reviews," Kaufman told Levant, "are not kind, but they are just." However, Theodore Strauss wrote a special feature on Levant's conducting of *The American Way* in *The New York Times,* and *The New Yorker* ran a piece on Levant called "Distant Music":

To keep Mr. Levant in touch with the action on stage six stories below, there are three signal lights: a blue one, a white one, and a red one. Blue means, "Get ready," white means "Go," and red means "Stop." In case these should fail, there is a supplementary mike, from which a tinny voice says "Go ahead." . . . When they're not playing, the musicians, who have already exhausted the stories of their lives, tell each other jokes that a mixed audience might find upsetting. . . .

At our visit the men smoked and played cards during these [inter-missions] and we chatted with Mr. Levant, who has never seen "The American Way" and probably never will unless he loses his job.

For Levant, *The American Way* was another job in the parallel universe he had been inhabiting since his friendship with George Gershwin had taken root, and the *coup de grâce* was his puny orchestra kept in a room far removed from the excitement of the theatre.

One afternoon during rehearsals for *The American Way,* Levant was walking on Fifth Avenue, hatless as usual, wearing Nick the Greek's castoff overcoat, when he bumped into Barbara Wooddell. The show at Loew's State was over: After five years of marriage, the flame-haired young actress with the bow-shaped lips had divorced Arthur Loew.

Levant was lonesome for June and nostalgic about seeing his former wife, and this accidental meeting seemed to revive his old feelings for Barbara.

Over coffee at the Shubert Alley drugstore, Barbara confided in Oscar that she had unsuccessfully auditioned for a part in *The American Way*.

Barbara didn't even have to ask. Levant immediately called Kaufman and got his ex-wife into the show. Grateful and at the same time a little remorseful over how she had treated him in the past, Barbara made a date with Oscar that she failed to keep. Later that evening Levant caught a glimpse of his ex-wife slipping into a cab with George S. Kaufman.

Soon thereafter Levant introduced Barbara to life at the Swopes'. The pool and tennis courts, the lawn at Sands Point with its omnipresent croquet paraphernalia, seemed an appropriate setting for Levant to become reacquainted with his beautiful ex-wife. He introduced her to Ottie and to Ottie's best friend, his dashing young uncle Bruce Powell.

During the run of *The American Way,* Barbara started to visit the Sands Point estate on her own every weekend for the tennis, the croquet, the fresh air—three of her irreconcilable differences with

Oscar. Soon Barbara became a fixture at the Swopes' and Oscar the occasional guest. Barbara remembered how sad and lonesome he seemed on those visits—"he never had a girl with him." Within a few weeks Bruce Powell was smitten with Barbara, and they began a love affair.

One month after the opening of *The American Way,* June Gale arrived in New York on a publicity junket for 20th Century–Fox. For the first time in over a year, the "gruesome twosome" (as Levant liked to call them) would be together again. A lot had happened to Levant in the intervening year—he was now famous, he was loved by millions as the bad boy of radio, the music expert who delighted and fascinated America. He had always been a personality; now he was a Personage.

It was the first time they had seen each other since their walk down Michigan Avenue at dusk when Oscar had rushed to Chicago to see June in the final performances of *Stage Door.* "We were happy to be together again, and I was relieved to find he hadn't forgotten me," June remembered. Levant, however, was a changed man. His confidence had been boosted by his tremendous success on *Information, Please!* and by the responsibility of conducting the orchestra for two Kaufman-Hart shows. His reunion with Barbara, although ultimately unrewarding, had also given Levant more leverage in his dealings with June Gale. He was now more reserved, more independent, more guarded. June recalled an incident that would never have happened before their break: She arrived late for a meeting with Levant but found that instead of waiting for her he had taken Barbara out to dinner. June was furious and refused to see or talk to Oscar for two days. "But paradoxically," she remembered, "I secretly admired his independent attitude."

Levant continued to see June during her publicity tour and to maintain his friendship with Barbara as well. June and Oscar still quarreled, though, and Levant would occasionally drag Barbara into their arguments for leverage:

"Barbara thinks I'm funny, June," Oscar said once when June gave him the cold shoulder.

"If Barbara thinks you're so funny, then why did she divorce you?" June retorted.

So confusing was Levant's love life at this point that Kaufman and Hart worked an inside joke into their next play, *The Man Who Came to Dinner.* When the play opened the following season, Barbara Wooddell appeared as the ingenue. The character she played was given the name of June.

...

After June's departure for Los Angeles, Levant returned to his full schedule of appearing twice monthly on *Information, Please!* and conducting *The American Way* from his seventh-floor closet. He also continued to orchestrate his Suite for Piano and Orchestra, which had now grown to include a dirge he had written for George Gershwin. It was the most painful and difficult piece of music he had ever written.

When *The American Way* closed in July 1939 and the freshly out-of-work actors and crew went into the sweltering summer heat to look for work, the organizers of the second Gershwin Memorial Concert, to be held at Lewisohn Stadium, came looking for Oscar Levant. But Oscar wanted no part of it. He recalled too vividly the weeks of anguish preceding the first concert and the vicious stage fright that had staggered him. The second movement of his orchestral suite, "Dirge," which he had just completed as an homage to Gershwin, had rekindled the memories of his friend's horrific death. How could he face all of that again? When the offer came, he refused.

It was Rose Gershwin, George and Ira's mother, who persuaded Levant to change his mind. Curiously, Rose Gershwin's name was linked, now, in Oscar's mind, to two of his most inexplicable losses—the early death of his young friend Rose and the death of the composer whose music had so influenced his life. He agreed to take part in the Lewisohn Stadium program.

Once again the public turned out in record numbers. They arrived by subway and by bus from the Bronx and Riverdale, from Mt. Vernon and Greenwich Village. Furriers, milk truck deliverymen, doctors and bookkeepers, secretaries and their dates, French teachers and music teachers—all came to hear Gershwin's music and to see for themselves who this engaging mystery man was they had been listening to on *Information, Please!*—this impudent, brilliant wise guy who seemed so New York, so cheeky, so smart. *The New York Times* had run a picture of Oscar at the piano, taken by Gershwin at his apartment late one evening, in an article announcing the concert.

By dusk, eighteen thousand people had filled the outdoor stadium. It was the largest turnout for a musical event that summer. "To the vast gathering Mr. Levant was more than a piano soloist; he was a celebrated radio personality," wrote Howard Taubman, who covered the event for *The New York Times*. Samuel Chotzinoff was also at Lewisohn Stadium that night, and he described Levant's playing as "gifted and enthusiastic." Levant played the Concerto in F "like an improvisation," Chotzinoff wrote in the *New York Post*. He then characterized Levant's performance of the Concerto as "a posthumous triumph" for Gershwin.

Levant had long ago given up his dream of having a concert career, but now savvy concert promoters would come to realize that his name was a draw—that the same audiences who attended Lewisohn Stadium's summer music programs also listened to *Information, Please!* Gershwin's death and Levant's tremendous success on the radio had joined to clear his path; after his performance that July 10, 1939, at Lewisohn Stadium, Levant finally arrived at the place he had set out for so long ago. He was now a pianist at the beginning of a real concert career.

Nineteen thirty-nine marked the beginning of the Second World War. By the end of the year, Hitler had begun the bombing of British towns. On September 8, 1939, President Roosevelt proclaimed a limited state of national emergency.

It was also the year of Irving Berlin's patriotic "God Bless America"; other popular songs were "Over the Rainbow" by E. Y. "Yip" Harburg and Harold Arlen, from *The Wizard of Oz*. Cole Porter, Rodgers and Hart, Buddy DeSylva, and Billy Rose all had popular songs that year; so did Andre Kostelanetz, in an adaptation of the second movement of Tchaikovsky's Symphony No. 5 with the title "Moon Love."

The House Un-American Activities Committee disbanded the Federal Theatre Project of the WPA relief program, which had employed more than 13,000 theatre professionals and had produced 1,200 plays. On Broadway, Howard Lindsay and Russel Crouse's *Life with Father* broke all existing box-office records. Lillian Hellman's *The Little Foxes* debuted in 1939, as did William Saroyan's *The Time of Your Life,* winning the 1940 Pulitzer Prize. Kaufman and Hart's *The Man Who Came to Dinner*—with Barbara Wooddell playing "June"—opened on October 16 at the Music Box Theatre. Oscar Levant's favorite sport, baseball, was reckoned to be one hundred years old by the official record keepers at Cooperstown, New York. Nineteen thirty-nine was also the year that Oscar Levant, at long last, was launched on a concert career.

Levant, who had made a kind of virtue out of failure, now had to deal with success. He did not know what to make of the offers that started to pour in from concert promoters and orchestras to appear as a guest soloist. From San Francisco, St. Louis, Cleveland—the letters lay strewn about his suite at the Park Central Hotel. "You'd be amazed at the many offers I've turned down," Levant wrote to June Gale.

> The hell with it. I like to play the piano like I haven't done since I was a kid. I got a Steinway Grand Piano—well, I won't give you the rest of this corny routine you'll think it's on the "tired" side.
>   Only this, this thing of always having to make good isn't for me. The hell with it . . .

Levant's instinct to be suspicious of his good fortune wasn't entirely without some basis in fact. The new demand for him that had sprung out of his radio celebrity was inspired in part by the calculated desire to increase ticket sales by spotlighting a popular figure. In 1939 orchestras were not oversubscribed. It was a hard sell to fill seats at the end of the Depression and the beginning of American involvement in the war effort. If audiences were to be developed for metropolitan and local orchestras, the orchestras needed a big draw. Levant was unquestionably an excellent pianist, but more than that, he was guaranteed to "put fannies in the seats," encouraging his vast radio audience to become supporters of symphonic music.

No wonder Levant was ambivalent about the new demand for his talents. Here was the career his mother had prepared him for. This was the career that had informed every aspect of his life until he realized that it would never happen, that debuts went to other musicians. Now that the offers were pouring in, the old pressure of having to make good returned to him with a vengeance.

Accompanying the old terrors were new ones: Was he well enough prepared to walk back out on the concert stage? He had stopped his formal training when he left Stojowski. True, he had studied composition, briefly with Schillinger and then with Schoenberg, but he had long ago given up the daily, rigorous practice a concert career demands. Could he ever in one year—in ten years, in a lifetime—retrieve what he had long ago abandoned?

In an interesting irony, earlier in the year an aging and nearly senile Paderewski had returned to make his twentieth concert tour of America. It was a chilling omen for Levant to be reminded again of Paderewski's ancient assessment—that Levant did not have the soul of a concert pianist. Now he would find out if he had ever possessed that soul, and if he had, if he could reawaken it. Or was it simply too late—was he making a Faustian bargain that would destroy him? "The hell with it," he wrote to June.

• • •

It seemed an unlikely romance between the seventeen-year-old, temperamental child star and the thirty-two-year-old terror of radio, but Judy Garland nonetheless had fallen for Oscar Levant.

"What do you think of me?" demanded the hopeful, high-strung star of *Love Finds Andy Hardy* soon after their first meeting backstage at the Capital Theatre in New York City.

"You're enchanting," Levant quickly answered her.

"Don't give me that! What do you really think of me?"

Levant, echoing Madame Derville in Stendhal's *The Red and the Black,* countered with "To me you are like a Mozart symphony."

The young actress was thrilled with this answer. Despite all her hard work and rough knocks, she possessed an acutely poetic nature. Her show business travails had left her sensitive to a fault. By the age of seventeen, she was a veteran not only of a grueling film schedule but of crash diets and the abuse of pep pills and Nembutal.

Inspired by Oscar's compliment, Judy Garland went out and bought all of the recorded works of Mozart—the symphonies, the piano concertos, the chamber works. Garland herself preferred music she regarded as more sensual and romantic, composers such as Debussy and Ravel. Levant would later comment that "she couldn't make contact with the purity of Mozart's music." Eventually she phoned Levant, furious with the comparison.

Their unfulfilled relationship began during the first year of Levant's fame on *Information, Please!* When Levant met the young actress, she was being cast in her seventh film as Dorothy in *The Wizard of Oz,* despite the studio's worry about the increasing dimensions of her bosom.

Levant soon began receiving letters from Garland full of heartfelt effusions, outpourings of adolescent angst—not unlike the letters Levant had once written to June Gale. She enclosed her own highly romantic poems, and Levant would write back, suggesting books for her to read and music for her to listen to. His were more letters of encouragement and support than love letters. "I thought she was a child," Levant remembered, "and I treated her as a child."

But Levant felt drawn to Garland. He especially loved hearing her talk about the MGM studio school, where she, Lana Turner, Ava Gardner, and other starlets would practice long division and take turns reciting John Donne's "The Flea." Like Levant, Garland was insecure and self-conscious about her looks. "Never in her lifetime," writes a Garland biographer, "did she consider herself a beautiful woman, always very conscious of the absence of two ingredients she equated with beauty: a good figure and lovely, thick, long hair." As far as she was concerned, Nature had gotten it all wrong: Her hair was thin and her waist was thick. Levant would later write about her, in words that could have been a description of himself:

> For a throbbingly emotional girl she must have felt overshadowed, not as far as talent was concerned—she always had that—but in other areas. She was the cute kid who never grew up (yet she grew increasingly harder to handle).

But Garland had grown up fast, and she knew what she wanted— she wanted Oscar Levant. She began to pursue Oscar the way he had pursued June Gale—extended phone calls, staying on the line for hours, pouring out her heart long distance, the poetry in her letters with their sad entreaties.

Garland's crush on Levant became even greater as the two were separated on opposite coasts. During the making of *The Wizard of Oz,* Judy sent Oscar a tenderly inscribed photograph of herself and a little gold cross on a chain, a treasured gift from her father, Frank Gumm, whom she had adored and who had died suddenly when Judy was twelve.

Oscar described the relationship in his letters to June Gale, recognizing why they were drawn to each other. Not long after their first meeting at the Capital Theatre, Levant wrote to June, with some insight:

> We unconsciously grasp each other's hand to combat this unconscious feeling of insecurity. We should have leaned on each other. . . . I am an authority on this form of oppression, and Judy Garland the gifted young sufferer . . .

Their affair would go no further than an embrace, but Levant later wrote that when Judy Garland embraced you, her need for love was so great that her embrace seemed to take you inside of herself, as if by force of will.

Their vulnerabilities kept them friends. Early on they shared their feelings about stage fright. Eventually they would share neurotic experiences. They would go from exchanging letters to exchanging prescription pills. "If we had ever married," Levant would one day joke, "she would have given birth to a sleeping pill instead of a child—we could have named it Barb-iturate."

• • •

One night June Gale was invited to attend a party at the Cocoanut Grove in Los Angeles, the popular dining room at the Ambassador Hotel that was favored by the movie colony. June recognized Judy Garland seated at another table. Three years earlier June had been a contract player in *Pigskin Parade* with the young star. On this night at the Cocoanut Grove, June remembered, Judy Garland was "dressed in white, looking cute and animated, surrounded by friends."

Toward the end of the evening, the young actress, who had by now completed making *The Wizard of Oz,* approached June Gale's table.

"May I introduce myself?" she asked.

"I know who you are. You're Judy Garland."

"We have a mutual friend," she told June.

"Oh, who?"

"Oscar Levant."

The two actresses spoke for a few minutes, looking each other over surreptitiously. June could hardly wait to get home to call their "mutual friend."

When June returned to the Olympic Boulevard apartment she shared with her mother, she dialed the long-distance operator and demanded CIrcle 6-9786. Oscar was home. He had just gotten off the phone with Judy Garland.

"What did she say about me?" June asked breathlessly.

"She said you have a pretty nose," Oscar reported, no doubt enjoying the potential rivalry brewing.

The evening at the Cocoanut Grove had given June a lot to think about. She wondered just how attracted Oscar was to Judy Garland. She worried that Garland's vulnerability appealed to Levant. That night at the Cocoanut Grove, something had clicked for June Gale. Garland's schoolgirl crush on Oscar had been a catalyst for her. Looking back on their courtship, June would later recall that Oscar had

> constantly reassured me about his love, when, ironically enough, what I evidently needed was a little doubt now and then. Just enough, I mean, not to feel so complacent about him. The idea that I might lose him to someone else gave me an awful fright.

June wrote to Oscar almost immediately after the Cocoanut Grove encounter, and Levant responded with surprise and enthusiasm. At last the two agreed to marry. June's option at 20th Century–Fox was coming up for renewal in November 1939, so if it wasn't picked up, she would be free to join Oscar in New York—a married woman. But if it was renewed, then June would have to decide all over again.

Soon after the first anniversary of *Information, Please!*, Dan Golenpaul decided it was time to present the program on the big screen in a series of movie shorts, produced by RKO-Pathé, that would run like a newsreel before the featured movie.

Clifton Fadiman was the first to arrive on the set, where he would rehearse the questions, giving every possible variation on lines like "Very good, Mr. Levant" for the sound track. Of the four participants, Fadiman was the only one who was rehearsed. The panelists were kept out of the studio so they would have no idea what the questions would be. A cast hired for the show acted out certain clues, such as a couple miming a popular song title or a W. C. Fields lookalike impersonating Micawber from *David Copperfield*.

The film shorts were enormously popular, and Levant would appear in five made in 1939. More would follow: He made eleven film shorts in 1941 and nine in 1942. The films were literate, but the spontaneity—except in Levant's case—was sometimes forced. Though they were very popular in their day, the film shorts have not aged well. The strain of recasting into a new medium shows. One problem was the panelists' lack of stage presence. What was appealing on radio looks stilted on film—Kieran comes across as pained, FPA is especially unphotogenic. "The close-up cameraman," observed Fadiman, "had a nerve-wracking job because he never knew who would speak next." He had to get his shots "by exercising what is almost mental telepathy." Only Levant—who, after all, had already had some stage and film experience—remains lively and interesting on film.

Levant was thirty-two, and his youth made him a refreshing contrast to his fellow panelists. Whereas Kieran and FPA sat upright in their chairs with their hands on the table like school examiners, Levant's way of slouching down and calling out answers as though he were in another room gave him a look of total relaxation and self-confidence. It was an irresistible film presence, and the moguls were watching.

By 1939 Levant had already begun to generate a small mountain of newsprint. His popularity on radio and now in the *Information, Please!* film shorts gave book publishers the idea of trying to capitalize on his growing reputation for impudent wit. It wasn't such a great leap from being quoted in the gossip columns to putting his own remarks and opinions down on paper. A Doubleday salesman suggested to editor Ken McCormick that he approach Levant about writing a book. McCormick recalled:

> So I went over to his hotel and said, "Would you write a book for Doubleday?" He said, "Interesting," and I said, "Would you write a biography of Victor Herbert?"
> He said, "Write one? I wouldn't even read one!"

If only they could find the right lion tamer to give shape to Levant's often brilliant but erratic way of thinking, a book could be written. McCormick felt much the way June Gale had: that making a contract with Oscar Levant would be a risky business, but it would be worth it.

Levant believed that literature was the highest of the arts. Though he never entertained the idea of becoming a serious writer and competing with the greats, he certainly must have been flattered by McCormick's offer.

Levant suggested to the editor that he write a handful of essays that would cover the subjects that interested him, such as George Gershwin, popular music, Hollywood, Harpo Marx, and his observations of various conductors. "So we got together," McCormick recalled,

> and he wrote a book called *A Smattering of Ignorance*. He had about forty titles for it. One of them was called "The Treble I've Seen," and [there were] a lot of really crazy titles, but *A Smattering of Ignorance* was a kind of lesson to me in titles. Because I realized that this combination of words really imparted the brashness of Levant, and that it also suggested, contrary to the reputation he had as a sort of know-it-all, that he didn't consider he knew it all.

Irving Kolodin was recruited to help Levant write his book. The two men worked in the afternoons. Kolodin shared Levant's enthusiasm for baseball, so they would often sit in Levant's Park Central Hotel suite, a portable radio on the grand piano tuned to a baseball game. Kolodin would sit at a card table with his typewriter; Levant practiced scales or played Bach on the piano, all the while talking out his ideas to Kolodin, who would write them down. Occasionally the two men would take a break at Lindy's, or, if things were going particularly well, they'd send out for sandwiches. One publishing secretary remembered that when the manuscript came in it had more stains on it than an old Lindy's menu.

Despite Kolodin's assistance, Levant was disappointed with the book's progress. No matter how well the writing was going, Levant couldn't help but compare himself to the great authors he had always admired—"He did more reading than playing the piano," Kolodin recalled.

"Don't be taken in," Levant wrote to June Gale. "I'm not crazy about the book. I will have to correct the manuscript for publication. The book will be released January 1st. I worry like hell for each thing."

It was during their collaboration that Kolodin first thought about Levant's friendship with George Gershwin. In Kolodin's view, Levant was more talented as a pianist and composer than he was given credit for, but he constantly set unrealistic goals for himself. If he couldn't be the best, he gave up the endeavor. "When he became acquainted with George Gershwin," Kolodin believed,

> that was again a part of his own inner destructive impulse, because he knew that his songs weren't as good as Gershwin's, so he stopped writing popular songs. . . . He had the impulse and talent to be a serious composer but he began to study with Arnold Schoenberg and that ruined him, because he couldn't function on the same level with Schoenberg. Every form of impulse that he had ran into obstacles, because he was aiming to exceed or excel on some very high level, and it wasn't working.

This helps to explain his despair over the progress of *A Smattering of Ignorance*. And now, with offers to concertize filling up his mail cubicle, Levant began to practice seriously again. Here was something at which he must excel.

"He began to seriously apply himself to developing the talent that he had in the earlier years, in the Twenties," noted Kolodin, "and he practiced seriously." Although even then he would occasionally fall into despair, groaning to Kolodin that perhaps it was too late, that he would never be able to play as well as Artur Rubinstein.

Among the requests for Levant's services as a guest soloist was an invitation to perform with the Pittsburgh Symphony in the birthplace of his discontent. Soon the prodigal son would return, not as George Gershwin's rehearsal pianist but as a soloist and composer in his own right.

Annie couldn't wait for her youngest son's arrival. She had always kept a piano in her apartment for Oscar to play, on his infrequent visits home. Oscar still marveled at how strictly his mother continued to observe the Jewish rituals. He asked her once why she did so, especially now that her serious heart condition kept her confined to her apartment. "I don't know if I still believe, but it's too late to change," she told her son. "And besides, I don't want to ruin a perfect record." Her constant reminders to keep up with Jewish orthodoxy had the usual effect of creating in Oscar "a violent dichotomy about the religious traditions." His failure to be an observant Jew was another area in which he felt he had disappointed his mother.

Though Annie Levant was now virtually incapacitated by her cardiac condition, she was still a force to be reckoned with. Hearing that Oscar was coming to Pittsburgh brought back the twinkle in her eye. Though she didn't show it in any demonstrative way, Annie was in fact proud of her youngest son's accomplishments. His radio fame delighted the sixty-eight-year-old matriarch. She listened on Tuesday nights as Levant matched wits with his fellow experts and managed to answer a high percentage of the questions correctly. Annie would get into the spirit of the program, calling out answers—such as the name of Lenin's wife—to her son from her living room, as if he could hear her over the radio waves.

But Annie was never very articulate about expressing her emotions or complimenting her children. She was of the generation that feared that praising your children was too much like praising yourself—it just wasn't done. Her praise was reserved for Tchaikovsky, Heifetz, and Paderewski.

The family planned to turn out in force for Oscar's concert with the Pittsburgh Symphony. He was scheduled to appear in the triple role of guest pianist, composer, and conductor. He would perform Gershwin's Concerto in F under the baton of Fritz Reiner and conduct the second movement of his unfinished Suite for Piano and Orchestra—"Dirge," dedicated to the memory of George Gershwin. So "Dirge" would have its premiere in Pittsburgh, where Oscar had first heard Gershwin play the piano for Nora Bayes a lifetime ago.

Two-year-old Oscar in the backyard of the Radin home at 9 Marion Street, in the Hill district of Pittsburgh, circa 1908. From left: brother Harry, grandfather Abraham Radin, brothers Howard ("Honey") and Benjamin (seated), grandmother Sarah Radin, Oscar (in her lap), uncle Mickey Radin. *(Courtesy of Oscar Radin)*

Annie Radin Levant, Oscar's mother. "You'll never be a Paderewski, but you'll never be lonely," Annie Levant frequently told Oscar, though she pushed her youngest son toward a concert career. Oscar felt that he never lived up to his mother's dreams for him. *(Courtesy of Oscar Radin)*

Oscar with his piano teacher, Sigismond Stojowski, at a student recital for Ignacy Jan Paderewski at the Hotel Plaza, May 5, 1924. Oscar's encounter with the legendary Polish pianist haunted his later years. Center: Paderewski and Stojowski. Oscar is second from left, last row.

(Courtesy of June Levant)

Seventeen-year-old Oscar (at right) with his brother Howard on the boardwalk in Atlantic City, 1924. Oscar left home at the age of fifteen and supported himself in New York City playing the piano in hotels and roadhouses.

(Courtesy of June Levant/USC Cinema-Television Library and Archives of Performing Arts)

Oscar was twenty-one when he made his acting debut in the Broadway stage play *Burlesque,* with Hal Skelly and Barbara Stanwyck. Paramount brought him to Hollywood to appear in the 1929 film version of the play, *The Dance of Life.* Oscar is pictured here with Hal Skelly in a scene from the film. *(Paramount Pictures and the Academy of Motion Picture Arts and Sciences)*

Oscar with his two collaborators on the score for the Broadway musical *Ripples,* 1930: Irving Caesar (at left) and Dr. Albert Sirmay. Oscar preferred to spend most of his time across the street listening to George Gershwin's music for *Strike Up the Band.* *(Courtesy of June Levant/USC Cinema-Television Library and Archives of Performing Arts)*

Oscar's New York debut as a concert pianist in Lewisohn Stadium's "all-American" program, August 10, 1931, he experienced his first bout of crippling stage fright. From left: Oscar, Otto Langley, George Gershwin, Robert Russell Bennett, Fritz Reiner, Deems Taylor, and William Merrigan Daly. *(Courtesy of June Levant/USC Cinema-Television Library and Archives of Performing Arts)*

Oscar's first wife, the actress Barbara Smith (stage name Wooddell). Their 1932 marriage lasted barely a year. "Besides incompatibility, we hated each other," Levant quipped about their divorce, though he got his ex-wife a role in George S. Kaufman and Moss Hart's *The American Way.* *(Courtesy of June Levant/USC Cinema-Television Library and Archives of Performing Arts)*

One of a series of photographs of Oscar taken late at night by George Gershwin at George and Ira Gershwin's adjoining penthouses on Riverside Drive, early 1930s. Oscar spent so much time at the Gershwins' that he described himself as a "penthouse beach-comber." *(Courtesy of the Gershwin family)*

Oscar Levant by George Gershwin. "I flowered as a buffoon, warmed in the sun of this amiable household." Levant's talent for unflagging conversation and dangerous wit was honed at Gershwin gatherings. *(Courtesy of the Gershwin family)*

Oscar at one of the two Gershwin pianos. While Gershwin often made use of Oscar's pianistic talents when sketching large works for two pianos, their friendship was uneven: hero worship on Oscar's part, aloofness on George's. *(Courtesy of the Gershwin family)*

Oscar Levant by George Gershwin. Oscar envied his friend's musical gifts and his apparent confidence, which bordered on arrogance. "An evening with George Gershwin is a George Gershwin evening," Oscar quipped. *(Courtesy of the Gershwin family)*

A sketch of Oscar, raccoon-eyed, by George Gershwin. "To use a feminine adjective, I was rather buxom in those early days—an epic in bloat," Oscar said about his appearance, but he treasured this sketch. *(Courtesy of the Gershwin family)*

Oscar

by George
Mar 27 '31

Arnold Schoenberg, one of the most controversial and influential composers of the century, in an inscribed photograph given to Oscar in 1936. While writing music for the movies, Oscar studied composition with the exiled composer in Hollywood. He considered Schoenberg "a great man," but they later had a falling-out. *(Courtesy of June Levant)*

A film-studio glamour shot of June Gale, circa 1936. "You have an unawakened face but your mouth has possibilities," Oscar told the young actress at the beginning of their tempestuous courtship. He first noticed June at a piano in the 20th Century–Fox film *Sing Baby Sing.*
(Courtesy of June Levant)

The Gale Quadruplets. June and her sisters (actually two sets of twins) were a popular vaudeville attraction, displaying acrobatic dancing and winsome good looks. The girls virtually grew up on the vaudeville circuit. From left: Joan, Jane, June, and Jean.
(Courtesy of June Levant)

Judy Garland had a crush on Oscar in the late 1930s (this shot was taken in the late '40s) "If we had married," Oscar joked, "she would have given birth to a sleeping pill. . . .We would have named her Barb-Iturate." Judy's interest in Oscar prompted June Gale to accept Oscar's marriage proposal. *(Courtesy of June Levant/USC Cinema-Television Library and Archives of Performing Arts)*

"Just Married": This Associated Press wire photo appeared in newspapers across the country when Oscar married June Gale on December 1, 1939. Oscar is wearing the inscribed wristwatch given to him by George Gershwin. *(Courtesy of June Levant)*

Oscar's July 5, 1938, guest appearance on the popular radio quiz show *Information, Please!* created such a sensation that he was invited back as a regular member of the panel. From left: Oscar, John Kieran, guest panelist Sir Cedric Hardwicke, F. P. Adams. Clifton Fadiman was the show's moderator *(The Bettmann Archive)*

As a result of his celebrity on *Information Please!*, *Life* magazine featured Oscar in its February 5, 1940, issue, describing him as "a Times Square Dr. Johnson . . . wandering from place to place on Broadway, wisecracking . . . to a group of devoted followers." *(Otto Hagel,* Life *magazine © Time Warner, Inc.)*

Composing at the St. Hubert Hotel, where Oscar and June lived in the early days of their marriage. Despite encouragement from Aaron Copland and Arnold Schoenberg, Oscar eventually abandoned his music-writing career. *(Otto Hagel,* Life *magazine © Time Warner, Inc.)*

"He smokes through the finest meals," noted *Life* magazine. Pictured here at Voisin's with June and with his companion of the early 1940s, the racetrack maven Alfred Gwynne Vanderbilt, Jr. Oscar chain-smoked and consumed an average of thirty to forty cups of coffee a day. *(Otto Hagel,* Life *magazine © Time Warner, Inc.)*

June Levant relaxing with Harpo Marx at the summer home of George S. and Beatrice Kaufman in Bucks County, Pennsylvania, circa 1940. Oscar loathed the outdoors but loved Harpo Marx, virtually moving into Harpo's Hollywood mansion and taking over his household in the mid-1930s.
(Courtesy of June Levant)

"What I love most are my children," Levant wrote in the opening of his memoirs. "I also told them they could do anything except bring me their problems." Oscar with two of his three daughters, circa 1943: Marcia (with the curls) and Lorna. The Levants' youngest child, Amanda, is not pictured.
(Courtesy of June Levant)

From left: Columbia Records president Goddard Lieberson, conductor Eugene Ormandy, and Oscar listening to a playback at a Columbia Masterworks recording session, circa 1944. Oscar's friendship with Lieberson survived his recording career, which came to an end in 1958. *(Yale Music Library, the Fred and Rose Plaut Archive)*

"I played an unsympathetic part—myself," Oscar joked about his role in the 1945 Warner Bros. film biography of George Gershwin, *Rhapsody in Blue*, but the experience of re-creating his friend's life was sometimes painful. Pictured here with Robert Alda (as George Gershwin). *(Warner Bros. and USC Cinema-Television Library and Archives of Performing Arts)*

A scene from the 1946 Warner Bros. film *Humoresque,* adapted by Clifford Odets from a Fannie Hurst story. Arguably Oscar's best work in the movies. From left: John Garfield, Oscar, Joan Crawford. Garfield based his early film persona on Oscar's wise-guy personality. *(Warner Bros. and USC Cinema-Televison Library and Archives of Performing Arts)*

Oscar moved permanently to Los Angeles in 1947 to serve as Al Jolson's pianist and sidekick on Jolson's *Kraft Music Hall* radio show. Oscar had long admired Jolson, but Jolson never really understood Oscar's brand of humor. The show was canceled after two seasons. From left: Oscar, Lucille Ball, Al Jolson. *(Courtesy of June Levant)*

"I knew Doris Day before she became a virgin," Oscar said about the star of the 1948 Warner Bros. film *Romance on the High Seas*. It was Day's first film role, and Oscar, as usual, played a version of himself: Here, he is Oscar Farrar, piano player. *(Warner Bros. and USC Cinema-Television Library and Archives of Performing Arts)*

Oscar with Gene Kelly in the Academy Award–winning film *An American in Paris* (MGM, 1951). Oscar devised the "ego fantasy" scene in which he imagines himself not only as the pianist but as the orchestra, conductor, and audience at a performance of Gershwin's Concerto in F. *(MGM and USC Cinema-Television Library and Archives of Performing Arts)*

Fred Astaire and Oscar on the set of Metro-Goldwyn-Mayer's 1949 musical *The Barkleys of Broadway*. Astaire was fond of Oscar and would make his television debut almost ten years later on Oscar's local televison talk show. *(MGM and USC Cinema-Television Library and Archives of Performing Arts)*

Just six weeks after his heart attack, Oscar barely made it through the filming of the strenuous "That's Entertainment" scene in *The Band Wagon* (MGM, 1953). Astaire threatened to carry him (literally) through the scene. From left: Jack Buchanan, Nanette Fabray, and Fred Astaire, with Oscar below. *(MGM and the Academy of Motion Picture Arts and Sciences)*

Oscar at the loom with Lauren Bacall in a scene cut from *The Cobweb,* Oscar's last film (MGM, 1955). Oscar's role again imitated life as he portrayed a patient at a private sanatorium. From 1953 to the early 1960s, Oscar was treated for drug addiction, mania, and depression at a series of private hospitals. *(MGM and the Academy of Motion Picture Arts and Sciences)*

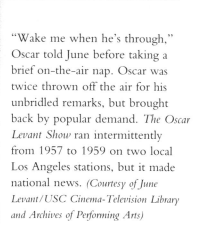

"Wake me when he's through," Oscar told June before taking a brief on-the-air nap. Oscar was twice thrown off the air for his unbridled remarks, but brought back by popular demand. *The Oscar Levant Show* ran intermittently from 1957 to 1959 on two local Los Angeles stations, but it made national news. *(Courtesy of June Levant/USC Cinema-Television Library and Archives of Performing Arts)*

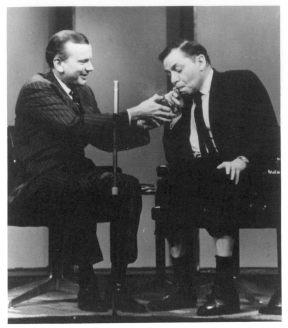

In November 1958, Oscar emerged from his sickroom to appear on *The Tonight Show* with Jack Paar, which gave Oscar a new kind of celebrity as "America's favorite neurotic." Paar was criticized for allowing the grimacing, obviously ill—but still witty—pianist on the air. (*Courtesy of June Levant/USC Cinema-Television Library and Archives of Performing Arts*)

Oscar Levant at fifty-seven. Within a few years he would become a recluse as legendary as Howard Hughes. In 1964, Julian Wasser took this and a number of other photographs for Levant's bestselling book, *The Memoirs of an Amnesiac* (G. P. Putnam's Sons, 1965).
(*Julian Wasser/USC Cinema-Television Library and Archives of Performing Arts*)

"He had a wonderful face," thought Roddy McDowall, who took a series of photographs of Oscar for a 1966 volume of pictures and commentary, *Double Exposure*. Dorothy Parker profiled Oscar for the book; it was her last piece of writing. *(Courtesy of Roddy McDowall)*

Oscar and June Levant in a photograph taken by Candice Bergen, 1972. Oscar's reluctant appearance at Walter and Carol Matthau's luncheon in honor of Charlie Chaplin became an event in itself. "Was I seeing a ghost?" Candice Bergen later wrote about her encounter with Oscar. *(Courtesy of Candice Bergen)*

Oscar at the Matthaus' luncheon, wearing his trademark dark suit, in this somber picture taken by Candice Bergen four months before Oscar's death on August 15, 1972. He was sixty-five. *(Courtesy of Candice Bergen)*

25

"The Future Mrs. L."

"You know, I only married you to get even."

THE DAY BEFORE LEAVING TO REHEARSE "DIRGE" WITH THE PITTS-
burgh Symphony, Levant, with barely three hours of sleep, rose at
eight in the morning to conduct a Hanns Eisler score for a short-
subject film directed by a young Joseph Losey. "That lousy short," as
he described it in a letter to June Gale, was an ambitious, animated
puppet film made for the Petroleum Industry's exhibit at the World's
Fair, and it was cornily titled *Pete (Roleum) and His Cousins.* At the
recording session Levant conducted Eisler's "horrifically modern and
difficult" score for the animated film. (The German-born Eisler had
been a student of Schoenberg's in Vienna twenty years earlier.)

Despite his complaint to June, Eisler's score truly interested Levant:

Not only was there pleasure in the brightness and clarity of his ideas,
there was also distinction in the clean precision of his orchestration,
the polish and finesse of his writing.

A few years later, Levant would conduct the recording of a second
Eisler score, this one for a five-minute black-and-white film on soil

conservation, *The Living Land,* made for the U.S. Department of Agriculture.

His conducting of Eisler's scores for the two film shorts, however, would ultimately get him into trouble with the House Un-American Activities Committee, which would cast a wide net in the 1950s during the McCarthy hearings. Eisler, who was Marxist-oriented, would be hounded by HUAC and linked to nearly every important musician who had sought sanctuary in the United States—Schoenberg, Tiomkin, Klemperer. A file would be opened on Levant in the fifties, but it would remain thin.

In Pittsburgh before the rehearsal, Levant worried about the reception his hometown would give to his Schoenbergian tribute to Gershwin. "Dirge" was very much a modern piece—perhaps "horrifically modern" to some tastes.

To June he described "Dirge" as "shrouded in a thick web and consequently it didn't always emerge."

> I was quite hostile about it to the orchestra. Despite this, there are some very rich expressive (deeply felt) moments and the audience will not only understand it but will, from their point of view, hate it. But that's my life—an even keel of hate, I guess. It does me in temporarily then I get by, turn angry, hurt, then (again then) I revive in customary resilient fashion.

"There was no light, no transparency in my composition. 'Dirge' was a study in murk," Levant told his musical friends. If he needed reassurance, he wasn't going to get it from the Pittsburgh Symphony's resident conductor, Fritz Reiner. Reiner, who had accepted the post after Klemperer had turned it down, was a soft-voiced tyrant.

Levant was also unsure of his skill as a conductor—it was a world away from his impromptu conducting of phonograph records in his hotel suite, which he used to do when he was married to Barbara. And so Levant asked Fritz Reiner to watch him rehearse. He had just written about Reiner in what was to be the first section of his book, *A Smattering of Ignorance,* in a comparative description of conductors entitled "Music in Aspic." He had observed about Reiner that the conductor had

> a facility for terrifying inferior orchestras unequaled among conductors of the present day. . . . A mere series of facial expressions can shade his degrees of contempt for a nervous oboist or a fright-palsied violinist.

. . . His passion for the least audible of possible sounds has created among violinists a new form of occupational ailment known as Reinerparalysis.

Though Levant concedes that Reiner "can achieve fabulous results" with a fine soloist or an operatic score, in essence he inspires in his orchestras "the full gamut of emotions [except] deep affection." Reiner, not unlike Max Levant, was a stern, imposing autocrat with a perfectionist's command of music. His sarcasm and short-fused intolerance eventually prompted the Musician's Union to reprimand him for his abusive behavior toward his musicians. With Reiner present at the rehearsal, Levant's contempt for his "Dirge" somehow deepened. He found himself insulting his own composition at the same time he was trying to communicate to the orchestra what the work was all about and how it should be played.

Nonetheless, Levant asked Reiner to advise him in his conducting. "Dirge" opened with a French horn pianissimo. Levant's gestures, Reiner felt, were too grand and intense.

"How are you going to conduct when it gets louder . . . gets forte?" he demanded.

And so Levant returned to Pittsburgh for the premiere of "Dirge" at the Syria Mosque, for two weekend concerts. Annie Levant would be there with Oscar's brothers Ben and Honey, her grandson Marc, and various Levant and Radin cousins. Oscar's mother would be a guest of one of Pittsburgh's socially prominent families, occupying a box with the rest of her brood.

It was, at first, a triumphant return. Reporters came up to Annie's apartment in the days before the concert to interview the composer's mother. Levant checked into the Hotel Schenley. A number of newspapermen congregated outside his hotel room, but hearing him practicing the piano they just stood by the door for a few minutes, listening to him play a Chopin étude, the notes filling the hallway "like brilliants from a broken necklace," as one of them later wrote.

When the gaggle of reporters, led by the orchestra manager, finally burst into Levant's hotel room, Levant began what had by now become a routine with him—bantering with the newspapermen, touching on *Information, Please!,* music, his famous friends, the book he was near to finishing, and his complaint that he wasn't taken seriously as a composer.

"It's warm in here," complained the orchestra manager.

"What do you want to do—breathe? I'm against breathing," retorted Oscar. "Leave the radiator on, please, because I want to feel enervated." (A difficult state for Levant to achieve, in light of all the caffeine coursing through his bloodstream. Three small silver coffee urns stood empty on his piano.)

Levant then told the scribbling reporters that John Kieran "got off a good crack about 'Dirge' the other day. He wanted to know if I had written it about the Pittsburgh [Pirates] baseball team." The team was in a serious slump that season.

The evening began with Aaron Copland's "An Outdoor Overture," followed by the "Romanza" from Dohnányi's Suite Op. 19. Levant then stepped out on the concert stage to play the Concerto in F, after having steeled himself to the presence of Annie and his brothers staring down at him from their exalted private box.

"It is certain," wrote music critic D. S. Steinfirst about the Saturday-evening concert, "that a more nervous soloist or one more anxious to please never stepped onto the stage of the Mosque than Levant last night." Levant's playing of the Concerto in F was warmly received: "Levant dashed through the Concerto in magnificent style, getting a smooth streamlined effect and a dashing activity that brought him many deserved curtain calls," Steinfirst wrote.

But "Dirge" would not receive that kind of praise. Levant's family was merciless. His younger cousin, Oscar Radin, remembered that it

> started, and it groaned, and it wailed, and it sighed, and it lumbered; it was the most horrible-sounding thing. . . . And he was absolutely the most awkward-looking man up there on the stage you can imagine. It was a caricature. . . . And his mother—she sat there; she couldn't smile, she couldn't grimace.

When it was all over, Annie was escorted to her son's side. Levant bent down to kiss the cheek of the heavy, white-haired woman with the imposing presence and a savvy glint in her eye.

"So," she said in front of all the assembled well-wishers, "you call that a dirge?"

Modern music was still a novelty for most audiences in 1939, and, with the possible exception of Stravinsky's, few modern pieces would have been heard—and even fewer applauded—by the typical Pittsburgh Symphony audience. The local press, however, was not as brutal as the family. One reviewer wrote, with sweet reasonableness,

> . . . most of the audience would have been satisfied to have Levant content himself with his pianism rather than hear his Dirge. An ultra modern work, full of some strange harmonies difficult to grasp at first

hearing, the Dirge is well orchestrated and has a certain drive that suggests the composer's teacher Schoenberg. But it will take several hearings to establish the work more firmly in the public's affection.

Despite the lukewarm critical reception and the disapproval of Levant's family, "Dirge" would endure. Of all his compositions, it is the least mercurial and surest in tone. The opening French horn evokes the fabulous clarinet slide that announces *Rhapsody in Blue,* immediately establishing Levant's homage to Gershwin. A felicitous, show-tune melody weaves in and out of slightly dissonant, serial progressions: The mood is both anxious and lush. There is *gravitas* in this music, and deep emotion, as it moves to its funereal, yet cathartic, ending.

"I've always had a resistance (deep-seated) to loving anybody," Levant wrote to "the future Mrs. L." after they had set a date for their marriage. In April 1939 Levant had moved into roomier accommodations at the St. Hubert Hotel on West Fifty-seventh Street. "Hurry up and come here. I await December 15th as the date of my rebirth. We'll be all things in life together."

> Don't worry about closet space. You and I will evolve a practical plan I'm sure. If you want to move, we'll move. Those things will be solved but not until you're here and we can discuss them.
> If you need money for fare, etc. please let me know for you are my problem now and don't hesitate.
> From now on you're my woman.

Whatever insecurities he had about his talent and career he would often take them out on the young woman who had agreed to become his wife. Levant's love for June Gale was a kind of Jekyll-and-Hyde love, made up of two faces: the beaming, idolatrous love for his "empty-headed picture actress" and the scowling, hurt, and insecure love for the woman who had the power to reject him.

June was still conflicted about giving up her contract at 20th Century–Fox. During Levant's two stressful days in Pittsburgh she had sent him a telegram informing him that the studio had picked up her option. On November 29 June got a casting call: "You have a part in a new picture. Report to wardrobe." She telephoned Oscar in New York and asked him if he'd mind if she did just one more movie before heading east—"the last one, the absolutely final one I'd ever consider," she told him.

His answer was unequivocal and right to the point; it left no doubt in my mind whatsoever. And I believed him. And admired him. And experienced a magnificent sense of relief. Sprung!

June marched into Sol Wurtzel's office and told him she couldn't do the picture.

"Why not?" asked Wurtzel in his pebble-crushing voice.

"I'm going to get married!"

"Really! And who are you getting married to?"

"Oscar Levant."

He was a little horrified, June remembered, but he regained his composure and congratulated the young actress, adding, "He'd better be good to you or else he'll have to answer to me!"

The next day, June Gale's plane landed in Newark, New Jersey, on a landing strip that wasn't much more than a field of clover. June looked out of the window and saw Oscar waiting for her. Irene Selznick was on the same plane, and as she and June were waiting to be let through the door, they looked out and surveyed the gathering below.

"Oh, there's Oscar Levant," Irene said. "He's combed his hair for a change!" (She, of course, knew nothing of their plans.)

June finally disembarked and was reunited with Oscar. Almost immediately she heard herself paged over the airport intercom.

It was a reporter from *The Daily News*. "Miss Gale," the reporter asked, "is it true you're going to marry Oscar Levant?"

"I've never heard of such a thing!" June told the reporter, keeping her promise to Oscar not to reveal their wedding plans.

The following day, December 1, 1939, accompanied by an assistant to Morris Ernst (Levant's divorce lawyer) and Oscar's screenwriter pal Charlie Lederer, June and Oscar flew to Washington, D.C. They then drove to Fredericksburg, Virginia, where they were married. In the car Oscar turned to Ernst's young assistant and jokingly asked him, "Confidentially, do you think I'm making a mistake?"

June requested a bunch of violets to hold during the ceremony. Sweet peas were all they could find in Fredericksburg, the historical site of some of the bloodiest fighting of the Civil War. Right after exchanging vows, Levant told his bride, "You know, I only married you to get even." June merely smiled. Mrs. Oscar Levant—it would be her most demanding role.

Their marriage did not remain a secret for long. By the time Oscar and June returned to New York from Fredericksburg, word of their nuptials had traveled from one end of the country to the other. If it was hard for June to imagine the extent of her husband's celebrity, the scope of the coverage must have changed her perspective. She started to keep a scrapbook of all the news stories covering their marriage. "Info, Please! Is Levant's Bride June Gale?" demanded one headline. "Musician, Wit of Radio Program Takes Scandals Star for Bride." A "Film Actress Weds Radio Quiz Expert." In its "Milestones" column, Henry Luce's *Time* magazine announced: "Oscar Levant, 32, composer, pianist, glib-libbing expert on Canada Dry's 'Information, Please!' program; and June Gilmartin, 24, cinemactress (June Gale); he for the second time, she for the first; in Fredericksburg, Virginia."

Nowhere was mention of the marriage more ubiquitous than in the gossip columns. Winchell, who hadn't spoken to Levant in years, wrote, "Oscar Levant, who knows most of the answers, explain[ed] that June Gale married him for his beauty, when everybody knows she married him for his theatre passes."

The story was carried all across the country. The *Star Times* in St. Louis, as well as dozens of other newspapers, featured a photo of June laughing and playing the piano while Oscar leaned over her, placing his hands on top of hers on the keyboard.

When the excitement wore off, however, June Levant was faced with the situation of figuring out what to do as the wife of a famous man. "He didn't want me to act," she recalled. "He didn't want me to do anything. He *did* want me to stay home and wait for him to come home. That's what I was supposed to do."

There were other adjustments to make. June had never learned how to cook or to run a household—"My mother never taught us anything [about housekeeping] because we were so busy working," June recalled. She finally called her mother to ask for help.

"Ma, how do you cook a leg of lamb?"

"Well, stick a little garlic here and there to give it a good flavor. Put a little lemon juice and put a little oil on it."

June learned, but at first she didn't enjoy managing a house. She was intimidated by some of Oscar's friends, like Kitty Carlisle Hart and Bea Kaufman, who were fabulous, stylish entertainers. Kitty Hart in particular "ran terrific houses and supervised everything," June remembered. It would take a few years before June gained the confidence to run her household the way she thought it should be run. Decorating was another problem she didn't know how to begin to solve, though she would have help in that department from a savvy expert—the elegant Dorothy Paley. But for the time being, June had nothing to decorate; it was time to find bigger and better quarters than the St. Hubert Hotel.

June recruited her twin sister, Jane Wood, who was married to

Barry Wood, a vocalist on the popular radio show *Your Hit Parade*. The two women began looking through the real estate advertisements and combing the better neighborhoods in search of an apartment. Wherever they went, no one would rent to them. "Then we realized," June recalled, "that they saw these two good-looking girls and they might have thought we were up to hanky-panky." So they took another approach.

"How do you do? I'm Mrs. Oscar Levant, and this is Mrs. Barry Wood" they told the next landlord they met. With that out of the way, and Oscar's name a key to the city, apartment doors were flung open.

June discovered the Alwyn Court building right around the corner from the St. Hubert Hotel, not far from Carnegie Hall. The Alwyn Court, a magnificent, ornament-encrusted residence house, had been built in 1909 as a luxury building with only two apartments per floor, each with fourteen rooms, five baths, and its own ballroom. The dining rooms had parquet floors, mahogany doors, and paneled walls. Floral ornamentation adorned the woodwork. All that has changed over the years, but its most remarkable feature—the magnificent façade—remains. Nearly every inch is ornamented in the glossy style of the French Renaissance. The apartment that would be the Levants' was watched over by a salamander, part of the decorative motif worked into the terra-cotta, and two seraphs—Comedy and Tragedy—perched like patron saints just beneath the apartment windows. By 1940 the outsized apartments had been broken into smaller quarters, but the three-bedroom, three-bath apartment with the large living room June saw was just right for them. And so June and Oscar, with his Steinway grand piano, moved into the Alwyn Court.

Levant loved the neighborhood—the area from Central Park South to the theatre district included Carnegie Hall, the Stage Delicatessen, Lindy's, and the Steinway showroom on West Fifty-seventh Street. The grand piano he had moved into the apartment alongside his old upright had been given to him by the Steinway brothers in recognition of his rising fame as the foremost interpreter of Gershwin and a concert pianist of more than promising stature. At last, with Oscar's two pianos in the great living room of the Alwyn Court apartment, his decade had arrived.

26

Ghost Music

"I played Gershwin music until it exuded from
my body like an excretion of a drug."

LEVANT WOULD LATER SAY THAT THERE IS USUALLY ONE DECADE IN A
person's life that defines him—for Oscar, that decade was the 1940s.
With his marriage, the continuing popularity of *Information, Please!,*
his book about to come out, and a blossoming career as a concert
pianist, Levant finally had all he could ask for. But beneath this surface
of happiness, his nerves were beginning to fray.

The stress of "Dirge" and the Pittsburgh trip, and the secret terror
that he would be found unworthy of the invitations to concertize,
exacerbated Levant's superstitions and luck-ensuring rituals. He became superstitious about cigarettes, which he continued to chain-
smoke at an alarming rate. He began to smoke Lucky Strikes when
that company became the corporate sponsor of *Information, Please!* in
1940. Levant complained that "they had a bad habit of putting the
packs carelessly into cartons. Some cartons had them upside down."
Those packs had to be discarded. He began to insist that all his shirts
be placed in the bureau drawer with the collar facing front—they
looked less like corpses that way. Not long after their marriage, Oscar
noticed that June had turned to page thirteen in a book she was reading. He leapt from his chair and knocked the book out of her hand.

The rules were contradictory and impossible to figure out—he considered it lucky to smoke his sponsor's brand of cigarette, but any word or suggestion of the work "luck" was anathema to him. LUX soap spooked him. A beer called "Lucky Lager" made him squirm.

It seems clear that Levant's behavior had gone beyond simply carrying out actions to ensure good luck but had developed into an obsessive-compulsive disorder, also called obsessional neurosis. "Rituals have taken the place of religion with me," he realized, and in the early years and around guests he tried to perform them covertly. Secrecy is often a part of the disorder. At first his rituals gave him a kind of comfort and security, but they would eventually tyrannize him.

On December 10, 1939, he was scheduled to play the *Rhapsody* with Wilfred Pelletier conducting for the CBS broadcast of the *Ford Sunday Evening Hour,* one of the most popular concert music programs in the country. Later in the broadcast he was to play Chopin's Waltz in C-sharp and Étude in C-sharp Minor. This would be the first time Levant would play a strictly noncontemporary program. He was terrified, though he managed to acquit himself without embarrassment.

In January of the new year, he and June traveled to Cleveland, where a sold-out crowd and an eager press awaited "the music expert of the Info radio show," who was to play Gershwin's Concerto in F and, bravely, once again conduct his "Dirge." June quickly learned that it was torture being around him in the dressing room before a concert.

> I don't care how many times he did the Gershwin program, it was still "hold your breath" time. . . . I wouldn't say a word. I didn't want to be the cause of any problems. He had tremendous stage fright and anxiety; it would really start the day of the concert. Everybody would walk out of his way because one wrong word—he was waiting to blow his top.

It was a vicious cycle. The more offers that came his way, the harder they were to refuse and the greater his anxiety. If the reviews were favorable, he would have to add a new ritual to keep the gods appeased.

In Cleveland, where *A Smattering of Ignorance* was first released to coincide with his two nights of performances, the notices were very good indeed. Cleveland—only eighty miles from Pittsburgh along the Monongahela River—had recognized "Dirge" for what it was: "a work of lamentation . . . dramatic in its intensity. It seems as if the clever Gershwin jazz contraptions . . . were saying good bye to their master."

"Dirge" attempts to forge an alliance between the approaches of the two men whose musicianship he most admired: Gershwin and Schoenberg. It is also a lament, an attempt to come to terms not only with Gershwin's death but with the other deaths carried within it: the death of Rose, the death of Max Levant. But its difficulties were not failures. A later generation of conductors would rediscover "Dirge"—Michael Tilson Thomas included the piece in a 1981 program, praising its "high seriousness." For Levant, who had been so haunted by the Kaddish, the Jewish prayer for the dead, "Dirge" was the only memorial form his grieving would take.

The Cleveland reporters lay siege to Levant's room at the Wade Park Manor, where he again gave the kind of interview almost unheard of for a performer of that time. Asked how he liked being a concert pianist, Levant answered, "I don't like it—it's not my racket. And I don't like being an author—that's not my racket either.

"I used to be a much better pianist, ten years ago," Levant added. "That's when I seriously studied music. It is very hard now. I like to compose and that is what I consider myself—a composer."

The trip to Cleveland also involved a book signing at Halle Bros. & Co., a local bookstore. *A Smattering of Ignorance* was released nationally in January 1940 by Doubleday, Doran & Co., Inc., of New York, and almost immediately it became their first best-seller of the year. The book carried a cheeky dedication to Oscar's collaborator, Irving Kolodin: "With whose considerable aid I have augmented my influence and diminished the circle of my acquaintances." Levant seemed incapable of straightforward gratitude.

The introduction by Oscar's closest friend, Sam Behrman, is written with affection and insight into Levant's personality. He describes Oscar as "a character who if he did not exist, could not be imagined." He continues, "this book does reveal Oscar as something new and completely 'underivative' in his humor and point of view, in his integrity also." Behrman had always been impressed with what he called Oscar's integrity—his inability to lie, even just a little bit, to gain an advantage.

Harper's magazine had run an excerpt in October. The chapter, "Music in Aspic," caused something of an uproar when it appeared. It was devoted to one of Levant's favorite topics: conductors and orchestras. Full of deep gossip and deeper opinions, no one is spared—Toscanini, Reiner, Stokowski, Koussevitzky, Klemperer—all the

European sacred cows are gored. "I would like to have been present," Levant writes, "when Stokowski suddenly became conscious of his beautiful hands. That must have been a moment."

"Music in Aspic" is not just about conductors and orchestras but a vivid, chatty, and rather brilliant description of the power struggle between these ultimate authority figures and the musicians who serve them. Oscar characterizes every orchestra's attitude toward any new conductor as "a hundred men and a louse." For the public, hardly ever privy to these power struggles, Levant's observations shed light on a subject that until then was mostly hidden from view.

Another feature of his candor is his willingness to show himself in a bad light. In a description of Otto Klemperer: "I have a special affection for the good doctor based on his chronological rejection of my compositions." As if anticipating rejection, he is determined to beat the reader to the punch. Nowhere is this more apparent than in the remarkable fourth chapter of the book, entitled "My Life: Or the Story of George Gershwin." From its witty, revealing title to its angry and tender final paragraph, Levant's memoir of his friend has stood for the last half century as perhaps the most vivid personal portrait of Gershwin we have. This is where Levant writes, in a bantering tone that allows him to tell a truth, "two characteristics I have nurtured as the dominating influences of my life—[are] jealousy and revenge."

It was Clifton Fadiman, whom the light-verse poet Ogden Nash had once described as "The Socrates of 'Information, Please!',," who offered in *The New Yorker* the most appreciative and knowing review of Levant's best-selling book. Fadiman wisely described it as being "only incidentally about music. For the most part," he observed, "this is a book of comic myths in which many of the leading characters happen to be musicians." Fadiman reserved his highest praise for Levant's memoir of George Gershwin, calling it "remarkable," and "Probably the oddest elegy ever written . . . it is funny, outrageous, and sad."

Of course there were dissenters, some who thought the book "pasted together out of notes on Levant's conversational patter"— which is not far from the truth, though Kolodin's piecework is fairly seamless. His writing style is at times ponderous and overwrought, drowning a *bon mot* in verbiage, but Levant's satiric bite and emotionally ambivalent, sometimes plangent, tone comes through. And Levant's editor, Ken McCormick, felt satisfied that despite Kolodin's role, the book was unadulterated Levant.

In a chapter titled "The Boys Are Marching," Levant devotes himself to the rising generation of American composers, touching on his appearance at the First Festival of Contemporary American Music at Yaddo. It's here that he avenges Marc Blitzstein's insult ("Now try to write a little *music*") with his critique of Blitzstein's own composition aired at Yaddo ("like a meal consisting entirely of stained glass, with different dressings").

Levant's book satisfied Fadiman's definition of what constitutes a good, reliable read: A book must have "magic and personality"; "it should be capable of holding your attention more than once, as these qualities, if they emerge once, will emerge for all time."

As much as he admired it, Fadiman didn't consider the book a classic. "While the book is brilliant," he observed,

> it is not as brilliant as Mr. Levant's conversation: he is a dinner table wit, not a library table wit. . . . I do not want to give the impression that 'A Smattering of Ignorance' is frivolous. It isn't; it's impudent. But behind the impudence one feels Mr. Levant's real concern for music and a serious interest in his development, not as a buffoon and chartered wit, but as a composer. . . . You wouldn't think it, but he has an almost over-developed faculty for admiration. Actually he is one of the most modest and sensitive men I know, but he has worked out an amazing technique for demonstrating the opposite . . . back of all the flip-flops, the insouciance, the wisecracks, the attitudes, is a core of ascetic integrity.

The publicity machinery chugged along. In January *Life* sent a photographer to spend a typical day with Oscar and his bride. The magazine ran eight photographs of the many taken that day and published them in the February 5, 1940, issue under the title "Oscar Levant, A Musical Know-It-All, Writes Book about Music and Himself." It was great publicity for his book, and it confirmed the popular image of Levant as a Broadway boulevardier and eccentric character.

In the first ten weeks, sales for the book Levant and Kolodin had knocked out between innings were running at nearly five thousand copies a week. The book would go into four printings before Doubleday, Doran & Co. had even settled on an advertising campaign.

Not all the advertising they came up with pleased Levant, who already felt like a literary charlatan. One advertisement in particular enraged the insecure author. Doubleday published an ad that ran on Tuesday morning, the day of Levant's *Information, Please!* live broadcast. The gist of it was "After you have heard Oscar Levant on *Information, Please!* tonight, read this book."

When Levant saw the ad appearing on the day of the broadcast, he panicked. He called McCormick, accusing his editor of trying to humiliate him by putting pressure on him to "get all the answers right" on the radio program. Edith Schick knew that the broadcasts were torments to Oscar. The growing demands on Levant to concertize added to his irritability, which grew in relation to his increasing popularity. But Levant's anxieties were groundless. He came through that night and in fact answered all the musical questions correctly for several weeks after the ad appeared. By the end of February, *Smattering* had sold over 33,000 copies.

Oscar and June traveled to San Francisco for his performance with the San Francisco Orchestra under the direction of Pierre Monteux. It was a triumphant concert, but Levant felt the strain of performing, even under ideal conditions and with a sympathetic conductor. He was beginning to resent the media attention as well, feeling pigeonholed by the repetitive news articles. He told one San Francisco reporter, with a kind of wistful bitterness,

> I have been in Hollywood some twenty times. I was steeped then in most unwilling obscurity. I want to play Mozart, but it needs serenity. When I sit down to the piano, I'm not [serene]. Don't worry about me being famous. I'll be through in six months.

But that was wishful thinking. There would be no serenity—and no Mozart—for Levant. His highly successful San Francisco concert set a course for the next several years. Symphony orchestras around the country soon began preparing for their all-Gershwin evenings with Oscar Levant. In Toronto's Massey Hall, Levant joined conductor Percy Faith to play *Rhapsody in Blue;* in July, the summer air was full of Gershwin music—in an open-air concert at the Robin Hood Dell in Philadelphia, two weeks later at the Hollywood Bowl, where Levant was greeted by a tremendous crowd of 19,000. One Hollywood Bowl reviewer enthused, "[Levant] undertook a miracle in his performance of the Rhapsody . . . [his] fine pianism sent one of the largest crowds in the history of the Bowl home with tingling nerves."

That summer, Levant played the Concerto in F and the *Rhapsody* for 22,000 at Lewisohn Stadium. His appearance at the Robin Hood Dell shattered all past attendance records—close to 10,000 music lovers "jammed every available seat and overflowed to establish squatter's rights on the side embankments. Another 3,000 were turned away . . ."

To most of these fans, Oscar Levant had been a disembodied voice on the radio, a brash, funny personality who seemed to know all the answers. Now they came to catch a glimpse of him, to see just how good this entertaining know-it-all really was. In time, however, the Gershwin repertoire would not be enough. Oscar had already heard from his mother on the subject—long before. What had begun as a tribute to his lost, youthful friend, turned into an Oscar Levant event. People flocked to his concerts to hear *Levant* play, not just to worship at the Gershwin shrine.

Of course, there was a danger in all of this, as Levant knew. In *A Smattering of Ignorance* he criticized orchestras for relying on big names with questionable musical credentials to sell tickets. Levant knew that the only way he wouldn't be gone in six months would be to expand his repertoire, to have the courage to play the music he had once had the skill, training, and desire to play—Bach, Chopin, Beethoven, Brahms. The old rivalry was still there, but now it was Gershwin's music—which had helped create Levant's popularity—that stood in his way. "What makes you, breaks you," George Kaufman had once warned Oscar, and now he was finding that out for himself.

After June and Oscar's stay in San Francisco, the couple took the train to Los Angeles, where Oscar was scheduled to appear on Bing Crosby's radio program. They settled into the Beverly Wilshire Hotel.

It was great to be back in Los Angeles among old friends. Charlie Lederer was the first to call, followed by Ira and Lee Gershwin. Their hotel suite filled up with flowers sent by Sol Wurtzel. June was relieved that the concert was over, Oscar could relax now, and she wouldn't have to worry so much about saying the wrong thing. And there was a happy secret they carried to Los Angeles with them— there was going to be a baby. But for now, Oscar was still the baby of the family—impatient, indulged, moody, needing to be the center of attention.

The movies have always loved a wise guy. So perhaps it wasn't much of a surprise when, in 1940, Paramount Pictures offered Levant a movie contract. "When I informed them that I couldn't act," Levant later joked, "my modesty beguiled them and I was signed for three pictures."

The offer came from William Le Baron, Oscar's former boss at RKO. Oscar had burned a few bridges in his youth with some of the Hollywood moguls, but Le Baron's memory was short when it came to cashing in on a good thing. A type was emerging in the movies that Levant embodied—a kind of resident cynic who's brilliant but intrinsically lazy, a nocturnal creature with a good heart who is nonetheless capable of turning on you, suddenly, but who is always harshest on himself.

One of the first things Levant did after arriving in Los Angeles was to head over to the Paramount lot, where director Victor Schertzinger had begun to film scenes for *Ghost Music,* which would be retitled *Rhythm on the River* and would be Levant's first screen acting role since Paramount's *The Dance of Life* twelve years earlier.

Levant was hired to play Starbuck, a piano-playing factotum to Basil Rathbone's Oliver Courtney, a dishonest, burnt-out songwriter who hires ghostwriters to compose his tunes and write his lyrics. The two "ghosts" are played by Bing Crosby and Mary Martin, who fall in love and end up ditching Courtney to collaborate on their own tunes. The songwriting team undergoes its romantic and musical struggles in a quaint Tarrytown inn called "Nobody's Inn," under the watchful eye of Bing Crosby's lovable, misogynist Uncle Caleb.

Levant's contract specified three and a half weeks of work, an amount of time Dan Golenpaul, back in New York, was not happy about. Paramount was obligated to provide *Information, Please!* with a substitute for the loss of Oscar's services. It was the beginning of contractual problems between Levant and Golenpaul, whom Oscar liked to call "Dan Golem Paul."

The script was a disappointment to Levant:

> They gave me the script when I got off the train. I looked through three pages and then I saw the role. Starbuck. Starbuck looks annoyed. So I turned to the studio assistant and said, "Listen, my gamut of looking annoyed is very confined."

Le Baron and Schertzinger agreed to let Levant supply much of his own dialogue—after all, that was partly what they had hired him for, his snappy one-liners. The script was based on a story idea by the young Billy Wilder, but they felt it could be enlivened by Levant's ad libs.

Levant, in fact, was given a great deal of latitude—in one scene he's filmed lounging on a sofa, clearly reading *A Smattering of Ignorance,* which he then puts down both literally and figuratively with the disdainful comment "An irritating book."

Levant was nervous on the set and quarreled with the assistant director. When he was asked if they could prerecord his piano playing, Levant refused. "I'd rather not. I'd like to play it when the scene is being filmed. You see, I never play a selection twice the same way."

The assistant director acquiesced. The crew decided to indulge Levant as much as possible, as long as he didn't get in the way of filming the rest of the picture.

Skeptics thought Levant would simply walk through his role, but when the film was released that summer several critics felt Oscar had walked off with the picture—had stolen it right out from under "Der Bingle's" meerschaum.

In one of his best scenes, Levant employs his skill as a musical impersonator, which he had honed at countless Gershwin gatherings— caricaturing guests in musical passages played on the piano. Levant plays a few bars from the Second Hungarian Rhapsody, varying the tempo to parody an animated conversation Basil Rathbone is having on the telephone.

Schertzinger was worried that when Levant's weeks of filming were over, some of the "edge" he brought to the film would disappear. In fact, it does; his presence greatly enlivens what is otherwise a fizzled soufflé. Mary Martin sings charmingly, but the songs provided for her are lackluster (a serious flaw in that she and Crosby portray gifted songwriters). Bing Crosby shuffles through, relaxed to the point of somnabulism. Basil Rathbone, effectively but without much pleasure, plays a stuffed shirt. "The special distinction of *Rhythm on the River*," wrote the *New York Herald Tribune*'s Howard Barnes,

> is not Mr. Crosby, nor Mary Martin, but Mr. Levant, who has the capacity to give a vital twist to the most obvious situation. Unless I am mistaken, his screen career should be something to watch. Give "Rhythm on the River" credit for introducing him to filmgoers, even if you agree with me that it is a sluggish show.

Despite the good reviews, Levant was under no illusions that he was an actor. What he contributed to the film was not a performance so much as an attitude, a persona, that he achieved simply by showing up.

When Bing Crosby walks into Basil Rathbone's office in an early scene, he finds Oscar Levant stretched out on the divan in his rumpled suit, smoking while trying to take a nap. It is a moment lifted from Levant's real life, as if he had been carried like an emperor on a litter and lowered onto the middle of a Hollywood sound stage. No Method actor in the 1950s could have achieved such verisimilitude.

27

The Talking Pianist

"It's more fun talking about music
than listening to it."

LEVANT WAS KEENLY INTERESTED IN BECOMING A FATHER, THOUGH HE joked to his friend Curly Harris that June was already poisoning their offspring against him: "She writes nasty little notes about me and swallows them." Marcia Levant was born on October 12, 1940. Over the next several months, Levant began bringing to the apartment friends and acquaintances he happened to bump into, to show off his new baby. "He was always dragging somebody home to me," June recalled. "He ran into Barbara one day and brought her home."

"I just want to see what Barbara looks like holding a baby," Levant told his wife, placing Marcia tenderly in Barbara Wooddell's arms.

One day he brought Charlie Chaplin in to see the baby—he had run into the great silent screen actor on Fifty-seventh Street and had immediately invited him over. Judy Garland would also be escorted to Alwyn Court. After taking one look at Marcia, with her sleepy eyes and shock of dark reddish hair, Judy sighed, "Oh, I want to have a baby so much, if only MGM will let me!"

June often greeted her unexpected guests with curlers in her hair and diaper pins in her mouth—not the ideal way to meet Charlie Chaplin for the first time, or your husband's former sweethearts. But soon the couple hired a nanny and a maid who came in for a half day, and things returned to a semblance of normalcy, Levant still rising at one or two in the afternoon to begin his day.

Levant had two more pictures to make to fulfill his contract with Paramount, so the family of three, plus nanny, bundled up and piled onto the 20th Century Limited. For his second film, Levant was again teamed up with Mary Martin and director Victor Schertzinger. *Kiss the Boys Goodbye* was filmed in the spring of 1941 for a summer release date. The script, which displeased Levant very much, was based on the 1938 play by Clare Boothe Luce, a political satire that uses Selznick's search for a southern belle to play Scarlett O'Hara in *Gone With the Wind* as a ruse for taking swipes at a number of well-known New York figures. Much of the satiric bite, however, was removed when the play was turned into a breezy film musical. Levant was brought in to supply some of the acid that had been leached out of the script.

Schertzinger, who wrote the musical score for the film with Frank Loesser, knew just what to expect from Levant and how to get it. Schertzinger told one Hollywood reporter, "He's so self-conscious before the camera that the only way to get spontaneity is to let him play the clown. . . . I'd let him ramble along . . . but somewhere you'd get a brilliant flash that repaid all the effort."

When Levant complained that he hadn't had a look at the script, Schertzinger reminded him that he didn't want to look at it—that he preferred to come up with his own lines. "His favorite crack," Schertzinger told the reporter, was "It's in the script, I don't like it."

Schertzinger realized it was caffeine that kept Oscar's engine roaring. "Give him his opiate, so we can get to work," the director would bawl at the crew whenever Oscar ambled onto the set.

Though Levant was noticeably more relaxed during the filming of *Kiss the Boys Goodbye,* he was fairly contemptuous of the final product. When he arrived back in New York after his five weeks of moviemaking, he horrified the Paramount executives by knocking the picture. When asked to describe the kind of part he had just played, Levant blurted out, "It's the kind of part they give you when they have you under contract and want to get rid of you. . . . I'd love to see the review it gets in *Time.*" (Clare Boothe was, of course, married to the magazine's founder, Henry Luce.)

The reviews were unenthusiastic about Levant's presence in *Kiss the Boys Goodbye,* though they gave Mary Martin high marks and generally approved of the Schertzinger-Loesser score. Levant didn't have much to do in the film, and his dour presence is dutifully noted in most of the reviews but without the warm praise his earlier film had received.

Levant's third film for Paramount was never made because Dan Golenpaul refused to give Levant time off from *Information, Please!* After his experience with *Kiss the Boys Goodbye,* Levant was relieved and he turned his attention full time to his real "racket"—concertizing.

Upon returning to New York, Levant continued his visits with his psychiatrist, Dr. Shoenfeld. Levant was trying to get used to success. Dr. Shoenfeld advised him to try to accept his many careers and simply to do what interested him. But Levant had felt like a failure for so long; now that success had come, it wasn't what he'd thought it would be. Why did he still feel like a musical fraud, like a freak held up for the public to laugh at?

He rededicated himself to practicing the piano in his Alwyn Court living room. He knew he had to develop an "indoor" repertory as well as his "outdoor" repertory—the Gershwin crowd pleasers he tossed off at the Lewisohn Stadium, the Robin Hood Dell, and other open-air venues. His friend Irving Kolodin remembered,

> He practiced more and more. He set new goals for himself. Some of them were realistic. He never performed any of the Beethoven or Mozart concertos in public, though he knew all of Beethoven's and many of Mozart's. Tchaikovsky, Grieg, Khachaturian, Honegger, Saint-Saëns—these were composers with a sufficiently broad popular appeal for the audiences he attracted. . . . They were also composers whose music required more exacting standards of execution than Gershwin's. Mothlike, Oscar was attracted to the brightest of them.

Kolodin recalled a time when he told his friend that no one—including Levant—could hope to pick up the thread of a performing career after fifteen years and hope to match the standard attained by men like Vladimir Horowitz and Artur Rubinstein, who had done little else but practice and concertize over decades.

Inevitably it was June on whom Oscar vented his frustration. She soon understood why Oscar was so dependent on Dr. Shoenfeld. "He needed a figure to tell his problems to," she explained, "somebody to say, 'Well, now you don't have to do that if you don't want to.' "

After one argument in which Levant began yelling at her, June marched off to one of the apartment's three bathrooms and locked herself in. "Nothing infuriates me more than a locked door," Oscar had once said, and he began to kick the door with his bare foot. This happened more than once; on one such occasion Oscar broke his toe.

Levant just couldn't take the pressure of his stepped-up concert schedule. He had little time for his own compositions, now that he had agreed to a tour and was making short trips to play one-nighters in nearby cities. "He was just mildly neurotic [then]," June remembered. "He wasn't all screwed up. He was easygoing; he was chubby; he loved to eat. His success changed his looks—he dropped twenty pounds, he had such a tight schedule."

Despite the demands on his time and his increasing sense of inadequacy, Levant managed to complete two new orchestral works, *Overture 1912* and Caprice for Orchestra, and a brooding little piece called "Poem for Piano."

He hid the significance of the *Overture*'s title behind a façade of jokes. For its premiere performance with the NBC Orchestra conducted by Frank Black, Levant simply called it "A New Overture." In a WNYC radio interview in January 1941, he explained that the work had had three titles, including *Polka for Oscar Homolka,* named after the gifted Viennese character actor known for his portrayal of "heavies."

Later that year, in April, Levant would more fully describe *Overture 1912* in a program note that accompanied its performance with the Minneapolis Symphony Orchestra under the direction of Dimitri Mitropoulos:

> This overture represents an effort to break away from a kind of highly complex, harmonically involved music that I had been writing for some time under various personal influences—predominantly those of Arnold Schoenberg. It was composed primarily for entertainment; mine, at least, if not the audience's.

Levant insisted that the title had no personal significance, that 1912 had been "an unimportant year." But, despite his disclaimer, Levant's *Overture* was an intentional and ironic salute to Tchaikovsky, his mother's favorite composer. "She used to torment me with Tchaikovsky," Levant remembered and he had been jealous of that music. The title is at once a funny, self-mocking comparison with one of Tchaikovsky's best-known works (a warning to the listener not to take the piece too seriously nor judge it too harshly) and an invocation of that day in Schenley Park when five-year-old Oscar was terrorized by a sudden thunderstorm. The *1812 Overture* was the music Annie had taken her young son to hear on that summer afternoon. Though he claimed in his program note that "nothing critical happened to me in 1912," being plunged into a state of panic while he listened to Tchaikovsky with his mother is one of the few early childhood memories Levant ever records.

The music captures some of the excitement and confusion of that long-ago event. Its opening phrases evoke a carnival-like atmosphere; one can readily imagine picnickers blithely taking their places on a great lawn on a beautiful afternoon. There is excitement in the lively tempo, with traces of a darkening mood. A note of anxiousness enters, and a slower, contemplative tempo alternates with the playfulness of the opening phrases. As anxiety and lightheartedness play hide-and-seek, the self-important horns join in, adding a portentous note. Rolling drums—thunder—are heard as from a distance, and the work moves toward a disturbing climax, ending suddenly.

Whenever one of Oscar's works was performed for an audience, he went out of his way to trivialize it. On another radio interview, when asked to describe the mood of his Piano Concerto, Levant answered, "It only hurts for a minute." As conductor Michael Tilson Thomas would observe when he undertook to perform Levant's "Dirge" in 1981, "despite creating many works of high seriousness, Levant refused to dignify his compositions with the same keen musical intelligence he brought to others' work, or the work of his contemporaries."

It took a commission from Robert Russell Bennett, and Frank Black's premiering of the two new works, to cut through the layers of Oscar's self-protective sarcasm.

Caprice for Orchestra was the second orchestral piece Levant composed in the fall of 1940. It was commissioned by his old friend Bennett for *Robert Russell Bennett's Notebook* on WOR. Levant described the somewhat quirky piece in a program note: "From my standpoint this is a tuneful and simply constructed work, with no elaborate formal structure." Later, in a January 1941 radio interview just prior to conducting Caprice, he admitted that he had written the piece "in about a week," and he explained that "the form is so loose that I can protect myself by calling it 'Caprice.' " When the program moderator assured Levant that he was invited as a composer and not as one of the famous panelists on *Information, Please!*, Levant replied tartly, "I doubt it. It seems no matter how bad the music is, it's all right if I talk."

Caprice for Orchestra begins ponderously, in a minor key full of anxieties. A lovely melody appears and disappears, lightening the mood. Halfway through Levant introduces a saucy show tune— something straight out of vaudeville—then reprises it with a jazz reading. The piece is mercurial—beginning in Schoenberg, restlessly moving through Gershwin, then becoming sweet and melancholy and ending on a disturbing note. As Michael Tilson Thomas has observed about Levant's compositions, Caprice is midway between the language of popular and serial music, reflecting Levant's ambivalence as to the kind of music he really wanted to write. Despite Levant's disclaimers, Caprice for Orchestra would be conducted by the controversial English conductor Sir Thomas Beecham, and it would be performed by the Minneapolis, St. Louis, Pittsburgh, and Rochester symphonies.

Levant premiered his "Poem for Piano" on Robert Russell Bennett's program, just after a performance of the Andantino from his String Quartet. "Maybe it should be called 'Insult for the Piano,' " Levant told Bennett about the short, moody, and rather haunting piece.

"There you have the typical Oscar Levant," Bennett explained to his listeners. "He can't resist poking a little fun at the deepest of his musical thoughts. He wrote this piece while lonely and much further under the influence of modern Viennese musical ideas than he felt like being. He said he was tempted to call it 'The Lone Ranger in Vienna.' "

Bennett's *Notebook* gave Oscar the opportunity to prove himself as a composer with deep, musical thoughts.

On the 20th Century Limited heading back to New York after performing in yet another Gershwin memorial concert in Chicago, Levant was seated in the dining car with Arthur Krock of *The New York Times* and James Farley, who had recently resigned as postmaster general to protest FDR's running for a third term. Farley was an acquaintance of Levant and had been a popular guest on *Information, Please!* After dinner the three men were about to return to their compartments when Levant was stopped in his tracks by "a little man sitting in the back of the dining car, alone," who asked the pianist to join him.

Levant didn't know the fellow, who was balding, with crooked teeth, and spectacles resting on a raw-looking, Roman nose. His name was James Caesar Petrillo. Petrillo looked up at Levant and said, "You're a newspaperman."

Levant, who was approaching the height of his fame and whose picture appeared almost weekly in the newspapers, replied, "No, I'm a musician."

Petrillo insisted that Levant had to be a newspaperman. He then proceeded to pour his soul out to Levant, dominating the conversation for the rest of the evening—an unusual feat in Oscar's presence.

Levant thought Petrillo rather endearing, and he enjoyed his loquacity. The two train companions discovered they had a few things in common besides their destination—Petrillo was a good friend of Harry Levant. They also had music in common. James Caesar Petrillo, Levant discovered, was the much-feared president of the musician's union, whose iron glove reached into every concert hall, opera house, nightclub, and gin joint in America. Cartoons of the time depicted him as bearing a resemblance to Benito Mussolini, Italy's Fascist dictator who, among other things, made the trains run on time. The two men would meet again under very different circumstances.

Levant's train companions, Krock and Farley, were returning from the Democratic party's national convention, which that summer had nominated Franklin D. Roosevelt to run for a historic and unprecedented third term. Levant had always regarded Roosevelt as "the ultimate father figure," and he greatly admired Eleanor Roosevelt. He would have voted for her for president if he could have. "He loved her," June remembered.

> He even mentioned that he was within walking distance of her once and he had such a reverence for her that he didn't dare spoil it by speaking to her. You know, he really idolized her. He thought she was everything good and wonderful.

Levant's growing concern with the developments in Europe made him twice as impatient with his own progress as a concert pianist—why slave so hard over the toil of daily practice when the whole world was going to hell? In 1940 the U.S. government had established the first peacetime military draft in American history. All male citizens up to the age of thirty-five received registration cards, including Oscar Levant, who turned thirty-four at the end of that year.

At the beginning of 1941, Levant signed a new contract with Golenpaul for another season of *Information, Please!* His salary was increased to $500 for each appearance on the show. The two men had never liked each other. Levant found Golenpaul's proprietary air suffocating. Though Golenpaul returned Oscar's dislike, he knew that Levant had made himself irreplaceable on the program. He resolved that Levant's blossoming film and concert careers would not prosper at the expense of his quiz show.

Something new was emerging in Levant's 1941 concerts. He enjoyed the camaraderie of joking with the audience—it relieved his tension to be able to disarm his listeners by being the first to dismiss his music. Just before conducting Caprice with the Pittsburgh Symphony, Levant gave a spontaneous ten-minute monologue of "very funny patter" reminiscent of his radio persona. He talked about conductors, Schoenberg, his aversion to exercise, and his well-known physical inactivity, ending by plugging his book. Though it undercut the dignity of the occasion, the audience lapped it up.

At the beginning of the next concert season, he announced that he would embark on a tour to be billed as a "program of piano music with comments." The concept was not entirely new: The Russian pianist Vladimir de Pachman had toured the country as a "talking pianist," but Levant would be the first concert artist to do so since Pachman had chewed the austere scenery in his 1915 recitals. (Pachman was a famous Chopin interpreter whose antic behavior onstage earned him the nickname "Chopin-zee of pianists" from the press; he liked to remove his socks during a performance, and his constant chatter was said to have delighted his audiences.)

Levant's next concert, at Philadelphia's Academy of Music, was billed as "a piano recital with comments." Levant announced, "as I was not a good enough speaker to give a lecture nor a good enough pianist to play a recital, I was going to give two inadequate performances for the price of one."

The minute he stepped onstage, he threw his music on the floor, rubbed his eyes and thrust his hands into his pockets. "I don't know why I'm here this evening," he told the standing-room-only crowd. "Despite my manager's penchant for making money, I've never done this sort of thing before." Philadelphia's famed Curtis Institute of Music came in for its share of jibes—"they turn out a pianist every hour," Levant complained.

Levant began with his encore piece, a Chopin waltz. "It will be my only chance to play an encore, and you get to think it's time to go home," he told the audience. He next announced that he was going out for a smoke; he returned to play a Bach Partita and the first movement of Beethoven's Sonata in D Minor, Op. 31, No. 2, which he promised to play with his "customary arthritic abandon." Of the Beethoven Sonata, Levant commented that "this has never had worthy interpretation. And it still won't."

Between cheeky comments Levant played a lively performance of Gershwin's *Rhapsody in Blue,* introduced by a disclaimer: "I feel a bit naked without an orchestra." In the second half of the evening he played Brahms's Rhapsody in B Minor and Intermezzo No. 13, Opus 118 in A Major, followed by the musical fireworks of two polkas by

Shostakovich, a composer in whom Levant had long been interested. He finished with Manuel de Falla's "Ritual Fire Dance."

Scattered throughout were references to such personalities as Bob Hope, Greta Garbo, Katharine Hepburn, Orson Welles, and Gracie Allen. There were anecdotes about pianists of the past—Liszt, Paderewski, and Pachman. Occasionally he would toss out public service announcements, informing the audience how long the piece he was playing would take, in case anyone wanted to woolgather or snooze. "Be back in nine minutes!" he cheerfully warned his audience as he began the Bach Partita.

His justification for such behavior, made in mock solemnity, was his theory that a piano recital—even a good one—is a rather bitter experience for a listener and that he should do his best to keep his audience's mind off the music as much as possible. Levant was only partially kidding in expressing this opinion. His friend Dorothy Paley, a frequent companion at Carnegie Hall, remembered that he had a hard time sitting through concerts and recitals. "It made him too nervous," she recalled. "He could only take so much, then he'd leave for long stretches and come back at the end. He could sit through rehearsals, but it was torture for him to sit through an entire concert."

At the concert's end, Levant leaned back on his stool and began to applaud himself. The audience joined in with thunderous approval. Whatever the music critics might say, the public found his recitals "with comments" refreshing, entertaining, and sometimes quite moving. The high point was often the Gershwin preludes, which he played with unrivaled authority and joy.

Levant's "concerts with comments" were played from the mid-1940s through the early 1950s. There were two constants: Most of his remarks were made at his own expense, and though he provided a printed program to accompany each concert, he would rearrange his selections to suit his fancy so the public never knew exactly what it was going to hear. By scrambling each evening's repertoire, Levant exercised complete control over what he would play. It was as if, at every recital, he felt the need to reassert his independence from his father's authority over his music. Critics sometimes complained when certain pieces announced in the program were dropped. "We were disappointed," wrote one reviewer, "that Levant did not play any Debussy. Claude was on the printed program, as was Schoenberg; neither found birth on Oscar's keyboard."

Not all of Levant's concert humor was intentional. In St. Louis he appeared with the St. Louis Symphony. Upon concluding the *Rhap-*

sody to great applause, Levant worried that he would miss the train to his next concert date. He ran back onstage for his bows, and the audience insisted on an encore. Levant held up his arm and pointed to the Gershwin wristwatch. He announced pleadingly, "I've got to catch a train," then proceeded to play a Gershwin prelude. The following day, the review of Levant's concert read: "For an encore [Levant] played one of those nostalgic melodies of Gershwin, 'I Have to Catch a Train.' "

Levant's "concerts with comments" risked degenerating into a handful of showpieces strung together on a necklace of self-denigrating jokes and pitiable excuses. But somehow they were more than that. He wasn't just pandering to an audience that had liked his brash wit on *Information, Please!* and who merely tolerated serious music; his unconventional approach to concertizing evolved as the only way he could comfortably perform the music he loved with the least amount of anguish. The self-lacerating jibes were a necessity for warding off the deeper demons inherent in the act of concertizing. Critics noticed his "intensity to the point of hysteria"—a quality that added depth and danger to what might have been just an evening of fun and games.

Levant was keenly aware of what the competition was capable of, and he felt he did not measure up favorably. In one concert, after playing the first movement of the Beethoven Sonata in D Minor, Opus 31, No. 2, he concluded with, "There are two more movements, but [Artur] Schnabel can play them for you."

Levant had once asked Artur Rubinstein for advice before embarking on his first transcontinental concert tour. "Always play to your strength," the great pianist instructed him. "Be satisfied with what you've got."

"I'd be much more satisfied with what you've got," Levant shot back.

In composer David Diamond's opinion, by temperament Levant preferred being backstage to being onstage. "He loved going backstage," Diamond said. "He was either at Lindy's or backstage or at the Stork Club or '21.' And he loved being backstage with Rubinstein and Horowitz, of course, or when the Pittsburgh Orchestra came." It was this "backstage" temperament, and eventually his abandonment of daily practice, that stood in the way of his forging a truly world-class concert career. Diamond felt that Levant

> was superb. If Oscar practiced every day, he could have gone on Carnegie Hall and played a mixed [repertoire]. That's what I wanted him to do. We had programs worked out. [But] the temperament was too

completely "ga-ga"—I mean, he'd make fun. . . . He played all French music beautifully. Debussy—unbelievable! I'd say, "Oscar, please, here is the program." (I still have them written out in pencil.) Here's a great program for Town Hall. And Scarlatti—how he played Scarlatti! My God, even Horowitz used to hear him, wouldn't believe it.

On December 7, 1941, Japanese warplanes attacked the Hawaiian port of Pearl Harbor, stunning the nation into action. The United States declared war on Japan; Japan's allies declared war on the United States. Rationing of gasoline, food, clothing and other articles went into effect in 1942, and air raid sirens and blackout drills were instituted. A war bond rally was held in Gimbel's department store in New York City, auctioning off such items as Jefferson's Bible, George Washington's letters, and Jack Benny's violin. A host of public figures—actors and actresses, opera stars, musicians, and radio personalities—went on nationwide tours selling war bonds.

Whenever he was available, Levant joined his *Information, Please!* colleagues in traveling across the country selling bonds. The members of the troupe, usually accompanied by Golenpaul and his assistant, Edith Schick, were hailed as conquering heroes wherever they appeared. Once in a while families would come along—June and their daughter, Marcia, held in her father's arms, appear in group photographs at the train station. A caravan of local dignitaries met them at every stop along the way. At Boston's Symphony Hall they sold $4,036,000 worth of war bonds. In Cleveland, Levant and company sold $50 million worth in a live broadcast at the Cleveland Music Hall.

Levant found the tours a necessary evil—they were exhausting, and they often took him away from his young family. The tours were treated as publicity stunts for many of the entertainers he traveled with. Levant, who had no press agent or personal manager, would avoid such star-making machinations throughout his entire career.

On his brief trips home to Alwyn Court, Levant began preparing one of the works he had completed under Schoenberg's benign tyranny, his Piano Concerto, for its first performance with the NBC Orchestra. This was the piece Levant had stubbornly refused to play for Klemperer that afternoon at a gathering at Salka Viertel's, instead breaking into a rousing rendition of "When Irish Eyes Are Smiling." It was the work into which he had inserted a jazz strain, purposely undercutting the Schoenbergian purity of the composition. But despite these attempts at sabotage, Levant cared deeply about his Concerto—it was the first piece he had written under Schoenberg, and it was his first attempt to break away from Gershwin's musical influence.

The premiere of Levant's Piano Concerto was scheduled for February 17, 1942, as part of the NBC symphony's live radio broadcast from Studio 8-H in Radio City. The conductor was Alfred Wallenstein, whose career, like Oscar's, had flourished on the radio.

Behind a glass enclosure which separated him from some of New York's leading music critics, like witnesses at an execution, Levant performed with the NBC Orchestra. The critics listened to the music through headphones while furiously scribbling notes. Among them, music critic and composer Virgil Thomson was there to review the NBC concert for the *New York Herald Tribune*. Thomson had collaborated with the avant-garde, expatriate writer Gertrude Stein on an opera entitled *Four Saints in Three Acts*. In 1948 he would win a Pulitzer Prize for his score for the documentary film *Louisiana Story*. During the fourteen years he served as music critic for the *Tribune*, Thomson established himself as one of the most respected critics of his day. Levant especially admired his score for the Pare Lorenz documentary film *The Plow That Broke the Plains*.

Thomson described Levant's concerto as "rather dramatic and dissonant" for conventional tastes, lacking an "essential musical idea," yet he perceived the muscularity of the music beneath its occasional confusions.

Oscar Levant's Piano Concerto is a rather fine piece of music. Or rather it contains fine pieces of music. Its pieces are better than its whole, which is jerky, because the music neither moves along nor stands still. The themes are good; and if they are harmonically and orchestrally overdressed, they are ostentatiously enough so that no one need suspect their author of naïveté. The rhythm is lively, too, and the expression, for the most part, direct and easily comprehensible. . . .

Maybe a too long working over destroyed its original unity. As music it is honest and charming and, for all its pseudo complexity, straightforward. At least, each passage is straightforward. It is the spiritual isolation of the passages one from another [that] gives the whole a reserved and compartmental quality that weakens its impact.

Nevertheless, the impact of Mr. Levant's battling personality is not absent. His music, like his mind, is tough and real and animated by a ferocious integrity. . . . Its off moments are like the Sunday afternoon of a pugilist, all dressed up and no place to go. . . .

[F]or all its not being, I think, a completely successful work, it is friendly music and good music, all of it. It is even, beneath its trappings of schoolboy homage to Gershwin and Schoenberg, hard and lonely and original music, full of song and solitude. I sometimes wish Levant would not work so hard at being a composer. He seems afraid to relax and let music write itself. But every man must scale Parnassus in his own way. Maybe the hard way is the only one he would feel right about taking.

Levant felt that Thomson "was not taken by [his] exercise in relentless atonality," and he misconstrued Thomson's review as entirely negative, though the critic clearly respects and admires the Piano Concerto despite certain limitations. It was difficult for Levant to accept any kind of approval of his work. However, the two men became friends and attended many Carnegie Hall concerts together.

Curiously, negative reviews of Levant's work—no matter how damning they might be—did not send him into a dark, raging mood. Perhaps because he had had enough self-criticism to last a lifetime, and because honesty was important to him—he couldn't abide phonies or pomposity—he appreciated honest criticism from those he respected. It was *praise* he couldn't handle.

Levant's Piano Concerto would be performed the following year, and it would have some half-dozen performances throughout the 1940s. Levant, however, would soon give up composing. He never wrote about why he stopped—it could have been that the favorable reviews put too much pressure on him. In any case, success did not breed success. Or, as Virgil Thomson intuited, Levant derived little pleasure from composing. It was something he felt he *ought* to do, but his perspiration too often left its mark on his compositions. Just as he once told a reporter in San Francisco that he did not have the serenity to play Mozart, he felt that his concert career had robbed him of the serenity to compose. And he had allowed his heavy concert schedule to make composing virtually impossible. After Caprice for Orchestra and *Overture 1912,* Levant would virtually end his composing career.

28

A Bargain for
a Dedication

"Talent's like a baby.
Wrap it up in wool and it goes to sleep."

ON LEVANT'S TRIP TO LOS ANGELES TO APPEAR IN *KISS THE BOYS Goodbye,* he met up with his former mentor. A few years earlier, in January 1939, Schoenberg had written to Levant to ask his help in getting into ASCAP, the American Society of Composers, Authors, and Publishers, which made sure that songwriters and composers were compensated when their works were performed. Schoenberg was broke, bitter that he was cut off from receiving German royalties for performances of his work abroad. His slightly peevish letters—in slightly broken English—indicate how much their relationship had changed since Levant had been Schoenberg's student, now that Levant was famous:

> Dear Mr. Levant:
> The only thing I heard from you was over the radio last week. Why don't you write me once in a time?
> Today I have to ask you something very urgent and serious, and I hope you will not deny to help me.
> Longtime ago you wanted [to] induce Gershwin to recommend the

ASKAB [sic] to accept me as a member. Either you forgot it or Gersh-win. Or have they refused to take me?

Now I want to ask you to do this yourself. You are a man of a great reputation now in New York and I am sure if you go immediately and talk to them, they would not refuse to accept me . . .

Schoenberg goes on to remind Oscar that "If you need details of my biography, you find them in Grove's dictionary."

Levant did not respond until March 6 to what must have been a painful letter for Schoenberg to write, but he did sponsor an application to ASCAP for his former teacher. Schoenberg wrote to him again, in April and finally in October of 1939: "How are you? Do you compose? Do you still remember that you studied with me? I hear you sometimes on 'Information, Please' which amuses me very much."

When they met up again in Los Angeles in 1942, Levant asked Schoenberg if he would write a piano piece for him, promising his old teacher a down payment of $500.

"Suddenly," Levant later described, "this small piano piece burned feverishly in Schoenberg's mind and he decided to write a piano concerto." Schoenberg wrote to Levant suggesting that for the commission of his Piano Concerto, now well under way—to be under exclusive contract with and dedicated to Oscar Levant—he would require $5,000. There was no doubt in Schoenberg's mind that his former pupil's fame and success had put him into a position to pay such an amount.

Levant was stunned. He had had no intention of commissioning $5,000 worth of music nor any idea how to extricate himself from the situation, so he said nothing. Six months later, Schoenberg wrote to Levant, on August 8, 1942, that he was mailing him "the first 132 measures of 'your' piano concerto."

Levant took this new complication back to Dr. Shoenfeld, whom he was still seeing regularly. "The negotiations had suddenly become frenzied," he felt, "and the familiar father figure was suffocating to me. I couldn't stand it."

The two men exchanged several letters trying to work out the negotiations; Schoenberg suggested Hanns Eisler to act as a go-between. Levant wrote that he "was delighted with the wonderful quality of the concerto" but felt the price was far too high. Schoenberg pointed out the advantage of the exclusive contract he was offering—no one but Levant would be allowed to premiere his Piano Concerto, and of course it would be dedicated to him.

Levant sent Schoenberg a letter on October 6 stating that $5,000 was out of the question and offering $500 instead. Schoenberg wrote back and suggested $1,000 as "a very good bargain for a dedication." Schoenberg felt that the theme of escape from the Nazis and finding safe harbor in Los Angeles would especially interest Levant, the son of Jewish immigrants; Levant thought Schoenberg might have inserted an anagram of his name into the main row of tones. But Levant felt trapped and overwhelmed, so he sent a telegram to his former mentor withdrawing "utterly and irrevocably" from the entire venture.

Ultimately, the Piano Concerto would have another patron, to whom the piece was finally dedicated—Henry Clay Shriver, a former student of Schoenberg's protégé Gerald Strang and a UCLA alumnus. Nonetheless, Schoenberg still hoped that Levant would premiere the piece with the NBC Orchestra under Leopold Stokowski on February 6, 1944, and he sent Levant the completed score. David Diamond remembers Levant practicing the Piano Concerto, trying to get it ready for the February 6 performance. Diamond helped Levant prepare, and the two men would often walk from the Alwyn Court to the Steinway brothers' showroom, where they would play Schoenberg's concerto, side by side, on two pianos. Levant played the first section in old Viennese waltz time, "with a marvelous kind of feeling, just delicate—beautiful," Diamond remembered.

"Oscar, it's beautiful," he told the pianist. "It's not . . . that dry Schoenberg."

"Yeah, it's better than the violin concerto. I agree. You think it's going to be okay?"

"Oscar, it's going to be a beauty because it opens this way. Schoenberg must have some sense of your playing and he knows how you play so it's going to be wonderful!"

"Well, let's hope so."

Levant continued to practice the Piano Concerto. But as the deadline approached, he found himself unable to continue. His usual hatred of deadlines and expectations paralyzed him. Though he respected Schoenberg enormously, his "boss-hating attitude" reared up to jeopardize the whole undertaking.

Once Schoenberg realized that Levant would not be ready for the premiere, he gave the piece to Eduard Steuermann, the gifted pianist who had studied with Schoenberg in Vienna and Berlin. Levant had always had rivalrous feelings toward Salka Viertel's brother, who was clearly a favorite of Schoenberg's. Levant's Concerto was now in Steuermann's hands, and Levant was unhappy about it.

"Oscar, don't get yourself into this tizzy!" Diamond had cautioned his friend. He was worried about the amount of coffee and cigarettes Levant was consuming, and how they made his hands shake. "Oscar, you're going to be a wreck. Stop this! Steuermann is giving all his time to the Concerto."

"So what? I do it in my own time. Gershwin never banged me on the head when I had to play anything."

"Look, Schoenberg is different. He's getting on in years. Please, Oscar, don't be angry with him. You commissioned it—it's wonderful."

"Schoenberg should be grateful to me," Levant groused.

Diamond felt that it was typical of Oscar to be unaware that when a composer is writing a work for you there is a deadline involved. And Stokowski, who would premiere the piece, was known to be obsessive about deadlines.

Schoenberg later asked Diamond, "Why should Oscar play the Concerto when Steuermann spent hours learning it and Oscar didn't even bother to tell me if he's ready to play it? Oscar's always away playing George's music!"

It is hard to know exactly why Levant backed away from the commission and the premiere of Schoenberg's Piano Concerto, given his high regard for Schoenberg and the status it would have bestowed on him. Certainly $5,000 was too stiff a fee for Levant to pay, but $1,000 was manageable—"a very good bargain," in Schoenberg's words, for a dedication. It's likely that Levant could not accept such grand approval from a father figure. Such a gift—exclusive rights to a great work dedicated to him—was not meant for Levant. His bitterness over Steuermann's appropriation of the Concerto caused him virtually to break off communications with his old teacher.

A few years later, during one of his junkets to Los Angeles, Levant ran into Schoenberg on the street in Beverly Hills. The first question out of Schoenberg's mouth was "Are you composing?"

"I have forgotten how," Levant answered.

"One never forgets."

Feeling, perhaps, a bit ashamed about abandoning his commitment to Schoenberg's Piano Concerto, Levant suddenly said, "I owe you some money."

The old man nodded in agreement, and Levant gave him a check for $100, which Schoenberg cheerfully accepted. Levant didn't really feel that the money was owed, but it was a way of ameliorating his bad conscience about the whole affair—"Christ, what a foul-up" was how he later characterized it.

• • •

On August 6, 1942, June and Oscar welcomed their second child into the world: another girl, whom they named Lorna. Oscar was now unquestionably part of a family again—not just the borrowed households he had haunted during the 1920s and 1930s but a family of his own. He was thrilled with both of his tiny girls—photographs show him doting over sloe-eyed Marcia, her thick, curly hair cascading around her pretty face, or holding both girls in their matching pinafores while they playfully squirm away from him. Because Oscar had married a Catholic, a decision which didn't seem to trouble his mother despite her earlier complaints about her sons' choices, Levant liked to refer to his wife and children as "the goyim." In truth, Levant was, deep down, a family man, and he reveled in his two lively daughters.

But there was trouble in Paradise. To begin with, Dan Golenpaul's suzerainty over *Information, Please!* and his intellectual pretensions were designed to antagonize Levant, who could barely conceal his contempt for the producer. Levant was getting tired of the numerous war bond tours they were booked on. He never did like to be away from his favorite haunts for long, and now he hated to be separated from his wife and daughters. Being away from home also fed Levant's possessiveness about his wife.

It started with his not wanting June to continue her acting career in New York. Soon it extended to his not liking her to go out with her girlfriends or sisters. Once he followed her, showing up in a restaurant to see whom she was meeting for lunch. It turned out to be an innocent lunch date with a girlfriend—but Levant still felt jealous. He wanted June entirely to himself. So it pained him to be away on tour; it filled him with all sorts of dreadful fantasies.

It had become a custom during the World Series to have "Lefty" Gomez, a pitcher for the New York Yankees and one of the wittiest fellows in baseball, appear as a guest on *Information, Please!* Gomez, in fact, was sometimes called "the Oscar Levant of baseball," for his rapid-fire delivery and sharp mind, and for his habit of belittling himself. Oscar, still a tremendous baseball fan, enjoyed Gomez's guest appearances.

After one such appearance, Gomez presented Oscar with a baseball autographed by all the New York Yankees. As he handed the treasure over to Levant, Golenpaul snatched the ball away. "You don't want this," the producer said.

Angered, Oscar grabbed it back and then hurled it, full force, at Golenpaul, hitting the producer squarely on the chest.

John Kieran and the others quickly stopped a fight breaking out between the two men. But Golenpaul was determined to strike the last blow. He went to the new agency that handled the program, which was now under the sponsorship of the H. J. Heinz Company, and told them Levant had to go. Unfortunately for Golenpaul, in his anxiousness to put a lock on Levant's services for *Information, Please!* he had written him into an ironclad contract that succeeded in binding Levant not only to the quiz show but to Golenpaul as well.

It wasn't a pleasant situation for either man. By 1943 *Information, Please!* had become a suffocating chore for Levant, despite the doors it had opened. It was like a genie who refuses to go back into the bottle after it has granted your deepest wish.

Throughout the 1940s, Levant's popularity on *Information, Please!* led to numerous guest spots on other radio broadcasts. He was all over the dial as almost every major program pressed him into service. In January 1943, he teamed up with George S. Kaufman as cohost of a show called *Carnival* on WOR radio. Kaufman and Levant presided over a variety show that, in the words of *Daily News* radio reviewer Ben Gross, "registered as the best new show to hit the airwaves in many months." The first airing of *Carnival* featured—what else?—*Rhapsody in Blue* with Levant at the piano and Benny Goodman on clarinet belting out that beautiful opening glissando. Kaufman and Levant abandoned the project after six weeks, however, as their busy schedules drew them in other directions. They also weren't getting along particularly well. Both men were hypochondriacs, and each complained that his symptoms and ailments were the real thing. "I'm sicker than you are!" Levant would tell Kaufman. Kaufman would show him his medications and say, "No, you're not!"

Levant also appeared many times on the *The Bell Telephone Hour,* and on programs hosted by Frank Sinatra, Jack Benny, and Fred Allen—an entirely new, post-Jolson generation of entertainers who came into their own on radio. Levant never thought of himself as a comedian; he never told a joke in his life. But the timing and delivery of his quips and insults earned him the respect of professional radio comedians. Jack Benny persuaded Levant to be his accompanist for his Carnegie Hall debut when the comedian was invited to play the violin as part of FDR's birthday concert.

Levant always thought that he was at his best on *The Fred Allen Show.* The two men, who were both living in the Alwyn Court at the time, would meet regularly for lunch in a nearby drugstore, where Levant would bring up all the great old names in show business, only to hear Fred Allen "rap them mercilessly." Levant reveled in Allen's curmudgeonly opinions—Allen was about the only personality on the radio Levant could stand to listen to.

In the early months of 1943, Levant seemed to have reached some understanding and acceptance of the direction in which his talent was leading him. His reluctance to return to composing hardened into a decisive break with that part of his life. Appearing as soloist with the National Symphony Orchestra at Constitution Hall, Levant told the *Washington Star,*

> I am finished. You can't dispense the kind of work I do—bond sales, radio talks, canteen performances, recitals—and create music. Composing is reflective. It is not as artistic as people think. It is hard work. . . .
>
> A serious composer cannot write popular music. It isn't that he is snobbish. It's simply not in his realm. His gift lies in only one direction, and he must pursue it.

Here was Levant turning his back on the road Gershwin had opened up for him: the possibility of composing for both Carnegie Hall and Tin Pan Alley. Maybe Vernon Duke had had the right idea, to split himself into two people and compose different music under two different names. Levant was not another Gershwin after all. He was finally what his mother had struggled for all those years: a concert pianist, no longer a composer or songwriter. But another door would soon open: Levant's pianistic gifts were about to be recognized in another arena.

"Yesterday, I finally enticed Oscar Levant into a studio," wrote Goddard Lieberson in a memo to a Columbia Records executive.

> And the expected happened. He wants to make records. I am quite convinced. . . . Levant is really an excellent pianist, and I think it would be commercially advantageous to do an album of small pieces and call it "An Oscar Levant Recital."

The idea of making a serious record with Levant had been kicked around at Columbia Records throughout the summer of 1942. The question was just how to present Levant as a recording artist and what material he should record for his Masterworks debut. Lieberson heard Levant try out his "concert with comments" in the studio that August and was convinced that his first album ought to be a "sort of compendium of Oscar Levant favorites through the ages, going back as far, let us say, as Bach."

Lieberson was thirty years old and had been at Columbia Records for just three years before he was tapped to become director of its Masterworks Division. William S. Paley had paid a mere $700,000 for the wobbly, Depression-battered company. In 1946 Lieberson would become the company's vice president.

Lieberson was a well-liked man who seemed to have gotten along with all sorts of difficult personalities. Both men were the sons of Russian Jewish immigrants, though Lieberson had been born in England and raised in Seattle, Washington. Both had been musical prodigies. But there the similarities ended. Lieberson was elegant, well mannered, a joy to work with, a great kidder who, like Fred Astaire, "[wore] the most cheerful looking combinations of suits and shirts and ties," as one writer observed. They were an incongruous pair to the casual observer—the sartorially splendid Lieberson next to the most negligently dressed man in New York.

Leonard Bernstein, who would become a close friend of Lieberson's and would have a tetchy relationship with Levant, said at one point that Lieberson possessed *rachmunos*, a Yiddish word meaning empathy or compassion. Lieberson saw through Levant's growing reputation for being difficult, insecure, and bad-mannered, and felt that his intelligence and humor were worth the sometimes harrowing price of admission. They became lifelong friends.

Levant's first album released by Columbia Records was called *A Recital of Modern Music,* and it comprised four ten-inch, 78-rpm records: a Shostakovich Prelude and the Polka from *The Age of Gold;* two études by a young Soviet composer named Valery Jelobinsky; two pieces by Debussy—"Les Collines d'Anacapri" and "Jardins sous la pluie"; the Minuet from Ravel's "Sonatine"; and the first movement—the only one he liked—of his own "Sonatina." The album begins with Gershwin's three Preludes, which had earned warm praise throughout Levant's concertizing.

Levant's recording career, like his careers in film, radio, and eventually television, would span the technical innovations in the medium. He began his recording career on the same kind of heavy, 78-rpm discs he and his mother had once listened to in the parlor behind the jewelry store back in Pittsburgh. And within a few years— by 1948—he would be recording music on the industry's most spectacular breakthrough—the development of the 33⅓-rpm long-playing record, an innovation championed by Goddard Lieberson.

Levant next recorded Gershwin's Concerto in F with Andre Kostelanetz conducting the Philharmonic Symphony Orchestra, which earned high praise from Irving Kolodin:

> he plays the music infinitely better than Gershwin ever did or could . . . there are several sections of the piece (especially in the first movement) which are essentially improvisatory in character; and Levant treats them as just that rather than trying to establish a false unity with conventional musical form.

In 1945 Levant and the Philadelphia Symphony Orchestra, led by Eugene Ormandy, recorded *Rhapsody in Blue.* The orchestra Oscar had heard as a young boy in Demmler's music appreciation class was now his recording partner in presenting the *Rhapsody* twenty-one years after its debut in Aeolian Hall. With these and subsequent recordings, Levant became identified, in a way unimaginable even to him, with Gershwin's music.

Almost instantly—by January 1946—Levant's album of *Rhapsody in Blue* became the number one classical recording in *Billboard*'s listing of best-sellers. It would remain one of Columbia's top-selling albums for the next ten years. But it was Levant's recording of the *Second Rhapsody* and the *"I Got Rhythm" Variations,* made in July 1949 with Morton Gould conducting his orchestra, that were considered "supreme," as Gershwin biographer and musicologist Robert Kimball has observed.

Levant's selections in these and subsequent recordings present him as a kind of Romantic modernist. In the fifties Columbia would release an anthology of *Levant's Favorites,* which included Falla's "Ritual Fire Dance" and "Miller's Dance" (from *"The Three-Cornered Hat"*), Lecouna's Malagueña (which he would later dismiss as a piece of fluff), Poulenc's "Pastourelle" and "Mouvements perpétuels," the Spanish modernist Albéniz's Tango in D Major, Op. 65, No. 2, and seven works by Debussy. By the fifties, Levant was trying to advance beyond his identification with Gershwin. His affinity for the almost brutal rhythms of the Spanish dance in the Falla selections showcased his power as a pianist and his superb mastery of tempo. And his clear preference for Debussy reflects not only his indebtedness to Sigismond Stojowski but his taste for limpid, Romantic delicacies.

Levant would turn out albums by the dozen, recording eight concerti and countless piano works of Liszt, Debussy, and Chopin. Lieberson's gamble had paid off. There would eventually be over one hundred recordings.

Though he could perform in the recording studio without stage fright, his nervousness and perfectionism derailed him in other ways. On one occasion, when he recorded Schoenberg's Six Little Pieces for Piano, Op. 19, he played perfectly until he came to the last chord, marked *pianissimo piano*. Levant became obsessed about playing the chord exactly as Schoenberg had intended; he struck the piano so weakly that no sound emerged. Everyone in the studio, including Levant, laughed, but the record was never released. He had become unbearably touchy—even an innocent mistake on an album cover was perceived as a personal affront, an attempt to humiliate him, and he responded with a wrathful phone call to the guilty party. Lieberson made sure it was changed in the next printing. Levant became unglued when an advertisement for his recording of the Gershwin Concerto made with the Philadelphia Orchestra was left out of the orchestra's program booklet. Levant put in a febrile call to Columbia Records and demanded that flyers be placed in all of the programs.

Overwhelmed by *Information, Please!,* his moviemaking, a tight concert schedule, and now his recording career, tiny fault lines began to appear all over Oscar's personality.

29

"Again, the *Rhapsody*?"

"It got very Pirandelloish."

THE WHOLE THING MADE HIM A LITTLE UNCOMFORTABLE. THE IDEA OF making a movie about the life of George Gershwin had been knocking around Hollywood as early as August 1937, just weeks after the composer's death. Now Warner Bros. was going ahead with it. In fact, no fewer than ten writers would work on the Gershwin movie, including Clifford Odets and Ira Gershwin himself, whose legal blessing was needed by the studio in order to move ahead with the project. Ira wrote to a friend during the early stages of the film:

Outside of our immediate family and an occasional character like Oscar Levant the rest of the cast is entirely fictional as is the love story.
There are great difficulties today in casting as the army has taken most of the possible leading men.
Odets seems to have caught the spirit of George and his work very well and I have my fingers crossed.

Clifford Odets worked on the script in a bungalow on the Warner Bros. lot, where the other scenarists complained about Odets's phonograph, which blared Gershwin music all day long. (Whether to

move Odets to another bungalow or to send him home to work became the subject of a flurry of memos between studio executive Hal
Wallis and Jack Warner, the tyrannical paterfamilias of Warner Bros.)

Despite Ira's vote of confidence, Odets's script turned out to be
more *Sturm und Drang* than the studio moguls had bargained for—over
eight hundred pages, more about Odets and the struggles of a suffering
artist than about the wildly successful composer. The left-leaning
Odets even went so far as to make Gershwin pro-Communist, which
couldn't have been further from the truth. When Levant read Odets's
script, he said to Ira, "You know what Cliff's done? He's written his
own life, but with song hits." Clifford Odets's script would not be used
at all, but it would be resurrected a few years later for another Warner
Bros. film, *Humoresque,* about a Lower East Side violinist who makes
good.

The greatest difficulty in coming up with a compelling story line
was the apparent lack of conflict in Gershwin's life. George's life was
the stuff of great music, not great drama, Oscar felt. He commiserated
with the writers who were searching for signs of angst. "There was
almost none," Levant believed. "He was the most extroverted person
I've ever known"—though Levant should have guessed that the
Gershwin family's lack of affection must have pained George. The
scriptwriters settled on two points of conflict: Gershwin's driven ambition to compose both popular and concert music before running
out of time (clocks and stopwatches occur as a motif throughout the
film) and two unhappy love stories developed to give Gershwin some
angst (both women reject him, not wanting to play second fiddle to
his career).

As soon as Warner Bros. received the go-ahead, the studio approached Levant. He was, ironically, at first under consideration to
play George Gershwin in the movie—just at the point when he had
given up composing either popular or serious music; that is, given up
all psychic claim to being another George Gershwin. But then the
studio heads hit upon the brighter idea of having Oscar Levant play
Oscar Levant, a role to which he already brought considerable experience.

Levant first asked Warner Bros. for $40,000 to appear in the pic-
ture. The studio balked. As the year wore on and Oscar's concert
schedule became more hectic, negotiations for his services reached
the boiling point. "He is now asking $25,000 for three weeks and five
thousand weekly thereafter" read one anxious memo to Colonel
Warner. (In April 1943, the movie mogul had been appointed a lieu-

.tenant colonel in the Army Air Corps, though he continued to work at the studio.)

Now, for the first time in his life, Levant was making good money. A listing of his various concert fees prepared by the studio during contract negotiations illustrates just how lucrative his concertizing was. Levant was one of the first pianists to play on a percentage take of the house. As his popularity soared, his concert fee went from $1,500 for a single concert in 1941 (giving him an annual income of $81,850 from concertizing alone) to his highest fee for a single concert, $4,630, in 1944. By 1943—the year he signed a contract with Warner Bros.—his concert fees exceeded those of Vladimir Horowitz and Artur Rubinstein. In addition, by 1943 he was being paid $1,700 for guest appearances on the radio. (Golenpaul, however, kept him to his contracted $500 per show.) Levant finally settled on a salary for appearing in *Rhapsody in Blue* of $4,166.66 per week for a guaranteed six weeks of work, plus an additional $2,000 for recording the Concerto in F for the sound track.

Appearing in *Rhapsody in Blue* would be a weird, unsettling experience for him. It would be like entering a hall of mirrors in which life imitates art imitating life. Levant was hired not only to play himself but to act as a source of information about Gershwin's music, his personality, how he dressed, what his last apartment looked like—the arrangement of his furniture, where the pictures were hung, and so on. He would also, as in past films, contribute dialogue to many of his scenes, mostly recounting the remarks and witticisms that had long circulated in Lindy's and the gossip columns and had made it into his book.

It was Oscar's task to re-create his Gershwin friendship for the director, Irving Rapper, and the film's producer, Jesse Lasky. The handsome, fresh-faced newcomer Robert Alda was signed to portray George Gershwin. With his sleek black hair and high forehead, he did indeed resemble Gershwin—with a nose job.

There was so much wrong with the picture that Levant didn't know where to begin. Even before he reported to wardrobe to be outfitted in a duplicate of the same dark suit he was wearing when he showed up, Levant tried to change the direction of the film, to force it to measure up to the life he had known with Gershwin. But it was an impossible task. Finally, the greatest verisimilitude the film would have would be Levant's performance as himself, although the film did get George's rather impersonal treatment of Oscar right.

Levant was skeptical about the script's many mutations. "Even the lies about George were being distorted," he complained. For example, Ira and George are shown clasping each other's hands toward the end of the picture, yet "The Gershwins were the most undemonstrative family I ever saw," Levant remarked.

Levant felt that most of the writers assigned to the picture were inhibited by the amount of music to be included in the film, leaving little room for dialogue or dramatic action. In going over the music, however, Levant was surprised to see that only a few of George's early songs would be used. He was further surprised that a lengthy sequence was devoted to Gershwin's *Blue Monday Blues,* the one-act opera that had been dropped from *George White's Scandals* because its melodramatic ending was deemed too depressing.

"Why are you giving so much attention to a forgotten work?" Levant asked Jesse Lasky about its inclusion.

"Well, we need a failure—a setback—for some contrast," he explained. It had been hard to find a filmable Gershwin flop. "Almost all of the songs in the Gershwin catalogue were hits."

"They wouldn't have that trouble doing *my* life story," Levant retorted.

"It got very Pirandelloish" was how Levant described the six weeks he spent filming *Rhapsody in Blue,* especially on his first day on the set. The first scene on the shooting schedule called for the re-creation of Paul Whiteman's 1924 "All Jazz" Concert at Aeolian Hall. The scene featured Robert Alda as Gershwin seated at the piano and Paul Whiteman conducting (he was among the host of characters conscripted to play themselves—Al Jolson, George White, Hazel Scott, Oscar Levant). For the sake of accuracy, Paul Whiteman shaved off his mustache in order to don a fake one made by the makeup department to resemble the skinny moustache he had worn in 1924. The once-corpulent Whiteman had dropped seventy-five pounds since that famous concert; he now had to conduct the orchestra wearing a specially padded suit to re-create the extra weight he used to carry around with him like the portmanteau of a traveling salesman.

Levant had previously recorded the Concerto in F for the sound track, and now he was being photographed in the balcony as part of the audience, reveling in Gershwin's performance of the Concerto. "The camera was supposed to catch me as part of the audience in the balcony of Aeolian Hall going nuts about the performance . . . there were those guys, Alda and Whiteman, on the stage, taking bows for music I myself had [recorded] and which I was applauding them for," he remembered.

Making the film involved an exhumation of Gershwin's era. The real-life characters—Whiteman and Jolson, for instance—literally hauled their paraphernelia out of mothballs to re-create their moments in the Gershwin story. Jolson (always a monumental pain on a movie set—he ended up being barred from the set of his own movie biography some years later for his relentless interfering and for conducting unbecoming a legend) was present to reenact the night he first sang "Swanee" in *Sinbad* at the Winter Garden Theatre in 1917. Jolson had been sick with malaria and pneumonia when filming began. He had just returned from entertaining troops overseas when he was stricken, but he managed to recover sufficiently to appear, in blackface, in *Rhapsody*.

Jolson applies his makeup in front of the cameras and wears the identical costume he wore in 1919, having kept it all these years for sentimental reasons. Jolson looks a trifle sad that the George Gershwin story isn't about him.

Rhapsody in Blue dominated the Warner Bros. lot that summer, with its fifty-eight different interiors and twenty-three exterior sets, including George and Ira's boyhood flat, Max Dreyfus's inner office, and the Harms reception room, where we first see Oscar Levant in the midst of a fruitless wait to show Max Dreyfus his stuff.

"You're fresh," Dreyfus's secretary, Irene Gallagher, tells Oscar when he presses her for an appointment with the music publisher.

"Unfortunately, you are not," Levant retorts. He lets out a wolf whistle that turns into the opening notes of Tchaikovsky's First Piano Concerto.

In this scene, the film takes a liberty with the truth as far as the Levant-Gershwin relationship is concerned. George enters the office and sits down next to Oscar, who introduces himself and takes a sneak look at Gershwin's score of "Swanee." Levant begins to hum the tune approvingly and says, "Hmm. Diminished ninth. If I had your talent I'd be a pretty obnoxious fellow."

Of course, Oscar didn't really meet Gershwin in the Harms waiting room. Phil Charig, the man who took a youthful Oscar up to the Gershwin flat to meet George while he worked on the Concerto in F with William Daly, is completely written out of the picture (just as Levant had completely supplanted him in the Gershwin circle).

Levant then leans toward Dreyfus's annoyed secretary. "How would you like to sponsor me through college?" he says to her before strolling nonchalantly out of the waiting room. And then, "You loathe me, don't you?"

Though the facts are bent to tell a story, this scene does capture Levant's picketing of booking agents and music publishers when he first came to New York. It also captures Levant's cheekiness and a lightheartedness that was missing in his first two Paramount films. And it captures his professional jealousy, which is neutralized by his candid humor. Levant is insouciant and confident in this scene and throughout the film as he ambles through the movie with an almost proprietary air.

The film was produced on a massive scale. Fourteen concert theatre interiors had to be constructed for *Rhapsody in Blue,* including Aeolian Hall, Carnegie Hall, Lewisohn Stadium, the Los Angeles Philharmonic auditorium, and the Comédie-Française of Paris, as well as the Winter Garden, the Music Box, and the Apollo Theatre. Times Square was also re-created, and three thousand dress extras were employed to appear as audiences in all of these venues. Over a thousand musicians were on the Warner payroll, appearing as members of the symphony orchestras and popular bands. Ensemble dancers and showgirls were needed for the various shows, musicals, and vaudeville production numbers. Le Roy Prinz was given his own production unit in which he directed the film's musical numbers while Irving Rapper directed the story. A hundred and fifty black performers found employment in *Blue Monday Blues* and *Porgy and Bess.*

The career of the director, Irving Rapper, was in its ascendancy. Originally a stage director, he had recently completed the Bette Davis–Paul Henreid film *Now Voyager* for Warner Bros. Levant got along well with the Englishman, a short, dapper man who appreciated Oscar's wit. Rapper would go on to direct many films for Warner Bros., though he would constantly fight with the dictatorial Jack Warner. He was put on suspension ten times during his career at the studio ("Cagney, [Bette] Davis, and Bogart had eleven amongst them"). "One more suspension," Humphrey Bogart once said to Rapper, "and you'll look like the Brooklyn Bridge."

Toward the end of Levant's first week on the set, his shooting schedule called for a scene in Gershwin's Riverside Drive apartment. Oscar was not prepared for what he saw during the scene, which opens with George and Oscar at the piano singing a spirited (but pretty bad) rendition of "Mine" from *Let 'Em Eat Cake.* (Oscar and Ira both admired the song's vocal counterpoint.) There on the set, with a fake New York skyline in the background, Oscar saw George's worktable—not a prop but the real thing. He had described it in *A Smattering of Ignorance* as an "incredible synthesis—of carpentry and composition." The silent piano keyboard with which George had always traveled was also on the set, and on the walls hung six of

George's paintings. Levant had not seen them since the day he had gone over to the Gershwins' and had helped Ira and Lee take them all down. It was a shock seeing so many of Gershwin's real effects among the faked Hollywood re-creations of his life.

Ira had in fact lent those cherished objects to Warner Bros. but had neglected to tell Oscar. It had always seemed that Oscar inhabited some universe parallel to George's. Now he had become a living embodiment of that world. After *Rhapsody in Blue,* Oscar Levant would become inextricably linked in the public imagination with George Gershwin. And now, thanks to radio and film, he was as famous as Gershwin ever was.

Making *Rhapsody in Blue,* however, was a kind of therapy for Levant. He was able to publicly express his envy of George's genius. Alexis Smith, as the love interest Christine Gilbert, tells Oscar, "Mr. Levant, you're not so ferocious as you sound."

"Don't let that get around," he tells her.

"I understand you compose, too."

"If it wasn't for George, I could have been a pretty good mediocre composer."

The words are spoken without bitterness. Though Levant's stock in trade is the self-deprecating remark, he seems to have accepted his role in life as a pianist and "personality" and not a composer. It's as though he has finally forgiven Gershwin for possessing the singular, creative genius he lacked; he can now revel in his status as "George Gershwin's friend."

Once Levant seems to make peace with his status of acolyte in the Gershwin circle, a curious thing happens at the end of the movie. The film concludes with Levant playing *Rhapsody in Blue* at the Lewisohn Stadium memorial concert after George's death, with Paul Whiteman conducting. The camera pans over the audience: we see a saddened Max Dreyfus, and then Julie Adams, the musical star girlfriend who was about to be reunited with George just before his death. She watches Levant at the piano, and, as tears fill her eyes, suddenly she sees Oscar Levant turn into George Gershwin.

Just as Levant had flourished in the Gershwin circle at Riverside Drive and later on North Roxbury, he took over the Warner Bros. lot during the filming of *Rhapsody in Blue.* He dominated through his nonstop palaver, his abundance of musical ideas, his obstreperousness, and his excitability.

Although the serious musicians, composers, and conductors who appear in the film—Ravel, Rachmanioff, Heifetz, Damrosch—are portrayed by actors, the set was a magnet for the real thing. One day Igor Stravinsky visited the Warner Bros. lot and dropped in on Oscar Levant during a break in the long workday. Wearing black tie and tails and balancing a cup of coffee on his knee, Levant received the composer of *Le Sacre du printemps* in a quiet corner of the movie set. Levant greatly enjoyed the spirited, fiercely opinionated Russian. Between takes he had been reading a life of Ferruccio Busoni, the Italian pianist and composer, so he knew that Stravinsky had met Busoni only once, despite the fact that they had lived just five miles from each other in Switzerland during the First World War.

"Why did you visit Busoni only once?" Levant asked Stravinsky.

"Because," replied the composer, bristling slightly, "he represented the immediate past and I hate the immediate past."

For Levant, who had done nothing but immerse himself in the immediate past for the last few weeks, Stravinsky's remark struck him as a kind of oblique comment on the musical world he was inhabiting. Might it not be wise to learn to hate the immediate past, just a little? Chastened a bit by Stravinsky's visit, Levant determined to further expand his repertoire and try to shake some of his Gershwin obsessions.

This new attitude may have been what contributed to his jaunty presence in the sometimes lachrymose, memorial film. Levant emerges as one of the strengths in *Rhapsody*—cheeky, confident, and refreshingly brash where others are merely reverential.

The reviews were mixed, though Levant was generally lauded for his role in the film. "The player who steals the show is Oscar Levant, whose acidulous wit gives one a feeling that one is close to the Golden Boy of modern music. More acid would have helped 'Rhapsody in Blue' no end," noted Howard Barnes of the *New York Herald Tribune*.

The film was a resounding success at the box office. Soon after its release, Mayor Scully proclaimed an "Oscar Levant Week" in Pittsburgh to honor Levant "as a pianist and prominent radio and movie actor." His success, the mayor announced, "should be an inspiration to our boys and girls"—an ironic accolade for a high school dropout and habitué of Colwell Street's brothels.

Rhapsody in Blue would prove a boon to Oscar Levant. Warner Bros. would sign him for two more films. Not only was it his most likable movie work to date, it had something of a cathartic effect on the pianist. Stravinsky's remark must have crystallized a process the film had set into motion: Levant seemed finally to have crossed a bridge, leaving his obsession with Gershwin behind. The only problem with loosening the leash that tied Levant to Gershwin, however,

was that Levant now opened himself up to new masters, more trenchant and more demanding than the composer of *Rhapsody in Blue*.

At the beginning of the new year, Arturo Toscanini invited Levant
to play the Concerto in F with the NBC Orchestra. The concert,
scheduled for broadcast the first Sunday in April 1944, was a bittersweet moment for Levant. Almost ten years earlier he had accompanied Gershwin to Samuel Chotzinoff's apartment, where they had
played Gershwin's music for Toscanini, who was considering including Gershwin in an all-American music program. Toscanini had
turned him down.

Levant paid his first visit to Toscanini's house in Riverdale, New
York, to discuss the Gershwin score and plan for the April broadcast.
Levant was not shy around the intense, volatile conductor who had
exercised his formidable will, unchallenged, over countless musicians.
He was quick to differ with the maestro over his interpretation of
several passages in the score.

"Mr. Gershwin wanted it *this* way," Levant insisted.

Toscanini raised the score to his weak eyes and pored over it with
great intensity. Suddenly he looked up at Oscar.

"That-a poor boy . . . he was a-sick," Toscanini replied in his
strong working-class Italian accent. "Poor man, he was a-sick when
he wrote this . . ." he responded every time Levant tried to explain
Gershwin's intentions. The fact that Gershwin had not been at all sick
when he composed the Concerto did not influence the maestro's ob-
tuse pity.

By the time Levant arrived with June at Studio 8-H for rehearsal,
the NBC Orchestra was in something of a turmoil. With Toscanini
and Leopold Stokowski as co-conductors of the orchestra, each of
them conducting about two dozen concerts, the orchestra was transformed into a two-headed monster. Stokowski sought a smoother,
plusher sound than Toscanini's; he reseated the musicians, and his
broadcast repertoire added a healthy crop of new works, including
Schoenberg's fateful Piano Concerto, which was supposed to have
had Oscar Levant's name on it.

Levant was never without a cigarette, particularly during rehearsals,
although such behavior was grounds for excommunication under
Toscanini. But Toscanini must not have noticed his pianist wreathed
in smoke, so Levant puffed away. The rest of the musicians stared in
envious wonder, too afraid of Levant's acerbic wit to tell him to stop
smoking.

During the rehearsal, Levant witnessed Toscanini's legendary rages with which the maestro bullied, shamed, and inspired his orchestra. Levant was no stranger to temperamental outbursts, yet he was shocked to see Toscanini attack one of his musicians: "He was so furious about this slovenly performance that he walked over and gave the score a knockout punch with his right fist and then started to shriek," Levant remembered.

Once the rather grueling rehearsals were over and the program aired, Levant's music with the NBC Orchestra was warmly received by the newspaper critics. There was, however, one noticeable mistake in the performance—the first clarinetist had come in at the wrong place in the second movement. "Should I killa him? Should I killa him?" Toscanini yelled after the concert was over. The maestro bellowed and raved until Levant finally mollified him by pointing out how truly remarkable the entire performance had been.

Annie Levant listened to the NBC broadcast from her home in Pittsburgh. Now seventy-four and seriously weakened by arteriosclerosis, she listened to Levant perform under Toscanini with unabashed pride. It was a triumph for Oscar's mother, who, like many of her generation, worshiped Toscanini. The son of a Palermo tailor, Toscanini had become a cult hero to millions of music lovers. Like Paderewski, he represented a generic idea of musical genius; he was regularly acclaimed in the press as "the greatest conductor of his time—even of all time." He was touted in newspapers and tabloids across the country; *Life* magazine deemed him "the greatest living master of music." He was as famous as Joe DiMaggio.

Just as he had been drawn to those other autocratic geniuses, Dreyfus and Schoenberg, Levant took a deep interest in Toscanini, and he and June became frequent guests at the old conductor's five-acre "Villa Pauline" overlooking the Hudson River. The first time June accompanied her husband to the Toscaninis' it was New Year's Eve. "Toscanini had a paper cap on with those little noisemakers," June remembered. "Oscar loved talking to him and getting information from him, you know. Oscar was a great interviewer—he loved getting information from people."

"I think Toscanini was consumed by envy more than any man I ever met," Levant later wrote, and Levant was no stranger to envy. "Sundays were particularly bad days." That was when Toscanini would tune in his radio and listen to the New York Philharmonic, which he had conducted from 1926 through 1936 with such brilliant results. During the broadcasts he snorted like a wounded bull, moving about the room in a kind of frenzy.

As he had with Schoenberg, Levant liked to pepper Toscanini with questions about the great conductors and musicians and to solicit his opinions on his contemporaries. Like Schoenberg, Toscanini had a harsh word for everybody.

Among the other frequent guests at Toscanini's Saturday nights were the pianist Vladimir Horowitz and his wife, Wanda, who was Toscanini's daughter. The most tragic figure in the household, in Levant's opinion, was Carla, Toscanini's wife. "She was bored beyond redemption" by the endless series of concerts she was forced to attend, Levant observed. Levant once sat in the Toscaninis' dress circle box as their guest at a Horowitz recital. With eyes nearly as weak as her husband's, Mme. Toscanini would bring the program booklet up to her nose as if she were smelling it. Rather than read the evening's program, she would peruse the advertisements. After she had studied every one, she sat back with a deep sigh, "an unwilling victim," Levant noted, of marriage to a great conductor. Not only did she have to attend her husband's concerts but, since Wanda's marriage in 1933, her son-in-law's as well. By the 1940s Horowitz had become the preeminent concert pianist of the age. Levant sympathized with Mme. Toscanini; it had always been difficult for him to sit through an entire concert if he weren't part of it—he preferred to drop in on rehearsals, where he could come and go as he pleased.

Throughout 1944 Levant hovered around the Toscanini circle. Both men were highly emotional and full of nervous energy, and both were highly superstitious. Levant once asked the maestro if he had any superstitions.

> A wild glint flashed into his eyes and he bellowed: "Superstish? . . . No superstish! What am I? A man or a no man?" This rather Talmudic confrontation went on for some time until he simmered down.

Horowitz then leaned over to Levant and whispered, "He's never given up one of his superstitions!"

They were both extremely sensitive about public opinion but could be ruthlessly critical, even mean, in their criticism of others. Toscanini must have had a soft spot for Levant. No one ever dared mention his rival Gustav Mahler around him—it was considered treasonous—but Levant once asked him if he had ever heard Mahler conduct *Tristan*.

"Poor man . . . he was a-sick," Toscanini replied.

The Cole Porter musical *Mexican Hayride* opened at the Winter Garden Theatre on January 28, 1944, with Harry Levant conducting.

Harry was regarded by many as one of the best musical directors on Broadway in the thirties and forties. His participation in a show was considered a guarantee of success. "Bad shows were successful when he took them, for as long as he had them," his nephew Marc Levant remembered. "He had a charm and he had a sense of stage music and he was a good orchestrator and a good conductor. . . . Harry was king of his hill."

In the first week of *Mexican Hayride* Harry Levant suffered a stroke. Oscar rushed to the hospital and was shocked by what he found. Harry could barely speak. He clutched Oscar's hand and yawned but could not utter a word.

In six weeks' time he was back in the orchestra pit of the Winter Garden, though the stroke had partially crippled his right hand, which made it difficult for him to conduct. His nephew Marc met him in the city, where they had planned to stroll down Broadway, but Harry found he could no longer make that walk. Three years later he would suffer another stroke, which left him even more debilitated. At forty-seven, Harry was a four-pack-a-day smoker, like Oscar, and had inherited a tendency to heart disease.

Levant was devastated by Harry's stroke. Harry was his eldest brother, his protector in New York during those lonely early years, even though he had been on the road touring so much of the time. Still, his success on Broadway had helped Oscar; it had made the Great White Way seem less intimidating. Oscar had worn Harry's cast-off suits and had read Harry's dog-eared books. He had been so happy during the months he'd lived with Harry and Pearl and Dossie at the Congress. To see his protector now felled was terrible. And it opened up a new terror in him—his father had been forty-seven when he died. The specter of death brushed over him like a shadow.

30

Endless Bleeding

"The hummingbird is psychotic. If there were
psychiatry for birds, they would have to
analyze every hummingbird."

A FEW DAYS AFTER HARRY'S STROKE OSCAR RECEIVED HIS DRAFT NO-
tice, commanding him to appear at the Delmonico Hotel at 5:30
A.M.—Oscar's usual bedtime. Virtually sleepless and extremely apprehensive, he entered Delmonico's lobby feeling as if he had already
been to war. He wanted to serve, but he had doubts about his eligibil-
ity.

Almost as soon as he arrived, the officer in charge commanded him
to play a recital for the other draftees. Levant had always hated to play
on command, but he sat down at the hotel lobby piano and dutifully
played a few Gershwin passages.

Word had leaked out about Levant's draft notice, and reporters
greeted the radio personality in the spacious lobby of the Delmonico.
Levant had a reputation as a wise guy; with the army as the ultimate
authority figure, reporters were anxious to record the inevitable
showdown. And the press was eager to know how the *Information,
Please!* expert would fare on the mental aptitude test.

Levant had made a virtue of his distaste for physical exercise. "I find
most forms of exercise repugnant and aimless; walking without an
objective, dull and pointless. Also fatiguing," he complained with

mock annoyance. Now he faced the most chilling physical challenge of his life. Despite his genuine patriotic feelings, fame had added a new terror to his possible induction into the army: Would he be mocked for being unathletic, knock-kneed, and pigeon-toed? For lacking the manly grace his three brothers displayed so effortlessly? Though he wondered how he could leave June and their two daughters, a 4F classification would be humiliating.

So Levant played the piano for the other bleary-eyed men who had been called up, all of them now listening to him play a Bach Partita. Some of them might never come back from the war. The officer in charge noticed how Levant's playing had calmed down the crowd of anxious and eager draftees. "You're a natural born leader," he told the pianist. "Go down to 46th Street and Lexington."

Levant led a phalanx of men marching in single file to Lexington Avenue, just as the sun started to rise over the city. Arriving at their destination, Levant led his men into army headquarters, where the medical examinations were to take place. Levant was treated differently from the rest. Every time a new doctor examined him, he was asked for tickets to *Information, Please!*

Finally, Levant was sent to the last physician, who carefully studied his medical chart. He looked up at Levant and declared in a loud voice, "According to your record, Mr. Levant, you should be dead." The remark must have horrified him.

A handful of reporters had followed Levant and his recruits from the Delmonico to the examining center. They were salivating to get the results of Levant's draft board intelligence test. Levant was always being challenged on his knowledge as a result of *Information, Please!* It was one of the distasteful hazards of his radio fame. Sensitive about having left school at the age of fifteen, Levant was somewhat embarrassed about being thought of as a know-it-all, a reputation that the press had helped to create.

But Levant finished first in the written test among all the other recruits. "My pride had overcome my fear," he said. He was then ordered to report to Governors Island for mental observation.

"All right," Levant replied. "This time I'll take a cab."

The officer in charge shook his head and told Levant that he would accompany the pianist by subway. Levant, who hadn't taken the subway in years, didn't like his first taste of being ordered around. He could feel his boss-hating attitude begin to rise.

At Governors Island, Levant was told to strip in a room with ninety other raw recruits. Another intolerable situation—but he did what he was told. He was kept under observation at Governors Island for three days, undergoing several sessions with a battery of psychiatrists. Levant told one of the headshrinkers that he was under analysis. "Do you think you can kill?" the doctor asked Levant.

"I don't know about strangers," Levant replied, "but friends, yes."

Levant was classified 4-F and sent back into the civilian world. "They must have been bumbling idiots to take three days to discover that I was neurotic," Levant joked. But it was probably his high pulse rate that disqualified him and the fact that he had two children and, at thirty-seven, was over draftable age. "It was all unnecessary," he would later write. "I was too old." Levant continued to make war bond tours as his sole contribution to the war effort.

One night at "21" Levant ran into the Hollywood producer Gottfried Reinhardt in his army uniform. Gottfried was having dinner with his father, Max Reinhardt, who had recently suffered a stroke. Levant—who was crazy about Max, once a regular at Salka Viertel's—gave the old man a boisterous greeting and joined the two at their table. When Gottfried was served a healthy portion of steak—"a beautiful Chateaubriand with sauce Bearnaise"—Gottfried laughed and told Levant, "You see, Oscar, this is how you'd be eating too if you were in the Army!" Levant took that remark as a veiled criticism that he had so far failed to serve his country.

Gottfried recorded Oscar's response in his diary entry for October 13, 1944:

> Never inaugurate fun with a funnyman. . . . He took my self-irony as a sting at him for not wearing his country's colors, slapped my face, sprinted across the room and down the stairs. . . . I shoved the table away, tugged myself free of my father's restraining hand and caught up with my "assailant" at the cloakroom, struggling into his coat while making a for-dear-life dash toward the exit. For the first and last time in my life I swung with a stiff uppercut to the chin.

The proprietor's brother, Mack Kriendler, separated the two men. They then shook hands and Oscar slunk off into the night.

In 1944 the Levants bought a summer home in Westport, Connecticut—a modern concrete-and-glass structure that sat on six acres of land, most of it wildly overgrown. "Who did you buy this from—" Levant asked the owner as they were shown around the property "—Lewis and Clark?" Levant would have to take a commuter train from the city, where they still kept their Alwyn Court apartment as their main abode. They bought the house for the children's sake.

Levant would try out being a country squire so his girls could have healthy, sun-drenched summers, while their father's heart burned for Lindy's.

The transition to country gentleman was not an easy one. The quiet, the sound of crickets, the animals rustling through the under-brush at night were a torment to Levant. The first day in their new house, he went out to take his walk, as was his custom in the city. Almost as soon as he stepped out of doors he saw two black snakes undulating along a rock. Certain they were poisonous, he scuttled back into the house, where he remained for three days.

The next time he emerged, the sight of a hedgehog terrified him. Insects gave him anxiety attacks. Even birds, with their restless flutter-ing, upset him. Levant, his nerves already unraveling, found that the most anxiety-producing creature in all the woods was the humming-bird.

"The hummingbird is crazy," he confided to the journalist Mau-rice Zolotow. "I make that statement flatly. The hummingbird is psychotic. If there were psychiatry for birds, they would have to ana-lyze every hummingbird."

The Levants occasionally visited with the Pittsburgh Symphony conductor Fritz Reiner and his wife, who also owned a house in Westport. John Steinbeck was another neighbor whose acquaintance Levant attempted to make. He asked the author for advice on what to do if he should encounter another "python" on his property.

"Just kick 'em in the belly," was the writer's manly advice.

Alfred Vanderbilt, Jr., Levant's wealthy, horse-racing buddy whose affable manner stood in startling contrast to Levant's nervous irrita-bility, visited Levant once or twice in Connecticut. If Al Vanderbilt were a literary character, he would have been written by Edith Whar-ton in collaboration with Damon Runyon. His is the story of an En-glish-born youngster, sickly and frail, who was fussed over by nurses and governesses and who placed his first bet on a horse when he was eleven years old. He received the daily racing form, mailed to him in a plain brown wrapper, so he could follow the racing season by any available light in his dormitory room at St. Paul's prep school. Oscar was very fond of the boyish, likable Alfred—the two became constant companions throughout the forties.

Vanderbilt preferred the company of jockeys and newspapermen to the high society he was born to. Levant once observed that Vanderbilt had been raised by hired governesses and nurses—"poor people, and that's why he doesn't know how to get on with rich ones. . . . Al

Vanderbilt is the poorest rich guy I know." He played Prince Hal to Oscar's Falstaff.

One of their favorite dining spots was "21." "They used to have a special sauce—'sauce 21,' " Vanderbilt remembered, "and they'd pass it around like you're being honored. Well, when it got to Oscar, he leaned back and, pointing to his tie, said 'Serve it directly onto my chest!' "

Country living had no appeal for Oscar Levant—it was a kind of banishment from everything he cared about. When he came out from Manhattan, he always carried the train schedule in his pocket to check the timetable back to New York.

One rule of their Connecticut household was that the radio could not be tuned in to *Information, Please!* Levant had finally had enough of the anxiety-producing show—he felt the other panelists had ganged up against him since Harry's stroke. Even Kip Fadiman had "turned against me," Oscar thought, "because I answered a question about Schopenhauer. . . . I finished by saying to Fadiman, 'He was a misogynist. He would have liked you.' "

> Fadiman thought that I had declared him a homosexual before an au-
> dience of millions. . . . That was the end. I left the show and I was glad
> to get away from the tyranny. It had become such an obsession and a
> fright that I didn't enjoy it.

Fadiman doesn't remember the panelists ever ganging up on Oscar, nor having responded to his remark in such a manner. It's not clear whether or not Levant actually quit or if Golenpaul had found a way to fire him. In any case, Levant got his wish: He no longer had to show up for the broadcasts (although two years later, in 1946, he would be asked back in an attempt to boost ratings, and he would return to the show for one more year).

Levant's concert schedule had become oppressively tight, demanding a great deal of train travel to dozens of cities. Fear and uncertainty over each performance had come to dominate his life. Just as the youthful Oscar had been dragged all over Pittsburgh by his mother to perform in Jewish community centers and private homes, he now transported himself across the country fulfilling concert engagements. Some were piano recitals billed as "concerts with comments," others were concerts with symphony orchestras. Levant traveled with a booking agent named Larry Fitzgerald whom Columbia Artists Management had sent to accompany him on tour. Fitzgerald had traveled with many temperamental musicians, going back to his days as a member of Paderewski's entourage.

As his concertizing continued, Levant's superstitions increased. Chief among them was his triskaidekaphobia, which had begun during *Information, Please!* Once in New York's Pennsylvania Station, Levant met Fitzgerald at the train, then he noticed that it was scheduled to depart from track 13. They boarded, but Levant was spooked; he prohibited Fitzgerald from speaking while the train slowly moved into the tunnel under the Hudson River. Fitzgerald sat in tense silence until they reached the New Jersey side.

Fitzgerald observed another superstitious ritual during one of their tours. In his hotel room preparing for a concert, Levant would take one of his soft white shirts and begin buttoning it from the lowest button to the top. When he removed the garment he would always unbutton it from the top down. This would never vary. If Fitzgerald tried to hurry him by buttoning his shirt for him, Levant unleashed a torrent of verbal abuse. Added to a pair of gloves he must touch, Gershwin's wristwatch he must wear, and his dread that someone might wish him "good luck" before a concert, this new ritual made not only performing but getting ready for the performance a trial.

Another constant annoyance to Levant was latecomers. Once, when a bejeweled woman came sweeping down the aisle in the middle of a piece, distracting the audience, Levant suddenly stopped playing Poulenc and began imitating her walk by playing in time with her gait. When she stopped, Levant stopped. When she hurried to find her seat, Levant played a flurry of notes, and so on. By the time the poor woman reached her seat, the audience was roaring and she was in a state of wild confusion.

Levant was scheduled to appear at the Hollywood Bowl in August 1944 with Artur Rodzinski conducting. When Rodzinski was suddenly forced to cancel, Sol Hurok, the concert promoter, insisted they allow Rodzinski's young assistant to step in and take his place. So a twenty-two-year-old Bostonian, whose name was Leonard Bernstein, replaced Rodzinski at the podium. It was Levant's first encounter with the brilliant young conductor. "A marriage of egomaniacs" was how Levant later described it.

The day before the concert, Bernstein had called Levant and begged him to let *him* play the solo piano part of *Rhapsody in Blue*, with Levant conducting the orchestra. Levant—known by now as the foremost Gershwin specialist in the country—"graciously, but with some horror, declined."

In revenge, Bernstein programmed Stravinsky's *Firebird* ahead of the *Rhapsody*. Stravinsky's magnificence smothered the *Rhapsody* in its crib.

It was the beginning of a relationship that was touchy, antagonistic, and at times nasty. There was jealousy on both sides. Bernstein's overbearing personality seemed to press all of Levant's hostility buttons, and over the course of the next decade Levant would make Bernstein a special target of his barbs. He recognized the younger man's immense talent and was envious of the success that had come to him at such an early age. "I like Lenny Bernstein," Levant would insist with mock sincerity, "but not as much as he does."

Another Bernstein insult Levant trafficked in over the years was "He uses music as an accompaniment to his conducting." On Bernstein's reputation as a pedagogue: "Leonard Bernstein has been disclosing musical secrets that have been well known for over four hundred years." On one of Bernstein's compositions: "It reflects a great knowledge—of other composers' music." On Bernstein's early fame: "I remember thinking then: Here is a young man who bears watching. Close watching."

Bernstein's flamboyant style, his exhibitionism and swaggering confidence, were like the red cape to the bull. It's possible that the ambitious young conductor reminded Levant too much of himself at a younger age, eliciting feelings both of sympathy and repulsion. He also feared that Bernstein was trying to emulate him:

> My flatfooted Renaissance figure pursuing many careers—composing, movies, concerts—touched off Bernstein's aspirations at a time when he was, as I recall him, an asthmatic Keats. If those metaphors are mixed, so was he.

Levant's opinion of Bernstein's overweening ambition is captured in his description of Bernstein's conducting at the Hollywood Bowl that night: "[It] had a masturbatory, oppressive and febrile zeal, even for the most tranquil passages." (This critique echoes a description of Levant's Piano Concerto made by Dimitri Mitropoulos a few years earlier. During dinner at the Alwyn Court apartment, in front of June, who was five months pregnant at the time, Mitropoulos characterized Levant's composition as being "full of hate and masturbation.")

• • •

On June 21, 1945, during the Levants' second summer at their West-port, Connecticut, home, their third child was born, a baby girl they named Amanda. Oscar was again thrilled—relieved in a sense that he wouldn't have to struggle with raising boys. "I wouldn't have known how to control boys," he said. "I seem to lack the required author-ity." There would be no tiny Oscar to compete for June's attention.

A month later, Oscar received a call from his brother Ben in Pitts-burgh. Ben was phoning his youngest brother to tell him that their mother had been hospitalized for her heart condition, which had been steadily deteriorating. Annie had reached the point where she could no longer do the simplest chores in her apartment—she could barely lift herself from her chair.

Levant canceled a booked appearance on *The Bell Telephone Hour* and went home to Pittsburgh to see his dying mother. He managed to visit her a few times in room 411 in the hospital, but on September 8, 1945, Annie Radin Levant, tired out and weak as a whisper, died.

Levant joined his three brothers in burying their mother. The smart, witty immigrant who had so dearly loved music would now be sealed away from all sound. Annie had lived to see all of her sons marry and become successful. Her life had been fulfilled, though she had left an ambivalence about success in her youngest son that no applause could assuage.

Oscar had been her favorite—her little genius. She had been the first one to recognize his gifts but also the first to warn him not to aim too high—"You'll never be a Paderewski" she had cautioned. She had been his severest critic, and her lack of sentimentality had some-times seemed cruel. She judged Oscar and seemed to love him. Her death brought all the brothers together again for the last time: Ben, Harry (still weak from his recent stroke), Honey, and Oscar. The funeral was an Orthodox Jewish funeral. Oscar sat in the same temple where he had been bar mitzvahed. As Oscar entered the cemetery, the first movement of the Brahms Violin Concerto came into his head. He couldn't get rid of the main theme. He knew this work was one of the favorite pieces of Jascha Heifetz, the celebrated violinist whom his mother had often held up as an example to Oscar. "Heifetz was the one that all Jewish families kept pointing out to their musi-cally gifted children," Levant remembered. "He was the great exam-ple of what could be done if the unfortunate kid merely kept playing his scale exercises." Annie Levant was buried in Section E, Row 1, Block 42 in a part of the cemetery called Beth Jacob, not far from her husband's grave eight rows away. Levant had always identified with the biblical Jacob, Esau's younger brother who had tried to cheat him out of his father's blessing.

Three weeks after his mother's death, on a Saturday evening, October 6, 1945, his friend Beatrice Kaufman suffered a cerebral hemmorhage and died in her New York apartment. When Oscar got the news from Moss Hart over the telephone, he broke down and wept. It was the first time June had ever seen her husband shed tears.

For many years Beatrice had had high blood pressure, which she did little to treat. Still, her death was a great shock, and her funeral, held at Frank Campbell's funeral home on Madison Avenue, was a kind of grand gathering of talent, genius, ego, and fame. George S. Kaufman, Bernard Baruch, former mayor Jimmy Walker, Mayor Fiorello La Guardia, Moss Hart, of course, who was as devoted to Bea as Oscar was, Bennett Cerf, who eulogized Beatrice in the chapel, and Oscar Levant were present. They sat in stunned silence as Beatrice's name was added to the death rolls.

Within less than a month, two of the most important women in Oscar's life were gone. Beatrice Bakrow Kaufman had championed Oscar Levant, tolerating his social dissonances and recognizing his special brilliance. She had gotten through to Oscar and had become his friend. He had loved her for it.

That Oscar's tears were shed for Beatrice and not for his mother suggests how much Levant had repressed his emotions toward Annie. From now on, anything that reminded him of his mother's death would fill him with dread.

31

Humoresque

"Frank Costello gets as sentimental as
a Chopin nocturne."

THE HOUSE OF THE DEAD WAS QUICKLY FILLING UP. WHILE ON TOUR IN
April 1945, Levant made a whistle stop in Texas. On the train plat-
form a newsboy held up a special edition of the local newspaper:
"FDR Dies" the headline shouted. The president had died in his
sleep at Warm Springs, Georgia. Although the idea of death took up
residence in Oscar's mind in 1945, he would refuse to acknowledge
it. He couldn't bear to have the word "death" mentioned in his presence. In fact, any object, word, or phrase that evoked the idea of
death was to be avoided. Funerals, coffins, wills, inheritances, ceme-
teries, the names of the dead, even insurance could never be mentioned around him without eliciting a wounded outburst.

By 1945 it had become customary for Levant to play in Washington, D.C., every winter. Most of the visiting soloists spent the night at
the Raleigh Hotel. Five of the suites were so-called "musical suites,"
named after well-known performers from the recent past, such as Lily
Pons ("those whose careers were over," Levant noted dismally). They
were numbered 411, 511, 611, etc., but Oscar's mother had spent her
last days in hospital room 411, so Levant couldn't sleep in any of those
numbered rooms. In fact, any constellation of numbers that was remi-

niscent of 411 was anathema to him. Eventually, Levant stopped staying on the fourth floor of hotels, just as he would assiduously avoid walking down the street Beatrice Kaufman lived on before her death.

His dread of the number thirteen also deepened after 1945. "It is Levant's most feared hex. He will have nothing to do with 13 in any way, shape or form," wrote one journalist profiling Levant at the end of the decade. Rather than say the word, he referred to it as "that number." When Levant arrived in Buffalo, New York, for one of his "concerts with comments," he wound up sleeping on a cot in the drafty waiting area of the concert hall rather than spend the night in the only hotel suite available to him, rooms 1301, 1302, and 1303. "That terrible number! You've ruined my concert! I'll never be able to come to Buffalo again. Why did you do this to me?" he wailed at the astonished hotel manager.

There were other phobias as well. Upon his return to New York, Levant met Ottie Swope, Jr., for dinner one night at the Cub Room of the Stork Club. During the course of the evening Swope noticed the sorry condition of Levant's cherished Gershwin wristwatch. It was yellowed and all the figures had worn off.

"Oscar," Swope said, "you really have to get that watch cleaned or get a new one."

Levant became furious at the remark. "Goddamn it," Levant yelled, dropping his fork. "Don't talk about that. Don't say anything about it." He threatened to leave the restaurant.

Swope was stunned that his innocent suggestion had unleased such a tirade. "You couldn't reason with him; he wouldn't tell you what the matter was," Swope later said about the incident. "So then I knew that there were areas you couldn't talk about."

Swope had no way of knowing that the very subject of wristwatches had become a sensitive issue with Levant. Not long after Annie's death, it had fallen to Oscar's brothers Ben and Honey—the dutiful sons who had stayed behind—to see to their mother's affairs and divide her possessions. Among her effects, Honey discovered an inscribed wristwatch Annie had left for Oscar, a watch meant, perhaps, to ameliorate his hurt at having never been given a gift for his bar mitzvah.

Oscar was "bemused, bitter, and touched" by the discovery, but he refused to accept the posthumous gift. It had come too late.

In 1946 Levant headed for Los Angeles to appear in his next film. *Humoresque* was the portrait of a brilliant young violinist, Paul Boray, played by John Garfield, from the Clifford Odets script that had been salvaged from *Rhapsody in Blue.* "I was let loose on this picture as though I were Franz Liszt giving a recital," Levant remarked about his work for Warner Bros. The studio signed Levant for a two-year contract, optioning the right to his services for one picture a year at a salary of $25,000 per picture.

Levant's film career was about to become another stroll through a hall of mirrors, not only reflecting his own life experience as a struggling musician in New York, but full of biographical doppelgängers as well.

Humoresque, which began life in 1919 as a short story by the popular novelist Fannie Hurst, became in 1920 the basis for a silent film. In the final version of the screenplay for producer Jerry Wald's 1946 production, the story of the Jewish immigrant family with the musical son had been turned into something vaguely Italian. One of the problems the Hurst novel raised with executives at Warner Bros. was what they indelicately termed "the Jewish problem." One executive wrote a memo to Jerry Wald mentioning his preference for keeping the atmosphere vaguely European but not specifically Jewish. The studio executives—most of whom were Jewish—were trying to anticipate what public tastes and reactions would be.

"In this outline I am doing Italian," Jerry Wald wrote in a memo to screenwriter Barney Glazer, who prepared an early treatment for the film. "But do not blame me too much if the Jewish creeps in. It is more than a choice between serving spaghetti or gefelte fish; . . . musically, it could well be a choice between Paganini's 'Perpetual Motion' or . . . the Kaddish death song."

A problem that needed immediate attention was getting Garfield to realistically portray a man playing a violin. Wald was a stickler for getting things right, and he delayed production to give Garfield more time at his violin lessons. Wald begged Warner Bros. for more time. "As you well know, learning to fake playing the violin is a much more difficult job than the piano," he wrote to a studio executive.

The violinist Wald hired from New York to prerecord the violin playing was twenty-five-year-old Isaac Stern. The lively, quick-talking young violinist was ecstatic to be in the movie capital of the world. Warner Bros. was paying Stern $25,000 to be a kind of musical Cyrano to Garfield's chevalier.

Stern coached Garfield, working with him patiently to show him the proper technique, but it turned out to be a disaster. Garfield just couldn't fake it convincingly. Finally, they hit upon a solution. For close-ups, Garfield's arms were pinned down, the violin was attached to his neck, and two professional violinists would crouch down beside the actor, out of camera range, one doing the fingering and the other bowing. The actual soundtrack heard by the audience was Stern's, with Oscar Levant accompanying him on the piano. After a couple of takes working in this strenuously awkward manner, Levant called out, "Why don't the five of us do a concert tour?"

Jerry Wald had started out as a journalist before making his mark as a writer-producer in Hollywood, where he would produce such classic films as *Mildred Pierce* (1945), *Key Largo* (1948), and *Johnny Belinda* (1948). By the forties, the aggressive, high-spirited Wald was considered one of Warner Bros.' hottest producers; his 1945 James M. Cain weeper *Mildred Pierce* earned Joan Crawford an Academy Award, though he had to talk Crawford into taking on the "matronly" title role. He had a driving, high-energy personality belied by his plump, six-foot-tall, over-two-hundred-pound frame. Many have speculated that Wald served as a model for Budd Schulberg's antihero Sammy Glick in *What Makes Sammy Run?*

Wald liked Levant. He appreciated his mind and his wit, and the two men, both lovers of literature and music, had much in common. The Levants were frequent guests at Jerry and Connie Wald's North Beverly Drive home.

Wald relied on Levant's judgment and musical knowledge to help authenticate the world of the struggling violinist who breaks through to a concert career with the patronage of a man-eating *grande dame* played by Joan Crawford. For example, Levant insisted that when Paul Boray makes his debut, the concert hall be only half filled, with no tuxedoes or formal wear in the audience. "People don't go to concerts in white ties. That still goes on only in the movies," he told Wald.

Whereas *Rhapsody in Blue* sentimentalized the musician–composer par excellence, *Humoresque* offered a more down-to-earth, flawed and angry artist in Garfield's biting portrayal of Paul Boray. Joan Crawford suffers magnificently as the rich, heavy-drinking Helen Wright who loves Boray but realizes she can't compete with his music. In her final scene she wanders the beach in tearstained alcoholic misery before plunging, like Virginia Woolf, straight into the sea to her death. Paul Boray's (that is, Isaac Stern's) lush violin playing is heard on the sound track as she sinks under the waves. (After the film was released, Warner Bros. received a petition signed by hundreds of women protesting Helen Wright's suicide as immoral and sending the wrong message to Crawford's many fans.)

Levant does his best acting in *Humoresque,* mostly in the first half of the picture. Once Crawford enters the story, it becomes a film about her, and as she dominates both Garfield and the storyline, Levant fades into the background. But in his first three scenes, he's a natural, appealing presence. Director Jean Negulesco had the good sense to allow Levant to light a cigarette, pour himself a cup of coffee, or play the piano throughout his early scenes, so he is physically engaged.

Perhaps because of the high caliber of the production and because Levant had the chance to work with pros like Wald, Garfield, Crawford, and Negulesco, there's a quality of seriousness underlying his performance, though many of his lines are comic. A lot of people dismissed Levant's acting efforts because his roles were so clearly versions of himself, but as many actors have observed, to "be yourself" on camera is extremely difficult. Levant had the ability to project his personality on film.

Wald encouraged Levant to come up with his own lines for his role as the wisecracking but gifted pianist Sid Jeffers who serves as Paul Boray's best friend, accompanist, and Greek chorus. Levant's own quickly souring view of the concert life provided an element of informed cynicism that helps cut through the film's melodrama.

In an early scene, Levant's Sid Jeffers meets eight-year-old Paul Boray (played by a snapping-eyed Robert Blake) in the Jeffers family store. Boray asks his recalcitrant father to buy him a violin. Later, when a grown-up Boray presses Jeffers for advice, the pianist replies, "You can't advise talent. Talent is a whole way of life." Jeffers launches into a definition of what makes for a concert artist:

> The whole point to me about an artist is the sound he makes. It's his own personal sound—on a violin or a piano or any instrument. That's what's communicated to the audience. That's what you call personality. If he's got that, nothing else matters very much; if he doesn't, he might as well quit.

When the subject of a debut concert comes up, Jeffers says, a little bitterly, "Who goes to debuts? Relatives and enemies."

"What about my playing?" the violinist asks. "Doesn't that mean anything?"

"Sure, you fill the lull between intermissions."

When Boray asks why he didn't tell him all this before, saving him years of practice and sacrifice, Jeffers answers with pure Levantian logic: "You weren't good enough to be disappointed ten years ago." And, a little later, in words Levant might have chosen for his epigraph, "It isn't what you are, it's what you don't become that hurts." The two men argue, and Boray prepares to leave. "Don't get sore at me," Jeffers tells him. "I didn't make the world. I barely live in it."

John Garfield lets Levant dominate the scene, and Negulesco keeps the camera on him, lit in the silky half-light of Jeffers's garrett. "You'll make it," Jeffers tells Boray. "You have all the characteristics of a successful virtuoso—you're self-indulgent, self-dedicated, and the hero of all your dreams."

"No matter how many concerts you play, you'll always have the penalty of not satisfying yourself," Jeffers tells Boray after his debut. "Preserve that feeling of dissatisfaction and you'll be okay."

"I envy people who drink," Jeffers tells Helen Wright late in the film as she wrestles with a hangover at Boray's apartment. "At least they know what to blame everything on."

"Why don't you drink?" Helen asks him.

"I have no character."

Levant was at the peak of his fame during the making of *Humoresque,* so much so that an establishing shot of an overflowing ashtray, a cup of coffee, and an alarm clock showing a late hour are all that's needed to announce we're in Oscar Levant territory. But he was growing difficult to work with. First of all, the contract negotiations had been problematical. Levant had to cancel a previously scheduled concert tour in order to appear in the film. Though he would end up with a salary of $4,166.67 per week for six weeks, he was insecure about money and suspicious to the point of paranoia about entering into contracts. He worked without an agent and negotiated on his own. (His book editor, Ken McCormick, had thought Levant "crazy about money," and felt that Levant hadn't paid Irving Kolodin enough for his role in writing *A Smattering of Ignorance.*) Now it seemed to him that contracts, the evidence of his success, concealed a secret humiliation ready to be sprung upon him.

Despite occasional run-ins with Negulesco, Levant felt good about his work in *Humoresque* and enjoyed the camaraderie of working with Odets and Wald. Good filmmaking experiences can turn a group of strangers into an intimate, close-knit family, but bad filmmaking experiences are like dysfunctional families. *Humoresque* seems to have been one of those families in which only the brothers got along. Jerry Wald was devoted to Oscar, and both men were fond of Julie Garfield. But Joan Crawford was another story.

Trying to be sociable with her colleagues, Crawford invited Oscar and June and the Levants' visiting guests, Al Vanderbilt, Jr., and his bride, Jeanne Murray, to a dinner party at her home. The presence of

a Vanderbilt at her table turned Crawford into a hysterical perfectionist. She became even more nervous and high strung than usual, so
anxious was she to show the Vanderbilts what a great lady she was.

June Levant remembered that fateful dinner party:

> The place was brimming with butlers, and the butlers were praying
> they didn't make any mistakes. . . . She was walking around like a jailer
> with keys hanging—clinking away. . . . She had a passion to be re-
> garded as a lady, because that's what she was playing. . . . That was her
> complex . . . her relationships went down the drain because there was
> no *there* there to make up a life. I mean, who was she? She wasn't real.
> She was playing a role . . . she was drunk with glamour.

After a tense dinner, Joan Crawford took her guests upstairs and
woke Christina and Christopher, her two adopted children.

"Out of bed, out of bed," she commanded like a top sergeant,
waking them up. They fell out of bed, and little Christopher quickly
hid his hand behind his back.

"Show them your thumb," she ordered the sleepy boy.

"No, no, Mommy dear," he pleaded.

Christopher reluctantly showed his mother's guests his thumb,
which was covered with a big rubber cap to keep him from sucking it.
Joan announced to everyone that he sucked his thumb.

"She humiliated the little kid in front of us," June remembered. "I
mean, everybody knew the terrible things she did to those children."

Levant had known Crawford when the actress was a slightly plump
flapper looking for steady work in the Jazz Age. He had met her once
backstage during the run of *Spice of 1922*. Crawford—born Lucille
LeSueur—had survived a mean, brutish childhood, and she seemed
desperate to scrub those memories from her life.

To Levant's mystification, Crawford always showed up on the set
carrying two raw steaks under her arm. She also had a habit of knitting
during the long hours between scenes—she was a compulsive knitter.
She even brought her knitting to dinner parties. Noticing this habit,
one of Levant's first remarks to her on the set was "Do you knit while
you fuck?"

There were "icebergs on the set for days" after that remark, according to Jean Negulesco.

Humoresque was released at the end of 1946, and the reviews were
mostly favorable. Levant was singled out for nearly unanimous approval. There was even, apparently, some talk about Levant being

nominated for an Academy Award for best supporting actor, but that was not to be.

"Anything that Oscar didn't do, I wasn't allowed to do," June remembered about the days and months that followed the making of *Humoresque*. The amorous fellow who could always make June laugh and who had promised her a life of "no more fights, just our love" had become moodier than ever. Now that he was off *Information, Please!* he felt he had to increase his concert schedule, a schedule that had already proved grueling. He could usually take his growing sense of frustration out on the piano, but when that failed to satisfy, he took it out on his wife.

"During 'Information, Please!'," June recalled, "he would get jealous and push me around." Edith Schick remembered running into June outside the NBC building right after a broadcast and noticing June's bruised arm in a sling. The talk around the studio was that Oscar had pushed June a little too hard.

On another occasion June showed up at a cocktail party after the broadcast where she was to meet her husband. She saw Kip Fadiman at the bar, and he invited June to join him in a drink.

"I was sitting at the bar talking to Kip Fadiman when Oscar came in, and he was furious. I mean here was his close friend and colleague, and the fact that I was just sitting and having a drink . . . would cause him to fly into a rage." Oscar hated to see June drink, and he hated to see her in the company of other men, even friends like Fadiman.

One day in 1946 David Diamond was visiting the Levants at the Alwyn Court. "He was playing Chopin mazurkas for me," Diamond recalled.

> I did not know them very well, but Oscar just ran through them all and I was fascinated with the music. . . . June made a martini and everything was fine and then we all decided we'd go to Lindy's for dinner afterwards.

The threesome got into the elevator where they ran into Clifford Odets going down at the same time. It was a small elevator, and the four of them were pressed tightly together. Suddenly, there was a loud rip as Oscar tore Odets's entire sleeve out of his coat. Levant then shouted at Odets to leave June alone.

"Now where Oscar got the idea that Cliff's hand touched her somewhere it wasn't supposed to," Diamond maintains,

I still believe that's all Oscar's pathological imagination. . . . When we hit the lobby, Cliff says, "Go away, Oscar," and Oscar went after him—and Oscar was no puncher, he was a grabber of clothes—and he started pulling. I never saw such hysteria.

Well, June was absolutely embarrassed and stood against the wall. . . . Cliff has taken off and gone wherever he was going. Oscar now begins to light into her. To me, it was the most awful shock because it was the first time I saw Oscar out of control.

For June, such scenes were horrible. Annie had warned her shortly after her marriage to be wary of Oscar's moods, but nothing had prepared her for this kind of behavior. June fought back. She had learned to do that in coping with the drunken behavior of her father. In some ways June had been a "parenting child," one who looked after and helped to support her mother, and that experience had shaped her character. So June struck out for independence. "I never drank unless he was crowding me about things and being unreasonable. Then I would purposely drink too much to have a good time."

One night Oscar and June had a terrible fight, and Oscar ended up telling June, in front of the children, that she was a falling-down drunk. It was one thing to accuse June of something that wasn't true—and that conjured up horrific memories of her childhood—but to do it in front of the children was unconscionable. "He just had to find something wrong with me," June felt, "to make what he did okay."

June announced she was going to sue Oscar for divorce. She knew how much Oscar doted on their three daughters—it would be like cutting off his hands to see June and the girls walk out of the Alwyn Court apartment forever. But she felt that threatening him was the only way to keep him in line.

On November 23, 1947, June's lawsuit for separate maintenance became a matter of public record. Within two days, however, she withdrew her suit. But she had found a way to keep her now-contrite husband in line, at least for a while.

Vladimir Horowitz understood what Levant was going through during those turbulent years of the forties. Horowitz himself had returned to the American concert stage in 1940 after having retired five years earlier, exhausted by the rigors—and boredom—of the concert life. During his absence, his formidable shadow fell across the path of every aspiring pianist who played the classical literature. As early as his first tour of the United States in 1928, Horowitz had achieved an almost legendary status.

What first endeared the Russian-born prodigy to Oscar Levant long before the two men ever met was a rumor that had circulated about the pianist: Horowitz was under the delusion that his delicate, sensitive hands were actually made of glass, and he lived in constant fear of shattering them. When Levant heard that apocryphal story, he felt a keen sympathy for the man. They met in Hollywood in 1942, the year Horowitz became a U.S. citizen.

In Horowitz, Levant found someone whose nervous system swung in and out of alignment as frequently as his own. The two men commiserated over the problems they were having with Columbia Artists Management. Horowitz was notorious for alienating concert promoters and driving record company executives to drink. He would treat them alternately with contempt or with consideration, depending on his mood swings.

Both men hated the grueling routine of concertizing, and they compared notes on the cities and towns they had performed in—the best places to eat or to sleep, the worst weather, the best and worst audiences, and so on. Like two long-haul truckers, the concert artists discussed hotels, restaurants, and characters they had encountered on the road. Once when Horowitz asked Levant where he planned on opening his next tour, Levant glumly told him, "Des Moines."

Horowitz rolled his eyes in commiseration. "Dostoevsky!" he groaned.

Horowitz and Levant later earned reputations as frequent cancelers (though Levant didn't make a habit of canceling concerts until his health failed around 1953). "Horowitz used to give me lessons in canceling concerts," Levant later announced. "I used to cancel as far ahead as two weeks when I was ill."

"Never do that," Horowitz explained. "Always cancel at the last minute."

When Horowitz canceled an appearance in Cincinnati, the concert promoter called Levant in New York and begged him to replace Horowitz. Levant indignantly told him, "But I already canceled Cincinnati."

While both men loathed the routine drudgery of the road, both felt that there was a sensual, almost sexual thrill to physical contact with the keyboard. Horowitz's breathtaking technique was certainly not lost on Levant. "Horowitz's octave playing was brilliant, accurate, and etched out like bullets," Levant would later write about his friend. "I once asked him whether he shipped them ahead or carried them with him on tour."

Oscar and Vlodya, Vlodya and Oscar. They were a funny pair, walking down Fifty-seventh Street together in New York toward Steinway & Sons and then on to the Russian Tea Room for lunch, like two difficult students cutting class: Horowitz with his deep, sonorous voice, thick Russian accent, and *commedia dell'arte* facial expressions, Levant with his dark moods, his euphoria, his acerbic tongue.

Despite their frequent depressions, both loved a good joke. Levant was one of the few men who could make Horowitz laugh when he was depressed. And Horowitz would sometimes indulge in outlandish behavior to get a rise out of Levant, such as playing a melody with his right hand on the piano and the bass with his derriere. Or he would elaborate the popular ditty "Tea for Two" with endless flourishes, arpeggios, and brilliant double thirds.

On their walks down Broadway, the two pianists were sometimes accosted by fans who would invariably stop Levant and ask him for his autograph. Radio and movies had made him far better known to the general public than his virtuoso friend. "Vlodya, don't you resent that they never ask you?" Levant wondered.

Laughing heartily, Horowitz answered, "I'm glad. I'm so happy. Let them ask you. Take his autograph. Take his. He is the greatest pianist!"

Though only three years Levant's senior and proud of his American citizenship, Horowitz had a nineteenth-century European sensibility. For Levant, Horowitz's friendship was a connection to—even a dispensation from—the great Paderewski, whose dismissal had long shadowed Levant's career.

Horowitz once took Levant aside and showed him a number of photographs of himself as a youth, looking like Franz Liszt with long brown hair. In one of them, Horowitz was clearly wearing lipstick. Horowitz looked at the photograph with Oscar and said with a sly smile, "Decadent." As he showed Oscar other pictures of himself as an older man, he added sadly, "Not so decadent."

As for Horowitz's gay side, Levant seemed to have respected Vlodya's privacy and his feelings. Levant was not above making homosexual jokes, but he never seemed to have done so at Horowitz's expense. Most of Horowitz's intimates knew of his status as a bisexual. June Levant remembered that he once left Wanda for a tall, blond, beautiful young man. "He was happy as can be," she said, "but he needed Wanda because of his career . . . he was like a man going off with a pretty showgirl for a while, and when he got through, he came back to Wanda."

Of all the things for which Levant admired Horowitz, chief among them was the fact that Horowitz had not altered his Russian Jewish name when he embarked on his concert career. Jewish musicians had often Frenchified their names or disguised their origins by using pseudonyms (Josef Levine became Josef Lhévinne, for example). But, as Levant pointed out, "Horowitz made his last name sound good because *he* was so good that he sanctified it." As far as Oscar was concerned, one of Horowitz's great achievements was simply in popularizing his Jewish name.

But there was another side to Levant's friendship with Horowitz. The uncontested master of the piano served as a kind of goad to Levant's ambition as a concert artist, just as Gershwin had fired his ambition to compose. "No matter how pure your outlook," Levant once remarked, "there is always someone who makes you feel guilty." Horowitz's superb technique was a touchstone of perfection that Levant felt ought to be within his own grasp. He was becoming concerned about just how he stacked up in the pantheon of concert pianists. It even crossed his mind that he ought to have studied with Nadia Boulanger.

"What is it that this woman's got that's supposed to be so fantastic? Do you think I ought to go?" Oscar asked David Diamond, who had studied with Boulanger in Paris. "I mean, after Schoenberg, isn't that enough? If this woman's anything like Schoenberg, I don't need it."

"No, no, really," Diamond responded. "I think she would be fascinated by you."

But despite the goad Horowitz provided, and despite his insecurity about his standing among other concert artists, Levant's own temperament got in his way. He could play beautifully at home, but he couldn't command the faith in his own technique to develop a more challenging repertoire for the concert stage. Again and again, he fell back on the old crowd pleasers his audience expected of him: mostly Gershwin.

Diamond made up a program for Oscar to rehearse for a possible Town Hall recital, but Levant would not practice it. Diamond took his case to Artur Rubinstein, a friend of Levant's and Horowitz's rival for the crown of supreme pianist in the Romantic tradition.

"Isn't it a shame that Oscar really doesn't want to buckle down?" he asked Rubinstein. "He would be so wonderful!"

"He has the same disease that I had when I was his age. I didn't want to practice. Now I pay a high price," Rubinstein said. Diamond felt that Levant had the genius to enter Horowitz and Rubinstein's class of pianists, but he lacked the discipline.

> What, after all, made Horowitz great? This ability to practice so many hours a day. When it comes to talent of the kind that Oscar had, I put him in genius category. Oscar had everything that genius had, the ability to read music immediately and make sense out of it and make you feel that he knows what he's doing . . . it didn't make him less of a genius in my eyes that it didn't mean enough to him. Gershwin's music he knew backwards and forwards. Even in Oscar's own music he'd fall apart, in the Sonatina or the Concerto . . . but when it came to Gershwin, never a note out of place. *There* he would practice.

But composers like David Diamond were not alone in their plaint that Levant was not living up to his potential as a concert artist. Goddard Lieberson, who through his Masterworks Recordings was aware of Levant's slowly expanding repertoire, seemed convinced that he was wasting his time appearing in the movies or plowing old ground on the radio.

It was a night for a little *Gebrauchsmusik*. Levant, who had made his name as court jester and pianist in some of the great houses of the twenties and thirties, was now about to perform at the greatest house of them all. Levant was invited to play at the White House on January 14, 1947, at the behest of President Truman.

No pianist better personified the Roosevelt-Truman years than Oscar Levant, the working man's genius. The cabbie who loved Tchaikovsky, the counterman at Woolworth's who listened to the Metropolitan Opera broadcast on Saturday afternoons, the Fifth Avenue physician who tuned in to the NBC Symphony on Sunday nights while visiting his mother in the Bronx—to that midcult audience, Levant was a hero. He was one of them—he personified the democratic, popular spirit of the age—and his music often, when he wasn't playing Gershwin, came from the Romantic piano literature which Americans held in high esteem.

Hofmann, Paderewski, Rachmaninoff had all played on the Steinway piano in the East Room of the White House. Now it was Oscar's turn.

Harry Truman was the perfect host for Levant's visit to Washington. The blunt, cagey, unpretentious Truman was the most musically literate president to occupy the White House. (He had strongly encouraged his daughter, Margaret, in her singing career, and would go so far as to publicly rebuke Paul Hume, the *Washington Post* music critic who would give her a bad review.) One of Truman's secret service agents recalled how the thirty-third president often wandered over to Blair House across the street, where he would play the Steinway by himself for an hour or more. Truman had often listened to Levant on *Information, Please!,* and he enjoyed the pianist's self-deprecating style of humor. Truman was not a fan of "noise composers," and the *Rhapsody* was one of his favorite contemporary pieces of music.

This command performance at the White House was a pinnacle of Levant's career, but it was off the scale as far as his nerves were concerned. As soon as the White House chief of protocol called the Levants, briefing them as to how things would proceed and advising them not to be late, Oscar began to panic. June put the studs in Oscar's shirt, combed his hair, and generally got him ready for his White House recital, which would be held in front of the president, eight justices of the Supreme Court, various invited cabinet officers, congressmen, and senators, and Mrs. Woodrow Wilson. (Oscar had proudly worn a Woodrow Wilson button when he was a boy in Pittsburgh's Hill district.)

The Levants arrived a full thirty minutes early. A naval aide greeted Oscar and June and escorted them down the long, portrait-lined corridors to the entrance of the East Room. The epauletted aide in dress whites drew himself up and announced, "Mr. and Mrs. Oscar Levant." Oscar and June walked through the folding doors into a completely empty room. For the next twenty minutes they stood looking at each other in the immaculate East Room until the next guests were announced and ushered in to join them.

Oscar's dinner companion was young Margaret Truman, who wore a blue chiffon dress. Margaret tried to relax the pianist, who seemed to her a bundle of nerves. Oscar couldn't take his mind off his upcoming recital, which, according to protocol, was supposed to run exactly twenty-four and a half minutes long.

After dinner Levant was escorted to the piano by another naval aide, who stood at arm's length, his rifle at his side, as Levant began his recital. "If I make a mistake, I'll be shot," Levant worried.

He began with the opening movement of Beethoven's "Moonlight Sonata." He played eight selections, closing with a spirited rendition of the *Rhapsody*. As they left the White House, Oscar turned to June and said, "Now I guess we owe them a dinner."

• • •

Levant would closely follow Senator Estes Kefauver's hearings on organized crime that began in 1950 and resulted in the extradition or jailing of many of the nation's most dangerous gangsters. But in the few years before the Kefauver hearings would, in Oscar's words, "ruin my social life," Levant hung out with a number of second-generation mobsters. These were men who modeled themselves on the popular image of gangsters in the movies, which were in turn modeled on the old-time mobsters Levant had known as a younger man in the twenties and early thirties. Some of the film impersonations were more recent, however; George Raft had been impressed by Joe Adonis's good looks and style and had patterned his debonair thug after the gangster known alternately as "Joey A." or "Mr. Fix." (Joe had changed his name when a reference to the Greek figure of Adonis struck his vanity.)

In the late forties, June and Oscar frequented a restaurant on West Fifty-fifth Street called Patio Bruno's. The restaurant, a genteel ladies' tearoom, was a favorite hangout for many of the underworld bosses of organized crime. It was the last place you'd look, among the scones and finger sandwiches, for a war council of the national crime syndicate. But it was here at Patio Bruno's that Oscar sometimes socialized with infamous men like Frank Costello and Joe Adonis, the successors to Al Rothstein, "Big Frenchy," and "Nigger" Nate. Moving among the dainty tables, sitting themselves down next to the Levants, waving their big cigars in the air, these crime bosses enjoyed associating with a man of Levant's celebrity. They also liked his sardonic wit and rough manners; like Oscar, they had all come up from the streets. Levant continued to count among his friends some of the country's most notorious hoodlums. But these gangsters were a little different from the old-style mobsters who had bootlegged in the twenties and thirties. The new-style hoodlum thought of himself as a patron of the arts, and he prided himself on his classical music collection and first editions, all the while fighting extradition as Kefauver stepped up his criminal investigations. These killers with social aspirations liked the fact that Oscar Levant was as comfortable as they were in pool halls and nightclubs but knew Horowitz and Stokowski. Every summer a fleet of black Cadillacs driven by bodyguards pulled up in front of Lewisohn Stadium to hear Levant play Gershwin. The men would emerge from the vast darkness of their cars to pay their respects to culture, Levant-style.

Frank Costello, head of the Gambino crime family, was known as "the boss of bosses," the "prime minister," the elder statesman of organized crime. He knew Oscar from his early bootlegging days, and whenever he bumped into Levant at Patio Bruno's, tears would come to his eyes as he waxed lyrical about the old days. "Frank Costello gets as sentimental as a Chopin nocturne," Levant would tell his friends.

June didn't like Oscar hanging around gangsters. They were dangerous, she was afraid of them, and she wanted to rid Oscar of these associations. But the Levants' imminent move to California would make his mobster associations a moot point. Levant had been invited by the William Morris Agency to be part of a new Al Jolson radio show, broadcast from the West Coast.

32

Romance on the High Seas

"I knew Doris Day before she became a virgin."

"How long is this going to take? I'm hungry," Oscar grumbled to the men in the Beverly Hills office of the William Morris Agency. They had gathered to talk about the *Kraft Music Hall,* a new radio show starring Al Jolson, to be broadcast over NBC on Thursday nights.

"Shall we send out for a sandwich for you?" one of them asked.

"Naw," said Oscar. "But what's this meeting for? I haven't talked a deal with anyone yet."

"No one has a deal yet," said the man who had offered the sandwich. "This is just to see if everybody likes one another."

"Suppose we hate each other to start with, then slowly grow fonder," Oscar suggested. Al Jolson got up from his chair. Nattily dressed, paunchy, and deeply tanned, the great Joley hardly resembled the agile minstrel of his youth.

"Oscar," Jolson began, his synthetic southern accent weaving in and out of his voice. "I was telling the boys. I don't want headaches. I'm nearing sixty. That's too old for trouble. We gotta work together on the show. We don't want to have any of that stuff just before the broadcast of someone saying 'This stinks!' Two days before the broadcast—that's not the time to say 'This stinks!' "

After a moment of silence, Levant spoke up. "I don't think we'll have any trouble."

"Can't have any," Jolson repeated, almost to himself. "At sixty a man don't want no headaches. No, suh! Time to retire."

"Toscanini is over eighty," Oscar said quietly.

"Over eighty?" Jolson asked, beginning to perk up.

"Yes. And he's the most dynamic man you've ever seen. . . . When he gets up in front of an orchestra to record, he becomes a young man again."

"He's really over eighty?" Jolson was quiet for a moment. "Maybe I'll stay in the business awhile."

"I'm going out to the studio," Oscar told Jolson and the other men. "Have someone call me about the business end of this deal."

"You'll do a little piano with Al, won't you, Oscar?" asked Charles Isaacs, who, along with his writing partner, Mannie Manheim, had just been hired to write the show. "I think the people will expect that."

"I'm not an accompanist," Levant insisted.

Jolson stood up again, as if he were about to scamper down the runway of the Winter Garden in the middle of *Sinbad*. "I had an idea you'd do a little noodlin' on the piano," he told Oscar, "then I come in with 'Toot, Toot, Tootsie,' you drop out, and the orchestra comes in."

"But I'm not that kind of a piano player," Oscar reiterated.

"You can noodle four bars, can't you?" Jolson asked impatiently.

"Oh, sure, sure. But I'm hungry." Levant left the office.

The youngest Levant to inherit Al Jolson, Oscar had come full circle. His uncle Oscar Radin had been the first in the family to be put through his paces as Jolson's music director. That was in the twenties, when Jolson was billed as "The World's Greatest Entertainer." And then Harry—poor Harry, who was now reduced to taking slow, rehabilitative walks through Central Park with his nephew Marc—had conducted the orchestra for Jolson back when Jolson was still a force of nature.

June remembers how important it was for Oscar that he, too, follow the family tradition and get his chance to work with the legendary performer, though Jolson was now long past his prime. At sixty years of age, he had outlived his era. But to Levant, he still represented the twenties and all they stood for: exuberant youth, high times, musical awakenings, "Swanee," George Gershwin. Jolson's career was undergoing a brief resurgence, thanks to *The Jolson Story,* which was the hit film of 1946. A whole new generation of postwar "bobby-soxers" went wild over Jolson, just because he reminded them of the film's star, Larry Parks, who was younger and better looking.

Jolson was not thrilled to be hosting a new radio program, but the Kraft cheese company trapped him like a rat by offering him $7,500 for each broadcast. "I didn't want to do it," Jolson would later confess. "I was swindled into it by this tremendous ego of mine. I'm like a child, I tell ya!"

When it was announced in the summer of 1947 that Oscar Levant was returning to radio after a two-year hiatus, it was widely thought that the two powerful egos could not work together. Scriptwriter Charles Isaacs didn't know exactly what to make of the volatile mixture. The program wasn't designed to showcase Levant's brand of wit but to feature Jolson and guest stars such as Charles Boyer, Lucille Ball, and Judy Garland. The scriptwriters gave Jolson little running jokes and gags to be used between songs, usually with Levant acting as straight man. It was a hard job: "Jolson was constantly torn between his pride at again being a prominent star and his dislike of reading jokes reminding him of his age," Isaacs remembered. The scriptwriters' jokes "bordered on the infantile," as Jolson biographer Herbert G. Goldman noted. They usually fell into four categories: (1) Jolson is old; (2) Jolson is rich; (3) Jolson is an egomaniac; and (4) Larry Parks.

Kraft Music Hall was a hit with the audience, especially the nostalgia buffs, in its first season; it was the number one musical variety show on the air that year. But its popularity didn't hold. By the second season, the show no longer clicked. As Goldman has pointed out, the combination of a slowed-down Jolson and an acerbic Levant was not pleasing. Jolson complained that his writers hadn't captured his personality the way, for example, Bing Crosby's writers had captured his.

Levant was little help. He had never liked working within the bounds of a script—he hated being told what to say as much as he bristled at being told what music to play. However, Levant would be kind to Jolson in his summation of the whole experience: "I loved being excoriated by Jolson," he would write in his second book. "His voice had such magic—an irresistible baritone beauty—regardless of what words he used."

Jolson never really understood Levant's brand of humor. Levant's level of cynicism was alien to the cantor's son turned Dockstadder minstrel. He used to tell Oscar, "Don't be cryptic," thinking it meant "sarcastic." Things became noticeably strained between the two men.

By the time Judy Garland appeared—on the first show of the second season—the tension was palpable. Jolson had aged noticeably in the past year, and he had begun to lose his hearing, a condition he covered up out of vanity. He'd often let remarks go by unanswered, with the devastating effect of dead air on the show. The jokes became even more banal, and Jolson's stamina gave out. His numbers were cut back to medleys of his old songs. The last show was recorded on May 18, 1949, and broadcast eight days later, on Jolson's sixty-third birthday. When it was over, the two stars and their writers gathered again at Jolson's dressing room for a postmortem. "The shows have been good. I don't know why they have to cancel us," Jolson complained.

"I'm just as happy," said Levant, slouching deep in his chair. "I won't have to shave on Thursdays anymore."

Oscar had brought his family out to Hollywood so they could be together during the summer of 1947 while he worked on his final film for Warner Bros., a lightweight musical called *Romance on the High Seas.* The film introduced a fresh, engaging newcomer with a thrilling voice and singing style, the young Doris Day.

The Levants rented a house on Camden Drive in Beverly Hills, one that nearly adjoined, by way of a back alley, the home of another Pittsburgher who had made it big—Gene Kelly.

The Levants held on to their Alwyn Court apartment, but they sold their Westport, Connecticut, home where they had spent the last three summers. The Levant children would now grow up surrounded by swimming pools, and June was back living near her mother.

The film's director, Michael Curtiz, was an indefatigable, painstaking workaholic who had been a distinguished director in Europe before coming to America in 1927. Curtiz, a handsome, gray-haired Hungarian, would direct seventy-four films for Warner Bros. during his two decades at that studio, winning an Academy Award in 1942 for *Casablanca.* Curtiz prided himself on some of his film discoveries, such as Errol Flynn and John Garfield, whom he directed in *Four Daughters;* Doris Day's name would be added to that list. The director was also known for his confused English. In one scene involving Levant, Curtiz suddenly stopped the filming and yelled, "I don't like the lighting. It's too Semitic." It became clear to Levant and the crew that Curtiz had meant the lighting was too symmetrical.

Jule Styne and Sammy Cahn had written the score for *Romance on the High Seas,* a musical bedroom farce whose main action takes place aboard a luxury cruiser bound for South America. The sets and costumes were indeed stylish and tasteful, but the only thing fresh and memorable about the film would be the young band singer new to Hollywood, Doris Day. Depressed about her recent divorce and skeptical about launching an acting career, Day had broken down twice in the middle of her audition while singing "Embraceable You," but Curtiz was not put off. He arranged to test her for the part, telling her, "I sometimes like girl who is not actress. Is less pretend and more heart."

"I was very aware of who Oscar was, and I was excited to be working with him," Doris Day said about the filming of her first motion picture. "I remember him smoking all the time and being covered in ashes. Wardrobe had to follow him around with a whisk broom. He was already having trouble breathing, and he always had a cup of coffee with him."

Day asked Levant why he smoked so much and told him he should quit, but he wouldn't hear of it.

It was a congenial set. Jack Carson, who played Day's love interest, helped the newcomer relax in front of the camera and gave her advice about film acting. "Oscar kept us all in stitches," the actress remembers.

Years later, during the height of Day's fame as a wholesome, girl-next-door type in a series of light comedies with Rock Hudson, Levant would tell people that he "knew Doris Day before she became a virgin." It was a remark that made the actress laugh, because she was annoyed by her squeaky-clean image. After all, she had been married twice and was raising a young son before she even appeared in her first film. And her onscreen romance with Jack Carson turned into a real, behind-the-scenes affair with her leading man.

What was surprising was that veteran director Michael Curtiz, with his European background and sensibility, didn't make better use of Levant, who is given fifth billing in the production (after having third billing in *Humoresque*). And Levant is oddly detached in the film, unconvincing as Doris Day's cast-off boyfriend. Though "Oscar Farrar" is clearly meant to be a takeoff on Oscar Levant, the character is interesting only when he has a chance to make wry, self-referential comments about the confusing status of his musical career.

Before the film was released, it had to go through the scrutiny of the Hollywood censors. There was little in this light comedy to offend, but the censors duly noted when Doris Day's outfits were too revealing. A letter to Jack Warner from Joseph I. Breen, vice president of the Production Code Administration, objected to one of Levant's lines:

Oscar's line, "Man cannot live by borscht alone," is unacceptable. The
reason for its unacceptability is that it paraphrases one of Christ's lines
in the gospel and will very likely give offense to patrons.

Only a Hollywood denizen would refer to Scripture as "Christ's
lines."

The film was a modest success when it was released in September
1948 (it was more successful in England, where it was released as *It's
Magic*).

A woman in Frederickstown, Pennsylvania, wrote to a Hollywood
fan magazine to comment on how sexy Levant was in the film. The
same phenomenon was noted in Earl Wilson's gossip column: "I've
seen girls in their late teens get giddy when they heard Levant, who's
forty and far from good looking, was in the joint." Levant's appeal to
young women, who probably found his unconventional looks non-
threatening and his sense of humor sexy, would be borne out some
sixteen years later, when a young Nora Johnson, daughter of screen-
writer-producer Nunnally Johnson, based her hero worship of a pianist on Oscar Levant, in her novel *The World of Henry Orient*.

It wasn't enough to be Oscar Farrar all summer long during the filming of *Romance on the High Seas;* he had to be Oscar Levant as well. It
was hard to imagine that it had been sixteen summers since Levant
had first appeared at the Hollywood Bowl with Robert Russell Bennett. Now he was preparing Tchaikovsky's Piano Concerto No. 1 in
B-flat Minor for the Bowl, in between filming scenes as Doris Day's
sidekick at Warner Bros.

This was the same piece of music his mother had so adored. Oscar
had taken the Mark Hamburg recording of Tchaikovsky's Piano
Concerto to Pittsburgh long ago, and Annie had been enraptured by
it. Now, two years after his mother's death, Levant would play the
piece in public for the first time. He was also scheduled to play Grieg's
Concerto in A Minor with Eugene Ormandy conducting.

The crashing chords of the Tchaikovsky Piano Concerto had rescued Horowitz from artistic oblivion in 1921. Levant was playing the
piece at the tender age of forty. He had a lot of catching up to do, and
he had to do it as an already famous pianist. But the Hollywood Bowl
concert was not an auspicious occasion. By the time Levant appeared
to play the Tchaikovsky, it was nearly eleven o'clock. Most of the
audience had already begun to head downhill. Levant felt somewhat
used by Ormandy, believing that the conductor had simply wanted

him as a soloist to boost box-office receipts and fill the Hollywood Bowl.

But within the next year, Levant and Ormandy's Philadelphia Orchestra would record the Tchaikovsky Piano Concerto for Goddard Lieberson on a "long-playing record"—three years too late for his mother to hear it.

Levant's favorite word for his career at 20th Century–Fox, where he had another three-picture deal, was "uninspired." Fox was the only studio to insist that Levant stick to the script rather than ad-lib or write his own lines, and it shows. In *You Were Meant for Me,* Levant again plays a self-referential character named Oscar Hoffman, manager of a band led by song-and-dance-man Dan Dailey. The band is called "Chuck Arnold and His Sophisticates." The picture seems to have been a remake of a 1942 film called *Orchestra Wives.*

Levant was unable to heed Stravinsky's veiled advice to break with the immediate past. The film is set in the twenties, and one of its strengths is its score of hummable, popular tunes from that era, including "Sweet Georgia Brown" and "Ain't She Sweet," two songs Ben Bernie and his orchestra had popularized with Levant at the piano. Levant also performs Gershwin's Concerto in F, providing one of the redeeming virtues in an otherwise silly, predictable film.

Since he had never had any real ambition to develop as an actor, Levant was dependent on the personalities involved in each production. When he found himself working with Jerry Wald or John Garfield or Clifford Odets, or in the Gershwin film biography with many of the men who had been part of Gershwin's life, Levant rose to the occasion and turned in a creditable and engaging performance. When the production lacked input from those whom Levant truly respected, he seemed to simply walk through the film.

But if *You Were Meant for Me* was a new low in Levant's inchoate film career, *The Barkleys of Broadway* would provide a fresh start. At Metro-Goldwyn-Mayer, with its well-oiled machinery, the American musical was undergoing an infusion of new blood, and Oscar Levant would be part of that process.

As if to remind himself that his true racket was serious music, during the filming of *Romance on the High Seas* Levant agreed to write a series of articles for *Saturday Review* called "Scratching the Surface with Oscar Levant." The title was accompanied by a small pen-and-ink drawing of a phonograph needle resting on a long-playing record.

With the dateline "Hollywood," Levant's first article appeared on

August 30, 1947, and its style reflects the pianist's own conversational interests. Here Levant writes mostly about the relationship between Hollywood and the record industry. Hollywood's machinations, bad taste, and pretensions were grist for his mill. He also used the column to pass along the witticisms he and his friends traded in.

But after his second article, Levant decided a monthly column was too much of a commitment. As with his experience on *Information, Please!*, the satisfaction of having an audience didn't outweigh the pressures of performing on cue, and he quit.

Despite a growing disenchantment on the part of the press, by the summer of 1948 Levant had been a national celebrity for a decade. But his fame had come at a high cost. By the end of the forties, Levant had nearly exhausted the tolerance of his wife and closest friends. His stage fright and irritability were worse after ten years of concertizing than they had been at his first Lewisohn Stadium performance.

His playing had never been better, but what his audience and the press could not hear was the private torment that concertizing inflicted on him. Oscar had learned to make jokes out of his neuroses, but his truly extreme behavior was still a secret to the public at large.

The forties, which had defined Oscar Levant, were now coming to a close. The new decade would cruelly redefine him.

PART V

The Fabulous Invalid

33

Freed at Last

"It's not a pretty face, I grant you.
But underneath this flabby exterior is
an enormous lack of character."

ABOUT TO BEGIN THE FIRST LEG OF A TOUR THROUGH THE PACIFIC
Northwest, Levant entered Union Station in Los Angeles. He collected an armful of magazines to read on the train and asked the newsstand clerk for the latest issue of *The New Yorker*. "You're out of luck. I just sold the last copy," she told the pianist.

To be told that he was "out of luck" minutes before boarding a train to begin a concert tour was more than Levant's network of superstitions could bear. He threw the magazines back onto the counter. "Now they're tainted by your remark! I'm going to memorize your name and throw my head away!"

Levant would never again go near that newsstand, no matter how many times he found himself in Union Station preparing for a journey. He also refused to ever buy or read *The New Yorker* again, and it had been his favorite magazine since its founding in 1925.

Levant continued to perform Gershwin's music for record crowds each summer at Lewisohn Stadium, and in concert halls throughout the country. His playing helped keep Gershwin's concert music before the public. Toward the end of 1949, Levant tried to reintroduce Gershwin's long-forgotten *Second Rhapsody* to his concert audiences, having just recorded it—brilliantly—with Morton Gould that summer. In fact, he would play the *Second Rhapsody,* along with Arthur Honegger's Concertino and Aram Khachaturian's Concerto for Piano and Orchestra at Carnegie Hall with Dimitri Mitropoulos conducting the New York Philharmonic on December 29, 1949—a program called "bizarre" by one critic. Playing at Carnegie Hall is the pinnacle of any musical artist's career. Hardly an unqualified admirer of Levant, Olin Downes of *The New York Times* took Levant to task for occasionally "whacking the keys" but leavened his criticism with warm praise: "His singing tone is melting and beautiful . . . he could go far as a virtuoso, farther than he went last night."

Many critics seemed to have been impressed by Levant's remarkable improvement and maturity as an artist. He continued to attract tremendous crowds throughout the 1949–50 concert season and to command their loyalty, a source of pride for the insecure pianist. While Levant was on a concert tour through Texas, his train was delayed and he was three hours late for a Houston recital. When he finally made it to the concert hall, he was astonished and deeply moved to find the audience of five thousand still waiting for him.

In 1948 Khachaturian's "Sabre Dance," recorded by Efrem Kurtz and the New York Philharmonic Symphony as part of the composer's Gayne Ballet Suite, had displaced Levant's Columbia recording of *Rhapsody in Blue* as the best-selling classical album in the country. American concert audiences delighted in Khachaturian's whirling, pulse-racing work, which never failed to bring down the house. Levant's last compositional undertaking would be to transcribe it for piano. When Levant completed the transcription and recorded it for Columbia, it shot up through the popular music charts like a Moiseyev dancer.

Since 1944, Levant had recorded Chopin études and nocturnes, Beethoven sonatas, and Brahms's Intermezzo. He recorded Gershwin's Preludes for Piano in 1941, Gershwin's Concerto in F in 1942, *Rhapsody in Blue* in 1945. With Morton Gould in 1949 he recorded the *Second Rhapsody* and the *"I Got Rhythm" Variations.* Liszt, Lecouna, Honegger, Grieg, Ravel, Schumann, Shostakovich, Poulenc—but, curiously, no Schoenberg.

Throughout the blossoming of his concert and recording careers, Levant's superstitions continued to mount. The very mention of his mother's name or his hometown caused him to lash out at the unsuspecting violator. His children learned to make sure that the Heinz catsup bottle was always placed on the table with the words "Pittsburgh, Pa." hidden from view.

• • •

From 1948 to 1954 Levant worked concurrently for 20th Century–Fox and Metro-Goldwyn-Mayer, with a three-film contract at each studio. *The Barkleys of Broadway* was Levant's first film for MGM. The Levants purchased a house at 905 North Roxbury Drive in Beverly Hills, not far from Ira and Lee Gershwin's home at 1021 North Roxbury, where George had spent part of the last year of his life. James Stewart lived next door and Lucille Ball across the street. Levant had once joked about "those snobs who lived on North Roxbury"—now he was joining them. It was a spacious, Spanish-style villa with high ceilings; all the rooms on the first floor opened onto a patio, including a special music room for Oscar's piano. There were avocado, fig, grapefruit, and peach trees in the backyard and plenty of room for the three girls to grow up boisterous and happy, especially once a swimming pool was put in and they could have grand little birthday parties at poolside. By now Marcia was an eight-year-old with a headful of glorious Titian hair. Lorna, now six and blond like her mother, was quieter than Marcia and very stubborn. Amanda, just three, had her father's green eyes, dark eyebrows, and wide, terrific grin. Their street was well known to tour buses, and whenever Levant saw a driver pointing out his house, he'd shudder.

Adolph Green and Betty Comden had written the part of Ezra Millar in *The Barkleys of Broadway* for Oscar Levant. During Levant's *Information, Please!* days, Comden and her partner would occasionally angle for tickets to the tiny studio where the program was being broadcast. Green shared two great passions with Levant. One was music and the other was the movies. But when Green first met Levant in Los Angeles in the mid-forties, he was a little afraid to speak to him. He would later write about Levant at this period in his life:

> Oscar was at the height of his national fame as a mercurial bad boy Renaissance man, with a far-ranging intellect and shattering wit. He had a quality . . . the mysterious ability to transmit to an audience a feeling of imminent danger—a sense that he was liable suddenly to do something totally unpredictable and devastating.

Thus was Oscar in real life, and no one ever felt quite secure around him. It was impossible to predict what would make him explode, as his category of taboo subjects, Green came to realize, seemed mysteriously to mutate and multiply. In the midst of a conversation about music, the writer and lyracist mentioned Prokofiev's Third Piano Concerto.

"What the hell did you have to bring that up for?" Levant demanded. "Now you've spoiled everything." He ordered his young friend out of the house.

Judy Garland was slated for the female lead in *Barkleys* opposite Fred Astaire. (Their May–December pairing in *Easter Parade* a year earlier had proved quite successful.) Levant was greatly looking forward to working with Garland. The two had recently appeared together on *The Bell Telephone Hour,* and Garland made a guest appearance on the *Kraft Music Hall.* Garland sang "Over the Rainbow," "Johnny One Note," and, with Jolson, "Pretty Baby," while Levant accompanied them on the piano. Garland was just twenty-six years old, but she was battling anorexia, an addiction to pills, and a crumbling marriage to the director Vincente Minnelli. She had become MGM's most brittle star.

The production was set to begin, but with Judy's weight now a mere eighty-six pounds and the actress again hooked on her only reliable diet cure, amphetamines, she failed to appear on the set. MGM gave Garland a three-month sick leave, and Ginger Rogers was called in to replace her. Suddenly, *The Barkleys of Broadway* had become an Astaire-Rogers picture, reuniting this most famous of dance teams for the last time.

Astaire and Rogers had often considered getting together again "for a rematch" as Astaire called it, but the right property had never turned up. Comden and Green had written the script for Judy Garland, but the slew of dance numbers would have been impossible for the eighty-six-pound actress, who now sometimes found herself unable to summon the strength to get out of bed.

Finally, production 1433—*The Barkleys of Broadway*—got under way. Then something awful happened. Garland appeared on the set where she had just been replaced, fitted in a dress designed for the picture. Levant felt heartsick to see this immensely talented young woman making such a sorry spectacle of herself "preening and parading around the set," flirting with the cameramen and crew. Ginger Rogers, who hated public squabbles, quickly retreated to her dressing room, slamming the door behind her.

Straws were drawn to see who would have to tell MGM's biggest star to go home. Garland was the jewel in L. B. Mayer's diadem, though it was said that he treated his racehorses better than his female stars. The role of Garland's executioner fell to Charles Walters, who had directed her the year before in *Easter Parade.*

Walters gingerly approached the actress and, amid fulsome praise, asked her to leave the set. She refused. Gently taking her arm, he began leading her away. She turned her head toward Ginger Rogers's dressing room and yelled, "Why, that no-talent bitch, that no-talent, fucking bitch!" as Walters guided her off the set.

Just then Fred Astaire appeared, puzzled by Garland's noisy imprecations. "What are they doing to that off-beat kid?" he asked innocuously. When shooting resumed, everyone on the set was visibly shaken. For Oscar, the scene combined his own two worst fears— rejection and public humiliation. He also felt sorry for Ginger Rogers, whose timing that day was thrown off by the unsettling incident.

The Levants and the Minnellis remained close throughout the debacle. The Minnellis' daughter, Liza, was the same age as Amanda, and the two girls were friends. Tiny, dark-eyed Liza was a frequent guest at the girls' pool parties on North Roxbury Drive. Oscar and June were both fond of Vincente Minnelli—"Vin-chen-tay" as Gene Kelly liked to call him, giving the name its Italian pronunciation. Oscar would often run into Judy at the Gershwins', where he had resumed his habit of dropping in unannounced just as he had as a brash kid commuting between the the the two wings of George and Ira's double penthouses.

The Barkleys of Broadway was Levant's first film working with "the Freed unit," as Arthur Freed's production crew came to be known. It would prove to be his most satisfying working relationship, producing three of his most successful films.

Levant had known Freed since his Tin Pan Alley days. Like Levant, Freed had entered the film industry in 1928, the first year of sound, when he was hired by MGM's Irving G. Thalberg to write songs (with Nacio Herb Brown) for the studio's first film musical, *Broadway Melody*. Freed and Brown wrote "Singin' in the Rain" for MGM's second musical, *The Hollywood Revue of 1929*. Freed became a full producer of musicals at MGM with *Babes in Arms* (1939), a Rodgers and Hart show that starred Judy Garland and Mickey Rooney. By the time Levant was working under him, Freed was considered the best producer of musicals in all of Hollywood.

Freed's great talent—besides his way with a lyric—was an ability to gather gifted individuals around him and let them go to work. It was Arthur Freed who gave Gene Kelly the chance to direct, who brought choreographer Michael Kidd to Hollywood, and who gave director Stanley Donen his start. Freed had brought Comden and Green to Los Angeles, where they flourished as screenwriters. He also brought Alan Jay Lerner to Hollywood. Freed respected Levant, and it shows in the three musicals they made together at MGM. "Arthur Freed would have cast Oscar Levant as Huckleberry Finn if he could've gotten away with it," Adolph Green observed.

Levant plays Ezra Millar, a Broadway composer. He is given two satisfying scenes at the piano: first, at a society party for the Barkleys on the opening night of their new show, he plays the "Sabre Dance." His second piano solo takes place toward the end of the film, at a benefit performance. Here he plays a truncated version of the Tchaikovsky Piano Concerto No. 1 in B-flat Minor, in formal dress surrounded by a full orchestra. Levant took credit for working out some striking camera angles for this scene so that the entire performance is dynamic:

> [Pianists] do their jobs, but they are always shot the same way. Usually they open up with a very big closeup of the twinkling hands of the player (always with a mirror where the piano trademark ought to be), then they pull back slowly into a decreasingly dramatic long shot showing him surrounded either by massed musicians or (if he is in love) nothing at all. I claim the responsibility for suggesting an entirely new shot: I reversed it so that at the climax of the piece the camera came in from a very long shot and ended on my hands.

Levant was proud of having worked out these innovative approaches, and he would follow through with their use in his next two Freed films.

On November 4, 1950, Harry Levant died. Another phone call, another solemn voice on the other end of the line, this time informing Levant that his eldest brother had succumbed to a series of strokes. Now Harry was gone. His final stroke had undone the fifty-year-old man, who had been reduced to hobbling around Central Park with his nephew, unable to stride through the city as in the old days. He had loved good food and women. He had been a voluptuary without guilt, with lots of bonhomie and a great deal of raffish charm. And he had been good-natured about his baby brother's fame, which had so eclipsed his own. "He's a bit of a genius," Harry used to say about Oscar. It was the last time June ever remembered seeing Oscar cry—the first was when Bea Kaufman had died. But this time Levant couldn't bring himself to attend the funeral. Death held too much terror for that.

It began over a pool table at the Gershwins', where Arthur Freed, a longtime friend of George and Ira's, was a frequent guest. There Ira

Gershwin agreed to sell Freed the film rights to the title of George Gershwin's orchestral suite *An American in Paris*. As with so many things of major significance in Levant's life, the film's presiding spirit was George Gershwin. The film critic Andrew Sarris once observed that if there were an *auteur* haunting *An American in Paris,* it was the ghost of George Gershwin. Agreements were made, Ira was hired as consultant for the film, and Freed's Culver City machinery went into high gear.

Alan Jay Lerner, whom Freed brought to Hollywood to write the screenplay, once said that Freed began a sentence on Wednesday and finished it on Friday. A heavyset man who was always on a diet, Freed used to drift onto the set during filming, his hands jingling the coins in his pockets, and not say two words. Despite his ponderousness, Freed knew how to get what he wanted, and he insisted that Lerner write in a part for Oscar Levant.

They decided that Levant would play Adam Cook, "a Dave Diamond type"—a kind of perpetual expatriate composer living in Europe on the largesse of foundation fellowships. "We thought of no one but Oscar Levant for the part of Jerry's sidekick, Adam Cook," Vincente Minnelli later wrote. "Including Oscar in the film lent the enterprise a sort of legitimacy . . . though he would have blanched if I'd told him that."

Fred Astaire and Gene Kelly were both under consideration for the part of Jerry Mulligan—an American studying art in Paris on the GI Bill—but plans to include a lengthy ballet tipped the scales toward Kelly, who was more of a balletic dancer than Astaire.

One thing Freed insisted on from the first was that there would be no concert music in the film. "I don't want any lulls in this picture," Freed told the assembled collaborators during a meeting at MGM. Levant, of course, felt differently, but it seemed that Freed only wanted Levant to play a medley of Gershwin's songs. After all, the "Freed Unit" was redefining the movie musical, ensuring that the story be as strong as the music, and at no point would the action stop just to showcase a star turn.

Levant felt instinctively that Kelly would not support his idea of including a concert sequence of any kind in *An American in Paris*. The vital, energetic dancer was becoming a powerhouse at MGM. His work as the star and codirector with Stanley Donen in *On the Town* the previous year had boosted Kelly to a major presence on the MGM lot.

After the meeting, Levant walked dejectedly into Minnelli's office and collapsed into a chair. He then blurted out an idea: that he, Le-

vant, be filmed playing all the instruments in the orchestra in a performance of the third movement of Gershwin's Concerto in F. At the
conclusion of the piece, he's sitting in a box seat cheering his own
performance. "That's a marvelous idea!" Minnelli enthused. He then
called Arthur Freed, reaching him just as he was leaving the Thalberg
building at MGM, and asked the producer to wait for them.

"Oscar's got a wonderful idea!" Minnelli told Freed. He described
Levant's concept, which Oscar had dubbed "the ego fantasy."

"Had Oscar not come up with that idea," recalled Saul Chaplin,
the film's orchestrator, "there's a chance that the Concerto might not
[have been] in the picture, because that's how the picture was approached. . . . There's not a single number where somebody just
stands by a piano and sings."

It was Gene Kelly who had brought the seventeen-year-old ballet
dancer Leslie Caron over from Paris to star as the gamine Lise Bour-
vier. Kelly had first seen her in a Roland Petit ballet in Paris called *The
Sphinx*. "[S]itting on top of a huge pedestal was a girl in a black wig
with long claws and heavy makeup. She was the sphinx . . . and she
moved very well," Kelly remembered. He was absolutely convinced
that she was ideal for the part of the young Parisienne with whom
Jerry Mulligan falls in love, though she had no acting experience.
When she tested for the part and was unanimously chosen, Caron
reluctantly left her bohemian dancer's life in Paris to come to Hollywood, accompanied by her eager American mother, Margaret Caron,
whose living expenses in Los Angeles would be covered by MGM.

Later, at a studio party to welcome Leslie Caron to Hollywood,
Oscar met the French teenager who would be turned into an American movie star with her first picture. June was anxious to know what
Gene Kelly's discovery looked liked. "She looks too much like me as
far as I'm concerned," he replied.

As preposterous as the remark sounded, there was truth in it. Caron
did indeed look like a feminized, fetching version of Oscar Levant,
with her full, pouty lips, round head, and wide, intelligent eyes. The
resemblance would be borne out later in Amanda Levant, the daughter who looked the most like her father and who would bear a striking
resemblance to Caron.

Caron, like Levant, was rebellious and tended to balk at the demands of her studio handlers. She was now thrust into the male world
of the MGM musical. "I was so revolted by all their emphasis on pink
and lace, and their idea of femininity, which was dumbness. So I
didn't play the game," she remembered. Her first act of rebellion was
to cut off her hair.

Caron thought her short hair looked great—modern and completely new. But Minnelli, Freed, and Kelly were all horrified. They stood around her, shaking their heads in disbelief at what the young actress had done. So shooting began with the French song-and-dance man Georges Guetary, Gene Kelly, and Oscar Levant, with Leslie Caron sitting beside her hairdresser, who every now and then gave a sharp tug on her hair.

June and the three girls visited Oscar on the set. The girls were particularly entranced by Caron, who was "so cute and friendly." Amanda remembered being present while they filmed the Beaux-Arts Ball, Levant dressed in a cowboy suit and Caron wearing a little tiara with tiny stars suspended on wires that seemed to shoot off in all directions.

Andrew Sarris has observed that Minnelli was a director with "an unusual, somber outlook for musical comedy," belied, perhaps, by his glorious use of color. Real fulfillment and contentment always seem just beyond his characters' reach. In *An American in Paris,* despite a happy reunion of the lovers in the film's final ballet, there are several instances of unresolved *tristesse:* Nina Foch as Jerry Mulligan's ill-treated, cast-off patroness; Georges Guetary's sympathetic role as the rejected suitor; Levant's status as a composer going nowhere, except in his fantasies. "I'm a concert pianist—that's a pretentious way of saying I'm unemployed at the moment. . . . I'm beginning to feel like the world's oldest child prodigy" is how he introduces himself in the film's opening scene.

There is pathos in Levant's Adam Cook, stemming perhaps from his portraying a composer, the "racket" he had already given up. Levant shared with Minnelli something of the successful man's fantasy of lost dreams and abandoned hopes—Minnelli himself had once aspired to be a painter. For Levant, the film had a slightly haunted feel to it anyway, because it was another celebration of Gershwin's music, from "(I'll Build a) Stairway to Paradise" (the first Gershwin song that Levant had fallen in love with back in Pearl Eaton's tap-dancing class) to "Love Is Here to Stay," the last, unfinished song George ever wrote, and one that Levant had helped Ira to complete after the composer's death.

It's hard to know which lines Levant contributed to Lerner's screenplay. He claimed credit for the remark "It's not a pretty face, I grant you. But underneath this flabby exterior is an enormous lack of character" and reprised it elsewhere, but he also records that Lerner was "apoplectic" about allowing him to write his own lines. Lerner, according to Levant, wasn't a "credit-sharer."

Freed was a Gershwin friend from the old days, as were Minnelli and songwriter Johnny Green, who was the film's musical director and head of MGM's music department. One of Green's prized possessions was an autographed picture of George Gershwin dated 1930. Green resented Levant's presence in the studio. He felt that while Levant had the public reputation of Gershwin's closest friend, he himself had been no less a friend and confidant of the legendary composer. In a word, Green was envious of Levant's professional reputation as a Gershwin intimate, and whenever the two men worked together, sparks would fly.

They fought over what "a Gershwin sound" really meant and what Gershwin's musical intentions were. During the recording sessions for the Concerto in F, the "ego fantasy" scene, the two men locked horns. Freed leapt into the fray to defend Levant, humiliating Green in front of his orchestra. "Never was there a conductor so put in his place," Green remembered. "Freed hit me with every Sherman tank, every Louisville slugger in the place . . . because Oscar was it." Minnelli also tended to side with Levant in these debates. Luckily, perhaps, for the morale of the set, Green's responsibilities as head of MGM's music department forced him to leave most of the orchestrating duties to the more congenial Saul Chaplin.

As film historian Stephen Harvey has observed, the "By Strauss" scene was one of three numbers "devoted to Kelly's strenuous notions of *fraternité*." It's interesting that *An American in Paris* is the only Hollywood musical in which all of the singing is done by men. Levant shared Minnelli's dislike of the scene. During rehearsals, Levant—who had learned his waltz time from Max Dreyfus—played the tricky Viennese afterbeat (a second beat that precedes the real beat). When Kelly stopped him and asked, "Where is that in the music?" Levant and Kelly got into a heated discussion over how the piece should be played.

When the film's final cut, completed in May 1951, was shown to the cast and crew, there was a great howl of pain from Levant. His final scene with Nina Foch at the black-and-white Beaux-Arts Ball had been edited out to make room for the seventeen-minute ballet.

Levant was crushed. The missing scene would have rounded out Levant's character with the suggestion that Kelly's jilted patron would go on to sponsor Adam Cook. It was also an important scene for Nina Foch, one she believed contained her best acting in the picture—possibly her best acting of all her screen roles. In the scene, Foch (as Milo) has just been abandoned by Jerry Mulligan; she now realizes that any emotion he felt toward her was just a cover for his feeling for

Lise. Foch has described the missing scene as providing a key to the character of Milo:

> [T]he thing that makes Milo so touching was in this last scene at the black-and-white ball, where I get drunk because I realize that I've lost Gene, and I'm sitting at the table with Oscar Levant, talking about men and why men don't love me. . . . I'm just buzzing, about to be a weepy drunk, half-laughing, and suddenly up comes this truly lonely, lonely little girl whose daddy never loved her. That's not in the lines, but you can see she's that kind of woman. A piece of confetti gets in my champagne glass, and I see it, take it out, and look at it. I stop in the middle of the scene, and Oscar takes the time to really look at it. I look up; then I think about it, what it is that's in my glass. "Oh, it's a pill," and I take it like a pill. It's a beautiful moment.

Minnelli thought the scene detracted from the love story between Caron and Kelly, but its absence does leave a slight hole in the picture. The scene would have fleshed out the characters of the discarded patron and the hopeful composer. Sarris has speculated that it was excised because of Minnelli's devotion to his "morbidly beautiful mise-en-scène"—in other words, the unresolved feeling we're left with at the end of the film is an expression of Minnelli's essential melancholy.

"Some may believe Oscar was a personality and not an actor, but you couldn't have proved it by his vanity-wounded roar" when he realized this scene had been cut, Minnelli remembered.

The reviews of *An American in Paris* were mostly ecstatic. The musical was a tremendous popular success, and it swept the Academy Awards the year of its release, being nominated in eight categories. Lerner's original screenplay was nominated, as was Vincente Minnelli's direction. Saul Chaplin and Johnny Green won their Oscars for musical direction and orchestration (Green getting some of his own back at Levant, who wasn't nominated for anything). Arthur Freed was given the Irving Thalberg Award for the body of his work as a producer, and Gene Kelly was given a special award for his contribution to dance on film. But when *An American in Paris* was named Best Picture, beating out such serious competition as *A Place in the Sun* and *A Streetcar Named Desire,* the audience was noticeably surprised. No Freed production had ever been nominated for that honor before, and few in the industry had expected it to win.

For Levant, the film's success was a mixed blessing. The overwhelming popular reaction to the movie furthered his public association with Gershwin's music at a time when his concert career de-manded that he move beyond his "Again, the *Rhapsody?*" image. And the film critics now pigeonholed Levant as a sidekick who could occa-sionally sit down to deliver a concert-level performance. Despite his great promise in *Humoresque,* they stopped wondering when Holly-wood would give him a major part in a film.

Not long after Oscar had completed work on *An American in Paris,* he and June joined Jerry Wald and his wife, Connie, for an evening out. The two couples were seated at a table in a popular restaurant on Sunset Boulevard, where Oscar regaled the Walds with stories about the making of his latest movie. George Jessel, the cigar-chomping vaudevillian who had recently become a Hollywood film producer, walked into the restaurant and made a beeline for Levant's table.

"Have you heard the news?" Jessel asked with a grave look on his face. "Al Jolson is dead." Jolson had died in San Francisco, in his hotel room, of a massive heart attack.

Oscar had never outgrown his idolatry of Jolson. He represented the old, lost era of Broadway show business, when "The World's Greatest Entertainer" pranced out into the crowd on that special run-way built for him at the Winter Garden Theatre. The two difficult years they had spent working together on the *Kraft Music Hall* had certainly tried Levant's devotion, but it hadn't changed his deeper feelings about the entertainer. He also represented the kind of com-plete, unquestioning self-confidence that had always eluded Levant—the absolute acceptance of one's own personality.

From that night on, George Jessel would represent to Oscar one of death's messengers. He couldn't bear to be in the same room with the old raconteur, whose very presence fed Levant's increasing terror of death.

34

Render unto Caesar

"I can stand anything but failure."

IN JANUARY 1951 LEVANT ANNOUNCED FOUR CONCERT DATES IN Michigan. The grueling schedule would turn out to be a means of self-destruction: Saginaw on the sixteenth, Ann Arbor two days later; Grand Rapids on the nineteenth, East Lansing on the twenty-second.

At a concert in Miami, Levant refused an invitation by a local student to visit his fraternity house. The snubbed fraternity men took their revenge by unloosing six cats into the Miami Beach Municipal Auditorium in the middle of Levant's concert. Visibly shaken, Levant walked off the stage during the fracas. In his private universe of bad omens, cats were definitely to be avoided.

Once he returned to Los Angeles, Levant set out to fulfill his contract with 20th Century–Fox. His next two films would be forgettable affairs. *The I Don't Care Girl* was the story of legendary showgirl Eva Tanguay and starred Mitzi Gaynor. Unfortunately for Levant, the film was produced by George Jessel, who would also appear throughout the film as himself, ponderously framing the story in his role as a producer trying to film the story of Eva Tanguay. It was a fairly miserable experience for Levant. He now hated Jessel because he had been the one to tell him of Jolson's death. And besides hating him, he didn't like the film. In spite of a few luscious production numbers, the lame script and overripe Technicolor make the film look like a B movie that got made at the wrong end of the studio.

His second 20th Century–Fox film had a more distinguished cast, including Oscar's longtime friend from his radio days and former Alwyn Court neighbor, Fred Allen. The film was based on a handful of short stories from the pen of O. Henry. Levant was to star alongside Allen in "The Ransom of Red Chief," in which two hapless kidnappers hold a hyperactive brat for ransom, only to find out that his parents are in no hurry to have the little tyke returned.

Despite Howard Hawks's direction of "The Ransom of Red Chief," Levant has one embarrassing moment on film when he's allowed to plug his old radio show: His character stops at a gas station and asks, "I'd like some information, please." The moment is jarring, suggesting that Levant would rather trade on his reputation than win the audience over with his comedic acting. It seems a low point in Levant's acting career and the first suggestion that his era had begun to pass.

Charles Laughton starred in one of the anthology stories, doing a heartbreaking turn as a dignified panhandler. His sequence is interesting for another reason: A young, inexperienced Marilyn Monroe has a few lines as a streetwalker.

During filming, the violinist Isaac Stern happened to be at the studio one day. He dropped by the soundstage where Levant and Fred Allen were filming "The Ransom of Red Chief" to deliver a piece of shocking news: Julie Garfield had just died of a heart attack in New York.

Garfield had been hounded by the House Un-American Activities Committee and by 1951 was virtually blacklisted by Hollywood. Even when a studio sent out word that they were looking for a John Garfield type, his agent was told, "We need a Garfield *type* but we can't use Garfield." The irony was that Garfield had once tried to join the Communist party in his youthful enthusiasm for left-wing causes, but they wouldn't have him—"They thought I was too dumb," he told a friend.

He had been experiencing a string of box-office flops, and in 1950 he suffered his first heart attack. Keeping his condition a secret, he returned to Broadway to appear in Clifford Odets's new play, *The Big Knife*. Both Odets and Garfield were brought up before the congressional committee. Garfield testified that he had never been a member of the Communist party, but no one really believed him, and a black cloud of doubt clung to his reputation. To add to Garfield's tale of woe, his marriage was breaking up. After three days of sleeplessness and drinking in his hotel room, Garfield ended up at the Gramercy Park apartment of a friend. The next morning, when she went in to check on him, Garfield was dead.

Like George Jessel, Isaac Stern was now taboo, because a messenger of death was almost as bad as the dreaded thing itself.

Between working on the two films for 20th Century–Fox, Levant continued his 1951–52 concert tour season. In order to keep to his punishing schedule, he began to rely on stronger barbiturates to ensure a night's sleep. They were beginning to affect his behavior.

When he appeared with Erich Leinsdorf to play the Tchaikovsky Piano Concerto in Rochester, New York, in a performance one critic described as "a blaze of tonal beauty . . . he had the singing tone which belongs with Tchaikovsky's lyrical ideas," Levant snapped. Someone had taken his picture at the conclusion of the performance, and Levant leapt into the audience, ready to pummel the photographer. He had to be restrained by members of the orchestra.

Levant appealed to Frederick Schang, one of the founders of Columbia Artists Management and Levant's manager, to get him out of a commitment to play in Fargo, North Dakota. The idea of playing Fargo in winter filled Levant with dread, and he couldn't put out of his mind what lay ahead of him. But he found no sympathy. Schang, in fact, disliked Levant and felt that he had gotten by on a puny talent. Levant would have to keep his scheduled commitments.

After a concert in Minneapolis was canceled due to a snowstorm, Levant arrived in New York in terrible condition. He was scheduled to perform Anton Rubinstein's Concerto in D Minor at Carnegie Hall under Mitropoulos's direction. The Concerto was a bravura piece well suited to Levant's resources and physical power; though it put a tremendous added strain on him, he practiced the Rubinstein Concerto every chance he got. Levant called his New York internist, Dr. Lester Tuchman, who examined him and found him to be in a toxic condition. Tuchman prescribed a liquid alkaloid called paraldehyde, a foul-tasting, foul-smelling barbiturate that is excreted through the skin's pores.

Despite Levant's jittery nerves and exhaustion, the Carnegie Hall performance of the Concerto in D Minor was a success. Levant was praised for conveying just the right mood and romantic atmosphere of the music. Immediately following the concert, Levant took his first dose of paraldehyde. On Sunday morning, he took another small dose. Later that afternoon, Levant repeated his concert program in a matinee performance that was simultaneously broadcast over the radio. By now he was feeling the effects of the paraldehyde, though he managed to run through the program without any noticeable difficulties. In fact, he played very well, despite feeling somewhat numbed from the drug he was taking. On Monday he met with Goddard Lieberson to record the Concerto in D Minor.

When June joined her husband in New York at the Alwyn Court apartment, she was frightened to see the toll his concertizing had taken. Levant retreated from all his social obligations and gave June strict instructions to field all telephone calls. When June went out and the phone rang, Levant would simply let it go on ringing. One of those insistent callers was no less than James Caesar Petrillo, head of the American Federation of Musicians, whom Levant had met on the train in 1940. Petrillo ruled over the union membership with absolute authority. "They're mine," Petrillo once said about the large numbers of classical artists he had brought into the union. "What's the difference between Heifetz and a fiddler in a tavern?" Petrillo wanted to convince Levant to make a radio endorsement for a piece of legislation under consideration in Portland, Oregon. Levant had no idea that Petrillo was seeking to enlist his endorsement, but if he had, he would probably have refused. He stayed out of union politics.

Two weeks later, June and Oscar left New York to play the rescheduled concert in Minneapolis. Oscar was already worn out from his tour. "Fatigued is an exhilarating word compared to the way I feel," Levant told reporters when he arrived in Minneapolis. The 1951–52 concert season had turned out to be a killer. Levant had made a tremendous effort to advance beyond the Gershwin repertoire, and, when he did play Gershwin, he tried to interpret him differently. Yet his advances only succeeded in making him feel guilty, as though he were abandoning his friend.

On Levant's first day back on North Roxbury Drive, James Petrillo was on the phone waiting for him. But Levant did not speak to him. Exhausted, faced with the prospect of going back to 20th Century–Fox to finish work on *The I Don't Care Girl,* which he detested, and woozy from paraldehyde, he continued to ignore Petrillo's calls. Being told what to do by one more authority figure was more than Levant could stand.

The next day, Petrillo's secretary called from union headquarters informing Levant that as of that phone call he was suspended from the musicians' union.

Levant had always considered himself a good union man, though he steered clear of union politics. He had proudly belonged to the union ever since he was a kid pounding the piano in Ben Bernie's band. Outraged, Levant tried to reach the union boss to protest the injustice of his dismissal. Now Petrillo would not return *his* calls.

But three days later, Petrillo reinstated Levant just before the start of his summer tour—the suspension was lifted now that Levant had been sufficiently humbled. During those three days, Levant had tried to soften the blow with paraldehyde. It didn't help.

Levant resumed his rigorous concert schedule. He had five concerts to play in one week. The Robin Hood Dell was the first stop on his summer tour. Levant arrived in Philadelphia late at night and checked into the Warwick Hotel around two A.M. Settled into his hotel room, he called down for a pack of cigarettes. When the bellboy showed up at his door with cigarettes in hand, Levant noticed that the number on the bellboy's uniform was thirteen. Panicked, Levant picked up the phone and told the desk clerk that he was checking out immediately.

He moved over to the Ritz but found he couldn't sleep due to the early-morning traffic on Broad Street's cobblestones, so he got up, dressed, packed his bags, and checked out of the Ritz. He moved back to the Warwick, but by now it was nearly six A.M. and Levant, sleepless, was scheduled to play the Rubinstein Concerto with Mitropoulos that evening in front of an expected audience of 20,000.

After an anxious but creditable performance, Levant next headed back to New York for a Friday night appearance at Lewisohn Stadium. On Saturday he was scheduled to appear in Westport, Connecticut. When his performance at the Westport concert was delayed, he found that he could no longer handle such unpredictabilities, which are often a part of touring, and he slammed his fist into his dressing room door. It wasn't the first time he had landed an uppercut against a wall or door while on tour—a dangerous practice for a pianist.

Levant played his five concerts mostly in outdoor stadiums in the summer heat. When his obligations on the East Coast were finally met, he took the train back to Los Angeles.

One day before having to leave for Milwaukee to resume his concert tour, Levant woke up with a severe pain in his back. He went downstairs to the music room to practice. Suddenly he was too weak to continue. He tried to get his physician on the telephone but was told the doctor had gone to the racetrack. Desperate, he remembered the name of a cardiologist his psychiatrist had recommended and called Dr. Morley J. Kert, who promised to appear on the Levant doorstep as soon as possible. June was used to Oscar calling up physicians day and night, so she wasn't overly concerned. She left the house to go to the market while her husband sat and waited for Dr. Kert to arrive. By the time June returned home, Levant had undergone an EKG and the doctor was studying the delicate lines on the graph. "You've had a heart attack," he told his bewildered patient, "a coronary occlusion."

The room was quiet, June remembered, except for the muffled sounds coming through the open windows.

"That's impossible. I had a test made yesterday."

"It usually takes a day to show up on the graph," Dr. Kert explained.

"But I'm leaving tonight for Milwaukee," Levant protested.

"Absolutely not. You must be hospitalized."

"What about my concert tour?"

"Cancel everything."

Dr. Kert told Levant that he needed complete, total rest for six weeks. Oscar and June looked at each other in a daze, trying to understand. "I've never been in a hospital in my life," Levant pleaded. "I'm not going. I'll stay in bed here at home."

Dr. Kert argued with his recalcitrant patient, but he finally agreed to allow Levant to remain at home. Kert sent for his nurse and then administered a shot of morphine to relieve Oscar's pain. Within a few days, Dr. Kert would switch to administering Demerol, a synthetic form of morphine.

The next day a truck arrived with a hospital bed and an oxygen tank, a day nurse, and a night nurse. For the next six weeks, Oscar and June's bedroom resembled a hospital room.

For the Levants' youngest daughter, Amanda, then six, the drama of Oscar's illness would be among her earliest memory of her father. "Your father's very sick," June explained to her daughters. "You're going to have to be very quiet because there are going to be nurses here to look after him. He'll be in bed for six weeks."

June put a sofa in a little alcove for the two nurses, who each had a twelve-hour shift. Kert permitted his patient six cigarettes a day, but Levant was used to six cigarettes an hour. His fear of death, however, made him a compliant patient.

Three days after his heart attack, Levant received his first visitors: Jean Negulesco, who had had run-ins with Levant when he directed him in *Humoresque,* and the set designer Oliver Smith. Smith was in the midst of creating sets for Levant's next film, *The Band Wagon,* which was scheduled to begin shooting at MGM in only six weeks. It was his third film for MGM, and it was going to be another Technicolor musical extravaganza produced by Freed, directed by Minnelli, and written by Oscar's friends Comden and Green. Oscar fretted that he would not be well enough in time to begin work on the film.

Levant was delighted to receive his guests, and for a time his old animation and volubility returned. In fact, he got so carried away with his visitors that he smoked an entire pack of cigarettes, oblivious to his doctor's orders and his oxygen tank standing nearby.

Demerol eased his pain and jittery nerves and helped him sleep. He was also allowed to continue to take his regular dose of sleeping pills at night. Alone with June, his veins coursing with numbing drugs, Levant would fall into a kind of truth-telling delirium. For the first time since the early months of their marriage, Oscar confided in June about his childhood and some of his lifelong fears. He talked about his father and his brothers and some of the humiliations of his youth. "He would talk about his father," June recalled, "and big tears would come."

Six weeks after his heart attack, Levant felt strong enough to report to work at the MGM lot where rehearsals were under way for *The Band Wagon*. The film was designed to showcase a number of Howard Dietz–Arthur Schwartz songs culled from past Broadway shows, including the original 1931 Broadway revue *The Band Wagon*, which had starred Fred and Adele Astaire. Comden and Green wrote a new story to accommodate its luscious Broadway score ("By Myself," "A Shine on Your Shoes," "New Sun in the Sky," "I Guess I'll Have to Change My Plan," "Louisiana Hayride," "Triplets," and one new song written for the film, the showstopping "That's Entertainment"). The plot, of the "backstage musical" genre, centers on the mounting of a disastrously arty play based on the Faust legend (complete with a "Damnation Ballet") that flops in New Haven and must be rescued by its comeback star, Tony Hunter, played by Fred Astaire. The film is a celebration of the well-made, mainstream Broadway musical with everybody pitching in to do their best. *The Band Wagon*—arguably Minnelli's best musical—is infectiously high-spirited and joyous. The irony is that all of its principals were suffering profoundly while the picture was being made; the exuberance on film couldn't have been further from the misery of its actors.

Throughout the making of *The Band Wagon*, Vincente Minnelli was having terrible personal problems with Judy Garland's emotional breakdowns. Judy was then married to Sid Luft, but there were still domestic problems concerning the children, and he continued to worry about Judy's frail emotional health. Jack Buchanan was in constant pain due to dental surgery he was undergoing, and the shooting schedule had to be arranged around his dental appointments. Fred Astaire's wife, Phyllis, was seriously ill, and Astaire was moody and distracted—he even uncharacteristically stormed off the set during the filming of the "I Love Louisa" scene, having suddenly snapped and completely forgotten his lines. Minnelli was so distracted himself that he didn't even notice his star's breakdown—he thought Astaire had just walked off the set to go to the men's room.

Nanette Fabray had been brought to MGM to become their next Judy Garland—they had promised her a bright future in MGM musicals, but, sadly, that was not to be. The studio would break up after *The Band Wagon,* and Fabray would miss out on her chance to star in other movie musicals, which she seemed born to. A veteran of ten Broadway shows but new to film, Fabray felt like an outsider among the film actors on the set. Cyd Charisse was self-absorbed and aloof, and Fabray felt there was no one there with whom she could form a close working relationship. To exacerbate matters, she felt that Levant had singled her out to be the butt of his sarcastic remarks. Tensions ran so high on the set that when it was all over, Fabray suffered a nervous breakdown.

And Levant was simply too weak and too ill to enjoy any aspect of performing. First of all, he felt he had to keep his recent heart attack a secret in order to keep the studio's insurers from dropping him from the picture. But it was obvious that he was not well. He could barely perform the big song-and-dance number "That's Entertainment." Fabray remembered:

> Oscar was down on the floor all the time on a chair. We would shoot two or three minutes of it, with a stand-in for Oscar, and they would arrange it so that it would be physically possible for him to do something and then he would do it . . . in one take. And then he would be popping pills—he was a very sick man.

Dr. Kert advised Levant that the number's finale, which entailed striding down a ramp at great speed, was too strenuous and he shouldn't do it at all. At the next rehearsal Levant refused to stride down the ramp, so Fred Astaire, in disgust, offered to carry him. "So I did it," Levant later wrote.

He was originally supposed to be one of the three cranky triplets in the musical number "Triplets," but Jack Buchanan had to replace him. It was just too strenuous because the performers had to dance on their knees in order to look like three toddlers in christening gowns and baby shoes. "That was physically the most difficult thing I've ever done," Fabray remembered. "If you ever want to try anything hard, get on the floor . . . and try just walking around on your knees and see how hard that is. They probably knew [Oscar] couldn't do it by then."

Rather than let it be known that he had suffered a heart attack, Levant played on his familiar reputation as a neurotic and told his colleagues he had been in a mental hospital. Fabray recalled:

[H]e didn't say anything about his heart. I think it was a secret. What he kept saying to everybody out loud was, "I need help. I need this because I just got out of a mental hospital . . . and you have to be patient with me." . . . We were all very put off with Oscar because of the way he was behaving. Well, he was legitimately not well, and if he had told us that we could have accommodated him. We could have all run around him instead of making him run with us or whatever . . . he was very, very difficult.

The trouble with being a hypochondriac is that when you're really sick, no one believes you.

Lester (Levant) and Lily Marton (Fabray) are the husband-and-wife writing team who author the musical-within-the-musical and recruit their friend Tony Hunter (Astaire) to star in it. The roles were based on Comden and Green (who aren't married to each other in real life) with a touch of the bickering, real-life married team of Ruth Gordon and Garson Kanin thrown in. Levant seemed to enjoy portraying his friend Adolph Green, and he jumps about and throws up his hands in an imitation of Green's boyish enthusiasm. It's quite a surprise to see Levant appearing without his usual sardonic composure. Occasionally he drops the Adolph Green impersonation and delivers a line in his typical deadpan manner, as in a remark that was tailor-made for him by Green, who knew him well: "I can stand anything but failure." Green was very pleased with Levant's impersonation of him and thought he gave "a terrific performance."

Halfway through the film, Lester and Lily squabble and stop talking to each other, which occasioned Levant's remark that in the film "I treated her atrociously—just as though she were indeed my real wife." Which shows that he was still able to joke throughout the making of *The Band Wagon,* but just barely.

Levant looks oddly unlike himself in the film; besides his frantic jumping around and throwing up his hands in his Adolph Green imitation, his face looks coarse and puffy and his eyes have disappeared into his face, which may have been a result of the drugs he'd been taking, coupled with the heavy makeup he was obliged to wear. He also uncharacteristically smiles a lot, which is so unlike the usual image of Levant that it's jarring; his bonhomie is a little ghoulish considering the condition of his health.

It is amazing how much vivacity and goodwill comes across on film given the low spirits and anxiety on the set. "My whole memory of my time with Oscar is totally unpleasant," Fabray recalled. "I kept wondering, 'Why does everybody love this man so? They must see something that I don't see because he obviously has friends.'" Though he manages to make a real contribution to the film, Levant the actor seems diminished in his role as Lester Marton, his intellect and his depth leached out of him. As film historian Stephen Harvey has noted, "*The Band Wagon* matches lyricism with high spirits, elegant surfaces, and an undertow of sadness." Levant's diminishment seems part of that sadness.

Frederick Schang was anxious for his star attraction to get back to work on the concert circuit—"If he can make a movie, he can play the piano." Levant himself was anxious to return to concertizing, to put as much distance as possible between himself and the sickroom. His illness had been costly in lost income, and his identity was inextricably bound up with being a concert pianist.

Levant again asked his managers to go easy on him, to schedule his concert dates—the first since his heart attack—so they wouldn't be so strenuous for him to fulfill. He asked for compassion. Schang told Levant that they had set up a limited tour for him, but in actuality it was hardly less demanding than the tour that had pushed him over the edge. "They [were] typical agents in that respect, and they were too hard on him," June felt. "Oscar was professional enough to show up once he agreed to do it. I guess he didn't realize himself how tough it would be on him. I mean, he was still a young man. Forty-five is pretty young as far as I'm concerned."

When Levant received the first dates of his itinerary, he knew his managers had failed in their promise to "go easy on him." By the end of the first week of his tour, in the beginning of March, Levant found himself in Chicago, freezing in the city's frigid winds. He was afraid he was going to have another heart attack, so he began sipping Scotch on Dr. Kert's recommendation. Levant, who had always prided himself on his disdain for alcohol, was soon making good headway on a fifth of Scotch. In Chicago he was scheduled to play two concerts, on March 7 and 8, with Thor Johnson conducting the Cincinnati Symphony. Levant later wrote that the local concert promoter had canceled the rehearsal in an attempt to cut expenses, but other accounts suggest that Levant simply was not up to rehearsing. In any case, the results were disastrous. During his performance of the Concerto in F at the Sunday concert, Levant got into a public altercation with his conductor.

According to the account in *Newsweek:*

> As Levant walked on the stage the first night to play the Tchaikovsky Piano Concerto, it was apparent to many that something was wrong. Hand over heart, he stalked to the piano gloomily. During parts of the concerto when he was not playing, he buried his face in his hands. Suddenly, he sat upright and gestured to Johnson to step up the tempo. Johnson turned his back. Levant then played on furiously, often playing with his right hand, and conducting with his left. Later, off-stage, Levant told Johnson off.

The following evening, Levant again became rattled by Thor Johnson's dynamics. Frustrated, Levant shouted at the conductor, "Diminuendo, diminuendo!" in an effort to get him to soften the orchestra. "Let them hear me for a change!" he yelled. A rehearsal would, of course, have worked out this lack of synchronization.

During a three-day stopover in New York, Oscar was looked after by Adolph Green. Green accompanied his friend to Pennsylvania Station, from which he was to depart for Toronto, the next leg of his tour. Green remembered that Levant, fearful of having another heart attack, arranged for a doctor to meet him at the station to give him a shot of Demerol. Now fortified for the trip, Levant steeled himself for the wintry days that lay ahead in Canada.

Frederick Schang, ever watchful of his pianist's ability to fulfill his concert dates, accompanied Levant on his trip north. He noticed how frightened Levant seemed, so he mentioned that the head of the committee sponsoring the next concert was married to a physician. Levant's eyes lit up. "Call him!" he cried eagerly.

Within an hour of reaching Toronto, Levant had been given another injection by another unfamiliar doctor. By the start of the evening's concert, Levant was floating high on Demerol.

The concert manager informed Levant that just before the performance it was customary to play "God Save the Queen." In his somnambulistic state, he couldn't remember how it went. With Demerol coursing through his bloodstream, he flubbed the anthem and then continued with the recital, which felt to him as though it were taking hours to complete. When it was finally over, he got out of town as quickly as possible.

His next destination was across the border in Buffalo. Levant fell into a deep sleep in the car driven by Schang. In the middle of the night, Levant was awakened at the border station by a uniformed customs officer.

"Where were you born?" the border agent asked.

"What do you mean, 'Where was I born?' The hill? The alley? The street? The country?" Levant demanded to know.

"Say any city," Schang muttered to Levant in the dark car. "It doesn't make a goddamned difference!"

Levant was placed under arrest until he could bring himself to utter the name of his birthplace. After ninety minutes, Levant shouted through the locked door, "Pittsburgh, Pittsburgh!" He was allowed to cross the border.

When June met her husband in New York she found his condition greatly deteriorated. She soon learned that in every town Levant had stopped, he had roused a local physician to give him a shot of Demerol. Levant knew how to be charming when he needed to, and his celebrity impressed even the most reluctant doctors into satisfying his craving for the drug. He insisted to his concert promoters that he couldn't go on unless he saw a doctor. And so a local doctor would be called in to give Levant yet another injection. "It got him through each concert," June said, "but it turned him into an addict."

In New York June insisted that her husband see Dr. Tuchman, who, it turned out, couldn't be talked or charmed into giving Levant more Demerol. He took one look at the nerve-racked pianist and gave him a temperance lecture on the dangers of addiction. Instead of Demerol he renewed Levant's prescription for paraldehyde as a bed-time sedative.

June was convinced that what remained of Levant's tour—five cities in western Canada in the middle of winter, followed by concerts in Portland and Corvallis, Oregon—would kill him.

"When Oscar had his heart attack," she recalled in later years, "the advice they gave him was 'get enough rest, don't get a chill,' things like that. But he was going to finish his tour—he [was] a professional. He was just going to die in the snow."

35

The Reign of Terror

"Self-pity—it's the only pity that counts."

WHEN A SECRETARY IN THE COPPICUS & SCHANG OFFICE TOLD JUNE, "Don't tell Mr. Levant, but he is to travel through Canada by bus," June immediately begged her husband to cancel the rest of the tour. She called Schang, insisting that her husband was too ill to travel through Canada, and she canceled for him. With a tremendous sense of relief, the Levants boarded the train and headed back to California.

When their train stopped at Albuquerque, a telegram was waiting for them. It was from Petrillo, and it was scalding. "Get off that train. Take a plane and fly to Canada and do the concert you're supposed to," is how June remembered it. But Oscar did not respond, and the two continued their journey. Within days, Herman Kenin, an ambitious union board member from Portland who had tried to involve Levant in their local music bond issue, called Levant at home and urged him to at least keep the Portland concert date.

"I'll play Portland but I think I'm going to be thrown out of the union," Levant told Kenin.

"You can be thrown out after Portland," was his answer.

Levant made the trips to Corvallis and Portland, fulfilling both concert dates. Upon his return to Los Angeles, a telegram from New

York informed him that he was suspended from the American Federation of Musicians for "unfair dealings . . . with his employers." Levant would henceforth be barred from the concert stage on grounds that he "failed to meet numerous recent engagements."

Levant's suspension was big news. Petrillo was out to get Oscar Levant, many believed; he was intent on making an example of the iconoclastic musician. He had purposely picked a fight with a nationally known artist in order to flex his muscle in front of the widest possible audience. If he could tame the *enfant terrible,* no one else would dare question his authority. So the union chief went public with his side of the story. "Oscar Levant's deft piano hands were rapped smartly yesterday by James C. Petrillo," reported *The New York Times.* Petrillo sent out word that no one was to book Levant. "This is unprecedented in our union," Petrillo announced at a news conference. "I have an idea that Mr. Levant feels he is bigger than the Federation. This we cannot tolerate." June leapt to her husband's defense, telling the Associated Press that she had canceled his Canadian engagements on doctor's orders, that he had a serious heart condition and his doctor had permitted him only to give two concerts in Oregon.

According to union regulations, Levant would have to answer to the executive board of the union, which had the authority to fine, suspend, or permanently expel him. His hearing was set for June 1953—two months away.

Some people thought Schang had gone straight to Petrillo, knowing of his antipathy toward Levant. This was far more serious than the three-day suspension Petrillo had pulled on him earlier. This was total warfare; Petrillo was out to finish him.

At long last it had caught up with him: humiliation at the hands of the father Oscar had always feared. His belief that every success merely cloaked a rejection was now vindicated by Petrillo's public shaming of him. He had been rebellious, and now he was being punished by the one authority figure who could finally ruin him: the Caesar he had met on the train. Like a Hollywood Philoctetes, the wounded pianist took to his bed.

By the time Levant returned to North Roxbury Drive, he was hooked on Demerol. "I became addicted to it with the same strong character with which I became addicted to my wife. Demerol became my cure-all, my panacea," he wrote in his memoirs.

Despite his feisty reputation, Levant didn't even have a lawyer to fight Petrillo's ban, which had begun to sink in. All he needed to do was to prove to the union's executive board and its pugilistic president that he was truly incapacitated and thus within his rights to cancel the Canadian dates. Meanwhile, Petrillo intensified the ban: He handed down another edict stating that all other union members in symphony orchestras were prohibited from joining Levant on any concert stage anywhere in the country. Those who violated the ban would be suspended.

"He just thought Oscar was being temperamental," June said about Petrillo. "From an early age Oscar was a union man, and he took it very seriously." But the press tended to side with Petrillo, portraying Levant as a cocky musician who disregarded the rules. "But he cared a lot about the music profession," June maintained. "No matter what he did, no matter that he was a wisecracking guy, he was first and foremost a musician. That's why when . . . his music career was cut off from him, it was like taking off his arms. It was a physical part of him, the piano."

In addition to hiring an attorney and securing an affadavit from Dr. Kert testifying to Levant's having suffered a serious heart attack, Levant had to make a public apology. Petrillo did more than take away Levant's livelihood; the public humiliation broke his spirit. The years he had spent trying to overcome his almost innate feelings of rejection were undone; his most atavistic fears about himself were now publicly confirmed. He was not fit to concertize, he was no longer a concert pianist. His rituals and superstitions, his courting of the gods, all had been for nought.

The whole Petrillo incident opened a wound in Levant's psyche, and he found himself falling deeper into addiction. He had long relied on Seconal and Nembutal to get to sleep, but now he was taking anything he could get his hands on: paraldehyde, sodium amytal, Demerol, chloral hydrate.

Whenever he was lucid, Levant wrote letters to Petrillo—the first letters he had written since his courtship of June—in an effort to be reinstated in the union. Many of Levant's old friends came to his defense—Leonard Lyons's column in the *New York Post* sought the assistance of Minnesota's Senator Hubert Humphrey, who promised to help the embattled pianist, though he never made good his offer. Lyons then tried to press George Meany, head of the AFL-CIO, the parent organization of the musician's union, into service on Levant's behalf. When Levant told Petrillo that George Meany was coming to his aid, Petrillo snorted, "Meany, hell! We hire him!"

After two and a half months of suspension, Levant received word that Petrillo was ready to ask the union's executive board to drop the charges against Levant and restore him to full membership in the union. But Petrillo was still not quite finished with Levant. There was one condition: Levant must ask Petrillo's forgiveness in person at union headquarters in New York.

So Oscar and June boarded yet another train and headed east. They arrived at Petrillo's office in an imposing building at 570 Lexington Avenue, where they were ushered into an empty boardroom. Petrillo entered the room and began making small talk with Oscar, asking him about his brother Harry. Since his death, his brother's name had joined the roster of taboo words, but Levant made a feeble attempt to reminisce about his brother with the union boss.

Petrillo was all smiles and graciousness for the press, which had gathered outside his office. "I'm going to take the charges and throw them out the window," Petrillo explained, "because Mr. Levant has promised to be a good boy in the future."

Petrillo then began a soliloquy about other artists who thought they, too, "were bigger than the union" and refused to be governed by union rules, including Yehudi Menuhin. Petrillo, who happened to be, like George S. Kaufman, a notorious germophobe, usually offered only his little finger in a handshake. But on this occasion he offered his whole hand to the grimacing pianist, posing for the photographers. During their private meeting, Petrillo had forbidden Levant to speak to the press. When *New York Post* columnist Murray Kempton requested an interview with the ousted musician, Levant was forced to refuse. The following day, Kempton's reportage of the event was noticeably negative:

> James C. Petrillo yesterday added to his already numberless contributions to our culture a short, totally decisive lesson in manners for Oscar Levant. . . .
> Yesterday he crawled in to render unto Caesar the apologies that are Caesar's, taking with him his wife, a remarkably fetching lady under any circumstances, let alone those of twelve years with Levant.

Levant had always liked Kempton's columns, and he considered the newspaperman a writer of "sinew and muscle." It was painful to see himself lampooned by a writer he admired. Once the press couldn't get enough of Levant's brashness, now they seemed to delight in his humiliation. From now on, there would be a definite shift in how the media viewed Levant. The new story angle would be "Oscar Levant—hypochondriac," or "canceler of concert dates." "Gershwin's friend" and "genius of the keyboard" would recede, and the image of an out-of-control neurotic would take its place.

Levant complained to Leonard Lyons, his friend on the *New York Post,* who mentioned Levant's displeasure to Murray Kempton. Kempton penned an apology to Levant shortly after his column appeared. He apologized for mentioning June in print: "I have been meaning all week to write you a personal apology for one thing I said in my column about you and Jimmy Petrillo. That was, as I am sure you know, that completely unforgivable reference to Mrs. Levant. . . . Any reactions I have to you are of course part of the game." Levant refused even to read the letter.

Within a few weeks of Levant's humiliation, Minnie Guggenheimer booked Levant for Lewisohn Stadium's annual all-Gershwin concert, which had become a tradition in New York's summer cultural life and a staple of Levant's concertizing. The night of the concert, crowds in excess of twenty thousand filled the stadium. Wearing a tuxedo, sitting tensely in a chair backstage waiting to go on, Levant suddenly felt he was having a second heart attack, but he later characterized the sensation as "unbearable neurotic hysteria, which included a psychogenic paralysis." Frightened, he ran rather than walked onstage. During the Concerto in F, Levant suddenly lost the coordination in his fingers, just as Gershwin had sixteen years earlier. For the first time in his concert career, Levant felt the terror that he was losing his ability to play.

Neither the critics nor the audience seemed to notice the marred notes or Levant's growing panic. "He still looks like a boy and oddly enough he acts something like one, too," observed one reviewer. "What I mean is his lack of inhibition has that relaxed spontaneity, almost always discarded by adults. When he wasn't playing he would spin around on his seat, so that he faced the orchestra."

Levant managed to finish the piece, but at its conclusion he did an inexplicable thing. He rose from the piano to take his bows, walked over to the concertmaster and his assistant, and kissed them both. Was it a kiss of gratitude for having gotten through the Concerto or a farewell to his life as a concert artist?

With Levant back at home to stay, Dr. Kert continued to monitor his condition. He seemed to have been a conscientious doctor, and the Levants trusted him, but like many of Oscar's physicians, he wasn't immune to his patient's celebrity status and the force of his personality. Many starstruck physicians worked the expensive real estate of Beverly Hills, and it was hard for them to deny their patients anything. If Oscar cried out for Demerol, Demerol he got. If chloral hydrate or paraldehyde seemed to appease him for a while, then it, too, was prescribed, in addition to his usual sleeping pills, which he kept by his bedside. He became bitter and full of rage, and he took those emotions out on the person nearest him. June Levant, against whom he held a grudge for loving him and staying with him, became the chief target of his frustration.

Levant was now in a constant state of confusion, imbibing paraldehyde and chloral hydrate chased by sleeping pills throughout the day. June often heard her husband trying to move into the bathroom and falling to the floor with a thud. (Chloral hydrate was known as "knockout drops" because it quickly rendered the patient unconscious.) It was impossible to raise him off the floor. For the next two months he alternated between nonstop talking jags and sleeping for twenty-four hours at a stretch.

June was becoming increasingly alarmed by her husband's condition. She herself was nearing a breakdown. She was going without sleep and was consumed with worry. She had been told that her husband's heart attack was a serious one and that he would probably not live more than another seven years at the most—that was the going rate for coronaries in those days. Whenever her husband collapsed in a heap onto the bathroom rug, June was terrified that he had suffered another heart attack. Desperate for help, June called in the well-known psychoanalyst Dr. Ralph Greenson.

At the time, Dr. Greenson was a highly respected psychiatrist who treated many Hollywood celebrities, including Marilyn Monroe. Trained in Vienna and Switzerland, Dr. Greenson was a strict Freudian analyst; he would later join the faculty of UCLA as Clinical Professor of Psychology. Arthur Miller would describe him as caring and sensitive, a good doctor. But his posthumous reputation has not fared as well: His unorthodox methods, such as involving his own family in the treatment of Marilyn Monroe and meeting with her at his home—what he called providing "protection" for his dangerously fragile patient—violated the basic tenets of psychoanalysis.

Greenson believed that Levant's "use of the drugs was an attempt to avoid acute anxiety . . . as well as an attempt to ward off a severe depression." It was clear to Greenson that Levant's drug taking was "a masked suicide attempt" and a "regression to an infantile helplessness."

From the outset, June did not like Greenson's bedside manner. When she called him to explain that her husband was completely out of control and violent, Greenson scheduled a nurse to look after the patient. June was at first relieved to have the efficient-looking nurse bring order to the chaos of their household. But what she then observed scared her: the frequency with which the nurse entered Levant's room with a hypodermic needle. Though Greenson claimed he was trying to reduce the amount of sedatives being pumped into Levant, the opposite seemed to be true.

A clinical chart for October 13, 1953, bears witness to the amount of opiates and barbiturates given to Levant under the doctor's instructions: "75 mg. Demerol to be given as far apart as possible. *No Placebos.*" Demerol was administered at 6:30 P.M., followed by an injection of paraldehyde at 7:45 P.M.; Demerol again at 10:00 P.M., with more paraldehyde at 11:30 P.M., more Demerol and paraldehyde administered together at 1:30 the next morning. This schedule of eight to twelve doses of Demerol and paraldehyde every twelve hours continued through October 26.

June called Greenson and demanded an explanation. The doctor explained that the Demerol was being given to wean him off paraldehyde (which had originally been prescribed to wean him off Demerol). But when the nurse withheld paraldehyde from Levant, he flew into a rage and hurled invectives at her. Soon they reverted to giving him the paraldehyde. "He was getting everything," June remembered, "Demerol, paraldehyde and handfuls of pills, when he couldn't even find his mouth."

"You've got to do something!" June again pleaded with Greenson. "You've got to get him off Demerol."

"He can get off it anytime he wants to," Greenson responded. He was not immune to the "VIP syndrome," in which physicians who treat celebrities are sometimes afraid of losing the reflected glory of their patients by going against their wishes. If Levant wanted drugs, drugs he got.

"I just got so sick and tired of doctors," June later admitted. "I finally lost all respect, and I even said to Dr. Kert, who was a bona fide good doctor, 'If you ever give him a shot again, I'll report you to the Medical Association.' I had to threaten him."

Dr. Greenson's visits seemed to embolden Oscar to go after June in a big way. "At times he was coherent, rational and cooperative, at other times, he became irrational, disoriented and erupted with . . . explosive violence toward his wife, to a point where he was dangerous both to his wife and to himself," Greenson wrote in an evaluation of Levant.

On one occasion Levant threw June down on the floor and tried to choke her. His fingers were unusually strong from years of playing the piano, and he pressed them against June's throat while she tried to struggle free. June moved into her daughter Marcia's room; she and the three girls all slept behind locked doors while Oscar raged like King Lear on the heath.

June finally called Oscar's brother Ben, the physician, who suggested that she call sanatoriums throughout the country that specialized in "people in Oscar's condition." In 1953 the drug addiction of a well-known figure meant ignominy for the family and ruin for the addict. "Sanatorium"—the very word suggested a misleadingly bucolic setting where dirty secrets were kept secluded from the rest of humanity.

In late October, Dr. Greenson finally told June that he had found the perfect place for Oscar: Westerly Sanatorium, a small, private hospital right there in Los Angeles.

"How are we going to get him there? He won't go voluntarily."

"I'll come tonight and we'll get him there," Greenson promised.

It was a cold night, colder than usual for Los Angeles, when Ralph Greenson arrived at the Levant home. He brought with him a gaunt physician in a raincoat—"cadaverous-looking," June thought, "he looked like the angel of death." Dr. Greenson introduced him to June as a doctor connected with Westerly Sanatorium.

The two doctors went upstairs and into Oscar's bedroom, where they gave him a shot to make him pliable. "Now we're going to take you someplace," Greenson told his patient. They managed to get him out of bed and onto his feet, and June draped an overcoat over his bathrobe. They walked him to the car and somehow eased him into the backseat without incident. Dr. Greenson told June to follow his colleague to Westerly while he excused himself and disappeared into the night, his work completed. June would have to drive Oscar to the sanatorium and register him there by herself.

Oscar was in a stupor when he arrived but he managed to shuffle along with help from his wife. He had no idea what was going on. Once inside, Levant was helped into a bed by a male attendant, who then turned to June and said, "You'd better go home now."

"No, I think I'll wait around a little bit," she told the attendant.

The whole setup disturbed her. The grim surroundings seemed wrong in some way she couldn't quite put her finger on. "It wasn't like a hospital," June remembered. "It was a tiny place with a few rooms, and that cadaverous-looking doctor, who was now nowhere to be found. I stayed there because they kept saying 'You can go home now, you'd better go home.' "

The harder they tried to dismiss her, the more adamant she became about staying. She realized her husband would be coming off the drugs and pretty soon he'd be yelling. She was right.

June placed herself like a sentinel outside of Oscar's room. Oscar was waking up from his drugged sleep and he began asking for a shot. June heard the nurse tell him that he couldn't have one. Thinking he was still at home in his own bed, Levant tried to wheedle the nurse into giving him another injection of Demerol. Meanwhile, other male attendants kept coming over to June and encouraging her to leave.

It was now close to midnight, but June had no intention of leaving. Her suspicions about how her husband would be treated compelled her to stay.

As Greenson's injection wore off, Levant began to fight with the attendant, becoming louder and fiercer in his denunciations. The attendant and nurse had a quick consultation and returned to Oscar's room with two large, powerful-looking men in hospital smocks. They lifted Oscar up out of his bed and led him down the hall.

June shot up out of her seat and followed them. "Where are you taking him?" she demanded.

"He's disturbing the other patients by his yelling," one of the attendants answered her.

"But where are you taking him?"

"Downstairs."

They took him to a cell-like room with three bars on the door and nothing inside but a bed. "This was their place of solitary confinement," June remembered. "They were just going to walk out and leave him there."

June demanded to know what they intended to do for her husband. "Aren't you going to give him anything to calm him? He's going to get more violent, and it can be very dangerous for him."

"Those are our instructions."

June ran to the nearest telephone and called the cadaverous-looking doctor who had seemed to be in charge. She let the phone ring until it finally roused him from sleep. Reciting the horrible occurrences of that night, June waited for the doctor's response.

"Well, that's the only way he can get over it."

"But they're going to lock the door, and he'll be like an animal! He's going to be clawing at the door. He could ruin his hands forever!" she shouted. "That can't be right! You can't do that to him!"

"We have to."

June announced that she wasn't going to leave her husband in this "snake pit" any longer. "I'm taking him out," she told him and hung up the phone. By the time June made her way back to Oscar's cell, she found herself face-to-face with the doctor.

"You can't take him out of this building," he told her sternly.

"This could kill him," she answered.

"That's the chance we have to take."

"That's not the chance I'm going to take!" June cried out.

"Do you or don't you want him cured?" he asked June in an exasperated voice, as though he had spent his whole life handling hysterical women.

"Yes, but not that way. Doctor, are you married?" she suddenly asked her grim opponent.

He nodded.

"Would you do this to your wife?"

He looked at her and said nothing, but when June placed Oscar's coat over his shoulders and started to lead him out of the building, the doctor didn't try to stop them.

At first light the following morning, June called Drs. Kert and Greenson and described their four-hour ordeal. Neither of them admitted knowing much about the practices of "that place," the small, private hospital with its basement cells.

June put Oscar to bed and watched the sun come up. After her small victory, she was more despairing than ever. "There's just no solution," she thought. "They fill him full of dope and then take him to that snake pit. There's no solution."

Paradoxical Excitement

"I was always humming my Demerol theme, which was
the second theme of Liszt's *Mephisto Waltz*."

IN THE WEEKS FOLLOWING LEVANT'S FOUR-HOUR INCARCERATION AT
Westerly, Dr. Greenson and Levant's Los Angeles psychiatrist, Dr.
Marmor, felt they could no longer treat him at home. A medical
history prepared around this time described him as

> very depressed and want[ing] to do away with himself at times . . .
> terrified that something is happening to him physically and . . . worried
> over every physical symptom. He has become abusive to his doctors,
> yet terrified if they do not respond to his call . . . his only aim is to be
> completely unconscious . . .

A verdant, spacious place in Pasadena, Las Encinas Sanatorium was
quite different from Westerly. But the authorities at Las Encinas were
at first reluctant to admit Levant without June actually committing
him. They were afraid that upon release he would turn around and
sue the hospital; commitment was the only legal way they could hold
him there long enough to effect a cure. But June refused. "I can't
commit him in this condition," she pleaded. "He's not able to stand
rejection. If I committed him, I would have to go to court and make

a public thing about it." Dr. Charles Thompson, the head doctor at the sanatorium, eventually decided to accept Levant for a ninety-day stay without commitment papers. June felt sure he would receive humane treatment there.

An ambulance took Levant to the sanatorium, where he was assigned to Cherokee Cottage. He arrived in a drug-induced stupor, occasionally crying out, at other times insisting on walking, which he did painfully, having injured his legs in a number of falls. In a letter to Dr. Thompson dated November 12, 1953, Dr. Greenson wrote that he considered Levant to be suffering from a toxic psychosis. "I might add parenthetically," he wrote,

> that Mr. Levant has had many years of supposed psychoanalytic therapy, which at this time is of no avail to him whatsoever. . . . I would like to add that I consider him an extremely worthwhile human being and I would like to urge you to give him your every consideration.

Levant first resisted his cure at Las Encinas, grappling with nurses and attendants and throwing doctors out of his room. He was being treated in the early days of his withdrawal with a kind of injection therapy, sequentially smaller doses of Demerol for the first few days, then glucose and insulin for his appetite, plus Benadryl and vitamin shots. The therapy pacified Levant, who was under the impression that he was still receiving his usual doses of Demerol. At first he hallucinated that he was in his bedroom at North Roxbury Drive, and he kept asking for his daughters, inviting them up as if he were still at home.

June visited Oscar at Las Encinas. She watched her husband go through withdrawal for the first time. During one visit, Oscar kept opening drawers in his bureau and rifling through their contents. "What are you doing?" June asked.

"I'm looking for the gold," Oscar told her. He was in a hallucinatory state, searching for Demerol. Other times she would find him sprawled out on his bed, having animated, imaginary conversations. During one interview with his doctors, Levant hallucinated the voices of children playing nearby, and he said, "Those are my children. They seem happy." He kept hearing June's voice and "seeing pretty girls on this side of the room." Levant thought there was a cat in his room: "It just crawled up there and urinated on my pillows. Right there! See!"

On one occasion he told Dr. Thompson, "You said my wife wanted to get rid of me," but Thompson had said that June was devoted to him and wanted him to have the best possible care so he could come home. Levant often remarked, "I just want to go home and sleep and sleep and sleep." Once he said his children were with him at Cherokee Cottage, and that he "did not like to leave them." He was quite concerned about the children, Thompson noted in Levant's medical records.

Levant would later describe his withdrawal at Las Encinas as "a mad Walpurgis Night . . . figures danced and charged at me."

At the end of two weeks, Levant was considered sufficiently recovered to be released. One of the doctors warned him, however, that if he ever took Demerol again, he would die.

Levant returned home free of his Demerol addiction but angry that June had hospitalized him in the first place. "He was furious about the whole thing," June remembered, "because he didn't want to be cured." Outraged by what he considered his wife's betrayal, Levant began to abuse her physically. He threatened to leave June and return to New York, but June had suffered enough and didn't care what he did. "I hope you go and never come back!" she told him, and she meant it.

Within a week Levant was in his old Alwyn Court apartment, alone. For three and a half months, Levant lived in the city, separated from June and his daughters. He spent most of that winter tracking down doctors willing to give him Demerol injections or prescriptions for paraldehyde. "I was always humming my Demerol theme," he later wrote of this period in his life, "which was the second theme of Liszt's *Mephisto Waltz,* a very narcissistic theme." Levant's drug abuse, hospitalization, and withdrawal had catapulted him into the manic phase of manic-depressive (now called "bipolar") illness. This would become a new pattern in his life: drug withdrawal followed by a false recovery characterized by manic symptoms. The sedatives he was consuming had the side effect of creating "paradoxical excitement"; that is, instead of sedation Levant's saturated nervous system sped out of control.

Two psychiatrists, Dr. John Urbach and Dr. James Levenson of the Medical College of Virginia, were asked to assist in a "psychological postmortem" of Levant. They felt that the co-existence of bipolar illness and obsessive-compulsive disorder presented Levant with unusually severe challenges, particularly in an era before the development of specific, effective medications. These disorders were compounded by Levant's rampant abuse of prescription drugs. Urbach and Levinson also suggested that Levant had some features of a Narcissistic personality disorder, which meant, among other things, that he went through life creating a series of "false selves," consistently avoiding coming to terms with his own fundamental emotions.

Levant's former analyst, Dr. Shoenfeld, was soon made aware of the terrible condition Oscar was in: the manic behavior, the craving for Demerol. What was new in all this was Levant's sudden infatuation with young women whom he would meet in the company of his old New York friends, inviting them to join him at Sardi's or the Russian Tea Room, where they would exchange numbers and Oscar would later flirt with them over the telephone. These "affairs" always remained flirtations. "Oscar was more interested in Demerol than in dames," recalled Oscar's old friend, Ottie Swope, Jr.

Ottie remembered Oscar visiting the Swopes during his weeks alone in New York. Upon arrival, Levant immediately raided the Swopes' medicine cabinets. "The old man had had an operation," Ottie remembered, "and there was some Demerol left over . . . Oscar was ecstatic that he found it. We told my father, 'Pop, you know you have to keep your medicine cabinet locked around Oscar.' "

Concerned for his patient, Dr. Shoenfeld called June in Los Angeles and convinced her to take Oscar back. Angry and resentful at her husband's ungrateful, violent behavior, she refused to meet Oscar at the train station when he arrived back in Los Angeles. Instead she sent their maid, a physically imposing woman named Dixie whom Oscar had always liked.

Dixie finally found him holed up in a luggage room in the train station, tattooed with bruises and welts and stinking in his disheveled, dirty suit. He had three fractured ribs and had not eaten during the entire train ride. In his weakened state, Levant had fallen repeatedly while trying to walk between the cars of the hurtling train, causing hairline fractures of his rib cage. Dixie was strong enough to lift him bodily into the car and bring him home. Dr. Shoenfeld's phone call had not adequately prepared June for the sight of Oscar in his sickness and squalor.

This time Levant made up his mind that he was going to withdraw from all medications on his own. He would make use of an extraordinarily tenacious resolve—the same resolve he had drawn upon in his early thirties, when he had grabbed his last chance to forge a concert career out of a specialty. The Levants' middle daughter, Lorna, remembered what it was like to be an eleven-year-old in that household:

> There was a long period when he was kind of a spooky figure in pajamas. . . . I was terrified what would happen while I was [at school]. You know, when you're a child, you think you can have some control if you're there.

One February morning in 1954, when June and her daughters had gone to her mother's home for sanctuary, Levant called June to beg her to come back. June had left the phone off the hook, a familiar ruse of hers on such occasions, and the steady busy signal aggravated Levant all the more. Frustrated, he dialed the local operator and asked her to check the line. The operator told an increasingly agitated Levant that the phone was indeed off the hook. "If you don't reach my wife, it will be too late!" he dramatically told her.

"I can try again in thirty minutes."

"I'll be dead in thirty minutes!"

"Please hold," she replied.

As Oscar held on, waiting for June's voice to miraculously appear, he began to get drowsy and he dozed off with the phone still in his hand. He had taken two teaspoonfuls of paraldehyde that morning, far less than his usual dosage.

Suddenly, Levant was startled out of his nap by the sound of sirens. The Beverly Hills police, led by Chief Clinton Anderson, had broken in through the back door and had bounded upstairs to Levant's bedroom. Anderson burst into the room. Noticing the fifteen empty paraldehyde bottles that Levant had compulsively saved and arranged in a special order, Anderson sniffed around like a police dog and announced with authority, "Paraldehyde!"

"You're a genius," Levant told the police chief. Anderson concluded that Levant had taken an overdose.

Levant tried to explain, saying that he had taken very little paraldehyde, but Chief Anderson and his officers escorted Levant from the house and took him by patrol car to the Beverly Hills Hospital emergency room, where they had his stomach pumped. By the next morning Levant's "attempted suicide" was carried in all the Los Angeles papers. Several newspapers, to their credit, duly noted Levant's denial and his insistence that it had all been "a police foul-up." Dr. Kert was called in to accompany Levant home from the hospital; he, too, went on record denying the suicide attempt. Two days after the incident the *Los Angeles Times* reported, "Oscar Levant Suicide Report Held Mistake." But the damage had been done.

Coming on the heels of Petrillo's humiliation the previous spring, the story only served to solidify Levant's new persona as the fabulous invalid of Beverly Hills. His celebrated past achievements were being wiped out by the image of his neurotic, self-destructive personality.

The reputation stuck. Ever since the Petrillo incident, concert dates had begun to dry up as booking agents were convinced that Levant's ill health and orneriness made him a risky bet. Levant's eccentricities and neuroses, which had once contributed to his celebrity, were now being held against him just when he most needed support. George S. Kaufman had been right: "What makes you, breaks you."

But not all concert managers and conductors abandoned Levant. Conductor Howard Mitchell came to his aid in 1954, inviting his old friend to play in Washington, D.C., with the National Symphony. Flattered by Mitchell's invitation at a time when few offers were forthcoming, Levant accepted the concert date. It was with a certain trepidation that June—bravely, doggedly—accompanied Levant on his trip to Washington. Levant, who had managed to withdraw himself from Demerol, nonetheless fortified himself for the trip with a remarkable array of pills.

It was not an auspicious journey. The train was eight hours late by the time it reached Kansas City. June insisted that they go the rest of the way by plane. The following morning, Levant appeared for rehearsals at Constitution Hall. As soon as he began to play, however, he felt that his coordination was seriously off. "I cannot play!" he moaned, and he jumped up from the piano and ran off the stage. Howard Mitchell, however, was sympathetic and did his best to soothe the anxious pianist. He told Levant that when Moritz Rosenthal had played at Constitution Hall, he had "played one out of every five notes." But Levant's fears could not be assuaged, and he canceled the concert.

In a despairing mood, Levant traveled with June to New York City on the next available train. "I failed again," he kept saying, repeating it like a mantra. At the age of forty-seven, he felt his concert career was truly over. He had expected and prepared for failure his whole life, and now it had arrived.

The National Symphony lost no time in replacing Levant in the wake of his cancellation. "Every time I appeared," Levant commented wryly, "there was always another pianist waiting." His reputation as a canceler preceded him even among friends.

A few days later, the two slowly made their way back to California on the 20th Century Limited. When they arrived at Union Station in Los Angeles, Levant ran into Noël Coward. "How are you?" Coward asked him.

"Not too well," Oscar muttered. "I'm slightly neurotic, you know."

Coward shrugged. "Oh, you Americans are all neurotic."

"But I'm not an American," Levant answered inexplicably. June's arm reached out and pulled him into a waiting cab.

For the next four months, Levant spent most of his time at home, in bed, cadging pills from physicians and friends. When he did manage to get out and see people, he usually made a beeline for his host's medicine cabinet. He stayed away from the piano for weeks at a time, convinced that his Washington failure was the end of his concert career.

While Levant nursed his wounds, Vincente Minnelli was making plans to turn *The Cobweb,* a critically acclaimed first novel by playwright William Gibson, into a film to be produced by John Houseman. The appeal of *The Cobweb,* besides its exotic setting within the grounds of a private psychiatric hospital based on the Austen Riggs Center in the Berkshires, was the opportunity to draw together an ensemble cast of major stars, along the lines of *Grand Hotel.* Minnelli initially wanted Robert Taylor, Lana Turner, and James Dean to play the important roles of the hospital's reigning psychiatrist, his pouty, neglected wife, and a sensitive young psychiatric patient. He wound up instead with Richard Widmark, Gloria Grahame, and John Kerr, a trio that lacked the star wallop of his first choices but turned out to be solid casting. Susan Strasberg made her film debut as a patient, and Lauren Bacall played an occupational therapist who falls in love with Richard Widmark's crusading Dr. McIver. Charles Boyer and Lillian Gish round out the cast as scheming hospital administrators. The hospital staff are as neurotic and disturbed as the patients, with whom they are often at odds, and therein lies the film's drama. "The sick look after the sick," is how one reviewer encapsulated it.

For the role of the neurotic patient Mr. Capp, Minnelli remembered his suffering friend. It was not a demanding role, and Minnelli realized it would be good for Levant to get out and accomplish something, in light of his recent, well-publicized troubles. Mr. Capp would be Levant's only film role in which he doesn't go near a piano—in the winter of 1954 he couldn't trust himself to play one. It would also be his final film appearance.

Never before had Levant's onscreen role meshed so perfectly with the life he was living: He would eerily re-create his emotional problems as he glided through the role of a bitter has-been recovering from a nervous breakdown in a mental hospital. Levant again provided much of his own dialogue, and to deepen the character he came up with his own twist: He gave Mr. Capp a mother fixation. In one horrendous scene Levant lies in a tub while a nurse pours water over him as he sings at the top of his lungs, "M is for the million things you gave me, O means only that you're growing old . . ."

Filming began in early December 1954 and continued for seven weeks. *The Cobweb* was actor John Kerr's first film. When James Dean had demanded too much money, Minnelli and Houseman had turned to the tall, lithe young actor who had just made a big splash on Broadway in *Tea and Sympathy*. John Kerr remembered Levant's first scene, in which he had to hit a croquet ball:

> Minnelli wanted it all in one [shot] . . . he wanted to see Oscar put his foot on the ball, hit the ball and then the other ball goes off. Oscar, for the life of him, couldn't hit the ball. He'd hit his shoe; he'd hit the dirt; he'd hit the ball and it would dribble away. It just wasn't working. . . . Oscar was getting more and more unhappy and angry and upset, and then he'd come back and slump in the chair and he'd ask me, "How do *you* prepare for a part?"

The Levants befriended Kerr and his wife during those eight weeks. When filming was over, Kerr would visit Levant, who received his guest upstairs in his bedroom, still dressed in his pajamas. He would recline in bed like a pasha and tell wonderful anecdotes, Kerr recalled.

Kerr noticed that Levant—even in his relatively debilitated condition—liked to flirt with women on the set. "He liked flirting. He liked having the attention of attractive women and pretty girls. He liked being thought of as an important person, and I think probably would rather have [attention] from a girl than from a man," Kerr recalled. "He flirted in front of June, but I doubt very much that he was a philanderer."

> I remember there was a young actress in *The Cobweb*. Dark hair. She was very attractive; she looked like she was a model; not a very great actress or anything. And he was very interested in her. . . . "What are you doing?" I remember he said to her. "Where do you lurk?" I mean, that was his style. He never asked me where I lurked!

Levant was often querulous on the set, and on several occasions he stalked off and threatened to quit. As much as he liked and admired Minnelli, the two argued about how the role should be played. Frustrated, Levant finally muttered to the assistant producer, "Who's crazy anyway—him or me?"

The film was released in June 1955 to mixed reviews. Though it was praised for its fine execution and the sincerity of its efforts, the consensus was that its entertainment appeal was far too narrow. The most shocking scene in the film is Levant's painful, off-key tribute to Motherhood while undergoing hydrotherapy—a scene that June Levant still finds so unsettling that she refused to attend a revival screening of *The Cobweb* thirty years later at the Los Angeles County Museum.

In June 1955, Howard Mitchell again invited Levant to appear with the National Symphony, a year after his last, disastrous attempt at concertizing. Touched by Mitchell's loyalty, Levant accepted the challenge and began to try to regain the coordination in his fingers. (Doctors at Las Encinas Sanatorium had noticed that Levant's hands were rigid, "held in a rather stiff position.")

With a few rudimentary yogic breathing exercises taught to him by the English novelist Christopher Isherwood, who had expatriated himself to Santa Monica, Levant tried to regain his former command. He managed to cleanse his system of all tranquilizers except Miltown. Accompanied by June and the girls, he arranged to meet his brother Ben and Ben's wife, Sarah, who planned to attend the concert to provide moral support.

The rehearsal went exceptionally well, to Levant's tremendous relief. He felt he had never played better in his life. He played so well that the orchestra stood up and cheered. They had all been there the year before when, in humiliation, Oscar had run off the stage.

The following night, a huge audience filled the auditorium, eagerly anticipating Levant's performance. His earlier cancellations during the previous two concert seasons had added a note of drama to the evening—will he or will he not perform? Levant waited in the wings as the Steinway concert grand was wheeled onstage. Suddenly, the piano's rear leg snapped, causing the tremendous instrument to come crashing to the floor. It was not a good omen.

June and the girls cringed at the thought of another embarrassing debacle. A wooden sawhorse was brought onto the stage and set firmly under the piano. Levant just laughed. It was that "pure gold" a concert artist waits for to break the unbearable tension before a performance.

When he set foot onstage he was met with tremendous applause. "And then," music critic Paul Hume wrote in *The Washington Post,* "with a look at the poor, up-ended Steinway, and a shrug that clearly indicated he couldn't do anything about it, he sat himself down and delivered a marvelous performance of the Concerto." Levant knew he was playing exceptionally well that night: "I played the slant of that piano like a Picasso painting. It didn't bother me . . . my playing that night had a deep expressivity and a rhythmic intensity."

During intermission Levant told Hume, who was Washington, D.C.'s leading music critic, that he had often talked with Gershwin about the Concerto in F, and Gershwin had told him that the middle movement was his favorite of all the music he had written—he felt it was "somewhat Mozartian."

"I felt moved by it this evening," Levant told Hume and conductor Mitchell during intermission, ". . . during the introduction before the piano comes in. It has wonderful form. I cried a little," Levant confessed.

Elated by the successful performance and Hume's glowing review, Levant headed for New York with his family. For a while, at least, he felt reborn.

Ben's presence in Washington represented the closest Oscar would ever come to having his father's approval and blessing. Ben had always been Max's favorite, the one who had stayed on the approved path. But Levant had always felt uncomfortable around Ben's wife, Sarah, though no one quite knew why.

In high spirits, the Levants embarked on a rare family holiday. In New York City Levant took his children to the movies and his wife on a shopping spree. Lorna remembers that her father "went out and bought us marionettes, and we were all thrilled. I remember I got the complete Cinderella. They were all traditional marionettes, the godmother and the stepmother and everything."

Levant felt confident enough to resume concertizing, but he decided he needed a new manager after having felt betrayed by Fred Schang—Schang's scheduling had nearly cost him his life. Levant set up a schedule of six concerts, all in the eastern part of the country. Despite his recent bad press and earlier spate of cancellations, the public welcomed Levant back onto the concert scene; all six dates were sold out in advance. And he was playing with a finesse and a power that seemed astonishing after all the punishment he had put his nervous system through. But with the resumption of his concert career came the resumption of his old superstitions; each appearance spawned new apprehensions about the next concert.

The last concert was scheduled for Milwaukee. In that city Levant's dread of the word "luck" reached its zenith. He had developed the habit of sprinting from his dressing room to the stage before each appearance to prevent anyone backstage from wishing him good luck.

By the time the Levants returned home, it was obvious that even a short tour was having a deleterious effect on Levant's health. His entire personality suffered under the anxieties of performing, warping his self-confidence and exacerbating his phobias and superstitions. After having withdrawn from Demerol twice, it no longer seemed worth risking that kind of pain.

"That's it," he told June. "We'll have to economize. I'm finished. I can't do it. It's over." At the age of forty-eight, he had made up his mind to never perform again. By way of comparison, Vladimir Horowitz would come out of retirement at the age of sixty-two and continue to perform for nearly a quarter of a century. Levant's life as a touring concert artist was over. One of the most famous pianists in America had gone home for good.

37

Chaos in
Search of Frenzy

"Shock treatments, anyone?"

A NEW GENERATION OF HOLLYWOOD PERSONALITIES WAS BEGINNING
to discover the aging *enfant terrible*. They saw in Levant a figure of
artistic integrity and independence, qualities the Hollywood establishment seemed to lack. He had not lost his power to entertain a gathering by the sheer brilliance of his conversation. Joe Hyams, a writer
and journalist who covered Hollywood for the *New York Herald Tribune,* befriended Levant and considered him "the most erudite man
I've ever met."

One evening, a group of young actors—Elizabeth Taylor, her husband, Michael Wilding, Joan Collins, and James Dean—visited the
Levant home. Joan Collins led James Dean up to Marcia's room,
where she hoped to surprise the teenager with her real-life idol.
"Marcia, Marcia, we're here to see you," Collins whispered to the
sleeping girl. "Now come on, wake up. We have somebody who
wants to meet you." Marcia slowly awoke to the sight of James Dean
lounging against her bedroom door. She screamed and put her head
under the covers.

"I knew she would be terrified," June remembered. But the next day, Marcia roped off the area in her room where James Dean had stood—it was now sacred ground.

"It was a strange thing," Levant later wrote about the incident, "but seeing my daughter's room (filled as it was with pictures of the young actor) did not seem to please James Dean. On the contrary, it depressed him." Dean told Oscar he felt crushed under the weight of such adulation. After the other guests had left, Dean stayed and discussed music with Levant, who was impressed with the young actor's knowledge of composers such as Bartók and Schoenberg. "James Dean and Oscar Levant," Joan Collins would write in her autobiography some thirty years later, "got along famously. Each relished the other's unusualness."

Collins was an occasional guest at the Levant home, and she invariably wore revealing outfits with plunging necklines, part of her English sex-kitten image. Her provocative attire did not go unnoticed by Levant. Observing that she always wore long, thick bangs that fell flirtatiously over her eyebrows, Levant was inspired to remark, "I have now seen every part of Joan Collins's anatomy except her forehead." But for all her provocative good looks, Collins was overcome by Elizabeth Taylor's beauty. She whispered to June Levant about Taylor, "Isn't she gorgeous! Isn't she beautiful!"

Levant remained friends with Elizabeth Taylor throughout her marriages to Nicky Hilton, Mike Todd, Michael Wilding, and Eddie Fisher. "Always a bride, never a bridesmaid," Levant quipped about her. "Her five husbands have absolutely nothing in common—except her." Levant's remarks had not lost their sting.

"I always thought of Oscar as both self-destructive and a survivor at the same time," Adolph Green said about his friend. Nothing illustrates this view more than the new course Levant's career would take. Levant had seen nearly every significant change and technological breakthrough in the popular media—radio, film, records. Television would be the last of these evolving forms with which he would become identified. And television would establish Levant's most enduring persona, to the detriment of his reputation as a serious artist.

Levant's first television appearances were in 1950, after he had moved to California but still commuted frequently to New York. He appeared on *Who Said That?*, a radio show produced by Fred Friendly that moved to television in 1950; a panel of four "experts" was called upon to identify the originators of famous quotations. "He was a brilliant man," producer and journalist Friendly said about Levant.

Friendly invited Levant onto the show despite the fact that his name was included on blacklists circulated in the industry, "not because he was a Communist but because he might just say anything [on the air]," Friendly recalled.

After Harry's death in 1950 Levant's death phobia had kicked into high gear. One afternoon Levant and Friendly were riding in a cab when the producer said that he would have to check with the NBC morgue for some newspaper clippings they needed for the show. Oscar was horrified at the word "morgue." "Why did you say that?" he demanded. "Why did you talk to me about death?" He stopped the cab and jumped out in the middle of traffic. It took Friendly a few days to figure out what he had done to offend him.

By 1955 many had tried to lure Levant out of bed and back to television. *New York Post* columnist Leonard Lyons, reviewing the glut of mediocre television game shows, reminded his readers about a wittier time: "No panelist working today," Lyons wrote, "is as gifted at it as Oscar Levant." Toward the end of the year, a bright young television producer named Al Burton was preparing a panel show for CBS-TV's local Los Angeles station, KNXT. The one-hour show was called *Words About Music* and it asked a panel of celebrities to sit in judgment while a string of guest songwriters showcased their newest tunes. Levant was suggested as a possible panelist.

At the height of his career, Levant had made $200,000 annually through his concert appearances and recording contracts. He had earned just under $5,000 per week at MGM only two years earlier. Now Burton offered him all the local studio could afford, a mere $44.50 to go on another panel show. Levant accepted.

America's taste in humor had changed since *Information, Please!* It was the Eisenhower era, and America had found its new role as a world power. The country had developed a certain prudery that had reawakened its Puritan conscience. America now presented a different image to the world: The suburbs, with their nuclear families, emerged everywhere from the potato farms of Long Island to the deserts of California. Was this newer, optimistic, no-longer-cynical America ready for the same old Oscar Levant? Nearly fifty, Levant would reenter American consciousness at a time when the pervading spirit of the country had changed, but he had not.

"Frank De Vol was the host of *Words About Music,*" producer Al Burton recalled, "and he was the star of the show until Oscar showed up." When the show premiered in January 1956, the "hit of the evening was not a tune, but panelist Oscar Levant," reported *Daily Variety*. On that first night, Frank De Vol asked Levant how he felt about being on the show. Levant answered, "Utterly degraded." His humor had turned darker since *Information, Please!,* and more personal. "I taught Mario Lanza how to have his nervous breakdown," he said on the air, and many of his remarks now centered around his experiences with psychiatry and drug addiction.

Herb Stein in the *Morning Telegraph* wrote that *Words About Music* was "a darned good package that oughta go nationwide. Levant is superb." He quoted a Levant answer to a query about his health: "It's too late for sweets, but too early for flowers." Burton remembered that Levant soon became the whole show; "People called it *The Oscar Levant Show* instead of *Words About Music.*"

It wasn't long, however, before his words began to get him into trouble. During the summer of 1956, when Adlai Stevenson challenged the incumbent president, Dwight D. Eisenhower, and Vice President Richard M. Nixon, Levant couldn't resist turning *Words About Music* into a forum for his political opinions. An admirer of Stevenson, Levant was "lovable about Democrats and shocking about Republicans." Vice President Nixon became a favorite target: "He swings a big mouth and carries a little stick," he said, and "I'd like to state now that I have a split personality when it comes to politics. Half of me is for Stevenson, half of me against Nixon." The CBS network lawyers decided that Levant's on-the-air jibes against the vice president were too risky, and they put pressure on the show. Levant was baffled by the network's ban on political subjects—"the whole purpose of the show is my boldness," he announced to a *Variety* reporter. When the network directive was handed down, Levant bolted. "It's not the way it used to be in radio years ago," Levant rued, "when there was no 'gag rule.' " In May, Levant quit the show. "Once Oscar pulled out," recalled one observer, "there wasn't much left." Three weeks later the show went off the air.

In June 1956, Al Burton revived the program on KCOP-TV, another local Los Angeles station, this time with Levant at the helm under the new title *Oscar Levant's Words About Music.* Levant asked for—and got—four female panelists, with whom he would discuss new songs and generally trade in his usual brand of uninhibited wisecracks and observations. Among his panelists was Eva Gabor. Levant had already gored her sister Zsa Zsa with on-the-air remarks like "Zsa Zsa Gabor has learned the secret of perpetual middle age."

Levant's at times bizarre train of thought and uncensored remarks became required viewing for the Los Angeles show business community, which came in for its share of abuse: "Strip the phony tinsel off Hollywood and you'll find the real tinsel underneath" he growled on one program. At home Levant prepared for his show by reading up on his guests and writing out questions in "the most pretentious polysyllabic language imaginable." During this period he found himself drawn to the French symbolist poets Charles Baudelaire and Arthur Rimbaud and "anybody who took opium in the nineteenth century." As a result, Levant's program was a bizarre mix of references ranging from *Les Fleurs du mal* to carpet advertisements for the sponsor.

Levant also prepared for the show in another way: Each week he took five Dexedrines and, "as a balance and check," ten milligrams of Thorazine right before going on the air. Mixing these pharmaceutical cocktails made Levant the speediest and most unpredictable talk show host in the history of television. He described the effect this mixture had on him as promoting a state of "chaos in search of frenzy."

Despite the show's popularity and the attention from the press, *Oscar Levant's Words About Music* lasted only a few short months. By August 1956 Levant's own uncensored wit would bring the show to a close. While on the air, Oscar commented on the marriage by a rabbi of Marilyn Monroe and Arthur Miller. "Now that Marilyn Monroe is kosher," Levant said, "Arthur Miller can eat her." A collective gasp escaped from the studio audience.

"I didn't mean it literally!" Levant later protested. "I just meant it in connection with the kosher dietary laws!" But KCOP's station manager had heard enough, and Oscar was taken off the air. But much later when he looked back on the incident, he recognized that his old pattern of sabotaging his success and antagonizing his bosses had reappeared in all its glory. "I suspect that my subconscious had led me into saying something outrageous enough to get thrown off the air," he wrote a few years later.

Levant's disappointment was mollified by the outpouring of audience support to have the program reinstated. Picketers showed up at KCOP protesting the cancellation. Oscar's audience took its cause to the press, where Levant's reputation was still undergoing a reassessment; Levant was now being described in print as out of control, in need of sympathy, not sarcasm. Again Levant turned to drugs to ease disappointment.

For the next year and a half, Levant sank deeper into the slough of despond. He would have a second breakdown, the beginning of a period in his life he would refer to as his "Bed of Nails." Levant's renewed paraldehyde addiction landed him in the new Mount Sinai Hospital in Los Angeles. There he came under the care of Dr. Lawrence Greenleigh, who had recently begun his affiliation with the hospital.

The third-floor psychiatric ward was one of the two best systems in the state. Dr. Greenleigh relied heavily on group therapy, getting patients to interact in an effort to re-create the family dynamic. In an era when strict Freudian psychoanalysis was in its heyday, Dr. Greenleigh was not a strict Freudian at all. He used his own strong personality and charisma to involve his patients in group activities. He had other celebrity patients such as Joan Collins and Judy Garland, but he seemed to have evaded the pitfalls of the "VIP syndrome." In fact, he bristled whenever his connection to a famous patient was made public.

Dr. Greenleigh was the first physician Levant encountered who seemed to have some understanding of his drug dependency. Dr. Greenleigh helped Oscar withdraw in a dignified and compassionate manner. Through therapeutic sessions Greenleigh began to learn something of the impossibly high standards that had been set for his patient, beginning in early childhood. Levant's failure to measure up—to be another Paderewski, another Gershwin, another Schoenberg—had produced not only intense anxiety but despair, giving rise to self-condemnation and self-destruction. Levant's addictions were a refuge from these imprisoning standards. Greenleigh also learned that Levant was guilt-ridden about his family, feeling he should have done more for them. Because his father had died of cancer on Christmas Eve, Levant was always disturbed around that time. He also expressed guilt about abandoning Jewish rituals.

Under Dr. Greenleigh's care, Levant successfully withdrew from paraldehyde during his stay at Mount Sinai, and he was sent home. But there were still obstacles to regaining any peace of mind. Without paraldehyde Levant was plunged into depression, and he began to abuse sleeping pills again. He would spend entire weeks in bed, rarely changing out of his pajamas. Figuring out ways to fill prescriptions for sleeping pills or to cadge them from friends became the only activity that interested him.

Levant's West Coast psychiatrist, Dr. Marmor, informed June that her husband was in deep depression and might therefore benefit from electric shock treatments. He recommended that Levant see Dr. George Wayne at Edgemont Hospital in Hollywood; electroshock therapy was his specialty. For the next eight weeks June drove her husband to Dr. Wayne's clinic, where Levant received eighteen treatments of electroshock therapy. He later wrote that the treatments had "one incalculable pleasure—each shock treatment was preceded by an intravenous injection of sodium pentothal." But the treatments did not seem to help. Levant continued to vegetate at home, a spectral presence in his bathrobe and pajamas haunting his own abode while his three daughters tiptoed around and tried to keep their friends from knowing about their father's condition. If anything, he had become even more lethargic and zombielike under Dr. Wayne's care. "I had an insatiable craving for unconsciousness. It was my only surcease," he later wrote about this period. "I wake up, and the feeling of terror is so knife-edged. . . . I see sadness everywhere; I could have written *Bonjour Tristesse*." Without much hope, Levant was admitted to Edgemont Hospital.

Edgemont was much less confining than Las Encinas or Mount Sinai had been. Levant was permitted free access to wander the premises as he wished. "Shock treatments, anyone?" Levant shouted on his first day in the recreation room of the hospital. But for the most part he continued in apathy, wandering around like a sleepwalker. Irene Kahn, the daughter of lyricist Gus Kahn, who had collaborated with Levant in the early thirties, was a volunteer at the hospital. She was shaken to see Levant haunting the grounds. She told her husband, Groucho's son, Arthur Marx, "Oscar Levant has been here for weeks and he's bearded and he hasn't shaved or taken a bath and he's walking around in a bathrobe."

Levant soon realized that the electroshock therapy was diminishing his memory, a devastating occurrence for a pianist. Throughout his lifetime Levant had been famous for his superb musical memory. Now he feared that those jolts of electricity had caused irreparable damage. Levant begged June to let him come home. Worried about the erosion of his memory, she arranged for his release from Dr. Wayne's house of pain, with the understanding that he would return three times a week for analysis.

Some of Levant's friends and family, especially his brother Ben, thought that Levant was addicted to analysis and the victim of bad psychiatry. Levant soon returned to Dr. Wayne and Edgemont Hospital. Despairing, June began to think seriously again about leaving her marriage, but as long as Levant was in the hospital, she knew she could not abandon him. But if he returned home in the same condition, unable and unwilling to help himself, she would call it quits. She had had enough.

Levant had a private nurse at Edgemont with orders to keep television and newspapers out of his sight. Any reminder of the outside world filled him with dread—the thought of a world going on beyond his suffering was more than he could bear. But encouraged by the nurses to take some exercise, Levant began to take walks on the hospital grounds.

One day while perambulating the lawns in a semiconscious state, Levant watched a smiling man being moved to another part of the hospital by white-coated attendants. Levant, standing with his nurse, saw the beatific man being wheeled toward him. "Thanks for a million laughs," the euphoric patient said to Oscar as the attendants hurried him away. As if he had been given a benediction by an angelic presence, Levant arranged to be released that week.

Irene Kahn and her husband, Arthur Marx, befriended Oscar when he was in Edgemont Hospital, and they frequently stopped by his house to "baby-sit" him when he was released. June was happy to have them come over and offer her some relief from the rigors of protecting Oscar from himself. "He was happy to see us," Arthur remembered.

> June liked to get out of the house and play poker in the evening, so Irene and I would be sitting with him once a week, which was entertaining . . . but wearisome because you didn't know when he was going to lose his temper. He used to lie on his bed in his bathrobe holding his heart and chain-smoking cigarettes, and the ashes would fall down the front of his clothes. But he was so amusing that you couldn't help be entertained and have a good time with him despite the miserable situation.

They noticed, however, that he was still bedeviled by superstitions. One day he ran up and locked himself in his room because June had asked if he'd like some Sara Lee cake. "He flew into a rage," June told Irene and Arthur when they arrived that evening, but she didn't know why. Levant apparently nursed a hatred of the name "Sarah," his sister-in-law's name. The mere mention of the name sent him to his room for two hours. Arthur recalled that on another occasion he drove Oscar out to a house in the Palisades. As they approached the driveway, Oscar noticed a flock of blackbirds on the front lawn. It filled him with terror: He flung himself out of the car and ran down the street at the sight of those funereal-looking birds.

"I'm leaving you," June informed her husband, in their bedroom crowded with pill bottles and paraphernalia that could not be touched or moved by any mortal hand save Oscar's. She had gone to Las Vegas with some friends, with Oscar's blessing. But when she returned a few days later, Levant was furious that she had gone away and left him alone.

Oscar knew June had used the threat of divorce to keep him in line on past occasions, but this time he felt she meant it. He also guessed that June would never leave him while he was hospitalized, so he volunteered to return to the psychiatric ward. Oscar begged June to wait until he signed himself into Mount Sinai before filing divorce papers. June agreed but was adamant that he not return to live at their North Roxbury Drive home upon release from the hospital. They accepted each other's terms and spent a melancholy night, his last at home before committing himself.

The next morning Levant got dressed quickly and secreted some pills in the pockets of his dark blue suit. He tremblingly signed himself into the psychiatric ward on the third floor at Mount Sinai.

It was one of the saddest times in his life. He was taken up to the ward by two attendants, who undressed him and discovered the pills he had carefully hidden before leaving home. That first night on the ward was chilling. He kept hearing a crescendo of blood-curdling screams. Levant, alone on his cot, listened to this constant noise, terrified that he would end up like that. At the end of seventy-two hours, Levant watched as a screaming patient was wheeled away on a cot, and he wondered how he would ever survive his stay.

Dr. Victor Monk, a young psychiatrist who was in training under Greenleigh, remembered Levant as "extremely arrogant and defensive." He resisted becoming part of the group, so his passes to the outside world were suspended and his visits restricted until he began to cooperate.

Dr. Greenleigh slowly withdrew Levant from his dependency on sedatives, just as he had the previous year. As he gradually emerged from the numbing haze of drugs, he began to experience his emotions more vividly, a condition that frightened him. His memory lapses were also disturbing—one night he lay in bed trying to remember the title of a play by one of his literary heroes, George Bernard Shaw, but he found he could not remember it. Finally the lost title came to him—it was *Heartbreak House.*

On the fourth day June made her first visit to the hospital. Levant was filled with conflicting emotions about seeing her. As he sat waiting for June to arrive, a man who had been admitted on the same day as Oscar sat down next to him. He told Levant that his son was supposed to see him that day, but the doctor had decided against allowing the visit. When he said this, the man broke down and began to weep. Levant then did something he had never done before. He put his arm around the weeping man and tried to comfort him. "Suddenly," Levant would later write, "I forgot all my troubles." For the first time he could remember, he embraced someone else who was in pain. "I let go of myself," he told Dr. Greenleigh. Slowly, Levant would begin to engage with the other patients, showing genuine interest in their situations.

June's visits, however, were not pleasant, especially during the early stages of Levant's withdrawal. He worried that the tremor he had developed and his fierce perspiring, caused by drug withdrawal, must surely repulse the still-beautiful and stylish woman who now dropped in on him like an emissary from a sweeter world.

As Levant grew stronger, he began something of an exercise regimen, which consisted of a game of croquet played with other patients on the hospital lawn. He took day trips with the patients, but they were often painful, especially when fans recognized him and tried to greet him, their look of surprise and pleasure turning quizzical at the sight of the company he kept.

Toward the end of his stay, Levant became protective of certain patients whom he thought were being treated too roughly by the attendants. When a woman who had pestered Levant at the beginning of his stay began to enter a manic phase, Oscar protested the use of physical force to restrain her. His behavior needled the attendants and earned him a reputation as a troublemaker, but it did Levant immense good to put others before himself.

"His vocational career, that of a concert pianist, has been a flourishing one," one doctor wrote in Levant's medical report, "and he has done extremely well. But he feels it is of no use now. He has lost everything. He didn't know why he ever tried to be a success." Perhaps he had only imagined the life of a concert artist and it had never really occurred. Jean Cocteau, the French poet and filmmaker, had once remarked that "Victor Hugo was a madman who imagined himself to be Victor Hugo." Perhaps that was true of Oscar as well: He was a madman who had only imagined himself to be Oscar Levant. "What ever became of Oscar Levant?" he liked to yell at the other patients. They looked back at him but had no answer.

One night, when most of the other patients had shuffled back to their cots, Levant returned to the dayroom, now empty but for one or two patients lost in their own thoughts. Levant went over to the upright piano and, with a tremor in his hands, played eight bars of "Apple Blossoms," a Fritz Kreisler waltz from the operetta he had always thought lovely and calming. After those eight stumbling bars, one of the patients who had been sitting quietly at the other end of the room looked up and said, "Would you play the 'Appassionata Sonata' by Beethoven?"

"In my condition that was quite a request," remembered Levant, and he ignored it. He was far from pleased with his playing, but at least he had broken the piano's hex. It occurred to him that if he could make friends with the piano again, maybe he could patch things up with June, that there might be a chance of a different kind of life on North Roxbury Drive. It was time to go home.

When June came to pick up her husband at Mount Sinai she could see instantly that he was a changed man. Something remarkable had happened up there on the third floor under Dr. Greenleigh's care. It seemed that by being with other patients and discovering a compassion for their suffering, Levant had turned a corner with his own severe neuroses. His transformation was so obviously a fact that June relented and accepted her husband back into their home. "It was the first time in my life that I ever saw him change so dramatically into being a nice guy," June remembered.

He returned often to the third floor of Mount Sinai to visit with the patients. Levant, who formerly had never risen before noon or one in the afternoon, now awoke at 6:30 in the morning, when he would start his day with a long, brisk walk in his Beverly Hills neighborhood.

June soon realized that her husband had no recollection of some of his more bizarre, violent behavior, such as trying to choke her on the bathroom floor or making plans to run off with one of Dr. Greenson's nurses. He was horrified when he realized how he had treated June and his children. He was contrite and deeply shamed.

But his drug addiction had taken its toll. He came out of Mount Sinai extremely gaunt, and he had developed a dreadful, constant blink and a Parkinson-like tremor in his hands. His drug taking and withdrawals had ruined his nervous system, which had already been battered by his caffeine and nicotine addictions. Sometimes his blinking contorted his whole face, making him grimace.

Levant's newfound tranquillity was about to undergo its first challenge. One February afternoon in 1958, the phone rang at the Levant home. It was Al Flanagan, the station manager of KCOP-TV, Channel 13, the station that had fired Levant nearly eighteen months earlier. Would Oscar consider returning to KCOP as a temporary replacement for the ailing Tom Duggan, a combative comedian on a local chat show? He accepted the offer.

Levant drove himself to the television station, but at first he couldn't remember where it was located. He finally walked into the building just as the show was about to begin.

"I've changed," Levant assured his audience. "I'm nice to people and I'm not so self-centered. What I'm trying to do now is think of the other person. The only trouble is," he added, "I've found that the other person thinks only of himself." Levant openly discussed his stay at Mount Sinai's psychiatric ward. Despite his initial nervousness and anxiety, he found these television confessions to be something of a catharsis. Flanagan brought Levant back on for a second night, and then for the following week.

"Everybody in town watches the show," Don Freeman wrote in the *San Diego Union*. Just in case the public thought the "new" Oscar Levant was all sweetness and light, he came out with the old familiar adder-tongued comments about Hollywood's celebrities. No one was spared: "Perry Como's voice actually comes out of his eyelids," he remarked about the casual, laid-back crooner. "I'm not allowed to watch Dinah Shore," he quipped about the eternally cheerful singer—"I have diabetes. . . . I'll have to give her lessons in sadness." About Jerry Lewis's weekly television show: "*The Jerry Lewis Show* has all the suspense of a Hitchcock thriller—the suspense of wondering when the first laugh will come." "John Wayne? He's too subtle for me."

Freeman noticed that when Levant surrounded himself with guests whom he liked and admired, such as composer Dmitri Tiomkin or actor Efrem Zimbalist, Jr., the son of the famous violinist, he was companionable and warm. "But when bores and exhibitionists are thrust upon him," Freeman wrote, "as they frequently are, [he] grows petulant, his wit turning into one of the deadliest, most corrosive instruments of insult . . . he can be unpleasant and just a little frightening to watch." Still, Freeman praised Levant as the kind of stimulant television sorely needed.

The overwhelming response to Levant's two weeks on the air pleased everyone but Tom Duggan. Before the ailing talk show host was even out of the hospital, Flanagan offered Levant his own weekly show on Tuesdays at nine P.M. Flanagan suggested that June join her husband as a cohost. Just three weeks earlier Levant had left Mount Sinai's psychiatric ward, and now he had his own television talk show.

Levant paced the set, furiously smoking, his face occasionally contorted by blinks, while he pressed his hand over his heart like Napoleon. "This is Oscar Levant," he announced to his studio audience, "who has made insanity America's favorite hobby. My show is now syndicated. It goes to the Menninger Clinic in Topeka, Bellevue in New York, and the psychiatric ward at Mount Sinai in Los Angeles." He called his show *Disgrace the Nation*.

It was therapeutic not only for Levant but for American audiences, who still regarded emotional and mental problems as shameful secrets never to be discussed in public. For the first time in the country's popular media, mental illness and its various treatments were coming out of the closet.

The serenity he had experienced when first released from Mount Sinai was beginning to give way to a manic phase, a situation Greenleigh had worried about when he first released him. He warned June to watch for signs of manic behavior.

Flanagan entreated Al Burton, Levant's former *Words About Music* producer, to come back as producer of *The Oscar Levant Show*. It turned out to be a fortuitous pairing. The plucky, crew-cutted young producer wasn't thin-skinned about Levant's wisecracks, and he didn't mind playing the underdog to Levant's bully. "I idolized Oscar," he remembered, "and he couldn't help himself. He knew he had my attention all the time, so it was a good meeting of spirits. . . . I was a victim often, but I got a lot out of it."

Levant continued to make his personal journey through the halls of psychiatry a prominent subject of his show. Once he brought on as his guest Dr. Wayne, the psychiatrist who ran Edgemont Hospital and who had given him eighteen electroshock treatments. "What kind of shape was I in?" Levant asked his doctor during the show.

"You were a basket case," Dr. Wayne replied proudly.

If *The Oscar Levant Show* was to be lauded for anything, it was the remarkable gathering of writers whom Levant brought into the tiny studio at KCOP-TV. One constant pleasure in Levant's life had always been his love of books, and he took great delight in inviting writers he admired onto his show.

Aldous Huxley agreed to be a guest. He told Levant that T. S. Eliot reminded him of "a doctor who lays patients out for surgery and then never operates." Levant asked the writer about a character in his novel *Point Counter Point* who commits suicide. Huxley reminded him that the character, Spandrell, commits suicide to Beethoven's String Quartet, Op. 132. "Why would he choose this to commit suicide [to]?" Levant demanded, clearly upset. "It's so slow. I would have committed suicide to fast music."

Toward the end of the hour, Huxley began to discuss hallucinogenic drugs such as mescaline, lysergic acid, and peyote, describing them as a potential key to understanding the symbolism of William Blake's poetry. That was daring, exotic stuff in 1959, and Huxley "not only made converts on that show," Levant recalled, "he made addicts."

Christopher Isherwood was another frequent guest. "Charming, warmhearted Christopher," as Levant liked to call him, was Levant's polar opposite in terms of temperament. "He looked like a tweedy Will Rogers and sounded like a poetic Huckleberry Finn," Levant later wrote about Isherwood. Sitting upright next to his slouching, blinking host, Isherwood would toss off verses by Baudelaire, Rimbaud, or his friend W. H. Auden. Levant liked to quote Baudelaire's passage "I cultivate my hysteria with terror and delight. / Today I have received a singular warning—the wind of the wing of madness has passed over me."

It was Isherwood who described Oscar as a character created by Dostoevsky—someone "completely unmasked at all times" who needed pain to survive. One night after Isherwood had appeared on Levant's show, he was taken by Oscar on one of his frequent trips back to Mount Sinai's third floor. Isherwood was fascinated by the patients' reverence for Levant and moved by Levant's obvious affection and concern for their welfare. Levant noticed that the patients had put up a handwritten sign with his name on it over his old room, a symbol he would take more pride in than having his own star on the sidewalk of Hollywood Boulevard.

The show continued to command a wide local audience. Levant's confidence grew and his enthusiasm swung wildly out of control. Just as Greenleigh had feared, *The Oscar Levant Show* rocketed Levant into a manic phase. It began with a feeling of invincibility. He became more and more voluble, eager to converse on any subject. What followed was a period of flirtatious behavior and skirt chasing. "Manic and full of life," he would later write, he began to "spread [his] good cheer among all the women of Southern California." To one young Hollywood actress, Levant tendered a pickup line that was a pretty good indication of his general health and state of mind in the late fifties: "Let's go to your apartment. We'll have an affair, I'll die of a heart attack, and you'll get a lot of publicity."

"They often ran away screaming," Levant recalled. "I don't know why I've so often been saved from having extra-marital sex since I've been married to June. Generally, some subconscious quirk protects me in the nick of time."

38

The Oscar Levant Show

"I wish I could please everybody,
but if you do please everybody, you're nothing.
You have to have some point of view."

"THERE WEREN'T ENOUGH HOURS IN THE DAY," JUNE RECALLED OF
Oscar's second spring, his 1958 renaissance. "There wasn't enough he
could do. He would get only three or four hours of sleep a night."
Oscar was by now so manic that it was a trial simply to go out with
him.

One afternoon Levant invited NBC television executive Alan Livingston to lunch at La Scala in order to persuade him to put his local
show on the network. Livingston, however, explained how that
would be impossible, given Levant's reputation as a loose cannon.
When they left the restaurant, Levant suddenly, inexplicably, put a
dime in a parking meter and proceeded to lie down on the sidewalk.
He urged Livingston to join him there. "It's very relaxing," he told
the surprised network executive, who chose to remain upright. What
Livingston did not know was that Oscar used to lie down on the
sidewalks of Pittsburgh when he was a boy and found it strangely
comforting.

Dr. Greenleigh became alarmed when he noticed symptoms of Levant's manic phase becoming manifest on *The Oscar Levant Show*. He

also detected signs that Levant had returned to abusing sedatives. His tremor and involuntary blinking seemed to have worsened.

Levant agreed to make his first concert appearance in three years, not to play Gershwin, but to give the West Coast premiere of a new work by Shostakovich, his Piano Concerto No. 2. Levant's *bête noire*, Leonard Bernstein, had given the composition its East Coast premiere just five months earlier, with Bernstein playing the piano solo. The pressure of performing after a three-year hiatus was increased by his rivalrous feelings toward the younger man. Levant spent much of that spring preparing the Piano Concerto for the Los Angeles Music Festival, which Franz Waxman would conduct.

Lorna remembered the telltale signs that her father's phobias were flaring up again. "He was preparing [the Shostakovich] and we were all tiptoeing around," she recalled. Levant's home life deteriorated as his state of exhilaration continued. The Second Piano Concerto had to compete with Levant's television show—now on three nights a week—and a series of articles he had undertaken to write for the *Los Angeles Mirror News* and *Hollywood Diary*. "Everything went from being very quiet," Amanda recalled, "to being inordinately busy and frenetic." June was nearly as busy as her husband, preparing for the show by reading a growing pile of fan mail; she usually selected a few letters to read on the air. Sometimes she would take over interviewing the guests, especially those whom Levant found boring. (On those occasions, he would sometimes stomp off camera, telling the studio audience he had to go lie down and leaving June alone with the guest.)

To be put down by Oscar Levant meant being part of an elite Hollywood club. Celebrities who came to converse, perform, and occasionally be insulted by Levant included the Irish playwright Brendan Behan and the angst-ridden William Inge, toward whom Levant displayed rather touching compassion, and Eddie Fisher and Debbie Reynolds (who would later substitute briefly for June as Levant's cohost). Levant joked that the feisty Miss Reynolds was "as wistful as an iron foundry." Many Hollywood performers were big fans of the show; Jim Backus left strict instructions with his wife to tape the show whenever he was away. Red Skelton made audio recordings of *The Oscar Levant Show*.

Levant continued to lampoon his own mental and emotional problems. "Suicide," he remarked on one show, "is the longest sleeping pill I know of."

Like the French Symbolist poets he admired, Levant was a great believer in juxtaposition. Probably the best example of this was when he had Jerry Lewis on his show doing an impersonation of T. S. Eliot. Levant handed him *The Waste Land,* and the madcap comedian rendered the poem of postwar angst in a falsetto, prissy voice. It was certainly no tribute to Eliot, but it was a rare moment in the annals of television history.

Levant was scheduled for six appearances on *The Eddie Fisher Show,* the first national network television program on which Levant would appear. At one point Levant became almost teary when he thanked Fisher for being the first to bring him onto a network show. "He seemed close to tears," one reviewer reported, "and turned to his keyboard to accompany Fisher in 'I Got Rhythm.' " His preparations of the Shostakovich Piano Concerto No. 2 for the Los Angeles Music Festival, scheduled for the first week of June, had made Levant more willing to play the piano in front of an audience.

John Kerr remembered the Royce Hall concert as a gala affair. It was the Twelfth Annual Los Angeles Music Festival, and there were a lot of important people in the audience who had come to root for Levant. A number of Levant's former colleagues from 20th Century–Fox were there, such as songwriter Johnny Green and composer Hugo Friehoeffer. His appearance at Royce Hall that Monday evening, June 2, 1958, was a sold-out affair. No doubt the popularity of his television show increased interest in his comeback performance.

The Second Piano Concerto is considered by some to be neither "a real concerto" nor "first-class Shostakovich." Music critic Robert Riley noted that Levant's pianism—which he had brought back from the brink by sheer force of will—was greeted with thunderous approval, and the audience's ovation brought him back onstage to repeat the particularly lovely andante. But Riley himself characterized Levant's playing as merely adequate.

Arthur Marx was in the audience that night. A strange thing happened, Marx recalled: "He played the first movement and he got through about half of it. He wasn't using music and he forgot completely where he was. He stopped, stood up, and said, 'I don't even know where I am. I'm going to start all over again.' " The second time he went right through it, completing the piece without mistakes.

"One day Fred Astaire asked to be on the show," June remembered. Since it was a tiny studio and Astaire was protective of his dancing, he wanted to come on the show and sing. He even agreed to appear for union scale—$82.50—for his first television appearance.

In some sense, *The Oscar Levant Show* was the perfect place for Fred Astaire to try out the new medium. Like Tony Hunter, the character he had portrayed in *The Band Wagon,* he found himself at a crossroads in his long career; 1958 was "a year of cogitation" for the great dancer. "I played a lot of bad golf," he wrote in his memoir, "took a few pleasure trips. . . . I had plenty of time to think over the past and to try to visualize the future."

Astaire would write that his appearance on *The Oscar Levant Show* on May 6, 1958, was "one of my most enjoyable experiences," a rather remarkable statement for a veteran of vaudeville, musical theatre, and some of the most memorable film musicals ever made. Here he was on the studio set, perched on a stool brought in from the Levants' living room while Levant prodded, encouraged, and embarrassed the shy master with his fulsome praises. It was an undeniable coup for Levant, and the network executives were beside themselves with envy. "I never expected to see the day," wrote Don Freeman,

> when Mr. Astaire would give in to any television offer, and . . . certainly not on a local program with not much in the way of a budget. It was . . . a true gem of a show, blessed with an intimacy no other 90 minute TV musical has ever remotely approached . . . with an altogether disarming blend of warmth and airiness. I can't remember when 90 minutes has slipped by so quickly.

Astaire himself denigrated his voice, but Levant knew how George and Ira, Irving Berlin, and a host of other songwriters felt about Astaire's singing style. "I wrote songs with Fred in mind," Irving Berlin once said. Levant's deep affection for Astaire was palpable that night. The singer recalled his days in vaudeville, when he remembered seeing June and her sisters in their acrobatic dancing act—"They were very good, too," he said. June beamed from her perch, radiant in a summer dress. At one point Astaire sang in a husky voice in imitation of movie mogul Sam Goldwyn—"it was a fairly inside joke," wrote Freeman, but one that a lot of Levant's regular viewers would have gotten. Levant's show had turned out to be a kind of private Hollywood party at which the public was invited to eavesdrop.

At one point Levant announced that he was going to lie down for a few minutes, turning the show over to June. "Fred," he admitted, his hand held over his heart, "I'm so suffocated by nostalgia and so unhappily happy that I cannot speak—which is one of the great public services of all time." He walked off camera, leaving June to take over, which she did by reading from a *Time* magazine description of the show while Levant kept up a running commentary off camera. June read from the article: "But for Oscar, success is hard."

Levant sputtered from offstage: "It isn't hard! It's nothing! Success is a stupid word. It's part of the American jargon, and I hate the word. Functioning is the important thing."

Toward the end of the program Astaire changed places with Levant and played a spot of jazz piano, while Oscar attempted to dance with knock-kneed abandon.

It was one of the highlights of Levant's television career and, curiously, one of only two episodes that have been preserved for posterity. Astaire's agent had made a kinescope of the entire program in order to have an idea of how the dancer came across on television. Except for a half-hour tape made by one of KCOP's technical crew, a show on which Hedda Hopper appeared, no other episode of *The Oscar Levant Show* now exists. All the other programs—Christopher Isherwood reciting poetry, Linus Pauling waltzing with June, James Mason, Aldous Huxley, José Ferrer, Johnny Mercer, writer Romain Gary, Dean Martin, Dmitri Tiomkin, Eddie Cantor, Brendan Behan, Levant's psychiatrist Dr. Wayne, composer Bronislau Kaper, boxers Archie Moore, Sugar Ray Robinson, and Jack Dempsey—Levant's experiments in juxtaposition have all but disappeared, taped over by cooking shows, matinees, traffic reports. "No one knew what we had in those days," Al Burton remembered. "Slapsie" Maxie Rosenbloom conversed with attorney general Pat Brown, who spoke of his son Jerry, who was studying for the priesthood. Even Walter Winchell and Vernon Duke, two emperors of a lost kingdom, were booked. The only full-length remaining show, Fred Astaire's appearance, can be read as a tribute to the Gershwin era that helped launch both artists. If Astaire came onto the show to take a look at the future, Levant used the occasion to revel in the past.

The *Time* magazine article June had read from was written by a young journalist named Bob Jennings. It ran on May 5, 1958, under the title "Frenzied Road Back," accompanied by a photograph of Levant seated at the piano, clutching his heart. The transformation of Levant's public persona was now complete. "Never before has KCOP had so much mail," Jennings's article noted; "some call it the 'sick-sick' show, but most rejoice at rediscovering Oscar, the dictionary, and good books as well. Says Huxley: 'He represents intelligence—something all of us can use more of.' "

By the end of 1958, Levant had become so identified in the public mind with mental illness that Jack Warner, Jr., son of the tyrannical producer, asked him to appear on a public service show promoting mental health. Levant did so, though he came close to getting into a fight with a security guard over fire regulations by threatening to light a cigarette onstage.

It was obvious to Dr. Greenleigh that Levant was beginning to crack under the strain. He simply couldn't manage his accelerated schedule: On one day alone, he taped two network shows and then arrived at KCOP that night for his own ninety-minute program. Levant was now relying entirely on sleeping pills and occasional shots of Demerol to get through his demanding schedule, and they wreaked havoc with his mood. On a televised interview for the Canadian Broadcasting Company conducted in Levant's home, the confident young interviewer who had done his homework asked the pianist, "What about the influence George Gershwin had on you?"

Somewhat startled by the question—no one had asked him that in years—Levant replied, "He had no influence on me whatsoever!" He kept repeating the phrase; then, after a moment of reflection, he suddenly burst into "a Niagara of tears." ("I suddenly remembered . . ." he would write a few years later about the incident. It had been his memory of Gershwin's inexplicable smearing of notes in the Concerto in F that had triggered Levant's tears.) "No influence whatsoever," he repeated softly to the interviewer.

After three months, *The Oscar Levant Show* was still one of the most-talked-about television programs in Los Angeles. But on June 21, 1958, Levant succeeded in once again getting himself thrown off the air.

Coping with Levant's increasing mania and the demands of doing a thrice-weekly television show took its toll on June Levant as well. Suffering from nervous exhaustion, June checked herself into Mount Sinai Hospital for a few days' rest. It was June who usually did the commercials for Philco, the television and radio manufacturer that was one of the show's most prestigious sponsors. With June absent, Levant was expected to read the commercials himself. He generally loathed having to do commercials, but when the Philco representative told Oscar just before the show went on the air that he had hired last year's Miss America to do the spot, Levant was annoyed. He insisted on doing the commercial himself—which was just what the anxious Philco representative wanted to avoid. Levant apparently didn't like the idea of another woman taking June's place on the show.

Levant proceeded to needle the Philco representative, telling him, "Philco promised me four TV sets months ago and I never got one. Two months ago they sent me a gramophone, which doesn't work too well." He then started to needle Miss America of 1957 until she fled the studio in tears. Right before going on the air, Levant was informed that Philco had just withdrawn its sponsorship of *The Oscar Levant Show*.

Levant immediately told his audience what had happened, and he launched into a tirade against Philco. "There's only one way to fight power, and that's with power!" he announced. "None of you buy Philco products until it returns to my show!" Oscar began to prowl through the tiny studio with a microphone in hand, looking for moral support.

But the next morning Flanagan suspended Levant indefinitely from KCOP-TV for making uncomplimentary remarks about one of their sponsors and two other television stations Levant had also managed to insult. (He had told his audience that his behavior would probably finish him at KCOP, but KHJ-TV and KTLA-TV would take him because "they'll take anybody.")

News of Levant's tantrum and suspension spread through Los Angeles like a prairie fire. What followed over that weekend was a deluge of letters and phone calls from fans. "From the upper reaches of the San Fernando Valley to the Mexican border," wrote Don Freeman, "Levant's legions rallied behind him in force." Support came from some unexpected quarters: Levant received a telegram that read, "HAVE JUST CANCELLED ORDER FOR MY 15TH PHILCO I DON'T NEED ANYBODY EITHER BUT YOU ARE A GOOD DEED IN A NAUGHTY WORLD . . ." from the architect Frank Lloyd Wright.

Levant and the station manager waged a kind of war in the press, with Flanagan defending his actions by asserting that the Philco incident was simply the latest in a growing list of troubles Levant had brought upon himself. "Everything depends on Oscar being well enough to continue," he said, invoking Levant's very real psychiatric troubles. "His sickness is a thing of the mind." Sounding like James Petrillo, he added that Levant would not be reinstated until he "learned some discipline."

"Flanagan is the one who is sick," Oscar fired back. "I'll admit I'm sick. . . . I'm a highly neurotic man. But my sickness gives me insight and makes me a better entertainer." Levant knew that part of his whole appeal lay in his unpredictable behavior, and he was not going to let those who profited by it pillory him for it.

Joe Hyams commiserated with Levant about his troubles with KCOP over dinner at Chasen's. He was writing an article about Levant's suspension for the *New York Herald Tribune.*

"I have the most intellectual and the most loyal audience in the history of television," Hyams would quote Oscar as saying. "I feel nostalgic in a bittersweet way about that audience. I hope you will forgive my humility, but I was doing the best show in the history of television."

39

Under Paar

"Someone once asked me where I lived and I said,
'On the periphery.' "

"Already the 'Affair Levant' has become a cause célèbre in Hollywood," wrote Joe Hyams. Because of the public outcry, Flanagan had little choice but to reinstate Levant within days of firing him. With June out of the hospital and joining him back on the air, Levant returned to KCOP, but before the week was out he jumped ship, abandoning KCOP for a more lucrative offer to take his show to a rival station, KHJ-TV on Channel 9. Flanagan's disciplining of Levant had ruined the show for him. Emerson Radios quickly wired Levant that they would like to sponsor his new show, joining the White Front Stores and the Jacuzzi brothers as his sponsors.

Soon after the move to KHJ, Levant received an offer from Steve Allen to appear on *The Steve Allen Show,* which was broadcast from New York. Levant braced himself to take a flight back east. He had become so worried about the condition of his health that on the day of his departure, he hired a private ambulance to pick him up at the studio and drive him to the airport. He even asked his cardiologist, Dr. Kert, to accompany him. Once they had boarded the plane, Dr. Kert administered another anesthetic, but it was ineffective. Levant woke up like clockwork every hour during the long flight to the East Coast.

During the show's rehearsal, Levant's free-floating anxiety and his renewed dependence on sedatives were noticeable. *New York Post* columnist Earl Wilson followed Levant around that weekend, and he reported that Levant "wouldn't allow anybody within 10 feet during rehearsals. . . . Oscar won't be forgotten by the Allen cast," wrote Wilson, "some of whom claim Levant's the new synonym for trouble."

The year 1958 saw a revival of Levant's recording career. On June 5, three weeks before his appearance on *The Steve Allen Show,* he went into the studio and made a second recording of several pieces by Debussy (Prelude No. 12, Prelude No. 6, "Jardins sous la pluie," and "Serenade for the Doll"). Five days later he recorded Federico Mompou's *Scenes of Childhood;* and Ravel's Sonatine, third movement, *Pavanne for a Dead Princess,* and two selections from *Le Tombeau de Couperin.* On the nineteenth he recorded Prokofiev's *Visions fugitives,* Op. 22 and Shostakovich's Polka from *The Age of Gold.* Lieberson and Levant decided to call the recording *Some Pleasant Moments in the 20th Century,* and indeed the selections are curiously serene. Contrary to the notion that modern music had progressed only toward dissonance, Levant chose to lull and be lulled rather than challenge his audience.

"I could never have a mistress," Oscar Levant once said, "because I couldn't bear to tell the story of my life all over again." He also said that the problem with having a mistress was "that second dinner you have to eat." But during his manic phase, and not long after the start of his "new" show on KHJ-TV, June and Oscar had their biggest fight yet, over Oscar's apparent philandering. Oscar had been overly attentive toward another woman at a Hollywood luncheon. He in fact had made a date to meet her later that night. When June discovered her husband's plans, she took off her high-heeled slipper and threw it at him. Their quarrel soon escalated into a shouting and shoving match.

Several of the Levants' neighbors gathered in front of the house. "That woman hit me with a shoe!" Levant yelled. "She's dangerous!" Levant had made a frantic call to Al Burton, who quickly arrived with his wife. Sally Burton went in to look after June while her husband went up to the second-floor bedroom, where Levant told him that

June had cracked one of his ribs, "near the heart." "I know the rib is broken!" Levant wailed, but he refused to go to the hospital for X rays. "Meanwhile," Burton recalled, "the Levant girls ran downstairs, gleefully saying, 'We taped the whole thing!' "

Chief Anderson, now on his second summons to the Levant home, became concerned about Levant's general appearance and his level of agitation. Oscar demanded police protection from June while he went upstairs to pack an overnight bag. He had decided to clear out and spend the night at a friend's house. Before leaving, Chief Anderson lectured the Levants on the necessity of keeping the peace.

Levant's North Roxbury Drive neighbors and the rest of California awoke to headlines announcing "Levant Says Wife Tried to Kill Him." The next morning—after eighteen years, seven months, and eight days of marriage—June again filed for divorce. Oscar had left the house that night, and no one knew where he was. "Levant Vanishes after Spat" read one headline. Reporters prowled North Roxbury Drive for clues.

For the next few weeks the Levants' battle royale was covered in the local press. "I never cheat, but I always get caught," Oscar complained to reporters who had found him hiding out at Vincente Minnelli's house. One newspaper ran a photograph of Oscar sitting on three-year-old Tina Minnelli's bed with an armful of fuzzy stuffed animals and a decidedly hangdog expression on his face.

At Minnelli's, Levant told a reporter, "I want to make it clear that I left my wife. . . . I don't like savagery. When a woman is in a rage it gives her terrific strength. I was terrified for my life." He claimed he was going to seek an injunction against June "to keep her from molesting me." Levant was quick to explain his side of the story. "You can say for me that I've never sexually cheated on my wife; I've never been intimate with anyone. Being out with them usually means buying them a cup of coffee."

June countered with "He should remember he has a wife and daughters, and shouldn't be acting like a fool by making dates with other women—even if they are only coffee break romances. Now he'll play Joan of Arc at the stake—he's bound to play the martyr, you know. But it's all over as far as I'm concerned."

Levant couldn't help making grim jokes about his situation, and June did her best to put the spat into its proper perspective. She recognized that Oscar was addicted not only to sedatives but also to publicity. It seemed that he had begun to feel that it didn't matter why he continued to have an audience as long as that audience continued to listen to him. But it was a steep path from George Gershwin's penthouse, from which his *bons mots* had been bandied about town, to his present cowering in Tina Minnelli's bedroom telling the press how terrified he was of his wife. By now, viewers of *The Oscar Levant Show* tuned in not for stimulating conversation and daring remarks but for the latest installment in the June-and-Oscar soap opera.

But Levant was not as full of *bons mots* and the hubris of wit as he appeared. He was, in fact, miserable, and he wanted to go home. He called June several times a day, looking for a pretext to come by the house, such as picking up a clean shirt or a book he intended to use on the show. But June would agree to see Levant only outside their home, with her lawyer present. This time she was serious.

In the document filed in Santa Monica by her lawyer, June Levant said that her husband was "now a prominent and well-established television personality capable of earning in excess of $100,000 a year." In her suit June charged "mental and physical cruelty" which caused her to "suffer mental and physical anguish." She asked that Levant continue to support and educate his children "in accordance [with] his status in life." Her attorney also sought a restraining order to keep Levant from entering the family home.

Meanwhile, Oscar took over Minnelli's household in the manner of the penthouse beachcomber he had once been. Often, late at night, after Minnelli had retired for the evening, Oscar would find himself unable to sleep and he'd pad into his host's bedroom and wake him up.

"He had to talk to someone," Minnelli later wrote in his memoirs. "He'd tell horrendous tales of misadventures and describe the demons who plagued him, who by this time were so familiar that he called them by pet names. Once he'd unburdened himself, he'd take a sleeping pill and go off to sleep in his room." It was Minnelli who would remain wide awake the rest of the night after listening to Levant's confessions.

He soon found himself wondering how much longer he could put up with Levant's "smothering presence." Levant had turned the Minnelli household into his own personal salon, calling his doctors to come over and give him sedatives at all hours and instructing the Minnellis' housekeeper as to when he wanted his meals. "The family maid worshiped Oscar," remembered Joe Hyams, who took to visiting him in his new quarters at the Minnellis', across from the Beverly Hills Hotel.

Over the next several weeks, Oscar tried to forge a rapprochement with June. Meanwhile, his performance on *The Oscar Levant Show* suffered noticeably—at times he would become lachrymose while he extolled June's virtues in her absence—"She's a wonderful woman— really!" Sometimes he would tell his viewers to "look at some other show."

June showed signs of weakening. What may have softened her atti- tude toward her estranged husband was the fact that KCOP-TV—the very station that had fired Levant for his bad behavior—offered her her own show. While the seat next to her husband remained empty, June became the host of an afternoon chat show that featured inter- views with celebrities, followed by a film.

It was Flanagan's idea. Not only did it give him a small revenge against Oscar, but it capitalized on the current media frenzy taking place around the Levant breakup. Their domestic troubles had become part of local television lore. In addition, June had proven herself an able sidekick on *The Oscar Levant Show*. She had received a slew of fan letters during her short absence from the program, when she had entered Mount Sinai for a much-needed rest. So two weeks after the first blow had been struck, June agreed to take Oscar back.

On his next show, Levant brought June on with him but an- nounced to the audience that she would no longer be his co-host but a frequent guest. They fleetingly embraced, and the audience ap- plauded. At the close of the program, he asked, "Anyone want to see my bandage?" June put her arms around her husband and told him that a cracked rib is better than a broken heart.

What Oscar probably didn't know about June's two weeks spent without him was just how close she had come to severing their ties. She had sought out the company of her women friends who were widowed or divorced. To June, making the rounds with her unat- tached friends, it seemed as if these women were living in purgatory. Their lives seemed empty to her, filled with shopping and bridge. "God, is this the way other people live?" she thought. "I was leading an exciting life, and I didn't realize it, even with all this bullshit. It was awful, but it was worth it." Years later, a line from Neil Simon's *Biloxi Blues* would sum up her complex feelings about her marriage: "At the end of the play, those boys had gone through such hell with the ser- geant. But when they got a new one, life was not as exciting. The last line is, 'Don't underestimate the stimulation of eccentricity.' That's true!"

Perhaps as a way to reclaim some of his lost glory, Levant began to prepare for his twelfth season with the Hollywood Bowl's all-Gersh- win program. In the weeks leading up to the concert he began to increase his sedation, arranging for Dr. Greenson and another physi- cian to come to the house to give him pentobarbital injections, which had become his newest solace. Now it seemed that Levant could meet the music of Gershwin only in the murky fog of drugged consciousness.

Levant traveled to the Hollywood Bowl that August 2, 1958, in the company of Dr. Greenson, who administered an injection of Demerol moments before his patient walked onstage. Levant's worries that his scandalous press coverage would discourage an audience from turning out were unfounded. A crowd of twenty thousand squeezed its way into the arena. Backstage, Levant noticed another nervous pianist waiting in the wings, dressed in black tie and tails. He was on hand in case Levant canceled or was too ill to perform. But the replacement would not be needed; Levant strode to the piano and began the Concerto in F.

During the somewhat lengthy opening of the piece, Levant sat with his head bowed and his arms at his side. By the close of the first movement, Levant's playing had gone so well that the audience burst into sudden applause. "This was the true Gershwin style," noted one reviewer. "There was the nostalgic tone, the incisive syncopations and profound feeling." But after the first movement, Levant got up from the piano, walked over to Andre Kostelanetz, and whispered to the conductor.

"I'm going to walk off the stage," Levant told him. He had suddenly panicked, and he felt he could not go on playing. Kostelanetz, sensing his soloist's desperation, immediately signaled the downbeat for the second movement, compelling Levant to finish the piece.

"He returned and played brilliantly to the end," Alma Gowdy wrote in her review in the *Los Angeles Herald Express* the following day. Levant received two curtain calls for his performance, and he played a Gershwin prelude for his encore. But before beginning the piece he shouted out, "I'm playing under the auspices of Mount Sinai!" The audience roared.

It was the last time Levant would perform in public as a concert artist. For many of his eighteen years of concertizing, he had been the highest-paid pianist in the country. Now it was over, ending with the same music that had first launched him. Four months before his fifty-second birthday, Levant took his final bow.

For the first time since the show's inception on KCOP, Levant was beginning to lose interest in his own television program. The truth of the matter was that he was taking so many pills and injections of pentobarbital—sometimes in the parking lot of the KHJ studio—that it had begun to affect his performance. One night when Emerson Radios asked Levant if he would demonstrate one of their new, unbreakable bedside radios by dropping it lightly on the desk, Levant hurled the radio at the floor, where its casing burst into smithereens, sending shrapnel throughout the studio. "Why should everything be unbreakable anyway?" he asked.

Levant became more and more uninhibited; his increasing pill intake gave his show a wild tilt. "I was the black tie and straitjacket Will Rogers," he liked to say about this period in his life. When he read in *Daily Variety* that the aging sex symbol Mae West was contemplating doing a television program in which she would give advice on romance, Levant told his audience, "Mae West is an old pro's pro; she couldn't give it away." John Mills, the president of KHJ-TV, made a formal apology to the film star. From then on, the decision was made to tape *The Oscar Levant Show* beforehand in order to be able to censor their star. "I said outrageous things that not only frightened me," Levant later wrote, "but the whole community. . . . Someone once asked me where I lived and I said, 'On the periphery.' "

Once again, June found herself in the intolerable position of trying to control her husband's pill intake, but her five-day-a-week television show made that almost impossible. He asked every visitor to the house if they'd bring him some pills. June started hiding his pills and warning friends like Lee Gershwin and Clifford Odets not to bring anything over for Oscar.

> I said, "Please, don't give him anything." They said, "Well, just one."
> I said, "It's just one from everybody." . . . I had to protect Oscar and
> to protect me and the kids. Judy [Garland] was coming around to steal
> pills from everybody, raiding our bathroom, and Oscar was doing the
> same thing.

By the end of August 1958, Levant asked KHJ for a leave of absence and it was granted. The official reason given was fatigue—"I'm just tired," Levant told his audience on the last Friday in August. "I don't feel good and I want to rest."

Toward the end of the year, in November 1958, *The Jack Paar Tonight Show* came to Hollywood for several weeks. The popular late-night talk show was usually broadcast from NBC studios in New York. Paar was a skilled conversationalist with a ready, affable wit who appreciated eccentrics and great talkers. His trademark was a folksiness that belied his sophistication and shrewd intelligence. Paar wanted Levant for his show.

The talk show host described his first visit to the Levant home:

[W]hen I rang the bell, the door opened slightly, and a maid asked nervously who I was. I said I was Jack Paar and that I had an appointment with Mr. Levant. She looked at me suspiciously, let me in, then locked the door, and put up a heavy chain. From upstairs I heard Oscar shriek, "Who's down there?"

"It's Mr. Paar," the maid squeaked in fright.

"Who let him in?" Oscar demanded. "I want nobody in this house but family."

He then shuffled in, clutching his heart, and told me all about his problems. "I've lost my voice," he said gloomily, "and my memory is completely gone . . ." He then proceeded to remember everything he'd done for the past thirty years. He also remembered to tell it to me. . . .

The truth was that Oscar Levant, the one-time great concert pianist, had become a drug addict.

Oscar agreed to one guest appearance on *The Jack Parr Tonight Show* scheduled for Wednesday, November 5, 1958.

Like that summer night twenty years earlier when Levant had first been heard on *Information, Please!,* his remarkable thirty minutes on *The Jack Paar Tonight Show* created one of the most controversial half hours of television. What the citizens of Los Angeles had taken in stride over the past nine months came as a shock to the rest of the country.

Seated in a chair beside Paar, puffing furiously on a cigarette, his crossed legs revealing a swatch of pale skin between his sock and pant cuff, Levant was a riveting sight even before he opened his mouth. He clearly lacked the groomed, unctuous, "cult of sincerity" manner that even in 1958 marked the average television personality. After he was introduced as "a man for whom living is a sideline," the audience was no doubt prepared for something dangerous.

"Oscar, you're a great wit," Paar began.

"Wits say two or three good things in their lives," Levant replied. "But humorists—like you—are the ones who are funny most of the time." He paused. "You know what a humorist is, don't you, Jack?"

Taking the bait, Paar asked, "What?"

"A humorist is someone like you. Someone with four writers who ad-libs a show."

"You're so full of charm," Levant then told his boyish host. "That's something I never stoop to."

The famous and the well-born came in for their share of Levant's verbal vampirism: Of Minnie Guggenheimer, the doyenne of Lewisohn Stadium, Oscar said, "She's a good friend. As long as you're on top, she'll stick by you."

Jack Paar beckoned the audience to come closer so he might confide in them. "I like him," he said about his guest, "but sometimes it's hard to be his friend."

Levant then touched on his ongoing treatment for mental illness, telling Paar with his customary candor, "I'm in the middle of a breakdown. It's my fifth in two years." The audience laughed nervously. When Paar brought to their attention the fact that Levant's hands were trembling, Levant looked down at the offending, though still beautiful hands. He stared at them for a moment, as if they belonged to someone else. "What is this? And I'm supposed to do surgery!" The audience laughed.

On well-publicized couplings, Levant said about Eddie Fisher's abandonment of Debbie Reynolds for Elizabeth Taylor, "How high can you stoop?" And when the subject of Joe DiMaggio's divorce from Marilyn Monroe came up, Levant commiserated with DiMaggio—"No man can excel at two national pastimes."

But nothing inspired greater laughter from the audience than Levant's recitation of his experiences as a mental patient at Mount Sinai. "I was thrown out of one mental hospital because I depressed the patients," he said. The audience enjoyed being shocked by his black humor.

Many viewers, including some television critics, felt that Levant's appearance on *The Jack Paar Tonight Show* raised questions of taste. William Ewald, a usually cantankerous television critic, wrote that he considered Levant's appearance "unquestionably one of the most provocative, fascinating, intoxicating, piquant, mad-brained, splendiferous half-hours of the TV year." But *The New York Times*' Jack Gould felt that Levant had not been invited to the program merely for purposes of innocent levity:

> It was his personal problems that Mr. Paar found much more interesting and exploited for all it was worth. . . . Let us hope that Mr. Paar is sensible enough not to try to make a running gag of mental health. The laughs cannot outweigh the dangers.

Levant's appearance on *The Jack Paar Tonight Show* restored his national reputation as a wit. "There is a fine line between genius and insanity," he said on the show, "and I have erased that line." Levant knew that he was mostly retailing remarks he had made on other occasions. Television was now beginning to recycle what was left of a brilliant era—Dorothy Parker and George S. Kaufman would have a fleeting acquaintance with the new medium; even *Information, Please!* would attempt to revivify itself as a television show. But for the most part television only succeeded in embalming an era it tried to embrace.

The enormous press attention and Levant's popularity on the show brought him back one week later for a second appearance. And the following year, Jack Paar beseeched Levant to come back on his show. Levant refused. "He just really didn't want to," June remembered. "I mean, he'd made the hit. Why should he take the chance and for what? He didn't want to waste himself for $320 anymore."

40

"Good Night, Oscar Levant, Wherever You Are"

*"More blankets! You see, I didn't get enough
affection when I was a child."*

ALTHOUGH LEVANT HAD NOT MADE A FILM SINCE 1955 NOR PER-
formed as a concert artist since 1958, he continued to crop up in the
collective imagination of the country. A personal ad in the *Los Angeles
Mirror-News* sought: "a husband. Must like Oscar Levant, drives in the
country, and music."

"I'd like to meet a man like that myself," Levant quipped when the
item was brought to his attention. Both Oscar and June were nominated for television's Emmy Award for "outstanding television personality" for the 1959–60 season. Whatever damage their domestic
troubles had wrought, it had brought them a loyal following. An announcement for a book review luncheon in Texas read, "Miss Louise
Constable [will give] interesting facts about the lives of: Oscar Levant,
Joseph Stalin, George Washington, and Christ."

As sick as Levant was in 1960—he was gaunt and pale and his hands
trembled—he still managed to attend a few parties and see people.
The writer Gore Vidal, a delegate that summer to the Democratic
National Convention, which would nominate John F. Kennedy for
president, had been an occasional guest on *The Oscar Levant Show.*
Vidal found that Levant was "wonderful company" in those days,

though "sometimes he was ga-ga from the pills or whatever he was taking."

Levant continued to sink into drug dependency throughout 1959 and 1960. While June was in New York visiting their daughter Marcia, who had begun to study acting at the Neighborhood Playhouse, he had discovered a truly disreputable Beverly Hills physician who would show up at their home every night to administer pentobarbital injections. The unscrupulous doctor informed Kert and Marmor that he was taking over Levant's case. The following day, Levant swallowed an entire bottle of chloral hydrate that he had gotten from a friend. At some point in the middle of the night Levant's legs started to twitch uncontrollably. "I was like a Russian dancer," he remembered, "running on my knees." Terrified, Levant began to scream, alerting the family maid, who called Dr. Marmor and begged him to come back and treat Levant.

It was clear that with this episode of locomotor ataxia Levant would have to be withdrawn from all medication. Dr. Marmor checked his patient into Mount Sinai for the third time. What was different about his third incarceration was that Levant had resumed appearing on *The Oscar Levant Show*. Producer Al Burton had the strange task of checking Levant out of the third-floor ward, driving him to the station to tape the show, and checking him back in again when it was over. Levant walked through the program like a shade, barely aware of who his guests were.

Citing fatigue and exhaustion—it was obvious to viewers that something was terribly wrong—Levant took a second leave of absence. In the interim, Al Burton had succeeded in getting the show syndicated and moved back to KCOP-TV, where it would be broadcast every Monday at nine P.M.

But there was a definite change in Levant: His manic phase had completely subsided, and he was now in the numbing fog of depression. He had lost his ardor for the show. Whereas before he would spend a few days reading up on each of his guests, he now told Burton that he didn't even want to know beforehand who his guests were going to be.

Pretaping and syndicating the show had indeed helped tame him— but it was no longer the live and dangerous enterprise it once had been. It had become a chore. After several months, Levant walked away from *The Oscar Levant Show* for good. He had now retired from his fifth career. Returning home from the studio, Levant went into his house, walked past the empty music room, went upstairs, and got back into bed.

Levant began to search for pills. One night he called his friend Joe Hyams, just before the two of them were to go out to dinner.

"What pills have you got?" Oscar asked.

"What do you mean?"

"Well, what's lying around the house?"

Hyams, who had already been briefed by June, answered patiently, "You've had one of everything I've got around the house."

"Well, what's your wife got?" Levant asked unabashedly. (Hyams, the softhearted writer with the tough-guy demeanor, was married to the beautiful German actress Elke Sommer.)

Hyams sifted through Elke Sommer's medicine cabinet and reported back to Oscar, "The only thing she's got here is something she takes for menstruation." (They were actually an old prescription of birth control pills.)

"Well, bring them over," Levant demanded of his friend.

Hyams brought over the birth control pills, and Levant greedily swallowed them.

Within a matter of months after leaving Mount Sinai, Levant was again admitted to the psychiatric ward to undergo a fourth attempt at complete withdrawal of all medications. However, after several days on the ward he suffered a convulsion and fell, fracturing a vertebra, so that he was moved to the orthopedic ward. To keep him still and calm while his fractured vertebra healed, the doctors on that ward saw fit to keep him under sedation. With three private nurses to supply him with sleeping pills, Levant was back in business.

His nightmare was far from over. The long period of sedated bed rest caused the muscles in his legs to begin to atrophy, and he was sent down to the second floor for physical therapy.

The wounded pianist eventually began to enjoy himself on the second floor. Tended by nurses, he felt secure there, safe from the strains and temptations of life on the outside with all its difficulties and potential hazards. When Dr. Kert told him he would have to leave the hospital in three days, he panicked. June arrived to take her husband home, but the fifty-three-year-old patient felt physically unable to walk out of the hospital and reenter the world. Afraid she wouldn't be able to handle Oscar once she got him home, June wanted to readmit him. But Levant refused, so June took her husband directly to another sanatorium in Westwood that was willing to accept him. His stay at the Westwood sanatorium, however, was brief, and he returned home.

After all he had been through, Levant was adamant about trying to withdraw from drugs at home. He called up all the physicians who had treated him—Kert, Greenson, Marmor, and Greenleigh—but they refused to continue to see him unless he checked himself into a hospital. He finally located the unscrupulous physician, who was more than willing to treat him. June gave Oscar a choice: Either he return to the third floor of Mount Sinai to be properly withdrawn, or she would simply withhold all of his nightly sedation.

Shortly thereafter, an ambulance pulled up at 905 North Roxbury Drive and two attendants tried to take Levant out of the house. His acquiescence had turned to fury and he lashed out at the two men, swinging roundhouse punches and threatening to bite them. As Levant punched, spat, and cursed, he was put into a straitjacket and carried out of the house.

Levant's fifth incarceration in Mount Sinai's psychiatric ward would be his longest, lasting nearly two months. He was reunited with some of the patients he had befriended during his earlier confinements. He didn't always remember their names, but he identified them by their ailments, such as "the moaning Jewish lady with the eczema" or "the young girl with the tracheotomy scar." Oscar would attend all the doctor patient meetings, enjoying these get togethers for their revealing and sometimes shocking character.

When Levant was discharged and returned to North Roxbury Drive, a persistent toothache revealed the presence of two rotted teeth that would have to be removed. The oral surgeon he consulted called the pharmacy and had twelve tablets of Seconal sent over to Levant's home to help him ease the pain of his sore mouth. Over the course of five or six hours he took all twelve tablets. He fell asleep with a cigarette still in his mouth. When he awoke he found himself in an ambulance headed back to Mount Sinai.

With Oscar out of the public eye, his viewers had begun to wonder what had become of him. Joe Hyams, who visited Levant at home throughout the summer of 1961, shared Levant's condition with his readers, describing him stretched out on his sickbed, unshaven, a hypochondriac of almost unbelievable proportions. "I haven't been downstairs for weeks or eaten a solid meal for months," Oscar rather proudly admitted to Hyams. Yet he was "keen, alert, and bouncing with his usual sarcastic opinions on a variety of subjects from President Kennedy, 'who has let me down,' to Brendan Behan, 'who was far funnier on my show than he ever was on Paar's.' "

Possibly as a result of Hyams's article, columnist Jack O'Brian went on a one-man campaign to bring back Oscar Levant. O'Brian, considered one of the more literate, thoughtful media critics, wrote in the *New York Journal:*

Oscar Levant should be back on television, where anyone with his sincere invective belongs. He's a proven champion in his edgy class of verbal lambasting . . . while lesser mentalities, more trivial talents . . . make a good if disreputable living just by sheer insistence. . . . He has given TV some of its brightest moments. He is a better interviewer than most give him credit for.

Levant's reactions to these articles were, as usual, mixed. While he told visitors that he hated the piano, never intended to go back on television, and couldn't stand to read about himself in the papers, Joe Hyams had noticed a pile of clippings by his bedside. He would occasionally rouse himself to go outside if there was someone he really wanted to see.

Harpo Marx's son Bill remembered the last meeting Levant and Harpo would have at Bill's small apartment in West Hollywood:

The meeting was for three o'clock, and my dad met Oscar, who was accompanied by a male nurse. Dad was in his underwear and the two of them sat across from one another and just started reminiscing. I don't remember any of the conversation except that it was completely about Oscar, who talked almost nonstop, because that was the way he was and Dad was a great listener. . . . Oscar would interrupt himself every five minutes by looking at his watch and saying to the male nurse, "Is it time for my pill?" . . . He was shaking. It was not a happy reunion. There was a sadness about Oscar my dad didn't want to deal with.

Having gone down the evolutionary scale of physicians who were willing to write prescriptions for him, Levant continued to see one of the most notorious doctors practicing in Los Angeles. Suspicious of his willingness to prescribe drugs for her husband, June contacted the American Medical Association to investigate him. The AMA told her that the doctor in question was not one of their members and therefore not subject to their regulations. They advised her to call the Board of Medical Examiners. When two investigators came out to the Levant home to speak with June, they informed her that the doctor was well known to the board; they referred to him as "a borderline physician." He knew how to operate just within the law, and they told June horror stories of how he had duped desperate patients out of fortunes. Yet he was clever; he always seemed able to defend himself, in effect by turning the Hippocratic Oath on its head: "I can't turn down a call from a sick person," he maintained. The authorities could do nothing.

June knew by their monthly bank statements that Oscar had been paying out hundreds of dollars to the unscrupulous doctor. He would make house calls whenever June was out or asleep, shoot Oscar up with pentobarbital or Demerol, and Oscar would pay with a check for $50 made out to cash. June found an average of eight checks per month, which confirmed her suspicions.

June called the doctor and pleaded with him to leave her husband alone. She told him how many times he'd been to the hospital to withdraw from drugs—six times—how ill he had been, how the injections were killing him. Her pleas fell on deaf ears. Levant continued to wake up in the middle of the night, tiptoe downstairs, call the doctor, and arrange for another house call. The doctor seemed to work best at night.

One night Levant discovered that the phone was dead. June had arranged for the phone to be turned off during the night to thwart Levant's efforts to attain drugs. Levant was furious. Forced to take drastic measures, he simply went outside and knocked on his neighbors' door. The astonished couple, new to the neighborhood, did not know Oscar, and they were shocked at the sight of this ghostly, pajamaed figure asking to use their telephone at five A.M.

One morning June awoke around 4:30 A.M. and found Oscar gone. She discovered him standing at the foot of the stairs with his physician, who was calmly preparing a hypodermic needle. It was like a scene from a bad television play, she later remembered.

"Don't you dare give him that!" June yelled. The doctor merely stared at her. "Get out of this house, you vulture! You're preying on a sick man! Get out of this house."

"My dear lady—" the doctor began.

"Don't talk to me. Don't say one word to me."

The doctor turned on his heel and walked out of the house, holding his hypodermic needle upright. Later that morning, June called the doctor and told him, "If you ever come back to this house, I'll kill you."

At least for a while it seemed to have worked. The doctor stayed out of sight. But June had only succeeded in frightening him out of the house; he now met his patient for "treatment" in his car outside of the Levant home. In the dead of night, Levant would creep downstairs in his bathrobe and meet this borderline doctor in his car parked just up the street, where the doctor would give him his pills and plunge a hypo into his arm while the rest of North Roxbury Drive slept—Lucille Ball, the James Stewarts, Agnes Moorehead, Ira and

Lee Gershwin, Jack Benny and his wife, Howard and Dee Hawks. The furtive affair, which took place three times a week, must have been humiliating, but Levant was powerless to jettison the unethical doctor. The injections kept him so weak and apathetic it would have been impossible for Levant to summon the strength to dismiss him, although June later discovered that some of the pills he was selling turned out to be baking powder poured into tiny capsules.

Finally, June found a lawyer willing to draw up a legal document ordering the doctor to ignore any calls from her husband—but that didn't work either; it was virtually unenforceable. Nothing worked. Oscar finally returned to Mount Sinai.

When he came home after several months, Levant discovered that June had purchased a portable lock that could be attached to their bedroom door. He would no longer be able to sneak out of the house at night. Out of sheer frustration, June had become her husband's jailer. "It gave me a feeling of desperation to be locked in every night," Levant later wrote. "I kept wondering, what if I have a heart attack?"

"Just wake me if anything happens," June reassured him.

Occasionally Oscar would wake June in the middle of the night, not because he feared another heart attack but to beg for pills, and June would become enraged, tossing an ashtray into his lap or clearing off his bedside table with one swipe of her arm. His precious empty pill bottles and newspaper clippings were swept to the floor.

Many of June's friends thought of her as a saint or a martyr. Some wondered if she wasn't being masochistic to stay with Oscar. Why did she do it? It was now going on ten years of dealing with Levant's addictions and illnesses. "I couldn't leave him when he was sick," June explained. There seemed to be little other motivation for her staying, that and the fact that she still loved him. Her experience of having an alcoholic father must have conditioned her to some extent for the role of caretaker.

After a year, the lock was removed. Levant seemed finally to have leveled out and overcome the more craven aspects of his barbiturate addiction, though at the time there was no cure for bipolar illness (lithium had not yet come into widespread use). He would occasionally return to Mount Sinai and check himself in, usually as a day patient. He missed his friends on the third floor, and it gave him a boost to see them. When the world seemed too demanding, the psychiatric ward was like Tahiti as far as Levant was concerned—a place he went off to, to protect himself from the world and from his past.

• • •

Now that Levant had finally and truly put his concert career behind him, some of the phobias associated with performing vanished. But others remained—there were still certain foods he would not go near or even allow on his table. A newly hired cook who served Levant a chicken garnished with little lemon wedges had to quickly remove the dish from the table. And there were still streets he could not bear to drive down on his infrequent forays into the world.

Levant and Joe Hyams sometimes went to the popular restaurant Chasen's for dinner. On one occasion, as they headed toward their table, Oscar spied George Jessel sitting at the bar. Levant balked. "No. I won't sit next to that man." Jessel looked up from his drink, saw Oscar creating a ruckus, and turned away again. The owner, Dave Chasen, wanting to avoid a contretemps, steered the two men into his private office, where they usually dined anyway, so Oscar "wouldn't be affronted by or affront any of the guests," Hyams remembered.

As far as Levant was concerned, Jessel had two strikes against him: Levant wrongly blamed the old vaudeville raconteur for having caused his heart attack by insisting that he return to the studio to do retakes of *The I Don't Care Girl;* and Jessel had been the one to inform him that Jolson had died.

Levant's daughters were usually pretty good about keeping up with their father's list of taboos, but Amanda was puzzled by Oscar's cringing any time her school friends mentioned college basketball sensation Oscar Robertson, known as "The Big O." When Levant first overheard Amanda refer to "The Big O," he "went into a snit for days," she remembered. The nickname was too much like "The Big C"—a euphemism for cancer, the disease that had left Oscar fatherless at fifteen.

And so Oscar began his years as an anchorite, a cave dweller in Beverly Hills, hidden away in his upstairs bedroom where sometimes the only event in the day worth noting was the occasional fluttering of wings at the windowsill. "It was sad—I remember visiting him in that room, [he was] sitting there in his pajamas," Betty Comden recalled of a rare visit to see Oscar at home. "He looked so . . . diminished."

The year 1962 began on a hopeful note. Oscar and June traveled to New York City by train to attend Marcia's Broadway debut in Felicien Marceau's comedy, *The Egg,* starring Dick Shawn. (Marcia had moved to New York City to study acting at the groundbreaking Actor's Studio there.) They checked into the Algonquin Hotel on West Forty-fourth Street.

The Algonquin, with its plush but faded tearoom elegance, was home for the Levants whenever they visited the city (they'd given up their apartment a few years earlier). It must have evoked some bitter-sweet memories for Levant, with Woollcott's corpulent ghost pad-ding the faded carpets. (Woollcott died in 1943, having suffered a heart attack while in the middle of one of his *Town Crier* radio shows.) Levant had been the youngest member of that set. "More blankets!" he said to the chambermaid making up their room. "You see, I didn't get much affection when I was a child."

Levant's return to New York set off a flurry of news items in the local papers, which made much of his return to the scene of his former glory. The columnists took to quoting him and telling their favorite Levant stories: "I remember a night with Oscar Levant at Lindy's . . ." began one such reminiscence. Levant's obvious pride at his daughter's opening night shines through in a photograph taken of the threesome backstage at the Cort Theatre.

At the Cort they ran into many of their old friends—Adolph Green and Betty Comden, Goddard Lieberson, Leonard and Sylvia Lyons. Levant had long since stopped enjoying evenings at the theatre— "you have to sit there and hear others talk"—but it was a tonic being out and seeing people. He reminisced with columnist Leonard Lyons about his own Broadway debut in *Burlesque* over thirty years ago. "I had one line to say—'Gee, Mazie, it's good to see you.' I never liked the way I said it. In fact, I'm still working on that line."

June would look back on their reunion with Marcia as particularly poignant. "It was the last time the three of us were out together as a family," she remembered.

No sooner did the Levants return to North Roxbury Drive than Oscar returned to his bed and to the kind of renouncement of life that June found almost more intolerable than his drug abuse. June told Hedda Hopper in an interview that she admonished Oscar:

> "Get out of that bed and bestir yourself." Why live like an old man? He even has a barber come in and shave him. He wants no responsibil-ities. . . . I'd like to build a bonfire under that bed. I can't even needle him into an argument any more.

Upstairs in his bedroom, full of sedatives he had hidden from June's periodic sweeps, Oscar would watch Jack Paar at night. During the three years since Oscar's first two, triumphant appearances on that show, Paar had taken to closing his program with the words, "Good night, Oscar Levant, wherever you are." Paar's sign-off never failed to bring a "paralyzed grin" to Oscar's lips.

41

The Memoirs of an Amnesiac

"So little time, so little to do."

THE LAST DECADE HAD INDEED WREAKED HAVOC ON LEVANT'S health. "He didn't age well, and everything caught up with him and showed on his face," June thought, as she accompanied her husband to New York for his reemergence on *The Jack Paar Show*. Paar had continued to salute his "old friend" on the air in the three years since Levant's last appearance, when he had mesmerized a national audience. Between 1963 and 1964, Levant would make four more appearances on Paar's new program, while a youngster named Johnny Carson took over *The Tonight Show*.

When he appeared on *The Jack Paar Show* on February 8, 1963, Levant was quick to announce to the audience that Paar had taken him "out of the darkness of the sickroom" and that he was grateful. Paar "knew he would be getting his money's worth from Oscar," June Levant believed, "because it would be publicized and people remembered Oscar, even though he didn't look great anymore—but he still had an impact. He still said funny things."

"How are you?" Paar asked his guest.

"Well," Oscar shrugged, "I'm not a promising astronaut."

"What do you do for exercise?"

"Oh, I stumble and fall into a coma." Levant recoiled into his chair during the long laugh that nearly smothered his remarks. "My usual formal attire is black tie and straitjacket," he told the enthusiastic audience, who now knew what to expect and who relished the pianist and wit who had risen, Lazarus-like, from his sickbed.

"On it went," Don Freeman wrote in the *San Diego Union,* "a typically Levant session climaxed by a touch of Gershwin at the piano, played grimly but with the fire and delicacy that has always been Oscar's hallmark as a concert artist. It was good having him back." Levant was paid $10,000 for his one night of renewed glory.

Levant appeared again on October 11 of that year; this time Paar introduced him as "Oscar Levant, American genius . . . one of the great natural resources of this country." When Levant ambled on-stage, blinking like a bull toad, he was greeted by a standing ovation that included the studio orchestra. "I do believe," wrote Freeman, "[that] Oscar, whose emotions reside close to the surface, was deeply touched."

"What have you been doing since you were on the show last?" Paar asked Levant.

"My behavior has been impeccable. I've been unconscious for six months—I've been doing intensive research into inertia."

"I'm appearing at a disadvantage," Levant then added.

I really do suffer from amnesia because I took shock treatments— which reminds me. I came back from the hospital and I was watching television, an old movie with Ralph Richardson in it where he's suffering from amnesia. And my wife came in—my wonderful wife, she really is—and said, "What are you watching?"

"I'm watching a movie with Ralph Richardson in it, and he's suffering from amnesia, and I want to see how it turns out." And she said, "But you saw it last week."

Paar asked his guest if he felt like playing the piano, to which Levant responded with a painful grimace, "I would play, but I have no coordination." The audience applauded, urging him on, and a look of distaste flitted across his face. However, he walked over to the grand piano. He played a few bars from the *Rhapsody* and then announced, "That's enough of the *Rhapsody.* I want to play a little piece. . . . Jack took me out of the sick ward and put me on the show, due to his generous nature. It's a rather sweet piece." He then launched into a brief passage from Federico Mompou's haunting "Scenes of Childhood." When it was over, he got up and started to walk offstage. Paar rushed over and tried to hug Levant, who visibly stiffened. Levant turned his back and left the set.

On April 3 and December 18 of the following year, Levant returned to New York to appear twice more on the Paar show. Paar insisted on clearing Levant's material beforehand. Levant wanted to use the line "I'm the only farmer in California growing organic marijuana."

"If you say that, I'll cancel your appearance. I don't think we'll be able to use your material unless you come up with something different."

"Oscar came up with different material," June remembered, "and snuck in a few that Paar didn't know about." When Levant came on, Paar took a risk and asked him what he thought about pornography. Oscar said simply, "It helps."

Levant's fee of $10,000 per appearance was the only earned income the Levants had in 1963 and 1964. June had made some wise investments over the years with the help of an unassuming little man who happened to be a shrewd investment adviser, discovered by June's mother, Sayde Gilmartin. Those investments had carried them through the years of Levant's inactivity. Paar had rescued Levant not only from obscurity but from financial difficulty. His hospitalizations had cost them approximately $300,000.

"Let's be honest—he wasn't very funny. You know, he'd lost the impetus to be original about things," said Ottie Swope about Levant's April 3 appearance on *The Jack Paar Show*. Some of Oscar's old friends found the Paar shows hard to watch. Television had never seen anything quite like him, his face a Kabuki mask of pain. The writer Jonathan Lieberson, one of Goddard Lieberson's two sons, wrote about Levant's resurgence as a television personality: "he had managed to create a ghastly new metier . . . by making jokes about his drug addiction and his declining mental and physical health . . . enumerating the sufferings his talents had imposed on him." Ottie Swope and Al Vanderbilt felt that Paar was simply exploiting Oscar for his shock value. "I felt so sorry for him," Swope said, "because Paar characteristically was unwilling to restrain him or keep him off the show. He never should have booked him." Vanderbilt found Levant so changed that it was painful and difficult for him to relate to his old friend.

Levant's final appearance on the Paar show on December 18, 1964, was the most difficult. Many of his remarks were cut out of the broadcast (the shows were pretaped before an audience). His appearance was cut to the point that some thought Levant had walked off the show entirely.

"No, I was cut," he told Hedda Hopper. "He let Richard Nixon play the piano [on an earlier show] and he cut me." Levant had said some brutal things about Judy Garland, and in retrospect he was glad they were excised. They left in his comment that Elizabeth Taylor (whose love affair with the married Richard Burton had made international headlines) should be named "the other woman of the year."

"Levant's rudeness is often embarrassing," Lieberson would write many years later. "He is constantly crying out for attention from his wife, his doctors, his critics, his vast television and film audiences. Yet there is something endearing and honorable about him. He is honest. His self-dislike is the result of measuring himself against a high standard."

Whatever the fallout, it was clear that Levant's appearances on the Paar show boosted his morale and gave him back what he had so sorely missed in the intervening years: an audience.

June and Oscar went to a few plays while they were in New York, seeing Uta Hagen's riveting performance in Edward Albee's *Who's Afraid of Virginia Woolf?* During their April trip, they had gone to see what would turn out to be Sam Behrman's last play, *But for Whom Charlie,* directed by Elia Kazan and starring Jason Robards and Faye Dunaway. The two men really hadn't seen much of each other since Oscar moved to Los Angeles. Behrman no longer wrote for the movies, and he had married one of Jascha Hiefetz's sisters. The big studios Behrman had worked for had broken up and the business had changed. This last play of Behrman's was a disappointment to Levant, who had always been so proud to have the author of *The Second Man* as his friend. He didn't have the heart to tell him that *But for Whom Charlie* had been better written thirty years earlier.

They saw many old friends and attended a concert of the New York Philharmonic conducted by Leonard Bernstein. Levant walked out before the performance was over, thus earning the emnity of Bernstein's wife. Bernstein, however, called up his old rival at the Algonquin and invited Levant out to lunch.

"I haven't had lunch outside the house for the last six years," Oscar informed Lennie.

"Then why not come to a rehearsal of the Philharmonic?"

"Lenny, I'd rather see you without your orchestra," Oscar told the conductor. The two men did not meet.

• • •

In the spring of 1964 Levant was only fifty-seven years old, but he couldn't stand to go to the theatre, the movies, the concert hall—they were all reminders of the life he had renounced. "Did it ever occur to you, dear old friend," Paar asked Oscar on his last appearance, "that a lot of your trouble or illness may just be in your mind?"

"What a place for it to be!" Oscar exclaimed, his eyes furiously blinking. At fifty-seven he began to write his memoirs.

William Targ, editor in chief of G. P. Putnam's Sons, approached Levant about writing his memoirs after seeing him resurface on the Paar show in 1964. He offered Levant an advance of $15,000 and a modest expense account. It had been a long time since Levant and Kolodin had knocked out *A Smattering of Ignorance* in Levant's New York hotel room. Its tremendous success had led Doubleday, Doran & Co. to ask for a second book, but Levant's other obligations had made that impossible. The publishers had reprinted *Smattering* during Levant's popularity on *The Oscar Levant Show,* a fact that seemed to cause him some embarrassment. "I'm not a writer—book writing isn't my racket," he told people. Targ realized that the best way to get Oscar to sit down and produce a book was to get him talking into a tape recorder. The transcript of Levant's reminiscences of his life would form the basis of the book.

There were problems from the beginning. As with his first editor, Ken McCormick at Doubleday, Levant and Putnam's editor in chief did not get along. Each was unhappy in his own way about their relationship, for his own reasons.

No sooner did Levant agree to Targ's proposal than he started to rail at the publisher about offering him "a shabby contract." Oscar had always complained about contracts and was deeply suspicious of them—they made him feel claustrophobic. He also perceived contracts as legal curtains behind which failure and humiliation lurked. Targ was not used to Levant's habit of testing authority figures—and in all cases the man with the contract was the boss. He probed their limits, poking them to find their weak points, testing their love and fealty. Targ's role as editor, critic, and potential censor of Levant's words made him into an untrustworthy authority figure. What followed was a power struggle over what could and could not be printed in Levant's memoirs.

For three months Levant worked on his book, speaking into a tape recorder. For the first time he found himself having to talk about his father and mother, his brothers, Pittsburgh—that whole trunk of memories that had been off limits for so many years. There were still subjects he could not bring himself to mention, such as the cause of his father's death. "A tragic and horrible death which I won't dwell on," he wrote in the early pages of his book.

He warmed to his subject when talking about the songwriters of the twenties and about Gershwin, to whom he returned in a chapter called "Hats Off, Gentlemen." It would have been hard to add anything to the long, eloquent chapter in *A Smattering of Ignorance* ("My Life: Or the Story of George Gershwin"), but in his new book Levant was aware of his own place in the Gershwin legacy. He bristled at other contemporary books on Gershwin, noticing that his place in the story had been nearly left out of Edward Jablonski and Lawrence D. Stewart's *The Gershwin Years*. "This biography is so controlled that they read me out of it," he complained. "I was the Trotsky of the Gershwin menage."

Whenever Bill Targ moved Levant's material around or suggested leaving something out, Levant would become enraged. He began to call Targ at all hours, in flagrant disregard of the three-hour time difference between Los Angeles and New York, sometimes calling his editor at three or four in the morning to tell him he wanted to insert a funny story in the book. Targ, more asleep than awake, would not laugh, so Oscar accused his book publisher of not having a sense of humor.

When Targ traveled to Los Angeles to meet with his author, he found himself greeted in the same fashion as Jack Paar, Gore Vidal, and nearly every other guest at the Levants': Oscar appeared in his pajamas at the top of the stairs, yelling at his guest to state his business. Targ, unused to this behavior, was unnerved. It was just as bad in New York. Levant spoke to Targ before his last appearance on the Paar show, telling him he didn't want him at the studio and ordering him not to show up. But when Targ stayed behind, Levant later accused his editor of not caring about him.

The publisher, who was always well groomed, even dapper, watched with distaste as Levant sprawled on his office couch and dropped ashes all over his rumpled suit. Finally Targ had enough when Levant called up his publisher on what happened to be Targ's wedding day to talk about the book.

"Oscar, I've just gotten married," he told Levant. "Can't this wait?"

"Congratulations. Now, about my book . . ." Levant began. But Targ refused to talk to his anxious author. He soon let it be known that he would no longer deal directly with him but only through June, whom he found much more agreeable.

Levant had already come up with his title: *The Memoirs of an Am-*

nesiac, which he may have gotten from another great title maker, the brilliant French composer Erik Satie, whose legendary eccentricities Levant found particularly appealing. Satie's mock-autobiographical writings—more like prose poems—were gathered under the title *Mémoires d'un amnésique,* written in 1912.

Levant was upset about material that Targ wanted kept out of the book. But Targ felt that the country was not yet ready for some of Levant's more candid revelations. When Levant wrote that Tennessee Williams had tried cannibalism, Targ deleted the playwright's name. In one omitted passage Levant repeated a remark made to him by a knowledgeable female friend that President Kennedy had inherited from his father a propensity for sexual adventurism. In 1964, with the country still in mourning for its newly martyed president, Targ removed that bit of information. A preface that was omitted from the published book exists now only in Levant's boyish longhand, written out on a sheet of yellowed typing paper. It reveals a particularly melancholy state of mind, as do several other excised passages in the first draft of the book. (Targ may have wanted to slant the book toward a sunnier point of view.) But it stands as a kind of credo. Levant had written,

This book is essentially an exercise in free association. It is not to be confused with the kind of formal autobiography that was written by St. Augustine, Henry Adams or Simone de Beauvoir. With the aid of the most lethal of devices, a tape-recorder. . . . Insomnia ruled the nights and the days were uniformly torporific. The Anatomy of Melancholy, the Book of Job, and Il Penseroso were my bedside companions.

I've tried to hew to the truth. . . . Truth is the writer's lancet—and when applied, blood is inevitable. For which I offer no further apology. If candor appears to be a sign of incorrigibility, I am willing to accept the verdict. I am even willing to furnish you with a certificate of my rectitude from my fifth ex-analyst.

One of the purposes of this book is to record, in a kind of mosaic form, the saga of Oscar Levant—and a world and a way of life that seem to merit preservation. . . . My contemporaries are vanishing fast from the scene. Who remains to tell the tale? So in this tassellated narrative . . . in the vale of neurosis, I offer you some of my friends and foes and moments from my past and present. . . . And choosing from the great Rousseau for a proper note to sound, "I mean to lay open to my fellow-mortals a man just as nature wrought him; and this man is myself."

Caveat emptor!

One month before the book's publication in August 1965, excerpts began appearing in major magazines, including an extended excerpt in the July 1965 issue of *Cosmopolitan* under the title "You Think You're Neurotic?"

Just four weeks after its release, *The Memoirs of an Amnesiac* appeared on *The New York Times'* best-seller list; Putnam's first printing quickly sold out. James Michener was at the top of the list in fiction that summer with *The Source,* and Theodore White's *The Making of the President* led the nonfiction column. "Anyone who doesn't like this book is healthy," blurbed Groucho Marx in the large advertisements run for *The Memoirs of an Amnesiac,* along with some of Levant's more memorable quotes.

Of the many reviews, the most perceptive was Clifton Fadiman's "Anatomizing Oscar: A Friend Looks at Levant" in the November issue of *Holiday.* Twenty-five years earlier Fadiman had reviewed *A Smattering of Ignorance* in *The New Yorker.* In a long preamble to his review, Fadiman wrote,

> About Oscar there are three obvious things to say. First, he has been immensely talented and could be again if . . . the locked horns of the elks fighting inside his head could only be separated. Second, he is that rarity, a natural wit, oral and uncontrollable rather than literary and calculated. Finally, he has suffered and still suffers far beyond what is proper to the human condition.

With his customary insight, Fadiman was quick to point out that no one had been able to help Oscar, including Levant's own legion of psychiatrists, with the possible exception of June ("smarter and tougher than the rest of us"). In describing the tone of *Memoirs,* Fadiman observed that it "mingles the anxiety of a sick man with the irony of a mocking mind observing the sick man. No wonder psychiatry has not helped him."

Fadiman understood that "Oscar had no boyhood, which may lie at the root of some of his troubles." He then echoed his assessment made twenty-five years earlier of Levant's essential integrity by noting, "Back of all the Broadway and Hollywood smartness, back of the bad temper, back of his seeming acceptance of the vulgar values of the entertainment world, there is something in him deeply innocent, pure, even on occasion gentle."

In 1964 Levant made a few television appearances besides *The Jack Paar Show.* In late May and early June, he appeared on three episodes of *The Celebrity Game,* a CBS game show hosted by Carl Reiner and clearly a forerunner of *Hollywood Squares.*

Levant is the only panelist slouching deeply in his chair and furiously chain-smoking, a dark scowl on his face. However, in all three appearances he manages to be outrageous and funny. It helped that he was sharing the panel with old friends like Hedda Hopper and those he seemed to like, such as Mickey Rooney and Rod Serling, though in one show he is seated next to Dale Evans and Roy Rogers—truly one of the oddest juxtapositions on television. They did not exchange one word.

On one show, the smoke from Levant's constantly lit cigarettes can be seen wafting across actress Ann Blyth's fur stole and lingering in her hair. Levant's fellow panelists over the course of the three shows included Dorothy Provine, Sal Mineo, Vic Damone, Lee Marvin, Robert Reed, a feisty, forward-thinking Gypsy Rose Lee, and Nanette Fabray—who, still bristling after all those years since *The Band Wagon,* manages to take Oscar to task for one of his remarks.

When he appeared on *The Joey Bishop Show* on October 11, 1964, Levant played a houseguest from hell, wreaking havoc on the Joey Bishop–Abby Dalton household and reveling in hypochondria and other eccentricities. The jokes capitalized on his reputation as a psychiatric patient, as when he arrived at the apartment laden with suitcases and told the superintendent, "Those are just my pills."

The Levants again traveled to New York in 1965 for the publication of *The Memoirs of an Amnesiac*—it would be Oscar's last visit to that great city where he had spent much of his life. He was scheduled to appear on *The Merv Griffin Show* to promote his book. He agreed to go through with it only if June accompanied him. He had come to rely on June for his most basic sense of security and found it difficult to negotiate the world without her. "Well," Merv Griffin asked a weary-looking Levant, "how do you like being in New York?"

"New York has everything, but you can't get in," Levant answered. As the conversation meandered, the genial talk show host asked Oscar what he would do if he had his life to live over again. "I'd talk my parents out of it." June then took over, smoothly launching into "a long stream of stories, talking her head off with all the aplomb in the world," as Levant later described it. While Levant had become more and more reclusive, June had developed into a witty, engaging raconteur in her own right. (Clifford Odets once told Levant that while he had "submerged June when they were first married, as the years passed, she had 'eclipsed' him, leaving Levant a 'captive audience' of his own works.") She talked while Oscar, like an exhausted mentor proud of his protégée, leaned back in his chair and smoked. Levant finally got in a word—"Why not plug my book?" he asked Griffin.

"It's a very good book," Griffin intoned, mugging at the camera.

"How do you know?" Levant barked, suddenly angry. "Since when are you a literary critic?" Levant was embarrassed by Griffin's compliment, which he felt was disingenuous—a condescending remark, perhaps even a put-down.

Levant later made a brief appearance on *The Les Crane Show* during his New York visit, creating a minor stir with his offhand comment that "every modern composer in this country save one is homosexual."

Finally, Levant appeared on *What's My Line?*, the popular quiz show in which a number of celebrity panelists (including Kitty Carlisle Hart and Dorothy Kilgallen, whose early column had helped launch Levant) try to guess the profession of a total stranger. Sometimes a celebrity was brought on, and the four panelists were masked as they tried to guess his or her identity. Levant appeared as the mystery celebrity. When the panel removed their masks, there was a collective gasp as they gazed upon the changes time and trouble had wrought on Oscar's face. "They were shocked, really, at Oscar's appearance—that it was really him," June recalled.

On what would be Oscar's last trip to New York, he had an emotional reunion with Vladimir Horowitz at the pianist's home on East Ninety-fifth Street. Horowitz was about to emerge from his self-imposed exile from the concert stage. Levant found his old friend in good health, "still looking boyish despite his age." He was surprised to learn that Horowitz continued to practice faithfully every day, playing for hours at a time. As their evening together wound down, Horowitz silently pointed to a bare wall that in earlier years had been hung with two Impressionist paintings. The empty wall testified to something Levant had learned all too well—the financial cost of inactivity. The two men stared at the wall without speaking. It was their last meeting.

Back in Beverly Hills, Levant became increasingly reclusive. With the exception of an occasional small social gathering attended at June's insistence, Levant remained hidden away in his bedroom. He still received visitors who knew that the only way to ever see their old friend was to make the pilgrimage to 905 North Roxbury Drive. Goddard Lieberson was always warmly received and sometimes brought his two young sons, Jonathan and Peter, with him.

"When I first met him at his house in Beverly Hills," Jonathan would write many years later in an appreciation of Levant,

> he looked as if he had just undergone a police interrogation. His face was puffy, pockmarked, with threatening black eyebrows and an exceedingly wide mouth. He shuffled his large body around the room as if he were looking for a place to sleep, and then crumbled onto a long sofa. I don't recall that he said very much. . . . But every so often he would . . . mutter an authoritative appraisal of his situation: "My home is a nice place to visit, but I'd sure hate to live here."

"It was the sixties," June remembered. "After all the big hullabaloo and everything else, everything stopped. He literally went back to bed. He wouldn't even touch the piano. It had turned on him, so he was going to turn [against] the piano."

June had gone back to acting in the early sixties, "just to get myself out of the house," she explained. In 1962 she appeared on an episode of *The Alfred Hitchcock Hour,* along with Tony Randall and Jayne Mansfield. The subject of acting held little interest for Levant, who for the most part found actors rather boring. At first he became upset and actually cried when June left the house to attend her acting sessions (June had become a member of the prestigious Actors Studio in Los Angeles). "I just stopped him cold," June remembered. "I was only going out once a week. I was devoting myself to him; I was working on his scrapbooks. He knew I was there on his behalf."

He missed June. In 1966 she appeared in two plays back to back that made Oscar feel more lonesome than ever. "I've grown unaccustomed to her face," he sang to a friend over the telephone.

In his last years Levant took to making many phone calls, talking to his friends from the old days and staying on the phone for hours. He called Sam Behrman, Goddard Lieberson, and Adolph Green, holding long discourses on anything that had caught his attention that he'd read or seen on television. But his coterie of friends had been sadly diminished. Clifford Odets, the angry young man whose playwriting career had peaked in the thirties, died bitter and unhappy in 1963 in Hollywood, a place he abhorred, "his big brave voice" reduced to a whisper. Herbert Swope, Sr., wrote his last byline in 1958. Max Dreyfus died in 1964 at his estate in Brewster, New York. He was ninety-one years old, and Levant had not seen him in over fifteen years. By 1968 the star of *Funny Girl,* Barbra Streisand, was better known to the public than Fanny Brice, upon whose life the musical was based. The great vaudeville crosier had pulled Fanny Brice and more recently Billy Rose off the stage. Toscanini—who seemed as if he might live forever—became sick and heard the music of the spheres in 1957. Jolson was gone. Schoenberg died on the dreaded thirteenth day of July, 1951, at the age of seventy-six, an age his numerologist had warned him about because its numerals added up to thirteen. Harpo had slipped quietly away in 1964. Aldous Huxley was now gone. Moss Hart died in 1961—he collapsed in front of his house in Palm Springs while waiting to be taken to the dentist. George S. Kaufman, who had once argued with Oscar over which one of them was sicker, died in his sleep in 1961. Death had been the one thing Kaufman could never joke about. Judy Garland would die on June 25, 1969, in London, emaciated and worn out at the age of forty-seven. Oscar's two remaining brothers were now gone: Ben had died in July of 1958 and Howard, known his whole life as Honey, had followed two years later. Even the vitally active Jerry Wald, who had had such high hopes for Oscar as an actor and who had entertained him in his projection room on so many occasions, died in 1963. Ira and Lee Gershwin, two of the constants in Oscar's dwindling world, still lived up the street. Ira made it his business to answer every piece of mail that came into the Gershwin home; he had turned himself into a kind of human *yahrzeit* candle to George's memory.

Each of these deaths chipped away at Oscar's interest in life. June moved out of the bedroom she shared with Oscar into Marcia's old room across the hall, "so I could turn on the television and put on a program I liked and he could put on what he liked. . . . We were within shouting distance of each other," June remembered.

Levant's hostility toward the piano pained his friends and occasional visitors and revealed to his family the severity of his abdication from the world. Even old friends like Lieberson and Green couldn't get him to play again. June coaxed, threatened, cajoled, but nothing helped. "Well, the piano knows where I am," Levant wrote. "I usually spend my days in my bedroom. . . . I sleep twenty hours a day and during the other four I have the happy faculty for taking cat naps."

One evening, when Oscar and June were completely alone—their three daughters had already moved out of the house—a troubled look passed over Oscar's face. He turned to June and asked her, "Did you ever have anything to do with Clifford Odets?"

"What are you talking about? How could you say such a thing to me?" June demanded. It was never mentioned again. Oscar's jealousy, and most of his phobias and taboos, seemed to abate once he had completely given up his concert career. Talking about his life, his obsessions, his rituals in the making of *The Memoirs of an Amnesiac* had been a therapeutic process for him, enabling him to shed many of his neurotic phobias. Now he was sleeping all day out of depression; he no longer needed barbiturates. "The comb and brush on my bureau seem heavy when I lift them," he told one visitor. Unwilling to get dressed unless June insisted, Oscar would spend a part of his aimless day waiting for the barber to come to the house to shave him. He began comparing himself to Firs, the old caretaker in *The Cherry Orchard*:

At the end of the play they forget to remove him from the house and the house is locked. You can hear his lonely pounding as the curtain goes down. You can hear the workmen with their hammering destroying the cherry orchard. That's the way it is around our house.

42

Remembering and
Forgetting

"I love songs more than anything."

ONE DAY WILLIAM TARG CALLED TO ASK LEVANT IF HE WOULD WRITE
another book. Levant refused, claiming that he had nothing more to
say, but Targ showed up at the Levant doorstep with a check in his
pocket. "Here's the advance for your second book," he told Oscar.

"Take it away. I'm not doing any more."

June took a look at the check and motioned to her husband to
follow her into the kitchen. "Oscar, can I see you for a moment?"
June asked her husband how he could turn down that amount of
money.

"But I have nothing to write about," he insisted.

"But we have a lot of stuff that wasn't used from the first book. I'm
going to sit down with a paper and pencil. I'm going to dig things out
of you." So Oscar accepted the check that Targ held in his hand, and
he began a third book.

Oscar's third and final book would be published in 1968, and
though it was received less enthusiastically than the previous ones, it,
too, became a best-seller. "These later books are little more than com-
pendiums of neurotic one-liners and inconclusive stories about famous
people he has known. The theme of self-loathing is the leitmotif,"

Jonathan Lieberson wrote in his essay on Levant. Occasionally there were flashes of the old wit: About Grace Kelly, Levant wrote, "She just married the first prince who asked her."

Levant's premature retirement from his lucrative concert career and his decade-long ordeal with doctors and hospitals had taken their toll on the Levant household. June fired the cook and the cleaning woman. One evening in their big, empty house they suddenly realized that with the children gone, this was the first time they had really been alone together since their marriage. "Well, what do you think about all that," June asked Oscar, "about having raised three girls?"

"It took care of twenty years," was his solemn reply. In 1964 Marcia married a young theatre critic named Jerry Tallmer, and they spent their first year of marriage on Tallmer's Ford Foundation grant. Lorna had moved to New York to work at Juilliard, the prestigious music conservatory, and she was saving her money to travel to the summer Wagner Festival held in Bayreuth. She had become close friends with Virgil Thomson, who adored Oscar's middle daughter. They would bake cookies together and listen to music. (In fact, Thomson was hurt when Lorna eventually decided to marry, refusing to speak to her for a time. He was crushed at her defection.) Amanda, whose physical attractiveness Oscar liked to boast derived from him, was a student at UCLA. Amanda did, indeed, resemble her father; Oscar referred to himself as "a Caliban-caricature of Amanda." She soon married and produced a grandson whom Oscar doted on.

Once upon a time Oscar had told his children that "they could do anything they wanted except bring me their problems." But the years had changed him, and now, whenever his children returned home, they were struck by how calm he had become, how much less tormented he seemed. It was no longer a high-wire act simply to have a conversation with him. "He started to relax about his [phobias]," Lorna noticed.

When Lorna began working at Juilliard, she was often told by members of the faculty how much they admired her father's pianism. Lorna would pass on those remarks. "He wanted to make sure people remembered him, and he liked to be told." Levant found an old, falling-apart copy of his Nocturne and sent it to his daughter, inscribed on the title page with "For Lorna, the jewel in my diadem. Your Daddy." And then, Lorna noticed, he'd written in parentheses "Oscar Levant." She wondered, "How many people put their names in parentheses after 'Daddy'?" But he was afraid of being forgotten; there were new recordings of the *Rhapsody* and the Concerto in F coming out every year.

Levant's old friend and former writing partner, Irving Kolodin, occasionally came by to see him on visits to Los Angeles. Once Kolodin arrived at the Levant home at ten P.M., and the two men reminisced for over an hour. "As I rose to go," Kolodin remembered,

> he exclaimed angrily, "You call that a visit!" I always went with trepidation, not knowing quite what to expect. I always left with an awareness that his mind—however disserved by memory lapses and sheer frustration at his lessened physical capacity to articulate—retained its sharp edge, its trenchant wit.

After one of these visits it dawned on Kolodin why Oscar had chosen to spend the rest of his days on North Roxbury Drive: "1019 North Roxbury Drive was the address of the house in which George Gershwin spent some of the happiest days of his life."

In 1966 the actor Roddy McDowall asked Oscar if he could include him in a book of photographs of famous personalities he was compiling and would publish under the title *Double Exposure*. McDowall had gotten other celebrities to write "portraits" to accompany his striking black-and-white photographs. Zero Mostel, for example, wrote about Ira Gershwin; Goddard Lieberson about Igor Stravinsky. McDowall asked Dorothy Parker if she would provide a short piece to accompany two photographs of Levant taken at his home. "He had a wonderful face," Roddy McDowall remembered, and he seemed pleased to have his picture taken for the book.

The four pages Dorothy Parker gave McDowall "were badly typed and full of typographical errors," wrote Parker's biographer Marion Meade; "actually not even well written, but they were pointedly honest. In paying tribute to Levant, she became defensive on his behalf, although it is possible to see how she may have been identifying with him":

> Over the years, Oscar Levant's image—that horrible word—was of a cocky young Jew who made a luxurious living by saying mean things about his best friends and occasionally playing the piano for a minute if he happened to feel like it. . . . They also spread the word around that he was sorry for himself. He isn't and he never was; he never went about with a begging bowl extended for the greasy coins of pity. He is, thank heaven, not humble. He has no need to be.
>
> He has no meanness; and it is doubtful if he ever for a moment considered murder. . . .
>
> Well. This was a losing fight before it started, this striving to say

things about Oscar Levant. He long ago said everything about everything—and what Oscar Levant has said, *stays* said.

It was the last piece Dorothy Parker ever wrote.

The curse of being the *enfant terrible*—always the youngest person
in the room—was that now he was condemned to see all of his friends
and colleagues fade from the scene. He was condemned to outlive
them.

Levant's taboos and rituals had lessened their hold on him; in his
final year he even gave up his entrenched caffeine and nicotine habits.
What remained were rituals and associations revolving around food.
Certain foods, especially desserts and sweets, would bring on an almost regressive, boyish zeal. One year it was chocolate, another it was
tapioca pudding. At one dinner, as Levant was served a dish of tapioca, he shrieked, "I love this more than anything in the world!" He
later quipped, "I was withdrawn from tapioca pudding gradually."

In the spring of 1970 Levant began writing letters. His chief corre-
spondent was Sam Behrman, one of his few friends from the late
twenties still among the living. Though he had seen little of his old
friend in the intervening years—Behrman had permanently settled in
New York—Oscar always thought of "Berrie" as one of the men he
truly loved. They had both lived through George Gershwin's terrible
death, just as they had lived through the glorious Gershwin years.
Now each was confined to his own room in deteriorating health,
feeling that they had outlived their era.

At the end of 1969, Behrman suffered a stroke that seriously weakened him and made it almost impossible for him to walk. It was too
exhausting for him to speak on the telephone, so the two men were
forced to rely solely on their written communication. "I would like to
show you my diaries of the 30's," Berrie wrote to Oscar on May 26,
1970. "They are full of you; there was not a day in which I was not in
close touch with you. You were then and are still an intimate part of
my life." Occasionally Behrman's letters made Oscar feel so nostalgic
that he would call Behrman up on the telephone, even though it was
a strain for his old friend to talk.

It was the most coveted invitation to a Hollywood event in recent
memory—a luncheon held in the spacious garden of Walter and
Carol Matthau's Pacific Palisades home in honor of Charlie Chaplin's
return to America. Chaplin had been twenty years in exile, ever since
business and tax problems and the specter of Congressional investiga-

tions had forced him out of the country. Facing a witch-hunt into his political affiliations, Chaplin had left America for good.

But now in his old age, old emnities were forgotten. America wanted to make amends to "the little fellow." The American Academy of Motion Picture Arts and Sciences had decided to present Chaplin with an honorary Academy Award, and the Film Society of Lincoln Center invited the Chaplins to travel to America to receive their tribute.

Carol Marcus, once married to the playwright William Saroyan and now married to the gifted, rubber-faced actor Walter Matthau, had been a girlhood friend of Chaplin's wife Oona O'Neill (daughter of Eugene O'Neill). Hollywood's elite began calling Carol Matthau, "waging their campaign for invitations," wrote Candice Bergen, then a photojournalist covering Chaplin's return to America for *Life* magazine. The invitation list was a roll call of some of the film world's leading figures—the "incomparables of the old Hollywood."

Levant received his invitation but refused to go. It had been an age since he had emerged from the house or had even gotten dressed. "I had to beg him to go to the Chaplin party," June recalled. Oscar finally agreed to accompany his wife to the Matthaus' to honor Chaplin, whom he had known since 1929, when he had first gone to Hollywood to appear in *The Dance of Life*. The last time he'd seen Chaplin was in New York just after Marcia was born, in 1940, when he had dragged Chaplin up to their Alwyn Court apartment to see his infant daughter. Levant had enormous respect for Chaplin as a filmmaker and a comedic genius, but if the truth be known he found the shy, inarticulate man rather tedious off camera. But it was enough of an occasion to force Oscar—with June's coaxing—out of his lair.

The luncheon was held on a balmy Sunday afternoon in April, the day before Chaplin was to receive his honorary award. "The weather was sublime," wrote Candice Bergen, who described the event in an article about Levant that she would later write for *Esquire*. "It was a day that made abandoning the East for the West a rational move."

Chaplin, eighty-two, dined at a special table inside the house to protect him from the sea breeze. He then moved to a small table on the flagstone terrace, wrapped in a cloth coat and looking frail and thin, to greet the guests. "Reminiscences abounded during lunch," wrote Hollywood reporter Joyce Haber, who covered the event for the *Los Angeles Times*. "George Burns started talking about 'the three greatest entertainers of all time. They are Chaplin,' he said, 'of course, and Al Jolson and Sinatra.' " Chaplin sat in his chair and "talked rather aimlessly to people" as they came up to greet him or to introduce themselves. One observer who attended the party felt that Chaplin knew very few of the guests, but he was good at faking it, calling them "dear old friend."

The party guests milled about on the lawn, which overlooked the Pacific. Pink, white, and blue hyacinths were planted around the garden. Cary Grant, William Wyler, Greer Garson, Danny Kaye and his wife, Sylvia, Rosalind Russell and her husband, Frederick Brisson, the Henry Fondas, Groucho Marx and his amanuensis, Erin Fleming, and Mrs. Sam Goldwyn, concealed by a brightly flowered hat, were among those present.

Oscar Levant's appearance caused a wave of surprise to ripple through the party of ninety-eight guests. Candice Bergen, who was the only photographer invited to the luncheon, moved through the crowd until she stumbled on Oscar seated in a rocking chair, observing the festivities with a fierce scowl on his face. "Sulking in the shadows, a spectral silhouette, loomed the face that launched a thousand analysts," she wrote. "Was I seeing a ghost? I thought Oscar Levant had been dead for years."

"He wore a dark and somber suit," she described, "that looked like it last saw action in the 1950s with Harpo Marx at '21' or Dorothy Parker at the Algonquin. His feet sat passively in slender wing tips reviewing the passing parade of patent leather boots and white Gucci loafers. It was as if he were a British colonialist struggling to maintain civility amidst savages."

Bergen was not the only one to notice Oscar in their midst. "Oscar Levant," wrote Joyce Haber, "the recluse second only to Howard Hughes, made a much heralded appearance. Those who had first greeted Chaplin strode to Levant, who reclined on a sofa or sat on a chair." Chaplin himself was delighted to see this familiar face; Oscar was one of the few guests he greeted with genuine warmth, grateful to recognize someone he had known and liked. Emerging briefly from his own self-imposed exile, Levant's presence at the luncheon became an event in itself. Like Chaplin, he, too, had citizenship in the country of the sick. The silent screen legend and the legendary talker briefly reminisced.

Bergen quickly offered to bring Levant a plate of food from the buffet table. "I was never so excited to meet anyone," she wrote. "What with his penchant for pretty girls and my fixation for ailing underdogs, we were instantly smitten."

Oscar clutched the arm of this willowy girl—daughter of the popular radio star and ventriloquist Edgar Bergen—and she led him out-side. "He seemed very ill, and had great difficulty walking," she re-membered.

"How old are you?" Levant asked Candice Bergen hopefully. "Twenty-five."

"I'm sixty-five," he said with pride. ("While he looked awful," Bergen wrote, "it was hard to believe. He seemed more like a little kid imitating a dying old man.")

"I've always been very boyish," Levant told her. "William Le Baron at RKO called me Peter Pan." His speech was interrupted by facial tremors, causing him to grimace as if in pain. Bergen asked Levant if he felt all right.

"My wife took me to the doctor and he treated me for Parkinson's disease," he explained, "which it turned out I didn't have. But the treatment gave me Parkinson's symptoms," he added bitterly.

After lunch, Bergen asked Levant if she could take his picture. "I pointed to a chair I had for Oscar. He had barely lowered himself onto it when June landed on his lap. His face went ashen and he limped into the house, cawing crazily, 'June's trying to murder me! She sat on my lap and almost killed me . . . she almost broke my legs!' " A short time later, just before leaving the party, Bergen bent down to give Levant a tender kiss on the cheek.

"I had one of those funny premonitions," Lorna remembered about a visit home she made over Easter break in 1972, "because I hadn't come out at Christmas. I stayed a week. He was so frail and thin and really very sweet, and he didn't have all those taboos anymore. You could sit and talk to him." Lorna remembered that her father never allowed his family or friends to say "good-bye"—it was a word that smacked of finality. "Okay, kid," Levant would say to his daughters at the end of a phone call, or he'd say "I love you" before hanging up. The evening before Lorna was scheduled to return to New York, Oscar shuffled out of his room to say good night to his daughter, who was leaving early the next morning.

> I went out and kissed him good-bye and then I started for my room. Then I had one of these feelings that this might be the last time I'd ever see him, so I turned around and went back and gave him a big hug.

Levant saw fewer visitors throughout 1972. Adolph Green dropped by for a brief visit in May. He was pleased to see that his old friend had resumed playing the piano, and the two men spent an enjoyable afternoon:

> I saw Oscar for the last time. . . . The setting was the same, but he seemed more fragile. He claimed to be out of touch with everything in the world, but that simply wasn't so. He was as brilliant, witty and informed as ever. He sat down at the piano, which he had recently resumed playing, and played his current favorite, the slow movement of Schubert's posthumous A Major Sonata. He was happy and we were happy.

In July Levant received his last letter from Sam Behrman, who had moved into a summer beach house in the hope that it would improve his health. Levant had sent the ailing playwright an article on the death of critic Edmund Wilson, written by Malcolm Muggeridge. He also praised Behrman's recently published book, *People in a Diary,* based on the journal he had kept since 1915.

> July 13, 1972
> Dearest Osc,
> . . . The air is more breathable here than it is in New York, but for the rest there isn't much difference, because I can't walk. I have simply exchanged one room for another. . . .
> The death of Edmund Wilson has deeply saddened me. . . . I read also a moving account of his funeral in the New York Review of Books. At the very end an old friend of his, with a gesture toward the grave, said: "Dear old friend, shalom."

Levant's last public act was to write a protesting letter to the *Los Angeles Times* in response to an article in which the author, Jon Coleman, bought a souvenir map of the "stars' homes" and went on a kind of treasure hunt for lost Hollywood. "I thought I had found 1935 all over again," Coleman wrote, "on North Roxbury Drive." He knocked on the doors of George Burns, James Stewart, and Polly Bergen, and he spoke to their maids and secretaries, sometimes through a peephole in the door. When Coleman knocked on the door of "Star No. 27" on the map, Oscar Levant, he was shocked to find "an old wrinkled man, dressed in crumpled pajamas and supporting himself on the doorknob."

> I understand why the maps read "do not intrude." They are not protecting the private homes of the stars of movieland. They're protecting that precious illusion. . . . Hollywood isn't 1935 anymore.

This article angered Levant, whose letter to the editor was published on August 13, 1972, under the heading "A 'Rich' Levant":

I deeply resent his scabrous attack. I do not have a staff of servants. I am perfectly able to open my own door. But I am far from pauvre. And in one way, at least, I am the richest man in town: My wife is still the most beautiful girl in the world who eats my candy, drinks my brandy. As for my maligned beauty, at least the amount and color of my hair are the same as ever and my teeth, for what they are, are still my own.

What Coleman had missed in his article was the fact that Levant had always stood in stark counterpoint to the illusions of Hollywood. His public breakdowns and unleashed tongue had always been a threat to the illusion business.

The letter salved Oscar's wounded ego, and it also served as his last love letter to his wife. It was, in fact, June who had brought about a truce between Oscar and his old friend and enemy, the Steinway in their music room. Playing the piano was still the one thing that could transport him beyond his suffering, and in the last weeks of his life, he had begun to play on a daily basis. Music was again heard throughout the Levant home.

The celebrated fashion photographer Richard Avedon called the Levants the day after the Chaplin party to ask if Oscar would sit for a portrait. Oscar wasn't interested. Avedon called back and asked again, telling June that he was photographing Chaplin and Groucho Marx. June thought the attention of the famous photographer fussing over her husband would be therapeutic; he would have an audience again. A few days later, on April 12, 1972, Avedon showed up at their house with his assistants. Oscar came downstairs for his photo session wearing his usual robe and pajamas, his hair uncombed, his face pale and puffy. "I didn't catch him in bed," remembered Avedon. "There was enough of the artist in him to want to give me the thing itself." Avedon took dozens of shots, but when June got a look at the proof sheets, she was horrified. The stark, black-and-white images showed a sick old man, his face betraying pain and dementia. She threw the proofs away.

But Avedon had been deeply impressed by Levant. He would later write that the session was "the best, most powerful sitting I ever had." For Avedon, Levant expressed that quality of ruined greatness, of life lived on the edge that formed the impulse behind many of his greatest photographs. Of course June hated them, showing as they did how badly Oscar had aged, but the portraits reveal something else. For Oscar even to have agreed to be photographed—unkempt, bundled in a bathrobe—showed his complete lack of vanity, a kind of plateau of personal honesty that he had striven for his entire life. It was as if all the psychological pain of his sixty-five years had been telescoped into a moment—a "study of drowning heroism" in the words of art critic David Ansen.

Four months after the luncheon in honor of Chaplin, Candice Bergen called Levant about setting up an interview for the following week. "Can't you come today?" Levant asked her. She agreed and a short time later arrived at the Levant home, where Oscar greeted her at the door in his pajamas and bathrobe, looking "like a kid home sick from school."

Levant sank into a chair in the living room and almost immediately began bombarding his young guest with old anecdotes that were already familiar to Bergen, who had read Levant's three books. Buoyed by the presence of a beautiful young woman, Levant pulled out all the stops in recounting his best stories and quips.

"You know what I said about Zsa Zsa Gabor? She not only worships the golden calf, she barbecues it for lunch. Judy Garland loved me. We met and she hugged me and I said, 'This is the greatest embrace of pharmacopoeia in history!'"

The barrage continued—it was like every television appearance, newspaper interview, radio broadcast, and Lindy's jam session crammed into one afternoon. "You didn't see my show," he continued. "I was brilliant on that show. It was after I had left all the mental hospitals. God, all the pills I took . . ." At one point he broke off abruptly and began to sing "It's very clear . . ." from Gershwin's last song, "Love Is Here to Stay," his voice trailing off into a whisper.

"My father was a great man," Levant went on. "He died very young. What of? I don't want to say the word. It's too terrible what he went through. I left it out of the book."

Levant's stream-of-consciousness began to lead him into deeper waters. With a pained look, he said, "One of my sisters-in-law [Sarah Levant] had the chutzpah to tell me that while my mother was carrying me, she tried to get rid of me during her pregnancy." He glanced at Bergen with an incredulous look on his face. "Isn't that a helluva thing to tell a young boy?" (No one had known why Levant dreaded the name Sarah.)

He suddenly stood and tightened his robe around him. He sat down again and asked his guest, "Does my blinking bother you? Is it pretty bad?"

Levant became aware that Bergen had not taken any notes throughout his monologue. "What's the matter? Don't you like my stories?" he demanded. "These are terrific stories."

Bergen reassured her disgruntled subject that of course they were terrific stories, but she wanted something "more personal than a performance. I want to hear something more personal about you."

"These are about me."

Bergen explained that he was one of the most special people she had ever met and she wanted very much to know him.

"Really? Help me into the den. I want to play you something. I can't play too long. I've got arthritis in my back and Morton's neuralgia in my feet and I've had this bacterial disease . . ."

Bergen described what ensued:

> He opened a piece of music and smiled softly. It was like finding his first love. "I love songs more than anything," he crooned quietly, almost to himself. Then, he said hastily, "half the keys don't play." And he began playing "But Not for Me" [from *Girl Crazy*], confiding happily, "these are lyrics no one knows—the third verse."
>
> And in his robe and pajamas and a faltering falsetto, he sang softly, "It all began so well, / But what an end. / This is a time a fella / Needs a friend. / He ain't done right by Nell. / However, what the hell / I guess he's not for me."

"I've had more than my share of moments in my life," Bergen wrote in the spring of 1973 for *Esquire*, "but this was one of the best." Levant then dove into a pile of sheet music and came up with Prokofiev's Third Piano Concerto—one of the pieces he had always loved but that had become taboo over the years. "Look what I found," he said triumphantly. As he played Prokofiev, Levant seemed transported. "Music was the miracle drug," Bergen wrote, "a magical time machine; the tremors and blinking disappeared, his ailments vanished." Levant looked up from the piano. "That's one of the pieces I played the night my mother died. I haven't played it in years." Prokofiev's Piano Concerto No. 3, written when the Russian composer was thirty years old and homesick, had become in Oscar's mind his mother's funeral march.

"Is it okay if I kiss you good-bye?" Levant asked Bergen as she prepared to leave. "I don't have any designs, you know."

Outside it was already dark, and Oscar turned on the porch light for his departing guest. "Can you see all right?" he asked after her as she walked down the path to her car.

During Bergen's visit a painful secret had leaked out. Despite all of his mother's efforts to turn him into a concert pianist, despite her faith in his abilities, perhaps she had not really wanted him after all. It may or may not have been true, but Oscar had been undermined by that fear. He believed that his mother's love was conditional: Only if he succeeded as a concert artist—if he became a great man—would he be loved by her.

The next day Levant became anxious that he had been too unguarded, that he had said too much or had made the wrong impression, and he called Bergen to ask if she would return for a second interview. They made a date for the following Monday.

It wasn't often that June and Oscar had breakfast together. June usually fixed her husband a tall glass of orange juice and left it for him in the refrigerator. She'd then prepare a bowl of oatmeal and leave it on the stove so it would still be warm when he got up a few hours later. But on this particular Monday, Oscar and June came down for breakfast at the same time. "What happened to the pictures of me with Adlai Stevenson?" he asked June, as he planned to show them to Candice Bergen later that day. He also wanted to give her a copy of his first book.

"I'll get them out for you," June said. She was about to leave the house to shop for two baby presents, one for the Sam Goldwyns and one for their friends the Prelutskys, whose new baby was named Max. June went over to the walk-in safe in the music room to retrieve the picture of Adlai Stevenson and a copy of *A Smattering of Ignorance*.

Candice Bergen called to confirm her appointment, but Oscar asked if she could come over right away. "Four o'clock—that's too late—come over now!" he wailed. He had always hated to wait. Bergen agreed, and Levant went back to the piano.

Half an hour later, June was on her way out the door when she saw Candice Bergen coming up the path. She told the young woman that Levant had gone upstairs to rest after practicing. She offered to go upstairs and tell him his guest had arrived.

June had checked on him earlier. She had heard him coming up the stairs, breathing heavily, tired from his workout at the piano. When she had last noticed he was lying peacefully on his bed, his hands folded on his chest. June had wanted to tell her husband how beautiful his hands looked, but she didn't want to wake him.

"Oh, God," June gasped from upstairs. Bergen heard her pick up the telephone and say, "Come right away. There's something wrong with my husband. I think he's dead."

Bergen went upstairs. She heard June talking excitedly on the phone. June had run into her own bedroom, afraid to call from Oscar's phone. In a panic, she made three calls, to Dr. Kert, to the fire department, and for an ambulance.

Oscar was lying in bed, his hands splayed out across his chest. His eyes were closed. His slippers were beside the bed. "I had never seen anyone dead before," recalled Bergen. "In the movies someone always feels for a pulse, so I felt for his pulse. My heart was beating so hard I could only feel my own." Bergen put the lifeless arm down gently.

"I never got the chance to tell him how beautiful his hands were," June said.

A police car and ambulance pulled up in front of the house. "What's the man's name, Miss?" a young policeman asked Bergen.

"Oscar Levant."

Bergen would write that the policeman showed no sign of recognition as he filled out his forms. The forgetting had begun. The noisy growl of a tourist bus could be heard from inside the house as they carried Levant downstairs. "The poor thing," June whispered.

In New York, Sam Behrman (who would die the following year) awoke from a nap the day before Oscar's death. He had dreamed that Oscar had been talking to him at a dinner table and had suddenly vanished. In the dream, Behrman searched for him all over the city until he saw a newspaper headline that said, "Oscar Levant Dies."

It was August 15, 1972. He was sixty-five years old.

Coda

"In some situations I was difficult,
in odd moments impossible, in rare moments loathsome,
but at my best unapproachably great."

AFTER OSCAR'S DEATH, JUNE IMMEDIATELY CALLED HER DAUGHTERS
and her sister in New York. "I have something important to tell
you," she said. Virgil Thomson and Adolph Green called, wanting to
attend the funeral. June told them not to come; she had decided to do
the least possible thing in order to spare the family, to make it easier
on the girls and herself. Barbara Stanwyck sent flowers. Marc Levant,
Oscar's nephew and the only surviving male to carry the Levant
name, arrived the following day.

"Oscar never could face the medieval agony of a funeral service,"
June told one reporter—one of the many who were saddened by the
news of Levant's death. New York mayor John Lindsay said that
reading Levant's lengthy obituary in *The New York Times*, which was
full of his anecdotes and wisecracks, was the only time he had ever
read the obituary page and laughed. Earl Wilson and Leonard Lyons
devoted their columns entirely to Oscar, and Clifton Fadiman was
asked to say a few words about his old friend. "In addition to being
the greatest interpreter of Gershwin's music . . . Oscar was a master of
the English language," he said. "In my wide acquaintance, Oscar Levant was the quickest wit I knew." Burt Prelutsky and Samuel Marx

wrote long columns celebrating Oscar's eccentricities as well as his warmth—that unexpected quality that had inspired devotion from so many. "For behind the façade of the world's oldest *enfant terrible* lurked the sweetest, warmest, most vulnerable man I've ever known. . . . I loved him," Prelutsky wrote. *The Hollywood Reporter* titled its obituary "A Wit's End," which angered June and her daughters and elicited a protesting letter from them. The *Los Angeles Herald Examiner* carried a bold headline above its masthead on August 15: "Pianist, Actor Oscar Levant Dies."

There was no rabbi and no religious ceremony, and no prayers were intoned over the body, which was privately laid to rest in a crypt at Westwood Memorial Cemetery on the Wednesday following Oscar's death. There were no fresh-cut flowers, no wreaths, just three sweet-smelling little plants. There were no strangers present, just June and her three daughters, Goddard Lieberson, and six members of their extended family. They sat on folding chairs in front of the crypt.

"There were no strangers, nothing funereal at all. We sat there and just said how much we loved him and told one another some of the things he would have liked to hear," June remembered. Then, when no one felt like talking anymore, they all got up and blew him a kiss.

When June left the cemetery and arrived at home, she happened to glance at Oscar's chair—the one no one else could sit in without triggering an outburst—and the tears came. In the days following Levant's death there were flowers and many phone calls; Irving Berlin called June every night for a week. Lee Gershwin, Vincente Minnelli, Sam Goldwyn, Emily Paley, and Fred Astaire stopped by the house. Even Leonard Bernstein called. But "the first few days were pretty bad and I was a little crazy," June remembered. Unable to sleep even with the help of a sleeping pill, June restlessly entered Oscar's bedroom one night soon after the funeral. The sleeping pill she had taken wasn't working, so she thought Oscar might have hidden away a stronger sedative. "I knew there was nothing in the bathroom," she thought. Oscar had stopped taking sedatives toward the end of his life, but she looked through the drawers in his room. Nothing. Once upon a time, it had been a house filled with pills; now it was clean as a bone. There was nothing to help her sleep.

Next to his bed, she found a number of handwritten notes her husband had jotted down so he could refer to them when he spoke to Adolph Green or Goddard Lieberson on the telephone. "I saw some kind of yellow newspaper and thought, 'What is he saving that for?' And I opened it up, and it was part of a *New York Times* that had reported the death of Eleanor Roosevelt. He loved her," June re-membered.

He knew everything about her. He thought she was everything good and wonderful, like you would feel about a mother. And I thought, "that's the sweetest thing to save as a remembrance . . ." And I opened up the yellow page and out fell a single pill—a prescription sedative. And you know what I did? I said, "Thank you, Oscar." It was exactly what I was looking for. Out of Eleanor Roosevelt's obituary. Isn't that something!

Notes

Oscar Levant's witticisms and remarks were often quoted in numerous magazines and newspapers throughout his lifetime. Since media accounts of Levant's remarks often vary, we have relied on Levant's own three books, *A Smattering of Ignorance*, *The Memoirs of an Amnesiac*, and *The Unimportance of Being Oscar*, as well as the unedited transcript of *The Memoirs of an Amnesiac*, for our main sources. Occasional undated and sometimes unattributed newspaper items are from June Levant's extensive scrapbooks of Levant press clippings, which she kindly made available to us.

Abbreviations of frequently cited works and archives:

Mem	Oscar Levant, *The Memoirs of an Amnesiac*
Sm	Oscar Levant, *A Smattering of Ignorance*
Un	Oscar Levant, *The Unimportance of Being Oscar*
Mtr	Unpublished transcript, *The Memoirs of an Amnesiac*, Oscar Levant Papers, Library of Congress (frequently unpaginated fragments or redundantly paginated manuscript pages; undated)
AMA	Academy of Motion Picture Archives, Center for Motion Picture Study
USC	Oscar Levant papers, Cinema–Television Library and Archive, University of Southern California
WB	Warner Bros. archives, Cinema–Television Library and Archive, USC
LPA	Library of Performing Arts, Lincoln Center
NYT	*The New York Times*
WP	*The Washington Post*
LAT	*Los Angeles Times*
PP	*The Pittsburgh Press*
NY	*The New Yorker*
NYP	*New York Post*

PRELUDE

xii   "high seriousness": Michael Tilson Thomas remarks on Los An- geles Philharmonic concert broadcast, Dec. 5, 1981.

xii   "a man of fragments": Clifford Odets, *The Time Is Ripe: The 1940 Journal of Clifford Odets*, p. 176.

CHAPTER 1: THE UNMENTIONABLE CITY

3   "I've always been": Un, photo caption following p. 98.

3   "I paid thousands": Mtr.

3   Information on the Jewish immigrant experience in Pittsburgh: Kurt Pine, *The Jews in the Hill District of Pittsburgh, 1910–1940, a Study of Trends,* and *By Myself I'm a Book, an Oral History of the Immigrant Jewish Experience in Pittsburgh.*

4   Family records and genealogy researched by Marsha Saron Dennis and from an excerpted letter giving family history written by Le- vant's uncle Maurice Radin, dated March 28, 1966.

5   "If Warsaw": Mem, p. 41.

5   Information on Levant's family and boyhood in Pittsburgh: Au- thors' interviews with Oscar Radin, March 3 and 4, 1991, and November 11, 1992; with Marc Levant, May 4, 1991; with Joan (Levant) Rodenberg, August 9, 1991.

6   "He ate ham": Mem, p. 44.

6   "That kind of": Ibid.

6   "My mother was inarticulate": Mem, p. 43.

7   "the most undemonstrative": Mem, p. 147.

CHAPTER 2: THE MAKING OF A *CHUCHUM*

9   "*Chutzpah*—that quality": Un, pp. 146–7.

9   "like bamboo shoots": Mem, p. 39.

10   "Are you still": Ibid.

10   Levant's letter to his mother, USC archive and Un, p. 98, photo insert.

10   "the eldest was given": "Oscar Levant Studied Piano against Will," PP, April 22, 1940.

11   "Sure, he could play": Kaspar Monahan, " 'Big Brother' Gives Lowdown on Oscar Levant," PP, August 11, 1941.

11   "I never quite overcame": Mem, p. 41.

11   "The thumb must never": Sigismond Stojowski, "Practice as an Art," *The Etude,* September 1937, p. 565.

12   "You'll never be": Mtr.

13   "A son murders": Mem, p. 42.

14   "Slap" anecdote: Oscar Radin interview, March 4, 1991, and Mtr.

15   "Balzac, Gilbert and Sullivan": Mem, p. 44.

16   "After one chorus": Sm, p. 148.

16   "Thus were established": Sm, p. 149.

CHAPTER 3: THE "PADEROOSKI" OF COLWELL STREET

17   "What did you want": Mem, p. 38.

18   Information on Fifth Avenue High School and Forbes Elementary School from the late Tom Baker, an authority on Pittsburgh's school system, and from "Finale for Fifth Avenue," PP, June 6, 1976.

18   "it was unheard of": "Finale for Fifth Avenue."

18   Levant's report card from Pittsburgh Public Schools.

18   Information on Oscar Demmler from PP, August 11, 1941.

19   "Do you want to hear": Oscar Radin interview, March 4, 1991.

19   "I got to know a great deal": Levant, "Odyssey of Oscar Levant," *The Etude,* May 1940, p. 316.

20   "Yes, he plays well": Harold C. Schonberg, *The Great Pianists from Mozart to the Present,* p. 284.

21   Information on cancer treatments and cancer in the popular imagination in the early 1900s: James T. Patterson, *The Dread Disease: Cancer and Modern American Culture* (Harvard University Press, 1987).

22   "My father was a great man": Mtr.

22   "a personal approach": Oscar Radin interview, March 3, 1991.

CHAPTER 4: THE MAIN STEM

27   "Integrity is a lofty": Mtr.

27   "a gentlemanly homosexual": Mtr.

28   "There are a certain": Sigismond Stojowski, "Practice as an Art," *The Etude,* September 1937, p. 565.

28   "Among the various": Ibid.

29   "As enthralled as I was": Mem, p. 53.

30   "There was much action": Mem, p. 64.

30   "He would urinate": Mtr.

31   Information about *Spice of 1922* and Florenz Ziegfeld and his *Midnight Frolics* and *Follies:* Randolph Carter's *The World of Flo Ziegfeld,* Charles Higham's *Ziegfeld,* and Allan Churchill's *The Theatrical '20s.*

31   "I always liked girls": Mem, p. 51.

31   "looked like the Louvre": Mtr.

31   "I ruined it": Mtr.

32   "the most Recently Invented": NYT, September 24, 1905.

32   "How does it go?" anecdote: Mtr.

33   "a livelier tune": Mtr.

CHAPTER 5: STAIRWAY TO PARADISE

34   "It didn't really affect me": Mem, p. 53.

35   "[At] the end of the piece": Mem, p. 64.

35   "As Paderewski patted": Ibid.

35   "he doesn't have the soul": Oscar Radin interview, March 3, 1991.

35   Information on Al Jolson from a variety of sources, most notably Herbert G. Goldman's *Jolson* and Michael Freedland's *Jolson*.

36   "emblematic of the energies": Irving Howe, *World of Our Fathers*, p. 566.

36   "Jolson and Brice": Gilbert Seldes, quoted in Howe, p. 566.

36   "Yiddish schmaltz": Howe, pp. 562–3.

37   "nearly all had rooms": Jimmy Durante and Jack Kofoed, *Nightclubs*, p. 232.

37   "a not too subtle": Mem, p. 63.

37   "I thought [it] would": Mem, p. 53.

38   "I loved Colwell Street": Mem, p. 60.

38   customers would wash their genitals: Oscar Radin interview, March 4, 1991.

38   "They charged $1": Mem, p. 59.

39   "Since I had been oriented": Sm, p. 149.

39   "a slothful": Ibid.

39   "beautiful hands": Sm, p. 7.

39   "his limitations are boundless": Mem, p. 56.

39   "one of the causes": Information on the early perception of jazz from NYT, January 30, 1922, and George Newell's "George Gershwin and Jazz," *The Outlook*, February 29, 1928.

40   "Jazz was considered": Aaron Copland and Vivian Perlis, *Copland, 1900–1942*, p. 95.

40   "febrile tornado": Mtr.

41   "I had developed": Mem, p. 66.

41   "a good deal": Sm, p. 266.

CHAPTER 6: THE EMPERORS OF BROADWAY

43   "When I was young": Mem, p. 26.

43   The Congress anecdotes: Authors' interview with Doris "Dossie" (Levant) Scadron, November 17, 1992.

45   "one of the ironies": Mem, p. 118.

45   "the realm of high audacity": Stephen Talty, "Inside 'Billy Bathgate,'" *American Film*, July 1991.

45   "If you had a graduate course": Jimmy Durante and Jack Kofoed, *Nightclubs*, p. 206.

46   "You were not only in": Mem, p. 72.

46   "The name of the piano player": Abel Green and Joe Laurie, Jr., *Show Biz, from Vaude to Video,* p. 217.

47   "This made me": Mem, p. 72.

CHAPTER 7: "SAX-O-PHUN"

48   "Long before I": Sm, p. 147.

49   "exposed, first hand,": Mtr.

50   "As good hosts": Mem, p. 84.

50   "leaning forward": Mem, p. 94.

50   "It was the scene": Howard Dietz, *Dancing in the Dark,* pp. 60–61.

50   "an unprepossessing": Mem, p. 84.

50   "a shambling Mercutio": Behrman's introduction to Sm, p. x.

50   "I was fond": Dietz, p. 61.

51   Information on Balaban & Katz: "Music in the Theatre," *Exhibitors Herald-World,* September 28, 1929; "Popular Novelties Feature the Pit Orchestra," by Lewis Adrian; further information from "Will Symphony, Opera and Film Join Hands?" *Musical America,* January 24, 1928.

51   "I'd love to": Mtr.

51   "My example of": Mem, p. 75.

52   "Can dance rhythms": Olin Downes, NYT, undated, June Levant clippings file.

52   "just one or two": Mtr.

52   "The place swarmed": Franklin P. Adams, "The Conning Tower," *The World,* January 30, 1926.

53   "a subject for": Sm, p. 154.

53   "orgy of rhythm": Mtr.

53   "the Paderewski of": "Saxophone Questions Answered by Rudy Wiedoeft," *The Metronome,* September 1929, p. 70.

CHAPTER 8: ONE OF THE BOYS

55   "I had an affair": Mem, p. 78.

55   "one of the spate": Mem, p. 77.

55   "It was . . . the supreme": Laurence Bergreen, *As Thousands Cheer: The Life of Irving Berlin,* p. 252.

56   "I always managed": Mem, p. 77.

56   "bear social and sexual": Mtr.

56   Information on the Forty-Three Club: Humphrey Carpenter, *The Brideshead Generation, Evelyn Waugh and His Friends,* pp. 77–8.

56   "The club was": Mtr.

57   "I couldn't": Mtr.

57   "I always felt": Un, p. 30.

57 "about as friendly": S. N. Behrman, "Profiles: Accoucheur," NY, February 6, 1932, p. 20.

57 "it was his early": Ibid.

58 "Change all of your": Lyrics from "Keep Sweeping the Cobwebs off the Moon," reprinted with permission of Warner-Chappell Music.

58 "Discussing his fondness": Behrman, p. 20.

58 "He was like": Undated letter from Levant to June Gale.

58 "I couldn't canter": Mem, p. 93.

59 "I could never get": Mtr.

59 "They printed the orchestration": Authors' interview with Stanley Adams, July 7, 1991.

59 "a little bit": Ibid.

59 "For a man" anecdote: Adams interview.

59 "Teutonic father": Mem, p. 90.

60 "because, among other": Mem, p. 95.

CHAPTER 9: *BURLESQUE*

61 "Gee, Mazie": Corruption of line from *Burlesque,* by George Manker Watters.

61 "the wandering minstrel": Marc Levant interview, May 4, 1991.

62 "bragging to me": Oscar Radin interview, March 3, 1991.

62 "You know, Ma": Mtr and Mem, pp. 43–4.

62 Information on *Burlesque* from Allan Churchill's *The Theatrical '20s* and "And Who Is Mr. Watters?" NYT, September 4, 1927.

63 "Maybe some of us": Watters, line from *Burlesque.*

63 "putty nose comedians": J. Brooks Atkinson, "Casting and Comedy," NYT, September 11, 1927.

63 "actors, [who] for once": Ibid.

63 Information on Hal Skelly: "The Rise of Hal Skelly," NYT, October 2, 1927.

65 "I always felt": Mem, p. 83.

66 "the maternal impulse": Behrman, introduction to Sm, p. x.

67 "half a dozen": Mem, p. 82.

CHAPTER 10: THE WIDENING CIRCLE

68 "Oscar, I've been hearing": Maurice Zolotow, "Lucky Oscar, Sour Genius of the Keyboard," *Saturday Evening Post,* October 21, 1950, p. 24.

68 "But of course": Damon Runyon, "Sense of Humor," *The Bloodhounds of Broadway and Other Stories,* p. 243.

69 "Lindy's sandwich shop prospered": "Lindy's Sandwich Shop," NYT, July 21, 1957.

69 "the same thing": " 'Original' Lindy's Closes Saturday," NYT, July 21, 1957.

69 "great bowls of": "The Passing Parade at Lindy's," NYT, August 4, 1957.

69 "Sandwiches in": " 'Original' Lindy's."

69 "Got an item?": St. Clair McKelway, *Gossip: The Life and Times of Walter Winchell*, p. 84.

69 "used to jeer": Ibid.

69 "a thrilling bore": McKelway, p. 30.

70 "baloney" etc.: Mencken on Winchell: H. L. Mencken, *The American Language*, pp. 331–2.

71 "I don't want": Michael Mok, "Here's Broadway's Herring Barrel Philosopher," NYP, June 27, 1938.

71 "George was tall": Un, p. 100.

72 "To a swell": Mem, p. 65.

72 "In the minds": Marion Meade, *Dorothy Parker: What Fresh Hell Is This?*, p. 320.

72 "Why, it got": Sm, p. 88.

72 "a tiny woman": Ibid.

73 "could not tolerate": Un, p. 104.

73 "arguing with you": Sm, p. 163.

73 "an orchestra on": Sm, p. 150.

74 "I like mine better": Mtr; account of Levant's visit to Gershwin after he had recorded *Rhapsody in Blue* differs slightly from his version in Sm.

75 "Levant hails from": "The Piano Player of *Burlesque*": NYT, June 17, 1928.

75 "If he likes": Ibid.

76 "a neurotic love affair": Mtr.

76 "an obsession": Authors' interview with David Diamond, December 12, 1991.

76 "There was nothing": Remarks prepared for the Medallion ML 310 recording *Oscar Levant for the Record*.

77 "[Gershwin's] music summed": Ibid.

CHAPTER 11: *THE DANCE OF LIFE*

81 "In 1929, every": Mem, p. 27.

82 "no boardinghouses": Harpo Marx with Roland Barber, *Harpo Speaks!*, p. 351.

82 "What do you know": Ibid.

83 "I had the two": Mtr.

84 "In his screen": Miles Kreuger, "The Roots of the American Musical Film (1927–32)," Notes, Museum of Modern Art Department of Film; and Ronald Haver's study, "The Selznick Style: The Dance of Life," 1979.

85 "Don't put your hands": Mtr.

85 "On Sunday nights": Mem, p. 97.

85   "girls denude themselves": Mtr.
85   "Pretty girls were": Mtr.
86   "intellectual baby": Un, p. 136.
86   Levant's love affair with Nancy Carroll: Authors' interview with June Levant, May 22, 1992, and Mtr.
87   "Inasmuch as": Sm, p. 95.
87   "However": Sm, p. 94.
87   "the man who": Mark A. Miller, "The Wild and Woolly Wit of Wheeler and Woolsey," *Film Fax,* October/November 1991, No. 29, p. 80.
87   Information about Levant and Sydney Clare collaboration from *The American Film Catalogue Index,* Vol. II, and authors' interview with Michael Feinstein, June 20, 1991.
88   "In *Shall We Dance*": Feinstein interview.
89   "There are only": Ibid.
89   "since RKO": Un, p. 132.
90   "My job had": Ibid.
90   "He was in a line": Un, pp. 132–3.
90   Information on Levant's affair with Virginia Cherrill: June Levant interview, May 22, 1992, and Un, p. 135.
90   "I'm sorry they": Un, p. 135.
91   "a little dull": Mtr.
91   "The one thing": Un, p.135.

CHAPTER 12: PENTHOUSE BEACHCOMBER

93   "An evening with": Sm, p. 170; when the remark first appeared in print, only Gershwin's last name was used; retellings used his full name.
95   "I . . . acquired": Sm, p. 156.
96   "How's your show": Ibid.
96   "After she had": Sm, p. 157.
96   "Like a missionary": Ibid.
97   "I escorted her": Ibid.
97   "Leonore was a": Ibid.
97   "Darling, please": Truman Capote, "The Muses Are Heard," *The Dogs Bark,* Part II, p. 232.
98   "Do me a favor": Howard Koch and Elliot Paul, *Rhapsody in Blue* (Warner Bros., 1945).
98   Lee Gershwin gave Levant his first sleeping pill: Mtr and June Levant interview, July 17, 1990.
98   "Gershwin couldn't run": David Diamond interview, December 12, 1991.
99   "My tactic": Sm, p. 155.
99   "The two pianos": Sm, p. 158.
100   "penthouse beachcomber": Sm, p. 159.

100   "There's a lovely": Mem, p. 102, and authors' interview with Barbara (Smith) Cornett, May 23, 1992.

CHAPTER 13: VARIOUS DEBUTS

102   "Who goes to": Clifford Odets, Zachary Gold, *Humoresque* (based on a story by Fannie Hurst; Warner Bros., 1946).

102   "the Beethoven of": Information on Robert Russell Bennett from *Current Biography,* NYT, August 19, 1981, NBC Music Research Files, and Mtr.

103   Information about the Hollywood Bowl: Carol Reese, "The Hollywood Bowl 1919–1989, Parts 1 and 3," *Performing Arts,* July 1989; and Herbert Glass, "The Hollywood Bowl and Its Performers, Part 2," *Performing Arts,* August 1990.

103   "the monotonous New York": LAT, July 21, 1930.

103   Information on Lewisohn Stadium, its summer music festivals, and Minnie Guggenheimer: *Time,* August 26, 1940; NYT, July 5, 1931, August 18, 1938, February 13, 1965, June 29, 1966, August 16, 1964, and April 7, 1973; and S. Willis Rudy's *The College of the City of New York: A History, 1847–1947.*

105   "Mr. Gershwin is": Olin Downes, "A Program of Native Works," NYT, August 9, 1931.

106   Ben Bernie anecdote: Mtr.

106   Marriage proposal anecdote: Barbara (Smith) Cornett interview, May 23, 1992, and Mtr.

106   "I said that": Mem, p. 40.

107   "a rather successful": Mem, p. 104.

107   "You're not in": Mtr.

108   "You can imagine": Mem, p. 104

108   "I could not": Ibid.

108   "apoplectically": Ibid.

108   "George, Barbara's forehead": Mem, p. 105.

109   "of skiing": Sm, p. 164.

109   "That's nice, Oscar": Mem, p. 105, and Mtr (slightly different wording).

109   "Barbara [Wooddell], who": Bob Thomas, *Winchell,* p. 119.

109   "Don't ever print": Un, p. 88.

109   "So I'm a": Ibid.

110   "As a hotel": Sm, p. 165.

110   "walk about three": Mtr.

110   "It relieved the": Ibid.

111   "Toscanini had never": Mem, pp. 119–20.

112   "George at the piano": Mem, p. 122, and Mtr.

112   Oscar Radin anecdote: Oscar Radin interview, November 11, 1992.

CHAPTER 14: OSCAR AMONG THE COMPOSERS

114 ". . . to the next": Sm, p. 226.

114 "miscellaneous evenings": Sm, p. 222.

114 "We *must* have": Aaron Copland and Vivian Perlis, *Copland, 1900–1942,* p. 130.

115 "The musical structure": Mtr.

115 Information on First Festival of Contemporary American Music at Yaddo: Alfred H. Meyer, "Yaddo—A May Festival," *Modern Music,* Vol. IX, No. 4, May–June 1932; "The Yaddo Music Festivals," Yaddo *Newsletter,* Spring 1980; and Copland and Perlis.

116 "A new generation": Sm, p. 221.

116 "There was on": Sm, pp. 221–2.

116 "You'll never be": Mtr.

116 "How strange the": Copland and Perlis, p. 177.

117 "I must recount": Sm, p. 223.

118 "All that saved": Ibid.

118 "Before the concert": Ibid.

119 "pure dross and": Mtr.

119 "Now try to": Eric A. Gordon, *Mark the Music: The Life and Work of Marc Blitzstein,* p. 75.

119 "Broadway (lower & noise)": Ibid.

119 "[*Serenade*] reflected": Sm, p. 224.

119 "surprisingly unsubtle": Ibid.

119 "the fairies' baseball": Mtr.

119 "This was a": Sm, p. 225.

119 "American music need": Alfred H. Meyer, *Modern Music,* May–June 1932, p. 172.

120 "The long-standing": Copland and Perlis, p. 206.

CHAPTER 15: A NEW YORK DIVORCE

121 "Besides incompatibility": Mem, p. 109.

121 "After I had": Sm, p. 230.

122 "I loved his": Barbara (Smith) Cornett interview, May 23, 1992.

122 "an unforgivable and": Mem, p. 125.

123 "I had my eye": Ibid.

123 "a beautiful lover": Barbara (Smith) Cornett interview.

123 "So the coat": Mem, p. 106.

124 "I can lay": Sm, p. 201.

124 "conditioned by the": Sm, p. 164.

124 "17,000 persons": NYT, August 17, 1932.

125 "The audience was": Ibid.

125 "a small boy": Sm, p. 166.

126 "It is by": Ibid.

126 "with a questionable": Mtr.

127   "little popular music": Sm, pp. 259–60.

127   "an indistinguishable": Mtr.

128   "Do me a favor": Authors' phone conversation with Artie Shaw, April 12, 1993.

128   "I refused his": Barbara (Smith) Cornett interview.

128   "I always felt": Ibid.

129   "I was a little": Mtr.

129   "What's playing at": Mem, p. 109.

129   "I roared": Barbara (Smith) Cornett interview.

CHAPTER 16: EXILES AND MOGULS

131   "Sorry, I didn't get": Mem, p. 110.

132   "the great house": Un, p. 130.

132   "Dmitri, that is": Un, p. 131.

133   "the 'enfant terrible' ": Salka Viertel, *The Kindness of Strangers,* p. 197.

133   "reserved, polite": Viertel, p. 161.

133   "I didn't know": Mem, p. 166.

133   "As for conversation": Sm, p. 71.

133   Greta Garbo anecdote: Mem, p. 110.

134   "When the inaccessible": Un, p. 126.

134   "mock French opera": Sm, p. 72.

134   "I found him": Sm, p. 110.

135   "I tell you": Sm, p. 111.

136   "a boor": Authors' interview with Jean Howard, June 30, 1991.

136   "incredibly boorish": Viertel, p. 134.

136   "an unbenevolent tyrant": Mem, p. 111.

136   "He was one": S. N. Behrman, "You Can't Release Dante's 'Inferno' in the Summertime," NYT, July 17, 1966.

136   "My duties were": Mem, p. 111.

136   "the music department," quoted in Otto Friedrich, *City of Nets,* p. 41.

137   "the direction was": Norman Sherry, *The Life of Graham Greene,* p. 408.

137   "She was warm": S. N. Behrman, *People in a Diary,* p. 138.

138   "That's a rather": Mtr.

138   "If you wanted": Mtr.

CHAPTER 17: CRIMES WITHOUT PASSION

139   "Mine was the": Sm, p. 232.

140   "the air of": Sm, p. 170.

140   "I adjusted myself": Ibid.

141   "reduction of all": Sm, p. 177.

141   "He wrathfully accused": Sm, p. 178.

141   "I chose him": Mtr.
141   "I was still": Mtr.
142   "so fulsomely": Mtr.
142   ". . . a beautiful song": Authors' interview with Michael Feinstein, June 20, 1991.
143   "is the better": Alec Wilder, *American Popular Song*, pp. 482–3.
143   "to sneer at": Sm, p. 231.
144   "orchestration was a": Ibid.
144   "tiraded eloquently on": Sm, p. 232.
145   "My association with": Sm, p. 113.
146   "With a generous": Sm, pp. 113–4.
147   "About five in": Mem, p. 115.
147   "as if Einstein": Otto Friedrich, *City of Nets*, p. 32.

CHAPTER 18: THE LION IN EXILE

149   "We had endless": Mem, p. 137.
150   "Ladies don't write": David Ewen, *American Songwriters*, p. 158.
150   "The Levant-Fields": "In Person" file, AMA.
150   "How did you" anecdote: Sm, p. 104.
151   "Brought finally to": Otto Friedrich, *City of Nets*, p. 33.
151   "Think of it!": Sm, pp. 127–8.
151   " 'What do you": Friedrich, p. 34.
152   "from the beginning": Mtr.
152   ". . . most of the": Sm, pp. 125–6.
153   "Airplane music?": Sm, p. 126, and David Raksin interview, May 16, 1992.
153   "You have a": Un, p. 152.
153   "I can see": Mem, p. 130.
153   "Who will play": Ibid.
153   "I do not": Ibid.
154   "the constant acerbity": Mem, p. 133.
154   "two innocent bars": Mem, p. 130.
155   "When I studied": Un, p. 147.
155   "This concerto": Draft of Program Note, NBC Symphony program, February 17, 1942, USC.
155   "The concerto is": Virgil Thomson, "Levant Tough and Tender," *New York Herald Tribune*, February 18, 1942.
155   "[your] relentlessly serious": Mem, p. 133.
156   "I didn't think": Un, p. 146.
156   "Schoenberg was very": Mem, p. 133.
156   "had once had": Mem, p. 131.
156   "sandwiches, little sausages": Salka Viertel, *The Kindness of Strangers*, p. 197.
157   "It's a right": Mem, p. 126.
157   "I have felt": Variant versions in Mtr and Mem, p. 126.

157   "Gershwin does not": Thomson, *Herald Tribune,* October 11, 1935.

158   "This opera is": Scott Darling and Charles S. Belden, *Charlie Chan at the Opera* (20th Century–Fox, 1936).

158   "This son-of-a-bitch": "Program Notes," Department of Radio/Television/Film, University of Texas, Vol. 15, No. 1, October 4, 1978, p. 117.

158   "Since this is": Sm, p. 118.

158   "I had heard": Sm, p. 117.

158   "The music had": Michael Feinstein, liner notes for *Oscar Levant, For the Record* (Medallion ML 310).

159   "it had a": Sm, p. 119.

CHAPTER 19: THE GREAT HOUSES

160   "During the Depression": Mem, p. 150.

161   "tea at six": Laurence Bergreen, *As Thousands Cheer,* p. 194.

161   "Let's all go": Authors' interview with Herbert "Ottie" Swope, Jr., February 29, 1992.

161   "Herbert wasn't the": Authors' interview with Dorothy (Paley) Hirshon, July 22, 1992.

162   "It was the": Ibid.

162   "almost fifty rooms": Mtr.

162   "He can afford": Interview with Herbert "Ottie" Swope, Jr.

163   "She used to": Ibid.

163   "nine tears" anecdote: Ibid.

164   "lamb girl": Howard Teichmann, *George S. Kaufman,* photo caption, photo insert.

164   "Idiot Boy": Mem, p. 166.

164   "undiscovered and": Scott Meredith, *George S. Kaufman and His Friends,* p. 50.

165   "the hardest job": Harpo Marx with Roland Barber, *Harpo Speaks!,* p. 346.

165   "a combination Retreat": Marx and Barber, p. 345.

165   "Harpo, I'm coming" and subsequent dialogue: Marx and Barber, pp. 347–9.

165   "He was a": Marx and Barber, p. 348.

165   "in reality a": Sm, pp. 54–5.

165   "the most beloved": Mem, p. 151.

166   "One can only": Sm, p. 54.

166   "C'mon, professor": Sm, p. 65.

166   "unable to enjoy": Marx and Barber, p. 349.

166   "He had wit": Ibid.

166   "The amount of": Ibid.

167   ". . . in the middle": Ibid.

167   "The rarest gift": Marx and Barber, p. 350.

CHAPTER 20: CONCERT OF MISSED NOTES

168   "Whenever anybody turns": Sm, p. 75.
168   "George was a": Mem, p. 129.
168   "subtlely spotted business": Sm, p. 187.
169   "His chest": Mem, p. 129.
169   "A lot of": Ibid.
169   "such men as": Sm, p. 183.
169   "It looks so": Sm, p. 185.
169   "string-quartet players": Sm, p. 187.
170   "the tallest conductor": Mtr.
171   "this was the opportunity" anecdote: Mem, p. 135.
171   "To this day": Ibid.
171   "That's like asking": Ibid.
171   "It was a": Ibid.
171   "Dr. Klemperer is": Sm, p. 74.
171   "When he had" anecdote: Sm, pp. 74–5.
172   "What's your hurry?": Sm, p. 75.
173   "I liked the": Mem, p. 136.
173   "Ordinary fogs are": Sm, pp. 137–8.
174   "If a composer": Sm, p. 142.
174   "play us a medley": June Levant interview, June 19, 1991.
175   "that's what *I*": David Raksin interview, May 16, 1992.
175   "He was programmed": June Levant interview, May 19, 1992.
175   "Ah, . . . here comes": Ibid.
175   "Oscar Levant was": Authors' interview with Kitty Carlisle Hart, September 9, 1992.
176   "I noticed that": Sm, p. 198.
176   "not terribly expressive": Mem, p. 145.
176   "When I made": June Levant interview, January 12, 1993.

CHAPTER 21: SOMEONE TO WATCH OVER ME

177   "You have an": Mem, p. 33.
177   "That's the best": Ibid.
178   "I'm standing waiting": June Levant interview, July 11, 1990.
178   "He would just": Ibid.
178   "We were always": Ibid.
179   "He's a crazy": Ibid.
179   "When I was": Ibid.
179   "In those days": Mem, p. 33.
180   "I guess I": June Levant interview, July 14, 1990.
180   "Oscar was sexy": Ibid.
180   "Something is going": quoted in Copland and Perlis, *Copland, 1900–1942,* p. 270.

180   "closed corporation": Ibid.
180   "It was hard": Copland and Perlis, p. 271.
181   "Copland expressed his": Sm, pp. 235–6.
182   "It was pure": June Levant interview, June 19, 1991.
182   "You don't know": Mem, p. 138.
183   "I remember how": June Levant interview, June 19, 1991.
183   "artistic temper tantrums": June Levant interview, June 14, 1991.
183   "When George came": Sm, p. 201.
183   "had lived all": S. N. Behrman, *People in a Diary,* p. 256.
183   "one-fourth or one-half": Mtr.
184   "It's disgusting": June Levant interview, June 14, 1991.
184   "People thought that": Mem, p. 146.
184   "its lack of": Sm, p. 204.
185   ". . . there is reason": Edward Jablonski, *Gershwin,* p. 326.
185   "In those days": Behrman, p. 251.
185   "All the time": Behrman, p. 252.
185   "Hollywood's parlor psychiatrists": Jablonski, p. 322.
185   "Oscar and I": June Levant interview, June 14, 1991.
185   "Oscar was playing": Ibid.
186   "George kept moving": Mtr.
186   "I stared at": Behrman, p. 253.
186   "I had to live": Ibid.
187   "George is dead": Mtr and June Levant interview, June 14, 1991.
187   "The time of": Mem, p. 147.

CHAPTER 22: "DEAR JUNIE"

191   "God knows, Christ": Undated later to June Gale (Levant).
191   "Promise me you": Mtr.
191   "seven conductors": Michael Feinstein and Celia Grail, liner notes, *The Historical George Gershwin Memorial Concert, Hollywood Bowl, September 8, 1937,* Citadel Records.
192   "ease his emotional": Mem, p. 138.
192   "Our" concerto: Sm, p. 153.
192   "Levant might profitably": Isabel Morse Jones, LAT, September 9, 1937.
192   ". . . one is no": Marcel Proust, *Remembrance of Things Past,* Vol. 2, (Random House, 1981), p. 43.
192   "when the flames": Edith Hamilton, *Mythology* (New American Library, 1969), p. 172.
193   "the most arrogant": Otto Friedrich, *City of Nets,* p. 18.
193   "He had a": Sm, p. 129.
194   "The beach was": Irene Mayer Selznick, *A Private View,* p. 83.
194   "If I appeared" anecdote: Sm, p. 128.

195   "He had enormous": June Levant interview, May 22, 1992.

195   All letter excerpts quoted in this chapter are taken from undated letters from Oscar Levant to June Gale (Levant), roughly September 1937–December 1939. Courtesy June Levant.

196   "I had a": June Levant interview, May 22, 1992.

197   "There was something": Ibid.

198   "The short Andantino": Quoted in Levant letter to June Gale (Levant), undated.

198   "one of the most": *Robert Russell Bennett's Notebook* broadcast, WOR, December 22, 1940.

199   "I wonder if": Ibid.

199   "a sweet lady": June Levant interview, July 4, 1991.

202   "the responsibility": Ibid.

203   "good enough to": Sm, p. 142.

203   "savage playing" and Prokofiev anecdote: Mem, p. 141.

CHAPTER 23: THE UNKNOWN CELEBRITY

204   "I was only": Mtr.

204   "conscience of a": William Gibson's introduction to *The Time Is Ripe: The 1940 Journal of Clifford Odets*, p. x.

205   "an unhappy, rambunctious": Clifford Odets, *The Time Is Ripe*, p. 176.

205   "Success is the": Ibid., p. xii.

205   "I am tired": Margaret Brenman-Gibson, *Clifford Odets: American Playwright*, p. 430.

205   "Everything he was": Mem, p. 188.

206   " 'Well, when I": "And It Was," Hedda Hopper file, AMA.

206   "the most startling": Bosley Crowther, NYT, August 19, 1938.

207   "He refers to": Dorothy Kilgallen, *New York Journal*, 1938 (undated, June Levant clippings file).

207   "In Hollywood I": Michael Mok, "Here's Broadway's Herring Barrel Philosopher," NYP, June 27, 1938.

208   "by reversing the": "Development of Radio Program 'Information, Please!' Described," NYT, March 12, 1939.

208   "The program was": Joan Shelley Rubin, *The Making of Middlebrow Culture*, p. 321, and authors' interview with Clifton Fadiman, August 13, 1991.

209   "People liked it": Rubin, p. 321.

209   "seemed to like": Clifton Fadiman interview.

209   "We talked with": Authors' interview with Edith (Schick) Engel, February 14, 1992.

211   "unpredictable . . . there is": Franklin P. Adams, "Inside 'Information Please,' " *Harper's Magazine*, February 1942.

211   "a bit of": Clifton Fadiman interview.

211   "its style belonged": Rubin, p. 323.

211 "That's Beethoven": Quotations from tapes of *Information, Please!* broadcasts at the Recorded Sound Collection, LC.

212 "It fits the": Mem, p. 159.

212 "The program will": Mtr, and a version appears in Mem, p. 159.

212 "I had to give": Mtr.

213 "at all hours": Edith (Schick) Engel interview.

213 "If there'd be": Ibid.

213 "He felt sympathetic": Ibid.

214 "Please pass the": Maurice Zolotow, "Lucky Oscar, Sour Genius of the Keyboard," *Saturday Evening Post,* October 21, 1950, p. 152.

CHAPTER 24: DISTANT MUSIC

215 "I'll have to": Herbert Swope, Jr., interview, February 28, 1992.

215 "I will probably do": Undated letter to June (Gale) Levant.

216 "The reviews": Mtr.

217 "To keep Mr. Levant": "Distant Music," NY, April 1, 1939, p. 14.

218 "he never had": Barbara (Smith) Cornett interview, May 23, 1992.

218 "gruesome twosome": June Levant interview, July 4, 1991.

218 "We were happy": Ibid.

218 "But paradoxically": Ibid.

218 "Barbara thinks I'm": Barbara (Smith) Cornett interview.

219 "To the vast": Howard Taubman, NYT, July 11, 1939.

219 "gifted and": Samuel Chotzinoff, NYP, July 11, 1939.

220 "You'd be amazed": Undated letter to June (Gale) Levant.

222 "What do you": Mtr and Mem, pp. 34–5.

222 "she couldn't make": Ibid.

222 "I thought she": Ibid.

222 "Never in her": Anne Edwards, *Judy Garland,* pp. 54–5.

223 "For a throbbingly": Un, p. 54.

223 "We unconsciously grasp": Undated letter to June (Gale) Levant.

223 "If we had": Un, p. 53.

224 "dressed in white" anecdote and dialogue: June Levant interview, July 4, 1991.

224 "constantly reassured": Ibid.

225 "The close-up cameraman": Authors' interview with Clifton Fadiman, August 13, 1991.

226 "So I went": Interview with Ken McCormick, August 5, 1992.

226 "So we got": Ibid.

227 "He did more": Dorothy Herrmann's interview with Irving Kolodin, undated.

227 "Don't be taken": Undated letter to June (Gale) Levant.

227 "When he became": Kolodin interview.
227 "He began to": Irving Kolodin, "The Trouble with Oscar," *Saturday Review,* September 9, 1972, p. 13.
228 "I don't know": Mtr.
228 "a violent dichotomy": Mtr.

CHAPTER 25: "THE FUTURE MRS. L."

229 "You know I": June Levant interview, July 21, 1990, and Mem, p. 35.
229 "That lousy short": Undated letter to June (Gale) Levant.
229 "horrifically modern": Ibid.
229 "Not only was": Sm, p. 144.
230 "shrouded in": Undated letter to June (Gale) Levant.
230 "There was no": Mem, p. 206.
230 "a facility for": Sm, p. 37.
231 "can achieve": Ibid.
231 "How are you": Mem, pp. 206–7.
231 "like brilliants from": "Levant Trains on Coffee for Concert with Symphony," *Pittsburgh Post Gazette,* November 24, 1939.
231 "It's warm": Ibid.
232 "It is certain": D. S. Steinfirst, "Oscar Levant Scores Hit in Concert Here," *Pittsburgh Post Gazette,* November 25, 1939.
232 "started, and it": Oscar Radin interview, March 4, 1991.
232 "So, you call": Ibid.
232 ". . . most of the": Steinfirst.
233 "I've always had": Undated letter to June (Gale) Levant.
233 "empty-headed": June Levant interview, July 14, 1990.
233 "You have a part": June Levant interview, July 21, 1990.
234 "His answer was": Annotations by June Levant of Oscar Levant's letters.
234 "Why not?": June Levant interview, July 21, 1990.
234 "Oh, there's Oscar" anecdote: Ibid.
234 "confidentially, do you": Mem, p. 35.
235 "Oscar Levant": Walter Winchell, "On Broadway," *Daily Mirror,* December 4, 1939.
235 "He didn't want": June Levant interview, July 21, 1990.
235 "Ma, how do you" anecdote: Ibid.
235 "ran terrific houses": Ibid.
236 "Then we realized": Ibid.
236 "How do you": Ibid.

CHAPTER 26: GHOST MUSIC

237 "I played Gershwin": Mem, p. 148.
237 "they had a": Mtr.

238   "Rituals have taken": Mem, p. 15.

238   "the music expert": Milton Widder, "For Your Information, Oscar Levant Can Wisecrack—off and on the Radio," *The Cleveland Press,* January 3, 1940.

238   "I don't care": June Levant interview, July 15, 1990.

238   "a work of": Elmore Bacon, "Levant's Jazz Makes Concert Hit," *The Cleveland Press,* January 5, 1940.

239   "high seriousness": Michael Tilson Thomas, Los Angeles Philharmonic concert broadcast, December 5, 1981.

239   "I don't like": Widder, *The Cleveland Press.*

239   "With whose considerable": Sm, dedication page.

239   "a character who": Sm, p. xi.

239   "this book does": Ibid.

240   "I would like": Sm, p. 47.

240   "a hundred men": Sm, p. 4.

240   "I have a": Sm, p. 39.

240   "two characteristics": Sm, p. 149.

240   "only incidentally": Clifton Fadiman, "The Audacities of Oscar," NY, January 13, 1940, p. 61.

240   "pasted together": Lewis Gannett, "Books and Things," *New York Herald Tribune,* January 13, 1940.

241   "Now try to write": Sm, p. 225.

241   "like a meal": Sm, p. 224.

241   "magic and personality": Fadiman, p. 62.

241   "While the book": Ibid.

241   "After you have": Ken McCormick interview, August 5, 1992.

242   "get all the": Mtr.

242   "I have been": "Levant, in S.F., Ends His Old Feud with Woollcott," *The San Francisco Examiner,* March 23, 1940.

242   "[Levant] undertook a": June Levant clipping file.

242   "jammed every available": "Levant's Crowd Sets New Mark," *Philadelphia Record,* July 2, 1940.

243   "What makes you": Mtr.

243   "When I informed": Mem, p. 180.

244   "Dan Golem Paul": Mtr.

244   "They gave me": Duncan Underhill, "Levant Keeps ahead of Critics by Criticising Himself," *New York World Telegram,* August 24, 1940.

244   "An irritating book": Dwight Taylor, *Rhythm on the River,* Paramount, 1940; probably an improvised line of Levant's.

244   "I'd rather not": "Levant's Ad Lib Livens Set, But Sometimes Delays Work," *Brooklyn Daily Eagle,* August 3, 1941.

245   "is not Mr. Crosby": Howard Barnes, "On the Screen," *New York Herald Tribune,* August 29, 1940.

CHAPTER 27: THE TALKING PIANIST

246   "It's more fun": Mtr.
246   "She writes nasty": Mem, p. 174.
246   "He was always": June Levant interview, July 4, 1991.
246   "I just want": Barbara (Smith) Cornett interview, May 23, 1992.
246   "Oh, I want": June Levant interview.
247   "He's so self-conscious": "Levant Doesn't Like the Levant Movie," *New York Herald Tribune,* August 25, 1940.
247   "His favorite crack": "Oscar Levant: Sourpuss," undated, June Levant clippings file.
247   "Give him his": Ibid.
247   "It's the kind": "Levant Doesn't Like."
248   "He practiced more": Irving Kolodin, "The Trouble with Oscar," *Saturday Review,* September 9, 1972.
248   "He needed a figure": June Levant interview, May 15, 1992.
248   "Nothing infuriates me": Mtr.
249   "He was just": June Levant interview, May 15, 1992.
249   "This overture represents": Levant's Program Notes, Minneapolis Symphony Orchestra, attached to a letter from Arthur J. Gaines, Secretary-Manager, April 19, 1941, p. 1, USC.
249   "an unimportant year": Ibid.
249   "She used to": Mtr.
249   "nothing critical": Program Notes, p. 2.
250   "It only hurts": *Robert Russell Bennett's Notebook* broadcast, WOR, December 22, 1940.
250   "despite creating": Michael Tilson Thomas, Los Angeles Philharmonic concert broadcast, December 5, 1981.
250   "From my standpoint": Program Notes, p. 2.
250   "in about a": N.Y.A. Symphony Orchestra broadcast and interview with Oscar Levant, January 12, 1941.
250   Performances of Caprice for Orchestra: Joseph Smith, liner notes for *Blue Monday,* Concordia, Marin Alsop, conductor. Angel CDC 7 54851 2 7.
251   "Maybe it should": *Robert Russell Bennett's Notebook* broadcast, WOR, December 22, 1940.
251   "There you have" anecdote and dialogue: Ibid.
251   "a little man" anecdote and dialogue: Mem, p. 236.
252   "the ultimate father": June Levant interview, May 22, 1992.
253   "very funny patter": June Levant clippings file.
253   "as I was": Max de Schauensee, "Oscar Levant Appears Nervous at Academy Performance," *The Evening Bulletin,* March 10, 1943.
253   "I don't know": Edwin H. Schloss, "Oscar Levant Jokes and Gives Piano Recital," *Philadelphia Record,* March 10, 1943.
253   "It will be": Ibid.
253   "I feel a": Ibid.

254   "Be back in": Ibid.
254   "It made him": Authors' interview with Dorothy (Paley) Hir-
        shon, July 22, 1992.
254   "We were disappointed": Paul K. Damai, "Radio Short Cir-
        cuits," [Hammond, Ind.] *Times,* January 28, 1942.
255   "I've got to": H.R.B., "Oscar Levant Received Here with En-
        thusiasm," *St. Louis Globe Democrat,* November 17, 1941.
255   "intensity to the": Hector Charlesworth, "Levant Persiflage
        Mixed with Rare Pianistic Art," [Toronto] *Globe and Mail,* April
        28, 1944.
255   "There are two": Ibid.
255   "Always play to": Mem, p. 220.
255   "He loved going": David Diamond interview, December 12,
        1991.
257   "rather dramatic": Virgil Thomson, *New York Herald Tribune,*
        February 18, 1942.
258   "was not taken": Mtr.

                CHAPTER 28: A BARGAIN FOR A DEDICATION

259   "Talent's like a": "Levantics," Warner Bros. publicity material,
        WB.
259   "Dear Mr. Levant": Schoenberg letter to Levant, January 38,
        1939. Archives of the Arnold Schoenberg Institute, USC. Cour-
        tesy of Lawrence Schoenberg.
260   "How are you": Ibid., October 2, 1939.
260   "Suddenly, this small": Mem, p. 136.
260   "the first 132": Schoenberg letter to Levant, August 8, 1942.
260   "The negotiations had": Mem, p. 137.
260   "was delighted with": Mtr.
261   "a very good": Schoenberg letter to Levant, October 9, 1942.
261   "utterly and irrevocably": Levant telegram to Schoenberg, Octo-
        ber 12, 1942, Archives of the Arnold Schoenberg Institute, USC.
261   "with a marvelous": David Diamond interview, December 12,
        1992.
261   "Oscar, don't get": Ibid.
262   "Are you composing?": Mem, p. 137.
262   "Christ, what a": David Diamond interview.
263   "the goyim": June Levant interview, June 19, 1991.
263   "the Oscar Levant": Mtr.
263   "You don't want": Mtr and authors' interview with Edith
        (Schick) Engel, February 14, 1992.
264   "registered as the": "Listening In with Ben Gross," *Daily News,*
        January 14, 1943.
264   "I'm sicker than": Mtr.
264   "rap them mercilessly": Mem, p. 177.

265   "I am finished": "Oscar Levant, Here for Concert, Bows Out as Composer," *Washington Star,* 1943, June Levant clippings file.
265   "Yesterday, I finally": USC, undated.
265   "sort of compendium": Ibid.
266   "[wore] the most": "Profile," NY, July 7, 1975, p. 20.
267   "he plays the": Irving Kolodin, "The New Records," *New York Sun,* July 17, 1942.
267   "supreme": Kimball and Simon, *The Gershwins,* p. 235.

CHAPTER 29: "AGAIN, THE *RHAPSODY?*"

269   "It got very": "Mr. Levant Discusses Mr. Gershwin," NYT, July 8, 1945.
269   "Outside of our": WB.
270   "You know what": "Mr. Levant Discusses Mr. Gershwin."
270   "There was almost none": Ibid.
270   "He is now": WB.
271   Levant's concert fees and film salary: Ibid.
271   "Even the lies": "Mr. Levant Discusses Mr. Gershwin."
272   "The Gershwins were": Mem, p. 147.
272   "Why are you": "Mr. Levant Discusses Mr. Gershwin."
272   "It got very": Ibid.
272   "The camera was": Ibid.
273   "You're fresh": Dialogue from Howard Koch and Elliot Paul, *Rhapsody in Blue* (Warner Bros., 1945).
274   "One more suspension": Irving Rapper, letter to authors dated September 17, 1991.
274   "incredible synthesis": Sm, p. 181.
275   "Mr. Levant, you're": Dialogue from Koch and Paul.
276   "Why did you": Mem, p. 181.
276   "The player who": Howard Barnes, *New York Herald Tribune,* June 28, 1945.
276   "as a pianist": "Oscar Levant Week," *Pittsburgh Sun Telegraph,* June Levant clippings file.
277   "Mr. Gershwin wanted" anecdote and dialogue: Mtr and Mem, p. 210.
278   "He was so": Mem, p. 210.
278   "Should I killa": Ibid.
278   "the greatest living": *Life* magazine, November 27, 1939.
278   "Toscanini had a": June Levant interview, July 4, 1991.
278   "I think Toscanini": Mtr.
279   "She was bored" and "an unwilling victim": Mem, p. 214.
279   "A wild glint": Mem, p. 215.
279   "Poor man . . . he": Mem, p. 213.
280   "Bad shows were": Marc Levant interview, May 4, 1991.

CHAPTER 30: ENDLESS BLEEDING

281 "The hummingbird is": Maurice Zolotow, *No People Like Show People,* p. 144.

281 "I find most": Mtr and Mem, pp. 177–8.

282 "You're a natural": Mtr and Mem, p. 177.

282 "According to your": Ibid.

282 "My pride had": Ibid.

283 "Do you think": Mem, p. 178.

283 "It was all": Mtr.

283 "a beautiful Chateaubriand": Gottfried Reinhardt, *The Genius: A Memoir of Max Reinhardt,* p. 310.

283 "Never inaugurate fun": Ibid, p. 311.

283 "Who did you": Maurice Zolotow, "Lucky Oscar, Sour Genius of the Keyboard," *Saturday Evening Post,* October 21, 1950, p. 82.

284 "The hummingbird is": Zolotow, *No People Like Show People,* p. 144.

284 "Just kick 'em": Un, p. 17.

284 "poor people, and": Authors' interview with Alfred Vanderbilt, Jr., July 11, 1991.

285 "They used to"; Ibid.

285 "turned against me": Mtr.

286 "A marriage of": Mem, p. 235.

286 "graciously, but with": Ibid.

287 "I like Lenny": Oscar Levant on *The Jack Paar Show,* April 3, 1964.

287 "He uses music": Mem, p. 235.

287 "Leonard Bernstein has": Mem, p. 236.

287 "It reflects a": Mtr.

287 "I remember thinking": Un, p. 14.

287 "My flatfooted Renaissance": Mem, p. 235.

287 "[It] had a": Ibid.

287 "full of hate": Mem, p. 225.

288 "I wouldn't have": Mtr.

288 "Heifetz was the": Un, p. 30.

CHAPTER 31: *HUMORESQUE*

290 "Frank Costello gets": Mem, p. 174.

290 "those whose careers": Mtr.

291 "It is Levant's": Maurice Zolotow, "Lucky Oscar, Sour Genius of the Keyboard," *Saturday Evening Post,* October 21, 1950, p. 82.

291 "That terrible number!": Ibid.

291 "Oscar, . . . you really": Authors' interview with Herbert "Ottie" Swope, Jr., March 27, 1992.

291 "bemused, bitter, and": Mem, p. 48.

292   "I was let": Mem, p. 182.

292   "the Jewish problem": WB.

292   "In this outline": WB.

292   "As you well": Rudy Behlmer, *Inside Warner Bros. (1935–1951),* p. 266.

293   "Why don't the": Mtr and June Levant interview, May 19, 1992 (another version in Mem, p. 183).

293   "People don't go": Mem, p. 182.

294   "You can't advise": Clifford Odets and Zachary Gold, *Humoresque* (Warner Bros., 1946). Many of Levant's own remarks were incorporated into the film.

294   "The whole point": Ibid.

294   "Who goes to" and following dialogue: Ibid.

295   "I envy people": Ibid.

295   "crazy about money": Ken McCormick interview, August 5, 1992.

296   "The place was": June Levant interview, June 19, 1991.

296   "Out of bed": Ibid.

296   "Do you knit": Jean Negulesco, *Things I Did . . . and Things I Think I Did,* p. 132.

296   "icebergs on the": Ibid.

297   "Anything that Oscar": June Levant interview, May 19, 1992.

297   "no more fights": Undated letter to June (Gale) Levant.

297   "he would get": June Levant interview.

297   "I was sitting": Ibid.

297   "He was playing": David Diamond interview, December 12, 1991.

297   "Now where Oscar": Ibid.

298   "I never drank": June Levant interview.

298   "He just had": Ibid.

298   June's lawsuit: "Wife Sues Levant for Support," NYT, November 25, 1947.

299   "Des Moines" anecdote: Un, p. 144.

299   "Horowitz used to": Mem, p. 217.

299   "Horowitz's octave playing": Mem, p. 218.

300   "Vlodya, don't you": Glenn Plaskin, *Horowitz, a Biography,* pp. 257–8.

300   "Decadent" anecdote: Mtr.

300   "He was happy": June Levant interview, May 15, 1992.

301   "Horowitz made his": Un, p. 144.

301   "No matter how": Mem, p. 219.

301   "What is it": David Diamond interview, December 12, 1991.

301   "Isn't it a": Ibid.

302   "What, after all": Ibid.

303 "noise composers": Elise K. Kirk, *Music at the White House, A History of the American Spirit,* p. 254.

303 "If I make": Mem, p. 242, and Mtr

303 "Now I guess": Ibid.

304 "ruin my social": Herbert Swope, Jr., interview, February 29, 1992, and alluded to in Mem, p. 172.

305 "Frank Costello gets": Mem, p. 174.

CHAPTER 32: *ROMANCE ON THE HIGH SEAS*

306 "I knew Doris": Authors' phone interview with Doris Day, May 16, 1992.

306 "How long is" and all other dialogue in William Morris Agency office: Charles Isaacs, "Swannie Song," *Park East, The Magazine of New York,* October 1951, pp. 29–31.

308 "I didn't want": Herbert G. Goldman, *Jolson, The Legend Comes to Life,* p. 281.

308 "Jolson was constantly": Phone interview with Charles Isaacs, December 12, 1992.

308 "bordered on the": Goldman, p. 282.

308 "I loved being": Mem, p. 193.

309 "The shows have": Isaacs, "Swannie Song," p. 32.

309 "I'm just as happy": Ibid.

309 "I don't like": Levant, "Scratching the Surface," *The Saturday Review,* August 30, 1947, p. 15.

310 "I sometimes like": A. E. Hotchner, *Doris Day, Her Own Story,* p. 93.

310 "I was very": Doris Day interview.

310 "Oscar kept us": Ibid.

310 "knew Doris Day": Ibid.

311 "Oscar's line, 'Man' ": Production Code Administration letter, Joseph I. Breen to J. L. Warner, June 13, 1947, WB.

311 "I've seen girls": Earl Wilson, NYP, undated, WB.

CHAPTER 33: FREED AT LAST

317 "It's not a": Alan Jay Lerner, *An American in Paris,* MGM, 1951.

317 "You're out of": Mem, p. 20.

318 "whacking the keys": Olin Downes, "Levant Is Soloist for Philharmonic," NYT, December 30, 1949.

319 "those snobs who": June Levant interview, May 19, 1992.

319 "Oscar was at": Adolph Green, "Oscar Levant, 1906–1972," NYT, August 27, 1972.

320 "What the hell": Ibid.

320 "for a rematch": Fred Astaire, *Steps in Time,* p. 294.

320   "preening and parading": Mtr and Mem, p. 196 (expurgated).

321   "What are they": Mtr and slightly different version in Sarah Giles, editor, *Fred Astaire, His Friends Talk,* p. 13.

322   "Arthur Freed would": Authors' interview with Adolph Green, November 23, 1991.

322   "[Pianists] do their": Un, p. 130.

322   "He's a bit": Hyman Goldberg, "Ever Hear of Harry Levant's Brother?," NYP, September 16, 1941.

323   "We thought of": Vincente Minnelli, *I Remember It Well,* p. 229.

323   "I don't want": Mem, p. 200.

324   "That's a marvelous": Donald Knox, *The Magic Factory,* p. 53.

324   "Oscar's got a": Ibid.

324   "Had Oscar not": Knox, p. 54.

324   "[Sitting] on top": Knox, p. 6.

324   "She looks too": Mem, p. 201.

324   "I was so": Knox, p. 85.

325   "so cute and": June Levant interview, May 19, 1992.

325   "an unusual, somber": Andrew Sarris, *The American Cinema,* p. 101.

325   "I'm a concert": Alan Jay Lerner, *An American in Paris* (MGM, 1951).

325   "It's not a": Ibid.

325   "credit-sharer": Mtr.

326   "Never was there": Knox, p. 89.

326   "devoted to Kelly's": Stephen Harvey, *Directed by Vincente Minnelli,* p. 102.

327   "[The] thing": Knox, p. 175.

327   "morbidly beautiful": Andrew Sarris's introduction to Knox, p. xi.

327   "Some may believe": Minnelli, p. 235.

328   "Have you heard": June Levant interview, May 19, 1992.

CHAPTER 34: RENDER UNTO CAESAR

329   "I can stand": Adolph Green (and Betty Comden), *The Band Wagon* (MGM, 1953).

330   "I'd like some": Nunnally Johnson (uncredited), *O. Henry's Full House* (20th Century–Fox, 1952). Probably Levant's ad-lib.

330   "We need a": Otto Friedrich, *City of Nets,* p. 383.

330   "They thought I": Friedrich, p. 381.

331   "a blaze of": Norman Nairn, "Levant Shares Ovation with Leinsdorf," undated review in June Levant clippings file.

332   "They're mine": "James Petrillo Dead: Led Musicians," NYT obituary, September 25, 1984.

332   "Fatigued is an": Mem, p. 246.

334   "You've had a" anecdote and dialogue: June Levant interview, January 12, 1993.

334   "Your father's very": Ibid.

335   "He would talk": Ibid.

336   "Oscar was down": Authors' interview with Nanette Fabray, June 25, 1991.

336   "So I did": Mem, p. 202.

337   "That was physically": Nanette Fabray interview.

337   "[H]e didn't say": Ibid.

337   "I can stand": Green, *The Band Wagon* (MGM, 1953).

337   "a terrific performance": Authors' interview with Betty Comden and Adolph Green, November 23, 1991.

337   "I treated her": Mem, p. 201.

338   "My whole memory": Nanette Fabray interview.

338   "*The Band Wagon* matches": Stephen Harvey, *Directed by Vincente Minnelli*, p. 116.

338   "If he can": Mtr. and June Levant interview, June 19, 1991.

338   "They [were] typical": Ibid.

339   "As Levant walked": "Battling Levant," *Newsweek*, March 23, 1953.

339   "Diminuendo": "Evening of Discord, Angry Pianist Levant Shouts at Conductor," undated, June Levant clippings file.

339   "Call him!": Mtr.

340   "Where were you born?" anecdote: Mtr and Mem, p. 250.

340   "It got him": June Levant interview, June 19, 1991.

340   "When Oscar had": Ibid.

CHAPTER 35: THE REIGN OF TERROR

341   "Self–pity—it's": *The Steve Allen Show*, NBC, June 29, 1958.

341   "Don't tell Mr.": June Levant interview, May 15, 1992.

341   "Get off that": Ibid.

341   "I'll play Portland": Mem, p. 250.

342   "unfair dealings": "Pianist Oscar Levant Suspended by Petrillo," undated, June Levant clippings file.

342   "Oscar Levant's deft": "Petrillo Accuses Levant of Run-Out," NYT, April 19, 1953.

342   "I have an": Ibid.

342   "I became addicted": Mtr.

343   "He just thought": June Levant interview, May 15, 1992.

343   "Meany, hell!": Un, p. 212.

344   "I'm going to": "Oscar Levant Swallows Pride and Squirms as Petrillo Calls Tune on Pianist's Future," NYT, June 10, 1953.

344   "James C. Petrillo": Murray Kempton, "Levant Terrible," NYP, June 10, 1953.

344   "sinew and muscle": Mem, p. 251.

345   "I have been": Letter from Murray Kempton to Oscar Levant, Wednesday, no date, June Levant clippings file. Courtesy of Murray Kempton.

345   "unbearable neurotic hysteria": Mem, p. 252.

345   "He still looks": Harriet Johnson, "Words and Music," NYP, no date, June Levant clippings file.

346   "use of the": Letter from Dr. Ralph R. Greenson to Dr. Charles Thompson, November 12, 1953, Las Encinas Hospital records.

347   "75 mg. Demerol": Oscar Levant's clinical chart for October 12–14, 1953.

347   "He was getting": June Levant interview, May 19, 1992, and Mem, p. 254.

347   "I just got": June Levant interview, May, 1992.

347   "At times he": Dr. Greenson letter to Dr. Thompson, November 12, 1953, Las Encinas Hospital records.

348   "How are we": June Levant interview, May 19, 1992, and Mem, pp. 256–8.

348   "cadaverous-looking": Ibid.

348   "You'd better go" anecdote and dialogue: Ibid.

350   "There's just no": Ibid.

CHAPTER 36: PARADOXICAL EXCITEMENT

351   "I was always": Mtr.

351   "very depressed and": Dr. K. P. Nash, Levant medical history taken November 11, 1953, p. 2, Las Encinas Hospital records.

351   "I can't commit": June Levant interview, May 19, 1992.

352   "I might add": Letter from Dr. Greenson to Dr. Thompson, November 12, 1953, p. 2, Las Encinas Hospital records.

352   "What are you": Mtr.

352   "Those are my": Levant's hallucinations at Las Encinas from Dr. Thompson, medical report, November 12–26, 1953.

353   "I just want": Ibid.

353   "a mad Walpurgis": Mem, p. 260.

353   "He was furious": June Levant interview, May 19, 1992.

353   "I was always": Mtr.

353   "defective Narcissism": Authors' interview with Dr. John Urbach and Dr. James Levenson, November 2, 1992.

354   "Oscar was more": Herbert Bayard Swope, Jr., interview, March 27, 1992.

354   "The old man": Ibid.

354   "There was a": Authors' interview with Lorna Levant, June 6, 1991.

355   "If you don't": "Oscar Levant Suicide Report Held Mistake," LAT, February 26, 1954.

355   "Paraldehyde!": Mtr.

356   "What makes you": Mtr.

356   "played one out": Mem, p. 262.

356   "I failed again": June Levant interview, May 19, 1992.

356   "Every time I": Mtr.

356   "How are you?" anecdote: Mem, p. 262.

357   "The sick look": Harold V. Cohen, " 'The Cobweb' Comes to the Harris," c. June 7, 1955, June Levant clippings file.

357   "M is for": William Gibson and John Paxton, *The Cobweb* (MGM, 1955).

358   "Minnelli wanted it": Authors' interview with John Kerr, May 16, 1992.

358   "He liked flirting": Ibid.

358   "Who's crazy anyway": Mtr.

359   "held in a": Las Encinas Hospital medical records.

359   "And then": Paul Hume, "Levant Thrills at a Canted Piano," *Washington Post and Times Herald,* June 25, 1955.

359   "I played the": Mem, p. 263.

360   "somewhat Mozartean": Hume.

360   "went out and": Lorna Levant interview, June 6, 1991.

361   "That's it": June Levant interview, May 19, 1992.

CHAPTER 37: CHAOS IN SEARCH OF FRENZY

362   "Shock treatments, anyone?": Mem, p. 267.

362   "the most erudite": Authors' interview with Joe Hyams, July 1, 1991.

362   "Marcia, Marcia, we're": June Levant interview, June 19, 1991.

362   "I knew she": Ibid.

363   "It was a": Un, p. 120.

363   "James Dean and Oscar": Joan Collins, *Past Imperfect,* p. 84.

363   "I have now": Mtr.

363   "Isn't she gorgeous!": June Levant interview, January 12, 1993.

363   "Always a bride": Un, p. 120.

363   "I always thought": Adolph Green interview, November 23, 1991.

363   "He was a": Authors' interview with Fred Friendly, September 10, 1992.

364   "morgue": Ibid.

364   "No panelist working": Lyons, NYP, undated, June Levant clippings file.

364   "Frank De Vol was": Authors' interviews with Al Burton, July 10, 1990, and January 13, 1993.

364   "hit of the": "Words About Music," *Daily Variety,* January 31, 1956.

365   "Utterly degraded": Al Burton interview, July 10, 1990.

365   "I taught Mario": *Daily Variety*

365   "a darned good": Herb Stein, *Morning Telegraph,* February 22, 1956.

365   "People called it": Al Burton interviews.

365   "lovable about Democrats": Mem, p. 265.

365   "He swings a": Ibid.

365   "the whole purpose": "Levant Almost Ankles Show When CBS Prohibits 'Words' About '56 Presidential Race," *Daily Variety,* April 30, 1956.

365   "Once Oscar pulled": Al Burton interviews.

365   "Zsa Zsa Gabor": " 'Words' Dickered for Net Showing," undated, June Levant clippings file.

365   "Strip the phony": Mtr and quoted in Leslie Halliwell, *Halliwell's Filmgoer's and Video Viewer's Companion,* p. 684.

366   "the most pretentious": Mem, p. 265.

366   "anybody who took": Ibid.

366   "as a balance": Ibid.

366   "chaos in search": Ibid.

366   "Now that Marilyn": Ibid.

366   "I didn't mean": Ibid.

366   "I suspect that": Mem, p. 266.

367   "one incalculable pleasure": Mem, p. 268.

368   "I had an": Mem, p. 15.

368   "I wake up": Mem, p. 27.

368   "Shock treatments": Mem, p. 267.

368   "Oscar Levant has": Author's interview with Arthur Marx, May 25, 1992.

369   "Thanks for a": Mem, p. 269.

369   "He was happy": Arthur Marx interview.

369   "I'm leaving you": June Levant interview, January 12, 1993.

370   "extremely arrogant and": Phone interview with Dr. Victor Monk, October 13, 1992.

370   "Suddenly, I forgot": Mem, p. 272.

371   "His vocational career": Dr. K. P. Nash, Levant medical history report, Las Encinas Hospital records.

371   "What ever became": Mem, p. 275.

371   "Would you play": Mem, p. 276.

372   "In my condition": Ibid.

372   "It was the": June Levant interview, January 12, 1993.

372   "I've changed": Mem, p. 277.

373   "Everybody in town": Don Freeman, *San Diego Union,* undated, June Levant clippings file.

373   "Perry Como's voice": Ibid.

373   "But when bores": Ibid.

373   "This is Oscar": Bob Jennings, "Frenzied Road Back," *Time,* May 5, 1958.

374   "I idolized Oscar": Al Burton interview, July 10, 1990.

374   "a doctor who": Mem, p. 278.

374   "Why would he": Mtr.

374   "not only made": Mem, p. 279.

374   "Charming, warmhearted Christopher": Un, p. 194.

375   "I cultivate my": Charles Baudelaire, quoted in Un, p. 194.

375   "completely unmasked at": Phil Jensen, "TV's Wackiest Genius,"
       p. 54, undated, June Levant clippings file.

375   "Manic and full": Mem, p. 286.

375   "Let's go to": Ibid.

375   "I don't know": Mem, pp. 286–7.

CHAPTER 38: *THE OSCAR LEVANT SHOW*

376   "I wish I": *The Oscar Levant Show,* KCOP-TV, May 6, 1958.

376   "There weren't enough": June Levant interview, June 19, 1991.

376   "It's very relaxing": Phone interview with Nancy Livingston,
       May 14, 1992.

377   "He was preparing": Lorna Levant interview, June 6, 1991.

377   "Everything went from": Amanda Levant interview, July 15,
       1990.

377   "as wistful as": Mem, p. 282.

377   "Suicide . . . is the": Joe Hyams, "Oscar Levant's Neurosis a TV
       Hit," *New York Herald Tribune,* April 28, 1958.

378   "He seemed close": "Looking Back," undated, June Levant clip-
       pings file.

378   "a real concerto": Robert Riley, "L.A. Music Fete Concert Wins
       Praise," *Citizen-Times,* June 3, 1958.

378   "He played the": Arthur Marx interview, May 25, 1992.

378   "One day Fred": June Levant interview, June 14, 1991.

379   "a year of": Fred Astaire, *Steps in Time,* p. 321.

379   "I never expected": Don Freeman, "Levant Program Wins Top
       Praise," *San Diego Union,* May 12, 1958.

379   "I wrote songs": *The Fred Astaire Songbook,* PBS Great Perform-
       ances.

379   "They were very": *The Oscar Levant Show,* KCOP-TV, May 6,
       1948.

379   "it was a": Freeman.

379   "Fred, . . . I'm so": *The Oscar Levant Show,* May 6, 1948.

380   "But for Oscar": Bob Jennings, "Frenzied Road Back," *Time,*
       May 5, 1958.

380   "It isn't hard!": Ibid.

380   "No one knew": Al Burton interview, January 13, 1993.

380   "Never before has": Jennings.

381   "What about the": Michael Feinstein interview, June 20, 1991,
       and Mem, p. 285.

382 "Philco promised me" anecdote: *The Oscar Levant Show,* KCOP-TV, June 21, 1958.

382 "they'll take anybody": Ibid.

382 "From the upper": Freeman, *San Diego Union,* undated, June Levant clippings file.

382 "HAVE JUST CANCELLED": Oscar Levant Papers, USC.

382 "Everything depends": " 'Bounced' Levant Bounces Right Back," undated, June Levant clippings file.

383 "Flanagan is the": Ibid.

383 "I have the": Joe Hyams, "Levant's Side of TV Dispute," *New York Herald Tribune,* June 23, 1958.

CHAPTER 39: UNDER PAAR

384 "Someone once asked": Mtr.

384 "Already the 'Affair' ": Joe Hyams, "Levant's Side of TV Dispute," *New York Herald Tribune,* June 23, 1958.

385 "wouldn't allow anybody": Earl Wilson, "It Happened Last Night," NYP, June 30, 1958.

385 "I could never": Un, p. 26.

385 "That woman hit": "Quarrel Over Other Women Brings Police," *Beverly Hills Citizen,* July 10, 1958.

386 "Meanwhile," Burton recalled: Al Burton interview, July 10, 1990.

386 "I never cheat": Un, p. 26.

386 "I want to": "Levant Feud Goes Legal; Oscar Sued for Divorce," *The Mirror News,* July 11, 1958.

386 "He should remember": "Levant's Wife Sues for Divorce," no date, June Levant clippings file.

387 "now a prominent": "Levant Feud Goes Legal."

387 "He had to": Vincente Minnelli, *I Remember It Well,* p. 324.

387 "The family maid": Joe Hyams interview, July 1, 1991.

388 "She's a wonderful": Radio Reports transcript, week of May 21, 1958, *The Oscar Levant Show,* USC.

388 "Anyone want to": Ibid.

388 "God, is this": June Levant interview, July 17, 1990.

389 "This was the": Alma Gowdy, "Levant Finds Pals at Bowl," *Los Angeles Herald Express,* August 4, 1958.

389 "I'm going to": Mtr.

389 "He returned and": Gowdy.

389 "I'm playing under": Albert Goldberg, "Gershwin Fans Fill Up Bowl," June Levant clippings file.

390 "Why should everything": Al Burton interview, July 10, 1990, and Mem, p. 291.

390   "I was the": Mem, p. 278.

390   "Mae West is": Mtr.

390   "I said outrageous": Mtr.

390   "I said, 'Please": June Levant interview, May 22, 1992.

390   "I'm just tired": Al Burton interview.

391   "[When] I rang": Jack Paar, *P.S. Jack Paar,* p. 170.

391   "a man for": *The Jack Paar Tonight Show,* NBC, November 5, 1958.

391   "Oscar, you're a" and subsequent dialogue: Ibid.

392   "unquestionably one of": William Ewald, November 7, 1958, June Levant clippings file.

392   "It was his": Jack Gould, "TV: Oscar Levant on Jack Paar Show," NYT, November 7, 1958.

392   "There is a": *The Jack Paar Tonight Show,* November 5, 1958.

393   "He just really": June Levant interview, May 22, 1992.

CHAPTER 40: "GOOD NIGHT, OSCAR LEVANT, WHEREVER YOU ARE"

394   "More blankets!": Leonard Lyons, "The Lyons Den," NYP, January 10, 1962, and Un, p. 226.

394   "a husband. Must": *Los Angeles Mirror News,* undated, June Levant clippings file.

394   "I'd like to": June Levant interview, May 22, 1992.

394   "Miss Louise Constable": Undated, June Levant clippings file.

394   "wonderful company": Authors' phone interview with Gore Vidal, January 18, 1993.

395   "I was like": Mtr.

396   "What pills have" anecdote: Joe Hyams interview, July 1, 1991.

397   "the moaning Jewish": Mem, p. 312.

397   "the young girl": Mtr.

397   "I haven't been": Joe Hyams, "Levant Loves to Adopt Ailments," *New York Herald Tribune,* June 27, 1961.

397   "keen, alert, and": Ibid.

398   "Oscar Levant should": Jack O'Brian, "Bring Back Oscar Levant," *New York Journal-American,* June 12, 1961.

398   "The meeting was": Interview with Bill Marx, May 28, 1992.

398   "a borderline physician": June Levant interview, July 21, 1990, and Mtr.

398   "I can't turn": Ibid.

399   "Don't you dare" anecdote: Ibid.

400   "It gave me": Mtr and Mem, p. 314.

400   "I couldn't leave": June Levant interview, July 21, 1990.

401   "No. I won't": Joe Hyams interview, July 1, 1991.

401   "went into a snit": Amanda Levant interview, July 15, 1990.

401   "It was sad": Authors' interview with Betty Comden, November 23, 1991.

402   "More blankets!": Lyons, and Un, p. 226.

402   "I remember a": NYP, October 10, 1952, June Levant clippings file.

402   "you have to": Lyons.

402   "I had one": Mtr.

402   "It was the": June Levant interview, May 22, 1992.

402   "Get out of": Hedda Hopper interview with June Levant, June 28, 1962, Hedda Hopper file at AMA.

402   "Good night, Oscar": Mem, p. 298.

CHAPTER 41: *THE MEMOIRS OF AN AMNESIAC*

403   "So little time": Mtr.

403   "He didn't age": June Levant interview, January 12, 1993.

403   "out of the": *The Jack Paar Show,* NBC, February 5, 1963.

403   "knew he would": June Levant interview.

403   "How are you?" and subsequent dialogue: *The Jack Paar Show,* February 5, 1963.

404   "On it went": Don Freeman, "To Oscar Levant—Welcome Back," *San Diego Union,* February 12, 1963.

404   "Oscar Levant, American" and subsequent dialogue: *The Jack Paar Show,* October 11, 1963.

404   "I do believe": Freeman.

405   "I'm the only" anecdote: June Levant interview and Mem, p. 317.

405   "Let's be honest": Herbert Swope, Jr., interview, March 27, 1992.

405   "he had managed": Jonathan Lieberson, "The Unimportance of Being Oscar," *The New York Review of Books,* November 20, 1986, p. 37.

405   "I felt so": Swope interview.

406   "No, I was": Hedda Hopper file, October 22, 1963, AMA.

406   "Levant's rudeness is": Lieberson, p. 38.

406   "I haven't had": Un, p. 152.

407   "Did it ever": *The Jack Paar Show,* December 18, 1964.

407   "What a place": Lieberson, p. 38.

407   "I'm not a": Dorothy Herrmann interview with William Targ, October 22, 1980.

407   "a shabby contract": Ibid.

408   "A tragic and": Mem, p. 52.

408   "This biography is": Mem, p. 142.

408   "Oscar, I've just": Phone conversation with William Targ, March 13, 1990, and the anecdote appears in Targ's *Indecent Pleasures,* p. 265.

409 "This book is": Mtr.
410 "About Oscar there": Clifton Fadiman, "Anatomizing Oscar: A Friend Looks at Levant," *Holiday,* November 1965, USC archive.
411 "Those are just": *The Joey Bishop Show,* CBS–TV, October 11, 1964.
411 "Well . . . how do": Un, p. 224.
411 "submerged June": Mtr.
412 "Why not plug" and subsequent dialogue: Un, p. 225.
412 "every modern composer": Ibid.
412 "They were shocked": June Levant interview, May 19, 1992.
412 "still looking boyish": Un, p. 145.
413 "When I first" anecdote: Lieberson, p. 36.
413 "It was the sixties" anecdote: June Levant interview, May 22, 1992.
413 "I've grown unaccustomed": June Levant interview and Mem, p. 19.
413 "his big brave": Mtr.
414 "so I could": June Levant interview, January 12, 1993.
414 "Well, the piano": Mtr.
414 "Did you ever": June Levant interview.
415 "At the end": Mem, p. 32.

CHAPTER 42: REMEMBERING AND FORGETTING

416 "I love songs": Candice Bergen, "Good–Night, Oscar Levant," *Esquire,* April 1973, p. 206.
416 "Here's the advance": June Levant interview, May 19, 1992.
416 "These later books": Jonathan Lieberson, "The Unimportance of Being Oscar," *The New York Review of Books,* November 20, 1986, p. 38.
417 "She just married": Un, p. 111.
417 "Well, what do": June Levant interview, July 4, 1991.
417 "a Caliban–caricature": Mem, p. 12.
417 "they could do": Mem, p. 11.
417 "He started to" and Nocturne anecdote: Lorna Levant interview, June 6, 1991.
418 "As I rose": Irving Kolodin, "The Trouble with Oscar," *Saturday Review,* September 9, 1972, p. 14.
418 "1019 North Roxbury": Ibid.
418 "He had a": Phone interview with Roddy McDowall, June 15, 1991.
418 "were badly typed": Marion Meade, *Dorothy Parker: What Fresh Hell Is This?,* p. 401.
418 "Over the years": Dorothy Parker, in Roddy McDowall, *Double Exposure,* pp. 43–5.
419 "I love this": Mem, p. 24.

419   "I would like": S. N. Behrman letter to Levant, May 26, 1970, USC.

420   "waging their campaign": Bergen, p. 88.

420   "incomparables of the": Joyce Haber, "Intimate Gathering for Chaplin Tribute," LAT, April 11, 1972.

420   "I had to": June Levant interview, May 19, 1992.

420   "The weather was": Bergen, p. 88.

420   "Reminiscences abounded during": Haber.

421   "Sulking in the": Bergen, p. 88.

421   "He wore a": Ibid.

421   "Oscar Levant . . . the recluse": Haber.

421   "I was never": Bergen, p. 89.

422   "He seemed very" and subsequent conversation: Ibid.

422   "I had one": Lorna Levant interview, June 6, 1991.

423   "I saw Oscar": Adolph Green, "Oscar Levant, 1906–72," NYT, August 27, 1972.

423   "Dearest Osc,": S. N. Behrman letter to Levant, July 13, 1972, USC.

423   "I thought I": Jon Colman, "A Tourists' Guide Through an Illusion," Los Angeles Times Calendar, July 30, 1972.

423   "I understand why": Ibid.

424   "I deeply resent": Levant letter to the editor, "A 'Rich' Levant," Los Angeles Times Calendar, August 13, 1972.

424   "I didn't catch": David Ansen, "Richard Avedon: A Life in Pictures," Newsweek, September 13, 1993, p. 53.

424   "the best, most": Ibid.

425   "study of drowning": Ibid.

425   "Can't you come": Bergen, p. 89.

425   "You know what" and subsequent conversation: Bergen, pp. 89 and 204.

425   "Isn't that a": Bergen, p. 204.

425   "Does my blinking": Ibid.

426   "What's the matter": Bergen, p. 206.

426   "more personal than": Ibid.

426   "He opened a": Ibid.

426   "I've had more": Ibid.

427   "What happened to": June Levant interviews, July 21, 1990, and January 12, 1993.

427   "Four o'clock—that's": Bergen, p. 206.

427   "Oh, God,": June Levant interview, January 12, 1993, and Bergen, p. 206.

428   "I had never": Bergen, p. 206.

428   "I never got": June Levant interviews, July 21, 1990, and January 12, 1993.

428   "What's the man's": Bergen, p. 205.

428   Behrman's dream: June Levant interview, January 12, 1993, and
        Behrman letter, USC.

CODA

429   "In some situations": Charles Maher, "Acid-tongued Levant May
        Get Show on Network," LAT, July 12, 1958.
429   "I have something": June Levant interview, January 13, 1993.
429   "Oscar never could": Ibid.
429   "In addition to": Clifton Fadiman, "Fadiman to Miss His Friend,"
        Santa Barbara News-Press, August 15, 1972.
430   "For behind the": Burt Prelutsky, "A Scream His Mating Call,"
        undated, June Levant clippings file.
430   "There were no": Amy Arched, *Daily Variety,* undated, June Le-
        vant clippings file.
430   "the first few": June Levant interview, January 13, 1993.
430   "I saw some" anecdote: Ibid.

Bibliography

Levant's papers exist significantly in two places: the Cinema-Television Archive at the University of Southern California and the Music Room at the Library of Congress in Washington, D.C. An invaluable source was the unedited transcript of taped reminiscences made by Levant in 1965, which formed the basis of his autobiographical *The Memoirs of an Amnesiac;* the transcript includes previously unpublished material.

Published Books and Articles by Oscar Levant

A Smattering of Ignorance. New York: Doubleday, Doran & Co., Inc., 1940.
The Memoirs of an Amnesiac. New York: G. P. Putnam's Sons, 1965.
The Unimportance of Being Oscar. New York: G. P. Putnam's Sons, 1968.
"Odyssey of Oscar Levant," ed. by R. Heylbut. *The Etude,* May 1940, pp. 316ff.
"Music at Home," *Good Housekeeping,* April 1940, pp. 34–5.
"Scratching the Surface," two columns in *Saturday Review,* August 30, 1947, p. 30, and September 27, 1947, p. 50.

Archives

American Academy of Motion Picture Arts and Sciences, Center for Motion Picture Study, Los Angeles, Calif.
Arnold Schoenberg Institute, University of Southern California, Los Angeles, Calif.
Columbia University Oral History Collection, New York, N.Y.
Manuscript Division, Library of Congress, Washington, D.C.
Motion Picture, Broadcasting, and Recorded Sound Divisions, Library of Congress, Washington, D.C.
Museum of Broadcasting Collection, New York, N.Y.
Music Library, Yale University, New Haven, Conn.
Oscar Levant Archive, Music Division, Library of Congress, Washington, D.C.
Oscar Levant Collection, Cinema Special Collections, Cinema-Television Archive, University of Southern California, Los Angeles, Calif.

The Performing Arts Research Center, The New York Public Library at Lincoln Center, New York, N.Y.

UCLA Film and Television Archive, University of California, Los Angeles, Calif.

Letters

Levant–S. N. Behrman, courtesy David Behrman.

Levant letters to June Gale (Levant), courtesy June Levant.

Levant–Schoenberg correspondence, Schoenberg Institute, USC, courtesy Lawrence A. Schoenberg.

Dr. Ralph Greenson's letters to Dr. Charles Thompson, courtesy Hildi Greenson.

Published Works

Adler, Polly. *A House Is Not a Home.* New York: Rinehart & Company, 1953.

Alpert, Hollis. *The Life and Times of Porgy and Bess.* New York: Knopf, 1990.

Anderson, Clinton H. *Beverly Hills Is My Beat.* Englewood Cliffs, N.J.: Prentice-Hall, 1960.

Anger, Kenneth. *Hollywood Babylon.* San Francisco: Straight Arrow Books, 1975.

Ansen, David. "Richard Avedon: A Life in Pictures," *Newsweek,* September 13, 1993, pp. 44–78.

Armstrong, William. "Sigismond Stojowski and His Views on Piano Study," *The Etude,* Vol. 24, No. 5, May 1906.

Astaire, Fred. *Steps in Time.* New York: Harper and Brothers, 1959.

Atkins, Irene Kahn. "The Image of Oscar," *Focus on Film,* No. 30, June 1978.

Atkinson, Brooks. *Broadway.* New York: Macmillan, 1970.

Bailey, Walter B. "Oscar Levant and the Program for Schoenberg's Piano Concerto," *Journal of the Arnold Schoenberg Institute,* Vol. VI, No. 1, June 1982, pp. 56–79.

Behlmer, Rudy. *Inside Warner Bros. (1935–1951).* New York: Viking, 1985.

———. *Memo from David O. Selznick, Selected and Edited by Rudy Behlmer.* New York: Grove Press, 1972.

Behrman, S. N. *People in a Diary, A Memoir by S. N. Behrman.* Boston: Little, Brown and Co., 1972.

———. "Profile" of George Gershwin, *The New Yorker,* May 25, 1929.

Bergen, Candice. "Good-Night, Oscar Levant," *Esquire,* April 1973, pp. 88–9, 204–6.

Bergreen, Laurence. *As Thousands Cheer: The Life of Irving Berlin.* New York: Viking, 1990.

Brenman-Gibson, Margaret. *Clifford Odets: American Playwright.* New York: Atheneum, 1981.

Cantor, Eddie, and David Freedman. *Ziegfeld, the Great Glorifier.* New York: Alfred H. King, 1934.

Capote, Truman. "The Muses Are Heard," *The Dogs Bark.* New York: Plume, 1977.

Carpenter, Humphrey. *The Brideshead Generation, Evelyn Waugh and His Friends.* Boston, New York, London: Houghton Mifflin Co., 1990.

Collier, James Lincoln. *Benny Goodman and the Swing Era.* New York and Oxford: Oxford University Press, 1989.

Collins, Joan. *Past Imperfect.* New York: Simon and Schuster, 1984.

Copland, Aaron, and Vivian Perlis. *Copland, 1900–1942.* New York: St. Martin's/Marek, 1984.

Daniel, Oliver. *Stokowski, A Counterpoint of View.* New York: Dodd, Mead & Co., 1982.

Dietz, Howard. *Dancing in the Dark.* New York: Quadrangle/The New York Times Book Co., 1974.

Dubal, David. *Evenings with Horowitz, A Personal Portrait.* New York: Birch Lane Press, 1991.

Durante, Jimmy, and Jack Kofoed. *Nightclubs.* New York: Knopf, 1931.

Edwards, Anne. *Judy Garland: A Biography.* New York: Simon and Schuster, 1975.

Ewen, David. *George Gershwin, His Journey to Greatness* (reprint). New York: Unger, 1970.

Fadiman, Clifton. *Any Number Can Play.* New York: Avon, 1957.

———. *Party of One.* Cleveland: World Publishing, 1955.

Fordin, Hugh. *The Movies' Greatest Musicals, Produced in Hollywood for the Freed Unit.* Revised edition of *The World of Entertainment.* New York: Unger, 1984.

Frank, Gerold. *Judy.* New York: Harper and Row, 1975.

Freedland, Michael. *Jolson.* New York: Stein and Day, 1972.

Friedrich, Otto. *City of Nets, A Portrait of Hollywood in the 1940s.* New York: Harper and Row, 1986.

Giles, Sarah, ed. *Fred Astaire, His Friends Talk.* New York: Doubleday, 1988.

Goldberg, Isaac. *George Gershwin, A Study in American Music.* New York: Unger, 1931, 1958.

Goldman, Herbert G. *Jolson, The Legend Comes to Life.* New York/Oxford: Oxford University Press, 1988.

Goldstein, Malcolm. *George S. Kaufman, His Life, His Theater.* New York and Oxford: Oxford University Press, 1979.

Golenpaul, Dan. *Information, Please!* New York, Simon and Schuster, 1939.

Gorden, Eric A. *Mark the Music: The Life and Work of Marc Blitzstein.* New York: St. Martin's Press, 1989.

Green, Adolph. "Oscar Levant, 1906–1972," *New York Times,* August 27, 1972. Section 2, p. 3.

Harris, Warren G. *Cary Grant, A Touch of Elegance.* New York: Doubleday, 1987.

Hart, Kitty Carlisle. *Kitty, An Autobiography*. New York: Doubleday, 1988.

Harvey, Stephen. *Directed by Vincente Minnelli*. New York: Museum of Modern Art, Harper and Row, 1989.

Herrmann, Dorothy. *With Malice Toward All*. New York: G. P. Putnam's Sons, 1982.

Heyworth, Peter. *Conversations with Klemperer*. London: Victor Gollancz, 1973.

"High-Brow, Low-Brow, Middle-Brow," *Life*, April 11, 1949, pp. 99–102.

Higham, Charles. *Ziegfeld*. Chicago: Henry Regnery Co., 1972.

Horowitz, Joseph. *Understanding Toscanini*. New York: Knopf, 1987.

Hotchner, A. E. *Doris Day, Her Own Story*. New York: William Morrow & Company, 1976.

Howe, Irving. *World of Our Fathers*. New York: Simon and Schuster, 1983.

Jablonski, Edward. *Gershwin*. New York: Doubleday, 1987.

————, and Lawrence D. Stewart. *The Gershwin Years*. Garden City. Doubleday & Co., 1958.

Kahn, E. J., Jr. *The World of Swope*. New York: Simon and Schuster, 1965.

Kaufman, Beatrice, and Joseph Hennessey, eds. *The Letters of Alexander Woollcott*. New York: The Viking Press, 1944.

Kimball, Robert, and Alfred Simon. *The Gershwins*. New York: Atheneum, 1973.

Kirk, Elise K. *Music at the White House, A History of the American Spirit*. Urbana and Chicago: University of Illinois Press, 1986.

Klurfeld, Herman. *Winchell, His Life and Times*. New York: Praeger Publishers, 1976.

Knox, Donald. *The Magic Factory, How MGM Made 'An American in Paris.'* New York: Praeger Publishers, 1973.

Kolodin, Irving. "The Trouble with Oscar," *Saturday Review*, September 9, 1972.

Lardner, Ring W. *You Know Me, Al*. New York: Charles Scribner's Sons, 1925.

Lieberson, Jonathan. "The Unimportance of Being Oscar," *The New York Review of Books*, November 20, 1986, pp. 36–8.

MacAdams, William. *Ben Hecht, The Man Behind the Legend*. New York: Scribner's, 1990.

MacDonald, Dwight. "Masscult and Mindcult: I," *Partisan Review 27*, Spring 1960, pp. 203–33.

————. "Masscult and Mindcult: II," *Partisan Review 27*, Fall 1960, pp. 589–631.

Mantle, Burns. *The Best Plays of 1927–28*. New York: Dodd, Mead and Co., 1929.

McDowall, Roddy, ed. and photographer. *Double Exposure*. New York: William Morrow & Co., 1966.

McKelway, St. Clair. *Gossip: The Life and Times of Walter Winchell*. New York: The Viking Press, 1940.

Marx, Harpo, with Roland Barber. *Harpo Speaks!* New York: Limelight Editions, 1961, 1985.

Meade, Marion. *Dorothy Parker: What Fresh Hell Is This?* New York: Villard Books, 1988.

Mencken, H. L. *The American Language.* New York: Knopf, 1945.

Meredith, Scott. *George S. Kaufman and His Friends.* Garden City, N.Y.: Doubleday & Co., 1974.

Minnelli, Vincente, with Hector Arce. *I Remember It Well.* Garden City, N.Y.: Doubleday & Co., 1974.

Mordden, Ethan. *The Hollywood Studios: House Style in the Golden Age of the Movies.* New York: Knopf, 1988.

Negulesco, Jean. *Things I Did . . . and Things I Think I Did.* New York: Linden Press/Simon and Schuster, 1984.

Newlin, Dika. *Schoenberg Remembered, Diaries and Recollections (1938–1976).* New York: Pendragon Press, 1980.

Odets, Clifford. *The Time Is Ripe: The 1940 Journal of Clifford Odets.* New York: Grove Press, 1988. Introduction by William Gibson.

"Oscar Levant, A Musical Know-It-All, Writes Book About Music and Himself," *Life,* February 5, 1940.

Paar, Jack. *P.S. Jack Paar.* New York: Doubleday & Company, Inc., 1983.

Patterson, James T. *The Dread Disease: Cancer and Modern American Culture.* Cambridge, Mass.: Harvard University Press, 1987.

Peyser, Joan. *The Memory of All That.* New York: Simon and Schuster, 1993.

Plaskin, Glenn. *Horowitz, a Biography.* New York: William Morrow and Co., 1983.

Rapoport, Judith L., M.D. *The Boy Who Couldn't Stop Washing.* New York: Dutton, 1990.

Reed, Kenneth T. *S. N. Behrman.* Boston: Twayne Publishers, 1975.

Reinhardt, Gottfried. *The Genius: A Memoir of Max Reinhardt.* New York: Knopf, 1979.

Robinson, David. *Chaplin, His Life and Art.* New York: McGraw-Hill, 1985.

Rogers, Ginger. *My Story.* New York: HarperCollins, 1991.

Rosenberg, Deena. *Fascinating Rhythm, The Collaboration of George and Ira Gershwin.* New York: Dutton, 1991.

Rubin, Joan Shelley. *The Making of Middlebrow Culture.* Chapel Hill: University of North Carolina Press, 1992.

Rubinstein, Arthur. *My Young Years.* New York: Knopf, 1973.

Rubsamen, Walter H. "Schoenberg in America," *The Musical Quarterly,* Vol. XXXVII, No. 4 (October 1951): pp. 469–89.

Runyon, Damon. "Sense of Humor," *The Bloodhounds of Broadway and Other Stories.* New York: William Morrow and Co., 1981.

Ruttencutter, Helen Drees. *Pianist's Progress.* New York: Thomas Y. Crowell, 1979.

Sanjek, Russell. *From Print to Plastic: Publishing and Promoting America's Popu-*

lar Music (1900–1980). New York: The Institute for Studies in American Music, 1983.

Sarris, Andrew. *The American Cinema, Directors and Directions, 1929–1968*. New York: Dutton, 1968.

Schoenberg, Arnold. *Style and Idea*. New York: St. Martin's Press, 1975.

Schonberg, Harold C. *The Glorious Ones, Classical Music's Legendary Performers*. New York: Times Books, 1985.

————. *The Great Pianists from Mozart to the Present*. New York: Simon and Schuster, 1963.

Schuller, Gunther. *Early Jazz, Its Roots and Musical Development*. New York: Oxford University Press, 1968.

Schwartz, Charles. *Gershwin, His Life and Music*. New York: Bobbs-Merrill Co., 1973.

Seldes, Gilbert. *The Seven Lively Arts*. New York: Harper and Brothers, 1924.

Selznick, Irene Mayer. *A Private View*. New York: Knopf, 1983.

Sherry, Norman. *The Life of Graham Greene*, Vol. I: 1904–1939. New York: Viking, 1989.

Smith, Joan Allen. *Schoenberg and His Circle*. New York: Schirmer, 1986.

Smith, Sally Bedell. *In All His Glory, The Life of William S. Paley*. New York: Simon and Schuster, 1990.

Smith: Steven C. *A Heart at Fire's Center, The Life and Music of Bernard Herrmann*. Berkeley, Los Angeles, Oxford: University of California Press, 1991.

Sobel, Bernard. *Broadway Heartbeat, Memoirs of a Press Agent*. New York: Hermitage House, 1953.

Spoto, Donald. *Marilyn Monroe: The Biography*. New York: HarperCollins, 1993.

Stein, Charles W., ed. and with commentary. *American Vaudeville, as Seen by Its Contemporaries*. Reprint. New York: Da Capo Press, 1984.

Stojowski, Sigismond. "Practice as an Art," *The Etude*, Vol. 55. No. 9, September 1937.

Stuckenschmidt, H. H. *Arnold Schoenberg*. New York: Grove Press, 1959.

Swindell, Larry. *Body and Soul, The Story of John Garfield*. New York: William Morrow and Co., 1975.

Targ, William. *Indecent Pleasures*. New York: Macmillan, 1975.

Tauranac, John. *Elegant New York, the Builders and the Buildings, 1885–1915*. New York: Abbeville Press, 1985.

Thomas, Bob. *Winchell*. Garden City, N.Y.: Doubleday & Co., 1971.

Thomson, Virgil. *Music Right and Left*. New York: Henry Holt & Co., 1951.

Teichmann, Howard. *George S. Kaufman, An Intimate Portrait*. New York: Atheneum, 1972.

Viertel, Salka. *The Kindness of Strangers*. New York: Holt, Rinehart and Winston, 1969.

Walker, Stanley. *The Nightclub Era.* New York: Blue Ribbon Books, Inc., 1933.

Wansell, Geoffrey. *Haunted Idol, The Story of the Real Cary Grant.* New York: William Morrow and Co., Inc., 1984.

Wayne, Jane Ellen. *Stanwyck.* New York: Arbor House, 1985.

Wieborg, Mary Hoyt. "The Three Emperors of Broadway," *Art & Decoration,* May 1925.

Wilder, Alec. *American Popular Song, The Great Innovators, 1900–1950.* London, Oxford, New York: Oxford University Press, 1972.

Zamoyski, Adam. *Paderewski.* New York: Atheneum, 1982.

Zolotow, Maurice. "Lucky Oscar, Sour Genius of the Keyboard," *Saturday Evening Post,* October 21, 1950, pp. 24–5 ff.

References

Bordman, Gerald. *The Concise Oxford Companion to American Theatre.* New York and Oxford: Oxford University Press, 1987.

By Myself I'm a Book, An Oral History of the Immigrant Jewish Experience in Pittsburgh. Pittsburgh: The American Jewish Historical Society, 1972.

Eames, John Douglas. *The Paramount Story.* New York: Crown, 1985.

Ewen, David. *American Songwriters, An H. W. Wilson Biographical Dictionary.* New York: The H. W. Wilson Company, 1987.

Green, Abel, and Joe Laurie, Jr. *Show Biz, From Vaude to Video.* New York: Henry Holt and Co., 1951.

Halliwell, Leslie. *Halliwell's Filmgoer's and Video Viewer's Companion,* 9th edition, New York: Harper & Row, 1990.

Jewell, Richard B., with Vernon Harbin. *The RKO Story.* New York: Arlington House, 1982.

Mattfeld, Julius. *Variety Music Cavalcade, 1620–1950, A Chronology of Vocal and Instrumental Music Popular in the United States.* Introduction by Abel Green. New York: Prentice-Hall, 1952.

Munden, Kenneth W. *American Film Institute Catalog of Motion Pictures Produced in the United States, Feature Film, 1921–1930.* New York and London: R. R. Bowker Company, 1971.

Nash, Jay Robert. *The Encyclopedia of World Crime,* Vols., I–VI. Wilmette, Ill.: CrimeBooks, Inc., 1989.

————, with Stanley Ralph Ross. *The Motion Picture Guide.* Chicago: CineBooks, Inc., 1985.

Pine, Kurt. *The Jews in the Hill District of Pittsburgh, 1910–1940, A Study of Trends.* Unpublished dissertation, University of Pittsburgh, 1943.

Rowd, Richard. *Cinema: A Critical Dictionary, the Major Filmmakers,* Vols. I and II. New York: The Viking Press, 1980.

Shatzkin, Mike, ed. *The Ballplayers, Baseball's Ultimate Biographical Reference.* New York: Arbor House, William Morrow, 1990.

Wolman, Benjamin B. *International Encyclopedia of Psychiatry, Psychology, Psychoanalysis, and Neurology.* New York: Aesculapius Publishers, 1977.

Interviews

Adams, Stanley. Phone conversation, July 7, 1991.

Allen, Steve. Los Angeles, January 12, 1993.

Bacall, Lauren. Phone conversation, January 6, 1993.

Behrman, David. Phone conversation, May 19, 1992.

Burton, Al. Los Angeles, July 10, 1990; January 13, 1993.

Caesar, Irving. Phone conversation, July 10, 1991.

Carmel, Amanda (Levant). Los Angeles, July 15, 1990.

Chaplin, Saul. Los Angeles, June 14, 1991.

Clements, Lorna (Levant). Mahopeck, N.Y., June 6, 1991.

Comden, Betty. New York, November 23, 1991.

Cornett, Barbara (Smith) Ojai Calif., May 23, 1992.

Day, Doris. Phone conversation, May 16, 1992.

Diamond, David. New York, December 12, 1991.

Engel, Edith (Schick). Larchmont, N.Y., February 14, 1992.

Fabray, Nanette. Los Angeles, June 25, 1991.

Fadiman, Clifton. Captiva Island, Fla., August 13, 1991.

Feinstein, Michael. Los Angeles, June 20, 1991.

Foch, Nina. Beverly Hills, June 1, 1992.

Friendly, Fred. New York, September 10, 1992.

Gould, Morton. Phone conversation, September 8, 1992.

Green, Adolph. New York, November 23, 1991.

Greenleigh, John. Phone conversation, October 12, 1992.

Hart, Kitty Carlisle. New York, February 26, 1991; September 9, 1992.

Herrmann, Dorothy. New York, March 14, 1991.

Hirshon, Dorothy. New York, July 22, 1992.

Howard, Jean. Los Angeles, June 30, 1991.

Hyams, Joe. Los Angeles, July 1, 1991.

Isaacs, Charles. Phone conversation, December 12, 1992.

Johnson, Nora. New York, September 24, 1992.

Kaufman, Dorothy. Los Angeles, July 2, 1991.

Kelly, Gene. Beverly Hills, June 17, 1991.

Kerr, John, Pasadena, Calif., May 16, 1992.

Kimmel, Joel. Los Angeles, June 19, 1991.

Klemperer, Werner. New York, December 13, 1991.

Kolodin, Irving (interview with Dorothy Herrmann), undated.

Lardner, Ring, Jr. Phone conversation, August 13, 1992.

Larson, Jack. Los Angeles, May 18, 1992.

Leslie, Joan. Phone conversation, January 14, 1993.

Levant, June. Los Angeles; July 11, 14, 15, 17 and 21, 1990; June 14 and 19, 1991; July 4, 1991; May 15, 19, and 22, 1992; October 31, 1992 (phone conversation); January 12 and 13, 1993.

Levant, Marc. Williamsburg, Va., May 4, 1991.

Levenson, James, M.D. Richmond, Va., June 11, 1992; November 2, 1992.

Livingston, Nancy. Phone conversation, May 14, 1992.

McCormick, Ken. New York, August 5, 1992.

McDowall, Roddy. Phone conversation, June 15, 1991.

Marx, Arthur. Los Angeles, May 25, 1992.

Marx, Bill. Los Angeles, May 28, 1992.

Monk, Victor, M.D. Phone conversation, October 13, 1992.

Peyser, Joan. New York, November 26, 1991.

Radin, Fran. Pittsburgh, Pa., March 4, 1991.

Radin, Oscar. Pittsburgh, Pa., March 3 and 4, 1991; New York, November 11, 1992.

Raksin, David. Los Angeles, May 16, 1992.

Rapper, Irving. Correspondence, September 8 and 17, 1991; phone conversation, September 13, 1991.

Rodenberg, Joan (Levant). Palm Beach, Fla., August 9, 1991.

Scadron, Doris "Dossie" (Levant). New York, November 17, 1992.

Shaw, Artie. Phone conversation, April 12, 1992.

Smith, Barbara. Ojai, Calif., May 23, 1992.

Swope, Herbert, Jr. Palm Beach, Fla., March 27, 1992.

Targ, William. Phone conversation, March 13, 1990.

Urbach, John, M.D. Richmond, Va., June 11, 1992; November 2, 1992.

Vanderbilt, Alfred Gwynne, Jr. New York, July 11, 1991.

Vidal, Gore. Phone conversation, January 18, 1993.

Wald, Connie. Beverly Hills, June 15, 1991.

Warner, Jack, Jr. Los Angeles, June 25, 1991.

Wilder, Billy. Phone conversation, August 10, 1992.

Acknowledgments

Whoever said (and it wasn't Oscar Levant) that "life is short, biography is long" must have known the debt of gratitude owed to those who helped. First and foremost, we want to thank June Levant, who graciously allowed two nascent snoopers into her home and into her life. She gave us hours of candid interviews and permitted us access to her extensive scrapbooks, which comprise a daily diary of Oscar Levant's long sojourn in the public eye.

Our deepest bows to the Levant daughters: Marcia, Lorna, and Amanda. To Michael Feinstein, our thanks for sharing his impressive archive of Levantiana, for his many insights into Levant's life and works, and for use of his Levant discography. To Gene Kelly, who greeted us in his doorway, a live monument to Gene Kelly. To David Diamond, for being there and for remembering. To Al Burton, producer of *The Oscar Levant Show,* for his time, his hospitality, and his gold mine of material. To David Raksin, for his reminiscences of Levant and the music community in Los Angeles during what was clearly a golden age.

To Oscar Radin, our heartfelt appreciation for his insights, opinions, and deep gossip about family life. To Marc Levant, who deserves his own book. To Joan Levant Rodenberg, for her hospitality, wit, and style during difficult times. To Doris "Dossie" Scadron, for her stories of life at the Congress.

To Clifton Fadiman, the Nereus of Captiva Island, "who thinks just and kindly thoughts and never lies." To Alfred Vanderbilt, Jr., who stands proudly in the winner's circle at all times. To Herbert "Ottie" Swope, Jr., one of the emperors of Broadway, for his incomparable recollections. To Barbara Cornett, who allowed us to track her down at her mountain retreat, for valuable pieces of the puzzle.

To Edgar Williams of the Music Department at the College of William and Mary, our gratitude and respect. To Drs. Jim Levenson and John Urbach at the Medical College of Virginia, our appreciation for their insights into Levant's character. In effect, they became Oscar Levant's final team of psychiatrists, analyzing him this side of Valhalla.

To our indefatigable research assistant, Arlene Hellerman, whose knowledge of the period was itself a kind of archive, for her resourcefulness and tenacity. To David Morrill, whose vast interests led him to Levantiana we would otherwise have missed. To Eva Burch, for her insights and her fierce intelligence. To Dorothy Herrmann, who opened up her heart and her files. To our genealogical researcher, Marsha Saron Dennis, who helped us discover the past Levant tried to forget. And to Lester Traub and Ben Browdy, for providing us with the only extant tapes of *The Oscar Levant Show*..

To Ned Comstock, the archivist tending the Oscar Levant Papers at the USC Cinema-Television Library and Archive, for his astounding knowledge and cheerful patience. To Ray White of the Library of Congress, for helping us gain access to the original transcripts of *The Memoirs of an Amnesiac.* To Charles Silver, of the film department of the Museum of Modern Art, for his encouragement and kind assistance. To Vivian Perlis and to Aaron Copland, *in absentia,* for their book of revelations. To Jeannette Bovard, Associate Director of Publications and Archives of the Los Angeles Philharmonic Association, for information on Levant's appearances at the Hollywood Bowl. And to the staff of Las Encinas Hospital for making Levant's hospital records available to Dr. James Levenson.

Our thanks to the many research librarians who gave us invaluable guidance: Don Welch, Coordinator of Reference Services; John Lawrence, Head of Interlibrary Loan; and reference librarians Bettina Manzo, Carol McAllister, Katherine McKenzie, and Hope Yelich at Swem Library, College of William and Mary. To Sherle Abramson, Janet Crowther, Jean Dovi, Betty Guernsey, Caroline Jordan, Mary Sawyer, and Benita Stockmeyer at the Williamsburg Regional Library. And to Sonya Minkoff and Bob Ludemann at the Merrick Public Library on Long Island, N.Y. To Wayne Shoaf at the Arnold Schoenberg Institute at the University of Southern California. To Sam Brylawski and Wynn Matthias, reference librarians at the Recorded Sound Division of the Library of Congress. And to Dan Einstein of the UCLA Film and Television Archive, a gentleman and scholar, who helped us enormously.

Our thanks also to Jack Fiske, who knew about Foulproof Taylor and who, as all Kashners know, is a good man to have in your corner. To Ellen Day, our hero and first reader, for her enthusiasm and encouragement. To Fred Mollin, the hardest-working man in show business, for his indefatigable faith in our project. To Gella and Bob Meyerhoff, that dynamic duo, who commiserated and encouraged.

To the eminent publisher William Targ, who published Levant's last two books, and to our unsinkable agent, Roslyn Targ, the Gioconda of the telephone, whose faith and tenacity kept us going. To Diane Reverand, our unimpeachable editor at Villard Books, and to Sally Arteseros, whose skills are legendary. To all those at Villard who helped: Melanie Cecka, Jacqueline Deval, Alex Kuczynski, and Amanda M. Murray. We are grateful to our gifted copy editor, Lynn Anderson, and to Benjamin Dreyer, our skillful and knowledgeable production editor.

Like the Lone Ranger, Jack Paar did not want to be thanked, but we thank him anyway for providing us with material from *The Jack Paar Show*.

To those who agreed to tell us their stories, recollecting Oscar Levant in tranquillity, our heartfelt appreciation: Stanley Adams, Steve Allen, Lauren Bacall, Irving Caesar, Saul Chaplin, Betty Comden, Doris Day, Edith Engel, Nanette Fabray, Nina Foch, Fred Friendly, Morton Gould, Adolph Green, John Greenleigh, Kitty Carlisle Hart, Dorothy Hirshon, Jean Howard, Joe Hyams, Charles Isaacs, Nora Johnson, Dorothy Kaufman, John Kerr, Joel Kimmel, Werner Klemperer, Ring Lardner, Jr., Jack Larson, Joan Leslie, Amanda Levant, Lorna Levant, Nancy Livingston, Ken McCormick, Roddy McDowall, Arthur Marx, Bill Marx, Dr. Victor Monk, Joan Peyser, Burt Prelutsky, Fran Radin, Irving Rapper, Artie Shaw, Gore Vidal, Connie Wald, Jack Warner, Jr., and Billy Wilder.

To David Behrman, for his kind permission to use his father's correspondence and for his conversations with us. To Mark Trent Goldberg, executor of the Gershwin estate, and to the Gershwin family for permission to reprint George Gershwin's photographs, sketch, and Ira's lyrics from "But Not for Me"—we remain grateful for his cheerful cooperation. To Lawrence A. Schoenberg, for permission to reprint excerpts of Arnold Schoenberg's letters, and to Murray Kempton, who allowed us to publish a personal letter. To Warner Bros., for permission to quote from Warner Bros. memos. To Irene Kahn Atkins, for her work on Levant in the movies. And to Candice Bergen, for her generosity and unerring eye and for permission to reprint her photographs of Oscar Levant, among the last taken before his death.

And, finally, our book is in part dedicated to the memory of Jonathan Lieberson, who first thought Levant's story worth telling.

Appendix

Filmography

As Composer:

My Man (Warner Bros., 1928): "If You Want the Rainbow (You Must Have the Rain)" (with Billy Rose and Mort Dixon).

Street Girl (RKO, 1929): "Lovable and Sweet," "My Dream Memory," "Broken Up Tune" (lyrics by Sidney Clare).

Side Street (RKO, 1929): "Take a Look at Her Now" (lyrics by Sidney Clare).

The Delightful Rogue (RKO, 1929): "Gay Love" (lyrics by Sidney Clare).

Half Marriage (RKO, 1929): "After the Clouds Roll By," "To Me She's Marvelous" (lyrics by Sidney Clare).

Jazz Heaven (RKO, 1929): "Someone" (lyrics by Sidney Clare).

Tanned Legs (RKO, 1929): "You're Responsible," "With You—With Me," "Love to Take a Lesson with You," "Tanned Legs" (lyrics by Sidney Clare).

Love Comes Along (RKO, 1930): "Night Winds," "Until Love Comes Along" (lyrics by Sidney Clare).

Leathernecking (RKO, 1930): "All My Life," "Shake It Off and Smile" (lyrics by Sidney Clare).

Crime Without Passion (Paramount, 1934): Background score (with Frank Tours).

Black Sheep (Fox, 1935): "In Other Words I'm in Love" (lyrics by Sidney Clare).

Steamboat 'Round the Bend (Fox, 1935): Title song (lyrics by Sidney Clare).

Music Is Magic (Fox, 1935): "Honey Chile," "Love Is Smiling at Me" (lyrics by Sidney Clare).

In Person (RKO, 1935): "Don't Mention Love to Me," "Got a New Lease on Life," "Out of Sight, Out of Mind" (lyrics by Dorothy Fields).

Charlie Chan at the Opera (20th Century–Fox, 1936): Opera *Carnival*—selections: Overture, Prelude, Marche, Marche Funêbre, Arias "Ah, Romantic Love Dream," "Then Farewell," "King and Country Call" (libretto by William Kernell).

Nothing Sacred (Selznick/UA, 1937): Background score.

Made for Each Other (UA, 1939): Title theme on which background score by Hugo Friedhofer and David Buttolph was based (lyrics by Harry Tobias for "Made for Each Other").

Romance on the High Seas (Warner Bros., 1948): *Cuban Rhapsody* (with Ray Heindorf).

Funny Lady (Columbia, 1975): "If You Want the Rainbow (You Must Have the Rain)" (with Billy Rose and Mort Dixon).

As Conductor:

Pete (Roleum) and His Cousins (1939): Directed by Joseph Losey. An animated film short made for the Petroleum Industry exhibit at the World's Fair. Levant conducted Hanns Eisler's score.

The Living Land (1939): A five-minute black-and-white film made for the U.S. Department of Agriculture. Hanns Eisler score.

As Screenwriter:

Orient Express (Fox, 1934): Screenplay with Carl Hovey (and Paul Martin). Adapted from *Stamboul Train* by Graham Greene. Director, Paul Martin.

Appearing In:

The Dance of Life (Paramount, 1929): Produced by David O. Selznick, directed by John Cromwell and A. Edward Sutherland. Screenplay: Benjamin Glazer, and George Manker Watters, based on the play *Burlesque* by Watters with Arthur Hopkins. Levant plays Jerry Evans, "Piano Player." With Hal Skelly and Nancy Carroll. B/w with Technicolor sequence.

Information, Please!: Produced by Fred Ullman, Jr., with Frank Donovan, supervisor; a series of thirty-eight one-reelers released from 1939 to 1942. Levant, Franklin P. Adams, John Kieran, and Clifton Fadiman appeared in filmed sequences of the popular radio quiz show. Among the guests appearing with the regular panel were Rex Stout, Gene Tunney, Ruth Gordon, Wendell Willkie, Boris Karloff, John Gunther, Christopher Morley, Deems Taylor. B/w.

Rhythm on the River (Paramount, 1940): Produced by William Le Baron, directed by Victor Schertzinger. Screenplay: Dwight Taylor (based on a story by Billy Wilder and Jacques Thery). Levant plays Billy Starbuck, a songwriter's assistant. With Bing Crosby, Mary Martin, Basil Rathbone. B/w.

Kiss the Boys Goodbye (Paramount, 1941): Produced by William Le Baron, directed by Victor Schertzinger. Screenplay: Harry Tugend, Dwight Taylor, based on a play by Clare Boothe. Levant plays Dick Rayburn, show composer. With Mary Martin, Don Ameche, Virginia Dale. B/w.

Rhapsody in Blue (Warner Bros., 1945): Produced by Jesse L. Lasky, directed by Irving Rapper. Screenplay: Howard Koch and Eliot Paul (story by Sonya Levien). With Robert Alda, Joan Leslie, Alexis Smith, Charles Coburn, Julie Bishop. Appearing as themselves: Oscar Levant, Paul Whiteman, Al Jolson. B/w.

Humoresque (Warner Bros., 1946): Produced by Jerry Wald, directed by Jean Negulesco. Screenplay: Clifford Odets and Zachary Gold (from a short story by Fannie Hurst). Levant plays Sid Jeffers, a pianist and best friend. With Joan Crawford, John Garfield, J. Carrol Naish, Ruth Nelson, Joan Chandler. B/w.

You Were Meant for Me (20th Century–Fox, 1947): Produced by Fred Kohlmer, directed by Lloyd Bacon. Screenplay: Elick Moll and Valentine Davies. Levant plays Oscar Hoffman, band manager and pianist. With Jeanne Crain, Dan Dailey. B/w.

Romance on the High Seas (released as *It's Magic* in Great Britain) (Warner Bros., 1948): Produced by Alex Gottlieb, directed by Michael Curtiz. Screenplay: Julius J. Epstein, Philip G. Epstein, and I.A.L. Diamond. Levant plays Oscar Ferrar, nightclub pianist and unsuccessful suitor of star. With Doris Day, Janis Paige, Jack Carson, Don DeFore, S. Z. Sakall, Eric Blore, Franklin Pangborn. Featuring the Paige Cavanaugh Trio. Technicolor.

The Barkleys of Broadway (MGM, 1949): Produced by Arthur Freed, directed by Charles Walters. Screenplay: Betty Comden and Adolph Green. Levant plays Ezra Millar, dyspeptic pianist and best friend. With Fred Astaire, Ginger Rogers, Billie Burke. Technicolor.

An American in Paris (MGM, 1951): Produced by Arthur Freed, directed by Vincente Minnelli. Screenplay: Alan Jay Lerner. Levant plays Adam Cook, expatriate American composer in Paris on a string of fellowships; best friend of star. With Gene Kelly, Leslie Caron, Georges Guetary, Nina Foch. Technicolor.

The I Don't Care Girl (20th Century–Fox, 1952): Produced by George Jessel, directed by Lloyd Bacon. Screenplay: Walter Bullock. The life of the vaudeville star Eva Tanguay. Levant plays Charles Bennett, an entertainer. With George Jessel, Mitzi Gaynor, David Wayne. Technicolor.

O. Henry's Full House (*Full House* in Great Britain) (20th Century–Fox, 1952): An anthology of several O. Henry stories. Produced by Andre Hakim, directed by Howard Hawks. Screenplay: Nunnally Johnson, based on the O. Henry story "The Ransom of Red Chief." Levant plays Bill, one of two hapless kidnappers. With Fred Allen, Lee Aaker. Narration, John Steinbeck. B/w.

The Band Wagon (MGM, 1953): Produced by Arthur Freed, directed by Vincente Minnelli. Screenplay: Betty Comden and Adolph Green. Levant plays Lester Marton, half of a husband-and-wife writing team. With Fred Astaire, Cyd Charisse, Nanette Fabray, Jack Buchanan. Technicolor.

The Cobweb (MGM, 1955): Produced by John Houseman, directed by Vincente Minnelli. Screenplay: John Paxton and William Gibson, based on Gibson's novel. Levant plays Mr. Capp, a mother-fixated patient at a private sanatorium. With Richard Widmark, Lauren Bacall, Charles Boyer, Gloria Grahame, Lillian Gish, John Kerr, Susan Strasberg, Paul Stewart. Metrocolor in Cinemascope.

Selected Discography, Scores, and Concert Works
Adapted from a complete discography compiled
by Michael Feinstein

I. *Selected Recordings of Songs by Levant:*
(all recordings in this section are ten-inch, 78-rpm records unless otherwise noted; ★denotes cassette tape or compact disc)

"Keep Sweeping the Cobwebs off the Moon"
Nick Lucas	Brunswick 3749–A
Vaughn DeLeath	Edison 52192
Fred Waring	Victor 21165
Ruth Etting	78 rpm: Columbia 1242–D
	33⅓ rpm: Take Two TT203

"If You Want the Rainbow (You Must Have the Rain)"
Fanny Brice	Victor 21812 (and 33⅓ rpm: VIK LX-997; Audiophile AFLP707)
Eva Taylor	Okeh 8665

"Lovable and Sweet"
Charleston Chasers	Columbia 1925–D
Sammy Fain	Velvitone 2014
Al Goodman	Brunswick 4488
Annette Hanshaw	Okeh 41292
Gus Arnheim and His Orchestra	Victor 22054

"My Dream Memory"
Al Goodman	Brunswick 4488
All Star Orchestra	Victor 22054

"Gay Love"
Bing Crosby	33⅓ rpm: Columbia CE2E201 (two 12″)
	Sony CK52855 and CSP A2 201★

"Lady, Play Your Mandolin"
Ben Selvin	Columbia 2367–D
The Revelers	Victor 22622
Al Bowlly	Saville CDSVL 150★

"Blame It on My Youth"
Jan Garber Orchestra	Victor 24809
Dorsey Brothers Orchestra	Decca 320
Gordon MacRae	Capitol 2196

June Rudell	33⅓ rpm: Vido 401 (12″)
Bing Crosby	33⅓ rpm: Spokane 12
Rosemary Clooney	33⅓ rpm: Columbia 6297; Harmony HL 7236
Frank Sinatra	Capitol/EMI 46572 and 99956★
Nat King Cole	Capitol CDP 7 48328 2★
Michael Feinstein	Elektra/Asylum 9 60743-4★
Chet Baker	Novus RCA 3054-2-N★
The Art Farmer Quintet	Contemporary Records CCD-14042-2★

"Don't Mention Love to Me"

Bobby Pittman	Supreme 101
Ishman Jones Orchestra	Decca 610
Ginger Rogers	Decca 638; 33⅓ rpm: Curtain Calls CC 100/21 (12″)
Kay Thompson	Brunswick 7564 and LP: Box Office JJA 197510
Bobby Short	CD-7 81715-2★

"Out of Sight, Out of Mind"

Kay Thompson	Brunswick 7564 and LP: Box Office JJA 197510
Ginger Rogers	33⅓ rpm: Curtain Calls CC 100/21 (12″) and 78 rpm: Decca F6822 (England)

"Pardon My Love"

Fats Waller	Victor 24889
Lud Gluskin	Columbia 3008-D CD: Take Two TT402★

"Afterglow"

Jan Garber	Decca 851
Dick McDonough	Melotone 61101

"Lazy Weather"

Nat Brandywine	Brunswick 7660
Don Redman	Meloton 60709

"Until Today"

Ted Weems	Decca 895
Red Allen	Vocalion 3292
Buddy Clark	Brunswick 7712

"Wacky Dust"

Chick Webb	Decca 2021 and Decca/GRP GRD 2-618★

Bunny Berigan	Victor 25872
The Manhattan Transfer	Atlantic CS19258★

"I Got a New Lease on Life"
Ginger Rogers	33⅓ rpm: Curtain Calls CC100/21 (12″)

"Asleep or Awake"
Tommy Dorsey Orchestra	Victor 26210

"Night Winds"
Bebe Daniels	Victor 22283-A

"Until Love Comes Along"
Bebe Daniels	Victor 22283-B

"Last Night a Miracle Happened"
Fats Waller	Bluebird B-10136

"After Dinner Speech"
Red Norvo	Brunswick 8171

"You Had an Evening to Spare"
Fats Waller	Victor 25834

The following two recordings are British original-cast performances from *Out of the Bottle* (6/11/32). Score co-composed by Levant and Vivian Ellis.

"We've Got the Moon and Sixpence"
Clifford Mollison and Polly Walker	HMV B4224

"Everything But You"
Frances Day and Max Kirby	78 rpm: HMV B4223 (England) 33⅓ rpm: Box Office JJA 19794 (two LPs)

"Out of the Bottle" Medley
Debroy Somers' Band	Columbia DX364 (England) 33⅓ rpm: Box Office JJA 1977-6
New Mayfair Orchestra/ Ray Noble	HMV C2439

II. *Selected scores for stage shows:*

1930 *Ripples:* "Is It Love?" "There's Nothing Wrong with a Kiss" "Lady, Play Your Mandolin"

1932 *Out of the Bottle* (London): "We've Got the Moon and Sixpence"

III. *Orchestral and chamber music:*

Orchestral:
Piano Concerto
Nocturne
Suite for Piano and Orchestra (including "Dirge")
A New Overture
Caprice for Orchestra†
Overture 1912 (A New Overture)

Chamber:
Sonatina for Piano‡
Sinfonietta
String Quartet
Two Pieces for Violin and Piano
Poem for Piano

IV. *Selected discography of Levant's recordings as pianist:*
(All recordings are Columbia Masterworks; unissued recordings are not included)

ALBÉNIZ: Tango in D Major, Op. 165, No. 2 (11/2/44)
78 rpm: 71638-D in Set M-560 (three 12″)
45 rpm: 4-72081-D in Set A-560 (three 7″)
33⅓ rpm: ML-2018 (10″); CL-1134 (12″)

BEETHOVEN: Sonata No. 8 in C Minor, Op. 13 (adagio cantabile only) (7/15/46)
78 rpm: 17043-D (10″)

Sonata No. 14 in C-sharp Minor, Op. 27, No. 2 (7/1 and 25/46)
78 rpm: Set X-273 (two 12″)

Sonata No. 20 in G Major, Op. 49, No. 2 (menuetto only) (7/3/46)
78 rpm: 71874-D in Set X-273 (two 12″)

BRAHMS: Intermezzo No. 13 in A Major, Op. 118, No. 2 (5/22/47)
78 rpm: 72372-D (12″)

Waltz No. 15 in A-flat Major, Op. 39 (5/22/47)
78 rpm: 72372-D (12″)

†Caprice for Orchestra is included in *Blue Monday,* a 1993 recording of Gershwin's one-act jazz opera, performed by Concordia and conducted by Marin Alsop (Angel CDC 54851).
‡The first movement, *Andantino,* of the Sonatina for Piano was recorded, in 1942, on his first album, *Oscar Levant in a Recital of Modern Music* (Columbia Masterworks, Set M-508). First, second, and third movements recently issued on CD: DRG 13113. Sonatina for Piano also recently recorded by Joseph Smith on *Rhythmic Moments* (Premiere CD 1028).

CHOPIN: Etude No. 3 in E Major, Op. 10, No. 3 (8/26/46)
(8/28/46—LP)
Etude No. 4 in C-sharp Minor, Op. 10, No. 4
(8/26/46) (8/28/46—LP)
*Etude No. 5 in G-flat Minor, Op. 10, No. 5 (7/19/46)
*Etude No. 12 in C-sharp Minor, Op. 10, No. 12
(7/19/46)
†Nocturne No. 2 in E-flat Major, Op. 9, No. 2
(8/26/46) (8/28/46—LP)
†Nocturne No. 5 in F-sharp Major, Op. 15, No. 2
(7/19/46)
Polonaise No. 3 in A Major, Op. 40, No. 1 (7/3/46)
Berceuse in D-flat Major, Op. 57 (7/18/46)
†Valse No. 7 in C-sharp Minor, Op. 64, No. 2
(7/25/46)
†Valse No. 11 in G-flat Major, Op. 70, No. 1 (8/26/46)
(8/28/46—LP)
78 rpm: Set M-649 (4-12″): *= issued separately on
71890-D (12″)
45 rpm: † = issued separately on A-1759
33⅓ rpm: ML-4147 (12″)

Valse No. 7 in C-sharp Minor, Op. 64, No. 2 (second
recording) (6/5/58)
Mazurka in A Minor, Op. 17, No. 4 (6/5/58)
Mazurka in B-flat Minor, Op. 24, No. 4 (6/5/58)
Mazurka in C-sharp Minor, Op. 63, No. 3 (6/5/58)
Mazurka in A Minor, Op. 67, No. 4 (6/5/58)
Etude No. 12 in C Minor, Op. 10, No. 12 (second re-
cording) (6/5/58)
33⅓ rpm: ML-5676 (mono); MS-6276 (stereo) (12″)

COPLAND: "The Open Prairie" (from *Billy the Kid*), arr. Lukas Foss
(9/1/49)
78 rpm: 72873-D in Set MM-867 (3-12″)

DEBUSSY: #*"Réflets dans l'eau" (*Images pour piano,* Set I, No. 1)
(5/16/47)
#"La Soirée dans Grenade" (Piano Estampes No. 2)
(5/8/47)
#"Général Lavine—eccentric" (Prelude No. 6, Book 2,
No. 18) (3/13/47)
†"Minstrels" (Prelude No. 12, Book 1) (3/13/47)
†*"La Cathédrale Engloute" (Prelude No. 10, Book 1)
(5/8/47)
†"Serenade for the Doll" (from *Children's Corner*)
(5/8/47)

#★"The Little Shepherd" (from *Children's Corner*)
(5/8/47)
†★"La Plus que lente"—valse (5/9/47)
Arabesque No. 1 in E Major (5/9/47)
Arabesque No. 2 in G Major (5/16/47)
78 rpm: Set M-710 (4-12″)
45 rpm: Set A-710 (4-7″); † = issued separately on
             A-1830; # = issued separately on A-1856
             (7″)
33⅓ rpm: ML-4277 (12″); ★ = issued separately on
             CL-1134 (12″)

"The Golliwog's Cakewalk" (No. 6 from *Children's
Corner*) (3/23/45)
78 rpm: 72080-D in Set M-560 (three 12″)
45 rpm: 4-72080 in Set A-560 (three 7″); 7-1222 in
             Set A-1537 (three 7″)
33⅓ rpm: ML-2018 (10″), CL-1134 (12″)

"Jardins sous la pluie" (Estampes No. 3) (1/20/42)
78 rpm: 17453-D in Set M-508 (four 10″)

"Les Collines d'Anacapri" (Prelude No. 5, Book 1)
(1/20/42)
78 rpm: 17453-D in Set M-508 (four 10″)

"La Fille aux cheveux de lin" (Prelude No. 8, Book 1)
(3/23/45)
78 rpm: 71637-D in Set M-560 (three 12″)
45 rpm: 4-72080-D in Set A-560 (three 7″)
33⅓ rpm: ML-2018 (10″); CL-1134 (12″)

"Clair de lune" (from *Suite Bergamasque*) (1/17/45)
78 rpm: 71637-D in Set M-560 (three 12″)
45 rpm: 4-72080-D in Set A-560 (three 7″);
             7-1222 in Set A-1537 (7″)
33⅓ rpm: ML-2018 (10″); CL-1134 (12″)

"Minstrels" (Prelude No. 12, Book 1) (second recording) (6/5/58)
"Général Lavine—eccentric" (Prelude No. 6, Book 2)
(second recording) (6/5/58)
"Jardins sous la pluie" (Estampes No. 3) (second recording) (6/5/58)
33⅓ rpm: ML-5676 (mono); MS-6276 (stereo) (12″)

"Serenade for the Doll" (from *Children's Corner*) (second recording) (6/5/58)
33⅓ rpm: ML-5324 (12″)

FALLA: "Ritual Fire Dance" (from *El Amor Brujo*) (11/22/44)
78 rpm: 71636-D in Set M-560 (three 12″)
45 rpm: 4-72079-D in Set A-560 (three 7″);
            4-4798 (7″);
            7-1222 in Set A-1537
33⅓ rpm: 3-530 (7″); 3-72079 (7″); ML-2018 (10″);
            CL-1134 (12″)

"Miller's Dance" (from *The Three-Cornered Hat*)
(11/22/44)
78 rpm: 71638-D in Set M-560 (three 12″)
45 rpm: 4-72081-D in Set A-560 (three 7″)
33⅓ rpm: ML-2018 (10″); CL-1134 (12″)

GERSHWIN: *Rhapsody in Blue* (1925) with the Frank Black Orchestra
78 rpm: Brunswick 20058 (12″)

(Abridged) Paul Whiteman conducting the Warner
Bros. Studio Orchestra (mid 1943) (transcribed from the
sound track of film *Rhapsody in Blue*)
78 rpm: V Disc 139A and B; WHI 7 and 8

(Abridged) Andre Kostelanetz conducting unknown orchestra. Includes Levant's spoken portrait of George
Gershwin
33⅓ rpm: Medallion ML 310
CD: Facet 8100

Eugene Ormandy conducting the Philadelphia Orchestra (5/20/45 and 6/2/45)
78 rpm: Set X-251 (two 12″); Set MM-1076
            (two 12″)
45 rpm: Set A-251 (two 7″); 7-1420 in Set A-1463
            (7″); Set B-2604 (7″)
33⅓ rpm: ML-4026 (12″); ML-4879 (12″); CL-700
            (12″);
            CS-8641 (12″) (simulated stereo)
            Excerpt: slow movement only: D-7 (12″)
CD: MK 42514; MPK 47681

Unknown conductor and orchestra (recently discovered
transcription)
CD: DRG 13113

Piano Concerto in F Major
(first movement only: 9/8/37) Charles Previn conducting the Los Angeles Philharmonic Orchestra
33⅓ rpm: Citadel CT7025

Movements 1 and 3 (abridged): Paul Whiteman conducting the Warner Bros. Studio Orchestra (mid 1943)
(transcribed from the sound track of film *Rhapsody in
Blue*)
78 rpm: V Disc 517A; WHI9

Andre Kostelanetz conducting the New York Philharmonic Orchestra (5/4/42)
78 rpm: Set M-512 (four 12″)
45 rpm: Set A-1047 (three 7″)
33⅓ rpm: ML-4025 (12″); ML-4879 (12″);
             CL-700 (12″)
             CS-8641 (12″) (simulated stereo)
CD: MK 42514; MPK 47681

Arturo Toscanini conducting the NBC Symphony Orchestra (4/2/44)
33⅓ rpm: Arkadia ARK 4 (Italy)
CD: Hunt CD 534 (Italy)

Three Preludes (12/17/41)
78 rpm: 17452-D in Set M-508 (four 12″)
45 rpm: 7-1483 in Set A-1047 (three 7″);
             A-1760 (7″)
33⅓ rpm: ML-2073 (10″); MS-7518 (12″) (simulated
             stereo)
CD: MK 42514; MPK 47681

Preludes No. 2 and No. 3 only (12/17/41)
78 rpm: 12125-D in Set X-251 (two 12″);
             72639-D (12″)
45 rpm: 4-12126-D in Set A-251 (two 7″)

Preludes No. 2 and No. 3 only (11/17/42)
78 rpm: V Disc 517B

Second Rhapsody (7/5/49)
Morton Gould conducting his orchestra
78 rpm: Set MM-867 (three 12″)
33⅓ rpm: ML-2073 (10″); Time-Life Records
             STL164
             P612418 (six 12″)
CD: MK 42514; MPK 47681

"I Got Rhythm" Variations for Piano and Orchestra
(7/6/49)
Morton Gould conducting his orchestra
78 rpm: Set MM-867 (three 12″)

45 rpm: Set A-1760 (7")

33⅓ rpm: ML-2073 (10"); Time-Life Records STL164

P612418 (six 12")

CD: MK 42514; MPK 47681

GRIEG: Concerto in A Minor for Piano and Orchestra (12/13/47)
Efrem Kurtz conducting the New York Philharmonic Orchestra

78 rpm: Set MM-741 (four 12")

33⅓ rpm: ML-4028 (12"); ML-4883 (12"); CL-740 (12")

P14192 (simulated stereo)

HONEGGER: Concertino for Piano and Orchestra (7/6/49)
Fritz Reiner conducting the Columbia Symphony Orchestra

33⅓ rpm: ML-2156 (10")

JELOBINSKY: Etude No. 1 and Etude No. 2 (1/20/42)

78 rpm: 17454-D in Set M-508 (four 12")

KHATCHATURIAN: "Sabre Dance" and "Lullaby" from *Gayne* (12/29/47)
Louis Bring conducting the Columbia Concert Orchestra (arr. piano and orchestra)

78 rpm: 17521-D (10")

45 rpm: 4-17521-D (7"); 4-4791 (7")

33⅓ rpm: 3-17521-D (7"); 3-524 (7")

Concerto for Piano and Orchestra (1/3/50)
Dimitri Mitropoulos conducting the New York Philharmonic Orchestra

78 rpm: Set MM-905 (five 12")

33⅓ rpm: ML-4288 (12")

P14162 (simulated stereo)

LECOUNA: Malagueña (1/17/45)

78 rpm: 71636-D in Set M-560 (three 12")

45 rpm: 4-72079-D in Set A-560 (three 12"); 4-4798 (7");
7-1222 in Set A-1537

33⅓ rpm: 3-72079-D (7"); 3-530 (7"); ML-2018 (10"); CL-1134 (12")

LEVANT: Piano Sonatina: Con Ritmo (first movement only: 1/20/42)

78 rpm: 17455-D in Set M-508 (four 10″)
CD: DRG 13113 (movements 1 and 2:
            2/28/40; movement 3: 11/18/40)

Piano Concerto (2/17/42)
Alfred Wallenstein conducting the NBC Symphony
Orchestra
LP: Medallion ML 310
CD: DRG 13113

Music for *Charlie Chan at the Opera* (1936)
Original sound-track excerpts (from studio 78-rpm
discs)
Singers: Tudor Williams, bass; Enrico Ricardi,
            tenor; Zaruhi Elmassian, soprano
LP: Medallion ML310
CD: DRG 13113

LISZT: *Sonetta del petrarca No. 104
         *Valse Oubliée No. 1 in F-sharp Minor
         Hungarian Rhapsody No. 4 in E-flat Major
         Hungarian Rhapsody No. 10 in E Major
         Hungarian Rhapsody No. 12 in C-sharp Minor
         Hungarian Rhapsody No. 13 in A Minor
         The above selections were recorded in April, May, and
         June of 1955.
         33⅓ rpm: ML-5094 (12″); *= issued on Odyssey 32
                    1601 69 (12″)

MOMPOU: "Scenes of Childhood" (6/10/58)
         33⅓ rpm: ML-5324 (12″)

POULENC: Mouvements Perpétuels (3) (3/23/45)
         78 rpm: 71638-D in Set M-560 (three 12″)
         45 rpm: 4-72081 in Set A-560 (three 7″)
         33⅓ rpm: ML-2018 (10″); CL-1134 (12″)

         Pastourelle (1/17/45)
         78 rpm: 71636-D in Set M-560 (three 12″);
                     71890-D (12″)
         45 rpm: 4-72079-D in Set A-560 (three 7″);
                     4-4798 (7″)
         33⅓ rpm: 3-72079-D (7″); 3-530 (7″); ML-2018
                    (10″); CL-1134 (12″)

PROKOFIEV: *Visions fugitives,* Op. 22 (Nos. 1, 3, 6, 10, 11, 16) (6/19/
           58)
           33⅓ rpm: ML-5324 (12″)

RACHMANINOFF: Prelude No. 7 in E-flat, Op. 23, No. 6 (11/12/47)
78 rpm: 12792 in Set MM-741 (three 12″);
72639-D (12″)

Prelude in D Minor, Op. 23, No. 3 (11/12/47)
78 rpm: 13075-D in Set MM-905 (five 12″)

Prelude in G Major, Op. 32, No. 5 (11/19/47)
78 rpm: 12910-D in Set MM-785 (five 12″)

18th Variation from *Rhapsody on a Theme of Paganini*
33⅓ rpm: ML-5324 (12″)

RAVEL: Sonatine: Menuet (second movement only) (1/20/42)
78 rpm: 17455-D in Set M-508 (four 10″)

Sonatine (complete) (6/10/58)
33⅓ rpm: ML-5676 (mono); MS-6276 (stereo) (12″)

"Pavanne for a Dead Princess" (6/10/58)
Forlane from *Le Tombeau de Couperin* (6/10/58)
Minuet from *Le Tombeau de Couperin* (6/10/58)
33⅓ rpm: ML-5324 (12″)

RUBINSTEIN: Piano Concerto No. 4 in D Minor, Op. 70 (3/31/52)
Dimitri Mitropoulos conducting the New York Philharmonic Orchestra
33⅓ rpm: ML-4599 (12″); Odyssey 32 1601 69 (12″)
CD: Palladio PD 4132 (Italy)

SCHUMANN: "Träumerei" (from *Kinderscenen,* Op. 15) (5/22/47)
78 rpm: 12372-D (12″)

SCOTT: "Lotus Land" (6/5/58)
33⅓ rpm: ML-5324 (12″)

SHOSTAKOVICH: Polka from *The Age of Gold* (12/17/41)
78 rpm: 17454-D in Set M-508 (four 10″)

Polka from *The Age of Gold* (second recording)
(6/19/58)
33⅓ rpm: ML-5324 (12″)

Prelude in A Minor, Op. 34, No. 2 (12/17/41)
78 rpm: 17454-D in Set M-508 (four 10″)

TCHAIKOVSKY: Concerto No. 1 in B-flat Minor for Piano and Orchestra (12/12/47)
Eugene Ormandy conducting the Philadelphia Orchestra
78 rpm: Set MM-785 (four 12″)
45 rpm: Set A-1063 (three 7″)

33⅓ rpm: ML-4096 (12″); ML-4883 (12″);
CL-740 (12″)
P14192 (simulated stereo)

WAGNER: Excerpts from *Tristan und Isolde* (arrangement for violin,
piano, orchestra)
Franz Waxman, Conductor; Isaac Stern, Violin (9/25/
46)
78 rpm: Set M-567 (five 12″)
33⅓ rpm: ML-2103 (10″)

V.   *Other albums featuring Levant:*

Al Jolson with Oscar Levant at the Piano
33⅓ rpm: Decca DL-9095   (12″)
Bing and Al (Contains complete *Kraft Music Hall* shows of 10/16/47 and
1/15/48)
33⅓ rpm: Totem 1017 (Levant plays Gershwin medley)
Bing's Party (contains *Bing Crosby Show* 11/10/48 excerpts)
33⅓ rpm: Artistic ART001 (England)(Levant plays Gershwin Prelude
No. 3)
The Marx Brothers (with *Kraft Music Hall* excerpts of 11/18/48, 1/13/49,
4/7/49, and 5/26/49)
33⅓ rpm: Murray Hill 931680   (four 12″)
Judy Garland on Radio (with *Kraft Music Hall* excerpt of 9/30/48)
33⅓ rpm: Radiola MR-1040   (12″)
The Band Wagon (sound track of the 1953 MGM musical film)
33⅓ rpm: MGM 2-ses-44-st   (two 12″) (simulated stereo)
The Golden Age of Comedy (Oscar Levant with Fred Allen, 1947)
33⅓ rpm: Murray Hill 900009   (two 12″); Longines Symphonette
SYS5277-5281   (five 12″)
Cut! Out Takes from Hollywood's Greatest Musicals—Volume Two (includes
"Sweet Music," cut from *The Band Wagon*, featuring Nanette Fabray and
Oscar Levant)
33⅓ rpm: Out Take Records   OTF-2
Ginger Rogers (includes sound track of "A Weekend in the Country" from
The Barkleys of Broadway, featuring Oscar Levant)
33⅓ rpm: Curtain Calls CC 100-21   (12″)
The Gershwins in Hollywood (includes Levant performing on sound tracks of
Rhapsody in Blue and *An American in Paris*)
33⅓ rpm: JJA Records JJA19773A-D   (two 12″) (includes deleted material)
Chase and Sanborn 101st Anniversary Show (NBC Radio, 11/14/65, 7:05–
8:00 P.M.), Fred Allen with Oscar Levant
33⅓ rpm: Issued as promotion by Chase and Sanborn   (no record
number)

That's Entertainment (sound track) (includes excerpt from *The Band Wagon*)
  33⅓ rpm: MCA 2-11002   (two 12″)
That's Entertainment, Part Two (sound track) (includes excerpt from *The Band Wagon*)
  33⅓ rpm: MGM-1-5301   (12″)

VI.   *Authors' Addenda:*

In 1981 Michael Feinstein produced an album of music by Levant titled *Oscar Levant: For the Record* (Medallion ML310). The recording featured Levant's Piano Concerto and music from *Charlie Chan at the Opera*, as well as Levant at the piano playing George Gershwin's music and speaking about Gershwin. It has been reissued with newly discovered material on DRG compact disc 13113.

Many of Levant's film performances are now available on videocassette and laser disc. Of special interest is the deluxe laser disc of *An American in Paris* (MGM/UA ML 102803), because it features several audio outtakes deleted from the final release print of the film, with characteristic brilliant, idiomatic piano and vocal performances by Levant. It includes Prelude No. 3, "Liza," a piano medley of songs, and "Bidin' My Time."

Grateful acknowledgment is made to the following for
permission to use both published and unpublished material:

David Behrman: Two letters from Samuel N. Behrman and excerpts
from *People in a Diary: A Memoir.* Reprinted by permission of the
Estate of Samuel N. Behrman.

Candice Bergen: Excerpts from "Good-Night, Oscar Levant,
Wherever You Are," by Candice Bergen, from the April 1973 issue
of *Esquire,* and photographs taken by Candice Bergen. Reprinted by
permission of Candice Bergen.

The Gershwin Family: Six photographs and one drawing of Oscar
Levant executed by George Gershwin. Reprinted through the
courtesy of the Gershwin Family.

Hildi Greenson: Letter from Dr. Ralph Greenson to Dr. Charles
Thompson. Used by permission of Hildi Greenson, Executrix of
the Greenson Estate.

Charles Isaacs: Excerpts from "Swannie Song," by Charles Isaacs
(*Park East,* October 1951). Reprinted by permission of Charles
Isaacs.

Murray Kempton: Letter to Oscar Levant from Murray Kempton.
Used by permission of Murray Kempton.

June Levant: Excerpts from Oscar Levant's written work, including
both published and unpublished professional and personal writings.
Used by permission.

Polygram Music: Excerpt from "Blame It on My Youth," by Edward
Heyman and Oscar Levant. Copyright © 1934 by Polygram
International Publishing, Inc. (renewed). International Copyright
Secured. All rights reserved. Reprinted by permission of Polygram
Music.

Lawrence A. Schoenberg: One letter and excerpts from another letter
from Arnold Schoenberg. Used by permission of Lawrence A.
Schoenberg.

About the Authors

NANCY SCHOENBERGER and SAM KASHNER are married and live in Williamsburg, Virginia. Schoenberger, who was the Writer in Residence at the College of William and Mary in 1989–90, now teaches creative writing there. Her book of poetry, *Girl on a White Porch,* won the Devins Award in 1987. Kashner occasionally teaches at the college and has worked as a writer in various media, including radio and television. Both are graduates of Columbia University's Writing Program, and each has published two books of poetry. This is their first collaboration.